ADMIRAL
ARLEIGH
BURKE

ADMIRAL ARLEIGH BURKE

E. B. Potter

NAVAL INSTITUTE PRESS
Annapolis, Maryland

Naval Institute Press
291 Wood Road
Annapolis, MD 21402

Charts in this book showing Disposition of Task Force 58 on 19 June 1944, Operations of
Task Force 58 in Support of the Iwo Jima Campaign, and the Track Chart of the Yamato Group
are based on similar charts in *History of United States Naval Operations in World War II* by
Samuel Eliot Morison, published by Little, Brown and Co., Boston, and in *Campaigns of the
Pacific* from the United States Strategic Bombing Survey (USSBS).

LIBRARY OF CONGRESS CATALOGING-IN-PUBLICATION DATA

Potter, E. B. (Elmer Belmont), 1908–
    Admiral Arleigh Burke / E. B. Potter.—1st Naval Institute Press pbk. ed.
    p. cm.
    Originally published: 1st ed. New York: Random House, 1990.
    Includes bibliographical references and index.
    ISBN 1-59114-692-5 (acid-free paper)
Burke, Arleigh A., 1901– 2. Admirals—United States—Biography. 3. United States. Navy—
Biography. 4. United States—History, Naval—20th century. 5. World War, 1939–1945—
Naval operations, American. I. Title.
E746.B87P68 2005
359'.0092—dc22
[B]

2004058190

Printed in the United States of America on acid-free paper ∞
11 10 09 08 07 06 05   9 8 7 6 5 4 3 2 1

PREFACE

IN EARLY 1943, Japan's World War II offensive came to an end with the ousting of its forces from Guadalcanal, far-eastern New Guinea, and the Aleutians. In June of that year the Americans with their New Zealand and Australian allies began a westward advance with a drive on the Japanese stronghold of Rabaul. The Allied offensive, after a slow start, picked up speed, and in November reached high gear with the invasion of Bougainville, followed by the cruiser-destroyer night victory of the Battle of Empress Augusta Bay, by devastating carrier raids on Rabaul itself, and by capture of the Gilbert Islands. Toward the end of the month the Americans won another victory in the Battle of Cape St. George, a night action brilliantly conducted by a navy captain nicknamed 31-Knot Burke.

Few nicknames have become more quickly and widely known to the public. In the buoyant mood generated by the Allied successes, the owner of the nickname became the embodiment of a new spirit of victory. So far as I can recall, no picture of Burke appeared in the newspapers at this time, but he was widely envisioned as a kind of modern Viking, pursuing the enemy at high speed through the night waters of the mysterious Solomons. The concept was not far from fact, but, as readers of this book will learn, the title "31-Knot" was not prefixed to Captain Burke's name in recognition of any high-speed operations. In fact, each of his ships, all destroyers, was designed for a top speed of 35 knots.

Early in 1944 the gallant but small-scale Allied cruiser-destroyer operations of the Solomons came to an end, and public attention became focused on the mighty carrier-spearheaded U.S. Central Pacific Force as it conquered its way across the Pacific, seizing the Japanese-held Marshalls and Marianas. Through no choice of his own, Burke transferred from the destroyers to the carriers—a promotion, as it were, from peanuts to the big time.

In common with most Americans, I became aware of Burke's change of duty from news stories of the Battle of the Philippine Sea, June 1944, in which he served as chief of staff to Vice Admiral Marc Mitscher, commander of the Fast Carrier Task Force. A photograph published at that time showed Burke seated on a kind of settee in flag plot with Mitscher and Captain Truman Hedding, whom Burke had relieved as chief of staff. The three officers, their brows furrowed with anxiety, were awaiting news of their aviators flying back through the night from their 20 June twilight attack on the retreating Japanese fleet.

I studied that photograph with interest, both for the drama of the situation and because it confirmed my notion of what a man called 31-Knot Burke must look like—lean, dark, with piercing eyes, a veritable hotspur. Unfortunately the picture was miscaptioned. The hotspur was in fact Hedding. I paid so little attention to the real Burke, labeled Hedding, that I quickly forgot what he looked like.

At the end of the war I shed my naval reserve officer's uniform and joined the civilian faculty of the U.S. Naval Academy. Through my navy connections I occasionally heard of the activities of 31-Knot Burke, whom I now visualized as hawk-faced and eagle-eyed. I saw him in person for the first time one summer in the late 1940s at Northwestern University, where officers were being prepared to serve in the NROTC units in various universities. The navy sent me there to address the officers on methods of teaching naval history, a subject on which I was acquiring some expertise. Before I began, the chairman announced that Captain Arleigh Burke was present, and that he would follow my speech with a discussion of the controversial subject of unification of the armed services, then being imposed by the president.

While speaking, I cast my eyes over the auditorium and tried without success to locate the lean, dark, sharp-eyed hotspur of my imagination. When I finished my speech, the chairman announced Burke, who rose from his seat and headed for the platform. I was dumbfounded. The approaching figure was plump and blond, with friendly blue eyes surmounted by a mass of gold ringlets. For a man approaching fifty, he was astonishingly youthful-looking. When he began his discourse, however, his command presence became manifest as he held the concentrated attention of his audience.

In the following years, I encountered Arleigh Burke many times, mainly because he often visited the Naval Academy, usually accompanied by his wife, Bobbie. The admiral and I served together on a panel at the Academy. At a Naval Institute dinner, my wife and I were appointed to act as hosts to the Burkes. He and I corresponded concerning a naval history textbook my colleagues and I were writing. When I published my biography of Admiral Nimitz, Burke sent me a gracious letter praising it. My wife and I were present at Burke's swearing-in as chief of naval operations and again at his relinquishment of that office.

Despite our numerous contacts, the relationship between Admiral Burke and me remained official or professional rather than social or personal. We were both fully occupied within our separate spheres, which only occasionally overlapped. Though Burke was always friendly and approachable, I kept my distance, partly because I knew he was a very busy man but mainly out of awe of his reputation and accomplishments.

When I published my biography of Admiral Halsey, I was approached by some of Admiral Burke's friends, who urged me to write the story of Burke's life. The admiral himself intimated that he would welcome such an undertaking. It was a tempting project. Burke was the world's most famous living naval officer, sometimes called a living legend. His life story was one of great variety and interest, in every respect worthy of emulation and of the widest publicity.

However, I had misgivings about writing a biography of a living person. Years earlier I had come under sharp criticism for my published comments on the wartime decisions or operations of officers still alive. I wanted no repeat of that experience, nor did I want to risk writing an "authorized" biography, one in which a person or persons besides myself would control, or attempt to control, what I wrote.

I need not have worried. On my own initiative, I sent each chapter as completed to the Burkes, and Bobbie read it to Arleigh, whose eyesight was failing. They limited their participation to encouragement, pointing out errors of fact, and in a couple of instances correcting my nautical phraseology.

So active and varied was Burke's career that a detailed story of his
life and work, based on his immense accumulation of papers, could
fill several volumes. I chose to write instead a selective, one-volume
biography. I hoped thus to attract general readers, acquainting them
with Arleigh Burke's character, his major achievements, and his
contributions to the navy and to his country. I wanted also to tell
them what I had learned about Bobbie Burke's far-from-inconsider-
able contributions toward Arleigh's accomplishments.

CONTENTS

MAPS
AND
DIAGRAMS

ADMIRAL
ARLEIGH
BURKE

EARLY YEARS
OF AN
AMERICAN
VIKING

ARLEIGH BURKE, famed destroyerman, carrier officer, and chief of naval operations, was born a thousand miles from the sea on a hardscrabble farm at the foot of the Rocky Mountains. His paternal grandfather, Anders Björkgren, apprenticed to a baker in Göteborg, Sweden, earned his journeyman's papers and in 1857, at the age of twenty-three, emigrated to the United States. Here, finding his American friends had difficulty pronouncing his surname, he changed it to Burke and adopted August for a new first name, all without benefit of legal process. As plain Gus Burke he attached himself as cook to a U.S. cavalry unit and journeyed west, at length fetching up in the pioneer town of Denver, Colorado. Here he met and married Mary Jane Harding, and together they established a bakery, the first in the area.

When they had acquired an adequate stake, Gus and Mary settled on a homestead near Boulder and took to farming while fighting grasshoppers and drought. They raised six children, four boys and two girls. The second son, Oscar, tried his luck as a cowboy and a gold miner before acquiring a wife and a homestead of his own.

Oscar's bride was Clara Mokler, a teacher in the grade school at Boulder. She joined him on the farm, which prospered. Their first-born arrived on 19 October 1901, a blond, blue-eyed boy, whom they christened Arleigh Albert. The name Arleigh was Clara's invention, probably derived from Raleigh—Sir Walter, that is. Five more

Burke children, four girls and a boy, were born on the family farm during the next eighteen years.

A few months before Arleigh's birth, Oscar contributed land on which he and his neighbors built a red brick schoolhouse. Named Baseline Elementary School, it consisted of one room, divisible into two by a sliding partition. At first one teacher taught all eight grades.

When Arleigh was ready to enter Baseline, more than a score of older children were enrolled there. He was by this time a handsome little fellow, his head covered with a mass of blond ringlets. Clara's teacher's instinct had long since told her that this boy was something special—quick, observant, and very, very bright. She was determined that he should have an education commensurate with his gifts. In a holiday mood she sent him off for his first day at Baseline School decked out in a Little Lord Fauntleroy suit, complete with white lace collar. His classmates were not favorably impressed. Arleigh, returning home for lunch with his suit muddied and his collar ripped off, demanded overalls. His father looked him over.

"You've been in a fight?"

"Yes, sir."

"Did you win?"

"No, sir."

"In that case," said Oscar, "I'll teach you to defend yourself."

While Oscar set about developing his son's combat-readiness, Clara devoted herself to nurturing his intellect. Under her tutelage he had already in his preschool days begun identifying printed words. At Baseline, stimulated by the competition of his fellow students, he made rapid progress and early began reading in his free time, mostly adventure stories. Clara, ambitious to have him read more substantial fare, obtained a library card for him, and each Saturday when family members went to town for shopping, she had him draw books. She encouraged him to read at least two a week, and when he had read three books of his own choosing, she insisted that he alternate with three she chose for him, often with the willing advice of his teachers. Thus she gradually raised his intellectual appetite so that his own selection of reading material steadily matured.

Oscar never interrupted his children's schooling, but before and after school each day and during vacations he expected each to do his share of farm work—endless, exhausting labor in the days before mechanization. Oscar assigned not only chores but times of completion, and no assignment was to be left unfinished. He thus imparted to his son the habit of systematic fulfillment of tasks.

Though the Burke youngsters worked hard under a demanding taskmaster, their lives were far from joyless. After supper and on weekends there was time for play. In the autumn a favorite game was constructing tepees of cornstalks and arranging the tepees into Indian villages. The Burkes, moreover, were a family of circus buffs. Whenever a circus came to Boulder, the taskmaster declared a holiday and took the whole family to town to watch the morning parade and attend the afternoon performance.

The Burke family also made much of holidays. The Fourth of July was an occasion for a picnic or a feast with homemade ice cream, followed by an afternoon in town, where the children played games, the women visited and chatted, and the men listened to patriotic oratory in the courthouse square. At Thanksgiving and Christmas the Burkes held open house, with bountiful meals for friends and relatives. On such occasions Oscar was likely to enliven the occasion with songs learned in his cowboy days, while Clara played the pedal-pump organ.

The Burkes were always glad to have company for dinner, but Clara was occasionally dismayed when her husband insisted upon inviting to the table passing peddlers and itinerant laborers hired for temporary jobs on the farm. Oscar's hospitality and openhandedness, however, never extended to extravagance. He shunned wastefulness and kept out of debt, rules of conduct reinforced by Clara, who managed the family's finances. Oscar used to boast, "I've got land, I've got kids, and I owe no man a dime."

The elder Burkes set a high standard of reliability for their children and held them sternly accountable for honesty in words and action. Just how sternly Arleigh learned when he was ten years old. Sent by his father one afternoon to bring home the cows from pasture, he dawdled along the way and got back late. When Oscar demanded an explanation of his tardiness, Arleigh, thinking fast, replied that he had stopped to mend a broken fence. That seemed reasonable enough, but some time later when father and son were in the pasture together, the elder Burke wanted to inspect the repairs. The boy admitted that he had nothing to show him. Having thus caught his son in a lie, Oscar on the spot gave the boy a whaling he never forgot.

A rare instance of irresponsibility brought Arleigh another licking. It was on a job he held toward the end of his years at Baseline.

For a dollar a month he served as schoolhouse janitor—emptying the trash baskets, cleaning the classrooms, and during the winter months tending the furnace and monitoring the steam radiators. One day somebody turned off the radiator in the cloakroom, and that was the radiator Arleigh neglected to check. As a result the pipes froze and burst. For this negligence Oscar again applied the rod. He paid to have the damage repaired, but made Arleigh reimburse him at the rate of fifty cents a month—half his salary.

In the spring of 1915, Arleigh's sojourn at Baseline came to an end. The relatives of the outgoing eighth-graders gathered to sit impatiently listening to erudite oratory by the county school superintendent, who then handed diplomas to young Burke and his fellow graduates. The ceremony was followed by a picnic on the chautauqua grounds and a baseball game between fathers and sons. The boys won.

That fall Arleigh enrolled at the high school in Boulder. From the farm he went to school by horseback, leaving his mount during the day in a nearby stable. Around the first of every month, on each of two days, Arleigh and his horse arrived in Boulder with a bale of hay, one for the horse and one for the horse's rent.

While still at Baseline, Arleigh had decided that farming with its tedium, frustrations, and dirt was not how he wanted to spend his life. His parents agreed that he should prepare to make better use of his talents. One probable means was at hand, the University of Colorado at Boulder. The Burkes had little cash for college expenses, but Arleigh could save money by living at home and continue riding to town on horseback.

To help his son earn money for future college expenses, Oscar gave him free time to work for pay on neighboring farms. Arleigh also trapped muskrats along Bear and Boulder creeks. He cleaned, stretched, and dried the skins and sent them to furriers in Denver, St. Louis, and Chicago, who paid a dollar for each acceptable pelt. The sums thus earned and put aside mounted so slowly that Arleigh wondered if he would be able to go to college after all.

Clara Burke was worried about Arleigh's association with the itinerant farm laborers, often rough, illiterate men. His closest contact with them came in the spring cleaning of the irrigation ditches, which in the course of a year became choked with sand, soil, and debris. Each ditch had to be emptied by temporary damming and then plowed down to its original depth to loosen the accumulated sediment, which then had to be shoveled out. Such hard labor formed a temporary bond among the laborers working shoulder to shoulder. A few days in the ditches were likely to infect Arleigh with a little of his coworkers' rough speech and manner. Clara began to wonder if her son might be better off leaving the farm and boarding at a more distant college where he would not associate with such rough fellows.

That was more than the Burkes could afford, but Arleigh came up with an apparent solution—West Point. There the students got free board and tuition and also received a small salary. The catch was that half the smart young fellows in Colorado at one time or another had their eyes on West Point. This had been true ever since the Indian wars, which brought to the state an army officered mostly by Military Academy graduates. These were impressive men, whom the boys had sought to emulate. The Indian wars were long over, but the old folks remembered and discussed them and the distinguished officers. Their reminiscences helped to steer Arleigh's reading toward military history and his ambitions toward a military career. The crowning stimulus was the ongoing World War I, in which some of Arleigh's only slightly older friends were serving as soldiers.

On inquiry Arleigh learned that the usual way to get into West Point was to be appointed by a congressman and then pass an entrance examination. To obtain such an appointment it helped to have political connections. The Burke family had no such connections, but their friend and neighbor Charlie Wilson did. He obtained an interview for Arleigh with the incumbent congressman of the district, Charles B. Timberlake. The congressman, an old gentleman, received Burke graciously but had nothing to offer him. His appointments to West Point, current and for some time to come, he said, were all filled or promised.

One of Arleigh's teachers, learning of his disappointment, inquired if he had asked Congressman Timberlake about an appointment to Annapolis. She explained that Annapolis was the navy's equivalent of the army's West Point, their actual titles being The U.S. Military Academy, located at West Point, and The U.S. Naval Academy, located at Annapolis. Both provided a college education at government expense. Arleigh promptly wrote a letter to the congressman, asking for an appointment to Annapolis. Again he was turned down. Timberlake had promised service academy appointments years ahead to sons of men and women who had done or could do him political favors.

In the late spring of 1918, on completing his junior year in high school, Arleigh took whatever jobs he could get, hoping against the odds to save enough money to enter college in the autumn of 1919. At the end of summer, however, Timberlake's naval appointees for the following year withdrew, and the congressman announced that his Annapolis appointments for 1919 were open. Any young man in his district, age sixteen to twenty-two, in good health and of good moral character, would be permitted to take the entrance examination, and Timberlake would appoint the two top scorers.

Arleigh was ecstatic. He signed up for the examination, to be conducted in April 1919. He promised himself that during his senior year in high school, in order to get ready, he would hit the books as never before. Then his hopes were dashed. At the height of the terrible 1918–19 influenza pandemic, which took twenty million lives worldwide, every public school and most private schools in the United States were closed for several months.

From his apparently hopeless situation, Arleigh was rescued by some of his high school teachers, among whom he had been a favorite. Three dedicated women instructors, having now no classes to teach, took him in hand and through the fall of 1918 drilled him in the subjects on which he would be examined. On their advice, he planned to finish off his instruction by attending one of the prep schools established specifically to get candidates ready to take the service academy entrance examinations.

Most of the prep schools for the Naval Academy were in or near the city of Annapolis, but on inquiry Arleigh learned of one closer, in Columbia, Missouri, and cheaper than most, one hundred dollars a month. Shortly after Christmas he headed for Columbia, his first long train ride, a 700-mile overnight journey. The school, he learned, was taught by a former congressman and his daughter. The course would last three months, ending just before the nationwide April examination.

After paying his $300 tuition fee, Arleigh had to find some way to stretch the amount he had left. He finally worked a deal with a boardinghouse that catered to Columbia College students. In exchange for kitchen and general cleaning work, he got room and board at a rate he could just barely afford.

The Columbia prep school course was no intellectual banquet. It consisted mainly of studying old Naval Academy entrance examinations. The exams, prepared by the Naval Academy faculty, consisted of math problems to be solved and questions to be answered in science, geography, and history. The format had not been changed in many years, and any question was likely to reappear in later examinations. The prep schools obtained copies of old exams and had their students take them one at a time. The instructor would then read aloud the various answers, point out errors, and discuss how the answers might be improved.

Thus when the candidate came to be examined for entrance, the examination handed him had a familiar look and probably contained questions he had answered in prep school. The schools, requiring no erudite, high-salaried instructors, thrived on the system and made their owners money. When West Point and Annapolis belatedly adopted a less primitive type of entrance examination, most of the prep schools couldn't cope and promptly folded—and fewer incapable young men entered the academies.

His cram course completed, Arleigh, feeling ill prepared to meet the coming ordeal, took the long train ride back to Colorado. Entrance examinations for the service academies were to be taken all over the country on the same day. Congressman Timberlake's candidates were to take them in the post office in Boulder. In later years Burke modestly attributed his success to very unusual weather. The evening before examination day, it began to snow—rare for Colorado in April, except in the mountains.

"Son," said Oscar, "you'd better get on your horse and get into town. You might not be able to make it in the morning."

Oscar was right. It turned out to be a bad storm, but Arleigh made it to Boulder, put his horse in a livery stable, and then to save money slept in the stable with the horse. The deep snow next morning deterred some candidates; not all were willing to make the journey for a long shot that would reward only two Annapolis appointees out of a considerable slate.

To Burke, not only was the 1919 entrance exam familiar in form, but about a third of the questions were ones he had seen before, and he had more or less memorized the answers. He felt a little like a cheat, but the prep course was lawful, accepted, and available to anyone with $300 and train fare, and it had paid off. Nevertheless, Burke doubted he had won one of Timberlake's two appointments until the good news arrived by mail. Then one of the first things he did was visit and thank the three teachers who had helped make his victory possible.

The good news was followed by bad. Oscar developed a fever, with spots on his face and body. The family doctor examined him and then drew Arleigh and his mother aside. He knew, of course, about the boy's appointment and that he was due to leave for Annapolis within a couple of weeks. He now advised Arleigh to leave at once. He wasn't sure, but Oscar appeared to have smallpox. If so, he would have to put the whole family under extended quarantine.

The normally unflappable Clara almost panicked—anxious about her husband's health and wondering where to find more money for her son. It had been difficult enough to provide his trainfare to Annapolis and the $350 down payment for his uniforms and textbooks. Clara now could scrape together only a little extra money, but Arleigh said he could make do with it.

Burke made the two-day trip to Washington by coach, managing a little sleep sitting up and subsisting mainly on handouts from Red Cross booths set up in railway stations to assist servicemen. From Washington he traveled by interurban rail to Annapolis and took quarters outside the Academy gates in one of the rooming houses catering to visitors. That left him so little money that Burke was a very hungry young man when his reporting date rolled around on 26 June 1919. By then he had heard from his mother and learned that his father's ailment was not smallpox but chicken pox.

Meanwhile Arleigh had thoroughly explored the Academy grounds. He never forgot his first view as he entered through what was then the main gate, with the academic group of buildings on his left and the impressive spread of Bancroft Hall, the dormitory, on his right—all constructed of granite and gray brick in monumental French Renaissance style. At the gate the gray-haired civilian guard, noting the gleam in Arleigh's eyes that proclaimed him a prospective midshipman who could hardly wait to report in, gave him a bit of avuncular advice: "Keep your back straight and your mouth shut. There's no room for wise guys at this Academy."

The great day finally arrived. Burke, after taking the oath that made him one of 709 new midshipmen, visited the Academy barber shop and had most of his curly blond hair clipped off. He next was issued "white works," a loose, pajamalike uniform with his name stenciled across the chest and a white sailor's cap edged in blue. Later he would receive an officer-type cap and more formal white service and navy blue uniforms.

The preliminaries attended to, the rigorous routine of plebe summer began. It was conducted mainly by junior naval and marine officers, including members of the Academy class of 1920, which through an accelerated wartime program had graduated in June 1919. These live-wire young officer instructors set out briskly to shape the rough material placed in their hands into acceptable facsimiles of midshipmen.

Under their exacting tutelage, Arleigh quickly learned to salute and say "sir" to his seniors and to respond to verbal orders with a prompt "Aye, aye, sir." He absorbed the basic naval traditions and the Academy concept of honor, which did not tolerate lying, cheating, or stealing. He learned to stand and sit straighter than ever before. He developed the habit of calling a floor—any floor—a deck, a wall a bulkhead, a ceiling an overhead, a stairway a ladder, and so on with the rest of the naval terms for familiar things. With his fellow plebes (freshmen) he marched everywhere, often shouting navy slogans. Under the hot summer sun, hour after hour he went through the intricacies of military drill.

The heat, the discomforts, the tough routine, and the stern discipline were expected to accustom the midshipmen to facing menacing situations and solving formidable problems. "This is a tough school," the young military instructors barked at them. "No skylarking. No funny business. Around here you've got to work. If you don't work, your throat's cut. There's no sympathy for you. You've got to be able to do what's expected of you, or you're out." In classrooms the professors conveyed the same message, albeit in cooler language.

It all proved too much for some of the plebes, who resigned and went back home. That was part of the system—to eject men who would make a greater contribution as civilians than as warriors. As for Arleigh, he found the Naval Academy, plebe summer and all, entirely to his liking. He was accustomed to strict accountability and to hard labor under a hot sun. He wanted to compete, he said later, "in just such an organization, in which the rules were strict, known, and observed."

What worried Arleigh was classwork. A country boy with only three years of small-town high school, he would be competing with much better prepared young men. These included graduates of big-city high schools and famous private schools. A fair number had been to college, and a few had bachelor degrees.

There had been some classwork in the summer, but the full curriculum got under way only in early September with the return to Annapolis of the upperclassmen. Then the fast-stepping summer drills were in part replaced by classwork and study periods. Outside of academic routine and athletics the plebes followed military regulations as before, but there was a difference. Burke missed the precision with which the summer duties had been carried out.

The Naval Academy, normally a temple of orderliness, was in some disorder. The regiment of midshipmen, having expanded threefold in the past three years, now numbered well over 2,000. Two new wings recently added to Bancroft Hall could house the additional men, but the rapid expansion coupled with the accelerated wartime curriculum had disrupted routines. Captain Archibald H. Scales, recently appointed superintendent specifically to lead the Academy back to normal, proved not up to the assignment.

Hazing, forbidden at the Academy by federal law but never entirely suppressed, had taken a nasty turn, with upperclassmen paddling plebes with broomsticks. Burke was spared that humiliation, possibly because would-be paddlers were discouraged by his large size and muscular build. Other indignities, such as being required to perform push-ups, Arleigh accepted with such grace that hazers generally sought less good-natured victims.

Proponents of such initiation rites, common in civilian as well as military schools of the period, claimed that they were needed to instill discipline. At the Military and Naval academies advocates argued that hazing was also an indispensable method for weeding out those psychologically unsuited to command in the armed services.

Burke, normally cheerful and friendly, was afflicted all his life with occasional spells of depression. During his first year at the Naval Academy these dark hours were intensified by homesickness and the sheer monotony of a plebe's existence. He was rarely allowed to venture outside the Academy gates, and he enjoyed few diversions inside.

Plebes were not permitted to attend the Academy's formal weekend balls. Their social life was largely confined to occasional Saturday- or Sunday-afternoon informal plebe hops, attended by an approved list of young ladies, usually local or from the Washington or Baltimore area. At the first few such gatherings Burke danced with different girls but made no lasting attachments.

For him the situation changed abruptly one weekend. His roommate, Bernard Duncan, had a Washington girlfriend, Annanora Gorsuch, who usually came over for the plebe informals. On one such visit she brought along her younger sister, Roberta, and Duncan asked Burke to see to it that "Bobbie" Gorsuch was properly entertained.

Arleigh and Bobbie made an odd couple. He was a big Swede, blond, blue-eyed, broad-shouldered, his rustic manners and plowman's lumbering gait not yet remedied by Annapolis. She, a brown-eyed brunette, the essence of daintiness, was a tiny creature, a little over five feet tall, weighing less than a hundred pounds.

Despite their differences, or perhaps at least partly because of them, they were attracted to each other. Her shyness, however, and his new lack of self-confidence proved impediments to lively conversation. Anyone overhearing their dialogue at this first meeting would scarcely have guessed that forty years later they would together host social gatherings that Washington's notables looked forward to attending or that Bobbie would be noted for her wit, sharp and sometimes sly but never malicious.

As a plebe, Burke was not allowed to "drag" (have dates), but when Bobbie visited the Naval Academy he managed to spend most of his time with her. At last, in June, on the eve of graduation day, the plebe restrictions were removed, and Arleigh attended the Farewell Ball with Bobbie on his arm as his acknowledged girlfriend.

With the graduation of the first classmen (seniors), the plebes became "youngsters" (sophomores), but they changed their shoulder marks only after a well-rehearsed group of them had climbed the Herndon monument and retrieved a cap that upperclassmen had placed there. This was no small achievement, because the monument was a smooth granite obelisk some 25 feet high. The plebes conquered it by joining arms in a series of rings around it, each standing on the shoulders of the ring below. In Burke's day, the upperclassmen had not yet fiendishly complicated the effort by greasing the monument and gluing the cap on top.

Out in Chesapeake Bay, in sight of the Naval Academy, a fleet of six battleships, *Minnesota, South Carolina, Connecticut, New Hampshire, Michigan,* and *Kansas,* lay at anchor prepared to take the midshipmen on their annual summer cruise. For Burke and his fellow youngsters this was to be a new and thrilling experience they had looked forward to for months.

The midshipmen were assigned duties that made them an integral part of the crews. Arleigh, with the hard luck that trailed him for some time, drew fireroom duty, an enlisted man's billet. It meant shoveling coal, which left him filthy, and tending boilers, which left him both sooty and bathed in sweat. He got the job because he was big and strong. He accepted it with pride, because he knew that not all midshipmen could stand it day after day. He also accepted it philosophically, because it taught him what it takes to make a big ship move and made him more tolerant of hardworking bluejackets.

After the ships transited the Panama Canal, Burke had his first liberty in the Port of Panama, which in his opinion had little to offer besides temporary relief from his black-gang stoking labors. Honolulu, however, was an entirely different proposition. The city was primed for the mids. As their ships rounded Diamond Head and paraded past the beaches of Waikiki, army and navy planes dropped on their decks leis of red and yellow flowers. The city received the visitors with open arms, sparing no pains to make their brief stay memorable.

Recrossing the eastern Pacific, the midshipmen continued cultivating their seagoing skills, and Burke and other unfortunates kept shoveling coal. Reaching the West Coast, the mids sampled the attractions of Seattle, San Francisco, Los Angeles, and San Diego, then steamed back through the canal and headed northward to Annapolis for a month's leave.

Back at the Naval Academy, Midshipman Burke paused only long enough to stow his gear and don civvies. Then he was away by train for Colorado. Clara and Oscar, waiting at home to greet their son, noted with pride the dignity of manner he had acquired to match the military bearing that by now had completely obliterated his plowman's gait. At their suggestion he wore his white service uniform with the stiff high collar and shoulder marks when making his duty calls and also when he escorted a local young lady to a Grange dance.

Whether the uniformed midshipman stirred any romantic interests among the young females of the Boulder area is not recorded. As for Burke himself, it is clear that his heart remained in the East. He had corresponded with Bobbie Gorsuch while on the cruise, and he wrote to her from Colorado. His letters were friendly, interesting, and informative, but they did little to further his courtship. Arleigh had not yet learned to express himself intimately, and it did not help when he signed himself "A. A. Burke."

In September 1920, Burke returned to Annapolis, rejoining his friends of the youngster class. High on their plan of operations was "initiating" the new crop of plebes into the regiment. Wanting to inflict as much rough treatment as they had endured, they early brought broomsticks into play against the posteriors of hapless plebes ordered to "assume the position." Burke protested such de-grading treatment. He did not altogether oppose hazing, but he thought it should be constructive, such as making the plebe exercise or memorize something or do some work that improved his naval knowledge or skills.

Keenly aware of the intellectual competition he had to meet, Burke never neglected his studies. His grades were consistently above average, but to keep them there he had, as he said, "to work like hell." He managed, however, to keep his activities in balance. In sports he engaged in boxing, fencing, and wrestling. He attended balls and other social activities, as often as possible with Bobbie. Visiting the Gorsuch home in Washington, he was treated to a concert by the three daughters, Bobbie playing the violin, her sisters the harp and flute.

When Burke attended the Naval Academy, most midshipmen acquired nicknames, which sometimes clung to them throughout their careers. Arleigh was no exception. In his plebe year, upper-classmen had saddled him with the name Satchel, with some vague reference to his ample fanny. The following year the famous movie star Billie Burke visited the Academy. Thereupon Arleigh's fellow mids dropped Satchel for Billie, a change of nickname Arleigh was glad to accept.

"Billie" was thenceforth the name with which he signed his let-ters to Bobbie, certainly an improvement. The letters were getting less stiff, too. In one he sent her in mid-January 1921, he began: "Dear Bobbie, The more I say that name the better I like it so don't be surprised if I keep repeating it when you come again."

A few days later he did still better: "Ever since Sunday, Bobbie, I've been seeing your eyes." He said he couldn't keep his mind on his duties. Thinking of her, he had gotten out of step on the parade ground and been bawled out before everybody. "I was made to realize that a man can't dream and drill at the same time."

On 1 February, Arleigh cracked his left shoulder while wrestling and went to the hospital. He had his roommate, Duncan, write Bobbie and explain why "Billie" couldn't write for a while. A week later, however, Burke was corresponding again. "I know well enough," he wrote Bobbie, "that the $210 a month of an ensign won't keep two." Not exactly a proposal, but he was raising the subject of marriage.

Arleigh was writing to Bobbie every few days. In March a letter began: "I should start with 'My fair love' but you might object and

I would be in a bad fix. Ah, I'm not romantic, I simply like you immensely." And in April: "I do love you even if I can't make you believe me. I shouldn't be very much surprised if you told me to pipe down along that line."

The midshipmen's 1921 summer cruise carried them to Europe. Their first liberty was in Christiania (soon to be renamed Oslo), which they found "neat, orderly, and busy but not hurried." The Norwegian capital, they later agreed, provided the most enjoyable stop of the summer. Burke was particularly happy to be visiting Scandinavia, home of his ancestors.

In contrast to superclean Christiania, the midshipmen found Lisbon filthy. They attended a bullfight and cheered for the bull. Next stop was Gibraltar, but to Burke's disgust his ship, dreadnought *Michigan,* remained behind in the Tagus with a fouled anchor. When at last this mishap was remedied, *Michigan* set out under forced draft and caught up with the other cruise ships just as they were dropping anchor in Gibraltar's inner harbor.

Burke now suffered a second bit of hard luck. He was assigned to shore patrol duty. He and his fellow patrolmen would be with, but not of, the liberty party. Their duty would be to oversee the midshipmen's behavior and make sure they were in the boats for return to the ships when liberty ended each day at sunset. Because the conduct of the visitors was exemplary, the shore patrol had little to do but stand around begrudging the freedom of their fellow midshipmen. Burke was particularly envious of those who took the ferry across to Tangier and came back with tales of the casbah with its narrow streets, robed men, veiled women, beggars, and little donkeys that carried on their backs monstrous loads of whatever had to be transported.

The admiral commanding the cruise was not unaware of the situation. When the shore patrol assembled on the pier the day before the scheduled departure from Gibraltar, his chief of staff announced: "We sail tomorrow morning at 0800. You fellows on shore patrol haven't had much of a liberty, so the admiral has arranged a treat for you. You will be allowed to stay ashore overnight. Reservations have been made for you at the Grand Hotel. After you've finished your duty this afternoon you can stay ashore if you wish and see Gibraltar tonight. You'll be on your own. Dismissed."

The patrolmen felt like shouting but contented themselves with broad grins. After an uneventful day, they stood on the pier at sunset watching the boatloads of midshipmen depart, gloating in the conviction that now *they* were objects of envy.

In the deepening twilight, the erstwhile shore patrolmen wandered the streets, entering the few shops still open. They dined at a restaurant, gratified at being able to order a meal of their own choosing. After dinner they wandered some more in the streets, now dark and generally deserted. They were realizing what the liberty party had found out days before, that there really wasn't much to do in Gibraltar, and the ferry to Tangier did not run in the evening. Rather earlier than they had anticipated, they turned in at the hotel, leaving orders that they were to be awakened at 0600.

The next morning, aroused, they breakfasted, shaved, bathed, and dressed and headed by foot and boat for the fleet. On their own, they had not bothered with the elementary precaution of taking muster, and nobody noticed that Midshipman Burke was absent.

Back at the hotel, Midshipman Burke woke, glanced at his wristwatch, and gasped. 0732! A check by telephone confirmed that he had grossly overslept. He threw on his clothes and practically tumbled downstairs, where he sought out the hotel manager and obtained from him a statement in writing that the blunder was the hotel's; the telephone operator had skipped Burke's name on the list of names to be called at 0600.

Thrusting the statement into the crown of his cap, Burke scooted for the harbor. What he saw from the pier tied his stomach in knots. *Michigan*, with steam up, was hauling her boats on board. Burke had a wild impulse to jump overboard and swim to the ship but scotched that recourse as too slow. Glancing wildly about, he espied secured to the pier a captain's gig. Drying off her nighttime dew was her coxswain in British sailor's uniform.

"Ahoy, the gig!" Burke shouted. "Can you set me on board *Michigan*, the U.S. battleship out there?"

"Sorry, sir," replied the coxswain. "I'm standing by for my captain."

"It'll only take five, maybe ten, minutes."

"Sorry, sir. Cap'n's orders are to pick him up at eight. He's due any minute now, sir."

Burke rapidly scrutinized the pier and adjoining shore. Nobody there. Taking a deep breath, he made a reckless, not to say outrageous, decision. "Coxswain," he said, injecting iron into his voice, "I *order* you to put me aboard *Michigan.*"

The coxswain, caught between orders to stay and orders to go, was clearly perplexed. Naval discipline had trained him to obey an officer's command without question, and only one officer was present. He made his decision.

"Why, sir," he said, "that makes things different! If you make it an order . . . well, tumble in, sir. I'll have you 'longside yon battle-ship in a shake or two."

Michigan was getting under way when the gig came alongside. Burke, clambering on board over the armor belt, proceeded at once to the bridge to report to the executive officer. The latter listened gravely to Arleigh's story, examined the hotel manager's statement, then on dismissing him quickly turned away to conceal his amuse-ment. As *Michigan* headed for the open sea, her captain apologized by flashing light to the British captain whose gig one of *Michigan*'s midshipmen had so loftily commandeered.

Later in the day Burke was startled to receive an invitation to dine that evening with the *Michigan*'s commanding officer, Captain Laws, in his quarters. Arriving in fresh whites, Arleigh was seated at table with the captain and several of the ship's senior officers. At an appropriate moment in the meal, Captain Laws asked Burke to tell the story of his last morning at Gibraltar. When Arleigh reached the part about ordering the British coxswain to deliver him to the *Michigan*, the captain and his guests nearly fell out of their chairs laughing.

During his second class (junior) year at Annapolis, Midshipman Burke won his class numerals in wrestling, one of the few distinc-tions that came his way at the Naval Academy. Anxious to have the numerals sewn on his sweater, he lost no time at all taking it to the tailor shop, which was next to the swimming-pool dressing room. The seamstress told him he could have it back by 1000 the next day. The following morning as soon as his formation for second-period class had marched back to Bancroft Hall and been dismissed, Burke made a dash for the tailor shop, taking a shortcut through the dressing room. Unfortunately, it had slipped his mind that this was ladies' day at the pool. Halfway across the room he realized he wasn't alone.

"When I looked up," he said afterward, "I saw a woman with one stocking on—and not another damned thing! And all around were others in various stages of nudity."

Leaving the room full of shrieking females behind him, he dashed through the tailor-shop door and slammed it behind him. He ex-plained his predicament to the seamstress, who, kindly soul, hid him behind a clothes rack. In due course when no posse came looking for a Peeping Tom in a midshipman's uniform, she scouted the dressing room. Finding it empty, she had Burke sign for his sweater and watched him till he had made it safely through the outside door.

Next morning the order of the day included the notice: "Will the midshipman who entered the women's dressing room about 1000 yesterday please report to the commandant"—words that threw Burke into a cold sweat. He did some quick thinking and reached the conclusion that the commandant was not especially anxious to find the errant midshipman or he would have interrogated the seamstress. On shakier grounds, he reasoned that the notice was not an order but a request. He did nothing and heard nothing more about the escapade. He noticed, however, that the outside door to the dressing room was nailed shut the next day. As of this writing, there is no door there.

The situation between Arleigh and Bobbie was settled forever during spring leave 1922, which Burke spent in Washington, chiefly with Bobbie. Of their last evening together before his return to Annapolis, he confided in a diary he was keeping, "We sat and looked at the moon ever so long."

In the weeks that followed, Arleigh and Bobby tried to see as much of each other as possible. The chief obstacle, aside from classes, was wrestling matches, in which Burke represented the Naval Academy at home and away. In his diary he confided, "If wrestling is going to interfere with my seeing Bobbie I'll give up wrestling. I may lose my numerals, but they're not worth *that* much!" During one of her visits to the Academy, Bobbie had left her watch with an Annapolis jeweler to be repaired, and Arleigh recovered it for her. "Oh," he wrote in the diary, "what a thrill I experienced when I touched it!"

In June 1922, Arleigh Burke's class of 1923 became first classmen (seniors), with all the privileges and responsibilities adhering thereto. The cruise that summer was less enjoyable, though perhaps more professionally instructive, than the two preceding ones. The midshipman were crowded into four vessels, battleships *Florida*, *Delaware*, and *North Dakota* and cruiser *Olympia*, which had been Commodore George Dewey's flagship in the Battle of Manila Bay.

The little fleet headed south through steaming heat and rain to Colón, then split up for visits to several West Indies islands, all ships finally assembling at the island of Culebra, which one mid aptly called "the 19th carbon copy of nothing." Here the midshipmen, still in oppressive heat, underwent landing drills, followed by dashes up steep, cactus-covered hills.

At last the unhappy, overheated mids cooled off in a run to the north with a stay at Halifax, Nova Scotia. All agreed that this visit was the high point of the summer. "The openhearted people had but one serious fault," noted the midshipman historian of the cruise. "It seemed positively rude and most horribly difficult to convince them and yourself that it was necessary to return to the ship."

Heading back south, the ships passed through the Virginia Capes for target practice in Lynnhaven Roads. That completed, the fleet maneuvered in Chesapeake Bay under a complete set of midshipman officers—"with an eager adviser ever-present at the respective elbows."

As a first classman, Burke was expected to take a major role in running the Naval Academy. Actually his participation was minimal. In view of the renown he richly earned during World War II and afterward, it is astonishing how little impression he made on the Academy and his fellow midshipmen. He held no rank in the regiment or office in the student body. He hoped and expected to be chosen manager of his class wrestling team and was crushed when the election went to somebody else. His classmates did not recollect him as a colorful character or an influential personality. What they did recall was that he was friendly and anxious to be helpful. Though Burke as a midshipman was in no sense a standout, he concluded his four years at the Naval Academy with the very respectable standing of seventy-first in a class reduced by resignations to 413.

Arleigh and Bobbie had long since decided that despite the poor prospects of an ensign's salary, they would not put off their wedding. They applied to the chaplains early enough to have their marriage scheduled in the Academy chapel on graduation day, 7 June 1923. Some time before that date, Arleigh received his orders for his first duty in the fleet. It was to be on board battleship *Arizona*.

Clara Burke came east to witness her son's graduation, commissioning, and wedding. Though her dresses were somewhat old-fashioned in comparison with those worn by most ladies gathering at Annapolis, they were well made and neatly fitted. She and Roberta, meeting for the first time, were cordial but reserved. There was nothing chummy about Clara. She was friendly to all but maintained her distance. If she had any special opinions about her son's marriage or choice of a bride, she kept them to herself. She had raised her son to think for himself, and now she respected his decision.

The graduation ceremony in Dahlgren Hall, then a great, bare armory, ended a little before noon. It concluded with the new graduates rising, hand upraised, to take the oath of office, Burke and most of his classmates for the navy, a smaller number for the marine corps, a few for the army. After the traditional exchange of cheers, "for those who are about to leave us" and for "those we leave behind," the new ensigns tossed caps into the air.

An hour later the chapel weddings began, each lasting about half an hour. Throughout most of the day the weather had been threatening. By the time the Burke-Gorsuch party had assembled, a thunderstorm with a heavy downpour had burst over Annapolis. The small, damp party included Bobbie's parents and two sisters, Arleigh's mother, and a few of Arleigh's classmates. During the ceremony, conducted by Chaplain Sydney Evans, the storm moved on. After the benediction the bride and groom walked the long center aisle and then down the front steps under the traditional arch of swords into a sunlit, newly bathed late afternoon.

Ensign Burke's orders authorized him to delay thirty days in reporting for duty. Thus he and his bride were vouchsafed sufficient interval for a long, lazy honeymoon. Many young officers would have made the most of the opportunity. But not Burke. He was on fire to begin serving the navy, "my navy," as he often called it. He already had railroad tickets for the long journey to the West Coast. Married life for him and Bobbie began with a three-day train ride.

2

JUNIOR OFFICER

AT THE END of their train ride across the continent, Ensign and Mrs. Burke paused in Seattle only long enough to catch the ferry to Bremerton, site of the Puget Sound Navy Yard. After crossing the sound, the ferry rounded a cape, and the Burkes caught their first glimpse of the yard—many low buildings amid a forest of cranes and derricks, with the huge broadside of *Arizona* looming over all. More than 600 feet long, displacing 33,000 tons, she would be home afloat for Arleigh Burke and over 2,000 other officers and men.

On landing, the Burkes proceeded at once to the navy yard, where Bobbie sought out the housing office, while Arleigh, tingling with excitement, made his way to *Arizona*'s wharf. Though he was not due to report till the end of the month, he went on board, identified himself to the officer of the deck, and simply explored.

Meanwhile, at the housing office, Bobbie had examined the list of apartments for rent. The Burkes, she found, were in luck. Having arrived in town ahead of schedule, they had a fairly wide choice. In addition to Bremerton's fixed population of shipyard workers and shopkeepers, the numerous navy families, usually renters, tended to come and go with the fleet. Most of the men being detached from *Arizona* had already left, and the bulk of the new arrivals were, like Ensign Burke, due to report at the end of the month.

Their stringent budget in mind, the Burkes rented a one-room apartment with a small bath attached and a bed that swung down from the wall. They were delighted to discover that a similar apartment in the opposite wing was occupied by old friends, Marge and Kenneth Walker, a young couple who like themselves were just setting up housekeeping after graduation. With the Walkers, the Burkes several times went in the early evening to the officers' club, situated on rising ground, and from the porch watched the sunset reflected off the snowcapped peak of Mt. Rainier, more than 60 miles to the southeast.

Though their Bremerton apartment was tiny and uncomfortable, Arleigh and Bobbie always remembered it with affection as their first home together. Arleigh celebrated their venture into housekeeping with a gift to his bride—*The Boston Cookbook,* a rather more practical token, thought Bobbie, than might have been anticipated on so sentimental an occasion.

Throughout the navy, the last day of June saw officers arriving for new assignments. Ensign Burke's entire Naval Academy class reported for sea duty that day. Fifteen of these freshly minted ensigns were assigned to each of the navy's battleships except the new *Colorado* and *West Virginia,* not yet commissioned, which received twenty apiece.

Among the older officers joining the Battle Fleet, which included *Arizona,* was Commander Chester W. Nimitz, fresh from the Naval War College at Newport, Rhode Island. He reported for duty as tactical officer on board fleet flagship *California* at about the same time Ensign Burke was reporting on board *Arizona.* Even inexperienced Burke would become aware of Nimitz's presence if not of his identity.

Right away Ensign Burke began getting assignments that would have discouraged a less determined and dedicated junior officer. He was given no fireroom duty this time, as in his youngster cruise, but the executive officer, looking him over and noting his size, apparent strength, and air of authority, assigned him to Division 4, to which all hard-case enlisted men were sent to be punished, straightened out, or otherwise dealt with. Second, he and about a dozen other freshly minted ensigns were assigned cots in the crew's quarters.

In late July, *Arizona* moved out into the sound and joined the Battle Fleet in time to participate in a salute to President Warren G. Harding, who had stopped in Seattle on returning from Alaska on a national tour. While the president stood at the bow of transport *Henderson,* the twelve battleships of the fleet filed past, each firing twenty-one guns. The fleet's flag officers then visited *Henderson* to pay a courtesy call on Mr. Harding and subsequently rode in the president's motorcade and heard his speech. Returning to their ships, they reported that Harding looked unwell and that his address had been poorly delivered. In fact, Harding was in a state of shock from having received information of corruption among friends he had imprudently appointed to high office.

After proceeding by train to San Francisco, the president became too ill to continue his tour. He died there on 2 August. When news of his death reached the fleet, all ships' colors were half-masted and flagship *California* fired a mourning gun every half hour the remainder of the day. For the next thirty days, officers and men of the fleet wore crepe on the sleeves of their dress uniforms.

The Battle Fleet regularly held summer maneuvers in the Puget Sound area. The presence of the big navy yard was a convenience, and the crews enjoyed the cool weather and relished the hospitality accorded them in Seattle, Bellingham, Tacoma, and Port Angeles. The citizens at these ports opened their homes and clubs to the officers and organized dances, barbecues, and picnics for the blue-jackets—all in eager anticipation of the boost to the local economies afforded by the visiting sailors' generous off-loading of the fleet's payroll.

For the senior officers, however, these amenities were more than offset by problems of the physical environment. Swift currents, poor holding ground, fog, and smoke from forest fires presented conditions in which loss of or damage to ships could be avoided only by constant alertness. Hence the fleet's captains and flag officers breathed more easily when on schedule at the end of August they transited Juan de Fuca Strait and rounded Cape Flattery, heading for San Francisco and then points farther south.

Bobbie Burke went directly by passenger steamer to San Pedro, home port of the battleship divisions. San Pedro and nearby Long Beach were the fleet's bedrooms. When officers and enlisted men drew Battle Fleet duty their wives or families usually made their homes in one or the other. This time Bobbie had to do considerable walking to find furnished quarters the Burkes could afford. For want of anything better, she finally rented a dark little furnished apartment in a shabby San Pedro neighborhood. The landlady showed her a photograph of the household china, with cracks clearly marked, and cautioned her that if any further cracks appeared the Burkes would be duly charged.

South of San Francisco there was no port spacious enough to

harbor battleships or any navy yard capable of servicing them. While the Battle Fleet's smaller vessels continued on toward San Diego, where they could be adequately berthed, the battlewagons turned landward at San Pedro and anchored outside the breakwater. Retaining minimum caretaker crews on board, they sent the rest of the men ashore in liberty boats. Bobbie, who made it her business to keep track of *Arizona*'s movements, was waiting to embrace her ensign. For Arleigh the dark little apartment was home enough when blessed by the presence of his adored Bobbie.

In fact, at San Pedro the Burkes were able to set up something like normal housekeeping, because the fleet was keeping regular hours. The battleships would leave their anchorage in the morning for maneuvers or target practice, often in conjunction with cruisers and destroyers out of San Diego. They would usually be back at anchor by 1630 with only the duty section remaining on board, and they seldom went to sea on weekends.

The fleet was thus deliberately curtailing its operations so as to allow its sailors more time with their families. This compromise with domesticity, deplored by some of the senior officers, resulted from congressional penny-pinching. Congress had in fact imposed such strict economy on the navy that its ships were undermanned. But this was a period of national prosperity, with plenty of jobs ashore. The naval service had to be made attractive enough to encourage sailors to ship over when their enlistments ended, or else the manpower shortage would get worse.

So far as Bobbie was concerned, the fact that their San Pedro quarters were conveniently near the boat landing did not compensate for its shortcomings. She soon began looking for something less seedy that they could afford, and she found another miniature apartment in the slightly less inelegant Long Beach. Her husband fully approved the move, neither he nor she taking seriously the local saying "If you love your husband, you live in San Pedro. If he loves you, you live in Long Beach."

Arleigh began hinting that Bobbie might make fuller use of *The Boston Cookbook* by inviting a few of his bachelor shipmates to dinner. With some trepidation, Bobbie welcomed them. They proved agreeable company, but Bobbie was taken aback when she heard one of them say to Arleigh, "How can you bear to leave the ship and come all the way out here every night?"

Out on maneuvers, Ensign Burke, thanks to Commander Nimitz's influence, was vouchsafed a preview of the circular formation, which had been developed at the War College. In a circle, except for ships directly ahead, astern, or abeam of the guide, keeping on station was a delicate, time-consuming task requiring almost constant changes of course and speed. At night, without radar, not yet invented, keeping on station in concentric circles was considered impossible and an invitation to collision. It is safe to say that in the fall of 1923 few officers of the Battle Fleet foresaw that the circular formation would in time become standard, particularly for daylight cruising.

The public was now being made aware of the scandals that had apparently hastened, if not caused, President Harding's untimely death. Nowhere were the exposés more avidly discussed than at San Pedro and Long Beach, because they concerned the navy, naval officials, and the deceased president with whom the Battle Fleet had recently had some contact. Secretary of the Navy Edwin Denby, though not accused of corruption, was hounded out of office for allegedly not having safeguarded the navy's interests with sufficient vigilance.

The Battle Fleet carried out maneuvers in the San Pedro–San Diego area only in autumn and spring. For winter operations it usually transferred to the waters off Panama or near the island of Culebra in the Caribbean Sea. Thus at the end of 1923 when the ongoing exercises were completed, the Burkes' Long Beach idyll was suspended. The lovers would be parted for several months, a prospect they dreaded.

When Arleigh learned that *Arizona* was scheduled to visit New York City in March, he and Bobbie hatched a scheme. She would move out of the little apartment, take a train to Washington, and winter there with her parents. When on leave from his ship, Arleigh would join her briefly, either in Washington or New York. Such an arrangement would break their long separation and give their budget some relief.

The twelve battleships left San Pedro on the first day of 1924, joined the cruisers and destroyers at sea, and proceeded westward far into the Pacific, then turned southeast and on 17 January transited the Panama Canal. In the Caribbean Sea the Battle Fleet joined forces with the Scouting Fleet. The latter, based on the East Coast, was built around the five oldest battleships of the U.S. Navy, veterans of 1910–12. Since these ships were smaller and less heavily armed than the West Coast heavy ships, the Scouting Fleet was less powerful than any one of the three four-battleship divisions of the Battle

Fleet. This disparity of force reflected the navy's emphasis on Pacific Ocean operations, and that in turn was based on the widely held conviction that with Germany defeated and apparently prostrate, the only likely antagonist the U.S. Navy would meet in any future war was Japan.

The combined fleet now participated with U.S. forces ashore in Joint Army and Navy Problem II, testing the defenses of the Canal Zone. A novelty of this operation was the participation of the navy's first and only aircraft carrier, little *Langley*, converted from a collier.

Arleigh was writing to Bobbie almost daily, though he knew his letters might take weeks to reach her. In them he poured out his love, his longing, and his loneliness without her. At the head of a letter dated 7 February he underlined the figure 7, the date of the preceding June when their wedding had taken place. "Dearest Wife," he began.

> Eight months ago, Dear, was the happiest day of my life. It was then that I waited in the chapel for my bride. It was a long time ago in my memories—there is a feeling as if we had been married for a long time. I miss you so very much when I am away and I am so happy when I am with you. Our wedding was not far enough away for me to forget even the slightest incident. That day is indelibly impressed on my memory. I am given to memories tonight for the mail didn't come and I am very disappointed. I should not have [been] so optimistic. I'm more than merely lonesome—but, honey, there is no way to tell you. You'll understand—I love you so much and being away hurts a lot. . . . Tonight I feel very close to you as if you wanted me there. Oh, how I wish I could be. . . .

Despite his spells of loneliness whenever he was away from Bobbie, Ensign Burke had acquired a reputation for both sunny friendliness and diligent efficiency. And as happened time and time again in his career, his hard work and effectiveness earned him not relief but tougher jobs. In the 1924 winter operations the tougher job was the task of inspecting, cleaning, and scraping rust from *Arizona's* double bottoms.

That was one of the duties regularly assigned to junior officers. It meant leading a working party down through a manhole into a compartment between the two hulls at the bottom of the ship. In this damp, dark space, with overhead so low one could not stand erect, they searched with portable lights for rust spots, which when found had to be scraped down to the bare metal and painted over. If there was much of this to do, the paint fumes in the enclosed space became sickening. In the circumstances, the officers responsible tended to inspect infrequently and get the inspections over with as hastily as possible. Hence when the admiral made his unannounced inspections he almost always found unscraped, unpainted rust spots, spots that could spread and eat through the steel hull.

One of the compartments, the ship's first lieutenant noted, was always free of corrosion, and a check showed it was the compartment for which Ensign Burke was responsible. The first lieutenant thereupon conferred on Burke, as a reward for his dependability, the dubious distinction of serving as permanent double-bottoms inspector for the whole ship. That meant keeping rust-free all the compartments from broadside to broadside and from stem to stern. On being notified of this assignment, Arleigh's face fell.

The first lieutenant said, "You don't like that job, do you?"

"No, sir."

"Why don't you like it?"

"It's one of the dirtiest, hardest jobs in the ship, and I don't see why I was assigned to do all the double bottoms."

The first lieutenant said, "You understand that those jobs have to be done."

"I understand, but not why I get so many of them."

"You will continue to get them, because those tough, demanding jobs are frequently the most important ones."

Arleigh recognized that the first lieutenant had paid him a compliment, albeit a left-handed one. He had also forecast Burke's whole naval career.

The work party of enlisted men sent to the double bottoms were tough fellows. Unlike Burke, who had been assigned to this dirty job because he did it well, the men were ordered down as a penalty for getting into trouble. Thus Burke was warden and overseer as well as officer in charge. Under his broader assignment, when he and his grudging workmen had made a compartment shipshape, they did not ascend to fresh air and light of day but proceeded to the next dark, stinking compartment by removing a watertight cover from a hole in the bulkhead and wriggling through.

It was a perfect stinker of a job, but Burke came to regard it with mixed feelings. After all, it was handed him in recognition of his efficiency, it was one hell of a challenge, and down here he was boss. In this black underworld he was the sole and reigning Pluto.

Burke insisted that his men keep steadily at work while they were down below, but when the paint fumes became stifling, he sent them topside a few at a time to catch a breath of air. He himself, though sometimes near suffocation, never left the job, thereby demonstrating his toughness and gaining a psychological ascendancy over the men.

"I am riding my men in the double bottoms," he wrote Bobbie. "They think I'm a slave driver. I worked them today until they were all in. Naturally they don't consider the fact that I stayed down there all the time while they came up for blows. They worked hard today, and if I can make them keep it up, all of my parts of the ship will be up to standard by admiral's inspection."

Luckily for Ensign Burke, inspecting the double bottoms, even all compartments, was by no means a full-time job. Like other junior officers, he was given a variety of tasks as part of his training. His proudest duty was taking the conn, which meant guiding the ship through maneuvers by verbal commands to the helmsman. That was a responsibility rarely placed in the hands of an ensign. Arleigh was glad to have a more experienced officer standing by to correct his errors, if any, and to witness his skill and reliability. He felt less pride, perhaps, but enjoyed greater satisfaction as turret officer. This was a fighting job, and he was in unsupervised charge of the enlisted crew. In a war situation he and his crew would actually be dishing out punishment to the foe via the turret's 14-inch guns.

In his view, shared by most officers of this period, the battleship was the queen of naval battles, and nearly everything else in the navy afloat and ashore existed to bring her guns and torpedo tubes within striking distance of an enemy. In 1924 he would have scoffed at the notion that within his lifetime tourists would visit a monument placed over his ship, *Arizona* herself, where she lay at the bottom of Pearl Harbor, put there by attacking naval aircraft.

As the first phase of the winter exercises drew to a close, Arleigh joyfully wrote to Bobbie: "A week from today we sail for New York. Two weeks from today we drop the hook in North River. 17 days from today I shall mount the elevated bound for [Washington] and my baby girl. I'll be so happy then—to see her, to love her, kiss her, caress her, and talk to her. I'm not sure when I'll reach [Washington] but, Sweetheart, I'm depending on meeting you at the nearest gate."

On 27 February the fleet scattered to various U.S. East Coast ports to permit the crews stateside liberty. On 4 March, *Arizona* anchored in the Hudson River opposite 103rd Street. For those desiring to travel outside New York City, the nine-day visit was divided into three leave periods, and Ensign Burke drew the middle one. On Thursday, 7 March, he left his ship at the earliest permissible moment and caught the El for Pennsylvania Station. He had wired ahead, and Bobbie was waiting for him when his train reached Washington's Union Station. The following Sunday, Arleigh took a late train back to New York. He and Bobbie had had only one full day together. She had crossed the continent for that.

As *Arizona* headed back south, Arleigh wrote despairingly, "Just one day away from the shore—yet it seems like dozens since I have seen you. I have missed you more after this last leave than ever before." He had made a mistake, he wrote, in not having met her in New York. Had she come there on Thursday and taken a hotel room, they would have had all of Friday, Saturday, and Sunday together—and he would not have had to share her with her family. Of course, he knew it had been out of the question. They could not have afforded the hotel bill. Again they were restricted by his meager service income. He began considering applying for naval air for the extra pay it would bring.

Further exercises off Culebra completed, the two fleets separated, and in early April the Battle Fleet passed back through the Panama Canal and anchored off Balboa. At dawn on the 12th as the ships were raising steam for an 0730 departure for San Pedro, *Arizona* was thrown into turmoil. A wild-eyed chief radioman had reported to the officer of the deck that he had seen a woman on board.

Within minutes the ship was in pandemonium. Hastily formed search parties clambered up and down ladders and probed quarters, passageways, and engine spaces. Reports of a distantly seen fleeing female came from all over the ship. Were there a dozen women on board? It seemed more likely that in the excitement the men's imaginations were working overtime. At any rate, only one stowaway was apprehended. She was sighted by one of the engine-room watches, which took off after the prey with a mighty "Tallyho!" and soon brought her to bay.

The officer of the deck sent an ensign to awaken and report the situation to the skipper, Captain Percy Olmstead, a man not noted for patient forbearance. The unfortunate young messenger caught the first blast of the skipper's wrath, couched in loud and opprobrious language. When the captain had let off enough steam to permit intelligible speech, he sent orders to remove the woman from the ship at once, hand her over to the shore authorities, and initiate measures to find out who was responsible for getting her on board.

Ensign Burke was topside when the stowaway was brought to the quarterdeck. A pretty little brunette, she was wearing dungarees, had her hair cut like a boy's, and was sounding off in language that made Captain Olmstead's invective seem mild. She was hustled down the accommodation ladder to the ship's motorboat.

Vice Admiral Henry A. Wiley, commander battleship groups, was not amused. When he hinted that *Arizona*'s officers and crew might be denied liberty at San Pedro, the senior petty officers launched an investigation. In a nighttime kangaroo court, they found means of eliciting from enlisted suspects full details of the affair, including names of the participants. The stowaway was a nineteen-year-old prostitute named Madeline Blair, and she had been on board a full month.

While *Arizona* was at New York some of her bluejackets had become friendly with the perky little dark-eyed hooker, whom they nicknamed Blackie. The girl, perceiving an opportunity to combine business with adventure, had her hair clipped short, donned a sailor's uniform and pea jacket, and at nightfall of a cold day boarded the battleship. With collar turned up and hat turned down and flashing a stolen or faked liberty card, she got past the guard and was waved below by the officer of the deck. Her sailor friends concealed her inside a generator room, where she made herself at home and opened shop. Certain cooks who were in on the plot participated in her income by providing her with board at ten dollars a day.

As the ship plowed southward into tropical waters, Blackie began seeking relief from the heat by nighttime strolls on deck, wearing dungarees furnished by her sponsors. As long as she kept out of direct light she attracted no special attention. Emboldened by the success of her masquerade, Blackie took increasing risks, including attendance at outdoor evening movies.

One night, as she was watching the show from the after searchlight platform, a young sailor, innocently unaware that there was a female on board, sat down beside her and quickly became absorbed in the picture. He took out a cigarette and fumbled in his pockets for a match. Not finding any, he casually reached over, eyes still on the screen, and felt for matches in Blackie's breast pocket. He hastily drew back his hand. "What I grabbed hold of," he said later, "didn't belong to no man."

The sailor, stunned by his discovery and fearful of what her sponsors might do to a whistle-blower, kept his mouth shut.

Blackie was finally caught as a consequence of staying outside too late on the busy April morning when the Battle Fleet, off Balboa, was preparing to weigh for San Pedro and an unusual proportion of *Arizona*'s crew was early astir. Out for a breath of fresh air, she was hastening toward her hiding place as the first rays of dawn grayed the sky. She paused at a scuttlebutt for a drink of water. Out of the main radio room nearby came a chief radioman, who stood behind her awaiting his turn for a drink. As she raised her head, the chief looked into her dark eyes and realized the shocking truth. They had a woman on board! Aghast, he sped to the bridge to report his discovery to the officer of the deck.

Even after Blackie had been captured and turned over to the police, Captain Olmstead and his officers had still not completely washed their hands of her. The guileful little hooker, released by the police, walked into the Panama office of the Grace steamship line and somehow convinced the agent that the U.S. Navy would subsidize a first-class passage for herself to New York. She thus departed Panama in style. The Grace Line sent the bill for her passage to the Navy Department, and the Navy Department sent it to Captain Olmstead, who sounded off in another blast of opprobrious language.

The next shock arising out of the Blackie affair came from Admiral Wiley. He sent word that, for their lack of vigilance, he was penalizing all of *Arizona*'s officers by entering a derogatory report to that effect in each of their fitness reports. For Arleigh Burke this was the first and last black mark ever placed in his professional record. To some extent he felt he deserved it. During the month that Blackie had been on board, in the course of some of his inspections he had noticed unusual stirrings and exchanges of glances among groups of enlisted men as he passed, and one of his bluejackets had told him he had heard there was a woman on board—a report Arleigh dismissed as too ridiculous to merit investigation. Luckily for him and his fellow officers, Rear Admiral William V. Pratt, commander Battleship Division 4, with his flag on *Arizona*, considered the censure unmerited. When he became chief of naval operations, he ordered Admiral Wiley's derogatory reports expunged from the records.

Arizona's enlisted plotters were less fortunate. Twenty-three of them were indicted as criminally involved in the Blackie infraction. In a court-martial held at Bremerton all were convicted, and they served terms of up to ten years in the naval prison at Portsmouth, New Hampshire.

Ensign Burke continued to attract favorable attention through painstaking performance of duty and readiness to accept responsibility. He displayed the latter most strikingly one night off San Pedro when he had the deck watch on board *Arizona* and a gale smote the battleship anchorage. Nearby ships began dragging their moorings and colliding. Without taking time to summon more experienced help, Burke on his own responsibility ordered a second anchor dropped, thereby probably saving his ship from heavy damage.

Shortly after leaving New York, Arleigh had written Bobbie, "I have definitely heard that I am to be torpedo officer next year." The following spring, instead of returning to the Puget Sound area for summer maneuvers, Ensign Burke enrolled in a four-month course at the Torpedo Training School at San Diego, and here he and Bobbie established another temporary home.

During the five years that Arleigh served in *Arizona*, Bobbie endeavored whenever possible to have a home ashore for him. "I'd get word when *Arizona* was returning from sea," she explained, "and find out where she was going to dock. Then I'd start walking."

Walk she did, many miles, in all the major West Coast ports, in search of acceptable and affordable accommodations, preferably on the waterfront where her husband could keep an eye on his ship. "Usually I found something, although now and again Arleigh just had to put up with being out of sight of his big canoe."

While Burke's dependability was winning him the plaudits of his superiors, he was also earning the goodwill of his shipmates because of his friendliness, genial good nature, and enthusiastic loyalty. In his view his country, his navy, his ship, and his ship's crew were simply incomparable and invincible. This cheerful conviction was put sorely to the test when once again *Arizona* lay off Panama.

The occasion was the arrival via the canal of cruiser *Concord*, which boasted the champion pulling-raceboat crew of the Atlantic-based Scouting Fleet. Since *Arizona*'s pulling-raceboat crew were the champions of the Pacific-based Battle Fleet, a prompt race for the two-ocean championship was in order. *Arizona* issued the challenge, the cruiser accepted, and the day and hour were scheduled.

Well-established naval custom required ships' companies to support their boat crews by betting considerable sums on them. *Arizona's* junior officers in particular felt that they should be represented by a substantial wager because the ship's oarsmen had been coached by one of themselves, Ensign Kirkpatrick, a classmate of Arleigh's and a member of the Naval Academy's victorious Olympic crew.

Unfortunately, the race was scheduled at the wrong end of the month—the farthest from payday. The junior officers were broke. Ensign Burke, newly elected mess treasurer for *Arizona's* junior officers, had just collected from each of them a last twenty-five dollars to cover the mess bill for the ensuing thirty days. Burke still had that money, and it was in cash.

That gave one of the officers an idea. "So far as I'm concerned," he said to a group of his young shipmates, "loyalty absolutely demands that we back our boat crew by betting the works—the whole mess treasury."

This was a startling proposal. He was talking about a month's eating money. "Do we know anything about *Concord's* crew?" asked one of the ensigns.

"Nothing to it!" he was assured. "We've scouted 'em. They've got a little, short stroke, no real power. We're a shoo-in to win."

Thus encouraged and reminded of the demands of loyalty, the junior officers voted to wager the whole liquid assets of their mess, and any of them who still had a dollar or so left tossed that in too.

The race was held, with the whole Battle Fleet as spectators. *Concord's* oarsmen, employing their "little, short stroke," attained astonishing speed, quickly outstripping their opponents. While *Arizona's* senior officers watched with disappointment, her junior officers looked on with shocked dismay. Their larder was nearly bare. The outgoing mess treasurer, Burke's immediate predecessor, had left behind only a few pounds of coffee, a couple of bags of rice, and, of all things, a barrel of mushrooms.

The juniors wouldn't altogether starve. The supply officer would extend a little credit, but for some time to come they faced dining on light, cheap rations, eked out by the leftover coffee and rice and the barrel of mushrooms. In the circumstances, each of them eagerly anticipated drawing watch-officer duty, which included inspecting and sampling the crew's meals with no specified limitation on the size of the samples.

Burke had a special problem. Along with his equity in the mess funds, he had bet money set aside for his wife's living expenses. In deep dejection, he wrote her confessing what he had done. Bobbie wrote back that he had done exactly what he should have done and that she had taken a job to tide her over till payday.

In accordance with the navy's policy of providing junior officers with broad training, Burke's seniors in *Arizona* continued assigning him a variety of tasks, duties as diverse as assistant engineer and ship's secretary. His principal interest, however, reflecting his warrior instinct, continued to be guns and torpedoes, the ship's direct means of assailing the enemy.

Arizona's gunnery officer, Commander Andrew Denny, aware of Burke's inclinations, advised him to specialize. Taking into account his ability and dedication, Denny urged him to train for one of the most complex jobs in a warship—controlling the big guns. This task had become far too complex to be performed in the turrets alongside the guns themselves. It was carried out instead by officer and enlisted specialists operating a battery of machines at a central station called the plotting room.

At battle ranges often in excess of 10,000 yards, hitting the target posed intricate problems involving correct elevation of the guns to cover the distance and allowances for the ship's roll and pitch, movement of the target during the flight of the projectile, air density and wind velocity, temperature of the powder, and wear of gun barrels (called bore erosion). The battery of machines, ancestor of the analog computer, did the required calculations, but its operators had to provide it with the correct input, or else its output would be worthless.

With his usual tenacity, Burke set out to learn how to operate the machines and then how to supervise their operators. At length, while still serving as torpedo officer, he qualified as head of the plotting room. As if that were not enough, he enrolled in the Naval War College correspondence course in strategy and tactics and prepared for his examinations for lieutenant (junior grade), a promotion he attained in the summer of 1926.

Early the next year, the Battle Fleet headed south for the usual combined winter maneuvers, and Bobbie once more headed east to winter in Washington with her parents and be on hand for a rendezvous with Arleigh when *Arizona* again visited New York.

In the following spring, while the combined fleets were operating out of Gonaives, Haiti, Lieutenant Burke picked up a bit of news that set his pulse racing. The navy was asking for junior-officer volunteers to attend a four-week course in New York to study the Ford Instrument Company's improved antiaircraft-gun system, which employed director-controlled fire, replacing the former barrage fire. Cruiser *Raleigh* was on hand to take the volunteers to the States.

Burke had been trained to control *Arizona*'s torpedoes and was being trained to control her big guns. If now he could learn how to control her antiaircraft guns from a central post, he would possess the skill to direct all the ship's weapons. He promptly volunteered for the New York school, submitting the proper form through channels. Then he impatiently waited. When the answer finally came back through channels, he was stunned. The quota of volunteers was filled. How could that be? He had submitted his application in plenty of time. Somebody or something must have delayed it in transit.

The deeply disappointed Burke did not content himself with sending a written tracer through channels. With one eye on *Raleigh*, which had not yet left the anchorage, he began a personal walking check up the chain of command, making polite inquiries at each step. He found the snafu in the captain's office. A yeoman had temporarily mislaid Burke's application.

Arleigh asked if he might go over to the fleet flagship and try to persuade the flag to increase the quota by one. Captain H. P. Perrill, Captain Olmstead's successor as *Arizona*'s skipper, replied that it was unnecessary. He would send over a dispatch explaining that a clerical delay was at fault, and that would be sufficient.

Burke doubted it, but he recognized that it would be disrespectful, if not nonregulation, for him now to go to the flag with a personal plea. That sort of action might well backfire. Instead, he went over to *Raleigh* and explained his problem to the executive officer.

"We're full up," said the exec. "There's no more room."

"Look, sir," Burke pleaded, "I won't even need a bunk. I'll sleep in a passageway and keep well out of the road."

"Will you stand watches?"

"Yes, sir!"

"Will you eat in the third mess?"

"Yes, sir!"

The three-striper added further discouraging stipulations, all of which Burke eagerly accepted. The exec was astonished. Could nothing daunt this fellow? At length he yielded. "All right," he said. "If you can get clearance from the flag I'll take you."

Arleigh lost no time making his way to the flagship to report that he had transportation to the States if the flag would clear him. Confronted by the impetuous Burke, the admiral also yielded.

Hardly had Arleigh returned to *Arizona* when he was ordered to report to Captain Perrill, who was unaware of his visits to *Raleigh* and the flagship.

"Burke," said the captain, "I have good news for you. I've received a dispatch from the flag that your request to attend that New York school has been granted."

The captain studied the young man with a mildly patronizing smile. "You've got to learn patience," he said. "A little while back you wanted to go over to the flag and do a lot of things that were entirely unnecessary. This dispatch proves that they were unnecessary. Now get your gear together and shove off—and in future don't be in such an all-fired hurry to take matters into your own hands."

"Yes, *sir!*" said Burke, who had the good sense not to tell the captain just how that permission had been obtained.

Arleigh used less sound judgment in his immediate stateside arrangements. Intending to surprise his wife, he neglected to tell her that he was coming. When *Raleigh* debarked him at Norfolk, he took the first train for Washington, and on arrival he telephoned Bobbie from the station with the news that they were going to New York. He was none too soon, for he had caught her as she was on the point of leaving Washington to visit an uncle. Instead, she joined him at the station, and they took the next train for New York. En route, Arleigh told her he had a hundred dollars and hoped that would last them until the end of the month, when the fleet would be in New York and he could draw some pay. Bobbie laughed, doubtless a bit wryly, for in four years of penny-pinching she had learned a few things about the cost of living, and she had heard that New York City was no bargain basement. She told Arleigh she had exactly twenty dollars. That's why she had been going to visit her uncle—part of an acquired policy of spreading her poverty around among relatives.

Arrived at the big city, the two innocents found themselves adrift in the roar of traffic and other street noises. Arleigh had to report to the Ford Instrument Company; Bobbie would look for cheap quarters, a skill she had honed to precision in four years as wife to an itinerant, underpaid sailor. When she had found something, she would call Arleigh at the Ford Company. Having heard of Greenwich Village as a possible site of inexpensive lodgings, she decided to try there.

Orienting themselves as best they could with a street map, they took the El near Pennsylvania Station and headed south. Bobbie, with vague notions about the location of the Village, got off at 25th Street, while Arleigh continued on over to Long Island. After he had matriculated and tended to other formalities at the Ford Company school, he waited five hours. When at last Bobbie called, Arleigh could tell by her voice that her mission had not gone well. She had been unable to find a place that would give them room and board within their means, but she had talked a landlady on 33rd Street near Fifth Avenue into renting them a room so tiny that there was no space for a chair. Arleigh and Bobbie moved in, making themselves as comfortable as lack of space would permit. They always remembered the next few weeks as among the happiest of their lives.

They subsisted mostly on day-old doughnuts from a nearby bakery. When Arleigh was not in class, they took walks together, or they visited the aquarium, the art galleries, and other free exhibits, avoiding the days when admission was charged. A fellow roomer, a widower who managed a hat store, was amused and intrigued by the Burkes' ingenuity at enjoying the pleasures of New York without funds. He offered to take them to shows and other entertainments, but the Burkes felt obliged to decline, since they would be unable to repay his kindness. He found a way, however, to help them at no cost to himself. Because his store was in the theatrical district, he received a good many complimentary tickets, and he insisted that the Burkes share these with him. Thus they saw a number of good shows. They missed some such opportunities, however, because after serious conferences they concluded that they really could not afford the twenty cents round-trip subway fare.

Throughout this delicate exercise in finance, Bobbie, more experienced than her husband in handling living expenses, served as treasurer. When the fleet arrived at New York at the end of April, with payday immediately following, it was none too soon. Bobbie had just two dollars left.

Arizona left New York with a Mark 1 Ford Antiaircraft Director installed, and Burke was in charge of the fire control division. In antiaircraft exercises his duty was, as he put it, to operate his Ford.

Burke was long overdue for a change of duty, but *Arizona*'s successive commanding officers held on to him because his experience in the plotting room made him an increasingly valuable officer. When, however, Burke put in a formal application for postgraduate training in ordnance, Captain W. T. Tarrant, who had relieved Captain Perrill, fair-mindedly gave it a strongly favorable endorsement. And Captain Perrill, now commandant of the Norfolk Navy Yard, sent in Burke's behalf a glowing recommendation to the chief of the Bureau of Navigation.

But in this heyday of the battleship, competition for special ordnance training was severe. There were fifty-four applications for the 1928 course. Only eight applicants were selected, and Burke was not one of them. Probably he was turned down because his only professional experience had been on board a battleship. Possibly the Bureau of Navigation wanted to observe how he handled other duties before assigning him to the Naval Postgraduate School. In April 1928 he received orders to report to fleet auxiliary ship USS *Procyon*.

About this time one of his shipmates made a remark that summarized the impression eager beaver Burke had created among his fellow officers: "Arleigh Burke will be dead before he's fifty, or he'll be the chief of naval operations."

3

THE ROAD
TO COMMAND

IT WAS FORTUNATE for Burke that *Arizona* and *Procyon* were both
at San Francisco when he left one for the other, because during his
five years in the battleship he had filled thirteen boxes with clothing,
books, instruments, and maritime curios. On 16 April 1928, accompanied by all these impedimenta, he reported for duty on board *Procyon*. An 11,450-ton cargo vessel, with a complement of fewer than
200, she was for him a jarring comedown from the majestic *Arizona*.
But *Procyon* was a flagship, the flagship of Rear Admiral William
W. Phelps, commander of the Base Force, comprising minelayers,
minesweepers, oilers, colliers, and hospital and repair ships. This
was the puny forerunner of Service Force Pacific, which in World
War II would support great fleets of America's fighting ships at sea
and by means of floating bases and underway replenishment maintain them there for the duration.

Two days after Burke's arrival the Base Force headed for Hawaiian waters to support the Battle Fleet's summer exercises. Burke was
at first appointed *Procyon*'s assistant navigator and education officer,
but in June the flag, possibly perceiving that it had an outstanding
young officer on board, assigned him to the Base Force staff as flag
lieutenant. In this capacity, sporting aiguillettes looped over his left
shoulder, he served as personal aide to Admiral Phelps.

At the conclusion of the Hawaiian operation, the Battle Fleet and
the Base Force returned to the States. The former headed for sum-

mer exercises in the Puget Sound area. Since in these waters it could be supplied through the ports and otherwise serviced by the Bremerton Navy Yard, the Base Force did not accompany it. *Procyon* anchored off Mare Island Navy Yard in San Francisco Bay. Here the Base Force settled down to a fairly unchallenging routine, mainly supervising and attending to the needs of its own ships.

Arleigh early became interested in the work of a small camera party on board *Procyon*, mainly because it concerned gunnery, his specialty. The objective was to determine the accuracy of ships' guns. The operators took simultaneous radio-controlled shots from various positions—the gunnery ship, the target-towing ship, and ships flanking the latter. By means of triangulation such photos would yield the exact position of the fall of shot relative to the target. With time to spare and energy to burn, Burke in effect joined the camera party. He developed sufficient skill that when the officer in charge went on summer leave he turned control of his camera crew over to Arleigh.

At the end of summer, Admiral Phelps was relieved by another rear admiral, who brought his own flag lieutenant with him and chose a different flagship. Relieved of his aiguillettes, Burke rejoined *Procyon*'s ship's company as assistant navigator and signal officer, posts that occupied so little of his time that he was able to continue a certain amount of camera work.

In December the routine was interrupted by an adventure that won Arleigh his first medal. One stormy night shortly after *Procyon* put to sea, her lookouts spotted wreckage of some sort with men on board, one waving. Burke, along with several enlisted men, volunteered to go to their relief, and the rescue party was lowered in a whaleboat into the tempestuous sea. As the boat approached the wreckage, Burke made out five men tied together on what appeared to be a raft. It was in fact the roof of a fishing barge, which had broken up in the storm the evening before. The man doing the waving was a strong swimmer who had somehow managed to haul his companions, all nonswimmers, onto the floating roof and tie them to himself.

Burke and his sailors hauled all five men into the whaleboat and hastened with them back to the ship, which headed for port at flank speed. Two of the men were found to be already dead. Two others, near death, were saved by prompt medical attention. For his rescue the Treasury Department awarded Lieutenant (j.g.) Burke the Silver Lifesaving Medal.

Arleigh's senior-officer friends had been urging him to renew his application to the Postgraduate School, and on his doing so, they rallied round with letters of recommendation. Admiral Phelps sent to the PG School on his behalf a really handsome letter that perhaps tipped the scales. A few days following the rescue mission a telegraph from a friend in Washington brought Arleigh the news that he had been accepted, and a couple of weeks later he received the official notice. In mid-May 1929, Burke was detached to the postgraduate course at Annapolis.

For a hundred dollars Arleigh had purchased a used car, a Chevrolet coupe with two seats under the roof and a fold-down rumble seat in the back. In this conveyance he and Bobbie crossed the country, pausing to visit their families in Colorado and Washington, D.C. On 17 June, Burke reported to the United States Naval Postgraduate School, located in the Naval Academy grounds in Annapolis.

Burke and the other young officers in the ordnance program, an obviously select group, now plunged into some of the toughest brainwork of their lives, involving courses in physics, thermodynamics, hydraulics, engineering, and mathematics. Burke calculated that he averaged fifty-eight hours a week in classroom exercises, practical work, lectures, and preparation. At the same time he boned up for his naval promotion examinations, which he passed, and in October he was promoted to lieutenant.

Several officers in Burke's ordnance course were to achieve flag rank, but not necessarily through application of their current studies, which were related to the battleship big gun. A small but growing minority in the navy was calling the battleship obsolete, because the range of its big guns was far less than the attack radius of a carrier's planes. These visionaries foresaw naval battles in which the opposing fleets, out of sight of each other, indeed hundreds of miles apart, would attack and counterattack with carrier planes.

The intensive study at the Postgraduate School was designed to prepare the students to undertake a year of graduate work at a civilian engineering school or university. Arleigh chose the University of Michigan. At Ann Arbor the Burkes took another tiny apartment, and the university provided Arleigh with a small office. Here or at home he studied his assigned courses in chemical engineering, fuels, and explosives every night until midnight, but he never forgot that he was preparing himself for his chosen profession of conducting naval warfare. A fellow student, puzzled at seeing the walls of Arleigh's office plastered with *National Geographic* maps of the Pacific and Orient, asked him why.

"One day, my friend," Burke replied, "our country will be at war with Japan. In that conflict it will be my mission to do my bit for my country in that theater of operations. When that time comes I intend to know that area of the world as intimately as possible."

Cramming for his promotion examinations and studying Pacific Ocean geography apparently interfered in no serious way with Burke's academic studies. On 22 June 1931 the University of Michigan awarded him a Master of Science degree in engineering.

Having exposed Burke to two years of scientific theory, the Navy Department next attached him to the Bureau of Ordnance, which sent him out for a year of visiting military and civilian factories and other installations dealing with design, production, and storage of explosives and other ordnance materials. At these locations he observed practical applications of the scientific theories he had been studying.

The Great Depression had now about reached its nadir. Decline of national income had obliged the navy to reduce allowances for quarters and subsistence by 10 percent and to require its officers to take a month's annual leave without pay. Despite the hard times, Burke seized the opportunity to become a homeowner when Bobbie's widowed mother, moving into an apartment, offered the Burkes her residence on Fulton Street in northwest Washington if they would assume the mortgage.

Coolidge economy had been followed by Hoover austerity. President Hoover believed the United States needed a navy capable only of defending its own shores. Shipbuilding came to a standstill, ship repairs were neglected, and naval forces remained idle in port longer than the commanders deemed advisable.

Admiral Pratt, as chief of naval operations, tried in some measure to offset the navy's deficiencies by streamlining. In the spring of 1931 the Battle Fleet and Scouting Fleet, both somewhat reduced, became respectively the Battle Force and Scouting Force. The latter moved to the Pacific, and Admiral Pratt announced that it would remain there. The navy and the American public soon ceased to think of two separate forces temporarily operating together. The combination had become simply the U.S. Fleet, permanently operating out of West Coast ports.

This was the situation when Lieutenant Burke received new seagoing orders. He had requested battleship duty. Instead he was ordered to heavy cruiser *Chester*. When Burke on 24 June 1932 reported for his new duty, *Chester* was resting on keel blocks in the Brooklyn Navy Yard's dry dock no. 4 undergoing overhaul. He was appointed main battery officer and served also as officer in charge of small arms, which included the responsibility of visiting the New York police department to identify several pistols missing from his ship.

In August, at last out of dry dock, *Chester* proceeded via the canal to the Pacific and rejoined the U.S. Fleet. Maneuvers in early 1933 carried her to Pearl Harbor, but she was soon back operating out of San Pedro. Here Burke received another set of orders. His services were required in ordnance-related photography, an expanding field with a shortage of experts. After less than a year on board *Chester,* he was directed to report again to the Base Force flagship, now auxiliary *Antares.* On 22 April 1933, the date specified in his orders, both *Chester* and *Antares* were at San Pedro. Thus, as in his previous transfer to Base Force, Burke simply shifted his gear from ship to ship and assumed the title of assistant Battle Force camera officer.

At the almost continual fleet maneuvers, the camera party were among the busiest men in the navy. During target practice they might be perched with their equipment atop battleship or cruiser turrets or swinging, camera in hand, from destroyer fantails. Between fleet operations they were usually on board *Antares* planning forthcoming undertakings or calculating the results of previous ones.

Burke not only carried out his photographic duties promptly and effectively but found time to engage in other activities and to spend time with Bobbie at their current San Pedro residence, 4002 Carolina Street. A workaholic's workaholic, he had developed the priceless capacity of eliminating waste motion. Bobbie and he had even reached a state of domesticity that permitted them to have a pet dog. Named Faffin, a Great Dane, he was a curious choice of breed for petite Bobbie, necessarily his chief custodian. He evidently made a hit with the Burkes, however, for they later acquired in succession two more dogs of the same breed.

In October, commander Base Force and his staff, including the camera party, shifted from *Antares* to the more commodious auxiliary *Argonne,* and *Antares* headed for her home port of Norfolk, carrying Burke's trunk, which the movers had overlooked. His boxes, containing possessions of less immediate concern, had all been properly transferred. In the trunk were uniforms and other clothing he would soon need. Local inquiry and a letter to *Antares* proving fruitless, Burke faced the problem of buying replacements—hard luck indeed for a low-pay junior officer on depression pay.

Argonne remained based on San Pedro until April 1934, when she headed south with the fleet. The men-of-war and accompanying auxiliaries together comprised a force of 110 ships, which transited the Panama Canal and headed for the Culebra area, where a full-scale battle exercise kept the camera party madly occupied. The maneuvers were followed by a welcome brief respite at Gonaives, Haiti. Here Burke and several other lieutenants from *Argonne* hit the beach to regain their shore legs and more particularly to sample the local dishes, which at their best were said to be very fine indeed.

Extensive inquiry in halting French brought assurances that the finest food in the region was to be had at a small place some miles out of town. Thither the young officers directed their steps, envisioning good barbecued roast pig or some even more exotic dish. When they arrived at their destination, they asked their native host if he could prepare them a meal fit to melt the heart of the late tyrant Henri Christophe. He assured them he could. After a long wait, he summoned the young men to the table and set before them the fruit of his labors—a hot bowl of soup followed by a hot dish of beans. These were no mere native dishes. He wanted his guests to have the best. He proudly showed them the source of his delicacies—cans, now empty, from the Campbell Soup Company of Camden, New Jersey.

Not long afterward the fleet headed for New York, where it arrived on 1 June to a tumultuous welcome. In three weeks some two million citizens visited the ships. Bobbie was in New York, where she had been awaiting Arleigh. At a series of parties to which officers and their ladies were invited they met such luminaries as Fannie Hurst and General Leonard Wood. They took in several shows and at one musical were amused at the antics of Fannie Brice.

On 20 June the fleet scattered to visit other coastal cities. *Argonne* drew Newport, where the summer homes were being opened, and these became the scene of more parties. After another visit to New York, *Argonne* proceeded to Norfolk, where she moored at the Naval Operating Base, and the camera party got to work carrying out triangulations for several ships. From Norfolk *Argonne* headed in September for New Orleans. Then, after rejoining the fleet for another series of maneuvers in the Caribbean, *Argonne* proceeded with it back to the Pacific, arriving at San Pedro in November.

Not long afterward, Arleigh received a letter from the executive officer of *Antares*: "On restowing the trunk storeroom on board this vessel, a trunk, apparently filled, marked 'A. A. Burke,' was found. As this is presumably your property, your direction regarding its disposition is requested." Having purchased replacements for the uniforms and other garments he assumed lost with the trunk, Burke now had duplicate sets, some of which would prove useless if he continued to gain weight. In the circumstances he could perhaps be forgiven exercise of a little intemperate language.

Arleigh had for some time been restless. He felt that he had learned about all he was likely to learn in ordnance-related camera work. For sea duty he preferred to get back to a combatant ship rather than stay with the auxiliaries he had been riding. First, however, he would try for a tour of shore duty, if possible at the Bureau of Ordnance.

From friends at Ordnance, Arleigh learned that his services were desired at the bureau, and that there was a place for him there whenever the commander Base Force was ready to release him and the Bureau of Navigation to transfer him—a combination that finally came about in the spring of 1935.

Toward the end of May, Arleigh reported for duty at the Bureau of Ordnance, and the Burkes settled down as residents of the nation's capital. During this period they initiated the practice, continued whenever Arleigh was stationed in Washington, of driving fairly regularly to the Naval Academy, 35 miles away at Annapolis, to witness football games and other sports events and to attend social and official functions.

Burke was concerned mainly with the purchase, storage, and distribution of ammunition and explosives. He also helped design a relatively safe arsenal for high explosives and conducted research toward attaining a more stable smokeless powder.

Though diligent as ever, Arleigh at BuOrd was no mere toiler, grim and unapproachable. On the contrary, he maintained a cheerful geniality that won him lifelong friends among his fellow officers and charmed the female secretaries. Months after he had left for sea duty, one of the latter added a postscript to a letter addressed to Burke: "Miss Hamm and Miss Clinton both say 'Hello.' We all certainly do miss your smiling face and curly hair." Nearly a year after that, at the time of his next promotion, among the letters he received was one from BuOrd signed simply "Mabel." It said in part: "Congratulations, salutes, salutations, and what have you on passing the examinations. . . . I'm awfully glad for you and know it must be a big relief. . . . Why don't you come sailing down the

Potomac? . . . We'd take the whole day off and come down to welcome you. . . . We still miss your laugh and jokes."

That Burke's performance was by no means all laugh and jokes is shown by his fitness report, written by the bureau chief, Rear Admiral Harold R. Stark, an officer not given to bestowing unearned praise. Burke, he wrote, had "a keen grasp of ordnance" and would "with additional experience in a position of responsibility become an officer of exceptional value to the service."

In May 1937 the Bureau of Navigation ordered Burke to the Bethlehem Shipbuilding Corporation at Quincy, Massachusetts, as prospective executive officer of destroyer *Craven*, being built and nearing completion. Detached from BuOrd on 15 June, he sacrificed half his month's leave in order to be present at the builder's trials of the ship.

The seagoing navy to which Burke now returned was experiencing a rebirth under President Franklin Roosevelt, who appreciated the close relationship between military strength and diplomacy. Roosevelt's National Industrial Recovery Act of 1933, designed to relieve unemployment, had authorized new construction of cruisers and destroyers to full treaty strength, and the Vinson-Trammel Act the following year launched an eight-year replacement program to provide 102 new ships.

Burke, who earlier had repeatedly requested battleship duty, had at length decided that for the sake of the naval service and for the advancement of his own career he should get experience in a variety of types. No doubt he had inspected and admired the sleek new destroyers coming off the ways to replace the tired old World War I flush-deckers and concluded that service in these ships would prove stimulating and also be the swiftest means of attaining his heart's desire, a command of his own. At any rate, the assignment to destroyer duty was in response to his own request.

At Quincy he met and conferred with *Craven*'s prospective commanding officer, Lieutenant Commander Watson O. Bailey. Likewise new to destroyers, Bailey was a submariner with postgraduate training in diesel engineering. His background thus complemented Burke's, so that the captain and his exec each had something to offer the other. From his new commanding officer, Burke was to acquire a better understanding of matériel, administration, and logistics, regarding which his long concentration on ordnance had left him deficient.

Craven's shakedown cruise, following commissioning, would require her to cross the equator, whereupon navy tradition decreed that the "pollywogs," who had never passed over the line, should be sternly initiated into the fraternity of the sea by the "shellbacks," who had. Captain Bailey, a shellback, dropped dark hints that Burke, who in his mid-thirties was becoming a trifle broad about the hips, was unusually well equipped to receive the ministrations of himself and his fellow shellbacks.

Craven, commissioned in the Boston Navy Yard, left port in early October, touched at Norfolk and Balboa, transited the Panama Canal, and on the 21st, off the coast of Ecuador, crossed the equator from the northern into the southern hemisphere.

On this solemn occasion, Lieutenant Arleigh A. Burke was served with a subpoena issued from the Domain of Neptunus Rex and signed by Davy Jones. The Bill of Particulars charged him with, among other offenses, assuming the duties and responsibilities of trusted shellback division officers while himself a mere pollywog.

There followed a period of horseplay, in which in the presence of a bearded "Neptune" and his court Burke and his fellow pollywogs, commissioned and enlisted, were tried, condemned, and subjected to various humiliations and punishments. The culprits, having endured their chastisement with proper humility, at last underwent a triumphant transformation into trusted shellbacks.

On her return to the States, *Craven* reported to the Boston Navy Yard for several months of alterations, adjustments, and tests, a not uncommon circumstance for a new class of ship after shakedown has revealed deficiencies and possible opportunities for improvement. Burke was kept busy overseeing, testing, and training, but he found time to study for his promotion examinations, which he passed triumphantly. Promoted to lieutenant commander, he was duly sworn in by Captain Bailey on 8 August 1938.

The following month, *Craven* at last joined the Battle Force on the West Coast and participated in fall maneuvers, scouting and screening for the battleships, including *Arizona.* "It's a good feeling to see the old ship," said Burke.

In October, a letter from a friend in Washington informed him that at the conclusion of his present tour, he was slated to command destroyer *Perry.* This was great news. "I'm all a-jitter," he replied.

In a sense this was the culmination of his dreams since his Naval Academy days—to command his own ship. Yet there was one small shadow in the rosy picture. *Perry* was an old flush-decker,* commis-

*Flush-decker. Destroyer of World War I design with weather deck extending unbroken the

sioned in 1922, hardly in a class with the new *Craven,* to which Burke had given his sailorman's heart.

At Christmastime the impatient Burke, trying to worm out information about when he might expect to assume his new command, was writing to Lieutenant Smith, former shipmate in *Arizona,* now in the Bureau of Navigation. The answer caught up with *Craven* in mid-January at Colón, where she was en route with the fleet to the Caribbean for winter maneuvers. It set off fireworks in Burke's head.

> Dear Arleigh [Smith wrote]: Your letter of 26 December has been received but since we have shifted your slating I can not answer your question. You are now down to command MUGFORD. I think you will agree that it is a much better billet. I do not know yet when you will be detached but it will be during the usual spring shift.

Mugford! Sister to *Craven,* she had been building at Boston while *Craven* was building at Quincy. Arleigh could hardly contain his joy. He promptly dashed off a letter to a fellow officer:

> One of your fat friends is completely bewildered. Just before leaving Colón, Smith of Bunav, in answer to a direct query of when I could expect to go to the PERRY, sent me a short snappy letter saying that I was now slated to go in command of the MUGFORD. Naturally I'm tickled a brilliant vermilion. In view of the difficulty of getting these new boats and the number of people angling for them, to get such information out of the clear blue sky takes me off my feet.

At the end of January 1939 the U.S. Fleet steamed across the Caribbean Sea and based the bulk of its ships in Guantánamo Bay, sending the overflow, including *Craven,* across the Windward Passage to anchor off the Haitian port of Gonaives, where five years earlier Burke had been regaled with Campbell's soup and beans. From these anchorages it carried out Fleet Problem XX.

It was apparent that neither Fleet Commander in Chief Claude C. Bloch nor Commander Battle Force Edward C. Kalbfus had any notion of the potential of the carrier as a weapon of attack. In part one, a mock battle, Kalbfus tried using the carriers as bait to lure the enemy cruisers within reach of his battleship guns. When the ruse

---

length of the ship.

failed, he sent Rear Admiral William F. Halsey ahead with two carriers to locate the enemy. Halsey did more than that. He "sank" the cruisers by air attack before the battleships could arrive within range. The clear lesson of this victory was apparently lost on Bloch and Kalbfus. The fourth and last part, witnessed by President Roosevelt and Chief of Naval Operations William D. Leahy in cruiser *Houston,* consisted of an antiquated Jutland type of battleship action.

Following this unimpressive conclusion of Problem XX, the participating ships joined *Houston* off Culebra. Here in the afternoon of 28 February the flag officers of the fleet, led by Admiral Bloch, called on Armed Forces Commander in Chief Roosevelt to pay their respects. Among them was Stark, now commander Cruiser Division 3. It was widely believed that this parade of the admirals was a sort of pass-in-review to aid Roosevelt in filling forthcoming vacancies in high commands, including the topmost, CNO, and the only slightly less prestigious billet of fleet commander in chief (CinCUS).

On 15 March, word reached the fleet that the top selections had been made. Admiral Stark would be the new CNO, Admiral James O. Richardson the new CinCUS.

Burke was delighted. His first impulse was to go over to Stark's flagship, *Honolulu,* and congratulate the admiral in person. He quickly discarded that notion, surmising that *Honolulu* would be inundated by well-wishing callers, including many seeking merely to ingratiate themselves with the prospective new chief. Burke also rejected the alternative of sending a letter, because the admiral would have to take time to answer it. There remained one more means of communication. It chanced that Stark's personal aide was Arleigh's Naval Academy classmate Lieutenant Commander Hal Krick. Through Krick Burke sent his felicitations to the admiral: "Will you please tell him that the President is to be congratulated on selecting the most suitable officer in the Navy for the most important position in the Navy."

Back came a note from Krick: "I have conveyed your good wishes to the next CNO. He was grateful and said the method used in getting the congratulations to him rated nothing short of a 4.0+." Krick confirmed what Burke had surmised: "He is very busy at the moment, and everyone and his brother are coming on board to make their numbers."

* *

Early on the morning of 5 June 1939 in San Diego's Coronado Roads, Lieutenant Commander Arleigh Burke, detached from *Craven*, crossed over and relieved Lieutenant Commander Marcy M. Dupre as commanding officer of *Mugford*. Under the able Dupre, *Mugford*, like her twin, *Craven*, had been maintained in top condition.

When the brief change-of-command ceremony was over and Burke had seen his departing predecessor to the gangway, he invited his inherited executive officer, Lieutenant Gelzer Sims, into the wardroom for a chat. Since they would be operating together hand in glove for some time to come, it was essential that they become acquainted without delay. In an earlier visit to *Mugford*, Burke had sized Sims up as a casual, relaxed Southerner and wondered how his apparently easygoing temperament would mesh with his own hard-driving, meticulous style.

Lighting his pipe, Burke opened the conversation with a few general observations, intending gradually to draw his man out. Presently he had the uneasy feeling that his exec was up to exactly the same game. In fact, Sims had drawn a major conclusion about Burke, which he expounded in a typically humorous, roundabout fashion.

"You know, Captain," he began, "you remind me of a little thing that happened down in my home town of Orangeburg, South Carolina. It's just a wide place in the road, you might say, but it's comfortable, and quiet, and lazy, and we like it. Well, sir, for years we had a character around the town—old Negro name of Sam. Everybody loved Sam; they'd go out of their way to help him, although Sam never got into any serious trouble. The thing was, Sam was what you might call shiftless. He didn't seem to like hard work, and people got concerned about keepin' Sam in greens an' grits. Not, of course, that you're lazy or shiftless, Captain; that's not the point.

"Well, came the time when the businessmen of the town got together and decided that something must be done about Sam. They didn't want him to starve. They didn't want him to suffer. But on the other hand they were perceptive enough to realize that Sam shouldn't be driven to hard, regular work. How to keep Sam became the burnin' question.

"Well, sir, I think it was Melton Melton—an improbable name, but he had it—who came up with the righteous idea. He was a young lawyer, an' sharp as a tack. His idea was this. We had an ol' brass cannon on the lawn in front of the city hall. It probably came from the Spanish-American War. An' it was pretty green an' dingy. This thing was a disgrace to the town, said Melton. Why don't we all chip in, and we'll engage Sam, on a monthly basis, to shine that cannon an' keep it bright so it's an ornament to the town.

"Everybody agreed; everybody chipped in; Sam was engaged for this light work—and for two years he really put his heart in it. Captain, I'm telling you, you never saw a prettier cannon in your life. Sam got so fond of that cannon he took to sleepin' under it on fair spring an' summer nights. An' then, all of a sudden, after two years, Sam showed up at Melton Melton's office. He waited patiently until Melton could receive him and then, hat in hand, he announced: 'Mr. Melton, I sure appreciate all you folks have did for me. I jes' came in t' tell you I'm resignin'.'

"Well, Melton Melton was struck full aback, Captain. But he didn't panic. He played it soft and easy; he told Sam what a good job he'd done keeping that ol' cannon sparklin', and, finally, he got around to the point. 'What are you going to do, Sam?'

" 'Well, Boss,' said Sam, 'I'm goin' in business for myself. Yes, sir! I've been savin' m' money, Mr. Melton. I been very particular. I been schoochin' meals here an' there, an' it don't cost me much t' live, an' I done bought my *own* cannon! Yes, sah, soon's you can fin' somebody t' take over mah work, I'm goin' in business f' myself, shinin' m' very *own* cannon!' "

"I remind you of *that* story?"

"Yes, Captain," said Sims. "I figure you're the kind of man who's got to have his *own* cannon!"

Lieutenant Sims, it turned out, was a very perceptive fellow. In the first hour of associating with his new captain at close range, he had uncovered one of the main goals of Burke's life—to be in charge, to run his own show. Another, he was soon to discover, was an aching urge to meet and sink the enemy. With war clouds gathering in Europe and the Orient, it was predictable that Burke might soon be called upon to satisfy both urges.

As for Gelzer Sims, Burke was to learn that he was as much a perfectionist as himself, the difference being that Sims took time to think his problems through, examine all aspects. In this regard he would occasionally serve as a brake to his captain's sometimes impetuous moves. He was, Burke soon found out, not easy to lead or drive. Sims was at his best when taken more or less into partnership.

Burke was not the senior officer on board his destroyer, a circum-

stance that at first lessened his satisfaction in being commanding
officer. *Mugford* happened to be the flagship of Commander F. E.
M. Whiting, commodore of Destroyer Division 8. But the presence
of "Red" Whiting, a destroyerman of long experience, proved a
spur to the ship's record-breaking ability and even more to Burke's
rise to fame. While Sims served as a brake to Burke, Whiting encouraged his impulsiveness. In night operations including simulated
torpedo and gunnery practices, Destroyer Division 8, eschewing the
customary cautious approach, closed in on the "enemy" at high
speed. Through unremitting training and constant drill under simulated battle conditions, Whiting helped Burke to prepare himself for
the feats of speed and audacity that were to become his hallmark in
the coming war.

Whiting properly left running the ship to Burke, who did so with
such boundless vigor that Red remarked to a colleague, "This is a
tremendous officer. He does all my work for me, and probably yours
as well." Burke, as if he were not busy enough, volunteered his ship
to serve as the fleet's destroyer gunnery school, with himself, his
similarly trained gunnery officer, Lieutenant Robert Speck, and his
gunners as instructors—his principal aim being to give his own
gunners additional practice.

Burke's relentless drive set the pace for his officers. "I will always
remember the speed with which he did things," one of them recalled. Burke expected them to be equally expeditious. He was
annoyed by ineptitude but fiercely intolerant of carelessness, even
in minor matters of protocol. Another *Mugford* officer remembered
keenly after twenty years the humiliation a moment's heedlessness
earned him at Burke's hands. On that occasion he had the deck when
getting under way and should have complied with the standard
practice of sounding the ship's siren three times and then testing the
whistle. Instead he absentmindedly tested the whistle first, whereupon Burke turned on him a glare of such blazing fury that the
officer averted his eyes in mortification and would have fled the
bridge had not that been an even graver offense.

Burke achieved a taut but happy ship by deft carrot-and-stick
strategy—the carrot being pride and praise. *Mugford*'s gunners, for
example, felt their months of toilsome exercises finally rewarded
when at the annual short-range battle practice their guns attained
the unprecedented score of thirty-six hits with thirty-six shots, after
which the ship steamed back into San Diego harbor with brooms
hoisted at every yardarm, proclaiming a clean sweep.

On another prideful occasion Burke declared to his assembled crew: "I couldn't wish for a better ship's company. I have been particularly well pleased by two things, two indispensable attributes for a man-of-war: your loyalty to your ship and your hard work. I have seen many ships, but I've never seen one that could excel the *Mugford* in these two characteristics. I have the utmost faith in you." *Mugford*'s engineering officer, recalling this statement long afterward, agreed that the ship's achievements were due in large measure to the high caliber of her officers and men. But, he added, Arleigh Burke "was the catalyst that welded the team and made it click."

The Japanese meanwhile had occupied the entire coastline of China and advanced far inland. In July 1939, U.S. Secretary of State Cordell Hull gave Japan the required six months' notice for the abrogation of the commercial treaty of 1911, thereby clearing the way for an embargo of American oil, iron, and other strategic materials on which the Japanese were heavily dependent. U.S. appeasement of Japan was clearly drawing to an end.

On 3 September, Britain and France declared war on Germany, which had invaded Poland. By the end of the year, German submarines, surface raiders, and mines had sunk 114 Allied and neutral merchant ships, and the United States had taken its first step toward entanglement in the European hostilities by establishing an Atlantic Neutrality Patrol of mostly U.S. men-of-war to keep belligerent naval forces out of American waters.

On 6 January 1940, Admiral Richardson relieved Admiral Bloch as commander in chief U.S. Fleet and promptly set in motion training exercises in preparation for Fleet Problem XXI, scheduled for April and May. In the exercises *Mugford* joined the Battle Force in extensive tactical maneuvers.

Though not so announced, even in classified orders, Problem XXI was to include two mock battles between "Japanese" and American naval forces. All Burke knew when *Mugford* departed San Diego on 2 April was that his ship was part of an antisubmarine screen of a force that called itself the White Fleet but that actually represented an American force. Its objective was to repulse and defeat a Black (Japanese) Raiding Force en route to attack Hawaii. After complex maneuvers, which mere destroyer commanders neither understood nor were expected to understand, the White Fleet interposed itself between the Black Raiding Force and a Black Covering Force and, by judgment of the umpires, succeeded in defeating both.

The preliminary moves leading to the second mock battle, between the Maroon (American) and Purple (Japanese) fleets, extended long past sunset and culminated in an unplanned and confused night engagement, with near collisions, objectionable illuminations, and missed gunnery and torpedo opportunities. This debacle hastened the navy's adoption of radar, then in its infancy, and stimulated Burke and a number of other officers into mentally devising tactical measures that they would later employ in wartime night operations.

Authorities in Washington assumed correctly that the Japanese would view the abrogation of their commercial treaty as a step toward an oil embargo. Without an ample supply of oil, Japan could not pursue its war in China. The obvious alternate source was the oil-rich Dutch East Indies. As a possible deterrent to a Japanese move in this direction, President Roosevelt ordered the U.S. Fleet to base itself on Hawaii.

Admiral Richardson, taking precaution against a surprise submarine attack, moved the fleet from its usual exposed anchorage at Lahaina Roads, off Maui, and concentrated the ships inside Pearl Harbor. From here *Mugford* emerged for escort duty and antisubmarine searches. During the last two weeks of July she participated in a patrol sweep along the Hawaiian chain to Midway, from there steaming to Johnston and Palmyra islands and so back to Pearl Harbor.

Here on the last day of the month Burke was relieved in command of *Mugford* by Lieutenant Commander Wyatt Craig of the Naval Academy class of 1921. When Burke took command the ship and crew were excellent; he left them in superb condition—having scored high in communications, standing third in engineering, and holding the Destroyer Gunnery Trophy.

Burke's relief after only a little over a year in no way reflected on his effectiveness as perceived by BuNav. The bureau was giving as many as possible of its more promising officers a period of command on the highest level commensurate with their rank. For each it was a time of trial and training to facilitate selection of commanders for the two-ocean navy then abuilding and leaders for naval personnel, including hordes of green reserves being inducted to help man the navy's ships and stations.

• •

Burke's new orders took him back to Washington as an inspector in the navy yard, then known as the Naval Gun Factory. Arleigh was delighted at the prospect of another spell of family life with Bobbie. He devoutly hoped, however, that if the United States got into the war he would then be back at sea. A warrior at heart, he had for nearly two decades been whetting his skills for a showdown with his country's enemies. He was ready and determined. Accordingly, when the 7 December 1941 Japanese air raid on the U.S. fleet at Pearl Harbor brought declarations of war, Arleigh lost no time submitting a request for sea duty. His commanding officer, Captain Theodore Ruddock, blocked it.

"Suppose you train a relief first," he told Arleigh.

"Aye, aye, sir!" answered Burke.

Ruddock liked Arleigh, but he had no sympathy with his itch to get into battle. Somebody had to hurl shells, bombs, and torpedoes at the enemy, to be sure, but somebody else had to provide, test, and forward the munitions to the fighters, and in the latter role Burke had few superiors. Burke in his opinion was where he was most needed and hence exactly where he should be. Thus when Arleigh showed up with an officer whom he had trained to the hilt to replace himself, the captain smiled pleasantly with just a touch of mockery.

"Arleigh," he said, "you've done such a good job of training that I am forced to use this man for another and more important duty. Train somebody else."

When Burke had done another thorough job of training and produced another well-prepared trainee, he got another turndown from the captain. Enraged and sounding the depths of frustration, Arleigh was tempted this time to do a sloppy job of training. But it was not in his nature. He brought Ruddock a third good man, again without obtaining his own release.

Arleigh was desperate. His captain appeared to have a ghoulish sense of humor, amusing himself at Burke's distress. A year had passed—a year!—since Arleigh had first asked for release. The battles of the Coral Sea and of Midway had turned the course of the war at sea. U.S. cruisers and destroyers were battling in the dark of night in the waters around Guadalcanal, sometimes with less-than-brilliant results. Arleigh longed to join them and try out strategic and tactical notions he had been working out in his mind and on paper since the night fiasco of Fleet Problem XXI. Under wartime conditions he had been promoted to commander without having to take an examination, but his duties had not changed in the least.

Finally in desperation he strode into Ruddock's office, pounded on the desk, and demanded to be let go. This was an act of mutiny, or at least of insubordination, and Burke knew it, but the captain, instead of taking well-justified offense, replied as if nothing unusual had happened.

"Arleigh," he said, "you've been trained for this job, and I can't spare you." Then, turning on the mocking half-smile that Burke had come to dread, he added, "But I'll tell you what I *will* do. You may have a standing appointment with me for 1600 every Friday afternoon to renew your request for sea duty. How's *that* for handsome?"

Burke brushed aside this meaningless offer and, with Ruddock's ironic permission, drove directly to BuOrd, a couple of miles away, and made his request to the admiral in charge of personnel. Ruddock must have telephoned ahead, because the admiral was ready for him. Nothing could be done, he said. Crestfallen, Arleigh left the great man's presence.

In the outer office, awaiting him was the admiral's secretary. Everybody called her Delores. Burke must have learned her last name also, but later, over the years, it slipped his memory. He never forgot the favor Delores did for him, however, and he never forgot his gratitude for it.

"Look, Commander Burke," she said, "if you will give me a telephone number at which I can reach you at any time, and if you promise to do *exactly* as I tell you, I'll get you to sea."

What strings Delores pulled on his behalf, Burke never knew, but two days later he was summoned back to BuOrd. "I have considered your request for sea duty," said the admiral. "Your request is granted." He handed Burke an official document—an assignment to proceed to the South Pacific and take command of Destroyer Division 43. Four destroyers! Burke pressed the admiral's hand delightedly and walked out of the sanctum on clouds. In the outer office Delores brought him down to earth.

"Look, Commander," she said, "if you don't move fast you're going to be a dead duck. When news of the admiral's softheartedness—some will call it softheadedness—gets around, there are going to be a lot of people trying to change his mind."

"What do you suggest?"

"Three things," snapped Delores. "First, get your assignment to sea duty."

"I've already got it."

"Good!" said Delores. "Now, can you operate a typewriter?"

"Sure. But what's that got to do with it?"

"Just this. It takes the Bureau of Navigation an average of four days to cut and process a set of orders. You can't afford to hang around Washington that long. Get over to BuNav and cut the stencil for your *own* orders—at once!"

"That figures," said Burke, now wide awake. "What else?"

"*Get lost!* As soon as your orders are processed, get out of town, and don't leave a forwarding address—because they're going to be out looking for you!"

"Honey, I'm on my way—and I don't know how to tell you how much I appreciate . . ."

"Skip it, Commander. You've got a job to do. I'll try to hold the home front meanwhile."

Burke fled, mimeographed and filed his orders at BuPers, dashed home, where he packed his bags, bade a tender farewell to Bobbie, patted their new dog, Schotz, and departed. On the way to Union Station, he paused at a florist's and ordered two dozen long-stemmed roses sent to BuOrd for Delores. Then he was off by rail for San Francisco.

During the change of trains at Chicago, Arleigh slipped into the station's USO room, "filled to the eaves with soldiers," and wrote a letter to Bobbie. At Boulder he paused between trains for a visit with his family. Headed again by rail for the West Coast, to Bobbie he wrote, "Mother is much older and isn't in very good health," and mailed the letter at Salt Lake City. He arrived at San Francisco nine hours later. From his hotel he telephoned Twelfth Naval District headquarters and was told to report at 0830 next morning. To Bobbie he wrote, "I shall know tomorrow whether I fly, go by transport—or walk."

The next morning he got the word. He was going by troop transport. Early on 17 January 1943 his ship put to sea, headed under radio silence for the South Pacific.

4

SOUTH
PACIFIC

THE GOOD SHIP *President Monroe*, built as a luxury liner, had been about to set out on a round-the-world cruise when the Japanese raided Pearl Harbor. The U.S. government took her over, stripped her of her grandeur, and assigned her to the War Shipping Administration as a troop transport. She had spent a year in that service when on the morning of 17 January 1943 she departed San Francisco with, besides her crew, 2,000 soldiers, 400 sailors, and Commander Arleigh Burke.

Burke had asked to be taken to the war zone in the first available transportation, and *President Monroe* was it. As the senior line officer on board, he was designated troop commander, which meant looking after the needs and maintaining discipline among the other passengers, mostly untrained reserves. A quick inspection of the passenger spaces revealed one distinct plus, a swimming pool retained from the ship's luxury-liner days. It also revealed some shocking deficiencies. The most critical of these, Burke discovered, was a shortage of cooks.

Calling the men together, Burke made a few announcements and then tackled the main emergency. "How many of you men were cooks in civilian life?" he asked. Two men responded. "Well," he said, "how many of you ever cooked on camping trips?" That brought a few more responses, but not enough. In desperation Burke said, "How many of you ever watched your mothers cook?"

A few naive souls raised their hands, and Burke quickly added their names to his watch bill for cooks.

When *President Monroe* paused at San Diego to take on a marine battalion, Burke rushed ashore and, with the help of a chaplain as guide, led a detachment of passengers in rounding up what was most needed: brooms, swabs, buckets, and other cleaning gear to keep the passenger spaces sanitary; soap, towels, and other toilet articles for the men themselves; and games—card, board, and dart—for pastimes when they were not otherwise occupied and the swimming pool was full.

When the ship was once more at sea, Burke set about organizing the passengers into sections with section leaders and devising and publishing watch lists and rules of conduct. To ensure prompt and undeviating compliance with his orders, he put on his "tough act," which his muscular build made highly convincing. He managed also to write Bobbie a daily letter to be mailed on arrival at his destination. By the end of the first week, he could report success in his project. "Everything is nicely organized and running smoothly," he wrote. "Everybody is working but me—which is the way to have an organization."

As they approached the equator, Commander Burke appointed a committee with instructions to prepare for a Neptune party. He was far from certain that a soldier was qualified to become a shellback, but he would let no mere technicality deny his men a party or exclude any of them from participation. On 26 January, the day of crossing, he welcomed on board a bewhiskered Neptunus Rex and his court, and the initiation began. There was insufficient humiliation to be meted out in equal measure among so many men, but at the end of the ceremony Burke declared them all shellbacks.

A few days later, as they neared their destination, *President Monroe*'s captain looked in on Burke to express his thanks. The passengers on this voyage, he said, were the best-organized and best-managed group of men he had ever had on board.

Arleigh Burke, during his enforced exile from sea duty at Washington's Naval Gun Factory, had read everything he could lay his hands on, including classified battle reports, about the conduct of the war—particularly the heartrending Allied retreat in the Pacific theater of operations. He followed with dismay the story of Japan's 7 December 1941 raid on Pearl Harbor and subsequent conquests of

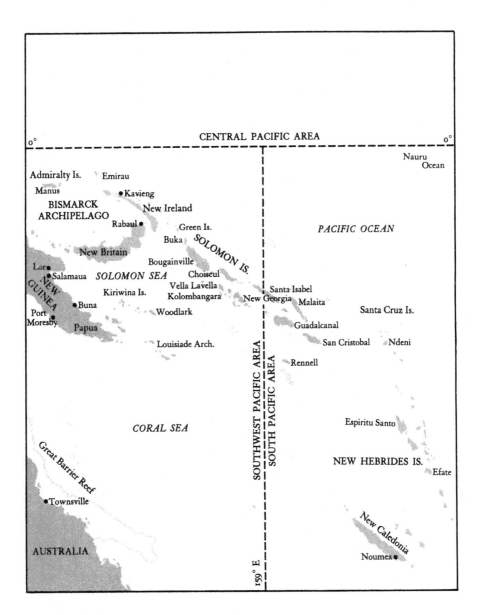

Scene of Early Operations in the South and Southwest Pacific Areas

Guam, Hong Kong, Singapore, and the Philippines—all carried out to facilitate its long-planned conquest and exploitation of the Dutch East Indies.

The Japanese conquest of the East Indies began on 17 December with a landing on Borneo and ended on 8 March 1942 with the surrender of Java. Thus ninety days after Pearl Harbor the Japanese had gained access to the rich oil wells of Borneo, Sumatra, and Java, thereby assuring themselves of an inexhaustible supply of fuel for their tanks, planes, and ships.

In January 1942 the Japanese had seized the Australian port of Rabaul in the Bismarcks and begun converting it into a major strongpoint. The Americans correctly assessed this move as the first step in a drive via the Solomons and New Hebrides to block any substantial flow of men and arms from the United States to Australia. It could be anticipated that Japan would undertake some such measure to prevent a buildup of American forces near its newly acquired and indispensable East Indies.

To counter the Japanese drive, the United States in concert with New Zealand established a command in the South Pacific with headquarters at Auckland and Nouméa and set up forward bases in the New Hebrides islands of Efate and Espíritu Santo. From these positions the Allies expected not only to block the enemy drive but to stage a counteroffensive up the Solomons to recapture Rabaul.

The predictable head-on collision between the Japanese drive and the Allied counteroffensive took place in the summer of 1942 at Guadalcanal Island in the eastern Solomons. Discovery that the Japanese had invaded and were building an airfield on Guadalcanal electrified the Allied South Pacific command into prompt action. A hurriedly assembled, hastily rehearsed naval force on the morning of 7 August put ashore on the island the amphibiously trained U.S. 1st Marine Division, which chased the Japanese construction workers into the jungle and took charge of the unfinished airstrip.

In the night of the 9th, before the transports had completed unloading supplies, a column of seven Japanese cruisers approached Guadalcanal from Rabaul. In an action called the Battle of Savo Island, they dashed through the Allied cover forces firing guns and torpedoes that sank four heavy cruisers and killed 1,000 men.

This was the beginning of the brutal and costly six-month struggle for Guadalcanal. Because the Americans soon had the airstrip operational—they named it Henderson Field—enemy ships approached the island only under cover of darkness. In a campaign to recapture the airstrip, Japanese destroyers and small transports brought in reinforcements and supplies with such nightly regularity that the marines began calling them the Tokyo Express.

Larger enemy ships approached from time to time to take the airfield under bombardment. To protect the field and derail the Tokyo Express, U.S. naval forces challenged the intruders, giving rise to battles in which so many ships were sunk in the body of water north of Guadalcanal that it was permanently renamed Ironbottom Sound.

In October 1942 the struggle for Guadalcanal reached a bloody climax, with operations turning increasingly in favor of the Japanese. At that point the aggressive Vice Admiral William F. Halsey arrived at Nouméa and on orders from Pearl Harbor relieved a defeatist U.S. South Pacific command. Under Halsey's leadership the Americans in the Guadalcanal area, on land, in the air, and at sea, took costly but calculated risks that in thirty extraordinary days and nights reversed the course of the conflict and threw the enemy on the defensive.

Even after the Americans had shifted to the offensive, their naval forces in the night Battle of Tassafaronga suffered another ignominious defeat, though this time it was the enemy who was taken unaware. A squadron of Japanese destroyers, recovering from surprise, fired a spread of torpedoes that sank an American heavy cruiser and severely damaged three others, and all but one of the enemy destroyers got away unscratched.

The American admiral, though assured by his destroyer commander that his destroyers had suitable targets, had withheld permission to fire torpedoes until the enemy, on an opposite course, had passed and was speeding away. The Japanese torpedo directors, with U.S. gunfire flashes as points of reference, aimed at the extended American track. The U.S. cruisers, instead of turning away after firing, maintained course and speed directly into the path of the oncoming torpedoes.

To Arleigh Burke, studying the campaign, it was obvious that the U.S. naval forces, despite their radar advantage, were sometimes clearly outfought. He blamed the American blunders on insufficient drill in night tactics. It was part of the pattern, faulty in his opinion, that included summer maneuvers in relatively cool Puget Sound, winter exercises in the warm Caribbean, and nights and weekends in port—all to keep the sailor happy so he would reenlist. Night operations presumably would make the sailor dissatisfied.

Nonsense, thought Burke. What satisfied the sailor was a sense of achievement, and he had proved it with *Mugford.* He was grateful for the hard night drills Red Whiting had put Destroyer Division 8 through. They had prepared him better to meet the Japanese, who were known to have executed fleet exercises in foul weather and darkness in the cold North Pacific so as to give themselves an advantage over less hardened enemies.

By the end of 1942, the Japanese were maintaining a garrison on Guadalcanal merely to keep the Americans occupied while they prepared a new line of defense in the form of a pair of airfields in the Central Solomons. Aircraft from those new enemy airfields attacked a U.S. troop convoy approaching Guadalcanal, sinking heavy cruiser *Chicago* with torpedoes. Two days later, bombers from the same fields sank U.S. destroyer *DeHaven.*

These losses generated considerable gloom and not a little frustration at South Pacific headquarters. Enemy planes originating from or staging through the new airfields repeatedly bombed Guadalcanal, occasionally bombed more distant Espíritu Santo, and were a constant threat to Allied ships in the area. Bombers from Henderson Field tried without much success to keep the fields too cratered for use. One night in early January an American cruiser-destroyer force

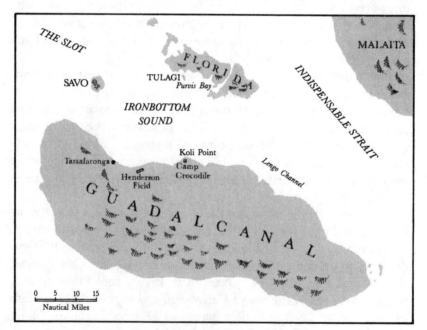

Guadalcanal and Nearby Islands

slipped in and gave the nearer field, at Munda on New Georgia Island, an hour's heavy bombardment. Toward the end of the month another U.S. cruiser-destroyer force, also at night, bombarded the other field, at Vila on Kolombangara Island across Kula Gulf from New Georgia.

During the first week of February, U.S. planes on three separate occasions flashed warnings of a score of Japanese destroyers headed toward Guadalcanal covered by swarms of fighters. Such reports drew planes from Henderson Field to attack the enemy ships and aircraft. In the resulting battles a good many Japanese and a few American aircraft were shot down and several Japanese destroyers were bombed but none sunk.

The renewed enemy activity caused a good deal of speculation and some anxiety among the Americans. Was the Tokyo Express operating again, bringing more nighttime reinforcements to Guadalcanal? Was the stubborn enemy, despite the odds, planning to build up force on the island for another grab for Henderson Field?

The Americans on Guadalcanal, under Major General Alexander M. Patch, had thrust the Japanese garrison into a corner of the island and virtually cut off its supplies. To seal off the enemy from the coast completely and shut him up in the jungle for annihilation, Patch had a battalion ferried around to the far side of the enemy's position. When these, advancing eastward along the shore, met the U.S. main body advancing westward, the truth dawned on all hands. There were no longer any living Japanese on Guadalcanal. Those destroyers seen approaching Guadalcanal were coming to evacuate troops, not bringing in reinforcements. In three high-speed night runs they had succeeded in carrying away the 12,000 half-starved survivors of the garrison that in November had numbered 30,000.

In the late afternoon of 9 February, South Pacific headquarters received with rejoicing General Patch's radio report to Admiral Halsey: "Total and complete defeat of Japanese forces on Guadalcanal effected 1625 today. . . . Tokyo Express no longer has terminus on Guadalcanal."

Four days earlier, troop transport *President Monroe* had rounded the southern cape of the French island of New Caledonia and entered Great Roads, the ship-filled harbor of Nouméa. With a mixture of regret and relief, Burke waved his troops farewell as they filed off the troopship and marched away to camp. He himself then went ashore and inquired his way through the generally lackluster city to the headquarters of commander South Pacific. Arleigh was entering the war at the precise time and place to engage in the destroyer offensives he was trained and yearned for. There were tough times ahead, but the early grim, almost hopeless fight was over.

Commander South Pacific was, of course, Admiral Halsey. This grizzled warrior had gained fame many months before he reversed the course of the war at Guadalcanal. He had first come into the public eye when in retaliation for the Pearl Harbor attack he led his carrier force in raids on Japanese bases in the Marshalls and on Wake and Marcus islands, exploits that in the press earned him the nickname "Bull."

On this his first visit to Nouméa, Burke did not meet the redoubtable Halsey, but, reporting to the staff duty office, he was delighted to encounter an old friend, Captain Ray Thurber, Halsey's operations officer. From him he learned that destroyer *Waller*, Arleigh's prospective flagship, was at sea en route to Havannah Harbor in the island of Efate, some 800 miles north of Nouméa. Burke was scheduled to proceed there as a passenger in cruiser *Denver*.

Denver arrived at Nouméa from Bora Bora on the morning of the 12th and departed the following day with Commander Burke on board. During the overnight run to Efate, Burke called on the skipper, Captain Robert Carney, another old friend, with whom he would be professionally associated later in the war and whom in the postwar years he was destined to succeed as chief of naval operations.

When *Denver* anchored in Efate's Havannah Harbor, Burke obtained passage to *Montpelier*, flagship of Rear Admiral A. Stanton Merrill, to whom he had been ordered to report. "Tip" Merrill, in his early fifties, had been admiral less than a week but was not unduly impressed with his new rank. Soft-spoken, friendly, he treated Burke like an equal, but Burke sensed under Tip's modest deportment a sharp intellect and an inflexible determination. He decided that this was an officer he would be glad to serve under.

Informed that *Waller* had arrived, Burke lost no time making his way to her berth. His heart gladdened when he caught sight of the graceful and powerful ship. A *Fletcher*-class destroyer, she and her sisters were at 2,050 tons the heavyweight champions of their type, armed with five 5-inch and five 40mm guns and ten torpedo tubes, abetted by depth charges. Burke promptly went on board and introduced himself to her skipper, Lieutenant Commander Lawrence H.

"Jack" Frost. In a short, simple ceremony, Burke read his orders and ordered his pennant broken at the mast. He was now Comdesdiv 43.

One of Burke's first official acts as destroyer division commander was to send a letter through channels to Admiral Halsey, asking to have all four ships of his division assembled at one place. To Arleigh that seemed a reasonable request and a necessary condition if, as he intended, he was to drill his team into the best damned destroyer division in the Pacific.

At South Pacific headquarters, however, Burke's letter was received with something approaching hilarity. Though destroyers, the workhorses of the fleet, were now sliding down the ways in almost assembly-line profusion, there were never enough to fill all the demands for raiders against enemy communications or escorts for carriers, tankers, and transports. Any destroyer not assigned to an immediate mission was sure to be snatched up and put to work. At area headquarters in early 1943 the notion of assembling all four destroyers of a division at one time in one place was likely to be considered ridiculous.

After *Waller* had undergone brief overhaul, Captain Frost took his new commodore to sea and put the destroyer through her paces. Burke was delighted with his flagship and favorably impressed by her skipper. To Bobbie he wrote: "I'm operating now and it's strenuous. We aren't in the balcony seats either. We're in the bald-headed row so it's sort of nerve-racking on a new fellow too. Fortunately my first couple of days were fair and I did well enough. . . .

"Could it be that I have been in here three days? It seems longer. Jack handles her well, and she's a good seagoing ship. She shoots well, steams well, has a good bridge force and so I think I'll take her."

Some of the cockiness with which Arleigh had approached his new assignment had become a bit diluted during the last couple of days—days in which he had been intimately associated with men just out of combat. He had yet to experience his own baptism of fire. He knew himself well enough to be sure he would not flinch. He had no doubts of his technical competence. What he had yet to learn was whether in the chaos of battle he would make the right decisions and give the right orders.

As for the general mood, the shift from concern to confidence that Burke had witnessed at Nouméa had preceded him to Efate. Throughout the South Pacific, earlier misgivings had been replaced by general optimism, a feeling among the Americans that they had at least reached the end of the beginning. This outlook was fortified by good news from General Douglas MacArthur, whose Australians and Americans in New Guinea had pursued invading Japanese back over the Owen Stanley Mountains and in several months of jungle warfare wiped out their foothold at Buna on the north coast.

Early 1943 provided rare opportunities for an officer of Burke's rank and training, because it was a period of minor operations in the Pacific, when small-scale victories, such as could be achieved by destroyers, would loom large in the national consciousness. In the Pacific war, major sea battles or amphibious assaults required the participation or support of fast aircraft carriers, the new capital ships, but by 1943 carriers were in short supply, because the war thus far had been destructive of this type. Of the six fast U.S. carriers at the outbreak, *Lexington* was sunk in the Battle of the Coral Sea, *Yorktown* in the Battle of Midway, and *Wasp* and *Hornet* while supporting the Guadalcanal campaign. *Saratoga* had twice been put out of action by submarine torpedoes but, patched up, was back in the South Pacific at the beginning of the year. *Enterprise* was with her but, bombed from the air three times in each of two battles off Guadalcanal, was in a state of such disrepair that she would soon leave for the United States. The Japanese had lost a carrier in the Coral Sea battle, four in the Midway battle, and one in a battle off Guadalcanal.

New U.S. carriers would soon be arriving at Pearl Harbor, together with new destroyers, cruisers, and fast battleships to screen them, but Admiral Chester W. Nimitz, commander in chief Pacific Fleet, had no intention of committing this expanding force to more than minor raids until it had become sufficiently powerful and coherent to be sure of victory over any ships and planes the Japanese could send against it. The successive commanders of Japan's Combined Fleet, aware of the growing threat to themselves, husbanded their strength, keeping their major warships at anchor at Truk, a ring of fortified islands 700 miles north of Rabaul.

Besides the campaign against Rabaul, the only extended U.S. Pacific action in the first ten months of 1943 was clearing the Japanese out of Attu and Kiska, a pair of bleak and barren Aleutian islands that the Japanese had occupied during the Battle of Midway. This operation concluded on a ridiculous note. After air force planes in six weeks had dropped 1,200 tons of bombs on Kiska, a hundred men-of-war bringing 35,000 invasion troops approached and gave the island a tremendous bombardment. When the troops went ashore they found nobody there. The Japanese had left unobserved some time before.

Interest in the Pacific war during these months, then, and later in the history books, was centered on the Rabaul campaign—a dual advance, with MacArthur's Americans and Australians in a mainly army operation advancing from the south via New Guinea and New Britain, while Halsey's Americans and New Zealanders in a navy-dominated operation advanced from the southeast via the Solomon Islands.

Thus for an American naval officer, service in the Solomons in 1943 was the place and time where he had the opportunity to perform the most outstanding service for his country and incidentally to enhance his own reputation. Had such worthies as Ainsworth, Merrill, Moosbrugger, and Burke participated in the Pacific war for the first time in 1944, a year of great battles between fleets and massive amphibious invasions, they might in the chronicles have been little more than four names in a list—names little noted by newsmen and historians and by senior officers responsible for appointments and promotions. That Arleigh found himself at war at the place and time most favorable for his career is part of the Burke luck, which became legendary. Fortunately for himself and his country he had the wisdom, the skill, and the fortitude to recognize and profit by his opportunities.

The Americans' first step up the ladder of the Solomons was their February 1943 invasion of the unoccupied Russell Islands, 30 miles northwest of Guadalcanal. Here they began construction of a pair of airfields that would extend the reach of their planes a little closer to Rabaul. Admiral Halsey would have preferred to make the really important 150-mile leap to New Georgia to capture the Japanese airfield on Munda Point, and he had ample means to do so. This conquest would remove a constant nuisance and menace to U.S. operations in the Guadalcanal area, and from Munda Allied aircraft could keep the nearby Vila airstrip pounded down while covering the final stages of the South Pacific advance on Rabaul.

There was, however, an impediment. The Rabaul campaign had been so planned that MacArthur's Southwest Pacific forces and Halsey's South Pacific forces would move step by step concurrently so as to be mutually supporting. Halsey's move to Munda was to coincide with MacArthur's invasion of Kiriwina and Woodlark islands off New Guinea to set up air bases. Because MacArthur was awaiting arrival of the modest naval force necessary for his move,

Halsey had to wait too. Meanwhile he put out an order to all South Pacific forces: "Keep pushing the Japs around."

U.S. and New Zealand planes based on Guadalcanal had been pushing the enemy around regularly, mainly by bombing the Munda and Vila air bases. With the Russell Islands occupation completed, the fleet prepared to join in the pushing with more bombardments. This time enough gunnery ships were available to hit both fields the same night. Halsey assigned the first such operation to Tip Merrill, who for the purpose organized a task force comprising light cruisers *Montpelier, Cleveland,* and *Denver* and seven destroyers, including *Waller.*

After fueling in safe southern waters, the task force early on 4 March assembled at Espíritu Santo. Here the commanding and flag officers, including Commander Burke, went on board *Montpelier* to receive instructions from Merrill and arrange coordination with the South Pacific air force, whose fighters would provide daytime cover and whose night-flying Catalinas, called Black Cats, would scout and carry spotters. In the early afternoon the task force got under way and shaped course for the Solomons.

From dawn on the 5th the force was under fighter coverage. In the afternoon beneath a cloudless sky the ships passed east and north of Guadalcanal via Indispensable Strait, Lengo Channel, and Iron-bottom Sound. Night fell as they approached the Russell Islands, and all hands went to general quarters. At 2000 the four destroyers assigned to the Munda bombardment detached themselves without signal and took a course that would carry them south of New Georgia. The rest of the force, heading for Vila, continued northwest to pass north of New Georgia via the broad passageway through the major Solomons known as the Slot.

In the calm, moonless night the Americans navigated by radar, changed course and speed at prearranged times, and maintained complete radio silence. Their radar detected their three assigned Black Cats passing overhead but picked up no other planes. Just as it began to appear that the task force would reach its destination undetected, Guadalcanal relayed a radio report that two Japanese ships, light cruisers or destroyers, were speeding down the Slot. Shortly afterward one of the Black Cats reported sighting them. Merrill suspected that these might be misidentified heavy cruisers en route to attack him.

The ships, actually a pair of destroyers, were in fact unaware of his approach. They were on a routine supply run to Vila via Vella

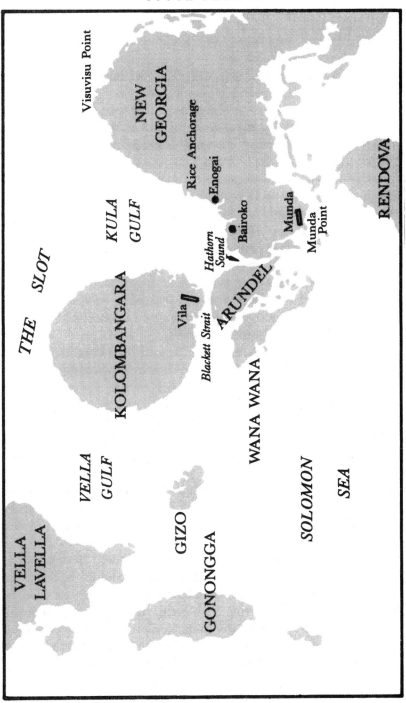

The Central Solomons

Gulf and Blackett Strait, west and south of Kolombangara. Their cargoes unloaded, they opted to return home the short way, via Kula Gulf, a choice that sealed their fate.

As the American task force neared its destination, Commander Burke took over command of *Waller* from her captain, thereby making himself a one-ship commodore. A few minutes after midnight, *Waller*, scouting 6,000 yards ahead of the cruiser column, rounded Visuvisu Point, northernmost cape of New Georgia, and entered Kula Gulf. Her mission was to sweep the gulf and give warning of any enemy ships inside. It was a hairy assignment. If Japanese ships were in fact waiting in the darkness ahead, *Waller*, without close support, would draw their first fire.

A little before 0100, *Waller*'s radar operator picked up and reported a ship moving slowly along the coast of Kolombangara. It was in fact one of the two destroyers heading home after delivering supplies to Vila. The other Japanese destroyer was nearby.

Burke was dubious. "Are you sure it's a ship—not just a rock?" he said. "We've got to be dead certain, you know."

"I'm sure, sir. It's a ship all right."

Still Arleigh was not convinced. He faced the cruel dilemma of risking a waste of expensive torpedoes or possibly letting an enemy ship escape. At last he gave the order to fire a spread of five torpedoes.

By that time *Montpelier*'s radar had picked up the target. Hardly had Burke's torpedoes left their tubes when the cruisers opened with gunfire. Under this double onslaught both Japanese destroyers went down.

The subsequent bombardment left the Vila runways, batteries, aircraft, and supply dumps a shambles. The victorious Americans, their ships unscratched, steamed jubilantly out of Kula Gulf and back down the Slot at 30 knots.

Only Burke was deeply dissatisfied with himself. In delaying to fire torpedoes despite the judgment of his trained radar operator, he had repeated the mistake of the admiral at Tassafaronga. Had he fired at once while reporting to Merrill, he might have sunk the enemy ships without the cruisers having to reveal their presence and position with gunfire. In the existing situation, Burke's tardiness had caused no harm, but a more powerful or more alert enemy might have used the flashes of cruiser fire as points of aim—precisely what had happened at Tassafaronga. Arleigh grimly resolved in the future to accept the reports of his trained subordinates and act upon them without dawdling.

His early lapse was on his mind eight months later when he had become a squadron commander with the rank of captain. Finding himself alone with a young ensign who had the deck, he said casually, "Son, can you tell me the difference between a good officer and a poor one?"

Caught unaware, the ensign hesitated, then, gathering his thoughts, went on at some length about aggressiveness, technical proficiency, command presence, knowledge of human nature—all leadership qualities he had been taught or had observed. Burke listened patiently, then gave his own concept. "The difference between a good officer and a poor one," he said, "is about ten seconds."

5

CENTRAL
SOLOMONS

TEN NIGHTS AFTER the bombardments of the Munda and Vila airfields by Merrill's force, four U.S. destroyers slipped into Kula Gulf and fired salvos at the Vila field without producing anything more spectacular than a few fires that soon died down. During the next few weeks the most effective U.S. naval activity in the Solomons consisted of sowing minefields, which sank three enemy destroyers before the Japanese swept the mines up. In the same period, warnings from scout planes or coastwatchers of the approach of enemy ships roused a cruiser-destroyer force under Rear Admiral Walden L. "Pug" Ainsworth into making a half-dozen night runs up the Slot without ever making contact.

Most of the "pushing the Japs around" that Halsey demanded was being done by Air Command Solomons (Airsols), operating from Henderson Field and nearby newer airfields and from a pair of airstrips in the Russells. Commanded by Rear Admiral Marc Mitscher, Airsols operated some 300 aircraft—bombers and fighters of the U.S. Army, Navy, and Marine Corps and of the Royal New Zealand Air Force. These regularly raided Munda and Vila airfields and shot down increasing percentages of the planes that came to attack targets in the Guadalcanal area.

By April the Allies had come to regard the enemy air attacks as mere nuisances, but beginning on the afternoon of the 7th the Japanese launched a massive series of raids, using at least 300 planes, some of which were observed to be carrier-type. They struck first at shipping in Ironbottom Sound, sinking a destroyer, a corvette, a tanker, and two transports, and then attacked Allied positions in New Guinea. The operation cost the Allies 25 planes, the Japanese 40.

This series of air attacks was planned and directed personally by Admiral Isoroku Yamamoto, commander in chief of Japan's Combined Fleet, who had recklessly stripped 200 planes from his carriers as temporary reinforcements for his decimated land-based naval air force. He hoped thus to check a deteriorating situation and blunt the forthcoming Allied advance. To raise morale and inspect equipment for further aerial offensives, he planned a quick tour of upper Solomons airfields. Rabaul, in a radio message that American cryptanalysts broke, ill-advisedly broadcast the date of the tour, 18 April, and the hour and minute of his arrival at each field.

Counting on Yamamoto's known passion for punctuality, a squadron of long-range P-38s took off from Henderson Field and shot him down as his plane was coming in for a landing in southern Bougainville. To the Japanese navy the loss of its most able and colorful commander was the equivalent of a major defeat. Admiral Mineichi Koga, his successor in command of the Combined Fleet, continued the fateful practice of committing carrier planes to the defense of Rabaul and the Solomons. Serving directly under Koga was the commander of naval forces at Rabaul, Vice Admiral Jinishi Kusaka, an officer with whom Burke would have unusual postwar dealings.

Meanwhile the U.S. Navy had reorganized its forces. Fleets in the Atlantic were even-numbered, those in the Pacific odd-numbered. Admiral Halsey's South Pacific Force became Third Fleet, divisible into task forces, task groups, and task units as operations required. For logistic purposes or when operating together, ships of the same type continued to be organized into squadrons and divisions.

Tip Merrill spent the spring of 1943 shaping up his task force, to which Burke's Destroyer Division 43 was temporarily attached. Operating out of Efate's Havannah Harbor, Merrill drilled his team in preparation mainly for the cruiser-destroyer night battles he hoped and expected to fight. At first he carried out the drills in daylight, simulating night conditions. Then, as his skippers became more skilled at operating together through complex maneuvers, he shifted to night exercises, with Rear Admiral Harry Hill's old battleships serving as "enemy." "We used 30 and 35 knots," he wrote afterward, "and were fortunate not to lose any ships."

By now dependable radar had become generally available in Allied ships, and fleet personnel were learning to use it effectively. The scopes were housed in a special compartment called radar plot, where contacts were plotted and analyzed. Other information, from radio and lookouts, began to be correlated here, and radar plot became the combat information center (CIC). Possession of the CIC gave the Allies an enormous advantage over the Japanese, whose radar, primitive by American standards, had at this time been installed in only their largest ships.

After most drills Tip got his key officers together, usually over beers, to discuss what they were doing and what they were trying to do. Those of his destroyermen who had served in the Guadalcanal campaign had a standing grievance—the tendency of task force commanders to keep the destroyers tied uselessly to the ends of cruiser columns. "When are they going to cut us loose from the cruisers' apron strings?" demanded the destroyermen. As they saw it, the destroyer, armed with torpedoes as well as shells, was a weapon of offense.

Merrill was sympathetic to their point of view. He agreed to release at least his van destroyers on night radar contact with the enemy and hold his cruiser fire until their torpedoes had exploded against enemy hulls. Arleigh Burke had been listening without saying much. Most of his fellow destroyermen had had far more experience in combat than Burke's own one belated torpedo launching. At last he spoke up, giving voice to an opinion he had held for some time. Why, he asked, should the van destroyers have to wait for the task force commander's release? If the destroyer division commander knew his business, and presumably he did or he wouldn't be a division commander, why should he not head for the enemy, without orders, the instant his ship, in the lead, made radar contact? It was a daring suggestion, but Merrill promised to give it some thought.

Merrill retained his four cruisers, but he had no better luck than Burke in holding on to his destroyers, which came and went unpredictably. He was sorry to lose officers whom he had indoctrinated in his tactics, but he recognized that the newcomers brought novel ideas and fresh points of view. One destroyer he went to almost any lengths to retain was *Waller*, mainly because it was Burke's flagship. Burke was not only his most hardworking and effective skipper, he also thought things out much as Merrill did, supplementing Merrill's thinking. Early in May he asked Burke to put into writing the doctrine they had worked out with respect to destroyers.

Applying himself diligently, Burke on the 7th submitted a typed doctrine, "Employment of Destroyers," which embodied the decisions reached in the numerous task force conferences. Under the heading "Use of destroyers with cruiser task force at night against enemy surface craft," he pointed out that a policy of immediate destroyer attack from the van of one's own forces requires (1) that the destroyers be ready for attack, (2) that the destroyer commander initiate the attack at the first favorable opportunity after contact, and (3) that the task force commander have confidence in the destroyer commander's ability to make a successful attack and retire with the least embarrassment to the cruisers. "The last of these is the most difficult," he pointed out. "The delegation of authority is always hard and under such circumstances as these, when such delegation of authority may result in disastrous consequences if a subordinate commander makes an error, it requires more than is usually meant by confidence—it requires faith."

Early in June, Merrill and Burke reluctantly parted company as the latter on orders from South Pacific headquarters transferred from commanding Destroyer Division 43 to command of Destroyer Division 44 and hoisted his pennant on destroyer *Conway*. Burke was disgusted to learn that his new division was assigned to the dreary business of convoy duty, escorting transports carrying supplies and reinforcements to Guadalcanal. In mid-June this type of duty became more hazardous, and for Burke more interesting, when the Japanese, spotting a buildup of forces in the Guadalcanal area as if for a major offensive operation, began a series of air strikes on shipping in the southeast approaches to the island.

On 30 June, timed to coincide with the invasion of Kiriwina and Woodlark islands by MacArthur's Southwest Pacific forces, Halsey's South Pacific troops stormed ashore in the Central Solomons for a four-mile drive through the jungle to capture Munda airfield on New Georgia Island. On the night of 4–5 July other South Pacific troops invaded New Georgia at Rice Anchorage on Kula Gulf nine miles north of the Munda area. Their mission was to advance inland and block reinforcements passing from Vila to Munda via the gulf.

The following night Pug Ainsworth at last engaged the Tokyo Express. With a force of three cruisers and four destroyers, he fought an Express of seven destroyers, sinking one with gunfire and losing a cruiser, sunk by torpedoes. A week later in another night battle, Ainsworth with three cruisers and ten destroyers tangled with an Express of one cruiser and five destroyers. He sank the cruiser, but torpedoes from the enemy destroyers sank one of Ainsworth's destroyers and heavily damaged all three of his cruisers.

While these battles were not exactly duplicates of the Tassafaronga debacle, they could hardly be called American victories. Obviously the Americans did not yet rival the Japanese in night surface tactics. In each of his battles, Ainsworth had come in close, making himself an easy visual target. He then waited too long to open fire, thus permitting the enemy to take careful aim and release torpedoes that reached his position just as he was belatedly turning away. Later, when Burke had an opportunity to study the battle reports, he was confirmed in his conviction that the difference between a good officer and a poor one is about ten seconds.

On 20 July, Commander Burke was given an assignment very much to his taste. While retaining his flagship *Conway* and his designation of Comdesdiv 44, he succeeded to the command of Task Group 31.2, with the informal title ComdesSlot. As ComdesSlot he would command whatever Third Fleet destroyers were available for independent missions in waters of the Central Solomons, supplementing Merrill's and Ainsworth's task groups. He would thus be commanding his own group in waters where he was sure to see action.

As commander of Task Group 31.2, Burke served directly under Rear Admiral Theodore S. "Ping" Wilkinson, commanding Task Force 31, the Third Fleet's amphibious force. Burke's first assignment from his new boss was to go to the relief of several hundred U.S. marines stranded at Enogai on Kula Gulf.

The marines had recently been sent to New Georgia to reinforce the American troops put ashore at Rice Anchorage on 4–5 July. For lack of artillery the newcomers had made little progress and had established themselves at Enogai, 4 miles down the coast from the Rice Anchorage landing area. Burke's mission was to escort transports to Kula Gulf to replenish the marines' depleted supplies and evacuate their sick and wounded. Tip Merrill's cruisers and destroyers would lead the way and operate up the Slot, providing cover.

In midafternoon, 23 July, Burke's convoy, four destroyers escorting four APDs (destroyers converted into high-speed transports), left Guadalcanal and shaped course for New Georgia. At midnight under a bright moon the convoy rounded Visuvisu Point and headed into the gulf, Burke's flagship *Conway* leading.

As they moved down the New Georgia coast, Burke puzzled over his chart with an eye on the radarscope. The chart showed two similar points of land, Enogai and Bairoko, about 2 miles apart. On the radar screen these were indistinguishable from several other points. It was important to know which position they were approaching, because at Enogai, their destination, the marines were waiting, whereas Bairoko was occupied by Japanese. For want of a more dependable guide, Burke used dead reckoning based on two known factors, the time of passing Visuvisu and the speed of his ship. When he reckoned his ship to be off Enogai he approached the coast and hove to.

The chronometer showed 0100. They were exactly on time, but where was the signal light the marines had been directed to display at Enogai Point? Until the marines made known their position by some means, there was not much Burke could do but wait. At last, twenty minutes late, the light flashed on. The convoy breathed with relief and promptly began to unload.

When unloading was completed and the last of the American wounded were being taken on board the transports, the destroyers moved down the coast according to plan and bombarded Bairoko. In the course of rapid ship movements to confuse the shore gunners and avoid their fire, Burke fell and broke two ribs. Though in considerable pain, he rose, and without mentioning his injury he resumed his command duties.

The Japanese batteries replied haphazardly to the American fire, achieved no hits, and were soon silenced. By that time the transports were buttoned up and departing the gulf at such speed that the destroyers had to race to catch up with them.

As dawn was approaching, Burke strolled out on a bridge wing of *Conway* and looked back at his column of ships. He was exasperated to note that one of his destroyers was swinging right and left out of line. Few things irritated him more than failure to maintain a tidy formation, and this time his irritation was aggravated by his aching ribs. Calling the offending skipper on TBS,* "Mister," he barked, "that's a destroyer you've got there, not a yo-yo!"

After breakfast Burke retired to the emergency cabin abaft the pilothouse and began his paperwork. Following any action in which guns were fired the officers responsible had to prepare and submit a stack of forms and reports. While he was thus occupied, the communication officer arrived with a decoded message from Admi-

---

* TBS: Talk Between Ships, short-range radio for voice communication at sea.

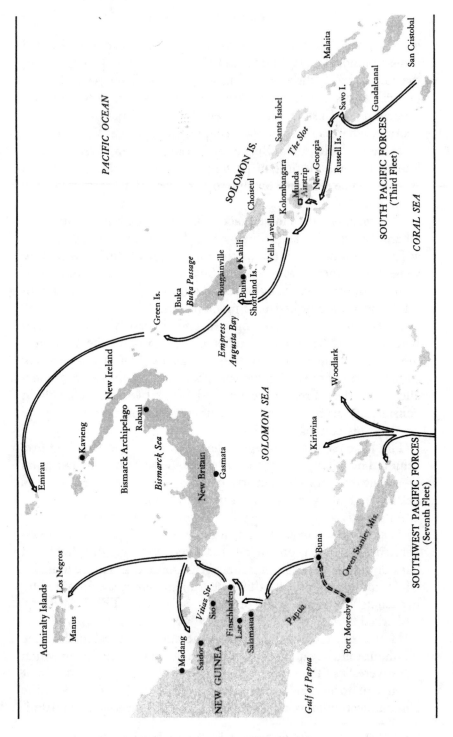

Rabaul Neutralized and Bypassed

ral Wilkinson: "You will be prepared to lead a force of eight destroyers up the Slot for a dawn bombardment of Munda tomorrow. The circumstances will be such that your bombardment must be delivered precisely at dawn, and your fire must register exactly on target."

Burke was perplexed. He had not been in a position to keep track of the campaign to capture Munda airfield. He had no notion of what "circumstances" required precise timing and pinpoint bombardment. Concluding that he'd better have more information, he dashed off a message requesting permission to have *Conway* bring him to Guadalcanal for a conference with Admiral Wilkinson. Permission granted, Burke's flagship in due course left the formation and steamed along the Guadalcanal coast to Koli Point, location of Camp Crocodile, Third Amphibious Force headquarters. Here Wilkinson was waiting for Burke with ground force and air force liaison officers, who explained the situation.

The drive on Munda had stalled when confronted by the Japanese in-depth defenses, including concrete pillboxes and underground fortifications. Major General Millard F. Harmon, Admiral Halsey's top army commander, had replaced the commanding officer and rushed in all reserves. The replacement commander, Major General Oscar W. Griswold, tightened his lines and proposed to resume the drive on the morning of 25 July. At his request the navy—that is, Burke's destroyers—would stage a bombardment of the Japanese positions beginning at dawn on the 25th, and that would be followed without interval by a concentrated bombing from dive-bombers. Because U.S. ground positions would be within yards of the enemy positions, the naval bombardment would have to be carried out with extreme precision, and the timing would have to be equally precise lest the aircraft fly into the destroyer fire. For Burke that was quite an order.

"What do you think, Arleigh?" asked Admiral Wilkinson. "Can you take this one on?"

"Without question, sir, but I have one request. If it's all right with you, I'd like to take a dummy run up there this afternoon and sort of case the situation. As you know, sir, our charts aren't much good, and I don't know a thing about Munda."

It was all right with the admiral, but he wondered when Arleigh expected to get some sleep. In fact, Burke had been awake and active for nearly twenty-four hours, part of the time under tense conditions and in considerable pain.

Disregarding fatigue, Arleigh stopped by sick bay to have his cracked ribs taped, then rejoined his task group, now anchored off Tulagi Island across Ironbottom Sound from Guadalcanal. After giving his skippers and gunnery officers precise instructions, he left on board *Conway*, which joined a convoy for mutual protection. En route he finally got a couple of hours' sleep.

Off Munda Point that afternoon Burke made good use of the skills he had acquired as camera officer on board *Procyon*, *Antares*, and *Argonne*. The target assigned for the naval gunfire was a strip approximately 1,400 by 400 yards parallel to the forward American line. Burke had been told range and bearing of the strip from a group of houses he could see, part of a peacetime coconut plantation. He carefully plotted the houses, using tangents of islands, so that they could be located accurately. From these he determined the range and bearing of the target strip from the ships. Since the strip, deep in the jungle, was of course invisible from offshore, the fire from Burke's destroyers would have to be indirect. That meant a high trajectory, all the more reason for a prompt cease-fire before the planes arrived.

When Burke had finished drawing his charts and making his computations, dusk had set in. As night fell he had *Conway*'s skipper head east-southeast to meet and join the rest of the bombardment group en route from Tulagi. During the southeasterly run Arleigh took another nap. After the meeting at sea, with *Conway* and the other destroyers heading back to the Munda area, he was too busy giving instructions, directly and via TBS, to think of sleep.

When first light grayed the sky, the bombardment group was steaming slowly off New Georgia, with Munda Point becoming gradually visible beyond the fringing reef. At 0609 on orders from Burke one of the destroyers opened a brief indirect fire. When no radio complaint followed, he knew that it was not hitting Americans. At 0615 *Conway* opened fire, and the other three ships joined in. In the short time allotted, the group hurled 4,000 5-inch projectiles into the target strip.

At 0644 with stopwatch precision the destroyer guns fell silent, and the men in the ships could hear the roar of oncoming aircraft. What followed was the heaviest air raid of the Central Solomons campaign—171 bombers and torpedo planes escorted by seventy-nine fighters.

When Burke got back to Tulagi he was handed an order for Destroyer Division 44 to head for Espíritu Santo for rest, recreation, and, as necessary, refit. The order was in conformity with Admiral Halsey's policy of relieving men in the combat zone at regular intervals, before unrelenting pressure impaired their efficiency.

Burke was willing to send his ships back to a rest area, but he himself was determined not to go if he could help it. The Tokyo Express was operating again, offering him, as he saw it, an opportunity at last to fight a battle at sea in command of his own force. Ainsworth's group was too depleted to do anything about the renewed enemy activity, and Merrill's was too far away. There were, however, half a dozen unattached destroyers in the Guadalcanal area. Burke proposed to Admiral Wilkinson that he organize them into a new Task Group 31.2 and offered himself as commander, since there was nobody else present and available with sufficient seniority.

Wilkinson accepted the offer, and Burke had his opportunity. Arleigh shifted his command pennant to destroyer *Maury*, where he was welcomed by her skipper, old friend Commander Gelzer Sims, his prewar executive officer in *Mugford*. Commodore Burke lost no time in indoctrinating his captains in his concept of fighting his ships in two mutually supporting divisions.

The plan was derived from his study of the Punic Wars. As he explained later:

> The tactics of Scipio Africanus particularly interested me as being sound, simple of execution, and adaptable to naval employment. The plan was based on hitting the enemy with one sudden surprise after another. This was accomplished by putting two destroyer divisions in parallel columns. One division would slip in close, under cover of darkness, launch torpedoes, and duck back out. When the torpedoes hit, and the enemy started shooting at the retiring first division, the second half of the team would suddenly open up from another direction. When the rattled enemy turned toward this new and unexpected attack, the first division would slam back in again. Of course, the Solomon Islands area was ideally suited to this type of tactic, with the many islands helping prevent radar detection of the second column.

On 1 August, anticipating an early encounter, Burke prepared and distributed his battle plan. On radar contact, one destroyer division, under cover of darkness, would approach the enemy on a parallel and opposite course, while the other division maintained station at maximum effective gun range from the enemy. The first division would fire torpedoes and turn away. As the torpedoes exploded against the enemy hulls, both destroyer divisions would open gunfire, a tactic that could be repeated as often as necessary to confound and destroy the enemy.

The expected encounter did not develop, but Task Group 31.2 patrolled the Slot each night, and Burke devoted much of the day to his paperwork, allotting himself little time for sleep. After each nightly patrol, Wilkinson reminded Arleigh that he was overstaying his time in the Slot and that he was to be detached as soon as a relief became available.

Arleigh devoutly hoped to have his battle before that happened, but the Japanese failed to accommodate. He still had not made contact with the enemy when Commander Frederick Moosbrugger arrived on 3 August to relieve him. His disappointment was somewhat offset by orders to proceed by air to Nouméa to take command of Destroyer Squadron 12 with the rank of captain.

Operating on nervous energy, Burke had ignored his state of exhaustion until the pressure was removed. Relieved of his command at last and waiting at Henderson Field for transportation to New Caledonia, he fell asleep sitting up and remained in that posture dead to the world for several hours. When space was found for him in a Nouméa-bound plane, he climbed stiffly aboard and stretched out on a fuel tank, where, disregarding the ridges that dug into his back, he remained soundly asleep until after the aircraft had landed and the flight attendant shook him awake.

Arleigh had scarcely got himself settled in his new flagship, destroyer *Farenholt,* and been sworn in as captain when he received news that filled him with wildly conflicting emotions. In the third night after Burke's relief, Moosbrugger commanded Task Group 31.2 in a striking victory over a four-destroyer Tokyo Express. In the action, called the Battle of Vella Gulf, six U.S. destroyers sank three of the enemy ships and came away unscathed. Americans had at last outperformed the Japanese in their own night-fighting specialty. Admiral Halsey, delighted at this turn of events, saw to it that details of Moosbrugger's virtuoso performance were widely disseminated as an example for other American tacticians.

Burke was envious of Moosbrugger's achievement but not bitterly so. He sent a letter warmly complimenting the victor. "Dear Moose," he wrote, "Your battle the other night will go down in history as one of the most successful actions ever fought. It was splendidly conceived and marvelously executed. . . . I would like to add my congratulations for a job well done to the hundreds of commendations that you will receive."

From details of the battle that Halsey had released, Burke strongly suspected that Moosbrugger had used the battle plan that Arleigh himself had drawn up. He was right. A couple of days after Commander Moosbrugger had taken over the task group, Admiral Wilkinson had ordered him to proceed with it south of New Georgia and Kolombangara and make a nighttime sweep of Vella Gulf, where there was a strong possibility of meeting enemy ships.

The commander had had time to confer no more than briefly with his captains and no time at all to indoctrinate them and drill them in his tactical methods. In the circumstances, Commander Rodger Simpson, who remained with the group as second-in-command, invited his new boss's attention to his previous commodore's battle plan. Moosbrugger perceived its merit and, after altering some geographic and navigational data to fit the situation, adopted and acted upon it.

"You probably know by this time," Simpson wrote Burke, "that Moosbrugger used your plan almost verbatim, a bit of a story on the necessity of the junior knowing how to support his boss, and I got them accepted. I knew it must be a swell plan when I saw it. Thanks a million. The result was too easy. Yet it will always be when you have your eyes open and know what you are going to do. I am looking forward to the time when the stakes are a lot higher and I can follow you in. Some may think, but I know your plans are tops."

Burke was delighted that his tactics had produced such spectacular success, but even the new silver eagles on his collar and his command of eight destroyers did little to relieve his disgust with his new assignment—more convoy duty. To Admiral Wilkinson he wrote: "Much as I like to have a squadron the shift did come at an unfortunate time for my morale. Every destroyer sailor hopes to serve in your active force and when I had to leave just as things were popping good, I was very disheartened.

"I do envy Moosbrugger, of course, but he did such a magnificent job that it couldn't be bettered. The whole situation was fine—good intelligence, staff work and decisions. It's good to know that destroyers can deliver the wallop they carry. It is reassuring to know that the attack plans worked so well."

In writing that last sentence, Burke was probably counting on

Wilkinson's being aware who had devised the attack plans that worked so well—a none-too-subtle hint that the author of such plans should be in the combat zone instead of hauling freight. At any rate, a short while later Destroyer Squadron 12 was transferred from convoy duty to the Slot patrol. For Burke, however, it proved a frustrating experience, because his squadron found nothing to shoot at but a few barges.

The fact was that the Tokyo Express of supply and reinforcement had ceased to operate in those waters because of a shift in Halsey's strategy. During the Munda campaign on New Georgia Island, the Japanese had been rapidly reinforcing Kolombangara, the adjacent island in the Solomons chain, obviously expecting the Americans to land there next and make a drive for the Vila airfield. Halsey decided not to play their game. He wanted no more costly, long-drawn-out Munda-type operations. Weeks before the fall of Munda, he decided to bypass Kolombangara entirely and have his forces occupy Vella Lavella, the island next beyond it, where the only Japanese present were half-starved survivors of the Battle of Vella Gulf, who had swum ashore from their sinking ships.

With the Allied occupation of Vella Lavella, the Japanese wrote off the Central Solomons, canceled the Tokyo Express, and turned their energies toward strengthening Bougainville, largest of the Solomon Islands and chief obstacle in the path of the South Pacific forces' advance on Rabaul. The Japanese made a considerable effort to get their men off Kolombangara and Vella Lavella, occasionally by destroyer or submarine but chiefly by barge. When slaughter of the barges became severe they postponed further major evacuations until the dark of the moon in late September. The Japanese destroyers, not looking for a fight, had acquired a means of eluding attack. Lacking radar themselves, they had a device that detected radar waves from Allied ships, which they thus easily evaded.

Allied aircraft staging through Munda generally controlled the air over the Solomons by day, but at night Japanese planes posed a continuing threat to Allied ships in the combat zone. There was considerable bombing by the former and shooting by the latter without much damage, except to the sailors' nerves. As Burke later explained: "There was no possibility of getting any sleep at night while we were under air attack, and there wasn't very much chance of getting sleep during the daytime because of the necessity for reading dispatches, getting into harbor, refueling fast, getting provisions, relieving ships, attending to a multitude of incidental chores, and getting going in time to take maximum advantage of the hours of darkness in the 'happy hunting grounds.'"

Toward the end of September, Desron 12 was ordered to Espíritu Santo for rest and recreation, a move everybody needed because of the strain of the air raids and nobody opposed because there was nothing worth hunting in the happy hunting grounds. Ordered to Espíritu at the same time was Tip Merrill's Task Force 39, temporarily comprising Cruiser Division 12 and Destroyer Division 45. When Desdiv 46, not yet assembled, was added to Desdiv 45, it would form Destroyer Squadron 23, an integral part of Task Force 39.

Everyone who had any appreciation of South Pacific strategy had a good notion of what was impending—nothing less than an Allied invasion of the big island, Bougainville. When that happened the lull would be over. Bougainville was the last major bastion defending Rabaul. The Japanese had been strengthening their positions on the island for two years. In all probability the Japanese Combined Fleet, so long quiescent at Truk, would emerge to hurl back the invaders.

Halsey was perilously short of naval forces to meet such a challenge. Many of his cruisers and destroyers had been lost in the Solomons campaign, and too much was happening or impending elsewhere—in Europe, in the Atlantic, in the central Pacific—for him to expect adequate reinforcement. While he had the advantage of Airsol's nearly 500 Allied planes based on Henderson, Munda, and a new field on Vella Lavella, his only carrier was *Saratoga*, damaged *Enterprise* having long since limped to the United States for repairs. At Halsey's urging, Admiral Nimitz lent him the light carrier *Princeton* with the proviso that both it and the *Saratoga* force must be available to support an invasion of the Gilbert Islands by the Central Pacific Force on 20 November.

Supported by Airsols and carrier planes, Wilkinson's Third Amphibious Force would land the invaders at the Bougainville beachhead. Because of the nearness to Rabaul, the Japanese were almost certain to counterattack by sea as well as by air, and the surface force would undoubtedly attack under cover of darkness. Only Merrill's Task Force 39 was available to fend it off.

In the circumstances, Merrill allowed his sailors little time for recreation. At dusk each day his ships went to sea for a night of maneuvers and rehearsal. To substitute for his missing Desdiv 46, he asked Burke for a loan of four destroyers from his Squadron 12, and Burke was happy to oblige, always including his flagship with himself on board in the loan. During these operations, which reminded Arleigh pleasantly of their inventive exercises of the preceding spring, Burke's immediate senior was Captain Martin J. Gillan, Comdesdiv 45 and Comdesron 23. Burke gathered the impression that Merrill, while pleased with the performance of his destroyer captains, had doubts about the aptitude of Captain Gillan. Burke shared his doubts but kept his opinion to himself.

As a special treat before combat, Admiral Halsey arranged for brief leaves in major ports for as many combatants as possible. Burke in *Farenholt* and Merrill in *Montpelier*, together with some of their other ships, drew Sydney, Australia, where they arrived on 19 October. It was a gleeful occasion for the crews. For them the recreation facilities of Espíritu Santo and Efate were well enough, but the big city offered something extra and very special indeed—namely, women.

Burke summoned his staff of three young officers. He told them he expected them to go ashore and stay there, with the exception that one of them, no matter which, must be back on board by 0800 each morning to read dispatches and be on hand for anything that had to be done. He himself would be on board from 0800 till early afternoon but would probably be ashore most evenings. He would leave word where he could be found, but, he added, "When I'm ashore I don't want to be disturbed about anything—not *anything*—unless it's really vital. Now get going and have fun, but try to stay out of trouble!"

That evening Captain Burke donned a fresh uniform and proceeded to a nearby officers' club, where Tip Merrill had reserved a room for a party to which he had invited senior officers. Like all Merrill's parties, it was a quiet affair, not the sort relished by officers who fancy a bit of uproar with their fun.

Arleigh, sipping a whiskey and soda, was talking with Tip when he became suddenly aware that one of his staffers was standing nearby, dispatch in hand.

Said Burke, "I thought I told you fellows not to bother me with ship's business when I was on the beach."

"Sir," replied the young officer, "you said not to bother you unless it was important. I think you'll find this dispatch important, sir."

As Burke ran his eyes over the message, he sat bolt upright. Captain Gillan, it said, had been relieved as commodore of De-

stroyer Squadron 23. Captain Arleigh Burke, detached as commander of Destroyer Squadron 12, would get earliest available air
transportation to Espíritu Santo, where he would take command of
Desron 23.

Arleigh's hand trembled with excitement as he passed the message
to Tip. As commodore of Desron 23 he would command the eight
destroyers of Merrill's Task Force 39, earmarked to provide night
cover for the forthcoming invasion. That would mean action at last,
probably a major battle.

Tip read the dispatch with satisfaction and handed it back. His
request had been granted. Burke, already on his feet, excused himself to go and seek air transportation. Merrill wished him good luck,
adding, "I'll be seeing you, Arleigh."

31-KNOT
BURKE

CAPTAIN BURKE boarded his new flagship, *Charles S. Ausburne*, at Espíritu Santo in the morning of 23 October. After meeting the ship's officers and hoisting his pennant, he summoned the skippers of *Dyson*, *Stanly*, and *Claxton*, which, together with the flagship, composed Destroyer Division 45, to a conference on board *Ausburne*. Desdiv 45, which Burke commanded directly, was half of Destroyer Squadron 23, of which Burke was likewise the new commander.

At the meeting also was Commander Bernard L. Austin, future commander, under Burke, of Desdiv 46, comprising four more destroyers, the other half of Desron 23. The ships of Desdiv 46 had been ordered to the Guadalcanal area, where they were being brought together for the first time.

To the officers assembled on board *Ausburne* Commodore Burke passed out a tentative version of a doctrine he had prepared for them and had had mimeographed during the delays en route from Sydney. Set forth in terse language it was the body of principles covering destroyer warfare that he had been developing since before his arrival in the South Pacific. The spirit of the document was summarized in five lines on the cover page:

If it will help kill Japs—it's important.
If it will not help kill Japs—it's not important.

Keep your ship trained for battle!

Keep your material ready for battle!

Keep your boss informed concerning your readiness for battle!

The last page contained only these words:

NON-BATTLE ORDERS: *NONE.* CORRECTIONS TO THIS SECTION WILL NOT BE PERMITTED.

In the ensuing conference the captains were strongly impressed by Burke's readiness in answering their questions. Obviously he had

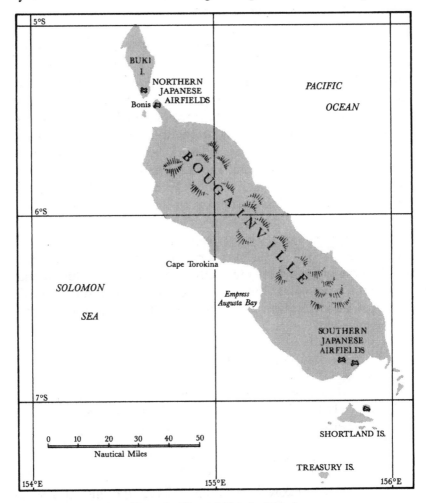

Bougainville and Nearby Islands

long since thought out a solution to every likely problem and formu-
lated answers that were succinct yet clear and complete.

Early the following morning, Desdiv 45 left Espíritu for Purvis
Bay, an indentation in Florida Island across Ironbottom Sound from
Guadalcanal. Burke went ahead separately by plane, summoned by
Admiral Halsey to a meeting at Camp Crocodile, where commander
South Pacific with his operations staff had arrived to confer with
major participants in the forthcoming invasion. Here Halsey and his
senior officers would be closer to the scene of action and able to
interrogate returning flyers and sailors. As for Burke, he was grati-
fied to note among the assembled officers old friends Rear Admirals
Tip Merrill, Ping Wilkinson, and Ray Thurber.

Admiral Halsey opened the conference with a few pithy remarks
and then turned the proceedings over to Thurber, who told the
assembled officers that after various scattered preliminary landings,
bombings, and bombardments, expected to perplex and it was hoped
disperse the enemy, the Third Amphibious Force, covered by Task
Force 39, would land 14,000 U.S. marines near Cape Torokina on
Empress Augusta Bay, halfway up the west coast of Bougainville.

All agreed that this would be a daring but logical move—daring
in bypassing the Treasury and Shortland islands and the airfields at
Bougainville's southern end, logical in that Cape Torokina was
lightly garrisoned and midway between the airfields at the northern
and southern ends of the big island. Here the Americans, instead of
fighting through the jungle to capture an enemy airstrip, as at
Munda, would build their own airstrip and let the Japanese fight
through the jungle and try to do the capturing, as at Guadalcanal.

The following afternoon, 25 October, for the first time Merrill's
Task Force 39 was assembled in one place, twelve ships together in
Purvis Bay, thus organized:

> Van Destroyers (Desdiv 45), Captain Arleigh A. Burke (Comdes-
> ron 23):
>   *Charles F. Ausburne* (flag), *Dyson, Stanly, Claxton*
> Main Body (Crudiv 12), Rear Admiral Merrill (CTF 39):
>   *Montpelier* (flag), *Cleveland, Columbia, Denver*
> Rear Destroyers (Desdiv 46), Commander Bernard L. Austin:
>   *Spence* (flag), *Thatcher, Converse, Foote*

By radio Commodore Burke called a meeting of his captains for
that afternoon, after fueling. Meanwhile he proceeded with his plan

to inspect each of his eight destroyers. Next in line was *Claxton*.

As the commodore came over *Claxton*'s rail, he was met by her captain, Commander Herald Stout, a bright and efficient but somewhat offbeat personality, whose whimsies were reflected by his ship and crew. An example was the destroyer's logo, painted across the front of her bridge: a pair of tumbling dice underlined with the words *Click with Claxton*.

Burke took that irregularity in stride, but he was brought to a standstill by what he saw painted on one of the torpedo tubes: a small Indian wearing only moccasins, a headband with feather, and an outsize G-string while firing an arrow into the posterior of a Japanese character labeled TOJO. Burke, who was not above occasionally amusing himself with the comics, recognized the Indian as Little Beaver, a sort of pint-sized chief of staff of one Red Ryder.

"You know, Stout," said the commodore, "that's what this squadron needs. We need an insignia—a trademark that all the ships can be proud of."

"Well, why not the Little Beaver, Commodore?"

"It's good enough for me," said Burke.

Arleigh had been casting about for something more colorful than a mere number to give his squadron identity and coherence. At the end of the afternoon meeting, in which Burke explained to his skippers their rather awesome duties of the next few days and nights, Burke asked them for suggestions for a distinguishing emblem. When nothing better was forthcoming, he offered Captain Stout's recommended symbol.

After all, as he pointed out, "We're the little beavers for those cruisers."

The proposal was unanimously accepted. Thenceforth the ships and men of Destroyer Squadron 23 were known, except in the most formal contexts, as the Little Beavers.

The following morning, Task Group 39.3, comprising cruisers *Cleveland* and *Denver* accompanied by *Ausburne* and three other Little Beavers, sortied from Purvis Bay and steamed up through the Slot. They were followed at some distance by eight troop-carrying APDs, escorted by three destroyers. Four additional transport units joined the procession at spaced intervals.

The function of Task Group 39.3 was to stand off after dark to the west of the lightly held Treasury Islands in a covering position to repel enemy surface forces seeking to interfere with the transport units. Unmolested, the units approached the Treasuries and landed

6,000 New Zealanders, who conquered and occupied the islands. In Allied hands they served for a small-craft staging station and at the same time forbade their use as a Japanese base for intercepting supplies en route to Torokina.

Shortly before the landing a float plane snooper found the cruiser-destroyer task group standing guard and dropped flares and float lights. "Fortunately," Burke reported, "the bogie became so interested in playing 'hide and seek' with the [covering group] that it is believed he did not see the landing forces coming up towards Treasury Island from the South."

The following night, 27 October, as a diversion for the ongoing Treasuries operation and for the forthcoming Torokina invasion, 725 U.S. marines landed on Choiseul Island, where they raided and created confusion for more than a week before withdrawing. On 1 November, the eve of D-day, Task Force 39 as a whole sortied from Purvis and shaped course for Bougainville. This force created further diversion by a midnight bombarding of two airfields northwest of Torokina—Bonis on Bougainville and another on nearby Buka Island.

Task Force 39 then raced southeast 200 miles down the Bougainville coast to carry out a dawn bombardment of the Shortland Islands airfield and other objectives southeast of Torokina. Already approaching the area were carriers *Saratoga* and borrowed *Princeton*, prepared to send their bombers in to complete the paralysis of the Buka and Bonis airfields.

While local Japanese air power was being thus enfeebled and Japanese attention drawn this way and that, Admiral Wilkinson's Third Amphibious Force made a dawn entry into Empress Augusta Bay and began landing marines at Cape Torokina. Some 300 Japanese at the beachhead put up a determined resistance, which the invaders quickly overcame, while Airsols scattered an air attack from Rabaul. By the end of the day Wilkinson's amphibians had landed 14,000 troops and 6,000 tons of supplies.

After bombarding the Shortlands, Task Force 39 retired to the vicinity of Vella Lavella to snatch a bit of rest and await developments—all the task force but Burke's Desdiv 45, that is. Because this division was dangerously short of fuel, Burke led it at high speed to Kula Gulf for a quick drink from an oiler and then back up toward Bougainville, catching up with and rejoining the task force at 2315. By this time Merrill was already heading for Empress Augusta Bay to intercept an approaching enemy cruiser-destroyer force reported by reconnaissance planes.

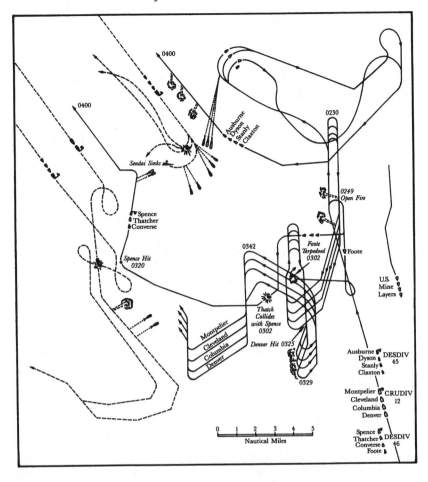

Battle of Empress Augusta Bay, 2 November 1943

The situation chillingly resembled the one preceding the Battle of Savo Island except that the U.S. scout planes were now providing "phenomenally accurate" reports, and Merrill had a winning battle plan. Mindful that his ships constituted the principal Allied surface force in the South Pacific, he aimed at no Nelsonian battle of annihilation. He would free his two destroyer divisions to carry the fight to the enemy while using his cruisers merely to repulse the attackers from the beachhead.

Burke's estimate, based on the scout plane reports, that contact would be made about 0230 proved impressively accurate. At 0229, *Montpelier*'s combat information center announced: "Contact bearing 306 degrees true at 32,000 yards. Believe this is what we want!" Admiral Merrill thereupon ordered a change of course to due north, placing his cruisers as a barrier across the approaches to the Torokina beachhead. This was the opening move in the Battle of Empress Augusta Bay.

Burke intently watched his radarscope. The moment enemy ships registered on it, without waiting for orders he led Desdiv 45 out of line and headed for them, announcing by TBS: "Contact bearing two-nine-one, 30,000. I'm heading in!"

On reciprocal courses, Division 45 and the enemy formation were speeding toward each other at better than 50 knots. Gradually other images appeared on the U.S. scopes until it became clear that what Division 45 was approaching was the northernmost of three enemy columns coming down from the northwest. It consisted of light cruiser *Sendai* followed by three destroyers. Designating this column as his division's target, Burke ordered his ships to prepare to fire half salvos of torpedoes. At 0245, when *Ausburne* was 5,600 yards on *Sendai*'s port bow, he ordered execute, and twenty torpedoes shot from their tubes.

"My guppies are swimming!" Burke shouted exultantly on TBS, then ordered his ships to make a simultaneous turn away to starboard. At that point the irrepressible Captain Stout ordered *Claxton* to fire her remaining five torpedoes at *Sendai,* the largest blip on his radar screen.

According to plan, the U.S. cruisers, and any U.S. destroyers in a favorable position, were to open fire as Burke's torpedoes exploded against enemy hulls. But none of the torpedoes found targets. A reconnaissance plane had dropped a flare over the U.S. cruisers. *Sendai* saw them, fired torpedoes at them, and flashed a warning to her own forces. All three Japanese columns then wheeled south to form a single line of battle. When Merrill was apprised of the enemy turnaway, he opened fire without further delay. Burke, realizing that his twenty-five torpedoes were wasted, could only moan, "My God, how do you like that!"

"That, Commodore," replied Commander Luther Reynolds, Burke's flagship skipper, "is what comes of a Swede expecting to have the luck of the Irish."

The forty-eight guns of Merrill's cruisers were now blazing away, taking as their target the northern enemy group, which by turning had just eluded Burke's torpedoes. Two of the Japanese destroyers collided while maneuvering to evade the concentrated American fire, and *Sendai* began to blaze and fell out of line with a jammed rudder. The Americans had handily won that round, but the ships of Desdiv 45 had become separated on the turnaway. It would take Burke an hour to locate and reassemble them and bring them back into the battle.

Meanwhile the South Pacific was witnessing a superb example of ship handling. Merrill, barking his orders by TBS through the roar of gunfire, maintained his cruisers in flawless formation while repeatedly reversing course so as to retain his blocking position while presenting the enemy gunners with constantly changing problems of range and deflection. Through thirty minutes of rapid maneuver he managed always to be somewhere else when enemy shells or torpedoes arrived. Japanese planes now appeared overhead and dropped red and white parachute flares. These, reflecting off the low cloud ceiling, combined with star shells to turn the night into an eerie twilight and thereby deprive Merrill of some of his radar advantage. Three shells, all duds, struck *Denver*, whereupon Merrill briefly turned away, making smoke.

Commander Austin's Division 46 was having one unlucky break after another. His destroyer *Foote* became separated and ran into one of *Sendai*'s torpedoes, which blew off her stern and left her helpless. Austin's flagship, *Spence*, collided with another of his destroyers and then took a shell hit at the waterline. Only momentarily slowed, *Spence* went after *Sendai*, which was turning in circles but still firing. A couple of Austin's destroyers launched torpedoes at her and apparently made hits, but the cruiser was still afloat as he headed northwest in pursuit of her two collision-damaged destroyers.

Burke, having cruised far and wide to reassemble his scattered division, was now also heading northwest. As he passed the battered *Sendai*, his destroyers sent her down at last in a hail of shells. Then, because radar recognition was working poorly that night, he set out in hot pursuit of what he took to be enemy ships but were in fact the remaining destroyers of Austin's Desdiv 46. Presently these opened fire on the Japanese destroyers, one of which, wreathed in smoke, caught Burke's attention.

As a precaution Burke warned by TBS: "We have a target smoking badly at 7,000 yards, and we are going to open up."

"Oh-oh, don't do it," replied Austin hastily. "That's us."

And so the two damaged Japanese destroyers got away, and Burke turned his fire on *Spence*. Austin, horrified to observe his ship being straddled, shouted into his microphone, "Cease firing! Cease firing! Goddammit, that's me!"

"Were you hit?"

"Negative," replied Austin, "but they aren't all here yet!"

"Sorry," Burke answered, "but you'll have to excuse the next four salvos. They are already on their way."

After such loss of opportunity and near disaster the two division commanders at length located each other and with special satisfaction joined forces in sending down the last of the crippled enemy destroyers still in their area. Except for the lost *Sendai* the remainder of the Japanese force was making best speed for Rabaul.

With dawn breaking, Merrill ordered his divisions to leave off the chase and rendezvous for better defense against the inevitable air attack. Leaving three destroyers behind to salvage the torpedoed *Foote*, he headed south with the rest of Task Force 39. A few minutes before 0800 about a hundred planes, all carrier aircraft from Rabaul, began to close Merrill's formation. Intent on bigger game, they passed over *Foote* and her escorts without dropping a bomb.

Merrill now had his formation in a clockwise-spinning circle, a maneuver that permitted maximum mutual support among ships and confused the attacking flyers as they corkscrewed down. Firing briskly, the Americans shot down seventeen attacking planes and suffered only two rather inconsequential bomb hits. Of the roar of battle, Merrill later reported: "It was an organized hell in which it was impossible to speak, hear, or even think, but we were happy to see the air full of enemy planes in a severe state of disrepair."

Ordered by Halsey to escort four slow transports, the last to finish unloading at Torokina, Task Force 39 did not reach Purvis Bay until late afternoon on 3 November. In response to the routine signal from the base "What do you require?" the flagship signaled, "Sleep."

The following day the temporary SoPac headquarters at Camp Crocodile was thrown into near panic by a scout plane sighting of one light and seven heavy cruisers and four destroyers approaching Rabaul from Truk. Intelligence estimated that this force would refuel at Rabaul and then proceed to Torokina to redeem the failure of the first Japanese cruiser-destroyer force. This was something Task Force 39 could not handle; not only were its crews exhausted, but it was also too far away from Empress Augusta Bay to get there ahead of the enemy. That left only Rear Admiral Sherman's *Saratoga-Princeton* carrier group, which by making a high-speed run northward might be able to attack the new force while it was at Rabaul.

The problem was that the Japanese during the nearly two years they had been in possession of Rabaul were believed to have developed it into the most strongly fortified position in the Pacific, and it had been thoroughly alerted by daily, though not notably successful, air raids from New Guinea. It was surrounded by airfields and bristled with antiaircraft guns. Sending carriers against such a base was thought to be near-suicide for the attacking aviators and perhaps for the carriers themselves.

Halsey, who had built his military reputation on calculated risks, called the current situation "the most desperate emergency that confronted me in my entire term as ComSoPac." He tried not to remember that his own son was serving on board *Saratoga*. All such considerations paled beside his clear duty and responsibility of protecting the marines at Torokina. "Let 'er go," he said and ordered Airsols to lend Sherman all the help it could.

The outcome of the raid, executed the following day, amazed and gratified both the participants and Halsey and his staff. While aircraft from Vella Lavella took over his combat air patrol, Sherman sent all his carrier planes, nearly a hundred, against Rabaul. At a cost of ten aircraft, the American dive-bombers and torpedo planes damaged six of the newly arrived cruisers and two of their accompanying destroyers, thus making sure that there would be no surface attack on Torokina or its amphibious shipping.

Elated by the success of his gamble, Halsey tried it again on a larger scale by borrowing from Admiral Nimitz a three-carrier group under Rear Admiral Alfred Montgomery. On 11 November, Halsey sent both Montgomery's and Sherman's groups to raid Rabaul. Sherman, north of Bougainville, was thwarted by foul weather, but Montgomery's planes, attacking from south of the island, raided shipping in Rabaul's Simpson Harbor. A 120-plane Japanese counterattack against Montgomery's carriers cost the attackers thirty-five aircraft without damaging a single ship. U.S. losses in both attack and defense amounted to eleven planes.

Having proved that carriers could attack powerful, fully alerted bases without unacceptable losses, Montgomery and Sherman sailed away to the central Pacific to participate in the forthcoming assault on the Gilbert Islands. What they did not realize was that they had rendered the assault far less costly. They had done so by actually paralyzing the Japanese Combined Fleet, rendering it incapable of counterattack. This was the end result of using the fleet's carrier planes to defend the Solomons. Many of the aircraft were shot down in that futile contest, and Sherman and Montgomery completed the destruction. Stripped of planes, the carriers were useless, and without air support the Combined Fleet was helpless.

Despite the attacks by U.S. carriers, Rabaul still had enough planes to harass the successive Allied echelons carrying supplies and reinforcements to Torokina. To provide cover for this shipping, Merrill's Task Force 39 alternated with a second cruiser-destroyer task force on loan from Admiral Nimitz. Merrill began the duty shorthanded, destroyers *Foote* and *Thatcher* having been ordered stateside for repair of damages suffered in the Battle of Empress Augusta Bay. Task Force 39 was further weakened off Torokina in the night of 12–13 November when *Denver* took an airborne torpedo in her after engine room. By that time 33,861 men and 23,137 tons of supplies and equipment had been landed at the beachhead.

Both the beachhead and support shipping were now further threatened by planes from the airfield on Buka Island. Knocked out along with the Bonis field by bombardment and bombing on 1 November, it was again operational. Since it was too distant a reach for effective neutralizing by Airsols planes, Burke's Destroyer Squadron 23 was ordered to give it another pounding from the sea. This was a tall order for a destroyer squadron, particularly one reduced to six ships, but sailors who had observed the Little Beavers in action were confident that they would at least give a good account of themselves.

Seeking surprise, as always, Burke avoided the usual and expected approach along the Bougainville coast. Instead he led his squadron west to the 154th meridian, rode it northward through the afternoon until he was abreast of Buka, and then headed east toward the target under cover of darkness. Surprise was lost when Austin's flagship made radar contact with a surfaced submarine and opened fire. The submarine dived and escaped, and the gunfire alerted the Buka airfield, which promptly launched bombers against the intruders. The only American ship so much as scratched was *Ausburne*. A near-miss heeled her over almost on her beam ends, and bombarding metal fragments poked dents in her hull, but there was no other structural damage, nor were there any serious casualties.

Two hours later a heavy formation of torpedo planes attacked the squadron, but Desron 23's sailors maneuvered their ships with such skill that all the torpedoes missed, and the Americans kept boring in toward Buka while advertising their progress with antiaircraft fire. When they reached the coast at 0418, Burke remarked to Reynolds, "This is some surprise! Those fellows on shore know who we are, what we are, where we are, and what we're here for."

Working in close among the reefs in the face of heavy defensive shore fire, the squadron blazed away at the airstrip till 0500 and then withdrew virtually unscathed. Spotting planes reported the airstrip well pitted, installations shattered and ablaze. The spotters got the almost incredible story back to Guadalcanal well ahead of Desron 23, which returned to Purvis on the afternoon of 18 November, greeted as the Lucky Squadron. For his success in this operation, Burke was awarded the Legion of Merit, his first of four.

Materially the squadron was less than lucky, all its ships being in dire need of overhaul. First to fail was *Stanly*. Her withdrawal from operations left three ships in Desdiv 45, two in Desdiv 46. *Spence* was in almost as poor condition, particularly after some numskull jammed a toothbrush into one of her boiler tubes. Rated at 35 knots, she could make barely 30, and the rest of the squadron was almost as enfeebled. In announcing compliance with orders requiring movement, Burke now added, "Proceeding at 30 knots."

When scout planes reported destroyers at Rabaul, South Pacific headquarters knew it had a job for Desron 23. It was deduced that the Japanese were reviving their Tokyo Express to reinforce, supply, or evacuate their bases on Bougainville and Buka. Through code breaking, SoPac learned that the first revived run was to transport troops to Buka, which the Japanese expected the Allies to invade next, and to bring away several hundred trained aviation personnel rendered useless by the bombarding of their airfield.

At noon on 24 November, Desron 23 was taking on oil at Hathorn Sound when it received orders to expedite fueling and get under way for Point Uncle, a reference point at sea west of Torokina, "further information and instructions to follow." That sounded like action. In their eagerness to get going, the men of 23 succeeded in clipping half an hour off usual fueling time.

Burke had been debating whether it was advisable to include *Spence* in the forthcoming operation. Austin thought so poorly of her capability that he had shifted his pennant to *Converse*. Burke decided while fueling was in progress to have another look at *Spence*. He found her skipper, his staff, and, as far as he could see, her entire ship's company ardent to go.

"Okay," he said to her captain. "With your plant cross-connected, what do you figure you can do?"

"Thirty-one knots."

Burke decided to take a chance, though he knew that in permitting *Spence* to operate with a cross-connected plant he was violating regulations which specified that when a ship was in combat or expecting combat her propulsion plant must be "split," so that if one side was knocked out the other could still keep the ship moving. To himself Burke excused his trespass on the grounds that his orders had not implied any prospect for combat.

At SoPac headquarters at Nouméa, Ray Thurber was directing operations, substituting for Admiral Halsey, who was in Brisbane for one of his periodic conferences with General MacArthur. Intelligence had just reported that the revived Tokyo Express had delivered the troops to Buka and would transport the aviation personnel from Buka to Rabaul that night. Thurber decided he had better check on Burke's strength and progress. His signal reached Burke at 1730 as his squadron was rounding Vella Lavella: "Report ships with you, your speed, and ETA [estimated time of arrival] Point Uncle."

Burke, in reply, named the five ships in his formation, gave his ETA Point Uncle as 2200 that night, and concluded: "Proceeding at 31 knots."

This conclusion produced some merriment at headquarters. For days Burke had been ending his reports with the statement that he was proceeding at a modest 30 knots, a kind of protest over the state to which his 35-knot ships had been reduced for lack of upkeep. Now, stimulated by action in prospect, he had managed somehow to bend on an extra knot. Thurber could not resist including a gentle gibe in his next transmission:

> 31-Knot Burke, get athwart Buka-Rabaul evacuation line about 35 miles west of Buka. If no enemy contact by 0300 love [local time] 25th come south to refuel same place. If enemy contact you know what to do.

He added a note to Comairsols:

> Get this word to your B-24s and Black Cats. Add a night fighter for Burke from 0330 to sunrise and give him day air cover.

Several commands to whom this encrypted radio dispatch was not addressed violated regulations by decrypting and reading it, a not uncommon practice, known as "eavesdropping." Because, like all dispatch orders originating at South Pacific headquarters, it was signed HALSEY, the message to Burke was generally thought to have been written by Admiral Halsey himself—all the more reason for calling attention to the amusing nickname "31-Knot Burke."

Reporters learning of the nickname used it in news items in the U.S. press and around the world. Thirty-one knots was a very moderate speed for a destroyer. Even the old World War I flush-deckers could make 35. But because the public generally supposed 31 knots meant high speed, they pictured Burke as a hotshot, hell-for-leather destroyerman, which of course he was. He thus gained worldwide celebrity, well deserved though based on a misconception.

For Burke the more important, immediate significance of Thurber's dispatch was that it provided the information he needed to win what turned out to be his most famous victory, the Battle of Cape St. George. He judged, however, that he had a better chance of intercepting the enemy at a point somewhat farther from Buka than the 35 miles suggested by Thurber. So he headed for waters nearer Rabaul than any Allied surface craft had penetrated since the Japanese had seized that port.

The night was dark with heavy overcast and frequent showers. At 0140, as the squadron reached the probable area of contact, it came to course due north, and Austin's Division 46 took station 5,000 yards from Division 45 on a 225-degree true line of bearing. Burke's division would launch torpedoes at the enemy, and both divisions would open gunfire as the torpedoes struck enemy hulls. It was the plan that worked perfectly at Vella Gulf but imperfectly at Empress Augusta Bay because of the enemy's turnaway.

Within a couple of minutes after the change of course, Desron 23 destroyers made radar contact with ships 11 miles away approaching from the east. Burke in *Ausburne* led his division toward the contact, which consisted of two new 2,000-ton destroyers. Austin, conforming to the battle plan, tagged along with his two ships on Burke's off side. Eager to get an early whack at the enemy, he contacted Burke by TBS: "I suggest I cross under your stern to cover your other side."

"Stay where you are!" snapped Burke, nettled by this proposal to scrap his proved plan.

"Okay," grumped Austin, "but that will keep me out of the show."

On reaching a point 50 degrees on the enemy's port bow, Desdiv 45 launched fifteen torpedoes at his extended track and then made a simultaneous turnaway to elude possible enemy torpedoes. Just before the American torpedoes were due to reach their targets, *Ausburne* made a new radar contact—three ships 7 miles away, approaching from the east. Evidently the destroyers they had launched against were escorts, and the new contact consisted of destroyers serving as transports, their decks crowded with the aviation evacuees from Buka. Burke immediately turned Division 45 toward them, signaling Austin: "We have second target bearing east from us. Polish off the first targets fired on. . . . We're going after new targets."

Just as Burke turned eastward the two escorts plowed unsuspectingly into the path of the American torpedoes. Three earsplitting explosions rent the night air. The leading destroyer burst apart in a blinding flash, from which burning fragments hurtled hundreds of feet skyward. The second, though on fire at bow and stern,

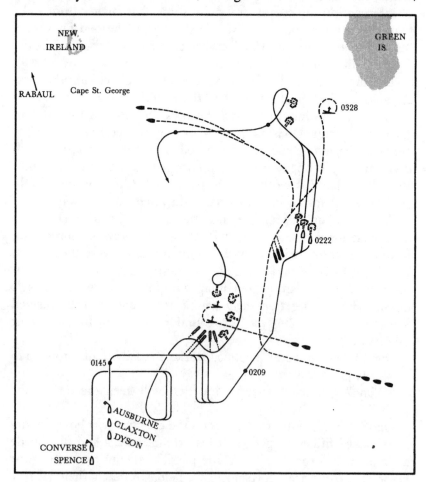

Battle of Cape St. George, 26 November 1943

remained afloat. Austin, who had turned away with Burke, now twitted him with the caustic report, "I'm coming north to finish off what you didn't finish," to which the commodore replied frostily, "Keep your transmissions short, please!"

On beholding the distant explosion of their escort, the three destroyer transports swung right and beat a hasty retreat northward, with Division 45 in hot pursuit. By radio Burke described the situation to Nouméa, adding, "Making 31 knots to intercept the enemy."

The second time he reported "making 31 knots," Thurber, who knew a thing or two about Japanese destroyers and their capabilities, snapped back, "31-Knot Burke, you've got to get up off your ass and make 33 if you're going to catch those boys." Thus spurred, Division 45, unencumbered by the slow *Spence,* built up speed to 33 knots and slowly closed the range to 8,000 yards.

Burke, acting on a hunch, now swung his formation 45 degrees to the right for sixty seconds, then swung back to his previous course, north by east. As his destroyers were steadying from their swing, they were shaken by three heavy explosions astern. These were Japanese torpedoes exploding in the American wakes. Burke's hunch and his zigzag had saved his ships.

Firing torpedoes at the fleeing Japanese would be futile, and turning to fire broadsides at them would open the range and permit them to escape. So Burke ordered his three ships to assume echelon formation and each to open fire with her two forward gun mounts. When the Japanese returned the fire, the Americans, darting expertly, confused the enemy gunners and avoided being hit but were buffeted by numerous near misses.

What Burke feared was that the enemy column would suddenly wheel right or left, crossing his T, and fire spreads of torpedoes. Such "down-the-throat" shots aimed at rapidly approaching ships would be difficult to evade. Instead, the enemy split, one destroyer continuing northbound while the other two turned west toward Rabaul. Burke, resisting the temptation to divide his own force, led it intact against the northbound loner, elatedly shouting, "Come a Ki-Yi-Yippee!" Under the concentrated gunfire of the three American destroyers, the loner quickly began turning in circles, then capsized and went down.

Meanwhile, Austin with *Converse* and *Spence,* conforming to Burke's orders, had remained behind endeavoring to sink the burning escort, which proved remarkably resistant. Twice Austin reported having set off more fires and explosions on board the embattled destroyer. Burke in his northward chase could have used the additional firepower of Austin's ships, but he insisted that they keep firing into the escort until the sea closed over her. He could not risk leaving her afloat, however helpless, so near an enemy base where she could be towed in, repaired, and used again against Allied forces. At last Austin's division succeeded in sinking her. As she disappeared with her dead beneath the surface, Austin radioed Burke, "One more rising sun has set. Joining you now."

Burke with Desdiv 45 was streaking westward in pursuit of the two remaining destroyer transports. Austin's Desdiv 46 was closing from the south. The Americans had seen nothing of the fleeing ships since the latter broke away to the west. The Little Beavers were nearing Cape St. George, which flanked the channel of the same name, passageway to Rabaul's Simpson Harbor. Dawn was approaching.

Burke on TBS addressed the squadron: "Does anybody think we can catch those babies?"

Replied Austin, "I don't think we can go much longer without refueling."

"Maybe we could refuel in Rabaul," suggested Burke deadpan.

"Okay," said Austin, "but we might have trouble with the fuel-hose connections."

A little past 0400, Burke broke off and joined Austin, and all headed for the Treasury Islands and home. The Little Beavers anticipated wrathful retribution from the air at first light, but Airsols complied handsomely with the orders to provide Burke cover. At break of day, instead of enemy bombers, fighters from Munda appeared overhead. Said Burke, "Never has the white star on a wing meant so much to tired sailors as those on these Lightnings."

During the battle Burke had made interim reports to ComSoPac. He now transmitted a more extended summary, concluding with a reminder that this was Thanksgiving Day. Thurber, still standing in for Halsey, acknowledged the report with commendations for Burke and Desron 23. When Halsey got back to Nouméa from Brisbane that afternoon and heard the good news, he flashed a stronger commendation, with copies to all South Pacific commands, and sent a personal report to General MacArthur and Admiral Nimitz, his two bosses.

Nimitz's Central Pacific Force was celebrating its recent reconquest of the Gilbert Islands, victory on a far larger scale than Cape St. George, but its triumph was tinged with grief over heavy American casualties, including 650 sailors lost with the sinking of an escort carrier off Makin and 1,000 marines killed or mortally wounded in the conquest of Tarawa. The Battle of Cape St. George, on the contrary, like Moosbrugger's Battle of Vella Gulf, was utterly one-sided—three Japanese ships sunk and many Japanese casualties, soldiers as well as sailors; American ships unscratched and no casualties at all. Only a few persons realized that both of these classic American victories were won with Arleigh Burke's battle plan.

When the Little Beavers steamed into Purvis Bay at 2200 that evening, Thursday, 25 November, a rare welcome was awaiting them. The cruisers illuminated and manned the rails, and the crews cheered and shouted their well-dones. In the eyes of all, the Lucky Squadron had become the Gallant Squadron. But Burke's iron rules did not permit the Beavers to rest on their laurels. "Keep your material ready for battle!" said the Doctrine. Before permitting themselves the rest and sleep they sorely needed, the crews of Desdiv 23 refueled and rearmed their ships.

During the next few weeks, Desron 23, usually as part of Task Force 39, was kept busy covering successive echelons of troops and supplies en route to the expanding beachhead at Torokina. After midnight on Christmas Eve, 1943, the task force bombarded Buka Island to discourage any Japanese notion of reestablishing the airfield there. On Christmas Day, Seabees and army engineers completed construction of a bomber strip inside the Torokina perimeter, a little over 200 miles from Rabaul. Shortly afterward, Comairsols shifted his headquarters from Munda to Torokina and increased his raids on the enemy base to one or more a day.

The U.S. Joint Chiefs of Staff had abandoned the plan to capture Rabaul as no longer worth the casualties and expenditure of effort and ammunition it would cost. While Airsols bombers kept it pounded down, MacArthur's forces would simply bypass it in favor of the Admiralty Islands, 300 miles farther west. MacArthur had counted on using Rabaul's superb Simpson Harbor as a base for his Seventh Fleet but was satisfied with the prospect of gaining the much more spacious Seeadler Harbor in the Admiralties.

To assure the continued impotence of Fortress Rabaul, Halsey and MacArthur proceeded to draw a ring of steel around it. On 26 December the U.S. 1st Marine Division, under MacArthur's command, invaded Cape Gloucester at the opposite end of New Britain from the bypassed base. In mid-February 1944, with Tip Merrill's Task Force 39 and Pug Ainsworth's Task Force 38 covering, Ping Wilkinson's Third Amphibious Force landed nearly 6,000 New Zealand and American troops on the Green Islands northwest of

Buka. After the invaders had destroyed the small Japanese garrison, Halsey's Seabees built a fighter strip on the main island, 115 miles due east of Rabaul.

Though the Joint Chiefs had concurred in the plan to bypass the rest of the Bismarcks, they opposed as too risky leaving both Rabaul and its backup base at Kavieng in Japanese hands athwart the Allied line of supply. If Rabaul was to be bypassed, they insisted, then Kavieng must be taken. Halsey disagreed, pointing out that an airfield constructed on the unoccupied island of Emirau, 70 miles northwest of Kavieng, would keep that base impotent, just as the combination of airfields at Torokina and the Green Islands was taking the fight out of Rabaul.

Between 17 and 29 February, Destroyer Squadrons 12, 22, and 23 underscored Halsey's argument that the Bismarck bases were no longer a threat by repeatedly bombarding both Kavieng and Rabaul. Admiral Koga had already transferred the bulk of the Japanese Combined Fleet from Truk to the Palau Islands east of the Philippines. The Central Pacific's Fifth Fleet, after capturing the Gilbert and Marshall Islands, on 17 February staged a devastating raid on Truk. This attack so convinced Koga that Rabaul and Kavieng were no longer defensible that he began pulling aircraft out of the Bismarcks to where they could be used more profitably.

In the course of these Bismarck operations, Desron 23, the Little Beavers, achieved a remarkable record. On the morning of 22 February, Burke with five destroyers sighted a large Japanese naval tug, *Nagaura*, engaged in evacuating aviation personnel from the Bismarck bases. Because Allied ships had not previously dared penetrate these waters, the captain of the tug assumed that the destroyers were Japanese, and because they were approaching bow-to, he could not recognize them as otherwise. Thus Burke, ordering his ships into echelon formation, was able to close the range before breaking the international flag signal demanding surrender.

Instead of capitulating, the Japanese captain ordered open fire with his one small gun. The destroyers, in echelon, turned their full broadsides simultaneously on the tug, which began sinking in seconds. Assigning two of his destroyers to antisubmarine guard, with the other three Burke set about picking up survivors. Most swam away, avoiding rescue, but the Americans would get one on board, give him a cup of coffee, and urge him to persuade others to let themselves be picked up. By such means they managed to rescue seventy-three men.

Before leaving the area, Burke, in an act of respect the rescued Japanese appreciated, held a one-minute prayer service for the gallant enemy captain who had opened ineffective fire against overwhelming odds. The captain was not among the survivors.

Squadron 23 now split into its component divisions, and Division 46 *(Converse* and *Spence)* moved in and boldly bombarded Kavieng. Burke with Division 45 *(Ausburne, Dyson,* and *Stanly)* took station off the strait between New Ireland and New Hanover to ambush shipping retreating from the bombardment. Thus just before nightfall Burke's division overtook and sank a minelayer in the shoals. After dark his three destroyers operating separately sank a small freighter and several barges.

These and slightly less spectacular exploits by the other two destroyer squadrons convinced the Joint Chiefs that the Allies could safely bypass Kavieng as well as Rabaul. Admiral Halsey had his way. On 20 March the Pacific Fleet's old battleship group, *New Mexico, Mississippi, Tennessee,* and *Idaho,* bombarded Kavieng and adjacent airfields, while 80 miles to the northwest the 4th Marine Regiment went ashore on the verdant island of Emirau, which the Japanese had never occupied. Construction of an airfield on this island would complete the Allied ring of steel around Rabaul and Kavieng. During the occupation the Little Beavers, with Burke in *Ausburne,* stood cover nearby to ward off any interference. This was Captain Burke's last service as commander Destroyer Squadron 23.

Since the beginning of 1944, Burke had passed two significant milestones in his career. The first was an outcome of his victory in the Battle of Cape St. George, following which Admiral Merrill had recommended awarding him the Navy Cross. The recommendation, gathering favorable endorsements, passed up the chain of command to the secretary of the navy, who concurred. On 30 January on board *Ausburne,* Merrill pinned on Burke the navy's second-highest award "for extraordinary heroism in operations against an armed enemy." The Navy Cross was outranked only by the Medal of Honor.

The second milestone was equally significant, though not recognized as such by Burke. It appeared in the form of dispatch orders from the Bureau of Naval Personnel:

You are hereby detached as Commander Destroyer Squadron 23 and Commander Destroyer Division 45. You will proceed via first available government transportation including government air to

the port in which Commander Carrier Division 3 may be. Upon
arrival report to Commander Carrier Division 3 as his Chief of
Staff.

In a letter to his old friend Gelzer Sims, Burke expressed his utter
bewilderment at this turn of affairs:

> A couple of days ago I received orders to be Chief of Staff to
> ComCarDiv THREE. They came out of the blue and since I
> know nothing of carriers or planes or little of big ships any more,
> I am at a loss to explain them. They are so sudden and so late in
> the game that I can't do anything about them, so within the next
> few days I expect to be whipped across to a carrier and start trying
> to be a good Chief of Staff. I am going to start by seeing if they
> won't let me be a tail gunner in a TBF. This isn't a job I will like,
> nor one which I am fitted for, but maybe it will be good for my
> soul. At least I'll have to work like hell for a year so that when the
> Admiral leaves he will feel kindly enough toward me that he will
> let me go to a surface ship again. I know now what the old
> quotation meant, "The ways of the Gods passeth all understand-
> ing." Fate is a darn funny thing.

Captain Burke had promptly addressed inquiries to what he
deemed the appropriate commands. What he needed to know was:
(1) Who is commander Carrier Division 3? (2) In what ship is he
presently embarked? (3) Where is that ship? (4) How do I get there?

In reply to his questions, Burke received some surprising information. Comcardiv 3 was, or had been, Rear Admiral Marc A.
Mitscher. Burke recalled that the preceding year Mitscher had
served on Guadalcanal as Comairsols and had a reputation as a tough
fighter and able administrator but was said to be of rather frail
physique. Within the last few days, he learned, Mitscher had been
promoted to vice admiral and fleeted up to commander Fast Carrier
Task Forces Pacific, spearhead of the great Fifth Fleet that had
recently captured the Gilberts and the Marshalls and raided Truk.
Burke, it appeared, was to be chief of staff to one of the navy's top
commanders.

Vice Admiral Mitscher was at sea with the Fifth Fleet in his
flagship, the new carrier *Lexington*. The fleet, Burke learned to his
amazement, would be off the Green Islands on 27 March, at which
time Destroyer Squadron 23 was to rendezvous with and be absorbed by it. Thus Burke had no travel problem. His own flagship
would carry him to his new job.

What he did not quite grasp was that these changes marked the end of a phase. The war of cruisers and destroyers had ended. In making possible the establishment of a ring of air bases around Rabaul, they had completed their function. Battles at sea would henceforth be fought between great fleets spearheaded by carriers. Burke, who suspected that somebody who wished him ill was railroading him out of his beloved destroyers, was in fact being transferred from peanuts to the big time. Admiral Halsey radioed him a fine sendoff:

> For Captain 31-Knot Burke. On your impending detachment from command of Desron 23 and from Sopac, I wish to express my appreciation and to repeat my many "Well dones" for the splendid contribution made by Comdesron 23 and by his fighting ships for the success of our campaigns against the Jap. Your intelligent aggressiveness has constantly set the enemy back on his heels and has sent many Japs to their proper resting place. All hands in the South Pacific are proud of the workmanlike job you have done. Well done indeed and good luck. Halsey.

On the 27th on schedule, Desron 23 rendezvoused with the Fifth Fleet just north of the Green Islands. Commodore Burke's tasseled, sennit-decorated chair stood on the deck hooked to a high line stretching between *Ausburne* and carrier *Lexington*. Before taking his seat to be transferred across, Burke addressed a few words of farewell to Captain Reynolds, speaking with unaccustomed brusqueness to conceal the emotion that his moist eyes betrayed.

"I don't want any cheers," he said. "I'll always keep track of *Ausburne*. Tell the boys if any of them ever is in Washington where I live to look me up. They'll be welcome! Goodbye now—and for God's sake don't drop me in the drink!"

7

BALD
EAGLE

THE U.S. JOINT ARMY-NAVY BOARD, established in 1903, had as a major function preparing and updating war plans. These were called the "color plans," because each nation included was assigned a color-code name: United States, blue; Japan, orange; Britain, red; Germany, black; Mexico, green; and so on. The first and most frequently revised of these programs was the Orange Plan, which specified military operations for relief or recapture of the recently acquired Philippines, should they be attacked by the Japanese. The original and the successive modifications of the Orange Plan all prescribed a drive by American forces across the central Pacific via the Marshalls and Carolines, groups of islands and atolls initially claimed by Spain, purchased from Spain by Germany, and, following Germany's defeat in World War I, mandated by the League of Nations to Japan.

Victory won by U.S. naval forces in the Battle of Midway early in World War II weakened the Imperial Japanese Navy enough to enable the Americans to shift to the offensive. The United States did not, however, at that time activate the Orange Plan, though by then Japan had already captured the Philippines. Instead, as we have seen, U.S. armed forces reacted to a more immediate threat by invading Guadalcanal and following up their victory there by advancing on, surrounding, and neutralizing the Japanese base at Rabaul.

Meanwhile, Admiral Nimitz was organizing at Pearl Harbor the

Central Pacific Force, to which new U.S. carriers were sent after commissioning. In March 1943, when Admiral King assigned numbers to the growing American fleets and Halsey's South Pacific Force became Third Fleet, the ships based on Pearl Harbor were designated Fifth Fleet. It was generally, and correctly, believed among knowledgeable officers that when the Third Fleet completed its mission against Rabaul it would be absorbed into the growing Fifth Fleet.

The naval force at Pearl Harbor was the subject of a good deal of speculation among informed, but not fully informed, officers. What was its mission? Who was to command it? Evidently it was being developed into the main U.S. fleet, destined to demolish all opposition and, far outstripping the small-scale advances of 1943, carry the war to the shores of Japan. Because the color code was still widely used on charts and in war plans to identify national armed forces, the Fifth Fleet came informally to be called the Big Blue Fleet.

Among high-ranking U.S. naval officers the question of who was to command the Big Blue Fleet was of immense concern. The appointee would face a supreme challenge, and he might go down in history as the chief victor over the enemy. Because the fleet would obviously be spearheaded by carrier forces, senior naval aviators took it for granted that one of themselves would be selected. When they learned instead that the Joint Chiefs had given the appointment to nonaviator Raymond A. Spruance, they were stunned.

Spruance, recently promoted to vice admiral, had earned an excellent reputation as commander of destroyers and cruisers, as professor at the Naval War College, and in other strictly surface and shore billets. At the outbreak of World War II, he had commanded a cruiser division of Vice Admiral Halsey's carrier task force and participated in Halsey's early raids from the Marshalls to Tokyo.

The Battle of Midway brought Spruance fame. Halsey, hospitalized, relinquished the senior command afloat to Rear Admiral Fletcher and the command of his own task force to Spruance. When Fletcher's flagship, carrier *Yorktown*, was disabled, Spruance assumed the overall command and brought home a victory that turned the tide of war at sea. Thereafter as chief of staff to Admiral Nimitz he helped plan the operations he was now to command.

The mission of the Fifth Fleet was specified in a Joint Chiefs directive of August 1943. The Big Blue Fleet, together with its attached amphibious force and shore-based air, was directed to execute the Orange Plan. Because no one yet knew whether carrier aircraft alone could provide adequate air support for assault on fortified enemy positions, the U.S. high command decided that the drive should begin not at the Marshalls but at the Gilberts, which could be reached by planes from existing Allied island air bases. In the Gilberts, when conquered, the Americans could establish bases to provide shore-based air support for the Marshalls invasion.

The August directive provided also for an element never contemplated by the various versions of the Orange Plan—a separate and parallel operation. While the Big Blue Fleet was driving across the central Pacific, the Southwest Pacific Force would advance westward the full length of the New Guinea north coast and from there invade the Philippines at the southern island of Mindanao—an operation called the New Guinea–Mindanao Axis. The Central Pacific Axis, commanded by Admiral Nimitz, and the New Guinea–Mindanao Axis, commanded by General MacArthur, would be in effect two separate wars within the same same theater of operations— mutually supporting, it was hoped, but potentially competing.

Nimitz's central Pacific drive kicked off in November 1943 with the reconquest of the Gilberts, including the bloody battle for Tarawa. Commanding the Fifth Fleet's Fast Carrier Task Force in this operation was Rear Admiral Charles Pownall, an aviator of wide and varied experience. He entered World War II with an unblemished service record, but in supporting the Gilberts assault and in a subsequent preliminary raid on the Marshalls he displayed what his subordinate carrier commanders regarded as insufficient aggressiveness. On their advice Nimitz replaced him with Rear Admiral Marc "Pete" Mitscher.

Mitscher, a pioneer aviator, had grown up with navy air and had flown planes from *Langley*, the navy's first carrier. In Admiral Halsey's task force he commanded carrier *Hornet* when Colonel Doolittle's B-25s took off from her deck and raided Tokyo and other Japanese cities, and he was her captain seven weeks later in the Battle of Midway. Admiral Halsey, dissatisfied with the performance of aircraft operating out of Guadalcanal, on 1 April 1943 sent Mitscher there as Comairsols. "I knew we'd probably catch hell from the Japs in the air," Halsey explained. "That's why I sent Pete Mitscher up there. Pete was a fighting fool, and I knew it."

Mitscher saw at once that among the aviators flying out of Guadalcanal were men who had no business in combat aircraft—some who didn't want to fight and some who tried but couldn't take it.

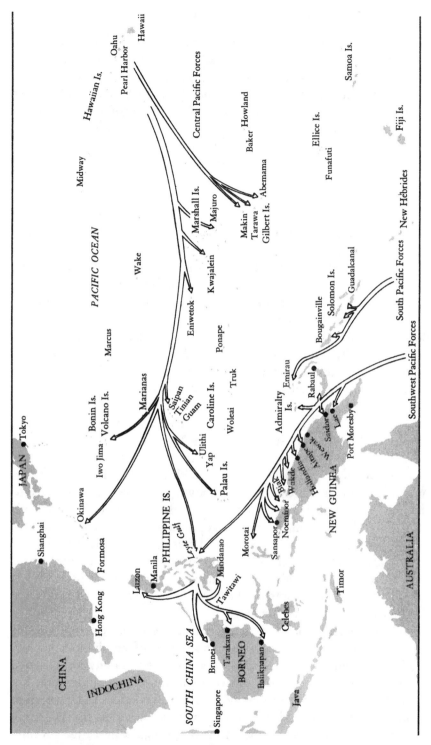

Across the Pacific

He had all such misfits cashiered or transferred to where their skills, if any, could be used to greater advantage. The others he made a little less uncomfortable by insisting on their being provided at least with decent food and with tents that didn't leak. Then in his quiet way he set out to turn them into enthusiastic professionals, able to size up a situation and take vigorous advantage of it. Before his first month on Guadalcanal was over, Mitscher demonstrated his own shrewdness by choosing the right men, the right planes, the right route to the target, and the right time of takeoff to ensure the shooting down of Admiral Yamamoto over Bougainville.

By July, Mitscher's aviators, in destroying nearly 500 Japanese planes and dropping more than 2,000 tons of bombs on the enemy, had ended the air threat to the Solomons, and since many of the planes they destroyed were from the Japanese Combined Fleet's carriers, they had also simplified the Fifth Fleet's task in conquering the Gilberts and Marshalls. But Mitscher's acute mind was lodged in a frail body. Tension, heat, and humidity and a bout with malaria so undermined his health that his weight dropped to 115 pounds.

Mercifully relieved as Comairsols, Mitscher was sent by the Bureau of Personnel to San Diego as commander Fleet Air West Coast. The move was made at Admiral Nimitz's request and was intended as a sinecure. From Pearl Harbor came informal instructions to Mitscher's inherited chief of staff to "keep him in the open and get him back in shape as soon as possible." In the next six months Pete got his fill of hunting and fishing, his favorite sports.

When Nimitz replaced Pownall with Mitscher, it was not without misgivings. Having been let down once, he was not ready to give Pete unqualified command of the fleet's carriers. Instead with Admiral King's concurrence he appointed Mitscher commander of only the senior division, Carrier Division 3. In this capacity, he would in fact be in temporary command of the whole Fast Carrier Task Force, but if his performance in the forthcoming Marshalls assault failed to measure up, he could be quietly shunted aside from the overall carrier command.

The Gilberts operation had seasoned Admiral Spruance and his task force commanders in the know-how of amphibious assault. They brought to the Marshalls attack better weapons and matured techniques. Mitscher had missed their experience under fire, but thirty years of intense devotion to naval aviation had fitted him uniquely to command the navy's roving air bases. In the brilliantly conducted Marshalls campaign his performance measured up fully to that of his fellow commanders.

The conquest of Kwajalein, the Marshalls headquarters atoll, was achieved with such economy of force that Spruance could push on without delay to assault Eniwetok Atoll, using the 10,000 uncommitted troops of the corps reserve. While one group of carriers provided close support, Spruance and Mitscher with the remaining three groups headed southwest to forestall interference by attacking the great Japanese island base of Truk.

Admiral Koga had withdrawn most of his Combined Fleet from Truk to the Palau Islands but left behind a few combatant ships to protect freighters and a quantity of aircraft for scouting and to defend the ships. In the American raid of 17–18 February, U.S. planes and gunfire destroyed 200 of the enemy aircraft and sank nineteen freighters, five tankers, and fifteen warships, including two cruisers—at a cost of twenty-five planes and heavy damage to one carrier.

Mitscher with two of his task groups next headed for the Marianas. Detected at dusk by snoopers while still distant, his ships, using radar-aimed fire, defended themselves successfully through the night from attacking enemy aircraft. After dawn on 22 February, Mitscher's planes destroyed about 150 bombers in raids on the islands of Saipan, Tinian, and Guam, all scheduled for assault in June.

For their achievement in conquering the Marshalls and in recognition of their increasing responsibilities in an expanding fleet, Vice Admiral Spruance; Rear Admiral Kelly Turner, commanding the Fifth Fleet's Fifth Amphibious Force; Marine Major General Holland Smith, commanding the V Amphibious Corps, the Fifth Fleet's amphibious troops; and Rear Admiral Marc Mitscher were each awarded an additional star, and Mitscher was confirmed as commander Fast Carrier Task Force.

Meanwhile, naval aviators continued to complain about a surface officer's commanding the carrier-centered Big Blue Fleet. Admiral King ignored them. "As to brains," he said, "Spruance is the best flag officer in the navy," thereby conceding that he was smarter even than King himself. He found merit, however, in the objection to Spruance's choice for his chief of staff, another nonaviator, Captain Charles Moore, an old friend and a workaholic who gladly handled the mountain of paperwork that Spruance detested. King agreed that a surface officer commanding a fleet with carriers should have an aviator at hand to advise him on aviation problems. Similarly, an aviator commanding a force that included surface vessels should have a surface officer adviser at hand. King's solution was to put out an order that a surface officer commanding a fleet or task force must have an aviator for chief of staff and vice versa.

Both Spruance and Mitscher were annoyed by the order. The former used delaying tactics, hoping to retain Moore at least through the upcoming Marianas campaign. Mitscher, regarding the order as contrary to the traditional prerogatives of sea command, treated it with silent contempt. He was, moreover, pleased with Captain Truman Hedding, the chief of staff he had inherited from Pownall. Hedding was a seasoned aviator, who had once served with Mitscher in the Bureau of Aeronautics.

When his admiral took no action, Hedding brought the order again to his attention. Mitscher brushed it aside. "I'm not going to do it," he said. "It's my privilege to select my own chief of staff."

"That's an order, Admiral. I don't see how you can do otherwise."

"If it's an order, Captain," snapped Mitscher, "you select the man."

He clamped his jaw shut, wanting no further discussion of the distasteful new policy. The Bureau of Naval Personnel had appended to the order the names of four surface veterans as suggested candidates. Hedding picked the last on the list: Captain A. A. Burke. He and Burke had been friendly associates at Annapolis when they attended the Postgraduate School together, and he had lately been hearing of 31-Knot Burke's fabulous exploits in the Solomons. Evidently this was a man of action and probably the least unfit of the choices to be his replacement.

Mitscher, at this time planning for the Marianas campaign, received unexpected orders to support General MacArthur. The latter, determined not to be outsped by Admiral Nimitz's central Pacific drive, had conceived Operation Reckless. This was his aptly named plan to make a tremendous 400-mile leap from the newly conquered Admiralties to Hollandia on the New Guinea north coast, a position considerably westward of the longitude of the Marshalls and westward even of the Marianas, the Fifth Fleet's June objective. Because Hollandia was almost beyond the range of his shore-based aircraft, MacArthur requested the support of the Pacific Fleet. The Joint Chiefs in a 12 March directive approved both Operation Reckless and the Pacific Fleet's participation.

Complying with the directive, the Fast Carrier Task Force on 23 March departed the lagoon of Majuro Atoll, its principal anchorage in the Marshalls. Designated Task Force 58, it would after absorbing additional ships at sea comprise eleven carriers, six battleships, thirteen cruisers, and forty-eight destroyers organized into three carrier task groups. Spruance was present in strategic command, while Mitscher in carrier *Lexington* exercised tactical command. Task Force 58's initial mission was to clear the way for the Reckless operation by attacking the Combined Fleet at its new anchorage in the Palaus. If the fleet should elect to come out and fight, so much the better. Concentrated, it could the more readily be annihilated, or at least rendered ineffective.

The greater likelihood was that Admiral Koga, apprised of the Americans' approach, would retreat, as he had previously retreated from Truk. Task Force 58 therefore avoided the direct course through the Carolines to the Palau group but made a wide sweep to the south, hoping to be beyond the search radius of aircraft based on Truk. The ruse failed. A scout plane out of Truk sighted the fleet on the 25th, and another saw and reported it the next day at a fueling rendezvous north of the Green Islands. Since Koga now knew that Task Force 58 was only 1,400 miles from Palau and closing, Spruance advanced the date of attack from 1 April to 30 March on the bare chance that his carriers still might get within attack range before the Combined Fleet could withdraw.

In the evening of 26 March, Destroyer Squadron 23, the illustrious Little Beavers of the Solomons campaign, arrived as ordered at the Green Islands fueling rendezvous and reported in by signal. This was part of the ongoing absorption of the Third Fleet by the Fifth. The squadron refueled next morning, and early in the afternoon its flagship, *Charles Ausburne,* eased up to *Lexington*'s starboard quarter. Sailors soon rigged a highline between the two ships, and presently across in a tasseled chair came Captain Arleigh Burke to relieve Captain Truman Hedding. The latter, neat, alert, and smiling, was waiting at the end of the line to greet his old friend. As Burke stepped on board they exchanged salutes and handshakes.

The newcomer's frown and knitted brows bespoke deep dissatisfaction. At that moment Burke was, as Hedding afterward recalled, "one of the maddest individuals I have ever seen." His khaki uniform, wrinkled and far from spotless, matched his mood. It was all he had. The rest of his uniforms, stored in a Purvis Bay warehouse while he was out on a raid, had been destroyed by an air-delivered Japanese bomb.

"What in hell am I doing here?" snorted Burke. "I don't know anything about carriers. Destroyers are my navy."

"Just relax, Arleigh," said Hedding, smiling. "Let's go to my cabin with your gear and have a cup of coffee."

Over coffee Burke continued to grumble. He had, he said, been promised a month's stateside leave, at the end of which he was to be given command of a squadron of new destroyers to bring back to the Pacific. That's what he had his heart set on, and then came this change of orders out of a clear blue sky. He repeated that he knew nothing about carriers.

Hedding grinned. "You're about to become knowledgeable about carriers, chum, whether you like it or not." He pointed out that Arleigh certainly knew a lot about the navy and thus would be a great help to Mitscher concerning problems of other types of ships. He was convinced, he said, that it wouldn't take him long to learn about carriers. He concluded, measuring his words, "You've got the finest job you could ever get."

"Well," said Burke dubiously, "we'll see."

Hedding told Burke he could use the room they were in, because he himself was occupying the emergency cabin on the bridge. That arranged, "Let's go up and meet the admiral," he said, and off they went.

They found Mitscher in his usual place and posture, on the flag bridge in a canvas-covered swivel chair facing aft.

"Admiral," said Hedding, "I'd like you to meet Arleigh Burke, your new chief of staff."

"Welcome aboard, Burke," said Mitscher, perjuring himself.

"Glad to be aboard, Admiral," said Burke with equal mendacity.

Arleigh was dumbfounded. Could this skinny, wrinkled little man be the nemesis of Japanese air power he had been hearing about? He looked like anything but a warrior, and the baseball-type cap on his bald head failed to add a sporting touch. In a less warlike setting he might have passed for a village grocer. His speech was mild, unassertive, and not much above a whisper. Arleigh felt instant dislike for the man.

The aversion was obviously mutual. Mitscher eyed Burke with the bleak stare Lord Nelson might have turned on a stagecoach driver in his driving togs reporting on board flagship *Victory* to advise his lordship how to combat the Napoleonic fleet at Trafalgar.

Mitscher's words belied his obvious distaste. "You look tired," he said. "Why don't you go down to my cabin and take a good shower and turn in and sleep it out? I live up here in my sea cabin. When you're rested, come back up to the flag bridge."

Arleigh was unacquainted with the bowels of a carrier, but he found his way down to the admiral's cabin all right. One thing at least he was sure of. Having been offered both the admiral's and his outgoing chief of staff's staterooms, he wouldn't lack a place to sleep and stow his gear. He looked at the admiral's bunk and thought what a beautiful bed it was and how fine it would be to sleep there. He could use some sleep, having been up and busy most of the night and the day before. Mitscher had invited him to "sleep it out." Did he mean it? His words were polite enough, but was he being courteous or sarcastic? His subdued manner of speaking made it hard to be sure. It occurred to Arleigh that it didn't matter. Going to sleep was no way to report in on a new job, particularly for a boss whose approval he obviously had to earn. If he turned in now, chances are he'd had it.

He sent for the messboy. "Go down and get me some clothes," he said. "Khaki britches and a couple of shirts." Off dashed the messboy, and presently a Supply Corps enlisted man arrived bringing the articles, for which Arleigh signed a chit. He then showered, put on the fresh uniform, and ascended to flag bridge. He had been away less than half an hour. He reported to Mitscher, saying he didn't want any sleep and was ready to go.

"Well," said the admiral, "you're on the job."

Burke felt very much alone. Hedding, whom he had counted on to show him the ropes, had gone over to *Saratoga,* sent by Mitscher to lend a hand to Carrier Group 4's Rear Admiral Samuel Ginder, whose chief of staff had been killed a couple of days before. Thus Burke stood outside on the bridge with only Admiral Mitscher, the latter still seated in his swivel chair. The admiral said nothing. Arleigh, uninformed about Mitscher's habitual silence, thought he was being pointedly ignored. In sheer discomfiture he fled the three-star presence.

"I went in," said Burke, "and looked at the op orders, and I talked to the staff watch officers, and I looked to see where all the equipment was—the TBS, the scopes, and all the other things I needed to acquaint myself with on the flag bridge. I didn't know anything about aircraft operations, so I sent for all the publications I could get on all the aircraft that they had aboard, or we'd be operating with, and I started to study."

In the next couple of days, Burke devoted every spare moment to his first rapid reading course, poring over orders, dispatches, instructions, aircraft operating manuals, and everything else a sympathetic staff could think of that might be helpful. Most daunting were the battle plans, thick volumes, filled with detail.

He asked questions by the score of the staff, the squadron commanders, and anybody else he could buttonhole. One thing he learned was that while each officer had read and understood his own duties as set forth in the battle plans, no one person had digested and mastered the plans in their entirety. That would be his task, and he found it discouraging. In the back of his mind he resolved to find means, when he had got on top of his job, somehow to shorten and simplify those plans without fouling them up.

Occasionally, when outside on deck and not under the admiral's baleful eye, Arleigh paused to marvel at the sheer magnitude of Task Force 58, the Fast Carrier Task Force. Seventy-eight ships in three huge circular formations stretched virtually from horizon to horizon. It was the greatest concentration of naval might in the history of the world, and in combat it was all controlled by the wrinkled little man in the swivel chair. Yet, as Arleigh knew, this was only the spearhead of the Big Blue Fleet. The assault component, called the Fifth Amphibious Force, though lacking the far-reaching punch of fleet carriers, comprised many more ships than these.

Task Force 58 was about to execute a raid for which planning had begun as soon as Admiral Koga moved his Combined Fleet from Truk to the Palau Islands. The Americans hoped to seal the enemy fleet inside spacious Palau Lagoon by placing submarines and airborne mines at the narrow exits. The enemy ships would thus have the unhappy choice of remaining in the lagoon to be destroyed by fleet planes and gunfire or attempting to get out and being sunk by torpedoes and mines.

American submarines had led the way to the target, several days ahead of the task force. The mining was to be done by specially equipped squadrons of torpedo-bombers operating from Mitscher's carriers *Lexington, Bunker Hill,* and *Hornet.* This was a trial employment of carrier aircraft, ordered by Nimitz. It was a mission, Burke gathered, that Mitscher and his fliers were reluctant to execute. The latter, wryly calling themselves the Flying Miners, had devised for themselves an emblem of crossed shovel and pickax.

The task force passed south of the Palaus so as be in position on 30 March to attack from the southwest, where they could steer into the prevailing east wind for carrier operations. Admiral Spruance ordered his ships to refrain from use of voice radio, at least until their presence had been discovered by the enemy. That discovery occurred on the evening of the 28th. Clear evidence that Palau had been expecting them appeared in the form of torpedo-bombers approaching from the north.

The Japanese planes staged their usual night fireworks display with flares and colored float lights. Guns of the task force added to the show with red and white tracers marking the flight of deadly proximity-fused shells that exploded as they neared the attacking planes and sent them flaming into the sea. The ships suffered no damage.

Several times during the attack Burke had heard voice radio orders beginning "This is Bald Eagle." It was Mitscher using his code name. Oral orders direct from the admiral were rare, Arleigh learned. He disliked using TBS. Hedding had always done it for him. Bald Eagle was acting as his own chief of staff. Arleigh had never felt less adequate, more desperately anxious to be somewhere else.

On 29 March, Burke, on flag bridge, caught sight of a particularly formidable flight of torpedo planes approaching—obviously heading in for a daylight attack. This was no novel experience for Arleigh. When he was with the destroyers he had had to contend with airborne enemy torpedoes and had set up a standard procedure of steering toward attacking aircraft in order to meet the torpedoes head-on and thread them—that is, pass between them. Similarly the ships of Task Force 58 were at that moment turning toward the enemy planes, but TBS was silent and no visual signals were being passed. Burke felt that somebody ought to lay it on the line with an order. When nobody did, he grabbed the TBS and, acting as Bald Eagle's deputy, began giving what he deemed necessary orders. The ships successfully threaded the torpedoes, and their guns splashed a good many of the attacking planes.

When the attack was over, Arleigh began feeling foolish. The practice of turning toward attacking torpedo planes was evidently not limited to Burke's destroyers. It was obviously standard operating procedure also for Task Force 58, requiring no command from the flag. Burke had been informed that Mitscher insisted on keeping orders to a minimum, and now Arleigh had given one that was superfluous. Stiffly he strode over to the port wing of the bridge and stood at attention before the admiral, anticipating a stern dressing-down. Mitscher looked him over. "Well," he said after a pause, "it was about time, Captain Burke."

8

SUPPORTING
MACARTHUR

"IT WAS ABOUT TIME, Captain Burke."

Arleigh was stung to the quick by Mitscher's words. They sounded to him like sarcasm, but chances are he had misinterpreted the admiral's meaning. Burke may have been a victim less of Mitscher's mockery than of his pixieish sense of humor. The admiral may have been both amused at his chief of staff's discomfiture and at the same time impressed that this destroyerman after only three days on board had the guts to grab and use a carrier flagship's TBS.

The next morning just before dawn, Task Force 58 reached the launching point, 100 miles from the nearest of the Palaus. Spruance relinquished the tactical command to Mitscher and became a spectator of the air battle about to begin. What sort of battle remained to be seen. The U.S. submarines now surrounding the Palaus reported numerous ships departing. Probably all or most of the Combined Fleet had escaped, but the submarines had succeeded in trapping quite a few ships inside the lagoon, chiefly noncombatants such as freighters, tenders, tankers, transports, and tugs.

In Mitscher's carriers the aviators had been breakfasted and briefed, and on each flight deck a deckload of aircraft had been emplaced. At first light all the carriers turned into the wind, and the planes began to take off, fighters first, some to serve as a protective shield over the task force, others to win command of the air over the islands. Next airborne was the attack force of dive-bombers and torpedo-bombers.

Mitscher and Burke watched the launchings from flag bridge. TBS was crackling with voices, but Mitscher's was not among them. All units had their printed instructions. The operation at this point was in the hands of the flight leaders, the ship captains, and the task group commanders. Mitscher would intervene only if required to by an unanticipated turn of events.

Japanese aircraft began approaching from the islands, but the American fighters pounced on them before they reached the task force. The enemy planes when struck by bullets or shell fragments generally streaked down in flames because, unlike American combat aircraft, they were not provided with self-sealing fuel tanks.

Eventually the bombers and torpedo planes of the American attack force began arriving back at Task Force 58 for refueling and rearming. *Lexington*'s flight leaders, as standing orders required, hastened to flag bridge to report personally to Admiral Mitscher. Burke eased himself over to listen. The aviators reported that they had succeeded in bombing or torpedoing many of the ships trapped in the lagoon. The antiaircraft fire posed a serious threat, they said, but the enemy aviators had handled their planes so poorly that Japan must have used up its best fliers and could not take time to give their replacements adequate training.

Burke was impressed to note how quickly and adroitly Mitscher extracted from the aviators the information he needed and how appropriate and without wasted words was the advice he gave. This little grocer, Burke was discovering, had command presence after all, but certainly not of the ostentatious sort. Arleigh began to understand a remark he had heard, that Mitscher was one of the few officers in the navy who could give an order without speaking, merely with a glance.

It occurred to Burke that if he was going to work with aviators during the next few months he ought to share their combat experience. The planes of the Flying Miners were at that moment being spotted on deck. On a sudden impulse Arleigh dashed below, sought out the group commander, and asked to be included in the mission. The commander doubted that he had the authority to take a passenger into combat, so they went up to consult Mitscher. The admiral asked Burke why he wanted to go.

"To get the feel," Arleigh replied. "I don't know anything about air combat, but I want to get the feel of it, and I can't do that sitting here in a ship or from listening to somebody else."

The admiral contemplated Burke with an expression slightly less bleak than usual and told him to go ahead. Down below, Arleigh donned flight gear, then dashed back up to the flight deck and climbed into the plane designated to carry him. En route to the target the squadron encountered no enemy aircraft, all having been destroyed or chased back to the Palaus by fighters from the carriers.

Eventually Burke made out a whitish line where waves were breaking over the reef that enclosed the lagoon on the south and west. Then the Palau Islands themselves came gradually into his view, stretching in single file 60 miles from little Angaur to much larger Babelthuap's northern tip. As the Flying Miners drew closer, Burke could see ships burning or smoking in the lagoon, but many had taken refuge in a landlocked harbor, where they were protected by massed antiaircraft batteries. Because ships could enter and leave the harbor only via a single narrow opening, the *Lexington* squadron's primary mission was to sow mines in this opening and its approaches. Here the mines would bottle up the ships inside and sink them if they tried to get out.

As participant in the operation, Burke could appreciate the fliers' reluctance. The pilots had to fly low and slow so that the mines they dropped would not be damaged when they hit the water. These conditions plus the planes' predictable line of approach simplified aiming by the antiaircraft gunners. Moreover, once the gunners had a bead on the first plane, they were on target for the rest of the squadron, which had to follow in column at the same speed and altitude as the leader. Remarkably, most of the squadron, including Burke's plane, made it through the gauntlet of fire. The survivors then joined the remnants of the other mining squadrons in sealing the exits from the lagoon.

The next day, 31 March, two carrier groups resumed operations against Palau, while the third worked over the nearby island of Yap. On 1 April, all three raided Woleai Island in the Carolines. In three days of air raids and fighting off attacking enemy planes, not a ship of Task Force 58 had sustained damage of any sort from enemy action.

In the course of those three days the task force had flown 2,645 sorties against the enemy. Its aircraft dropped 35 torpedoes, 78 mines, and 616 tons of bombs. They destroyed 114 aircraft in the air and 46 on the ground and sank nearly 130,000 tons of shipping. The mines the Miners had planted subsequently sank many additional ships.

Twenty-five American aircraft had been lost in combat. Of the forty-four men who went down, twenty-six were rescued by cruiser float planes, submarines, and destroyers. The percentage thus saved was the highest of the carrier war to date, but Mitscher was far from satisfied. For him no activity was more imperative than rescuing his downed airmen. He insisted on resolute conduct of lifesaving missions, even under perilous conditions that might produce more casualties, and he could never be satisfied with rescue of fewer than 75 percent of the men lost.

During flight operations Admiral Mitscher sat facing aft in his chair attached to the port wing of flag bridge. "Only a damned fool would ride with the wind in his face," he explained, but Burke was reminded of the mythical whifflepoo bird who always flew backward because he didn't give a hoot where he was going but was curious to see where he'd been.

Burke was present, as his duty required, at every flight operation. Since combat air patrol and reconnaissance flights took off prior to first light, he rose each morning about an hour before dawn. It was not incumbent upon the admiral to be there too, but Mitscher was never absent. Burke, judging he should be on the bridge before the admiral arrived and remain after he left, began rising an hour and a half or two hours before dawn and turning in only after everything was over and the admiral had retired.

Burke did nearly all his work in flag plot or on the flag bridge. He abandoned the comforts of the flag stateroom to rough it in a narrow sea cabin next to the one the admiral bunked in. In event of an emergency or surprise attack they could hit the deck and be on battle stations in ten or fifteen seconds. Burke established a rule that whenever the staff duty officer called the admiral, he would call him also. Certainly Bald Eagle could not fault his chief of staff for lack of diligence. He was simply unable to forgive him for not being an aviator, or so it seemed to Arleigh, to whom the admiral spoke only when necessary.

Task Force 58 reentered Majuro Lagoon on 6 April, and staff officers immediately began drawing up plans for its next assignment, direct support of Operation Reckless, General MacArthur's invasion of Hollandia. Captain Hedding now returned on board *Lexington* to participate in the planning on task force level.

Burke was delighted to see him, and not for professional guidance only. Here was an opportunity to unburden his grievances and seek advice on what to do about Mitscher. He told Hedding bitterly how he would come out on the bridge before dawn each morning, hoping that at last the admiral's ice would melt. He would greet Mitscher with all the pleasantness he could muster and elicit no more than a grunt in reply. He had finally concluded that the admiral was trying to cold-shoulder him into requesting another billet. "I'm not going to put up with this much longer," said Burke.

Hedding assured Arleigh that he was mistaking Mitscher's taciturnity for cantankerousness. The admiral, he said, rarely bothered to use words when a grunt, a nod, or a glance would serve his purpose. He was, to be sure, annoyed at being ordered to take a nonaviator as chief of staff, but he was basically a kind and considerate man and certainly not the sort of officer who would vent his resentment on a drafted appointee. "He's hard to understand at first," Hedding concluded, "but he's a great man."

Burke, who had learned patience in his years in the service, puffed silently on his pipe awhile, then agreed to stick it out a bit longer. He trusted Hedding, but when the latter asserted that the admiral had a lively sense of humor, Burke decided he was pulling his leg. Yet a couple of days later, he had reason to believe that Hedding was right again. Burke and Mitscher were together on the bridge when a destroyer on some mission or other came alongside *Lexington*. With a straight face, the admiral said to his marine orderly, "Secure Captain Burke until that destroyer casts off."

Burke discussed with Hedding an idea he had been hatching for shortening, simplifying, and clarifying those massive op orders he had been sweating through. The idea may have been inspired by that turn of the ships together to thread torpedoes. This was a standard operating procedure. Why not more standard operating procedures? Not to put tactics into a straitjacket, but to have clearly worded, well-understood plans of operation, to be deviated from as conditions required. Burke had waded through so many op plans in which procedures were explained at length, repetitiously, and sometimes in muddy language that he had longed to have them described once and for all, perhaps in a separate document, and thereafter recalled merely by title or other reference.

Hedding, who also had been working toward something simpler and clearer, was impressed by Burke's solution. There was not enough time to experiment with it before the Hollandia operation. All the staff could do now was draft a rough-and-ready plan for achieving Mitscher's objectives. Later, in working on the Marianas plan, Hedding said, they could make more extensive use of standard operating procedures, and he assured Burke that Mitscher would welcome any workable system that could shrink the growing mountains of paper apparently needed for controlling operations.

Task Force 58 departed Majuro on 13 April and shaped course for Hollandia, New Guinea. Admiral Mitscher was in undivided command, Admiral Spruance having gone to Pearl Harbor to supervise planning for the Marianas campaign. Captain Hedding remained with the task force a little longer, serving as deputy chief of staff, mainly to help Burke acquire the knowledge and skills required in his new job.

The naval assault force with the duty of landing the invaders at Hollandia was the Seventh Fleet, not part of Nimitz's Pacific Fleet but of MacArthur's Southwest Pacific Force. Task Force 58 having demonstrated at the Marshalls, Truk, and Palau that it could blast enemy defenses into impotence, MacArthur wanted it to administer the same treatment to Hollandia before his troops went ashore.

Admiral Nimitz was glad thus to have a part of his Pacific Fleet support a Seventh Fleet operation, mainly because it would presumably contribute to the war effort. But it would also demonstrate his readiness to cooperate with General MacArthur despite the competitive nature of their parallel campaigns, and it might at last lure out the Combined Fleet for a showdown battle. Judging from the op order the staff had drafted for Task Force 58, this last objective was Mitscher's chief concern. "This force," it specified, "will destroy or contain enemy naval forces attempting to interfere with the seizure of Hollandia" and would "without prejudice to the foregoing task" support the invasion itself.

When Task Force 58 arrived off Hollandia, Rear Admiral Dan Barbey, commanding the Seventh Fleet attack force, invited Admiral Mitscher or his representative to attend a conference the next day to coordinate the attack. To Burke's intense surprise, Mitscher told him to go in his place. Arleigh was no stranger to high-level conferences and had no doubt he could make a useful contribution, but he had about concluded that Mitscher regarded him as a prize dunce concerning carrier operations.

Burke's inward glow at this hint of the admiral's growing approval, or at least of his declining disapproval, was dimmed by Hedding's explanation that Mitscher didn't like conferences, never attended them, and considered them useless. Hedding, however, felt otherwise and advised Arleigh to prepare himself by making an aerial reconnaissance of the invasion area.

That struck Burke as good advice, and off he went to find a plane and pilot. Hedding, who liked to mingle a little humor with the stern business of waging war, drew up a mock announcement to be published on Arleigh's return. He took it to Mitscher, who with a twinkle in his eye read and initialed it.

Burke, occupying the rear seat of a dive-bomber piloted by Ralph Weymouth, the squadron commander, took off from *Lexington* and headed inland. No enemy planes were in the air, confirming a growing impression that MacArthur's air commander, General Kenny, had made good his promise that his land-based bombers and fighters would wipe out Japanese air power in western New Guinea.

Burke and Weymouth flew over the airfields in the area. There was nothing on them. They looked for front lines. There weren't any. They saw enemy troops but only in small detachments and none close to Hollandia. MacArthur's 400-mile leap forward along the New Guinea coast had obviously carried him well past enemy concentrations. There wouldn't be much opposition to the forth-coming landings.

Suspecting that they were missing something, Burke asked Wey-mouth to drop lower. He did, over an airfield close to the main proposed landing beach, but still there was no opposition. "You know," said Weymouth, "it would be nice if we were the first airplane to land in Hollandia."

Burke thought that was a great idea, so they descended, just touched down, took off, and started climbing. When they got above the end of the runway, a 40mm or other small-caliber gun opened up and smashed a hole through their starboard wing. As they con-tinued to climb, Weymouth, looking ruefully at the damage, said, "That was a stupid damned thing we did."

Burke heartily concurred. "Flathatting* always is," he said.

Because of cut wires, their rudder control was impaired and their aileron control lost altogether. Weymouth gave Burke ditching in-structions, then radioed *Lexington* his position, course, speed, and altitude and, without specifying the nature of his trouble, said he might have to ditch. They made it back to the carrier, but by the narrowest of squeaks.

Hedding meanwhile had communicated his mock announcement to the ships of the task force, to be broadcast on signal from him. He was now watching and gave the signal just as the wheels of the damaged bomber hit the flight deck with an ominous thud. The plane, out of control, rolled forward so fast that the hook catching

*Flathatting: Slang for flying low and stunting.

the wire produced a terrific jolt that ripped off part of the punctured starboard wing and threw the fuselage sideways. As Arleigh sat pale and shaken in the midst of this wreckage, squawk boxes in all the ships began sounding off: "The task force commander is pleased to report the safe return of his chief of staff, 31-Knot Burke, from a harrowing flight over enemy territory. Captain Burke announced when he landed back aboard, 'I believe the airplane is here to stay.' "

Above on the port wing of the flag bridge, Bald Eagle was watching the proceedings from his swivel chair. Arleigh climbed out of the damaged plane and went up to report.

"You're grounded," said Mitscher. "You must have flathatted."

"Yes, sir. We did."

"You couldn't get that kind of damage unless you had. It wasn't big stuff. It was small stuff and it got you."

"Yes, sir."

"You're grounded. No more flying for you for a while. Did you get the dope you wanted?"

"Yes, sir."

"All right. You get a destroyer to take you over to the conference tomorrow."

Later Burke learned that the conference was being held in Admiral Barbey's flagship, which happened to be a destroyer. He could not get there by air even if he had not been grounded. It dawned on Arleigh that Bald Eagle had been pulling his leg.

The conference next day was held in the captain's cabin on board the flagship destroyer. The cabin proved much too small. The admirals and generals squeezed in, but Burke, still a mere captain, was obliged to remain outside and confer through a porthole. The generals and surface admirals wanted to know what sort of support they could expect from the carriers and were gratified by Burke's replies. When he reported the findings of the navy scout planes, including his own, that there were few Japanese in the area, the conferees were skeptical. They believed there might be large numbers of enemy troops back in the hills prepared to spring a trap, and they complained of the scant information the navy aircraft were sending them.

"They've sent all the information there is," said Burke. "There isn't any information because there's no enemy. There are only a few stragglers."

Burke was correct. There were only about 1,000 Japanese in the area, mostly service troops, who took to their heels on 21 April when the shore bombardment began. MacArthur had executed a classic example of "hitting 'em where they ain't."

The support of Task Force 58 had not been needed, and the Japanese Combined Fleet did not respond to the challenge of its presence. Admiral Koga, killed in an airplane accident, had been succeeded as commander in chief by the more aggressive Admiral Soemu Toyoda, who planned to join battle but only when he had sufficient carrier aircraft and trained aviators.

Hollandia having proved a pushover, Task Force 58 still had on board plenty of bombs and a great deal of ammunition, but the ships had to return to Majuro for replenishment of supplies. As the staff studied the course back to base, already laid out on the charts, Burke noted that it passed temptingly close to Truk, now abandoned by warships but again being developed into a powerful Japanese air base. Arleigh was not at all surprised when Mitscher said, "Let's hit Truk again."

That remark threw the staff into a frenzy of planning, in the course of which they decided, with Mitscher's hearty approval, to strike also the islands of Satawan and Ponape. They would pass those too on the return to Majuro, and both had airfields situated, like those on Truk, on the flank of forthcoming central Pacific advances.

By this time the frost in the Burke-Mitscher relationship was beginning to thaw a little. The more Burke observed the admiral controlling operations or discussing plans, the more he was impressed by his mastery of warfare and of carrier warfare in particular. Burke began to feel a degree of warmth for Mitscher and was gratified to note that the admiral now usually listened to what he had to say.

What Burke had to say at this juncture was that the approaching raids could give the fast new battleships and cruisers an opportunity to exercise more of the functions for which they had been built and their officers trained. Hitherto their duties had been limited chiefly to escorting the carriers and protecting them and themselves with antiaircraft fire. If they did no more than that, they would get stale. Why not let the gunnery ships go on ahead and bombard Satawan and Ponape with minimum air support? It would give them useful exercise with their heavy armament. Mitscher approved the idea, and Burke drew up a rough plan, which the admiral sent over to his battle line commander, Vice Admiral Willis A. Lee, instructing him to draw up his own battle plan.

At dawn on 29 April, Task Force 58, standing 150 miles southwest of Truk, launched an 84-plane fighter sweep to seize command of the air over the atoll. The Japanese, warned by radar, managed to get 62 planes into the air. As usual by this stage of the war, the hurriedly trained Japanese fliers were quickly overwhelmed by the American aviators, who on this and the following day shot down 59 enemy planes and destroyed 34 on the ground. The Americans also heavily damaged or sank more than 20 freighters and small craft in the lagoon, and wrecked nearly all installations ashore.

At about 0815 on 30 April, half the U.S. carriers, including the flagship, had their flight decks covered with rows of gassed and armed bombers and torpedo planes about to take off. While the carriers were in this state of extreme vulnerability, eight Japanese bombers eluded the Hellcat fighters and approached the task force. A single bomb or machine-gun bullet from one of them could set off an explosion or start a fire in one of the parked aircraft that would spread to the others and turn the ship into a pyre.

As the enemy planes bored in through a torrent of flak, one of the officers on *Lexington*'s flag bridge yelled hysterically, "Why the hell don't they use their machine guns?"

From his swivel chair Mitscher called back, "Shut up! They might hear you."

One of the enemy planes, hit by the flak, plunged flaming into the sea less than a hundred feet from the flight deck. Another dropped a bomb not quite close enough to do any damage. When the officers caught their breath and surveyed the scene, all the Japanese planes were in the water or fleeing with Hellcats in pursuit.

Not all of the Japanese aviators shot down had been killed. One of the destroyer skippers presently announced that his ship had picked up a couple of prisoners. Mitscher signaled back, "Why?"

While the Japanese aircraft had been ineffective, their antiaircraft fire was fierce and well aimed. It accounted for most of the 26 U.S. planes destroyed. Of the 47 airmen shot down, 28 were rescued, some spectacularly from inside Truk Lagoon. Nevertheless Mitscher was deeply distressed that the percentage of rescues was not greater.

On the 30th, conforming to Admiral Lee's plan, nine heavy cruisers detached themselves from Task Force 58 to bombard the island of Satawan. The next day six new battleships worked over Ponape, largest of the Carolines, with their 16-inch guns. One of the carrier groups stood by to fend off possible air attacks on the gunnery ships.

The other two groups, including *Lexington,* proceeded on to Majuro Lagoon, which they entered on 4 May. In little over a month of operations, Task Force 58 had destroyed hundreds of enemy aircraft and a good many enemy ships. It had lost some of its own planes and airmen, but not one of its ships had been damaged by enemy action.

For most of the men and many of the officers there followed an interlude of rest and relaxation with minimum duties, but for the staff officers and division commanders it was a period of intense concentration as they planned for the Marianas expedition, scheduled to begin in mid-June.

Hedding was detached, to report to Pearl Harbor to assist Admiral Spruance's planners. Burke bade him farewell with heartfelt gratitude for his tireless exertions in helping the new chief of staff to master his duties. Hedding's leave-taking with Mitscher was no less cordial. In the months they had served together they had developed mutual friendship and admiration.

"Well, Truman," said the admiral apropos of nothing in particular, "it looks like this Burke's going to turn out to be real good."

Hedding smiled. In praising the student, Mitscher was praising the teacher.

9

ASSAULT
ON THE
MARIANAS

A MAP OF Japan's chief World War II southward communication routes would look like an inverted V with the home islands at the apex. The left-hand or western line ran past the Ryukyus and Formosa (Taiwan) and down west of the Philippines through the South China Sea. This was the route taken by ships to supply the early Japanese southern conquests and to convey to Japan raw materials from the East Indies and Southeast Asia—the so-called Southern Resources Area, which the Japanese seized at the price of war with the United States, the Netherlands, and the British Commonwealth. Because the indispensable East Indies oil was shipped via this western waterway, the route was sometimes called Japan's oil line.

As Japanese operations expanded southeastward they had to be supplied via a more direct route. This was the right-hand branch of the V, consisting of the Bonin, Volcano, and Mariana islands extending southward from Tokyo. Along this line of islands Japanese planes moved from airfield to airfield, and Japanese ships sailed a parallel route under protection of planes based on the airfields. From the southern Marianas the planes and ships in 1942 and 1943 continued southward via Truk and Rabaul. After these were neutralized, they followed a variety of routes through the Carolines.

Admiral King recommended blocking both lines of communication, thus depriving Japan of oil and raw materials from the south and denying munitions and other supplies to Japanese armed forces deployed in the Pacific islands. His fellow Joint Chiefs of Staff agreed that the two lines of Allied advance—General MacArthur's New Guinea–Mindanao Axis and Admiral Nimitz's Central Pacific Axis—should drive toward and converge at the Luzon-China-Formosa triangle, the choke point of the Japanese oil line. They were less ready to back King's proposal to block Japan's other main line of communication by capturing Saipan, Tinian, and Guam, large islands in the southern Marianas. King insisted that these should be taken, not only to block southward-flowing enemy supplies and reinforcements but also to remove a threat to future Allied communications to the western Pacific.

Geography dictated that conquest of the Marianas would have to be done by the central Pacific's Fifth (Big Blue) Fleet, and Admiral Nimitz at first fully endorsed King's strategy. Bloody Tarawa changed his mind. Taking flat, two-mile-long Betio, the fortified island in Tarawa Atoll, had cost a thousand American lives. What might it cost to take Saipan, Tinian, and Guam, all mountainous, many times the size of Betio, and far beyond the reach of Allied land-based air? A Nimitz recommendation to bypass the Marianas, however, brought a blistering letter from King, who was sturdily backed by Joint Chief Henry H. Arnold, commanding general of the Army Air Forces. Arnold wanted the islands as bases from which his newly developed long-range B-29 bombers could reach Japan.

To make definite decisions on forthcoming strategy, the Joint Chiefs of Staff summoned General MacArthur and Admiral Nimitz to Washington. The former declined to leave his theater of operations, sending instead his chief of staff, Lieutenant General Richard Sutherland. Nimitz came in good spirits, his shaken confidence restored by the comparatively easy conquest of the Marshalls followed by Mitscher's carrier raids on Truk and the Marianas.

The Washington discussions culminated in a directive of 12 March 1944 that gave Nimitz his schedule of operations. The Big Blue Fleet would invade the Marianas on 15 June and the Palaus on 15 September. Beginning 15 November it would support MacArthur's forces in their invasion of the Philippines at the southern island of Mindanao. Target date for gaining control of the Luzon-China-Formosa triangle was tentatively set at 15 February 1945, but left open was the decision whether this was to be achieved by invading Luzon or by invading Formosa.

On 23 April, shortly following the Hollandia invasion, Cincpac issued Operation Plan 3-44 for conquest of the southern Marianas.

Admiral Spruance's mission as commander Fifth Fleet was stated thus: "capture, occupy and defend SAIPAN, TINIAN, and GUAM and develop bases in those islands." That was all—capture, occupy, defend, and develop. Nothing was said about *how* the islands were to be defended. Nimitz was adhering to the old leadership rule: Tell your man what to do but not how to do it; if you have to tell him how to do it, you have picked the wrong man for the job. Nimitz had selected Spruance to command the Big Blue Fleet in complete confidence that he would exercise sound judgment in attaining his assigned objectives.

For the Fifth Fleet planners, Task Force 58's demonstration that it could pound such enemy strongholds as Truk and the Palaus into at least temporary impotence was immensely reassuring. They knew, however, that the Marianas assault would be no Hollandia-style pushover. As part of Japan's inner defense perimeter the islands were known to be strongly fortified and heavily garrisoned. By far the major part of the population was Japanese, and all Japan had come to think of the Marianas as an extension of the home islands. Soldiers and citizens could be expected to defend them with special ferocity, taking every advantage of obstacles imposed by the coral-rimmed beaches and the rugged interiors. The Task Force 58 staff concluded that the Japanese fleet, ready or not, would intervene.

Fresh ships and green hands were arriving for service in the task force. Conforming to a rotation plan inaugurated by Nimitz, air groups with six months of combat operations were relieved by groups from the States. Additional ships reporting for duty included carrier *Essex*, returning from overhaul, new carrier *Wasp*, and new light carrier *San Jacinto*. Mitscher did not integrate the new arrivals into his three existing four-carrier groups but instead organized a three-carrier fourth group with Rear Admiral W. K. Harrill in command. To give the newly arrived men, ships, and air groups seasoning under fire, and incidentally misdirect Japanese attention, Mitscher formed a temporary task group under old hand Rear Admiral Montgomery and sent it on a practice raid on Wake and Marcus islands.

Mitscher next called a meeting of his staff and told them what he expected with regard to surprising, getting the jump on, and isolating the enemy. He relied on them to prepare plans likely to achieve these goals to best advantage. He then retired to his swivel chair, and Burke took over.

Burke listened attentively to the opinions and suggestions of his

fellow staff officers. Most of them knew more about carrier operations than he did, but all soon recognized that Arleigh had a highly
dependable intuition about what would and would not work. In
writing up the op order he strove for clarity, simplicity, brevity, and
decentralization—and even a little humor, including a couple of
cartoons cribbed from a magazine and recaptioned.

The decentralization he was most intent on was independence of
action among the four task groups, provided the operations of each
group contributed to the common goal and did not embarrass the
others. A major key to all the qualities he sought was standard
operational procedures, so thoroughly understood that when it became desirable to deviate from them, all commands would understand what they were deviating from.

To achieve coordination of the various facets of the battle plan,
a steady stream of radio messages winged between Task Force 58 at
Majuro and the fleet and amphibious force planners at Pearl Harbor,
and Burke visited each of the four rear admirals commanding Task
Force 58's task groups. Aside from attaining uniformity of objectives, Burke's visits gave him a better understanding of the four
subcommanders, their strengths and weaknesses, and what methods
might inspire each to top performance.

At intervals Burke consulted Mitscher about some point in the
planning and usually received a quick and practical answer. Most of
the time, however, the admiral sat quietly in his swivel chair watching or, when nothing much was happening, reading a book, usually
a detective story, the only form of reading he really enjoyed. He was
in one of his silent periods. Operations of the past three months had
exhausted him. This was his way of recharging his batteries.

All the staff understood that the admiral didn't want to be disturbed, and only one officer besides Burke intruded into his solitude.
That was Charles Sims, a naval reserve junior lieutenant. Sims from
time to time went out onto the bridge wing and talked to Mitscher
without bothering to check with Burke. The admiral never seemed
to resent these intrusions. He and Sims would confer in low voices,
or Mitscher would get off his chair and they would go together into
the privacy of his office.

The Mitscher-Sims conferences at first aroused Burke's curiosity,
then his ire. What, Burke wondered, gave this little junior grade
reserve lieutenant access to the admiral, bypassing the chief of staff?
How could the chief of staff fulfill his duties denied the information
these two apparently shared? Finally the indignant Burke decided

to have it out. He went to Mitscher and asked what Sims did. As chief of staff, he said, he needed to know.

"He has orders to report to me only," replied Mitscher. "I have orders not to discuss this with anybody who's not already cleared." He thought for a minute, then added, "You can't operate here without knowing too, so I'll have to get you cleared."

They sent for Sims and went into the flag office. Request for clearance had to go out in a code and via a radio frequency to which, in the task force, only the lieutenant had access. When Sims arrived and was told what the admiral had in mind, he objected strongly. Open the gates once, he said, and you'll open them again. The more people are made aware of secrets, the greater the likelihood of loose talk, from which newspaper correspondents with the fleet would ferret out the facts and hint at them in their published stories.

However much Sims might object, he could not refuse to transmit Mitscher's request to Cincpac. Back came the clearance for Burke, who now learned that Sims was a Japanese-language specialist who had been trained at Pearl Harbor in codebreaking and keeping his mouth shut. He was on board *Lexington* as an agent of the Pacific Fleet intelligence officer. His function was to exercise his linguistic and cryptanalytic skills as needed and to serve as a conduit for highly classified information.

Burke was now cut in on the vital intelligence Sims was reporting to Mitscher, facts gathered by radio-traffic analysis, cryptanalysis of Japanese radio messages, captured documents, prisoner interrogation, plane and submarine observation, and a variety of other sources. Admiral Koga, Burke learned, had been killed in a plane crash and been replaced as commander in chief Combined Fleet by Admiral Soemu Toyoda. All but about 10 percent of the Combined Fleet had been reorganized into the carrier-centered Mobile Fleet, a carbon copy of Task Force 58 but with less than half its strength. Commander Mobile Fleet was Vice Admiral Jisaburo Ozawa, reputed to be one of the ablest officers in the Japanese navy.

The Mobile Fleet had recently been observed at Tawitawi, an island southwest of the Philippines, between Mindanao and New Guinea. Because submarines were decimating tankers on the oil line en route to Japan, the Americans assumed the enemy fleet was at Tawitawi to be near the Borneo oil wells. To observe and report the fleet's movements, if any, the U.S. Navy had stationed submarines off the Tawitawi anchorage, north and south of the Philippines, off the Philippine straits of Surigao and San Bernardino, and in the Philippine Sea, between the Philippines and the Marianas.

When other staffers observed that Arleigh had been admitted into the mysterious fraternity of Mitscher and Sims, some of them hinted that they too deserved to be let in on whatever was going on. "Look," said Burke, "this fellow's got a job to do, and he can only do it if he does it in the way that it's supposed to be done, and you can't know about it. I know about it, but just lay off."

Toward the end of May the drafting of the Task Force 58 Operational Plan was completed. The staff officers involved in its preparation said they thought it was the best they'd seen—and certainly the funniest. Burke didn't consider it perfect, but it was short and clear and lacked the usual jargon and redundance. At any rate it was better than those dense, forbidding documents he had waded through when he first came on board *Lexington*. It was prepared under his guidance, and he felt he had a right to be proud.

Arleigh stepped cockily out onto the bridge wing, handed the op plan to his boss, and beamed while awaiting expected praise. The admiral handed the document right back. Burke was stunned. "Don't you even want to look at it?" he asked.

"No, Captain Burke," replied Mitscher, "I'm just going to sit here and watch it unfold." Then, observing Burke's utter deflation, he added, smiling, "I'm going to rely on you to tell me all that I need to know."

Captain Hedding now returned to *Lexington*, having completed his temporary assignment on Admiral Spruance's planning staff, where he was regarded as an emissary speaking for Admiral Mitscher. His current assignment, as deputy chief of staff to Mitscher, was another temporary billet. At the end of the Marianas campaign or earlier he would take permanent duty on the Cincpac staff. Burke was glad to have Hedding's assistance and sage council through the critical period ahead.

As Task Force 58 was getting up steam to depart Majuro, a document flown out from Pearl Harbor was delivered to Mitscher and the other Fifth Fleet flag officers. Mimeographed, it bore the title "Combined Fleet Ultra Secret Operation Order No. 73" and outlined a series of what it called "Z Operations," whereby the Japanese fleet would advance and annihilate any segment of the U.S. Pacific Fleet should it enter the waters west of the Bonin, Mariana, and Caroline islands.

Burke later learned how this top-secret Japanese op order got into

American hands. The storm that had brought about Koga's death also caused a plane bearing his chief of staff to crash. The latter survived, was captured by Filipino guerrillas, and was recaptured from them by the Japanese occupation forces. But the guerrillas kept the chief of staff's briefcase containing important papers and radioed MacArthur that they had it. MacArthur sent a submarine, which brought the briefcase to his headquarters at Hollandia. Found among the papers was the Ultra Secret Operation Order. MacArthur sent it by plane to Pearl Harbor, where Nimitz had it translated and copies run off and flown out to Fifth Fleet flagships in or approaching the Marshalls, the general assembly area for the Marianas.

The "Z Operations" outlined in the Ultra Secret Operation Order were expected to offset Japanese inferiority in carrier air power by participation of Japanese land-based air power, operating from the islands. The air superiority thus obtained was to be directed first against the enemy carriers. When these were put out of action, it was to be directed against the enemy landing forces. "In some situations," the outline specified, "the landing forces will be attacked and destroyed first. . . . Every effort should be made to destroy the major element of the enemy landing forces." Admiral Spruance, studying the op order, noted the emphasis the Japanese placed on destruction of landing forces. It undoubtedly influenced his strategy in the upcoming Marianas campaign.

U.S. participation in World War II was approaching a climax. On 27 May, MacArthur landed a first echelon of 12,000 troops on Biak, a large island in New Guinea's Geelvink Bay. On 4 June, American troops occupied Rome. Just before noon on 6 June, in a rainstorm, Task Force 58, comprising 15 fleet carriers, 7 fast battleships, 21 cruisers, and 69 destroyers, weighed anchor and headed to exit Majuro Lagoon. It took nearly five hours for the 112 ships to file out. Hardly had the last one cleared the lagoon when loudspeakers throughout the task force began announcing exciting news from the other side of the world: British and American forces had crossed the English Channel and were invading Normandy.

As Task Force 58 on 9 June was passing north of Eniwetok, heavy cruiser *Indianapolis*, Admiral Spruance's flagship, approached and joined Group 58.3, at the center of which was *Lexington*. Spruance had been inspecting shore installations and conferring with the principal commanders of Admiral Turner's Joint Expeditionary Force, which had come from Hawaii and Guadalcanal and assembled in the Marshalls. This force, practically identical with the Fifth Amphibious Force, comprised 535 ships carrying 168,000 assault troops. On putting out to sea again it trailed at some distance behind Task Force 58.

By destroyer Captain Burke sent a copy of his op plan, which Admiral Mitscher had refused to read, over to Admiral Spruance, who also refused to read it. Spruance passed the document to his nonaviator chief of staff, Captain Moore, whose services he had managed to retain a little longer. Moore's specialty was paperwork. He read the plan carefully and recommended that Spruance approve it. This was normal procedure in Fifth Fleet flag country, because Spruance detested reading and writing official documents as much as Mitscher did. Spruance thought mainly on his feet; Mitscher, mainly in his swivel chair.

In the evening of 10 June, Sims brought Mitscher and Burke information that the closely watched Mobile Fleet had made a move. U.S. submarine *Harder* reported a battleship-cruiser force departing Tawitawi on a southeast course in the Celebes Sea. This movement indicated that the Japanese were not yet aware of the Fifth Fleet's approach to the Marianas. Their battleship-cruiser force appeared to be headed for Biak Island, where General MacArthur's troops were still trying to make good their foothold. The move deeply concerned the Americans, because MacArthur's Seventh Fleet had no battleships.

Task Force 58 was originally scheduled to open the Marianas assault on 12 June with a morning fighter sweep of enemy airfields. In the past, carriers had almost invariably attacked shore targets in the morning. They would hold off beyond the reach of the long-range land-based bombers till nightfall, then offset the long-range advantage by racing in under cover of darkness to bring their own attack aircraft close enough by dawn to reach the targets. But snoopers from the Marianas were bound to sight so gigantic an armada as Task Force 58 on the 11th or even earlier. The Japanese, anticipating a morning air raid, could be expected to give the raiders a hot reception and possibly get the jump on the raiding force by attacking the carriers themselves before they could launch.

To forestall this unfavorable turn of events and surprise the Japanese, Commander Gus Widhelm, the task force air operations officer, and his assistant, Lieutenant John Myers, devised a variation from the old attack pattern. It was a variation that Burke and Mitscher quickly accepted, naming its two parts for its inventors.

Part One, called Plan Gus, consisted of detaching several destroyers and sending them 20 miles ahead for early radar contact, fighter direction, and rescue of downed flyers. Plan Gus was devised partly to facilitate Part Two, Plan Johnny, an *afternoon* fighter sweep of the Marianas on the 11th.

On the 10th, a misty day with limited visibility, no Japanese scout planes got within 50 miles of the oncoming carriers, but American fighters searching out ahead shot down four would-be snoopers. The 11th dawned bright and clear. At midmorning, Lieutenant Sims, who was monitoring transmissions from enemy planes, announced that the task force had been sighted and reported. By then U.S. destroyers, executing Plan Gus, were moving out ahead to form their picket line.

At 1300 when Task Force 58 was 225 miles east of Saipan, the carriers launched a deckload strike of 211 Hellcat fighters accompanied by eight torpedo-bombers. The bombers' mission was to spot aviators downed at sea, drop life rafts for their use, and report their location for rescue by destroyers or float planes.

Eleven Hellcats and six U.S. pilots were lost in combat that afternoon. Estimates of how many Japanese aircraft were destroyed vary widely, but the losses must have been considerable, for during the next three days American planes, flying through intense antiaircraft fire, met no air opposition at all as they went about their business of cratering airfields and harassing shipping. The surviving Japanese fliers were evidently conserving their planes to hurl back the coming invasion or to support their fleet in the possibly approaching sea battle.

During the night of 12–13 June, two of Mitscher's task groups passed around north and west of Saipan. After sunrise, Vice Admiral Willis Lee's seven new battleships detached themselves and began bombarding Saipan's west coast. The bombardment achieved nothing of consequence. The battleships, long limited to escorting the carriers, were untrained for this sort of work. Moreover, too valuable to risk, they had stood off 10,000 to 16,000 yards from the shore. One wag of a sailor aptly described the proceedings as "a navy-sponsored farm project that simultaneously plows the fields, prunes the trees, harvests the crops, and adds iron to the soil."

Radio intercepts indicated that Admiral Toyoda had replaced Admiral Koga's Z Operations with a new ultrasecret op plan comprising so-called A Operations. The Pacific Fleet intelligence conclusion that the new plan was merely a modification of the old seemed confirmed by a report from submarine *Redfin*. Within hours after Mitscher's two task groups had entered the Philippine Sea by rounding Saipan, the main body of the Mobile Fleet shoved off from Tawitawi—evidently the trip wire of the Z Operations was also in the new op order. *Redfin*, which surfaced and got off its report in the evening of the 13th, had observed at least six carriers and four battleships in the departing Japanese fleet.

The American attack on the Marianas had taken the Japanese by surprise and at a severe disadvantage. They had assumed, after Task Force 58 supported MacArthur's invasion of Hollandia, that the New Guinea–Mindanao Axis was the sole line of Allied transpacific advance and that the Pacific Fleet would continue to support it, operating in southern waters. So they based their Mobile Fleet on Tawitawi not only to be near Borneo oil wells but also to be in position to sally forth and annihilate Task Force 58 when it crossed the trip wire of the western Carolines. To provide land-based air to cooperate with the fleet, the Japanese drained their central Pacific bases of many planes and sent them to New Guinea. On arrival some of the fliers were killed in battles with Allied aircraft. Others from the more healthful northern latitudes succumbed to malaria and other tropical diseases. Instead of the several hundred island-based aircraft the Z Operations counted on to cooperate with the Mobile Fleet, Ozawa could count on no more than fifty based on Guam and nearby Rota.

Admiral Spruance found *Redfin*'s report of Ozawa's sortie immensely interesting, but of more immediate consequence was information provided by his Japanese-language officer. Monitoring enemy radio transmissions, he reported that aircraft were assembling in Japan to island-hop southward to reinforce the Marianas. Spruance directed Mitscher to send two of his task groups north to pounce on the planes at their refueling stops, the islands of Iwo and Chichi Jima.

Mitscher passed the order to the two groups remaining east of Saipan, Rear Admiral J. J. "Jocko" Clark's Task Group 58.1 and Rear Admiral W. K. Harrill's Task Group 58.4. While these groups were refueling for their northward dash, both commanders raised objections. Clark, part Cherokee Indian and all fighter, didn't want to chance missing the big battle with the enemy fleet. Captain Burke, who knew his man, faked befuddlement. He said that Mitscher's staff understood and sympathized with Clark's reluctance to undertake such a dangerous mission. The ploy worked. Clark, his mettle thus impugned, hotly asserted that he wanted nothing better than to head north and blast the daylights out of the assembled enemy air power. Cautious Harrill objected for a different reason. He opposed going so close to Japan with less than half of Task Force 58 to challenge a concentration of possibly 200 planes. Mitscher cut him short with an order to get going. In view, however, of the Mobile Fleet's sortie, he instructed Clark and Harrill to complete their mission on the 16th and head back to rejoin the other two task groups on the 18th.

Eight old battleships, four of them veterans of the Pearl Harbor attack, had taken over the bombardment of Saipan's west coast. Too slow to move with the carriers, they now specialized in shore bombardment. Accompanied by eleven cruisers and more than a score of destroyers, they were presently joined by seven small escort carriers. Admiral Spruance arrived in *Indianapolis* to observe.

The next morning, 15 June, the marines stormed ashore on Saipan against heavy opposition. Late in the day, Task Groups 58.2 and 58.3, remaining nearby to lend support, came under air attack from the planes based on Guam. While the ships were throwing up a barrage of antiaircraft fire to fend off bombers, they were simultaneously heeling over to thread torpedoes. One torpedo passed so close to *Lexington* that Burke leaned over the bridge railing to watch it. The air attack ended as abruptly as it had begun. No ship was damaged, but flak from other ships accidentally killed three men and wounded fifty-eight. Clearly Task Force 58 for its own protection would have to take measures to keep Guam's two airfields unusable.

At 1835 on the 15th on the far side of the Philippine Sea, submarine *Flying Fish* sighted a Japanese force including carriers and battleships emerging from San Bernardino Strait. An hour later, submarine *Seahorse* 200 miles east of Mindanao observed a battleship-cruiser force coming up from the south. Neither submarine attempted to attack, being under orders from Vice Admiral C. A. Lockwood, Admiral Nimitz's submarine officer at Pearl Harbor, to report first. *Flying Fish* surfaced after dark and made its report. Japanese radio jamming delayed *Seahorse*'s report till next morning.

Admiral Mitscher and his staff identified the force debouching from the strait as the Mobile Fleet main body that had departed Tawitawi on the 13th, an identification confirmed by belated radio reports from Filipino coastwatchers, who had observed the force threading its way through the islands and counted nine carriers. The ships coming up from the south were correctly identified as those sighted in the Celebes Sea on 10 June apparently headed for Biak and now drawn north by the U.S. attack on the Marianas. This switch has been cited as an example of mutual support between the two lines of Allied advance, but in fact it was entirely fortuitous. Had the Marianas assault occurred a few days later, the Japanese battle-ship-cruiser force might not have been diverted before inflicting a major setback on MacArthur's forces at Biak.

There was no indication whether the two Japanese segments intended to rendezvous or to operate separately. Spruance was inclined to believe the enemy would again employ the tricky strategy of divided force, as in the battles of the Coral Sea and Midway. He estimated that Ozawa's main body would attempt to lure Task Force 58 westward, away from the Marianas, while the battleship-cruiser segment got in behind it and smashed the U.S. landing force at the Saipan beachhead.

Mitscher and Burke, confirmed in their estimate that the Japanese would contest the American invasion, had been planning how to offset Ozawa's three major advantages—his downwind position, the greater range of his carrier planes, and expected support from Japanese island-based aircraft. If the easterly trade wind held, Ozawa could advance on Task Force 58 while launching and recovering planes, whereas the Americans would have to turn back into the wind for air operations. Japanese carrier planes, unencumbered by the weight of such lifesaving American devices as built-in armor, self-sealing gas tanks, and bulletproof canopy glass, could carry more gas, giving them an attack radius of 300 miles, compared to 200 for U.S. planes. Not only could Japanese planes based on Rota and Guam supplement the Japanese carrier planes, but the carrier aircraft could stand off far outside the range of American aircraft and make use of the islands to shuttle-bomb the Americans—that is, send their bombers to hit the American ships, then rearm and refuel on the islands and hit the ships again on the return flight.

Mitscher and his staff had dreamed up a single, simple plan of operation that would cancel out all three of Ozawa's advantages: Head west by night away from the Marianas and toward the oncoming enemy fleet; head east by day, back toward the Marianas. The return trip, into the wind, would permit unlimited launching of search planes. When these had sighted the enemy fleet and reported its position, bearing, and speed, the Americans could calculate a final nighttime approach that would bring their task force at dawn close enough to the enemy fleet to attack it with carrier planes and too far away from the islands to permit land-based air support or shuttle-bombing. With luck, Admiral Lee could open the engagement with a predawn attack on the enemy fleet with his battleships, and the U.S. carrier groups could outflank it under cover of darkness, seize the downwind position, and block its line of retreat. Meanwhile, Task Force 58 planes repeatedly attacked the airfields on Rota and Guam, destroying aircraft and cratering landing strips.

In the afternoon of the 17th, Vice Admiral Lee began withdrawing from Task Groups 58.2 and 58.3 seven battleships, four heavy cruisers, and thirteen destroyers to form Task Group 58.7, a circular battle line. While this operation was in progress, Spruance in *Indianapolis*, accompanied by a reinforcement of eight cruisers and twenty-one destroyers from the Expeditionary Force, rejoined Group 58.3. On Mitscher's inquiring, via Burke, whether he intended to assume tactical command of Task Force 58, Spruance replied: "Desire you proceed at your discretion, selecting dispositions and movements best calculated to meet the enemy under the most advantageous conditions. I shall issue general directives when necessary and leave details to you and Admiral Lee."

Spruance, by reserving to himself authority to "issue general directives when necessary," could and might countermand any order of Mitscher's he disapproved of. Rather than be thus humiliated, Mitscher decided to submit all tactical orders to Spruance in advance, which meant that the latter would in effect be exercising tactical command after all.

When the sun set on the 17th, no U.S. plane had sighted the Mobile Fleet, though many scouts from Task Force 58 and from the Admiralties and New Guinea had searched the waters to the west. Japanese carrier and island-based aircraft had seen and reported Task Force 58, however, and some of the snoopers had been shot down by American planes.

Luckily Admiral Lockwood's submarines were on patrol and well distributed. Late that evening, submarine *Cavalla* sighted and reported the Mobile Fleet steaming eastward at 19 knots. Lockwood thereupon ordered his submarines in the Philippine Sea, after identifying ships sighted as enemy, to attack first and report afterward. He also moved his main patrol, a four-submarine "invisible trap," 100 miles southward into the path of the oncoming Japanese.

On receiving *Cavalla*'s report at 0345 on 18 June, Burke awakened Mitscher, and he, the admiral, and Hedding went into flag plot and did some fast figuring. Task Groups 58.2 and 58.3 were westbound in accord with the west-by-night plan. If these two groups and the Mobile Fleet maintained course and speed through the hours of darkness, they would be 500 miles apart at 0530. If the Americans continued on course west thereafter through the day they could be in position to attack the enemy fleet before sunset. But they were scheduled to rendezvous at noon with Clark's and Harrill's task groups coming down from the raid on the Jimas. The wise course, they decided, was for 58.2 and 58.3 to turn back east, keep the rendezvous, head back west again, and hit the enemy with everything they had early the next day, 19 June.

The ideal plan, concluded Mitscher and his staff, would be to advance on the Mobile Fleet through the night of 18–19 June. Before dawn Lee's battle line, leading the way, would engage the enemy fleet. At first light the carriers would launch an attack to complete its destruction. They got off a dispatch to Lee, explaining the situation and asking, "Do you desire night engagement?" Burke expected a vehement "Yes!" in reply. What came back was disheartening: "Do not, repeat *not*, believe we should seek night engagement." A battleship night action battle Lee had fought in 1942 off Guadalcanal had left him with the unshakable conviction that not even well-handled radar, at which he was expert, could unscramble the chaos of night combat.

On top of Lee's discouraging reply came a disturbing communication from Spruance. He had reliable intelligence that there were at least forty combatant ships in the Mobile Fleet. *Cavalla* had counted only fifteen. That was not bad for night observations at periscope depth, but the count buttressed Spruance's conviction that in addition to the Mobile Fleet there was a force of Japanese ships seeking an opportunity to get behind Task Force 58 and attack the amphibious forces at the Saipan beachhead. Mitscher's west-by-night, east-by-day scheme might provide the opening the Japanese were seeking.

"Task Force 58 must cover Saipan and our forces engaged in that operation," he reminded Mitscher. "Consider that we can best cover Saipan by advancing to westward during daylight and retiring to eastward at night so as to reduce possibility of enemy passing us during darkness." Spruance thus reversed Mitscher's operational plan for canceling Ozawa's three advantages.

Clark's and Harrill's task groups joined the others on schedule at noon. Mitscher lost no time in heading the reconstituted Task Force

58 westward to close with the oncoming Mobile Fleet. At 1330 he
launched searches. These ranged out more than 300 miles but did
not come quite within sighting distance of the enemy. At sunset,
1829, he recalled all planes. Subsequently he had Burke announce by
TBS that at nightfall, 2030, Task Force 58, in compliance with
Admiral Spruance's directive of that morning, would reverse course
and head back east.

Mitscher did not regard the change of course as necessarily disad-
vantageous, since the last report locating the enemy was *Cavalla*'s
of early that morning. He preferred to avoid an encounter with the
Mobile Fleet in darkness, particularly in view of Lee's reluctance to
fight a night battle. A message from Admiral Nimitz to the fleet,
which Mitscher received at 2245, gave him something tangible to
work with. Ozawa had broken radio silence, enabling U.S. high-
frequency direction-finder stations to get a fix on him.

Working with this fix, the task force staff concluded that the
Mobile Fleet was 355 miles away. If both fleets continued heading
east at about the same speed, the enemy would remain at that distance till daylight, too far for U.S. planes to attack and return to
their carriers. Further calculations showed that reversing course at
0130 the next morning, 19 June, would put Task Force 58 at the
optimum striking range of between 150 and 200 miles from the
enemy at 0500, dawn. Mitscher decided at once to seize the opportunity.

"It might be a hell of a battle for a while," he said to Burke, "but
I think we can win it."

Confident that ComFifthFleet would approve the change, he told
Burke to inform Spruance of his intention. To forestall any misunderstanding, Burke wrote out the message in terse, telegraphic language and read it at 2325 on the TBS: "Propose coming to course
270 degrees [west] at 0130 in order to commence treatment at 0500.
Advise."

When word of Burke's message drifted down to the pilots of Air
Group 16 who were still awake, they responded with enthusiasm.
"We came ten feet off the deck," said one.

Up in flag plot, Admiral Mitscher and his staff anticipated a quick
and affirmative reply. Instead, after a routine acknowledgment there
was only silence. That meant Mitscher's proposal was under discussion by Spruance and Fifth Fleet staff, and their approval could not
be counted on. Whatever the answer, extensive preparations had to
be made for the coming battle. In silence some of the staff stirred

about restlessly. The admiral and his chiefs of staff sat together on the transom, Burke puffing on his pipe, Mitscher and Hedding smoking cigarette after cigarette.

Midnight passed and still no answer. At last at 0038 on the 19th the TBS speaker hummed into life followed by the words "Bald Eagle—Bald Eagle, this is Blue Jacket." Next came Admiral Spruance's heartbreaking reply, read by his chief of staff: "Change proposed does not appear advisable. Believe indications given by *Stingray* more accurate than that determined by direction finder. If that is so continuation as at present seems preferable. End run by other carrier groups remains possibility and must not be overlooked."

Spruance's distrust of the direction-finder fix was understandable. Everyone knew about the ruse of sending a destroyer off to a distance to break radio silence as a means of tricking the direction finders into establishing a false fix on the main body. Mitscher and his staff had not heard about *Stingray*. *Indianapolis* radio operators had intercepted a dispatch from Admiral Lockwood to this submarine asking it to repeat a message received at Pearl Harbor in garbled form. The Fifth Fleet staff, knowing the recently changed location of *Stingray*, one of Lockwood's invisible-trap submarines, put two and two together and got ten. *Stingray*, they concluded, must have sighted the Mobile Fleet, which had jammed its report, producing garbles.

If indeed the unreadable message was a sighting report, the Mobile Fleet and Task Force 58 must be much closer together than the direction-finder fix indicated. Hence, if the latter reversed course at 0130 and headed west, as Mitscher suggested, it might easily run past the Mobile Fleet in darkness. That result would be entirely to Mitscher's satisfaction, since it would place him downwind in position to block the enemy's retreat. For Spruance it would be a nightmare situation, because it would place the Mobile Fleet between Task Force 58 and Saipan. Turner's transports had taken refuge east of the Marianas, and the U.S. invasion forces were now well established ashore. Most of their supplies, however, were piled up at the beachhead and moving in slowly. If the Mobile Fleet or some other enemy force could blast its way through the old battleships and jeep carriers on guard and destroy the piled-up supplies, the drive might be delayed. To prevent that setback, Spruance denied Mitscher attainment of his grand objective—nothing less than destruction of Japan's Mobile Fleet.

Mitscher believed, and his staff shared his belief, that in view of his numerical superiority in ships and aircraft, the far more extensive training of his aviators, and the combat experience of his officers and men during the many months that Japan's ships idled at anchor, he could so devastate the enemy fleet that there would be no more battles at sea in this war. He could do nothing of the sort, however, unless he was permitted to get close enough to the enemy ships to attack them with his torpedo planes and bombers.

It was a matter of priorities. Spruance's job was to "capture, occupy, and defend Saipan, Tinian, and Guam." Everything else, including destruction of the enemy fleet, was strictly incidental. When aviators argued that the far-seeing eyes of fliers could detect amply betimes any Japanese force trying to slip around behind Task Force 58, Spruance could point out that these same far-seeing eyes, whether based on airfields or carrier decks, had not in three days espied the main Japanese fleet, though the Americans knew from submarine reports in what general area it was operating.

Several officers in *Lexington* burst out angrily on hearing Spruance's negative reply. Some of them suggested points to be argued. Mitscher had no intention of arguing with commander Fifth Fleet. Without saying a word, he left flag plot for his sea cabin.

The staff pitched in and spent the rest of the night making plans for the coming battle. Mitscher, unable to sleep, presently rejoined them. They knew the enemy was getting ready too, and they imagined they could hear him arming his planes and coming toward them.

"We knew we were going to have hell slugged out of us in the morning," said Burke later, "and we were making sure we were ready for it. We knew we couldn't reach them. We knew they could reach us. And we were preparing plans, throwing most of them in the wastebasket, to get set as early as possible for an air attack which was bound to develop."

BATTLE
OF THE
PHILIPPINE
SEA

ON MONDAY, 19 June 1944, the sun rose shortly before 0600 and soon burned away scattered mists and night clouds, leaving the sky an immaculate azure dome. Admiral Mitscher, seated on his swivel chair, could see 20 miles. Task Force 58, which had steamed steadily eastward through the night, reached a point roughly 90 miles northwest of Guam and about the same distance southwest of Saipan.

The task force now consisted of five circular groups of ships arranged like a reversed F. Four of the circles, each about 4 miles in diameter, had carriers in the center and cruisers and destroyers in the circumference. Carrier Task Groups 58.1, 58.3, and 58.2 were in column north to south in that order, 12 miles apart. Fifteen miles west of Task Group 58.3, in the presumed direction of the enemy, was Admiral Lee's Task Group 58.7, comprising seven fast battleships, four heavy cruisers, and thirteen destroyers. Carrier Task Group 58.4 was stationed north of the battleship group to furnish it air cover. Twenty miles west of Group 58.7 steamed a pair of early-warning picket destroyers. Spruance's flagship *Indianapolis* and Mitscher's flagship *Lexington* were both in Group 58.3.

Task Force 58 usually endeavored, not always successfully, to move as a unit, and unless otherwise ordered or when threading torpedoes, ships and groups remained in position relative to each other. In 1942, U.S. carriers under air attack had maneuvered independently to evade bombs. In 1944 they generally relied on fighter

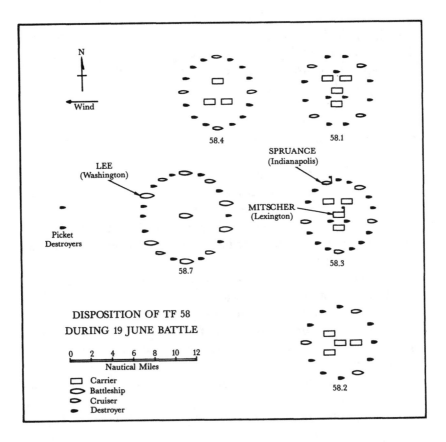

Disposition of Task Force 58 During 19 June Battle

aircraft and on antiaircraft guns firing radar-triggered shells that exploded with deadly effect when they came within lethal distance of a flying target. Such guns were most highly concentrated in Lee's battleship group, which aircraft attacking from the Mobile Fleet were expected to encounter first.

After launching dawn search, combat air, and antisubmarine patrols, Mitscher at 0619 changed course to west-southwest, hoping at last to bring his carriers within profitable striking range of the Japanese Mobile Fleet. But because he had repeatedly to head back into the east wind to launch aircraft, he was no farther west at 0900 than he had been at dawn. He had, however, gained a little extra sea room for eastbound combat operations.

Task Force 58's dawn search failed to locate the enemy fleet, but snoopers from Guam and possibly also from the Mobile Fleet had scouted the task force. Thus Ozawa obviously knew all he needed to know about the Americans and was bound to attack, employing his advantages of downwind position, superior attack range of his planes, and cooperation of island-based aircraft. "It was apparent by this time," wrote Burke, "that we were probably due for a working-over by both land-based and carrier-based planes."

That is exactly what Spruance was thinking. By TBS he advised Mitscher to send bombers to crater the airstrips on Rota and Guam. Bald Eagle replied that the raids on the Marianas had about used up his instant-contact bombs, normally employed for cratering. He had an ample supply of armor-piercing, but these were unsuitable for that job, and he hoped for an opportunity to use them against enemy ships. Instead of bombers to crater the airfields, he sent thirty-three Hellcat fighters to attack any aircraft launched from them. By a little after 1000, the Hellcats claimed to have disposed of thirty fighters and five bombers.

Task Force 58 was making 24 knots westbound when *Alabama*'s radar at 0957 picked up approaching bogeys at a distance of 140 miles, bearing 260 (west-southwest), altitude an estimated 20,000 feet. Within minutes a number of other ships, including *Lexington*, had the contact. Mitscher said to Burke, "Get those fighters back from Guam."

Burke passed the order to Lieutenant Joe Eggert, task force fighter director: "Give your fighters over Guam hey rube," and Eggert sounded off with a lusty "Hey, Rube!" to the fighter pilots. This old circus cry for help in a fight with townspeople had been adopted by the navy to signal "Come back over the ship."

By this time the whole task force was sounding general quarters. On board *Lexington* the bugler's call was all but overwhelmed by the bong-bong-bong of the warning bell. As this pandemonium subsided Captain Burke via TBS ordered all ships, "Stand by for action."

Mitscher, seated on his swivel chair, was observing the bustle on the flight deck below with his usual air of calm detachment. *Life* photographer J. R. Eyerman paused to take the admiral's picture, marveling at his apparently unruffled composure at this moment of furious action with battle imminent.

Mitscher, glancing at the photographer with the raised camera, said calmly, not raising his voice, "Are you excited?"

Taken aback, Eyerman lowered his camera. "I guess so," he said.

He suddenly noticed that the admiral's eyes were dancing, lending his face unwonted animation as he said, "Well, *I'm* excited!"

At that moment Eyerman snapped the picture, sure he had captured the admiral's suppressed excitement, but when he developed the negative Mitscher's photographed countenance wore only its usual expression of calm detachment.

Burke, TBS in hand, was giving orders in Mitscher's name. With Hedding's help he had learned the Bald Eagle system. Some orders were so obviously in line with Mitscher's style of command that Burke gave them without hesitation. When in doubt, he indicated his intention in a few words to the admiral, who replied with a slight nod or shake of the head or an approving or disapproving grunt.

For a few minutes the task force continued heading westward. Burke ordered "Steady as you go," knowing Bald Eagle preferred having his fliers expend gasoline in combat rather than in flying out to engage the enemy. At last at 1023 he ordered a radical change of course, and all 92 ships turned together and headed into the wind on course east-southeast, with Lee's 58.7, the battleship group, now following, not leading as before.

"Prepare to launch all available fighters," Burke ordered. Nine minutes later the task force heard his command: "Stand by . . . Execute." At 1023 the first of the blue-winged Hellcats rose from the flight decks. Eggert was already vectoring the Hellcats of the combat air patrol. While launching of fighters was in progress, Burke warned the ships to expect repeated attacks. "Keep fighters available to repel these attacks," he said, "landing planes as necessary."

As the decks were cleared of Hellcats, Burke had the dive-bombers and torpedo planes brought up and launched, with orders to orbit to the east, on call, till the air battle was over. By removing them from the carriers, he reduced the fire hazard and their probable destruction should the carriers be damaged in combat. He also kept the decks clear to recover the fighters and refuel, rearm, and re-launch them continuously as necessary.

Japanese-language expert Sims, as usual when action impended, had snapped on headphones to monitor the enemy aviators' voice radio channels. Often the chatter gave hints of what to expect next. This time Sims hit the jackpot. The oncoming 69 enemy planes, which the Americans called Raid I, closed to 72 miles and began to circle. Their air coordinator then began giving his ill-trained fliers a lecture, on which Sims eavesdropped and reported. Adequately trained, experienced aviators would have picked their targets and attacked without coaching, but these neophytes were being told exactly what to strike and how, including the extraordinarily poor advice to concentrate against the nearest group. This was the battle-ship group, which with far more antiaircraft guns than the others had been stationed to westward to serve both as a magnet for the enemy planes and a shield for the American carriers.

The quarter hour the coordinator spent briefing his fliers gave Eggert the time he needed to get his fighters stacked for the kill. He erected a wall of defense by sending most of the fighters up to 24,000 feet, with others at levels ranging down to 17,000. Some he kept near the surface to intercept any enemy aircraft, particularly torpedo planes, attempting to slip in at low altitude. As the last of the Hellcats left their carrier decks, the first of the fighters that had been called back from Guam with a "Hey Rube!" began landing on board for refueling and rearming.

When the Japanese planes broke out of orbit and headed for their target, the Hellcats swooped down upon them and sent dozens plummeting into the sea, usually with long comet tails of flame. The enemy planes that eluded this ambush soon ran into another, which destroyed a dozen more. The speakers in the ships were tuned to the chatter of the air battle—a cacophony of orders, acknowledg-ments, and reports:

"Vector two six five, angels twenty."

"Vector two four zero, bandits ahead, eleven o'clock, low."

"Tallyho! Tallyho! Many bandits, Zekes and Kates."

"Splash one Zeke!"

"Splash two Kates!"

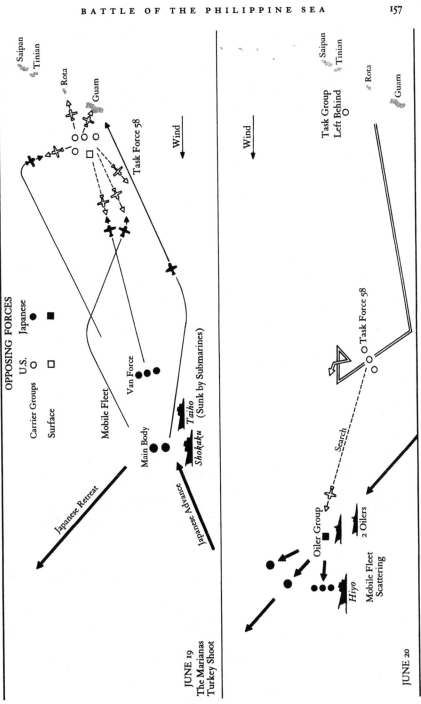

Battle of the Philippine Sea, 19–20 June 1944

Plus such less specialized phraseology as "Got the sonofabitch!" and "Look out, Joe! You've got one on your tail!"

Three or four enemy bombers broke through to the battleship group. Two achieved near misses on a pair of cruisers. Another attacked *South Dakota* and scored the only bomb hit of the day. The explosion killed and wounded several men without slowing the tough old battlewagon or impairing her fighting efficiency.

At 1057, Eggert reported that the radar screens were clear. Raid I had been broken up. Its few surviving planes were streaking back toward the Mobile Fleet. A check made as the Hellcats returned to their carriers showed that four American pilots were missing. Several of the fighter aircraft that got back were pushed over the side as too shot up to be worth salvage.

While undamaged Hellcats were being rearmed and refueled, flight leaders dashed up to Bald Eagle's perch on the flag bridge to report their almost unbelievable one-sided victory over the fragile enemy planes flown by inexperienced aviators. Among the Japanese flyers, they said, there was little mutual support; individuals fought bravely but each for himself.

The discussions were cut short when at 1107 *Lexington*'s radar detected approaching enemy aircraft, distant 115 miles, more than a hundred in one huge group. Like Raid I, Raid II began circling to receive instructions. The coordinator, the original or a successor, used the same frequency as before, but he had reached a greater altitude, perhaps 30,000 feet, from which he evidently could see all of Task Force 58, for he advised his fliers how to locate the American carriers.

Again the pause for instructions gave Eggert and his task group assistants time to stack their Hellcats for effective attack. The first clash cost the Japanese about seventy planes, but some twenty broke through to the task force. They first attacked the two picket destroyers, formerly in the lead, now trailing behind Task Group 58.7. The destroyers successfully fought off the attacks, and one reported: "The battleships, cruisers, and destroyers ahead put up a tremendous barrage which, together with the burning planes all around the horizon, created a most awesome spectacle."

Most of the Japanese planes reaching the task force were shot down by antiaircraft fire before executing their attacks, but one torpedo-bomber crashed into *Indiana* at the waterline, scratching her paint work; and near misses damaged and caused casualties in *Wasp* and *Bunker Hill* without slowing either down. Just before noon a small group of torpedo-bombers attacked Task Group 58.3, providing both Spruance and Mitscher a ringside view. Bald Eagle even slid down off his swivel chair and followed the action with binoculars. A torpedo intended for *Enterprise* exploded in her wake. Three planes gliding in to attack light carrier *Princeton* were blown to pieces by antiaircraft fire from *Lexington* and from the intended victim herself.

Throughout the fray, Burke, Hedding, or Widhelm periodically darted out from flag plot to bring Mitscher a bit of information or to get a decision. At 1215 the American radars were once more clear of bogeys, and all hands could take a breather. Fewer than a quarter of the planes of Raid II returned to their carriers.

Raids III and IV, powerful when they left the Mobile Fleet, were sent against contacts incorrectly reported by Japanese search pilots who apparently did not understand compass deviation. Most of the planes of Raid III, finding nothing at the reported locations, returned to their carriers. Most of Raid IV's planes went on to Guam. A few aircraft of each of the raids found and attacked carriers of Task Force 58 but achieved nothing of consequence while taking heavy losses.

The forty-nine planes of Raid IV that headed for Guam were in for a surprise. Mitscher, perceiving that he did not need all his fighters to intercept planes from the Mobile Fleet, had sent some Hellcats back to Guam to keep that base neutralized. They were joined by dive-bombers, which had abandoned their useless orbiting, with or without orders. The pilots, realizing that their planes could not remain airborne much longer while burdened with heavy bombs, decided there was no better place to get rid of the bombs than over Guam's two airfields. Lacking the instant-contact type, best for cratering runways, they dropped their 1,000-pound armor-piercing bombs. These, intended for use against ships, achieved little damage but apparently rattled the defenders. They also dropped 500-pound bombs with delay fuses, and these did a better job of making the runways unusable.

The Raid IV planes en route to Guam were detected by radars in Task Force 58, which vectored out about sixty fighters to attack them and a reinforcement of seven bombers to make sure the Guam airfields were freshly cratered. As the Japanese planes approached the island they jettisoned their bombs and headed to land at Orote Field. When they were circling the field with wheels down, the Hellcats fell on them and shot down thirty. The others were so battered in the fight or cracked up upon landing on the cratered strip as to be beyond repair.

With the virtual destruction of Raid IV, the Mobile Fleet had shot its bolt. Ozawa's desperate gamble to regain command of the sea had met disaster. Task Force 58 search planes winging out through the scene of the day's air battles reported the sea surface stained by a 12-mile stretch of oil slicks littered with floating and burning airplane parts. More carrier planes had been involved than in any other action of World War II. For the Americans it was an extraordinarily lopsided victory; for every U.S. plane shot down, more than thirteen Japanese aircraft were destroyed. It was a triumph for the Hellcats, which achieved 95 percent of the kills. Antiaircraft fire effected the rest.

It was a victory of well-trained over inadequately trained aviators, but the Japanese in a measure had talked themselves into defeat. On the strategic level it had happened before; preceding the Battle of Midway they had used an undependable code for radio communications that the Americans had intercepted, decoded, and acted upon. This time the loquacious air coordinators from their lofty perch in the sky had provided the Hellcats and their fighter directors priceless tactical information that gave the Americans the advantage at every interception.

There had been at least two coordinators, one relieving the other before his gas ran out, but the task force staff envisaged a composite little yellow man called Coordinator Joe, for whom they developed a wry affection as he continued unknowingly to shower them with helpful data. Burke assigned Eggert the task of conveying to his aviators that the coordinator was off-limits, not to be attacked. It was a tricky job. Eggert had to pass the word to his own fliers without letting on to the enemy that he knew Joe was there.

Burke had insisted all along that as a reward for his help Joe should go unmolested even when he had no more information to impart. Gus Widhelm, who held that the only good Jap was a dead Jap, branded such sentiments softheaded. When the remnant of Raid IV had been eliminated on Guam, he turned to Mitscher, no admirer of the Japanese. "Shall we get him now?" he asked.

"No indeed!" replied the admiral. "He did us too much good!"

During the break after Raid II, pilots had assembled in ready rooms for debriefing. To an inquiring air-intelligence officer one exultant young fighter pilot explained, "Why, hell, it was just like an old-time turkey shoot down home!" The apt expression circulated, and the action of 19 June 1944 became known around the world as the Great Marianas Turkey Shoot.

While the battle over the sea had been concentrated in the four raids, fighting over or against the enemy islands had been almost continuous. After the extinction of Raid IV, action for the rest of the day was chiefly over Guam. Nightfall at last brought the Turkey Shoot to an end.

At Pearl Harbor, Admiral Nimitz's Pacific Fleet headquarters had followed the day-long battle through radio intercepts. Early in the evening the official Fifth Fleet report came in. Expressed in Spruance's usual understated style, it said in part:

> Air attack on Task Force 58 commenced at 1045 coming in initially from westward and continued for several hours. Some enemy planes landed at Guam and Rota but these fields were hit by Task Force 58 planes several times to prevent their use. Over 300 enemy planes are reported destroyed by our planes and AA fire. Own aircraft losses not yet reported. Only known damage to our ships: 1 bomb hit on *South Dakota*, which does not affect her fighting efficiency.

Cincpac staff reacted to the report with relief and consternation—relief that the task force had suffered so little damage, consternation that the Japanese carriers had evidently sustained none at all. Almost exactly two years earlier, in the Battle of Midway, three lightly escorted American carriers had sunk four Japanese carriers backed by the whole Combined Fleet and in so doing had turned the tide of the war at sea. On this occasion the staff had anticipated an even more decisive victory by fifteen heavily escorted U.S. carriers with nearly 900 planes opposing Japan's nine carriers armed with fewer than half as many aircraft.

Later that evening the somber mood at Pearl Harbor was brightened by a dispatch from submarine *Cavalla:* "Hit *Shokaku*-class carrier with three out of six torpedoes. . . . Heard four terrific explosions in direction of target two and a half hours after attack. . . . Believe that baby sank."

During this fateful 19 June, in which Japan had lost so many planes, Task Force 58, barely scratched, was backing up against the Marianas. At 1023 that morning when it turned into the wind to launch fighters against Raid I, *Lexington* had been more than 100 miles from Guam. Because of repeated launchings and recoveries the course made good thereafter was east by south. In midafternoon when the remnant of Raid IV was wrecked at Guam, the task force flagship was just 20 miles from that island.

Now that the enemy's wings were clipped, and he was obviously attempting no end run, Spruance ordered a course change to west to close the Mobile Fleet. To recover all planes, however, took nearly five hours, during which time Mitscher thrice turned back into the wind, so that at 2000 the force was little farther west than it had been in midafternoon.

Meanwhile, Admiral Mitscher had received two requests. The first was from cautious Harrill, who reported that his destroyers were short of fuel and asked that his Task Group 58.4 be left behind. Sourly, through Burke, Mitscher granted permission, ordering Harrill to support U.S. forces on Saipan. Before the Turkey Shoot the other rear admirals had somehow managed to top off their destroyers. Harrill must have been dragging his heels. Mitscher recalled his foot-dragging when ordered north to bombard the Jimas. His days as a task group commander were numbered.

Fiery Jocko Clark, ardent for battle, radioed a different sort of request: "Would greatly appreciate remaining with you. We have plenty of fuel." Mitscher had Burke reply promptly, "You will remain with us all right until the battle is over."

At 2000, Task Force 58 headed due west. Spruance radioed Mitscher: "Desire to attack enemy tomorrow if we know his position with sufficient accuracy. . . . If not, we must continue searches tomorrow to assure adequate protection of Saipan."

At 2207, the task force changed course to 260 degrees, a little south of west, on the theory that if the Mobile Fleet was retiring, as seemed likely after such drastic loss of planes and aviators, it would retreat the way it had come. The new course carried Task Force 58 within an hour into the region of the afternoon battle. Here destroyers picked up several U.S. airmen. Though numbers of Japanese had parachuted into the sea or survived water landings, the force's combat mission forbade delays for further searches. In any event, Japanese warriors generally resisted rescue, having been taught that any sort of surrender was disgraceful. Those who remained in the water or on rafts might come to envy their brethren who had gone down in flames to a mercifully quick death.

Toward midwatch, Admiral Mitscher slid off his swivel chair, entered flag plot, and looked over the night orders Burke had prepared. He decided not to launch a search before dawn, a decision made partly out of concern for his aviators, whom he recoiled from sending out possibly to be shot or forced down in darkness without hope of rescue. Moreover, his pilots and crews needed their sleep, having gone through an exhausting day of battle and anticipating a similar day on the morrow. Lastly, in this downwind-chase situation, he could not afford to lose distance by turning back into the wind for launching and recovering more often than was absolutely necessary.

The admiral stood up and stretched. Then apropos of nothing in particular he said, "Tomorrow I'm going to get a haircut. Personally I hate barbers. I hate them like hell. But all the same, tomorrow I'm going to get a haircut." Then, drawing the blackout curtains aside, he disappeared in the direction of his sea cabin. Staff officers on first watch left behind were presently diverted by broadcasts from Tokyo claiming that in the day's battle Japanese aircraft had sunk many U.S. ships, including eleven carriers.

At first light, 0530, while Mitscher and Burke watched from the bridge, Task Force 58 turned back to launch the first search of 20 June, a routine 325-mile probe, due west covering a wide 120-degree arc. As hours passed with no sighting reported, it became clear that the probe had fallen short, since the Mobile Fleet could hardly have reached a point north or south of the broad coverage.

Admiral Spruance had a theory. The carrier that *Cavalla* had torpedoed, which Spruance identified not as *Shokaku* but as her sister *Zuikaku*, might not have sunk, and the Mobile Fleet could be shepherding her toward a shipyard in home waters. He signaled Mitscher: "Damaged *Zuikaku* may be still afloat. If so, believe she will be most likely heading northwest. Desire to push our searches today as far to westward as possible. If no contacts with enemy fleet result, consider it indication fleet is withdrawing, and further pursuit after today will be unprofitable. If you concur, retire tonight towards Saipan. Will order out tankers in vicinity Saipan. *Zuikaku* must be sunk if we can reach her."

Gus Widhelm became excited over Spruance's theory, not only for professional reasons but because in an incautious moment he had bet two air-group commanders a thousand dollars that Task Force 58 would intercept the Japanese fleet. He proposed sending Hellcats carrying jettisonable belly tanks with extra fuel on a 475-mile, ultra-long-range probe in the general direction of the great Japanese naval base at Sasebo.

When Commander Ernest Snowden, skipper of *Lexington*'s Air

Group 16, learned of Widhelm's proposal, he went bounding up to flag bridge and offered to lead the long-range search for the enemy. Mitscher looked him over admiringly. "They're a long way off," he said.

"I'll use volunteers."

"I've got a search out that should be back about 1100. If I don't get anything, I'll send you out." Concerned about navigation on such a long flight, he suggested taking along a radar-equipped bomber.

Snowden descended to the fighter ready room and chalked a column of twelve numbers on the bulletin board with his own name beside the first. Turning to the pilots, he said, "Gentlemen, this is strictly voluntary. Chances are less than fifty-fifty you'll get back. I need eleven people. My name is on top of the list."

He left the ready room. When he returned half an hour later, all the numbers had names written beside them.

When the 0530 search was back on board, and Snowden learned that the mission had been fruitless, he again dashed up to the bridge. The admiral nodded his assent. Then, as Snowden turned back toward the ladder, Mitscher called after him, "I want you to go back and tell those boys that if you make contact and anybody gets shot down, I'll come and pick them up even if I have to steam the whole damn fleet up after them."

At noon the twelve volunteer-piloted Hellcats took off and headed on course 340 degrees, just a little west of due north. On Mitscher's orders, Burke brought Task Force 58 from course 261 to 330 degrees. The force was now committed to Spruance's theory that the Mobile Fleet was somewhere off to the northwest.

Mitscher had no intention of restricting his hunt for the enemy to Snowden's long-range, and therefore necessarily narrow, probe. At 1330 he launched eight Avengers, six Hellcats, and two dive-bombers for a search between 275 and 315 degrees out to the usual 325 miles. Lieutenant Robert S. Nelson, piloting an Avenger, participated in covering the center sector.

At midafternoon Snowden's distant probe, having found nothing, was en route back to *Lexington*. The planes of the 1330 search were approaching the end of their outbound leg without reporting anything. In Task Force 58 the long wait begat tense nerves and low spirits. The mood in *Lexington*'s flag plot grew surly. Chewing the stem of a cold pipe, Burke muttered over and over, "Damn! . . .

Damn!" Hedding picked up a book, noted its title, *Action at Sea*, and hurled it aside.

In a low voice the flag navigator asked Gus Widhelm, "What'll you take for that bet of yours now?"

"Me? What bet?"

"You know what bet—that thousand-buck bet that we'd intercept the Jap fleet."

"I'll sell out for fifty."

"Fifty? I wouldn't give you—"

The radio loudspeaker broke in, "I see 'em!" Somebody recognized Nelson's voice.

Widhelm dashed out onto the bridge. "They see 'em!" he shouted to Mitscher. "We've got 'em!" He was grinning broadly, cheered by the happy turn in the strategic situation and in his own financial prospects.

The admiral slid off his swivel chair. "Get me the whole message," he said. Widhelm plunged down the ladder toward the radio shack. Burke grabbed the TBS and shouted, "Indications are our birdmen have sighted something big!"

Nelson's voice on the loudspeaker had faded out, but his radioman was transmitting the report in Morse code. In the radio shack, the monitor typed out the dots and dashes in plain English. When he finished typing the message, Widhelm snatched it and dashed back up to flag plot, where he spread it out on the chart table: "Enemy fleet sighted. Time 1540. Long. 135-25E. Lat. 15-00N. Course 270. Speed 20."

While Burke was relaying the report to the task groups, the navigator was making measurements on the chart. On a slip of paper he wrote "220," meaning distance in nautical miles from Task Force 58 to the reported position of the Mobile Fleet.

As we have seen, American carrier planes could not attack much beyond 200 miles and have enough fuel left for defensive and offensive operations. Mitscher conferred with Burke and the other staff officers, though all were sure that he knew the answers and had already made up his mind. The admiral was less concerned about the distance to the target than the fact that the pilots on returning to their carriers would almost certainly have to land in darkness, an operation for which they were not trained. Nevertheless, here was an opportunity he must not forgo—probably his last chance to come to grips with the Japanese fleet. He had to launch an attack, and he counted on his planes so damaging and slowing the enemy ships that

Lee's battle line could close and finish them off at daylight. "Launch 'em," he said firmly.

Burke addressed the task group commanders by TBS: "Launch first deckload as soon as possible. Prepare to launch second deck-load." To Admiral Spruance he reported, "Expect to launch every-thing we have. We will probably have to recover at night."

In ready rooms, loudspeakers barked, "Pilots, man your planes!" and pilots and crewmen, admonished to hit the carriers, dashed for the flight decks. On each of the decks, aircraft had been spotted for hours, armed and tuned, their engines warmed from time to time, following which their fuel tanks had been topped off. When signal flags were hauled down from *Lexington*'s yardarm, meaning "Exe-cute," the ships of Task Group 58.3 began turning simultaneously into the wind. Within minutes the other task groups turned simi-larly.

The first of the Hellcats lifted off at 1624. It was followed by 229 more planes, the shorter-range types carrying belly tanks. Malfunc-tions forced 14 aircraft to turn back, but 85 Hellcats, 54 Avengers, 51 Helldivers, and 26 Dauntless dive-bombers made the flight. Most of the planes were armed with 500-pound bombs, but 21 of the Avengers carried torpedoes.

As the last of the planes were being launched, a messenger from the radio shack handed Burke a shocker. It was a dispatch from Lieutenant Nelson correcting his previous report. The Mobile Fleet was at longitude 134-30 E, instead of 135-25 E, as stated in his earlier message. The enemy was thus 60 miles farther west than they had supposed. Because Task Force 58 had headed east while launching and the Mobile Fleet was heading northwest, the planes that took off last from the task force carriers would have to fly more than 300 miles.

Admiral Mitscher, deeply shaken, rechecked the charts. Then he made the heart-wrenching decision not to recall the planes already airborne. He did, however, tell Burke to cancel the second deckload and to notify Spruance that the planes on board would be held till morning. Burke next ordered the task force to change course back to northwest and increase speed in order to shorten the flight of the returning U.S. planes.

If, as seemed certain, the planes had to return to their flight decks after dark, the carriers would turn on running lights, truck lights, and glow lights to guide them to a safe landing. In 1944 this proce-dure was routine, having been initiated two years earlier in the

Battle of Midway by Admiral Spruance. Now at Mitscher's behest Burke directed each group flagship to be prepared, if necessary, also to turn searchlight beams straight up into the air as guides to the homing aircraft. Lastly, a measure previously planned but never before executed, he arranged to have a few communication planes fly out toward the Mobile Fleet and orbit, with the mission of relaying radio messages from the distant attacking planes to the task force.

Many of the pilots now airborne had intercepted Nelson's revised contact report, and Burke took measures to make sure that all were aware of the corrected position of the enemy fleet and of the extraordinary distance they were expected to fly. He would not have been surprised to hear proposals from them to abandon the attack. None came. Instead there was a good deal of advice from the more experienced pilots to the others on how to conserve fuel. As the planes drew farther away, the radio chatter, relayed via loudspeakers, grew fainter and at last faded away.

Admiral Mitscher ordered the night fighters in the task force to be serviced and spotted, their pilots on standby, ready to take off. Remaining on the bridge, he had his dinner brought to him on a tray. Every few minutes he would glance at the sun's position and check with his wristwatch. He and his staff had been figuring the odds. The pilots would be flying slow enough to conserve fuel, fast enough to get over the Mobile Fleet before sunset, which would come at 1900. As the sun, blood-red, neared the horizon, Mitscher had Burke order the three carrier groups to open intervals between groups to 15 miles to provide more maneuvering room for recovery operations.

At 1840, just as the sun's lower limb touched the horizon, the speakers came to life. The communication planes, orbiting out to the west, were beginning to relay radio transmissions from the U.S. attack aircraft, which had just arrived over the Mobile Fleet. In all the ships of Task Force 58, men whose duties permitted paused and listened. Only a few Japanese planes had risen to repel the attackers, but the antiaircraft fire was intense. The Americans reported hits on three carriers and two oilers set afire. Most of the enemy planes had been destroyed, but some twenty American aircraft were shot down over the enemy fleet.

It was all over in twenty minutes. As the sun sank below the horizon, the American air groups headed back in the gathering dusk toward their own carrier decks. Lieutenant Commander Ralph

Weymouth, commanding *Lexington*'s bombers, transmitted the final report: "Attacks completed. Two CV sunk." Hopeful message! How could he know? Aircraft carriers do not sink in twenty minutes.

In the long wait that followed, tension mounted in the task force as twilight turned into a moonless, pitch-black night. The admiral, seated in darkness on his swivel chair, repeatedly consulted his watch's luminous dial. Radio began picking up transmissions between returning pilots—at first routine, then increasingly anxious. Some had seen lightning to the south and apparently mistaken it for lights of their own fleet. At 2024 the leading planes, now 124 miles away, began appearing on task force radars. Burke, who had kept the night fighters in readiness, now ordered them launched to fly out and guide the planes in.

Confused by the lightning, their fuel tanks nearly empty, some of the pilots panicked and began calling for help:

"Can anyone tell me where I am?"

"Give me a vector. Can anyone give me a vector?"

Others had disciplined themselves to handle such a situation:

"Hey, Joe, how much gas have you got left?"

"About a gill."

"I've got about two gills. How about you, Tom?"

"It reads five gallons less than empty."

"Let's put 'em down together while we still have power."

Burke went out onto the dark bridge wing. He could see the luminous dial of the admiral's watch and knew Mitscher was consulting it. Burke sensed the depth of his anxiety for his fliers. Having no children of his own, he had in effect adopted them as his sons. Arleigh had admired Mitscher almost from the beginning of their association. Later, as he began to tolerate and even find amusement in his quirks and quiddities, he developed a liking for him. Tonight, sharing a common apprehension, he began to feel affection for the skinny little guy with the wrinkled face, bony hands, absurd long-billed cap, and matchless command of naval aviation.

The new disposition of the groups placed Admiral Clark's 58.1 somewhat nearer than the others to the oncoming aircraft, which thus had registered on his radarscopes first. After listening to their radio transmissions for ten minutes, Jocko could stand the pressure no longer. Without waiting for the signal, he ordered his flagship illuminated, including searchlights pointing skyward. The rest of his group followed his incandescent example, destroyers focusing searchlight beams on the carriers to render them more visible, and cruisers and destroyers turning the night into day with geysers of star shells.

This premature illumination took Mitscher by surprise, but he did not disapprove. To Burke he said, "Turn on the lights."

It was a command the fleet had been awaiting. Hardly had Burke given the word when the task force lighted up like a Mardi Gras spread over 60 square miles of mid-Pacific. Notified by air plot that the first of the returning planes were approaching, Burke turned the task force into the east wind and stepped up the speed to 22 knots.

Within minutes, firefly points of lights appeared in the northwest and grew brighter until the roar of motors, becoming audible, announced them as aircraft. Soon the leading plane was dead astern of *Lexington*. The landing signal officer, gesturing with fluorescent batons, waved it in. When it had come to a stop a deck crew hurriedly disengaged its tailhook and waved it forward to make way for the next plane, already being waved in.

"Whose plane was that?" Mitscher asked Burke.

"*Hornet*'s, sir."

"*Hornet?* She's not even in our task group. If the boys are having that much trouble finding their ships, we might as well tell them to land wherever they can. Just so we get them down tonight, we can unscramble them tomorrow morning."

At 2052 the pilots heard Burke's voice on their radioes: "All planes, from commander Task Force 58. Land on any base you see."

On most of the carriers the first few planes landed smoothly and quickly taxied forward, but these were followed by batches of aircraft so swarming into the landing circles that the LSOs, to avoid smashups as two or more tried to hit the flight deck together, had to wave off more than they landed. At length the task groups were surrounded by whirling masses of planes, their paths marked by lights flickering against the black sky. Some pilots shopped through the task force seeking an uncrowded landing circle. As planes exhausted their last drops of fuel and hit the water, destroyers turned their searchlight beams down to the surface and moved about picking up survivors. One desperate pilot disregarded a wave-off from *Lexington*'s LSO. High, he cut his engines, hit the deck, bounced over the barrier, and crashed into four newly landed planes, killing two men and injuring half a dozen others.

The pilot of the rogue plane was unhurt. Mitscher sent for him. Numb with nerves and fear, the fellow mounted to the flag bridge wing and approached the officer in the swivel chair.

Mitscher said, "Do I understand you refused a wave-off?"

"Yes, Admiral. My hydraulics were shot away. I didn't have enough gas to go around again."

Mitscher looked at the pilot a full minute, then said gently, "Son, you always could have gone into the drink."

Recovery was completed at 2232. After taking the last plane on board, the task force tightened formation and shaped course toward the scene of the sunset battle. Since that engagement, eighty U.S. aircraft had ditched or crashed on landing. Through the night the task force proceeded at 16 knots along the route the returning aviators had taken, while the destroyers, released from screening duty, busied themselves hunting for and rescuing waterlogged aviators. Using their searchlights, they found some bobbing in their Mae Wests, others on their inflated rafts, a few of the latter bound two or more together, for company and for greater likelihood of being seen and rescued. At dawn, seaplanes summoned from partly captured Saipan took over the hunt until all but forty-nine of the 209 aviators in the lost planes had been picked up. Presumably most of the forty-nine had been killed or knocked unconscious on ditching or trapped inside and had gone down with their planes, but there was always the heavyhearted realization that some luckless fliers might float undiscovered until dead of starvation or dehydration.

On Wednesday, 21 June, the bearded, unwashed men of Task Force 58, unless performing indispensable duties, simply went to sleep. Two days and a night of fighting off enemy attacks and launching and recovering one of their own had left them too exhausted to keep their eyes open. They fell asleep on decks, on tops of ammunition lockers, in corners or passageways—wherever they found a little empty space.

Burke and Mitscher stayed on the job. Arleigh profited by a strong body, sound nerves, and immense stores of energy that at the height of his career would be the envy, and sometimes the despair, of his colleagues. Mitscher, who lacked Burke's strength and steel nerves, apparently surmounted fatigue by sheer force of will.

The two hours Task Force 58 had spent on an easterly course recovering aircraft, followed by slow speed westward to facilitate rescues, had permitted the Mobile Fleet to get beyond reach of a second U.S. air strike. Early on the 21st, long-range Avengers observed the enemy fleet making 20 knots on course northwest 360 miles from the American task force. Hellcats searched fruitlessly all that day for possible enemy cripples. An hour after sunset, Spruance ordered the search abandoned, and Task Force 58 turned back east, thus ending what came to be called the Battle of the Philippine Sea.

In terms of aircraft destroyed, it was an overwhelming American victory. In the battles of 19–20 June, Ozawa lost 395 (92 percent) of his carrier planes and well over 400 aviators. American losses in the same period were 130 (14.6 percent) of their carrier planes, including the eighty that ditched or crashed following the sunset battle, and seventy-six aviators. Task Force 58, moreover, had fulfilled its stated assignment of covering the beachhead. That was all very gratifying, but it fell far short of what most informed Americans, particularly the aviators, had expected. In view of the great U.S. superiority in ships, planes, and highly trained aviators, they had anticipated something like a clean sweep of the Mobile Fleet. Now the Americans would have to fight at least one more naval battle to eliminate the Japanese navy.

So far as the Americans knew at the end of 21 June, not a single enemy carrier had been sunk. In fact, they had sunk three. In the morning of the 19th, the Mobile Fleet entered Lockwood's four-submarine "invisible trap." *Albacore,* one of the four, fired a torpedo into a large carrier and then went deep to elude destroyers that came charging. *Albacore*'s target was in fact Ozawa's flagship, *Taiho,* newest and largest carrier in the Japanese navy. The torpedo ruptured gasoline tanks and oil bunkers, releasing fumes that exploded and sank the ship. Four torpedoes from *Cavalla* similarly did in *Shokaku.* Two oilers and carrier *Hiyo,* victims of the American sunset attack of the 20th, sank that evening.

FROM THE
MARIANAS
TO THE
PHILIPPINES

AFTER FUELING ON 23–24 June 1944, Task Force 58 operated under new orders from Admiral Spruance. Lee's battle line was reabsorbed into Task Groups 58.2 and 58.3, which with Jocko Clark's 58.1 were to proceed to Eniwetok for rest and replenishment. Until 4 July, Harrill's 58.4 would continue to operate in support of the Saipan campaign. Spruance in his flagship, *Indianapolis,* together with the borrowed cruisers and destroyers, rejoined the amphibious forces at Saipan. On the island two marine divisions and an army division had captured the main airfield, had occupied the relatively flat southern third of the island, and were wheeling for a drive up the rugged north peninsula.

Clark was content to retire temporarily from the combat zone—but not right away. His Japanese-language listener had informed him that planes were piling up at Iwo Jima awaiting a break in the weather before continuing southward to attack U.S. shipping off Saipan. Clark notified Mitscher by dispatch that "unless otherwise directed" he would give Iwo a working-over. Mitscher enthusiastically approved what he dubbed Operation Jocko, and Clark took his group north and had a junior-grade Turkey Shoot of his own, destroying sixty-six enemy planes at a cost of six Hellcats but with no damage to his ships. He then proceeded to Eniwetok, where he arrived on 27 June.

On 4 July the three task groups that had retired to Eniwetok returned to support the Saipan campaign, relieving Task Group 58.4. Mitscher had intended this relief to mark the end of hesitant Harrill's career with the carriers, but nature anticipated him. A few days earlier an attack of acute appendicitis, requiring surgery, had removed Harrill from the fleet.

During the break at Eniwetok, Burke with the assistance of other staff members began preparing the action report of the Battle of the Philippine Sea. He himself wrote the narrative portion. When he had finished he took it to Mitscher.

"Is it all right?" asked the admiral, who had no intention of reading it. Having fought the battle, he assumed he knew what was in it.

"Yes, sir."

"Fine!" said Mitscher and reached for his fountain pen.

"Admiral," said Burke, "you'd better read the last two pages. This report is critical of Admiral Spruance, and you shouldn't sign that unless you agree with it."

"Is it true?"

"Yes, sir, it's all true."

"Well, let it go then."

"No, sir, I won't send it unless you read it."

"All right," said Mitscher grudgingly, "I'll read it."

He took the document, read the last few pages, and remained seated in his swivel chair thinking it over. When Burke figured Mitscher had cogitated long enough, he went out to him.

The admiral looked up. "It's all true, all right," he said.

He looked out across the lagoon, then turned to Burke and asked, "Do you know Admiral Spruance very well?"

"Yes, sir."

"What do you think of him?"

"I think he's a mighty good man, but he made a mistake this time, Admiral. He made a big mistake. I don't know why he did it, but it was a big mistake. This is true."

"Yes, it's all true," said Mitscher, "but what good is it going to do to send in a report like this?"

"It tells the truth."

"You don't think the truth does more harm than good sometimes?"

"No, sir."

"Well, it does." Another pause. Then Mitscher continued, "You and I have been in many battles, and we know there are always some mistakes. This time we were right because the enemy did what we expected him to do. Admiral Spruance could have been right. He's one of the finest officers I know of. It was his job to protect the landing force. Anyway, the ultimate outcome of this war is decided by now, and it's not going to make that much difference. Don't you think you ought to take it back and rewrite those last two pages?"

"No, sir," replied Burke, "but I will."

Arleigh rewrote the pages, deleting the criticism, but he could not resist concluding the report on a bitter note: "The enemy had escaped. He had been badly hurt by one aggressive carrier air strike, at the one time when he was within range. His fleet was not sunk."

Admiral Mitscher signed the final version without reading any part of it. Generations of historians later quoted portions of the report, attributing them to Mitscher as his own words.[*]

Few aviators were as generous as Mitscher concerning what some of them branded the blunder of the century. In various versions they expressed their common complaint: "This is what comes of placing a nonaviator in command over carriers." Even in the unlikely event a segment of the Japanese fleet had made a successful end run and got between Task Force 58 and Saipan, they said, it could hardly have harmed the transports, which had temporarily withdrawn to the east. The segment would, however, have encountered off the Saipan beach seven old battleships and six escort carriers, plus cruisers and destroyers. If not defeated by these, it would at least have been sufficiently damaged and slowed by the encounter that Task Force 58, after defeating the main body, could have pursued and destroyed it.

Admiral John H. Towers, deputy Cincpac, demanded that Nimitz fire Spruance for incompetence in handling carriers and permitting the enemy fleet to escape. Nimitz ignored the demand and defended Spruance's strategy then and later. He supported it in 1959 in a discussion with this writer, and he endorsed the defense of the Spruance strategy in the 1960 naval history textbook *Sea Power*, which he helped to edit.

Admiral King also commended Spruance's strategy. When he visited Saipan in July following the battle, his first words as he

---

[*]Concerning Mitscher's decision to launch the long-range strike against the Japanese fleet in the late afternoon of 21 June, Samuel Eliot Morison in *New Guinea and the Marianas*, page 291, introduces a long quotation from the action report with these words: "The danger inherent in this decision, and the reason why it was made, cannot be better stated than in Mitscher's own words."

stepped from his plane were addressed to Spruance. "You did a damn fine job there," he said. "No matter what other people tell you, your decision was correct." He praised Spruance's strategy in his 1945 report to the secretary of the navy, published in 1946, and in his autobiography, published in 1952.

Sharp-tongued Admiral Kelly Turner, sparing of praise and blunt critic of mistakes, said in a speech before the General Line School in 1949: "To capture Saipan, we needed the transports afloat and not sunk. Suppose at 0800 on June 19th, Admiral Mitscher had been 600 miles away with all his planes in the air! Admiral Spruance's decision to adhere strictly to a course of action that would *ensure* the accomplishment of the major objective of that great military adventure was sound and wise."

Spruance himself confessed some frustration that in his view the strategic situation had not permitted him to attack the Mobile Fleet. "As a matter of tactics," he wrote, "I think that going after the Japanese and knocking their carriers out would have been much better and more satisfactory than waiting for them to attack us; but we were at the start of a very important and large amphibious operation and we could not afford to gamble and place it in jeopardy."

Spruance's stoutest defenders, including the doyen of naval historians, Samuel Eliot Morison, had no such misgivings. They applauded his tactics as well as his strategy. By remaining near the Marianas on 19 June, Task Force 58 kept Guam and Rota unusable for shuttle-bombing, and Mitscher had all of its Hellcats available for interception. Had the task force divided its aircraft between attack and defense, the planes could hardly have achieved so spectacular a score. Because they had destroyed all but a hundred of Ozawa's 430 carrier planes on the 19th, the Americans no doubt took far fewer losses in their sunset attack of the 20th.

At the end of the war, Spruance's supporters found another reason for defending his tactics. They learned that the Mobile Fleet on 19 June was divided, but not the way Spruance suspected. Like the Americans, Ozawa placed a vanguard of gunnery ships between his main body and the enemy, but the Japanese vanguard, four battleships, one light and eight heavy cruisers, eight destroyers, and three light carriers for air cover, was a hundred miles east of the main body, which included one light and five heavy carriers.

If Mitscher had moved westward to attack the Mobile Fleet on the 19th, his planes would have encountered the intense antiaircraft fire of the vanguard, while the heavy enemy carriers were still a hundred miles away. The Japanese deployment, counted on to protect the big carriers from air attack, left them so lightly screened that U.S. submarines got past the escorts and sank *Shokaku* and *Taiho*.

Though most of the Japanese carriers escaped destruction, the Combined Fleet in mid-1944 was less capable of replacing lost pilots than it had been even following the disastrous Solomons campaign. The Japanese now lacked both the skilled aviator instructors and the fuel needed to support an adequate pilot-training program. They had fruitlessly expended their aviators in the Solomons, and U.S. submarine sinkings of tankers had reduced Japan's oil imports to a trickle.

As Admiral Mitscher suggested, Spruance's conduct of the battle, sound or unsound, made little difference, because the outcome of the war had been decided. As it turned out, the most significant effect of the Spruance strategy, or the discussion of it, was the influence it had on a newcomer to Pearl Harbor.

The newcomer was Admiral William F. Halsey, Burke's former area commander in the South Pacific. With the neutralizing and bypassing of Rabaul, he had worked himself out of a job. Admirals King and Nimitz, eager to make active use of his extensive experience and demonstrated skills as a leader, hit upon the idea of having him alternate command of the Big Blue Fleet with Admiral Spruance. Thus neither would have to be fighting and planning at the same time. So Halsey, relieved of his command of the now-peaceful South Pacific but retaining his title of commander Third Fleet, reported to Pearl Harbor with orders to relieve Spruance at the end of the Marianas campaign.

Arriving at Pearl on 17 June, Halsey followed the progress of the Battle of the Philippine Sea from Cincpac headquarters and subsequently was immersed, if not involved, in the discussions and controversies concerning Spruance's conduct of the battle. Almost certainly he discussed the subject with his old friend Jack Towers, who had relieved him in command of *Saratoga* in 1936 and as commander Air Force Pacific Fleet in 1942.

Towers as Naval Aviator No. 3 had been a true pioneer of naval aviation. In later years, as Rear Admiral John H. Towers, chief of the Bureau of Aeronautics (1939–42), he became an insistent and persistent advocate for giving senior commands to naval aviators. High-ranking nonaviators long resisted such demands on the ground that the aviators' experience having been limited largely to flying, they lacked the training to command ships and stations. In general, senior nonaviators were appointed to command air stations, seaplane tenders, and carriers after preparing themselves by taking a stiff course in aviation, including everything except solo flight. Halsey, when a fifty-two-year-old captain with experience practically limited to destroyers, had taken such a course at Pensacola and uniquely learned to fly solo.

To get Towers and his persistent demands out of Washington, Admiral King offered him the post of commander Air Force Pacific Fleet, with the rank of vice admiral. Towers took the bait, relieving Halsey, and established himself at Pearl Harbor as a thorn in Nimitz's side. Backed by Under Secretary of the Navy James Forrestal, a former naval aviator, he had some success and was eventually appointed deputy Cincpac, Nimitz's second-in-command.

Towers was indignant when at Nimitz's recommendation nonaviator Spruance was given command of the carrier-spearheaded Fifth Fleet. Thereafter he repeatedly criticized Spruance's practice of keeping his carrier force close to the beachheads during amphibious operations. Towers insisted that the function of the carriers was to protect the landing force by striking at enemy fleets and bases, the source of counterattacks. Tying carriers to beachheads, he said, nullified their mobility, which was their sole advantage over fixed airfields.

Halsey certainly agreed with Towers, but there is no record that he put his agreement into words, probably because he and Spruance were friends of long standing. They had become acquainted in 1921, when Lieutenant Commander Ray Spruance commanded the outstanding destroyer of Commander Bill Halsey's outstanding division of the outstanding squadron of the Pacific Fleet destroyers.

Besides skill in seamanship, Bill and Ray shared fearlessness, integrity, and utter devotion to duty. They were both great leaders, but their styles were strikingly different. Bill, garrulous, flamboyant, dashing, won and fully reciprocated the affection of his subordinates. Ray, quiet, reserved, introspective, won the respect and ready cooperation of his subordinates through competence, intellect, and what might be called his mystery. Bill could shout orders and, when necessary, invective. If there was shouting to be done, Ray had others do it for him. Bill was a skillful improviser. Ray thought things through. Bill's fighting-cock stance, barrel chest, and beetle brows fitted the popular conception of an old sea dog. Ray, lean, distant, somewhat otherworldly, looked rather like a professor, which in fact he had been—at the Naval War College. This dissimilar pair, this odd couple, each recognized the other's special gifts and developed an enduring friendship based on mutual respect.

Their current handling of forces developed to a great extent out of their past achievements. Spruance's victory in the 1942 Battle of Midway, which turned the tide of war at sea, resulted partly from luck, but it was precisely calculated timing that enabled at least some of the U.S. dive-bombers to strike the Japanese carriers at their most vulnerable moment, with planes on flight deck about to take off. Later in the action, Spruance twice turned away to evade what he correctly suspected were Japanese attempts to initiate night battles. In the dark his carriers, unable to use their planes, would be at a hopeless disadvantage attacked by Japanese battleships. He was criticized for his withdrawals, but his caution in this instance was amply justified.

A few months later, Admiral Halsey, in his struggle for Guadalcanal, won even more decisively. He took appalling risks, resulting in heavy losses of ships and men, but he emerged victorious, throwing the Japanese on the defensive, from which they never recovered.

Spruance, the meticulous planner and War College professor, based his preparations not on what he or his staff guessed the enemy *was going to do* but took into account everything the enemy *could do*. Spruance's critics called him overcautious, but he never let himself be paralyzed into a permanent defensive posture. "In making war," he said, "we try to minimize rather than to avoid danger."

Halsey, master of the calculated risk, operated largely on hunches, which were in fact educated guesses about what the enemy *was going to do*. He followed plans, but these were mostly in the form of what he called dirty tricks, schemes to harass and bewilder the gullible enemy. Or he fought by imaginative improvisation, conceived in the heat of battle to meet each changing situation. His admirers pointed out that if they, and perhaps Halsey himself, never knew what he was going to do next, his operations must utterly bewilder the enemy. His critics, on the contrary, called his conduct of battle sloppy and reckless.

The Japanese made a careful study of American military and naval leaders. To devise means of misleading, undermining, or otherwise getting the better of them in combat, they went to great lengths to gather information about their personalities and combat techniques. By mid-1944 they acknowledged both Spruance and Halsey as brilliant sea fighters, but in their opinion each had a trait of which the Japanese could take advantage. Spruance was cautious; Halsey, rash.

The summer of 1944 was a busy time for Task Force 58. Even when it was at its temporary home base of Eniwetok, it was undergoing reorganization as ships, including carriers, departed for upkeep and replacements arrived, and as officers, including task group commanders, completed their tours of duty and were relieved.

Throughout the Marianas campaign, some or all of the task force was operating in support of the fighting ashore, sending its planes in bombing sweeps over the islands before and during assaults and destroying enemy planes heading for the Marianas from the south via the Carolines or coming down from the north via Chichi Jima and Iwo Jima, which because of Clark's interest and his several destructive raids became known in the force as the Jocko Jimas.

Mitscher, in *Lexington,* participated in one Jima raid. On this occasion a combination of air attack and cruiser fire sank 20,000 tons of Japanese shipping, shot up a couple of dozen grounded planes, and destroyed many shore installations. As the two U.S. task groups involved were about to withdraw in order to maintain a tight operational schedule, Mitscher learned that one of his fighter pilots was down in Chichi Jima harbor. The pilot had bailed out of a burning plane, and his wingman had dropped him a raft. Heavy automatic crossfire from the beaches precluded the usual expedient of sending in a cruiser float plane to pick him up.

Burke watched Mitscher sitting silently on the transom, thinking over the situation. He knew the admiral was facing a tough decision. The force was slated to depart within a quarter of an hour to keep a rendezvous at sea and proceed on a major mission, but Arleigh guessed the choice his boss would make. Very gently he said, "Well, what about it, Admiral?"

"Jesus Christ," said Mitscher softly, "I can't leave that fellow in there. It'll be dark in an hour. Keep the fighters circling until dark. Then get a submarine to come in close to the reef and send their rubber boat in after him."

The pilot was rescued.

In late July, planes from Task Groups 58.2 and 58.3 photographed the Palau Islands, westernmost of the Carolines, in preparation for the forthcoming American invasion. At the same time, Clark's 58.1 photographed neighboring islands, seeking possible anchorages. The U.S. aircraft preceded each photography mission with bombing and strafing to send antiaircraft gunners scurrying for their foxholes.

The Marianas campaign was drawing to a close. Saipan was secured on 10 July, adjacent Tinian on 1 August. The American invasion of Guam, largest of the Marianas, was preceded by a thirteen-day bombardment, longest of the war to date. On 10 August, after three weeks of savage fighting, the island, seized by the Japanese in the first days of the Pacific war, was reconquered by the Americans.

The conquest of the three islands had cost more than 5,000 American and nearly 60,000 Japanese lives. The emperor and other high Japanese officials recognized that defeat was now inevitable. The Tojo government, which had launched the Pacific war, was succeeded by a less bellicose cabinet to whom the emperor made known his desire for early peace negotiations. But so rigid was the Japanese military code that no official in Japan yet dared initiate steps to end hostilities.

By this time Admiral Mitscher's attitude toward Burke had changed strikingly. The Turkey Shoot was the main turning point. Until then the admiral's communication with Burke had been limited almost strictly to business, and often he would simply bypass him, consulting or dealing directly with Hedding or Widhelm. But since the big battle Mitscher had become increasingly cordial to his chief of staff, addressing him no longer formally as Captain Burke but as Burke and occasionally Arleigh. When there was no immediate naval business to be attended to and the admiral felt like talking, which was not often, he would discuss with Burke such nonmilitary matters as Mitscher's favorite sport of fishing. "He decided I was trying to do a good job, and that I could be his chief of staff all right," Burke recalled. "He realized that what I was trying to do was help him have the most effective battle organization there was."

Arleigh, after months of discontent, feeling out of place and downright incompetent in Task Force 58, had now mastered his job and become accepted and valued by his admiral and by his fellow staffers. He had reason to be satisfied, but he was not. Back in *Mugford* days, Gelzer Sims had accurately sized Arleigh up as the kind of man who had to have his own cannon. In Task Force 58 he was not boss. He could not be satisfied unless he was boss, and he would not be entirely satisfied until he was boss of the entire navy.

On 9 August, Task Force 58 entered Eniwetok lagoon for a two-week breather before taking up the cudgels again. Hedding now left, as planned, to join the Cincpac staff, and Gus Widhelm was relieved as operations officer by Commander James H. Flatley. Burke had learned a good deal from Hedding and Widhelm, and he liked them both, but now he was not sorry to see them go, since their absence left him freer to exercise his chief-of-staff role. Flatley, a short, dark Irishman, proved no barrier between Burke and his admiral. He took an instant liking to Arleigh and attached himself to him as colleague and disciple.

Shortly after Task Force 58 began its rest period at Eniwetok, Admiral Nimitz arrived to discuss the upcoming Philippines campaign, of which the Palau operation was a preliminary. For Mitscher he had a Gold Star in lieu of a third Distinguished Service Medal. Rising to read the citation, Nimitz remarked, "Ninety-one years ago a naval officer [Matthew C. Perry] opened up the ports of Japan, and now another officer is doing his damnedest to close them."

It was at this point that Mitscher showed Burke two letters that left the chief of staff dumbfounded. The admiral had written them both: one to the secretary of the navy via Cincpac, recommending Burke for rear admiral; the other to Rear Admiral James L. Kauffman, commander cruisers and destroyers Pacific Fleet, asking him to push the recommendation. Arleigh had not dreamed he had progressed so far in winning the admiral's approval. He was gratified but also alarmed. He didn't want the promotion, at least at that time. He urged Mitscher not to send the letters, but the admiral told Burke he was a damned fool, and he let the letters go.

Fortunately for Burke's peace of mind, Admiral Nimitz had not yet left Eniwetok. Arleigh sought and obtained a meeting with the commander in chief, who received him courteously and heard him out. Burke presented three reasons for wanting to avoid flag rank at this time: (1) he did not need flag rank for the post he held, (2) he would be winning promotion not on his own merits but by virtue of being chief of staff to a very successful commander, and (3) at the end of the war he would probably revert to captain, and as a former rear admiral he would be something of an oddity, unlikely to get a desirable captain's billet. It would be better for his career, he said, if he attained flag rank in due course based on his own achievements. Nimitz appreciated Burke's point of view. He said he could not refuse to forward Mitscher's letter, but he would refrain from adding a favorable endorsement, and that should have the effect of nullifying it.

In a letter to his wife, Bobbie, Arleigh gave a fourth reason for avoiding promotion so far ahead of schedule—jealousy of his peers, which would be hard to live with. As an additional precaution he sent a letter to Admiral Kauffman, asking him to do no pushing on his behalf. He concluded:

> I deeply appreciate Admiral Mitscher's thoughtfulness in his letter. I have tried to dissuade him from sending it but he insists. Nobody has a better boss than I have now and I feel very humble about this recommendation. Perhaps I would do better to keep my big mouth shut but I doubt that I would be of any more value to the Navy as a Rear Admiral than I am as a Captain or, as far as that goes, as I would be as a Lieutenant.

Not long afterward Burke was informed that he had been promoted to commodore, apparently a compromise between Mitscher's recommendation and lack of favorable endorsement by Nimitz. Arleigh received the news with a notable lack of jubilation. Commodore was a mere honorary title with no increase in pay and was commonly considered a dead end, a pat on the back for a senior captain who was a good fellow but would never rate a higher promotion.

On 26 September, Admiral Halsey relieved Admiral Spruance as commander of the Big Blue Fleet, whose official designation thereby changed instantly from U.S. Fifth Fleet to U.S. Third Fleet, conforming to Halsey's title. At this highly atypical relief there was no ceremony, because Spruance was at Guam, Halsey was at sea on board battleship *New Jersey*, and the Fast Carrier Task Force was still at Eniwetok. Relieved of his command, Spruance in *Indianapolis* headed with his staff for Pearl Harbor. Though the Big Blue Fleet remained the same, except for the change of fleet flagships, *New Jersey* for *Indianapolis*, the Japanese, and a great many Americans, soon came to believe that the United States now had two mighty fleets taking alternate jabs at what remained of the Japanese empire.

When the Fifth Fleet became the Third Fleet, the Fast Carrier Task Force changed its name from Task Force 58 to Task Force 38, but Pete Mitscher remained serenely seated in his swivel chair. Vice Admiral John Sidney "Slew" McCain, late deputy chief of naval operations for air, had come out from Washington to unseat him, but Bald Eagle had compelling arguments for staying on for a while longer. For one thing, he considered himself not due for relief, having been in command of the carrier force only seven months.

More important, now that he had gained experience with the carriers, he insisted they should remain in his hands at least through the upcoming crucial Philippines invasion, which was likely to draw out the Japanese fleet for battle. His arguments prevailed with King and Nimitz. Slew McCain was an able and experienced aviator, but he had never commanded so much as a single carrier. Grumbling, he took charge of Jocko Clark's Task Group 38.1 as a makee-learn,* and Jocko remained on board for a while to teach him the ropes.

Concurrently with the forthcoming Third Fleet assault on the Palaus, scheduled for 15 September 1944, forces under MacArthur would occupy Morotai Island between New Guinea and the Philippines. Capture of these points was deemed necessary to clear the flanks of the invasion forces scheduled to land on Mindanao on 15 November and on the central Philippine island of Leyte on 20 December. To pave the way for these operations, three groups of Task Force 38 sortied from Eniwetok on 29 August, while as a diversion to distract Japanese attention Rear Admiral R. E. Davison's Task Group 38.4 headed northwest for another raid on the Jimas.†

Groups 38.1, 38.2, and 38.3, commanded now respectively by Vice Admiral McCain and Rear Admirals G. F. Bogan and F. C. Sherman, bombed the Palaus on 6–8 September with special attention to the small southern Palau islands of Angaur and Peleliu, the ones the Americans planned to occupy. Admiral Mitscher now conformed to Admiral Towers's strategic plan—but not entirely. He did not keep his whole task force near the Palaus to support Vice Admiral Wilkinson's approaching Third Amphibious Force, which was to stage the invasion. With his three groups at hand, Mitscher headed for the Philippines, from which, or by way of which, enemy interference was likely to come, and on 9–10 September sent his bombers against Japanese airdromes on Mindanao. He had arranged, however, for Admiral Davison's Task Group 38.4, after raiding the Jimas, to head south and arrive off the Palaus in time to supplement the D-day air coverage provided by Wilkinson's eleven escort carriers, and he intended to detach McCain's 38.1 to provide air cover for the assault on Morotai.

Like Spruance, Admiral Halsey chose to attach himself to the

---

*Makee-learn: Navy lingo for apprentice or apprenticeship.
†In Davison's raid on Chichi Jima, 2 September, one of his bomber pilots, Lieutenant (j.g.) George Bush, the future U.S. president, was shot down and subsequently rescued by an American submarine.

carrier force rather than to the much larger amphibious force. His flagship, *New Jersey,* escorted by three destroyers, arrived off Mindanao in the early hours of 11 September. He sent word to Mitscher to skip the usual courtesy call to the fleet flagship. He himself would do the calling in order to inspect *Lexington* and her planes. At 0745, Halsey and members of his staff came alongside in a destroyer and crossed over to *Lexington* by high line. Among the visitors was Burke's old friend Rear Admiral Robert B. Carney, late captain of *Denver,* now Halsey's chief of staff.

Speaking for Admiral Mitscher, Burke reported the astonishing fact that Mindanao, bigger than the state of Indiana, was virtually without air defense. Only a few Japanese planes had risen to repulse the Task Force 38 aircraft. Allied planes based on western New Guinea had already blasted the airdromes. If the New Guinea–based air force could keep Mindanao neutralized, he concluded, there was no point in wasting time, lives, and ammunition conquering it. Why not bypass Mindanao and invade Leyte, the next scheduled objective? Halsey listened with interest. Specialist at calculated risks and veteran bypasser, he was captivated by the suggestion but decided to steam up along the coast and feel Leyte out before sounding off.

On the morning of 12 September, Task Force 38 was abreast the central Philippines. That day and the next its planes flew 2,400 sorties, shooting down or destroying on the ground some 200 Japanese planes, sinking a dozen freighters and a tanker, and smashing installations—at a cost of eight U.S. planes. Halsey's conviction that the central Philippines were "a hollow shell" was confirmed by information from a U.S. pilot shot down over Mindanao and later picked up by PBY seaplane. The Filipinos had told the pilot (overoptimistically, as it turned out) that there were no Japanese on Leyte.

"I'm going to stick my neck out," Halsey said to Carney. "Send an urgent message to Cincpac." To Nimitz he recommended canceling all preliminary operations—against Morotai, the Palaus, the Talauds, Yap, Ulithi, and Mindanao—and using the shipping, amphibious, and ground forces thus made available for the earliest possible invasion of Leyte. Task Force 38 would be on hand to cover the landing until airfields could be established ashore.

Admiral Nimitz insisted on taking the Palaus and Ulithi, the former as an air base, the latter as an anchorage, but for the Leyte invasion he was prepared to place at General MacArthur's disposal the Third Amphibious Force and the XXIV Army Corps, the latter then loading at Pearl Harbor for Yap. Nimitz forwarded Halsey's recommendation together with his own offer to the Joint Chiefs of Staff, then meeting at Quebec with President Roosevelt, Prime Minister Churchill, and the British chiefs of staff.

General Marshall radioed Halsey's recommendation and Nimitz's offer to MacArthur to get the general's reaction. MacArthur was at sea maintaining radio silence with forces en route to invade Morotai, but his chief of staff, General Sutherland, at Hollandia, was as ready as Halsey to stick his neck out. Acting for MacArthur, he agreed to bypass the Talaud Islands and Mindanao and stated that with Nimitz's reinforcements and Halsey's support MacArthur's Southwest Pacific forces could invade Leyte on 20 October. The U.S. Joint Chiefs—Admirals Leahy and King and Generals Marshall and Arnold—were called out from a formal dinner to read Sutherland's message, gave the changes their okay, and went back in and finished dining. Within ninety minutes of Sutherland's dispatch, Nimitz and MacArthur had their orders, and the schedule of the Pacific war had been advanced two months.

There were few Japanese on either Morotai or Angaur, which the Americans occupied with light losses. On Ulithi Atoll were only friendly natives, who welcomed the Americans. Ulithi, a ring of islets surrounding an immense, deep lagoon, provided the Third/ Fifth Fleet an invaluable anchorage and logistic base for naval operations of the final phase of the Pacific war.

Peleliu proved an entirely different proposition. It was manned by 5,300 elite troops and as many construction workers, who had turned the small island into a fortress. After a three-day bombardment by Third Amphibious Force gunnery vessels, marines of the veteran 1st Division headed for the beach anticipating a rapid conquest. Instead they were met by heavy fire from well-sited, generally concealed artillery that by the end of the day cost the invaders 210 killed and 900 wounded. These losses had been inflicted by the defenders' outer defenses. The Japanese had learned that their doctrine of "meet and annihilate the invaders at the beachhead" invited disaster when used against the power-packed American ship-to-shore movement supported by fleet guns and aircraft. They had now supplemented it with a carefully calculated defense in depth, locating the main line of resistance far enough inland to escape the full power of the naval bombardment. Behind this line the main body of Japanese troops had withdrawn into a labyrinth of more than 500 natural and artificial caves, heavily armed and largely interconnected. Gouging the enemy out of this fortress was a slow, bloody process that lasted until February of the following year and cost the Americans more than 1,000 killed and 5,000 wounded. The only value of this ill-considered project was the preview it gave the U.S. armed forces of the horrors they would meet at Iwo Jima and Okinawa.

Following the revealing attack on the central Philippines that led to speeding up the war, Halsey signaled to the task force: "Because of the brilliant performance my group of stars has just given, I am booking you to appear before the best audience in the Asiatic theater." He was referring to Manila, Manila Bay, and nearby airfields. Halsey now turned the tactical command over to Mitscher and in *New Jersey* headed for the Palaus to observe progress and confer with the senior U.S. commanders there.

McCain's Task Group 38.1, after completing its support of the Morotai assault, rejoined Bogan's 38.2 and Sherman's 38.3 off the Philippines. Davison's Group 38.4, having raided the Jimas and supported the Palau attack, with high-speed runs to each, now withdrew to Manus for upkeep and replenishment. Mitscher, after refueling, began moving his three remaining task groups in on Luzon, the northernmost Philippine island.

How he moved in was crucial, because the wind off the east coast of the Philippines tends in the morning to blow either north or south. It is important to foresee which, so as to be downwind at dawn and thus have the carriers moving into the wind to launch and recover planes. The wind direction was something the fleet aerologists could rarely predict, but Mitscher generally had it right.

"Admiral Mitscher's ability to predict exact changes in weather conditions," Burke recalled, "drove the aerologists up the wall, for they couldn't do it. At first they argued—and when it turned out the Admiral was correct, they declared it was luck. After several such 'lucky' decisions they conceded he had a weather instinct. The admiral called it a seaman's eye based on a lifetime of weather watching."

The first raids on the Manila area were scheduled for 21 September. Halsey was back with Task Force 38 by that date but left Mitscher in tactical command. Arleigh, up before dawn, saw that the weather had turned foul, with heavy seas, low clouds, and dense fog. The pilots were in their ready rooms, and the planes were spotted on deck, but Burke had no intention of ordering launch until the weather improved. Flatley agreed. It would be difficult to launch in this weather, and if it was foggy in the target area the fliers couldn't see what to hit.

Summoned by the admiral, Burke went out on the wing of the bridge, where Mitscher was seated as usual. "What are you going to do?" he asked.

"I don't know, Admiral," replied Burke. "We've got to wait till the weather clears up."

"How are you going to know that—in the target area?"

"I guess we'll just have to depend on the aerologist."

Mitscher snorted. "The hell you do," he said. "Keep our radars going, and as soon as we see enemy air in the air, we launch."

It hadn't occurred to Burke or Flatley that if it was clear enough in the target area for the Japanese to fly from their fields, the Americans could fly there too, and see their targets.

Task Force 38 planes made four raids on the Manila area on the 21st and planned to make as many more the following day. At noon on the 22nd, however, Mitscher, citing the approach of foul weather and dearth of suitable targets, ordered Burke to cancel the last two strikes and recall all aircraft. Another, unmentioned reason, Burke suspected, was to spare his aviators, some of whom appeared near exhaustion. In two days they had damaged or destroyed 405 planes and 103 ships. American losses were fifteen planes and twelve men. No enemy planes had come near the task force.

The 23rd was fueling day. Admiral Carney invited Burke over to *New Jersey* for a conference. Admiral Halsey's staff had reason to believe that ships fleeing or evading the air raids on Manila Bay had taken refuge in Coron Bay in the Calamanian Islands on the far side of the Philippines. Presumably the Japanese considered themselves safe at this distant anchorage, but—Carney wanted to know—could Task Force 38 planes reach them there?

Burke studied the charts. From Coron Bay the nearest point in the Pacific Ocean was at San Bernardino Strait, some 300 miles away. He thought about the long flights of 20 June, especially Snowden's long-range probe. Yes, Hellcats with belly tanks could make it, each carrying a 500-pound bomb. Since most of the flight would be over the Sibuyan Sea, any pilot who went down had a fair chance of being picked up by a float plane.

Fueling completed, Task Force 38 headed for the strait. At 0550, 24 September, the Hellcats took off, followed presently by shorter-range bombers, which attacked ships and airfields in the central Philippines. The Hellcats sank or damaged several destroyer types and numerous tankers, transports, and freighters and shot down thirty-six planes. The bombers destroyed additional shipping and heavily damaged wharfs and shore installations. Carney celebrated the day's achievements in another congratulatory message sent to the task force in Halsey's name: "The recent exceptional performance yielded gratifying gate receipts, and although the capacity audience hissed very loudly, little was thrown at the players. As long as the audience has a spot to hiss in, we will stay on the road."

Task Force 38 now withdrew from Philippine waters for rest and replenishment. Task Group 38.1 went to Manus, whence Jocko Clark, having completed his coaching of McCain, departed with his staff for Pearl Harbor. Bogan's task group, including *New Jersey*, went to Saipan. From there Halsey and his staff flew to Hollandia to confer with MacArthur's staff concerning the Leyte operation. The men of Sherman's group, including *Lexington*, grumbled because their ships were replenished by an at-sea logistic group while anchored in Kossol Roads in the Palau Islands, where shore leave was out of the question.

Mitscher's periods of silence were lengthening, sure sign that the pace of operations in the past month was taking its toll. He climbed onto or down from his swivel chair rather gingerly. If nothing much was happening on deck he would sit inside on the transom or retire to his sea cabin. He looked at least a dozen years older than his fifty-seven years. Burke and Flatley agreed that in the coming battles they would take as much of the burden as possible off his shoulders.

Replenishment completed, Sherman's group moved on to Ulithi, where it joined Bogan's group from Saipan. On 1 October, Halsey with staff members flew in from Hollandia via Angaur and Peleliu and promptly convened the first of several conferences on board *New Jersey*.

Halsey had now received his operation plan from Cincpac. He was to "cover and support forces of the Southwest Pacific in order to assist in the seizure and occupation of objectives in the central Philippines" and "destroy enemy naval and air forces in or threatening the Philippines area." The plan was in sentence outline form, and each sentence was preceded by a number or letter, with a single exception. Unnumbered, unlettered, it stood alone, apparently a late insertion:

IN CASE OPPORTUNITY FOR DESTRUCTION OF MAJOR PORTION OF THE ENEMY FLEET OFFER OR CAN BE CREATED, SUCH DESTRUCTION BECOMES THE PRIMARY TASK.

It was obviously added to preclude the unlikely possibility that Halsey, presented with an opportunity to smash an enemy fleet, would consider himself tethered to the beachhead as Spruance believed he was the preceding June.

The forthcoming operations presented two unusual command problems. First, there was to be no officer with overall authority at the scene of action. Halsey, as commander Third Fleet, was responsible to Nimitz at Pearl Harbor, and Nimitz was responsible to the Joint Chiefs of Staff in Washington. Vice Admiral Thomas C. Kinkaid, commander Seventh Fleet, was responsible only to General MacArthur, who was responsible to the Joint Chiefs. As if to emphasize the independence of his command, MacArthur forbade Kinkaid to communicate directly with Halsey.

The other problem was almost opposite in nature—two officers sharing the same authority. Wilkinson's Third Amphibious Force was already moving piecemeal from the Palaus to Manus. Here and in the forthcoming invasion it would be part of the Seventh Fleet. The Third Fleet shorn of its amphibious element was simply Task Force 38. In the Leyte campaign Third Fleet and Task Force 38 thus would be identical, with Halsey and Mitscher commanding the same ships and crews. Both, moreover, were aviators, authorized to command air operations.

Halsey by virtue of his fourth star could simply have assumed the overall command and left Mitscher a mere passenger, and some writers have assumed that is what happened. In fact, old friends appreciative of each other's special skills, they reached a sensible compromise. Mitscher, as commander Task Force 38, would command all air operations when the force maneuvered as a unit. Halsey, as commander Third Fleet, was to control fleet movements and assign targets. If the situation demanded, he would form battle line, to be designated Task Force 34, under Admiral Lee.

To weaken the Japanese, particularly in the air, and to isolate the beachhead, U.S. bombers out of bases in western China battered Japanese positions in Formosa and on the Chinese coast. Bombers based on New Guinea, Biak, and Morotai took care of the southern flank, hammering away at enemy airfields in Mindanao and the East Indies. The Third Fleet was to batter the northern flank, an arc extending from the central Philippines through Formosa and the Ryukyu Islands to southern Japan.

The two groups at Ulithi sortied on 6 October and were joined at sea the next day by the other two, McCain's from Manus, Davison's from the Palaus, where since replenishment at Manus it had been covering the Peleliu operation. Task Force 38 now comprised nine large and eight light carriers, six battleships, four heavy and ten light cruisers, and fifty-eight destroyers.

Advancing behind a typhoon dubbed Task Force Zero and preceded by long-range scout planes out of Saipan that sank picket boats and shot down enemy search planes, the task force arrived undetected off the Ryukyus on the night of 9 October. Launching early next morning, the carriers sent planes raiding along a 300-mile arc, with emphasis on the big island of Okinawa. In the course of the day they sank a submarine tender, a dozen torpedo boats, two midget submarines, and four freighters and destroyed about a hundred planes at a cost of twenty-one aircraft, five pilots, and four crewmen. No U.S. ships were damaged.

On the 11th, Halsey had two of his groups raid Aparri airfield in northern Luzon. The raids on the Ryukyus and Luzon were intended to isolate the main target, Formosa. Instead, as Halsey ruefully admitted, the first alerted the Formosan Japanese, and the second vouchsafed them a day of grace to bring in more planes from Japan.

On 12 October, the first day of the attack on Formosa, there was a good deal of fighting in the air, battles in which the Americans destroyed about 200 enemy planes at the heavy price of 48 of their own. On the 13th and 14th the U.S. planes concentrated their attacks on airfields, hangars, and other installations ashore and on ships in the harbors. Aware that Formosan industry was heavily dependent on waterpower, Burke had Avengers fire torpedoes into dams and bombers blast flumes conveying water to the power plants. By the end of the three-day Formosa air battle, Task Force 38 planes and bombers out of the U.S. bases in western China had destroyed nearly 600 enemy aircraft and about 40 freighters and small craft, and had savagely battered hangars, shops, barracks, ammunition dumps, and industrial plants.

No American ships had been sunk, but heavy cruiser *Canberra* and light cruiser *Houston* had been torpedoed and were dead in the water. A cautious commander would have abandoned and scuttled these helpless ships, so near enemy airfields and 1,300 miles from Ulithi, the nearest U.S. base. But Halsey was not a cautious commander. He had *Canberra* and *Houston* taken in tow and made use of their hard luck to devise one of the most ingenious of his famed "dirty tricks."

At this time Radio Tokyo was announcing with great fanfare that Japan's intrepid aviators in a series of attacks had virtually wiped out the U.S. fleet. The broadcasts quoted a triumphant imperial proclamation and congratulations from Hitler and Mussolini and announced mass celebrations of the "glorious victory of Taiwan." A Japanese fleet, stated the broadcast, was en route from Japan to destroy the American remnant.

Halsey had heard some wild claims from Radio Tokyo before but nothing to touch this. He concluded that the enemy high command now really believed that the U.S. fleet had been overwhelmed. Japanese aviators must have sighted damaged *Canberra* and *Houston* under tow, now escorted by cruisers and destroyers, and identified these ships as the poor remnant of the Third Fleet—the remnant that a Japanese force was coming to destroy. Nimitz's op plan said, "In case opportunity for destruction of major portion of the enemy fleet offer or can be created, such destruction becomes the primary task." Here was the opportunity, obligingly offered by the enemy.

Humorously designating the *Canberra-Houston* group Baitdiv 1, Halsey told its commander to keep sending fake distress messages by radio. Aircraft from Formosa several times attacked Baitdiv 1, which shot down several, but one of the enemy planes succeeded in firing another torpedo into *Houston*. Halsey with the bulk of Task Force 38 had now hauled off to the east, he hoped beyond air searches out of Formosa, prepared to pounce on the enemy fleet as it advanced to take the bait.

The ambush came close to success. U.S. submarine *Besugo* reported a cruiser-destroyer force heading south out of Japan's Inland Sea. The ambush carriers to avoid detection had air patrols fan out and shoot down every plane that approached, but one at least must have broadcast a warning. At any rate, the Japanese cruiser-destroyer force never found Baitdiv 1. Halsey assumed, correctly, that it heard the warning and prudently retired.

Baitdiv 1 reached Ulithi, and Task Force 38 took station east of Leyte to cover the Seventh Fleet invasion force, now approaching. On 17 October in a message to Pearl Harbor, Halsey gave his reply to Japan's extravagant claims, and Cincpac promptly released it, to the amusement of the American public: "Admiral Nimitz has received from Admiral Halsey the comforting assurance that he is now retiring toward the enemy following the salvage of all the Third Fleet ships recently reported sunk by Radio Tokyo."

BATTLE
FOR
LEYTE GULF

USING HIS DAMAGED cruisers as bait and then guarding them from air attack obliged Admiral Halsey to change his plans. He radioed Vice Admiral Kinkaid that the Third Fleet might not be able to carry out its scheduled support of the Seventh Fleet's 20 October invasion of Leyte. Fortunately an adequate replacement was at hand. Near the van of the approaching invasion force were three task units of escort carriers, code-named Taffy 1, Taffy 2, and Taffy 3. These took station off the mouth of Leyte Gulf and substituted for the Third Fleet by raiding the central Philippines while the old battleships under Rear Admiral Jesse Oldendorf entered the gulf and began the shore bombardment.

When the Third Fleet's raids virtually on Japan's doorstep failed to draw out an avenging Japanese fleet for battle, Halsey and Mitscher suspected that loss of planes and aviators had again paralyzed the Combined Fleet. Yet Japanese naval forces were on the move. Submarines as well as aircraft based in China and New Guinea reported heavy surface units under way in the Singapore-Borneo area and southbound along the China coast. These reports provoked lively discussion in the Third Fleet and Task Force 38 staffs. The consensus was that the ships were converging on the South China Sea west of the Philippines, probably intending to base on Coron Bay or Manila Bay. From either position they could set up a 1944 version of the Tokyo Express to supply and reinforce the Japanese on Leyte.

One vital element was missing: the carriers. Nobody had yet sighted Japanese carriers. It was generally agreed that the enemy would not be so foolhardy as to send surface ships without carrier support against an American carrier fleet. The Japanese carriers, having been sighted nowhere else, must be in home waters to the north, whither they had retreated following the Battle of the Philippine Sea. Halsey relied on the dozen U.S. submarines on watch off southern Japan to warn him of any sortie.

Despite Halsey's notice to Kinkaid of possible nonsupport, Third Fleet managed to have one or two carrier task groups off the Philippines each day, pounding down enemy airfields to ward off attacks on the invasion forces and on Baitdiv 1, which was now inching past Luzon. On 20 October all four Third Fleet groups were on hand to support the invasion, and ships' loudspeakers carried General MacArthur's address to the Filipinos, spoken into a microphone set up on the Leyte beachhead. "This is the voice of freedom, General MacArthur speaking," he began. "People of the Philippines, I have returned! By the grace of Almighty God our forces stand again on Philippine soil." Burke and his fellow staffers thought it a bit bombastic but perhaps just the thing to inspire a downtrodden people.

Halsey, having seen the general safely ashore, turned his gaze farther westward. On the morning following the invasion he sent a dispatch to MacArthur, with Admirals King, Nimitz, Kinkaid, Mitscher, and McCain cut in as information addressees: "Since the South China Sea may suddenly become a critical area, information is requested as to what is the earliest estimate for a safe route to that sea via Surigao and Mindoro straits for (a) well escorted oilers and (b) major combatant ships."

By "safe route" he meant mainly absence of mines. The implication of the message was that since the Japanese fleet was apparently unwilling to come into the Pacific to confront his Third Fleet, he would take the Third Fleet to the South China Sea to do the confronting—not by the direct route via San Bernardino Strait and the Sibuyan Sea, which would mean passing close to the Manila airfields, but roundabout via Surigao Strait, the Mindanao Sea, and Mindoro Strait to reach the presumed enemy anchorage.

Halsey's readiness thus to abandon support of the invasion in order to entrap the enemy fleet or to track it down in the South China Sea clearly demonstrates that he regarded his order to destroy a "major portion of the enemy fleet" as superseding every other responsibility. He wrote later, "The Third Fleet was offensive. It prowled the ocean, striking at will with its new battleships and fast carriers."

Cincpac, however, imposed some limits on the prowling. In response to Halsey's inquiry about a safe route via the straits, Nimitz reminded him that the op plan requiring him to "cover and support forces of the Southwest Pacific" was still in effect and forbade him to move major units of the Third Fleet into central Philippine waters without orders from Cincpac. Commodore Burke, reading this message, was reminded of the night four months earlier when Spruance denied Mitscher's proposal to head west to engage the enemy.

Restrained by Nimitz, Halsey set in motion another project—that of at last providing much-needed rest for his men and replenishment for his ships. For ten months the men had been operating in the tropics, living between steel decks, often under combat conditions, setting foot on shore if at all only on some barren atoll. In the recent three-day Formosa air battle, fighter pilots and ships' crews had withstood the heaviest series of air attacks the enemy thus far had hurled against the fleet. In *Bunker Hill* so many pilots were suffering from combat fatigue that Halsey sent her to Manus escorted by two battered destroyers to pick up relief pilots. He began rotating the rest of the ships by task groups to Ulithi to reprovision, rearm, and rest their crews. McCain's group left for the atoll in the evening of 22 October, with Davison's due to follow on the 23rd. On their return on the 29th, Bogan's and Sherman's groups would head for Ulithi.

Such was the plan, but it was disrupted by a series of reports from U.S. submarine *Darter* operating in Palawan Passage west of the Philippines. The first dispatch, received in Third Fleet at 0518, 23 October, reported contact on three probable battleships. The second, intercepted at 0620, indicated contact was being maintained and increased the estimate to at least nine ships. A third, at 0745, upped the figure to a minimum eleven ships.

Halsey's and Mitscher's staffs concluded that the contact consisted of at least eleven enemy ships, comprising two or three battleships and the rest cruisers and destroyers. The positions stated in the three successive reports indicated that this force, undoubtedly the one sighted earlier in the Singapore-Borneo area, was on course northeast at a speed that would bring it to Coron Bay by sundown.

Halsey's reaction was to cancel his order for Davison's group to retire to Ulithi. He directed it and Bogan's and Sherman's groups to refuel and then move in closer to the Philippines to launch dawn searches on the 24th. He issued no change of orders to McCain's group, which continued on toward Ulithi, with five of the Third Fleet's sixteen carriers bearing 326 of the fleet's 921 carrier planes.

When simultaneously setting a trap, protecting Baitdiv 1, and supporting the Leyte invasion obliged the four task groups of Task Force 38 to operate separately, Admiral Halsey automatically took over the tactical command from Mitscher. This shift was in accord with their earlier agreement, but Halsey began ignoring the chain of command by giving orders directly to the task group commanders instead of via their immediate superior, Admiral Mitscher.

Commodore Burke, Commander Flatley, and other Task Force 38 staffers worked up quite a bit of indignation over this disregard of normal procedure, but Mitscher took no umbrage at being bypassed. Since Halsey had definite ideas of what he wanted done, were Mitscher included in the chain he would be a mere relay, a function in which he took no delight. Giving orders directly to the task groups reduced radio traffic, particularly since Halsey and Mitscher were in separate groups, often far apart. An example, Mitscher pointed out, would be Admiral Halsey giving an order to Bogan's group 2, which included Halsey's flagship *New Jersey*. A direct order could be transmitted by flashing light, flag hoist, semaphore, or short-range TBS. Adherence to the chain of command would require a radio dispatch to Mitscher's *Lexington* in Sherman's group 3, which might be several hundred miles away, and a return message from *Lexington* to Bogan's group. Such a procedure, involving a double breaking of radio silence, would give Japanese radio direction finders two fixes and enemy cryptanalysts two messages to attack.

Unknown to Third Fleet, the great Battle for Leyte Gulf had already begun. More than an hour before *Darter*'s third report had been relayed to Halsey, *Darter* had joined submarine *Dace* in an attack on the Japanese force in Palawan Passage. Their torpedoes sank two heavy cruisers and put a third out of action. These were the opening shots in an operation that was to involve more ship tonnage and cover a wider area than any other naval battle in history. The operation called the Battle for Leyte Gulf was in fact composed of several separate but interconnected actions, the major ones being the battles of the Sibuyan Sea and Surigao Strait and the engagements off Samar and off Cape Engaño. It ended the Imperial

Japanese Navy as an effective fighting force and established the United States Navy in command of the Pacific.

Having fueled, groups 2, 3, and 4 moved through the night of 23–24 October toward the Philippine east coast, fanning out so that by dawn they were about 140 miles apart. From north to south, Sherman's group 3, including *Lexington*, stood off central Luzon; Bogan's group 2, including *New Jersey*, off San Bernardino Strait; and Davison's group 4, off Leyte Gulf. All three launched search teams of Hellcats and Helldivers to comb the interisland waterways and the seas to westward for enemy naval forces, particularly the ships *Darter* had reported the preceding day.

In *Lexington* Mitscher was on his swivel chair, and Burke and Flatley were with him observing the group 3 search planes take off. There was little else for the task force officers to do, because Admiral Halsey was commanding the fleet, Admiral Sherman was commanding the task group, and Captain E. W. Litch was commanding *Lexington*. On 24 October Mitscher and his staff were mere passengers. They kept themselves fully informed, however, prepared to take over the tactical command whenever they were so ordered or circumstances required.

In the predawn darkness as Sherman's group 3 was approaching Luzon, enemy snoopers had found and continued to shadow it. Night fighters kept the snoopers at a distance, but at dawn five were still on the radar screen. All hands were curious to know what the enemy had to throw at them. Since the Formosa air battle the Japanese had been oddly, even ominously, passive. Had they shot their bolt and been rendered incapable of counterattack in the air? Or had they been bringing in planes from Japan via the Ryukyus and Formosa and preparing to spring a trap of their own?

It began to rain, lightly and intermittently, not enough to impede flying but offering some cover to ships if a squall happened to be nearby when an air attack arrived. The sky above the rain clouds was sufficiently overcast to provide concealment for attacking or retreating planes.

In the Third Fleet it was assumed that the Japanese force reported by *Darter* was now in Coron or Manila bay. A little after 0820, however, all three task groups were electrified by a report from carrier *Intrepid*'s search planes. En route to scout Coron Bay, they had sighted the Japanese force, much larger than reported, rounding the southern tip of Mindoro Island and entering the Sibuyan Sea. They counted nearly thirty ships—battleships, cruisers, and de-

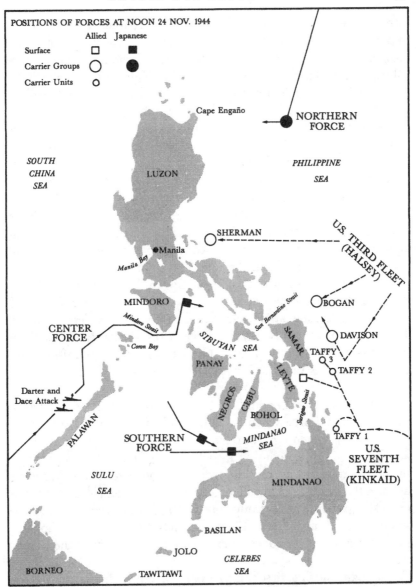

*Battle for Leyte Gulf, Position of Forces
at Noon 24 November 1944*

stroyers. This armada, which the Americans later called the Center
Force, was evidently heading to transit San Bernardino Strait in
order to bombard the Leyte beachhead and attack the shipping in
Leyte Gulf.

Forbidden by Nimitz to take his ships through San Bernardino

Strait to meet the oncoming enemy, Halsey rebroadcast the contact report, summoned Sherman and Davison to close at best speed on Bogan, who, being off the strait, was nearest the enemy, and gave all three groups their combat orders in the single word: "Strike!" He directed McCain, 600 miles away to the east, heading for Ulithi, to reverse course, refuel, and stand by for further orders.

Before the first strike could be launched against the Center Force, search planes from Davison's carriers sighted eastbound in the Sulu Sea another, smaller group of Japanese ships, which the Americans labeled the Southern Force. The search planes attacked this new group, damaging a battleship and a destroyer without slowing either. Evidently the Southern Force was headed for Leyte Gulf via Surigao Strait to cooperate with the Center Force in a double envelopment. If both forces maintained their reported speeds, they would arrive at the gulf at dawn the following morning.

As Davison continued closing on Bogan, his aircraft could ever more readily reach the Center Force while the Southern Force lay at last outside their attack radius. Halsey was thus depending on Kinkaid to block the Southern Force, a responsibility Kinkaid acknowledged by listing Halsey, Nimitz, and King as information addressees in his radio orders to Oldendorf to prepare for a night engagement.

To the north, off Luzon, Sherman was about to launch an attack on the Center Force when his ships' radars showed a large group of planes approaching from the west. The radars soon revealed another large group coming in behind the first, then a still larger group 60 miles away closing from the southwest. The Japanese apparently were hurling all of their available land-based aircraft against Sherman's task group on the assumption that this was the whole U.S. Third Fleet. They thus left Davison's and Bogan's groups free all day to concentrate their air power against the Center Force.

Sherman, putting first things first, postponed his attack on the Center Force and scrambled all his available fighters to repulse the oncoming air raid. As soon as the Hellcats were launched, the ships headed for cover into a nearby rainsquall, which they entered, said Sherman, "like soldiers going into their foxholes." The attacking Japanese pilots appeared even more poorly trained than the others the Americans had encountered lately. Sherman's 58 Hellcats, in a new edition of the Turkey Shoot, made short work of them, shooting down a reported 76 planes. The enemy remnant fled, and Task

Group 38.3 turned into the wind, emerged from the rain, and began recovering fighters in need of fuel and ammunition.

During the battle of the Hellcats, Sherman's carriers had been arming their dive-bombers and torpedo-bombers for the postponed attack on the Center Force. In order to recover the returning fighters, the carrier crews temporarily struck the newly armed bombers below on the hangar decks. A little after 0930, as the first of the Hellcats were landing, a lone Japanese bomber, which had been orbiting above the overcast awaiting an opportunity, streaked down out of the clouds. Although several ships immediately took it under fire and a returning Hellcat soon shot it down, the bomber managed to hurl a 550-pound bomb amidships through the flight deck of light carrier *Princeton*.

Mitscher and Burke instantly put their glasses on the carrier. The admiral was of the opinion that *Princeton* could easily survive and not be greatly disabled by a single relatively light bomb, but Burke reminded him that she was carrying fueled, armed aircraft on her hangar deck, a condition Mitscher endeavored to avoid. As if to illustrate Burke's point, gasoline fumes from planes the bomb had damaged in *Princeton*'s hangar suddenly ignited with a loud "whoof!" and there followed a series of deafening thunderclaps as overheated torpedoes exploded, hurling the carrier's forward elevator masthead-high and ejecting a column of black smoke hundreds of feet into the air.

As the wounded carrier fell out of formation, Sherman ordered cruisers *Reno* and *Birmingham* and three destroyers to stand by her to help fight the fires and protect her from air attack. The remaining seventeen ships of Task Group 38.3, instead of closing on Bogan as Halsey had ordered, remained off Luzon in support of the burning *Princeton*.

Out of habit, *Lexington*'s flight leaders came up to flag bridge to report to Mitscher. From them he and Burke learned with surprise that the enemy raid they had just repulsed had been carried out by carrier planes. Yet all evidence indicated they had come from Luzon airstrips. Could the raid have been the tail end of a bungled attempt at shuttle-bombing—launched originally from carriers that had eluded the submarine pickets off Japan?

Reassuming a little of his divested authority, Mitscher ordered Sherman to launch a search to the north. The latter had by this time managed to send his strike against the Center Force and at 1245 was readying a second strike against it when radar showed a large group of enemy planes at a distance of 105 miles approaching from the northeast. Thinking fast, Sherman launched the second strike and then scrambled all his remaining fighters to ward off the new threat. The search to the north would have to wait.

The oncoming enemy raid became divided. The Hellcats took on one of the segments and easily dispersed it, shooting down a good many of the planes. The American pilots noted and reported that the raiding aircraft were all carrier-type and that many retreated not back to the northeast whence they had come but toward the Luzon airfields.

When radar showed the other segment boring in toward group 3, the fighter director on orders from Burke radioed "Hey, Rube!" for all unengaged Hellcats to come to the rescue. Fighters thus called home shot down a dozen or more of the raiders and sent most of the rest fleeing toward Luzon. Some six or eight bombers, however, evaded the Hellcats and, hurtling in through cloud cover, dived on the American carriers. One dropped a bomb within 50 feet of *Lexington* and then, pulling up from its dive, flashed across the violently maneuvering ship, spitting machine-gun bullets.

Mitscher leaped from his swivel chair and bolted into flag plot. "What kind of deal was that?" he sputtered. "That fellow was actually firing at us!"

The staff, surprised at this lively bit of footwork by the usually unhurried Mitscher, watched open-mouthed, then burst out laughing. Said one, "That's the first time I've seen you jump up like that."

Mitscher, who had rather surprised himself, grinned.

All of the attacking bombers were shot down, either by Hellcats or by ships' gunfire. They made no direct hits but had slightly damaged carriers *Essex* and *Langley* with near misses.

Meanwhile, aircraft from Davison's, Bogan's, and Sherman's task groups, in an operation titled Battle of the Sibuyan Sea, were repeatedly attacking the Center Force. By a little past 1500 they had staged five massive raids on the hapless ships, which were getting little cover from the nearby Japanese airfields. Evidently the aviators from those fields believed their best contribution was to attack Sherman's group, which they obviously continued to believe was the entire Third Fleet. The only ship they damaged, however, was the still-burning *Princeton*.

The Japanese ships endeavored to protect themselves by sending up great geysers of antiaircraft fire, including shells from their big guns, but they succeeded in shooting down only eighteen of the hundreds of attacking planes. The Americans concentrated on the big ships, particularly two enormous ones believed to be superbattleships *Yamato* and *Musashi,* rumored the world's largest, most heavily armed combatant ships. By midafternoon one of these, later identified as *Musashi,* had fallen far behind. Listing and trailing oil, she was apparently sinking. Pilots reported four additional battleships severely damaged. A heavy cruiser with steering difficulties had departed the area on a retirement course.

The consensus of the American pilots was that the Center Force was now too battered to pose any serious threat. Its ships, maneuvering to evade bombs and torpedoes, had by the end of each raid become scattered, apparently in irreparable disarray. Yet the force showed surprising powers of recovery. Subsequent U.S. raiders arriving over the Sibuyan Sea found the ships back in formation and ever nearer San Bernardino Strait.

The Center Force was clearly bent on transiting the strait and was apparently capable of doing so. Admiral Halsey, on the chance he had a surface action impending, at 1512 radioed his battle plan to Vice Admiral Mitscher, Vice Admiral Lee, and his task group commanders, with Admirals Nimitz and King as information addressees. The plan specified that four battleships, two heavy and three light cruisers, and two divisions of destroyers, all drawn from Bogan's group 2 and Davison's group 4, now together off San Bernardino Strait, "will be formed as Task Force 34 under Vadm Lee, commander battle line. Task Force 34 engage decisively at long ranges. Commander Task Group 38.4 conduct carriers of Task Group 38.2 and Task Group 38.4 clear of surface fighting."

Admiral Kinkaid read the dispatch with satisfaction. It was not addressed to him, but his communicators had intercepted it. To keep himself informed he had them listen in on communications between all major commands, an unauthorized but widely practiced form of radio eavesdropping. He expected Oldendorf's Seventh Fleet battleship force to block any attack on Leyte Gulf from the south. Now he believed he could count on Halsey's Third Fleet to bar any enemy incursion via San Bernardino Strait or from Japan.

Not long after the sending of the 1512 dispatch, a U.S. scout plane reported the Center Force now heading west, in either temporary or final retreat. In view of this uncertainty, Halsey notified Davison and Bogan by TBS: "If enemy sorties Task Force 34 will be formed when directed by me"—a short-range transmission that was intercepted by no other commands.

Task Group 38.3, still off Luzon, was at last preparing to launch the long-delayed search to the north. Instead of taking time out to recover, rearm, and refuel the Hellcats that had repulsed the raid from the northeast, Sherman with Mitscher's consent at 1405 sent off bombers in single-plane search missions unaccompanied by fighters. "We were fighting again on a shoestring," Burke afterward remarked.

Sherman's group was still chained to damaged *Princeton*, whose stubborn fires refused to be extinguished. Only her skipper and a fire-fighting party were still on board. At 1523, *Birmingham* was alongside helping fight the fires and attempting to take the carrier in tow. Suddenly the carrier's torpedo stowage exploded with a shattering blast that blew off her stern and the after section of her flight deck. Every man on *Princeton* was killed or wounded, but far greater casualties were suffered on board *Birmingham*, where all the men not on duty elsewhere were topside, handling lines, manning hoses, or rigging the tow. Against *Birmingham*'s open decks the explosion hurled tons of debris ranging from steel splinters to great sections of plating. Virtually every man on the decks was hit. More than 200 were killed almost instantly, and twice that number were wounded, half of them severely. Her captain, himself painfully injured, reported, "From the main deck up, the ship was a veritable charnel house of dead, dying, and wounded."

From contemplation of this horror Admiral Mitscher's staff had its attention diverted at 1540 by the first of several contact reports from the bombers sent north on search missions. The bombers reported battleships, cruisers, and destroyers but, oddly enough, no carriers some 75 miles northeast of Sherman's group 3. Not until 1640 were carriers reported: at least three, accompanied by cruisers and destroyers, 60 miles northeast of the previously reported battleship group and 190 miles north of Sherman's group. All the Japanese ships to the north and northeast Flatley lumped together as the Northern Force.

All day the need to guard the burning *Princeton* had restricted the movements of group 3. Now by TBS Mitscher suggested to Sherman that "in view of contact to north" the crippled carrier should be sunk. Sherman, agreeing, regretfully sent in cruiser *Reno*, which sent her down with torpedoes. Mitscher told Burke to inform Halsey of the contact reports and of the sinking.

The pattern of the Japanese counterattack was now clear. Three forces were to converge on Leyte Gulf: the Southern Force via

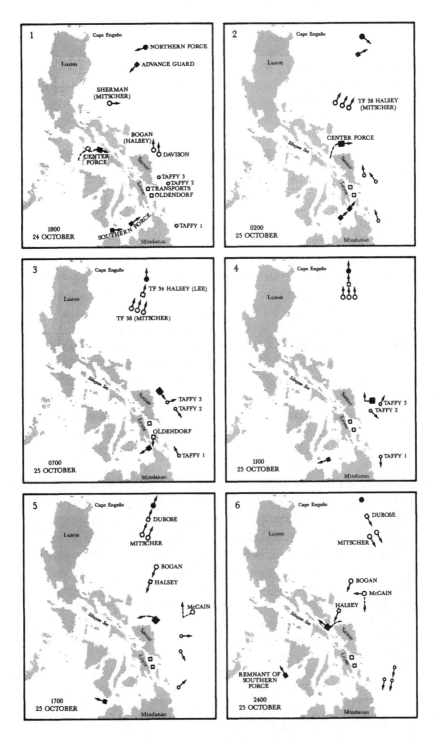

Battle for Leyte Gulf, Fleet Movements

Surigao Strait, the more powerful Center Force via San Bernardino Strait, and the Northern Force coming down from Japan. All hands recognized that the Northern Force's carriers, the warships with the longest reach and the hardest punch, had superseded the retreating Center Force's battleships as the Third Fleet's main target.

"The carrier forces to the north were our meat," said Admiral Sherman; "they were close enough so they could not get away." Mitscher considered at once launching Sherman's planes for a strike against the enemy carriers but decided it was too late in the day. The returning pilots would have to make night landings, for which they were not trained.

As the search planes returned to *Lexington,* Mitscher summoned the pilots to flag plot, where he and Burke put them through a thorough grilling. The admiral and his chief of staff concluded that there was only one Northern Force, operating currently in two sections, and that it included at least three carriers, four to six cruisers, six or more destroyers, and just two battleships, the easily recognized *Ise* and *Hyuga,* unique conversions with flight decks aft. Each was known to have retained eight of her 14-inch guns.

Old night fighter Arleigh Burke now had a brainstorm. Why not detach Sherman's two battleships, *Massachusetts* and *South Dakota,* each with nine 16-inch guns, and send them up with cruisers and destroyers to demolish the Northern Force in a night battle? Mitscher bought the idea at once, passed it on to Sherman, and ordered him to prepare to execute it after dark.

Before the Burke-Mitscher plan could be put into effect, however, Halsey initiated one of his own. By radio a little after 2000, with all affected parties as information addressees, he ordered Davison and Bogan to head north at 25 knots. Sherman was to join them as they sped past, and McCain, far out in the Philippine Sea, was to race to catch up with the rest of the Third Fleet. A separate message to Kinkaid read: "Strike reports indicate enemy force Sibuyan Sea heavily damaged. Am proceeding north with three groups to attack enemy carrier force at dawn."

This message was subject to more than one interpretation. Kinkaid construed it to mean that Halsey was taking three *carrier* groups north while leaving Task Force 34 behind to guard San Bernardino Strait. Mitscher and Burke understood it to mean that Halsey had scrapped the battle plan set forth in his 1512 dispatch and was taking every ship and plane of the Third Fleet north, leaving the strait unguarded. The latter interpretation was correct. The 1512 dispatch had listed "Batdiv 7" among the participants assigned to Task Force 34. Mitscher and Burke knew that Halsey's flagship, *New Jersey*, was in Battleship Division 7. Kinkaid did not, but knowing Halsey, he might have surmised that he would place his flagship and himself in the midst of any impending fight.

Halsey's Third Fleet staff had been studying the situation quite as thoroughly as had Mitscher's Task Force 38 staff but had reached somewhat different conclusions. Third Fleet accepted its aviators' reports that the Center Force was battered to the point where it was no longer a serious menace. It could safely be left to the Seventh Fleet. Oldendorf's old battleships after defeating the small Southern Force in Surigao Strait could swing about and, with the support of aircraft from the newly captured airstrip at Tacloban and from the three Seventh Fleet jeep carrier units, Taffies 1, 2, and 3, finish off the Center Force, which Halsey's air operations officer predicted would never enter Leyte Gulf.

Even if his prediction proved untrue, what sort of victory, the Third Fleet staffers asked themselves, could it achieve in the gulf? Most of the shipping had already departed, and the rest with adequate warning could skip out to sea. The Japanese surface forces, unaccompanied by transports with assault troops, could not consolidate their position. They could only hit and run, and the Guadalcanal campaign had demonstrated that such tactics could not dislodge a determined occupation force.

Halsey had a special reason for taking all his available strength against the Northern Force. He was determined to make a clean sweep of the carriers. In every preceding carrier battle of the Pacific war, the Japanese had got home with a considerable remnant of their fleet. He wanted to make sure that nothing of the sort happened this time. He still did not know how many carriers he was going to find, but he intended to sink them all and if possible their escorts as well. Should the Center Force choose to linger in the gulf area, Third Fleet would return in time to reverse any advantage it might have gained.

While the Third Fleet staff was downplaying the Center Force, Burke was puzzling over the Northern Force. He decided there was something suspect about it. It must have been sent down to cooperate with the other two enemy forces, but how? Surely the Marianas Turkey Shoot had taught the Japanese they could not defeat the U.S. carrier fleet. That lesson was reinforced by the air battles of the day. Arleigh believed, incorrectly, that planes from the Northern

Force had participated in the morning's attack on Sherman's group. Its heavy losses could account for the small number of planes in the midday air attack from the northeast. Many survivors of the midday raid had headed not for their flight decks but for airfields on Luzon. But the virtually planeless carriers were still up there to the north. Why?

The answer came to Burke in a flash. Those carriers were decoys, sent down to lure Halsey into doing precisely what he was doing— clearing the way for the Center Force to reach Leyte Gulf via San Bernardino Strait. The Japanese had reason to be confident Halsey would take the bait. He was famed for taking calculated risks that paid off. In the spring of 1942 when Japan's armed force far exceeded America's, he had daringly led his carriers into Japanese waters and launched an air raid on Tokyo.

Burke excitedly turned to Mitscher, explained his theory, and suggested that he pass it on to Halsey. Mitscher pondered the suggestion. "Well," he said at last, "I think you're right, but I don't know you're right." He recalled the times he had been annoyed by subordinates butting in with gratuitous criticisms of a tactical plan he was executing. "I don't think we ought to bother Admiral Halsey," he concluded. "He's busy enough. He's got a lot of things on his mind."

Admiral Lee, who like Burke had been puzzling over the odd activities of the Northern Force and its planes, had come to the same conclusion—that the force was there to lure the Third Fleet away from its covering position off San Bernardino Strait. Less reticent than Mitscher, he communicated his theory to the flag by flashing light. His message was acknowledged with a perfunctory "Roger." Halsey and his staff had discussed that possibility and rejected as absurd the notion that any navy would expend carriers as bait to clear the way for an attack by obsolescent battleships.

Mitscher, all too familiar with the aviators' tendency to overrate the damage they inflicted, did not share Halsey's low opinion of the Center Force's fighting potential. Seeking some means of attacking both it and the Northern Force, he devised an improved version of Burke's night battle plan. He proposed having the joint force proceed north at high speed, form and detach a super Task Force 34 including not four but all six Third Fleet battleships, and send it forward to attack the Northern Force at night, with the Third Fleet aircraft taking over at dawn to sink whatever enemy ships remained afloat. That done, the Third Fleet could hurry back south, possibly too late to bar the Center Force from entering Leyte Gulf but at least in time to shatter it when it emerged. The staff, enthusiastic over the proposal, urged Mitscher to suggest it to Halsey. He refused lest it disconcert the latter's tactical thinking, but he told Burke to work out the details and have the plan ready for use if an opportunity arose. Then, bone-tired, he withdrew to his sea cabin to rebuild his stamina for the next day's battle.

At 2045 a night search plane from light carrier *Independence* reported the Center Force on an easterly course, again headed in the direction of San Bernardino Strait, but the turnaway had put it so far behind schedule that it could not possibly achieve its supposed dawn rendezvous with the Southern Force at Leyte Gulf.

Burke was alarmed but not much surprised by this second reversal of course. He had conjectured that its commander had withdrawn temporarily in the futile hope that Japanese planes could whittle down American air strength enough to weaken the attacks on his ships. Burke discussed the situation with Flatley. They decided not to awaken Admiral Mitscher unless and until it was certain that the Center Force was steering to transit the strait. Meanwhile, Burke penciled several messages from which Mitscher could choose one to send to Halsey. With some variation in the ships to be included, each of them recommended forming Task Force 34 at once and sending it back south together with one of the carrier groups.

A little after 2300 another report came in from an *Independence* search plane. The Center Force was definitely heading into San Bernardino Strait, which now had its navigation lights turned on. On the chart Flatley drew a large X off the strait, and he and Burke headed for Mitscher's sea cabin. Awakened, the admiral raised himself on one elbow as they told him about the search plane's report and Burke's recommendation.

With a shade of exasperation in his voice, Mitscher asked, "Does Admiral Halsey have that report?"

"Yes," replied Flatley.

"If he wants my advice he'll ask for it," said Mitscher, putting the final quietus on his staff's urge to send Halsey unsought counsel. Then he turned over and went back to sleep.

Around 2330, when eastbound Task Group 38.3 was maneuvering by radar to join Task Groups 38.2 and 38.4 coming up from the south at 25 knots, Burke was handed a copy of a dispatch from commander Third Fleet ordering the three groups to join, slow down to 16 knots, and head north together. Burke was surprised and annoyed, because this was a situation in which by prior agreement commander Task Force 38 or his representative was to take the tactical command. He telephoned Mitscher and asked, "Do we have tactical command when we join?"

"Yes, we always do. We are the tactical commander. Why do you ask?"

"Well, Admiral Halsey is giving tactical orders."

"Take it over," said Mitscher.

As soon as the three groups were within TBS range of each other, Burke ordered them to form east-west line of bearing and head north. When there was no reaction from the fleet flag, he assumed that Halsey had surrendered the tactical command. Seeing this as an opportunity to carry out Mitscher's proposal for a night surface battle followed by a dawn air strike, Burke ordered the fleet to resume its 25-knot speed. Presently another dispatch arrived from Halsey ordering the fleet to slow back down to 16 knots. Obviously he had not entirely surrendered the command.

Halsey's main concern was to avoid passing the Northern Force during the night. If the enemy slipped past on the offshore side, it could use Luzon airfields to shuttle-bomb the Third Fleet. If the Northern Force passed between the Third Fleet and Luzon, it might join the Center Force in its attack on Leyte Gulf.

Burke, uninformed of Halsey's grounds for maintaining slow speed through the night, tried again to set up a tactical situation for executing Mitscher's plan. He inched the fleet forward by a series of brief TBS commands. When it was again racing ahead at 25 knots, he sat in a chair, put his head back, and promptly went to sleep—a knack he had acquired in his destroyer days.

Around 0100 Burke was brought abruptly to his feet by Admiral Carney's voice on TBS barking a command to bring the fleet's speed back down to 16 knots. Admiral Halsey, now more concerned than ever lest he overrun the Northern Force, had Carney order a new night search launched from *Independence*. When Burke heard this order, he respectfully recommended its cancellation. The Japanese might detect it and dart away, he pointed out, so that by dawn their ships would be beyond the attack radius of the American planes.

"Have you any information that we don't have?" asked Carney.

"No, sir."

"Launch the search," said Carney.

The sound of planes taking off awakened Mitscher, who arrived in *Lexington*'s flag plot wearing a dressing gown and his long-billed cap. Nearly an hour passed before the planes made radar contact with the enemy. The Northern Force, they reported, was still in two sections, now evidently heading for a rendezvous. Halsey was shocked and Mitscher and Burke were elated to be informed that the enemy surface section, with *Ise* and *Hyuga*, was only 80 miles away. Apparently Burke's speedups had set the stage for inevitable employment of Mitscher's plan.

A quick calculation forecast a night surface action at around 0430. Speaking for Mitscher, Burke recommended forming Task Force 34 and sending it ahead. Halsey approved at once. If there was going to be a night battle, he didn't want his carriers involved in it.

Burke passed the word to Admiral Lee, specifying inclusion of six battleships, seven cruisers, and eighteen destroyers. Lee, bearing in mind the perils of withdrawing scattered ships at night from a fleet under way, sacrificed speed for safety by ordering the specified ships to slow down. The rest of the ships steered past them, leaving the ships of Task Force 34 behind. Officers on watch throughout the fleet, observing Lee's operation on their radarscopes, assumed that Task Force 34 would now dash southward to cover San Bernardino Strait. Instead, to the surprise of all and the consternation of some, the newly formed task force sped northbound on past the reduced Task Force 38 and took station 10 miles ahead of *Lexington*, the fleet guide.

Mitscher ordered Burke to have all the carriers arm first deckloads for prompt takeoff when ordered. Hours passed with no such order. When 0430 came and went with no surface battle developing, Burke concluded that the Northern Force had indeed detected the *Independence* search planes and had at once begun to open the range. He was mistaken. The Third Fleet had never been closer than 200 miles to either section of the Northern Force. The 80-mile figure that led to the formation of Task Force 34 was apparently a transmission error.

At first light, around 0600, Mitscher sent out another flight of search planes and, without waiting for these to regain contact, launched combat air patrol, followed by a 180-plane first strike. He counted thus on getting the jump on the enemy without exposing his carriers to the fate of *Princeton*, which had come under air attack with armed planes on board. When passage of time with no contact reports indicated that the enemy was not so near as supposed, Mitscher ordered his striking planes to orbit until the enemy was found. Having thus set his attack in motion, Mitscher, utterly exhausted, retired to his cabin, leaving its final execution to Burke.

At 0710 the search planes from the U.S. carriers made a fresh contact with the Northern Force, now united and northbound, 142 miles north of the Third Fleet. For the first time Burke learned the approximate makeup of the force he was expected to destroy. It comprised one large and three light carriers, the carrier-battleships *Ise* and *Hyuga*, several cruisers, and a few destroyers—some seventeen Japanese ships being pursued by sixty-five American ships, including five large and five light carriers.

Burke ordered the orbiting planes to strike, and the search planes coached them to the target. A little after 0800, pilots' chatter indicated they had the enemy force under attack and were making hits. Before the chatter died down, Burke had a second strike launched, some thirty-six aircraft from Sherman's and Davison's task groups.

Then, mindful that Halsey had ordered Task Group 38.1 to catch up with the rest of Third Fleet in its attack on the Northern Force, Burke radioed McCain some helpful information: "Attacking enemy force 4 carriers plus cruisers and destroyers who are in lat. 20 north, 126–30 east, course northerly, speed 20 plus."

As in previous actions, returning flight leaders dashed up to flag bridge to make their reports. Burke received them standing, never presuming to occupy Bald Eagle's perch, the swivel chair. The aviators brought cheering news. Hardly more than a dozen fighter aircraft had risen to protect the Japanese ships, and the Hellcats shot down most of them. The American bombers and torpedo planes meanwhile bored in through intense antiaircraft fire and drove home their strike. They torpedoed the heavy carrier, which began steering erratically and developed a list, and they bombed two of the light carriers and a destroyer. The destroyer sank at once, and one of the light carriers appeared to be sinking. Strike No. 2, arriving over the target around 0945, found the Northern Force widely scattered and observed the final plunge of the light carrier left sinking by Strike No. 1. The fliers now heavily bombed a light cruiser and left another light carrier dead in the water, afire, and listing.

The extreme shortage of planes in the Northern Force convinced Burke that his theory was correct; those carriers were bait, being sacrificed to lure Halsey out of the path of the Center Force. If so, Halsey was still being lured—barreling ahead in *New Jersey* with Lee's Task Force 34. A few hours earlier, when the night ended without surface contact with the enemy, Task Force 34 took as its function supplementing the work of the U.S. carrier planes by sinking cripples and stragglers and any other Japanese ships it could overtake.

Toward 1000, Burke was handed a dispatch that validated his forebodings. It was from Admiral Halsey to Admiral Kinkaid with Cominch, Cincpac, and Third Fleet as information addressees. In reply apparently to a message from Kinkaid, Halsey signaled: "Am now engaging enemy carrier force. Task Group 38.1 with 5 carriers and 6 CAs [heavy cruisers] has been ordered to assist you immediately. My position with other three carrier task groups lat. 17–18 north, long. 126-11 east."

Evidently the Center Force had entered the Pacific Ocean and was either in or threatening Leyte Gulf. There had been a series of radio messages that morning between Halsey and Kinkaid, but Task Force 38 communicators had not eavesdropped. Mitscher forbade the practice both because it was contrary to regulations and because "gentlemen do not read each other's mail."

Toward 1100, McCain sent in his report. A stickler for regulations, he conformed to normal practice by addressing it to his immediate superior, Mitscher, with Halsey and Kinkaid as information addressees: "Strike one launched at 1030 against enemy's BBs off Samar." If the Japanese battleships were off Samar, at least they were not in Leyte Gulf.

At 1115, Halsey detached from Task Force 34 four cruisers and ten destroyers under Rear Admiral Laurance DuBose to carry on the mission of sinking Japanese cripples and stragglers. With the rest of Task Force 34, including the six new battleships, he changed course from due north to due south, picked up Bogan's Task Group 38.2 in passing, and headed for San Bernardino Strait.

Burke wondered what crisis had at last prompted Halsey to do what he had tried to advise him to do twelve hours earlier. Though Mitscher's battle force had now been stripped down to considerably less than half the strength of Task Force 38, Burke was confident he had ample means to complete the destruction of the four bait carriers. Nevertheless he felt uneasy, having neither Halsey nor Mitscher to supervise him.

With Davison's and Sherman's carrier groups and with DuBose's surface group out ahead, Burke continued on course north till 1145, when he turned his carriers into the northeast wind to launch Strike No. 3, more than 200 aircraft, the largest of the day. The planes passed over the cripples of the morning strikes, leaving them to DuBose, and found the heavy carrier and a light carrier together with one of the converted battleships, a cruiser, and three destroyers steaming north at 20 knots, their damages, if any, apparently under control.

On receiving the target coordinator's report, Burke radioed, "Get the carriers!" The light carrier, quickly set afire by bombs, managed to extinguish the blaze and kept going. The attacking pilots concentrated on the heavy carrier, hitting her with at least a dozen bombs and three torpedoes. They were gratified to observe as, flying an enormous battle flag, she rolled slowly over to starboard and went down. She was identified as *Zuikaku*, last survivor of the raid on Pearl Harbor and veteran of every carrier battle of the Pacific war except Midway.

Strike No. 3 suffered no casualties to planes or pilots. The fliers returned to their carriers with a glow of accomplishment. One young Helldiver pilot leapt from his plane and scampered up the ladder of *Lexington*'s island shouting, "I gotta hit on a carrier! I gotta hit on a carrier!"

The planes of Strike No. 4 attained a few near misses on *Ise*, causing minor damage, but the main achievement of this strike was the sinking of the last operational carrier of the Northern Force, the light carrier that Strike No. 3 had set briefly afire. Several half-ton bombs and a pair of torpedoes finished her off at about 1500. There now remained one enemy carrier, still afloat but by no means operational. That was the light carrier that Strike No.2 had left dead in the water and listing. Somewhat earlier, Sherman, believing the crippled carrier abandoned, had suggested taking her in tow as a souvenir. Mitscher, who was paying one of his several brief visits to the bridge, was intrigued by the idea but turned it down in favor of sending DuBose's surface force north unaccompanied to sink this and any other enemy stragglers he could overtake.

For DuBose this was quite an order, for the Northern Force still had its two battleships, *Ise* and *Hyuga*, and Halsey had taken all six Third Fleet battleships south. By radio he expressed doubt that his cruisers "could handle the situation" to the north, because if the Japanese "should be able to get those two battleships together, it is going to be tough on the cruisers. However," he conceded, "if you think it possible, we will do it."

Mitscher thought it possible and told DuBose to get going. He would not, however, risk his carriers in a night battle, in which they would be at a hopeless disadvantage against surface forces. He ordered Burke to haul off to the east, try to destroy the enemy battle-

ships by air attack, make every effort to rescue downed U.S. aviators, and promptly on recovery of the last of his airborne planes head
south at best speed.

Burke sent two strikes against *Ise* and *Hyuga,* but the tough old
hermaphrodites by use of heavy, accurate antiaircraft fire and expert
maneuvering preserved themselves from serious damage from
planes flown by pilots who were near exhaustion at the end of two
days of battle. DuBose had the good fortune not to overtake the
battleships, which he would then have been obliged to engage.
Pausing to sink the derelict, last of the four bait carriers, he was
outsped by most of the retreating Northern Force. After nightfall,
however, he overtook three destroyers and sank one in a running
gunfire-torpedo battle. By that time Task Groups 3 and 4 were
heading southeast for a dawn fueling rendezvous, and the powerful
frame of former Naval Academy wrestler Arleigh Burke had at last
reached its limits. Having set the watch, he retired to his sea cabin
and went to bed for the first time in three nights.

Fueling completed on 26 October, Mitscher's two task groups
received dispatch orders from Halsey to move in toward Leyte Gulf
and be "prepared to make strikes or furnish cover over Leyte area."
On the 27th, Sherman's group 3 sent fighter sweeps over the central
Philippines and provided fighter cover over the gulf. Planes from
Sherman's flagship, *Essex,* attacked an enemy convoy in the South
China Sea with bombs and rockets, sinking two destroyers. The
following day, groups 2 and 4 took over the Leyte patrol, and group
3 headed for Ulithi, whither McCain's group 1 had already proceeded.

During his brief stay at Ulithi, Burke began to learn something of
the confusing activities elsewhere on 25 October while he was chas-
ing the Northern Force. Years passed, however, before he became
acquainted with all the details.

The enemy group sighted by Davison's pilots in the Sulu Sea on
the morning of 24 October consisted of two battleships, one heavy
cruiser, and four destroyers. This was the leader of two groups of
ships that together formed the Japanese Southern Force, heading
toward Leyte Gulf from the south. Ordered by Kinkaid to "prepare
for night engagement," Oldendorf lined the sides of Surigao Strait
with his destroyers and PT boats and placed his battleships and
cruisers on T-capping courses across the northern end.

In the early hours of 25 October the leading Japanese group blundered into Oldendorf's trap and was nearly annihilated. The second group, observing what had happened to the first, prudently withdrew. At 0623, Kinkaid announced the U.S. victory in the Battle of Surigao Strait to Halsey, who was then with Lee's Task Force 34 pursuing the Japanese Northern Force. Because the dispatch was not addressed to Mitscher, his communicators did not decode it.

Gratified by the victory in Surigao Strait, Halsey believed Oldendorf's old battleships could now swing about and in a few hours be in position to block the Center Force's entry into Leyte Gulf, should it venture so far. It fact, the Center Force had already arrived. Emerging from San Bernardino Strait a little after midnight, it had steamed unchallenged along the north and east coasts of Samar until at 0659 a little north of the gulf it encountered and opened fire on escort carrier unit Taffy 3—just thirty-six minutes after Kinkaid had announced the victory over the Southern Force.

Taffy 3's commander radioed a call for help against the overwhelming odds, and Kinkaid repeated the call to Halsey, adding, "Request Lee proceed top speed cover Leyte. Request immediate strike by fast carriers"—fairly impractical requests to forces 300 miles away. When Kinkaid continued to call for help with increasing stridency, Halsey, as we have seen, ordered McCain's Task Group 38.1 to go "at best possible speed" to the aid of Taffy 3—though by then McCain was almost as far from Leyte Gulf as Halsey was.

Toward 1000, when Kinkaid's appeals had reached a nerve-wracking crescendo, Halsey was handed a message from Admiral Nimitz, with Admirals King and Kinkaid listed as information addressees. The message read: WHERE IS RPT [repeat] WHERE IS TASK FORCE THIRTY-FOUR RR THE WORLD WONDERS.

To Halsey, whose stomach was already tied in knots, this looked like a piece of heavy-handed sarcasm with King and Kinkaid called in to witness his humiliation. The tough old warrior, whom the press called Bull Halsey, slammed his cap onto the deck and broke into sobs.

It was a mistake, of course. Nimitz was incapable of such sarcasm or of humiliating Halsey, whom he liked and admired. The Cincpac staff had been urging Nimitz to do something about the situation off the Philippines, but he was reluctant to interfere with officers at the scene of action. At last he agreed to a simple inquiry, asking

Halsey where Task Force 34 was. Nimitz knew it was nowhere near San Bernardino Strait, or it would long since have engaged the Center Force. Where else could it be unless with Halsey, who was known to have blood in his eye where enemy carriers were concerned?

Nimitz intended the message WHERE IS TASK FORCE THIRTY-FOUR as a nudge, to make Halsey pause and consider: "Where *ought* it to be?" The staff officer entrusted with the message added the information addressees, the yeoman who wrote it up added the RPT, and the ensign who encoded it added THE WORLD WONDERS.

This last was "padding," added to foil enemy cryptanalysts. Because the Allies were regularly breaking and reading Japanese and German encoded radio messages, Americans were especially careful about their own. Because opening and closing phrases of messages tended to be routine and hence could provide points of attack for cryptanalysts, U.S. regulations required cryptographers to insert nonsense padding phrases fore and aft, separated from the text by double consonants.

The Pearl Harbor encoder in attaching THE WORLD WONDERS at the end broke the rule that the padding must not be readable as part of the message. It fooled the decoder on board *New Jersey*, who tore off the opening padding but left on the end padding and shot the strip via pneumatic tube to flag plot, trusting someone to point out the RR. Nobody did, and Halsey had the shock of his life.

A communication officer explained to Halsey about padding, which he had never seen before, but the shock and the rage remained. He and many of his officers had been fervently anticipating an old-fashioned fire-away-Flanagan gun battle directed against enemy stragglers just over the horizon. Instead, after detaching DuBose and his surface units to fight the gun battle, Halsey dejectedly ordered the rest of Task Force 34, including *New Jersey*, to turn around and head back south.

"I turned my back on the opportunity I had dreamed of since my days as a cadet," he afterward wrote. "For me, one of the biggest battles of the war was off, and what has been called 'the Battle of Bull's Run' was on."

Meanwhile in the Leyte Gulf area the Americans were putting up a historic defense in the Battle off Samar. The Center Force, opening fire on the six little carriers of Taffy 3, sank one and heavily damaged three others. The unit's destroyers in an act of extreme courage charged in through heavy-caliber fire and attacked the big ships of the Center Force with torpedoes. Three of the destroyers were sunk, but their suicidal charge threw the enemy into confusion. Aircraft from the three Taffies, from Leyte, and from the approaching Task Force 38.1 struck, sinking three of the Center Force cruisers and inducing the remainder of the force to retire the way it had come.

In this battle the Japanese introduced a new, ominous weapon, the Kamikaze Special Attack Corps of suicidally inclined young aviators. Lacking the skill to hit ships with bombs or torpedoes, they made up in guts what they lacked in competence by flying their bomb-loaded planes and themselves into their targets. Kamikazes crashed into three carriers of Taffy 1 and nearby Taffy 3, sinking one and heavily damaging the others.

Halsey had interrupted his southward dash to spend several hours fueling his destroyers. Informed that the Center Force was on a retirement course, he detached his two fastest battleships, *New Jersey* and *Iowa*, three light cruisers, and eight destroyers and with these raced to head it off. When he reached San Bernardino a little after midnight, all of the Center Force had passed back through the strait except one destroyer that had lingered to pick up survivors of the Battle off Samar. Again dividing the force he had erstwhile so zealously kept united, Halsey sent forward his cruisers and destroyers to sink her with gunfire and torpedoes. He witnessed the sinking from the deck of his distant *New Jersey*. It was the only surface action he beheld in a long and bellicose career.

During the voyage to Ulithi, Mitscher spent most of the time resting in his sea cabin, and Burke saw to it that he was not disturbed. On their arrival at the atoll base on 30 October, Slew McCain in conformity with the rotation plan relieved Mitscher in command of the task force, and their staffs rotated with their chiefs.

Mitscher invited Burke to fly with him to Pearl Harbor in his seaplane, departing Ulithi in the morning of 1 November. The admiral had decided to leave before dawn so as to attract as little attention as possible. He told Burke when to be ready and admonished him to keep it under his hat. Burke did, but somehow the word got around in the late afternoon of 31 October that Bald Eagle would leave early the next morning.

At about 0400, Mitscher and Burke were making their way aft

along *Lexington*'s dimly lighted hangar deck when they made out many figures standing near the after brow.

"What the devil are all these people doing here?" asked Mitscher.

"I don't know, Admiral," replied Burke.

It was the pilots of *Lexington*'s air group, nearly all of them, about a hundred men, some in uniform, others in bathrobes and pajamas. Few of them had had a decent night's sleep in weeks. Nevertheless, when their commander, Hugh Winters, proposed to set his clock at 0330 and see the admiral off, the pilots asked him to get them up too.

Winters stepped forward. "Well, Admiral," he said, "they just wanted to be here when you left."

Bald Eagle, embarrassed, darted away quickly. The men watched him down the ramp. As he reached the barge, chugging alongside the wharf, they saw him take out a handkerchief.

IWO JIMA
AND THE
TOKYO RAIDS

THE OFFICERS OF Admiral Mitscher's staff accompanied or followed him to Pearl Harbor. From there most of the staffers proceeded directly to the United States for several weeks' leave. The admiral, Commodore Burke, Commander Flatley, and Captain W. A. "Gus" Read, staff administrative officer, remained at Pearl a few days for consultation and planning.

Burke found the officers at Cincpac headquarters eager to discuss the recent naval battle and especially Admiral Halsey's tactics. Most were critical of his leaving San Bernardino Strait unguarded when he knew a powerful enemy fleet was headed that way. Some ridiculed Halsey's leading the Third Fleet's six battleships 300 miles north and then 300 miles back south without their making contact with the enemy at the end of either run. While praising the Third Fleet's sinking of four carriers, they deplored the fact that ten of the enemy's thirteen accompanying surface ships returned safely to Japan and that all four Japanese battleships that debouched from San Bernardino Strait in the early morning of 25 October passed back through the strait the following evening and regained the South China Sea.

Burke would not let himself be lured into any criticism of his fleet commander's tactics. When courtesy required him to say something, he emphasized the destruction of the Japanese carriers. He refrained from pointing out, however, that three of them were sunk by a stripped-down Task Force 38, in which Admiral Halsey was not present and of which Admiral Mitscher was not in direct tactical command.

Admiral Nimitz invited Mitscher to attend a Cincpac morning conference, a courtesy he extended to all senior officers on or visiting Oahu. Mitscher accepted and brought along Burke and Flatley. Word that he was to be present attracted an unusually large officer turnout that morning. On his arrival, some who had not seen Mitscher before were surprised by his unprepossessing appearance, but all respected his record. In the months he had commanded the fast carriers he had been unfailingly aggressive. Not even Halsey was readier to take calculated risks. If he had made any mistakes, the officers present had not heard about them.

There was some feeling that Mitscher had been let down by Spruance in the Battle of the Philippine Sea and by Halsey in the more recent battle. Perhaps this morning he would seize the occasion to voice a few complaints. Burke expected nothing of the sort. That was not Mitscher's way. He could be ruthless in removing an incompetent subordinate, but he did not criticize a senior, particularly to his peers.

After Nimitz had opened the meeting with greetings and a few introductions, Captain Edwin Layton, Pacific Fleet intelligence officer, took the floor and presented the morning's intelligence summary. It was grim. Enemy suicide planes had so damaged Third Fleet carriers *Franklin* and *Belleau Wood* that they would have to be sent to major shipyards for repair. Inside Leyte Gulf, Japanese planes, not all kamikazes, had sunk one Seventh Fleet destroyer and damaged five others.

Admiral Nimitz then asked Mitscher if he would care to make a few remarks concerning the battle of 24–25 October. Some of the officers present doubtless expected an extended lecture on this most complicated of U.S. naval conflicts, but Burke and Flatley knew better. They had found that about the only subject on which Mitscher was ready to sound off at length was fishing. This time the admiral surprised even them. Within a few minutes he sketched, without comment, the main operations of the battle as he saw them, and that was all he had to say. He presented no facts the officers present had not already gleaned from the preliminary reports.

On leaving the conference room, Flatley, though well acquainted with Mitscher's exceptional reticence, could not resist remarking, "Admiral, you didn't tell them very much."

"They're all after my job," replied the admiral with a twinkle. "If I told them everything I knew, they'd be as smart as I am."

Later in the day, Admiral Mitscher and staffers sat with Admiral Spruance and some of his staff. The visitors were informed that the question of whether to invade Formosa or Luzon had been decided in favor of the latter—partly to rid the friendly Filipinos of the hated Japanese occupation forces and partly to profit by the guerrilla warfare the Filipinos were already waging against the conqueror, but mainly because enough invasion and support forces to wrest Formosa from its hostile population could not be assembled before mid-1945.

The Joint Chiefs had tentatively scheduled General MacArthur's invasion of Luzon for 20 December. If he could make that date, he should by the end of the year have a sufficiently firm foothold on the island to release both Task Force 38 and the Third Amphibious Force. Accordingly, Admiral Halsey could be expected to hand the Big Blue Fleet back to Admiral Spruance on or about 1 January 1945, at which time it would resume its title of Fifth Fleet. Admiral Mitscher would resume his command of the carrier groups, again designated Task Force 58, and Admiral Turner would take command of the Third Amphibious Force under its original name of Fifth Amphibious Force. The Joint Chiefs had assigned to the reassembled Fifth Fleet the tasks of occupying Iwo Jima, midway between Saipan and Tokyo, with a target date of 20 January 1945, and the much larger Okinawa, midway between Formosa and Japan, target date 1 March 1945.

Mitscher and his staffers were given charts and intelligence material on Iwo Jima to study in preparation for further meetings and discussions. They were provided with office space and the services of a yeoman for writing the official report of commander Task Force 38 on the recent battle, which newsmen were beginning to call the Battle of the Philippines or the Second Battle of the Philippine Sea and which later would be designated the Battle for Leyte Gulf. Burke had barely finished the official narrative for Mitscher's signature when dispatch orders arrived for him and Mitscher to report to the navy commander in chief, Admiral King, in Washington.

They departed promptly by seaplane for San Diego, taking along Read as a passenger and leaving Flatley behind to work on Fifth Fleet plans with Spruance's staff. It was an overnight flight, and because the plane had no bunks the travelers sat up talking and drinking coffee. About an hour out of San Diego, Mitscher asked Burke what he'd like on the flight to Washington. Burke said he hoped there would be someplace where they could catch a little shut-eye before bearding the lion in his den. Then, not entirely for laughs, he added, "I'd like some tomatoes and fresh milk and ice cream and a pretty girl to serve them."

"That's fine," said Mitscher. "I'll set it up for you. We'll have a plane waiting for you when we land, and you go on to Washington."

"Admiral," said Burke, taken aback, "what are you going to do?"

"I'm going fishing."

"But, Admiral, you're ordered back to Washington."

"No but anything—I'm going fishing."

Mitscher drew an envelope out of his pocket. "Here is a sealed envelope," he said, "and if, in your judgment, you have to know where I am, it's in here, but don't open it unless you have to know."

"What do I tell Admiral King?"

"Tell him the truth—I've gone fishing someplace, you don't know where."

They had been descending for some time. As the plane touched ground they shook hands in farewell, and Burke began collecting his gear. Sure enough, when they came to a stop there was another plane all warmed up waiting nearby. With his gear Burke dashed across and boarded it. The lieutenant who greeted him seemed not at all surprised that he was alone. After a "Welcome aboard, Commodore," the young man took his suitcase and conducted him to a bunk, prepared and waiting. Burke, gratefully removing his jacket, collar, and tie, flopped down on the bunk and was asleep by the time the plane was airborne.

The transcontinental flight in this plane of vintage 1944 took nearly ten hours. Before it was halfway to Washington, Burke was awakened by someone gently shaking his shoulder. Opening his eyes, he saw that he had been aroused by a pretty Wave holding a tray.

"I've brought your tomatoes and milk, sir," she said. The ice cream came later. Burke wondered when and how the dickens Mitscher had managed to make such arrangements.

Arleigh approached his first Admiral King interview with curiosity, awe, and trepidation. The commander in chief had a reputation for intellect and competence but also for arrogance and severity. Burke had heard him called everything from a sundowner* to a

---

*Sundowner: An extremely strict naval officer, inclined to be sadistic in enforcement of regulations.

hardheaded, coldhearted son of a bitch. Subordinates, including flag officers, were known to emerge both pale and sweating after a session with the big boss. Burke had a theory that King made a practice of putting his interviewees on the defensive as a means of eliciting information without waste of time. A man on the defensive has to defend things rapidly and concisely.

When Arleigh reported to Cominch headquarters in the Main Navy building on Constitution Avenue, his uneasiness was heightened by the reaction of King's aide, Captain McDill, to Mitscher's absence. Informed that commander Task Force 38 had ignored the boss's summons, McDill uttered a soft, shocked whistle. Then, leading the way to King's office, he implied darkly that Burke himself was in for a rough time.

As Burke entered the inner sanctum, the commander in chief rose from his desk. Tall, his lean frame made him seem taller than he was. High-domed, with aquiline nose and piercing eyes, he looked formidable. He extended a hand to shake, then motioned Arleigh to a seat. Burke sat down on the edge of the chair.

King asked, "Where's Admiral Mitscher?"

"He's gone fishing, sir."

"Good," said the commander in chief. "Mitscher's got sense." Burke was dumbfounded. This was not at all the sort of reaction he had been led to expect.

After a couple of general questions, King picked up from his desk a copy of commander Task Force 58's operation order for the Marianas invasion. Burke recognized it and felt more at ease. If King, looking for something to quibble about, had been obliged to dig up an order written five months earlier, Task Force 38/58 must have a pretty clean record. Besides, this was a document Burke felt he could defend. Admirals Mitscher and Spruance, who rarely read op orders, had finally read this one with approval.

"Did you write this op order?" asked King.

Burke had just about sized up the admiral's style. He decided to have some fun. "Admiral Mitscher signed that op order," he said.

"I said, did you write this op order?" repeated King, his voice rising.

"You are holding Admiral Mitscher's op order," replied Burke, keeping a straight face.

"Dammit," roared King. "I asked you if *you* wrote it."

"Yes, sir."

"Well, just look at this thing. It's unseemly, it's not in proper form, it doesn't use correct naval terminology, and look at these cartoons. They have no place in an operation order!"

"But it's short, Admiral."

"I'll hand you that—but it's no way to write an operation order."

"Have you read it—and did you understand it?"

"Yes, I did, but . . ."

"Did you read that long, detailed op order that Admiral Turner issued to the amphibious force?"

"No."

"That's how it is, Admiral. Nobody can wade through those wordy, repetitious orders that officers used to write, and some still do. Everybody could take time to read this one."

King, frowning, pondered this observation a few moments. "Okay," he said at last. "Let it go, let it go." Then, relaxing his features slightly, he added, "Why don't you take some leave?"

"I'd like to," Burke said.

"Fine. You go home."

Before he left the Navy Department, Burke learned that on Mitscher's recommendation, strongly seconded by King, he was being awarded a Gold Star in lieu of a second Legion of Merit.

Burke at last had met the commander in chief, and he liked what he found—an officer intolerant of stupidity, inefficiency, and laziness but fair, reasonable, and prompt to recognize and reward achievement. Henceforth anyone calling the Cominch insulting names in Arleigh's presence could expect anything from a polite correction to a sharp dressing-down.

His official business completed, Arleigh hastened to join Bobbie. They had been apart now nearly two years, during which they had corresponded almost daily. They had eagerly looked forward to being together again for a few weeks of happy union and undisturbed domesticity.

Arleigh's professional duties permitted them no such respite. On 7 November he was called to the Navy Department to give a talk to officers concerning lessons learned from what was by then generally called the Second Battle of the Philippine Sea. From Secretary of the Navy James Forrestal came a letter saying that Vice Admiral Aubrey Fitch, deputy chief of naval operations for air, would represent Forrestal at a 16 November luncheon in Boston of the New England Council, at which the governors of the New England states would be present. "I wonder," the secretary wrote, "if you would be good enough to accompany Admiral Fitch and tell the governors and the other guests very briefly some of your impressions and experiences in the Pacific War."

Burke, taking the secretary's request as an order, obediently went to Boston, taking Bobbie with him. He had decided to confine his speech to remarks about the Second Battle of the Philippine Sea. At the Pearl Harbor conference, Mitscher had covered that time-demanding subject in a matter of minutes. At Boston, Burke erred in the opposite direction. "That was the most horrible speech I've ever made." he said afterward. "First, it was an hour and a half long, I think. I didn't know how to stop. I knew that something was wrong. I bored the hell out of them."

Burke's verdict on his speech is refuted by a letter from the executive vice president of the New England Council. It said in part, "You must have realized from the close attention and warm response of your audience that your talk was a great success." Arleigh was not, however, invited to make any more speeches during his stateside leave.

On 20 November, Burke was attached to the Cominch staff for temporary duty. With no definite tasks assigned, he made it his business to visit around the Navy Department promoting closer and more dependable liaison between operations and intelligence in Washington and the fleets in the Pacific. One particularly worrisome subject was weather. Since weather usually travels from west to east, it was important that the Pacific fleets be in early receipt of information from the weather-reporting network of the military Sino-American Cooperative Organization (SACO), based mainly on Chungking, China.

Burke persuaded the authorities to give the Big Blue Fleet access to the code and radio frequency that would enable it to read the SACO weather messages directly instead of waiting for them to pass through several commands in the United States for recording and interpretation. By means he never revealed, he also made direct contact with Commodore Milton Miles, senior American officer with SACO, who contrived to send Arleigh private weather information concealed in the padding at the ends of encoded messages.

In mid-December, Commodore Burke was back at Pearl Harbor with other Task Force 58 staff members deeply involved in planning. Their mission was to spell out in detail the means of covering and supporting the assaults on Iwo Jima and Okinawa. There would be insufficient time between these operations to permit detailed planning for the latter.

Iwo in American hands would in several ways assist Saipan-based
B-29s that had begun raiding the Tokyo area. Weight of fuel for the
3,000-mile round trip limited their bomb loads to 30 percent of
capacity, and since the distance was too great for fighter-plane escort, they had to make fuel-consuming climbs to about 28,000 feet,
an altitude that precluded precision bombing. Moreover, enemy
bases, including Iwo Jima, in the Bonin and Volcano islands between Saipan and Japan could warn Tokyo of the B-29s' approach
and send up fighters to attack them going and returning.

U.S. possession of Iwo would enable aircraft based there to end
this nuisance and also provide fighter escort for the big bombers.
Moreover, the island could serve as a refueling station, a refuge for
damaged aircraft, and an air-sea rescue base.

While awaiting its capture, the Marianas-based XXI Bomber
Command of B-29s appealed to Cincpac for seaborne fighter support. Nimitz passed the request to Halsey, who would gladly have
taken his Third Fleet to the shores of Japan and helped blast Tokyo,
but MacArthur remained desperate for carrier support. Hampered
by bad weather and kamikazes, the general had to postpone his
invasion of Luzon to 9 January 1945, which required delaying the
next two operations a full month—Iwo Jima to 19 February,
Okinawa to 1 April.

In seeking to repulse MacArthur's January landing in Luzon's
Lingayan Gulf, the enemy's kamikaze tactics reached a sort of grim
climax. While foul weather at first thwarted support by Third Fleet
carrier aircraft, the suicide planes, operating under any sort of conditions, damaged forty-three Allied ships, eighteen seriously, and
sank five. One cruiser was hit by five planes. In ten days the kamikazes killed 738 men and wounded nearly 1,400.

The skies at length cleared, whereupon Task Force 38 so blan-
keted the Luzon airfields that few enemy planes arrived over Lingayan Gulf, and most of these were shot down. Then, to seal off the
Philippines from Japan, Halsey took the task force north and raided
Formosa and the Ryukyus.

The kamikaze phenomenon bewildered the Americans. Combat
by deliberate suicide was utterly alien to their psychology. The U.S.
fighting man, however brave, seldom undertook a mission that did
not promise at least an outside chance of survival. Japanese pilots,
on the contrary, all obviously volunteers, were hurling themselves
by the hundreds to certain death. The Americans found the new
tactics frustrating as well as perplexing. Just when they had reduced

Japanese air power to little more than a nuisance, suddenly it flared up as the principal menace. At Lingayen Gulf virtually all Japanese resistance had come from Luzon airfields, there having been no fleet opposition.

Burke and his planners at Pearl Harbor concluded that the new menace required the carrier force to take a leaf out of Halsey's book. Instead of standing off Iwo Jima during the pre-assault bombardment, it should approach the coast of Japan and attack the Tokyo airfields, from which suicide strikes on the landing forces would most likely originate. This decision accorded with the views of Admiral Nimitz, who for several months had been seeking an opportunity for a carrier raid on the Japanese capital. The planners recognized that in thus shielding the amphibious force, Task Force 58 would be exposing itself to suicide attack. To minimize this risk, they counted on surprise and on heavily increasing the number of fighter planes in proportion to bombers.

Burke kept the planning staff at work well into each evening, seven days a week, including Christmas. He had set the end of 1944 as the deadline for completion of their task. But when New Year's Eve arrived, there was still work to do. Flatley shook his head. Burke looked at his weary assistants. "Aw, hell," he said at last, "go out and have fun tonight. Then finish up."

Soon after New Year's Day, Admiral Mitscher arrived at Pearl, and Burke and his staff subordinates handed him an elegant set of plans. There followed several days more of conferences, adjusting the task force plan to fleet and amphibious force plans. As usual, Burke had kept the carrier force op plan short and general. It delegated as much authority as practical. Also as usual, Admiral Turner's plan for the amphibious force, dictated largely by himself, was as fat as a New York telephone book.

Kelly Turner had the most inventive and retentive mind of any flag officer in the navy. His intelligence and energy had so impressed Spruance that on his appointment to command the Fifth Fleet he at once asked for Turner to head his amphibious force. In that capacity Kelly, driving himself and others mercilessly, had planned and conducted his series of brilliant amphibious assaults, from the Gilberts to the Marianas.

Turner lacked only the ability to delegate authority. Supremely assured of his own competence, he planned every phase of his operations, neither expecting nor wanting advice from anybody. He tried to foresee and provide for every contingency. His subordinates, not encouraged to think for themselves, were sometimes at a loss when confronted with the unexpected. To take up the resulting slack, Kelly stormed about, sweating and swearing. His hot-tempered impatience, fired by intemperate drinking and monumental hangovers, had earned him the nickname Terrible Turner.

Burke pored over Turner's voluminous, detailed Okinawa op plan with both admiration and distaste. He was fascinated by its insights and ingenuity, offended by its lack of confidence in subordi-

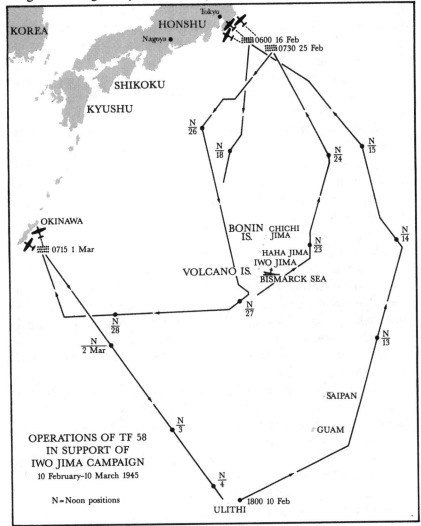

Operations of Task Force 58 in Support
of the Iwo Jima Campaign

nates—the attribute of *faith* that Arleigh had preached during his Solomons campaigns.

One item in the plan brought old destroyerman Burke up short. It called for stationing a ring of early-warning, fighter-director picket destroyers around Okinawa, a single destroyer at each station. Oncoming kamikazes, nerves aquiver in the face of death, would see one of these ships first, and probably many of the pilots would strike at once instead of searching out more profitable targets. The picket destroyers, so threatened, should not be solitary, Burke believed, but operate in division strength at each station. A single ship could not possibly shoot down a simultaneous attack of planes coming in from several directions, and it might need help in repulsing even a one-plane attack.

Burke pointed out to Mitscher the order to station single picket destroyers. "You know," he said, "I think Admiral Turner's wrong on this."

"Well," said Mitscher, "go over and see Admiral Turner and tell him about it."

Burke went over to where Turner was working in a nearby building and suggested to him that he station the destroyer pickets by divisions. The admiral listened with obvious impatience, then replied coldly, "I know about amphibious warfare."

"Yes, sir, I know you do," said Burke, "but one destroyer can't handle a large air attack. A division can do so most of the time."

Turner turned back to his work, as if paying no further attention. Burke, disregarding the cold shoulder, persisted. "We've got some destroyers that we could put up there for a little while," he said, "if we could get them back again when we need them. They can help, but only if you put them on stations in divisions."

The offer caught Turner's attention. "We want the destroyers, all right," he said. "I need them very badly. Send the destroyers over to us, and we will run them the way we think they should be run."

Burke murmured a polite noncommittal farewell and left. "Nothing doing," he said to himself. He told Mitscher he hadn't got to first base with Admiral Turner.

"You've done what you can do," said Mitscher. "If he doesn't want them he doesn't want them."

"Well," replied Arleigh, "he'll lose his ships."

At last the various plans were made to mesh. Where commanders could not agree, Admiral Nimitz made the decision. He also gave the plans his final review and approval.

On 14 January, Admiral Spruance and his staff left Pearl Harbor
in *Indianapolis* and headed for Ulithi, where they arrived on the
morning of the 25th. That afternoon *New Jersey* entered Ulithi
lagoon with Admiral Halsey on board. Other ships of Task Force
38, which had completed its support of the Luzon invasion, soon
followed. Two days later, without ceremony, Spruance took over
command of the Big Blue Fleet. Mitscher, with Burke and other staff
members, arrived at Ulithi by plane on January 30 and relieved
McCain on that date.

Spruance and Mitscher had decided not to go at once into action
but to give the ships' crews, exhausted after their exertions under
Halsey, a few days of rest and relaxation at Ulithi. It was no longer
the undeveloped atoll the Americans had taken in September. Now
boasting an airstrip and repair and logistic facilities, it had succeeded
Eniwetok as the Big Blue Fleet's advanced base. The northernmost
island, Mogmog, was the atoll's recreation center. No Riviera or
Waikiki, it was nevertheless joyfully invaded by the fleet's sailors
and aviators, who had been at sea too long and faced death too often.
Mogmog had a swimming beach, horseshoe pitches, basketball
courts, baseball diamonds, even a football field. Soft drinks were to
be had, enlisted men were allowed two bottles of beer a day, and for
officers there was a bar dispensing Scotch or bourbon for twenty
cents a shot.

While the crews were relaxing on Mogmog, the senior officers,
including Burke, were pondering bad news about Iwo Jima. When
Spruance first proposed invading the island, he and Nimitz had
anticipated no special difficulties for their forces, which so far had
not been repulsed from any beachhead. Subsequently photorecon-
naissance had made them apprehensive. It appeared that this eight-
square-mile heap of lava and volcanic ash might be rendered
extraordinarily defensible. B-24s from the Marianas had been raiding
Iwo since August, and beginning in early December they bombed
the island daily. Five times, cruiser-destroyer groups had approached and bombarded its defenses. Through it all, the garrison
had maintained two airfields and begun construction on a third. By
mid-January 1945, aerial photographs showed more than 700 major
defense installations, and there were doubtless many others well
hidden.

General Holland Smith, after studying the photographs, som-
berly predicted that taking Iwo would cost 20,000 American casualties. Admiral Spruance was beginning to wonder if capture of the

island would be worth the cost, but Major General Curtis LeMay, commander of the XXI Bomber Command and its B-29s, assured him it would. "Without Iwo Jima," he said, "I couldn't bomb Japan effectively."

Task Force 58, Tokyo-bound, sortied from Ulithi on 10 February and, taking an indirect route to the target, began to refuel a hundred miles east of Saipan. As planned, it now carried more than twice as many fighter planes as dive-bombers or torpedo bombers. Because half the newly arrived fighter pilots, though superbly trained, were entering combat for the first time, Burke, working with other staffers and battle-experienced aviators, prepared a paper of tactical advice, "Air Combat Notes for Pilots," to be posted in every ready room. It stressed the importance of teamwork, which inexperienced flyers tended to neglect. Mitscher read the paper with approval and inserted a stirring forecast. The forthcoming operation, he predicted, would be "the greatest air victory of the war for carrier aviation."

Because Task Force 58's mission was to launch air raids, Mitscher had the tactical command, but Burke, having mastered his boss's style, usually conducted operations, with Mitscher's approval. Burke took extensive measures to achieve surprise. He steered a course 500 miles east of Iwo Jima. Though this was beyond any likely air scouting from the Bonin and Volcano islands, he had taken the precaution of requesting aircraft from the Marianas to patrol for snoopers. The ships' long-range radio transmitters had maintained silence from the start. On 15 February, the eve of the strike, Burke ordered radar turned off and even TBS silenced. He detached five destroyers and sent them ahead as a scouting line to sink picket boats and warn of air and surface threats. Pacific Fleet submarines were already off Japan on a similar mission.

Thanks to Burke's efforts in the Pentagon, Task Force 58 now had regular and direct weather reports from China. Reports came in also from submarines and B-29s near Tokyo. To Burke's disgust, radio receivers in Mitscher's flagship, carrier *Bunker Hill,* functioned so poorly that he had to rely almost entirely on Spruance's meteorologists to interpret the reports. Their forecasts, however, enabled him to approach Japan undetected under a weather front. In the morning of the 15th, rain drenched the carrier decks, but the ocean was calm. Spruance told Mitscher he expected reasonably good weather over Tokyo the next day.

Mitscher had been in these seas before, in carrier *Hornet* bringing

Doolittle's long-range army B-25s for the April 1942 raid on Tokyo. At that time, when 620 miles from the coast of Japan, the American carrier force, daring to approach no closer, launched its planes toward Tokyo and turned away, speeding east out of danger. Now in early 1945, Task Force 58 had passed the 620-mile mark and was still heading toward Japan, confident of its ability to defend itself against anything the enemy could send.

During the day the weather worsened, and by nightfall a strong northeast wind was building mountainous waves. Mitscher, however, was not to be deterred from his plan. At 1900 on Burke's orders the force began its high-speed run-in toward launching position, plowing its way through heavy seas and rain mixed with snow. At dawn the 116 ships of Task Force 58 were 60 miles off the coast of Japan, 125 miles from Tokyo. Despite continuing rain and heavy overcast, Burke launched the attack. Fleet radio operators picked up routine radio broadcasts from Radio Tokyo, indicating the Japanese were unaware a hostile fleet was in their home waters. At the time predicted for the first wave of U.S. planes to cross the coast, Radio Tokyo suddenly went silent.

At the same time, at Iwo Jima, 600 miles to the south, the gunnery ships, jeep carriers, and support ships of the expeditionary force, having approached through the night, opened the pre-assault bombardment. Not far behind was the main body, bringing a three-division marine landing force and Vice Admiral Kelly Turner, who would take personal command of the assault. The bombing of Tokyo and the bombardment of Iwo were timed to coincide, so that neither alerted the enemy against the other.

Up north, the first of the U.S. carrier aircraft arriving over Japan were attacked by about a hundred fighters, nearly half of which the Americans shot down. That was the only major attempt by the Japanese to defend their capital. Like the Americans, they were hampered by low overcast and rain, but some of the enemy fighters were obviously evading combat, thus verifying Burke's hint to the pilots that "he is probably more afraid of you than you are of him." The enemy's apparent reluctance tempted some of the green Hellcat pilots to break formation to seek dogfights. Several Americans who thus rejected teamwork for individual combat were shot down.

A major U.S. objective was destruction of aircraft-engine factories, but because of cloud cover the only one the bombers found and attacked on 16 February was the Nakajima Aircraft Company 40 miles northwest of Tokyo, which the B-29s had bombed the preceding week with meager results. For the most part, the American planes spent the day cruising over the city and surrounding airfields, hitting whatever targets they could find while encountering little opposition from gunfire or interceptors. At sunset, Burke, after recovering all the task force's daytime planes, sent a sweep of night fighters over the airfields. Thereafter the force cruised unmolested through the night off the Japanese coast.

On the 17th, despite continuing miserable weather, Burke resumed launching before dawn. Mitscher's bombers damaged three aircraft frame and engine factories on the outskirts of Tokyo and sank several ships in Tokyo Bay, the biggest being a 10,600-ton freighter. When Spruance's meteorologists predicted even worsening weather, commander Fifth Fleet, judging that Mitscher was not likely to call off the attacks on his own, decided to intervene. He explained to a staffer, "No subordinate likes to tell his boss that he is afraid to do something."

To Mitscher, Spruance signaled that continued bad weather "made launching of further sweeps inadvisable." Burke directed strikes already airborne to complete their missions but launched no more strikes that day. In the late afternoon, when all the U.S. raiders had been recovered, Task Force 58, according to plan, turned bows southward toward Iwo Jima.

Carrier aircraft had not achieved the great victory Mitscher had predicted, but despite wretched weather conditions they had done very well, having damaged four aircraft plants, sunk a number of ships and small craft, and destroyed a great many enemy aircraft. The claim was 332 planes shot down and 177 destroyed on the ground. The task force lost 49 planes in combat. As with the 1942 raid on Tokyo, however, the most important outcome was the contrasting effect on Japanese and American morale. Under banner headlines the *New York Times* called the 1945 attack "the most daring operation of the Pacific war to date."

Spruance flashed a message of praise and congratulations to the force, and he asked Mitscher what he recommended doing after supporting the American landing on Iwo. Mitscher proposed raiding Tokyo again, then Okinawa. "Approved," Spruance replied. "Make your plans accordingly."

Southbound, Task Force 58 in the night of 17–18 February crossed the line of Japanese picket boats it had avoided two nights earlier by advancing on Tokyo from the southeast. Task force destroyers now sank four of the boats, one of which fought back, killing three

American sailors with gunfire. In the following afternoon, while passing Chichi Jima and Haha Jima, Burke had one of the carrier task groups send fighter sweeps and strikes that destroyed a number of small craft and cratered the Chichi Jima airfield.

Spruance next detached from Task Force 58 two light cruisers and two new battleships armed with bombardment ammunition and with them headed in *Indianapolis* for Iwo, where they joined the bombardment force of old battleships, escort carriers, cruisers, and destroyers. While two of the carrier task groups continued southward for a rendezvous with oilers, the other three, including Mitscher's *Bunker Hill,* took station 65 miles northwest of Iwo Jima to provide additional air support for the landings, scheduled for the next morning.

Pre-H-hour bombardment of Iwo Jima, the heaviest of World War II, began at 0640 on 19 February. For the first eighty-five minutes, fire was deliberate, aimed at selected targets. Then at 0805 the naval guns lifted their fire to permit air strikes from the carrier task groups to the northwest.

Down from 10,000 feet swept the first strike, seventy-two Corsair and Hellcat fighters and Dauntless dive-bombers, four abreast, firing rockets and machine guns and hurling bombs at the landing beaches, at the armed ridge above the beaches, at the heavily fortified high ground to the north, and at Mount Suribachi, a dormant volcano, to the south.

As the first-strike planes headed back to their carriers to refuel and rearm, in roared the second, forty-eight additional fighters, including twenty-four marine-piloted Corsairs. Dropping napalm and firing rockets and machine-gun bursts, they came in low, very nearly obeying their flight leader's order: "Go in and scrape your bellies on the beach."

At 0825 the bombardment ships resumed fire, this time at an immensely increased pace. In the next half hour they hurled more than 8,000 shells into the beach area. They then lifted fire again so that the returning fighter planes of the second strike could strafe the beaches. As the pilots turned away, they could see the sixty-eight landing craft of the first assault wave approaching the shore in an orderly line abreast as if on parade.

On board *Bunker Hill,* Mitscher with Burke and other staffers tried to follow progress of the assault through radio intercepts. They learned that as the orderly line touched the beach it broke up in confusion. The shore, rising steeply from the sea, was composed of soft volcanic ash, affording such poor traction that few of the amphibious landing craft were able to crawl up onto the slope. Succeeding waves could not be beached at all, and many had their screws damaged or their bottoms stove in by the wreckage of earlier arrivals.

The marine landing force, intending to go ashore on the run, was slowed as feet sank into the ash. At first the invaders could advance only by crawling up a series of terraces under heavy fire. By nightfall some 30,000 troops had landed, but more than 2,400 were casualties, and the beachhead was far short of the projected phase line—circumstances that confirmed General Holland Smith's prediction that Iwo Jima would be no pushover.

Bombs dropped by planes from the Task Force 58 carriers and from the escort carriers nearer Iwo, together with continued heavy bombardment from the gunnery ships, played an indispensable part in the conquest of the island. The Japanese commandant radioed Tokyo that his men could defend against the three divisions of U.S. marines ashore but not against the marines supported by bombardment from aircraft and warships. There were, however, many well-concealed Japanese strongpoints that neither bombs nor shells could reach. These had to be taken one at a time by infantry with rifles, machine guns, flamethrowers, and close-range tank support.

Planes from Japan could readily reach Iwo Jima by flying down the Bonins and refueling at one or more of the islands en route. At dusk on D-day some twelve or fifteen enemy aircraft approaching from the north sighted Task Force 58 to their right and turned to attack. Two of the planes were shot down by antiaircraft gunfire, and the rest were chased away by fighters from the night carrier group. This was Task Group 58.5, consisting of the venerable carriers *Saratoga* and *Enterprise* and their escorts. It provided Iwo and the amphibious force with dawn and dusk combat air patrol, night fighter cover, and night observers for naval gunfire.

On 21 February, on orders from Spruance, Mitscher split Task Group 58.5, retaining *Enterprise* with three cruisers and seven destroyers while sending *Saratoga* and three destroyers in closer to Iwo. Except for his early underrating of Burke, sending in old "Sara" too lightly protected was possibly Mitscher's only serious mistake of the war. As ill fortune would have it, the Japanese chose that evening to send to Iwo their only major and last kamikaze attack of the campaign, and the pilots sighted *Saratoga* while most of her fighters were on dusk CAP duty over the amphibious force.

Six of the suicide planes dived on *Saratoga* out of a cloud. Three slammed blazing into the carrier, one struck her with a bomb, and one splashed. She suffered 123 men killed and 192 wounded and lost forty-two planes and was out of action for the rest of the war, undergoing extensive repairs. That same evening the kamikazes sank escort carrier *Bismarck Sea,* killing 218 of her ship's company, and damaged two other ships.

Mitscher now ordered *Enterprise* with her escorts to take *Saratoga*'s place in close night support, thereby depriving Task Force 58 of night fighter cover. Meanwhile, the other groups of the force had reunited. *Indianapolis* with Admiral Spruance on board joined on 23 February, and that evening, after refueling, the reassembled task force began another high-speed run toward Tokyo to finish the task that had been curtailed by bad weather the preceding week.

This time Spruance's meteorologists, again basing their estimates on reports from Chungking, again predicted an impending period of fair weather over Tokyo, but when Task Force 58 arrived off Japan at dawn on the 25th, it found the weather quite as bad as it had been on the 16th. Burke began to wonder if he had done the fleet a service by arranging for direct reports from Commodore Miles at SACO.

Despite rain with heavy overcast and low ceiling, Burke at 0715 launched first sweeps against Tokyo. Most strikes hit secondary targets or were based on mere estimates regarding location of such major targets as aircraft plants. Such guesswork was bound to result in hits on nonmilitary targets, including homes, schools, and hospitals. This was a form of warfare to which Spruance and most other naval officers strongly objected.

Worsening weather convinced Mitscher around noon to cancel all further operations for the day. Seeking better operating conditions, he headed for Nagoya, a port and manufacturing center 170 miles west of Tokyo and Japan's third-largest city. High winds and heavy seas so slowed the task force, however, that it could not reach the Nagoya area in time for an early-morning launching; so Mitscher terminated the operation, and Task Force 58 headed back south to its refueling area west of Iwo Jima.

Fueling completed, Task Force 58 again split. *Indianapolis* with Spruance and his staff on board and accompanied by destroyer escorts headed east to rejoin the amphibious force off Iwo. Task

Group 58.4 headed south to Ulithi, while the other three groups headed west toward the Ryukyus.

The three groups arrived off Okinawa in the early morning of 1 March in perfect weather. The carrier planes spent the day bombing and strafing likely targets throughout the 60-mile-long, 465-square-mile island and, more important, thoroughly photographing it and nearby smaller islands. As soon as the carriers had recovered their planes that evening, the task groups shaped course for Ulithi.

No air opposition had developed over the Okinawa area that day, and none developed against U.S. forces in the Iwo Jima area after the attacks of 21 February. Had Japan used up all its suicidally inclined pilots? Whatever the cause, this lack of Japanese air activity seemed a good omen for the forthcoming Okinawa campaign.

The three task groups entered Ulithi lagoon on 4 March. The next day, Spruance in *Indianapolis* left Iwo Jima and headed for Ulithi, followed on the 9th by *Enterprise* and her escorts. Also on the 9th, Turner and staff headed for Guam, leaving Rear Admiral Harry Hill in command of the small naval force remaining at Iwo.

Major General Harry Schmidt, commanding the marines on Iwo Jima, declared the island secured on 16 March and the operation completed ten days later. Of the Japanese garrison of 21,000 elite troops, all but 200 prisoners of war had been killed. For the Americans it was a costly victory won by an agonizing, month-long, yard-by-yard advance. Their casualties outnumbered losses among the defenders; on the island and in the fleet, 19,000 Americans were wounded and nearly 7,000 were killed or died of wounds.

Admiral Spruance had proposed and undertaken the assault on Iwo mainly to provide a base for fighters to escort the B-29s so they could eliminate military targets by daytime precision bombing from low altitude. In fact, however, by the time the island was conquered, the B-29s no longer required escorts. General LeMay had learned the effectiveness of night raids with incendiary bombs. On the night of 25 February, following the morning when Mitscher off Tokyo had been frustrated by foul weather, 200 B-29s soared over the city dropping firebombs indiscriminately through the clouds and setting fire to the highly inflammable Japanese houses. They thus in one night burned out a square mile of the enemy capital.

Encouraged by this result, LeMay tried it on a larger scale. On the night of 9 March more than 300 B-29s, unaccompanied by fighters, dropped over 2,000 tons of firebombs on Tokyo from low altitude. They thus burned out nearly 16 square miles of the city, incinerating 83,000 men, women, and children and burning or otherwise injuring 14,000 others. This was clearly not the outcome Admiral Spruance had in mind.

Iwo Jima did, however, prove valuable as a haven for planes damaged or short of fuel. By the end of the war, 2,400 B-29s, with crews numbering nearly 27,000, made emergency landings on the island. Experience preceding the conquest of Iwo suggests that some of these planes could have reached the Marianas and that, if forced down, a good many of the crews would have been rescued. But availability of the emergency landing fields added to the peace of mind of the army aviators. Many naval and marine officers, however, must have wondered if it was worth the sacrifice of so many brave, well-trained sailors and marines.

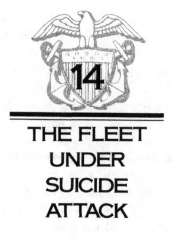

THE FLEET
UNDER
SUICIDE
ATTACK

THE MID-1944 U.S. conquest of Saipan made Japan's defeat inevitable, but the Japanese had demonstrated on a dozen isolated islands that certainty of defeat did not make them surrender. American leaders therefore weighed other means of inducing them to lay down their arms.

The army ground forces' view was that occupation of the home islands could break the Japanese will to resist. In the past, nations capitulated after invaders had occupied a substantial portion of their territory, usually including the capital. But when the Americans were completing their conquest of Saipan, even Japanese civilians living on that island committed suicide in wholesale numbers rather than surrender. When Iwo Jima was otherwise completely in U.S. hands, surviving Japanese soldiers preferred to await death in caves rather than yield to promises of humane treatment. The inference was that invasion and occupation of Japan would prove an extraordinarily prolonged and bloody operation, to be undertaken only as a last resort.

The navy proposed defeating Japan by means of blockade. An island nation, overpopulated and lacking internal resources for carrying on modern warfare, it was absolutely dependent upon imports. The U.S. reconquest of Luzon had already blocked the "oil line," the principal route for materials flowing north from the Southern Resources Area. Further disruption of Japan's communications, including aerial mining of its harbors, would at length leave the Japanese starving and incapable of further resistance.

The army air forces operated in the belief that Japan could be defeated by continuous bombing of its cities and industries until it lacked the will and means to make war. In February 1945, General LeMay learned of a possible new dimension for his bombing plan when a U.S. Navy commander arrived in the Marianas as an emissary from the Joint Chiefs of Staff to inform him, Admiral Nimitz, and a few other officers that an atomic bomb was under development, expected to have an energy yield equivalent to about 20,000 tons of TNT, enough to destroy an entire city. The bomb, they were informed, should be available in the Pacific theater about 1 August.

The recipients of this startling news, men accustomed to explosives that blasted in accordance with principles they understood, received the message with some skepticism. "Young man," said Nimitz, "this is very interesting, but August is a long time from now, and in the meantime I have a war to fight."

When Admiral King at last faced the fact that an early American conquest of Formosa was out of the question, he and the other Joint Chiefs and their immediate subordinates were willing to accept Spruance's suggestion that Okinawa would be the appropriate objective to follow Iwo Jima. Leaders of each of the armed services saw the proposed occupation as forwarding their particular goals. The army advocated use of Okinawa as a staging base for what General MacArthur considered the inevitable invasion of Japan. The army air forces wanted airfields from which their planes could reach and ignite more Japanese cities. Spruance wanted Okinawa as a base from which U.S. ships and planes could tighten the blockade by interdicting the last lines of communication into Japan. To that end, he proposed seizing points on the China coast and entry into the Sea of Japan as steps toward surrounding and completely isolating the Japanese home islands.

The objectives of the services were not mutually exclusive, nor was each objective fully supported within its originating service. Since the navy and air forces would necessarily be heavily involved in an invasion of Japan, they joined the army ground forces in planning for Operation Olympic, the proposed invasion of the southern Japanese island of Kyushu, scheduled for 1 November 1945, and Operation Coronet, the invasion of the main island of Honshu with a drive on Tokyo, tentatively scheduled for the following March.

The air forces cooperated with the navy's blockade by sending B-29s to sow mines in Japanese harbors and other waterways. Spruance, while continuing to deplore the saturation bombing of cities, saw Okinawa as a valuable base from which to bomb military targets in Japan. Halsey applauded all the proposed campaigns but one—capture of bases on the China coast. He thought that would lead to an endless series of peripheral operations his war-weary country would not stand for. Not yet informed about the atomic bomb, he believed that if the blockade, the occupation of Okinawa, and the bombing of their cities did not drive the Japanese to their knees, there was no alternative to Operations Olympic and Coronet.

While their seniors were debating such high strategic matters, Mitscher, Burke, and Flatley were planning tactics—mainly what to do about the kamikazes. Thus far none of the three had observed a suicide plane in action, but what they had heard from men who had been under kamikaze attack was chilling. The fact that there had been no enemy air activity over Iwo Jima after 21 February and none at all during the recent raids on Okinawa could not be accepted as evidence that the danger had ended or even abated.

One exercise Mitscher ordered for Task Force 58 was plenty of gunnery practice. His flagship, *Bunker Hill,* in her turn moved out to the gunnery range for a day's workout. Because this was not a danger area, Mitscher abandoned his usual practice of having his meals brought on a tray to the bridge and joined his staff in the gallery-deck flag mess.

While Mitscher and staff were at lunch, the *Bunker Hill* gunners took aim at a low-flying target and opened up with 5-inch guns directly across the flight deck. The roar was earsplitting and jolted flag mess, just below. The dishes went up into the air and fell back on table and deck chipped and broken. All the officers, including Mitscher, leaped to their feet.

"For Christ's sake," said one, "can't they wait until we have lunch?"

"I don't give a damn what they do," replied Mitscher, "so long as they learn how to shoot."

On 9 March, *Indianapolis* arrived at Ulithi from Iwo Jima, and Spruance promptly called a council. Mitscher went over with Burke and Flatley. Admiral Lee arrived with some of his staff. All hands realized that the forthcoming operation was to be the most powerful

Midshipman Arleigh Burke as a plebe (1920). Burke, the grandson of a Swedish immigrant, grew up on a hardscrabble farm at the foot of the Rocky Mountains. He went to the Naval Academy for a free education. In spite of his poor academic background, he graduated respectably in the top 20 percent of his class.

Burke's first duty as ensign was on board battleship *Arizona*. There were fun and games on board the old battlewagon, such as racing a peanut by blowing on it. He remained with *Arizona* five years, an exceptionally long tour, but the ship's successive commanding officers held on to him because of his expertise, particularly in gunnery. When at last eager-beaver Burke was relieved, one of his shipmates remarked, "Arleigh Burke will be dead before he's fifty, or he'll be chief of naval operations."

Burke developed an interest in the new technique of using photography to determine the accuracy of ships' guns. In 1934–35 he was officer-in-charge of the Battle Force camera party, here shown on board a heavy cruiser.

At the Naval Academy, Arleigh Burke had acquired a wife, Roberta, known as Bobbie. They married on his graduation day. During the next few years, they rented a series of apartments in the West Coast ports out of which Arleigh operated and also got themselves a pet dog. Named Faffin, a Great Dane, he was a curious choice for five-foot two-inch Bobbie, necessarily his chief custodian. The Burkes even acquired two more Great Danes, and Bobbie controlled the big dogs as deftly as she dealt with Arleigh, her Big Swede.

"31-KNOT BURKE"

Burke's first combat experience in World War II was commanding destroyers in the Solomon Islands. Here Captain Burke, as commander of Destroyer Squadron 23, is reading on the bridge wing of his flagship, USS *Charles Ausburne*. Arleigh acquired the nickname 31-Knot Burke, and his crews adopted the name Little Beavers after the Indian boy comic-strip character. Note the squadron's Little Beaver insignia on the side of the bridge.

Captain Burke having a beer with Commander Bernard L. Austin, who commanded one of Burke's destroyer divisions. Together they fought in two night naval battles as well as other combat operations in the Solomons.

OFFICIAL U.S. NAVY PHOTOGRAPH

Vice Admiral Marc Mitscher, commander Fast Carrier Task Force, was indignant on receiving orders from Washington that he had to replace his aviator chief of staff with a surface officer. Captain Arleigh Burke was shocked on receiving orders that he had to leave his beloved destroyers and serve in the carriers as Mitscher's chief of staff.

Thus Mitscher and Burke were ordered into an intimate command relationship that neither desired. As they served together, however, their attitude underwent a profound change, from mutual hostility to friendship and mutual respect.

Bomb hits on carrier *Franklin* blew up her armed, fueled planes and exploded her gasoline and ammunition, killing 724 and wounding 265 of her crew. Yet she made the 12,000-mile voyage to New York under her own steam, a record matched by no other capital ship so ravaged.

Wrecked planes aft on what was left of the flight deck of Mitscher's flagship, *Bunker Hill*, after a kamikaze attack. Mitscher and staff members, including Burke, transferred to *Enterprise*, which in turn was disabled by kamikazes. Mitscher, along with Burke and staff, then shifted to carrier *Randolph*, his third flagship in four days.

U.S. NAVAL HISTORICAL CENTER

In Japanese waters, June 1951, during the Korean War, Rear Admiral Burke greets retired Admiral Kichisaburo Nomura as he boards Burke's flagship *Los Angeles* for a dinner party. Nomura was ambassador to the United States when his countrymen attacked Pearl Harbor.

Off Korea, July 1951. Burke invited Lieutenant General James Van Fleet, commander U.S. Eighth Army, to *Los Angeles,* for a dish of ice cream, a favorite of the general's. Their helicopter crash-landed on board, but Van Fleet enjoyed his ice cream.

U.S. NAVAL HISTORICAL CENTER

The UN negotiating team rests on the steps of the conference house at Kaesong, Korea, during armistice talks with Chinese and North Korean officials. Left to right: Major General Laurence Craigie. vice commander of Far East Air Forces; Major General Paik Sun Yup, representing President Syngman Rhee; Vice Admiral Turner Joy, USN, senior delegate; Major General Henry Hodes, deputy chief of staff of the Eighth Army; and Rear Admiral Arleigh Burke, USN.

Burke outside his tent at the delegates' base camp near Munsan, Korea.

Burke and Hodes, feeling let down by their own State Department, glumly dine on Thanksgiving turkey shortly before departing for the United States.

GETTING READY FOR THE BIG JOB

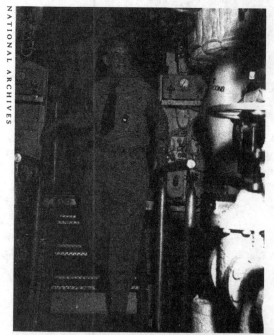

Admiral Burke, appointed chief of naval operations, set out to prepare himself before taking office. Here he is inspecting the engine spaces of *Nautilus*, the world's first nuclear-propelled submarine.

Burke also visited bases and potential trouble spots around the world. In Taiwan, threatened by communist China, he was greeted by President and Madame Chiang Kai-shek.

CHIEF OF NAVAL OPERATIONS

Admiral Burke served an unprecedented six years (August 1955 to August 1961) as chief of naval operations. He expected extraordinary accomplishments from his subordinates, and his own labors extended usually from early morning until well into the evening seven days a week, with time out for little else besides navy-connected social or other activities.

His penetrating blue eyes often twinkled with mirth…

but could turn glacial with disapproval.

LIGHTER MOMENTS OF THE CNO

Arleigh and his adored (and ador-
ing) Bobbie attending the Navy
Day Ball at the Coconut Grove,
Los Angeles, 22 October 1960.

In the evening of 23 November
1960, Arleigh at the Naval Academy leading midshipmen in a pep
rally before the Army-Navy game.

The fleet ballistic missile Polaris, because it could be launched from a submerged submarine, was considered the most nearly invulnerable deterrent to nuclear attack. Burke initiated the Polaris project during his first two-year term as CNO. Four years later, in the middle of his third and final term, Polaris was successfully launched. It was the achievement of many men, but it was Burke who set the project in motion and who promoted, guided, financed, goaded, encouraged, and defended it.

The Joint Chiefs of Staff in session, October 2, 1960. Left to right: General Lyman Lemnitzer, army chief of staff; Admiral Arleigh Burke, chief of naval operations; General Nathan Twining, USAF, chairman of the JCS; General Thomas White, air force chief of staff; and General David Shoup, commandant, U.S. Marine Corps.

LAUNCHING ARLEIGH BURKE (DDG 51)

On 16 September 1989 at the Bath Iron Works, Bath, Maine, Mrs. Burke smashed a bottle of champagne on the bow of Aegis guided missile destroyer 51 and christened her with the name of her husband. The destroyer then went gliding majestically down the ways into the Kennebec River.

With the newly launched *Arleigh Burke* afloat, visible in the distance between them, Bobbie poses with roses; Arleigh, with his jacket stained by champagne from Bobbie's bottle smashing.

assault thus far of the Pacific war, on a scale equivalent to the 1944 invasion of Normandy but with far longer and more vulnerable approaches and lines of supply. It would also be the most audacious, executed within easy flying distance of enemy airfields in the Japanese home islands and on Formosa.

As at Iwo Jima, Spruance would command the Fifth Fleet; Mitscher, Task Force 58; and Turner, the expeditionary force. The landing force was the Tenth Army, comprising three marine and four army infantry divisions, to be commanded on Okinawa by Lieutenant General Simon Bolivar Buckner of the U.S. Army.

The Task Force 58 carriers were to raid Kyushu and Japan's Inland Sea on 18 and 19 March and then launch air strikes on Okinawa from 23 March through D-day, 1 April. Thereafter it would remain on call for air support throughout the campaign, with the special mission of protecting supplies en route to U.S. forces on the island.

The next day, 10 March, Mitscher conferred with his task group commanders on board *Bunker Hill.* He said he could not predict what the Japanese would do in response to a landing so near their homeland. They would certainly attack from the air and probably launch air, surface, and subsurface suicide raids. For all he knew they might even employ poison gas.

As if to underline Mitscher's warning to expect the unexpected, a pair of suicide pilots raided Ulithi in the evening of the 11th, incidentally providing Burke and Mitscher with their first sight of a kamikaze attack. Burke was on *Bunker Hill*'s flag bridge when two irregularities caught his attention: first, on board carrier *Randolph*, a cargo light still shining despite the general blackout, then the sound of an approaching aircraft. The pilot, obviously drawn by the light, crashed his plane into *Randolph*'s starboard quarter. The aircraft exploded and instantly enveloped the ship's stern in flames that set off a series of further explosions. The second suicide plane, its pilot evidently unable to find a suitable target, crashed on Mogmog Island. Fortunately most of *Randolph*'s ship's company was watching a movie amidships on the hangar deck. Even so, 25 were killed and 130 wounded. On Mogmog, 14 men were injured by the crashing plane.

The task force was in the last stages of being armed, fueled, replenished, and reorganized for the coming campaign. Burke now had little to do. Everything had been planned in advance, mostly in late 1944 and January 1945 at Pearl Harbor.

"Much of the fighting leaves me as on onlooker," Arleigh wrote to Bobbie. "Usually by the time a fight starts, my work is done."

Arleigh's state of temporary freedom permitted him to accept an invitation to a destroyer sailors' beer party on Mogmog. He went joyously, as to a family reunion.

"It was good to be among friends again," he wrote Bobbie. "It was good to sit on a smoky, dirty island and throw beer bottles about and not have anybody to wear me down. Mostly it's good to be among people whose language I understand."

After a year with the fast carriers, which at times he had commanded in his admiral's name, Burke would still have exchanged his gold-braided commodore's cap for a destroyer command.

On 14 March the sixteen carriers of Task Force 58 and their escorting battleships, cruisers, and destroyers sortied from Ulithi lagoon and shaped course for Kyushu 1,700 miles to the north. After refueling on the 16th, the force began its final run-in. Because their ships had come away unscratched from the raids on Tokyo, Mitscher and his staff had become less wary. In this approach to Japan they employed fewer measures to achieve surprise, and there was no weather front to hide behind. Inevitably, snoopers shadowed the ships and reported their coming.

At dawn on 18 March the force reached launching position 90 miles southeast of Kyushu's southern capes. The first strike, taking off in fine weather, met little opposition in the air and found few planes on the ground. Alerted, most Japanese aircraft were airborne, en route to attack the carriers. The American bomber pilots had to content themselves with striking airfields, barracks, and hangars.

Of the many enemy planes that went after the carriers, only three eluded the skillful CAP pilots and the practiced ships' gunners. One of the three hurled at *Enterprise* a bomb that failed to detonate but struck her flight deck and bounced along spraying fiery jets that seared three men, killing one. A bomber trying to crash *Intrepid* was shot down at such close range that hot fragments of the exploding plane killed two men, wounded forty-three, and started a fire on the hangar deck. A bomb aimed at *Yorktown* hit her signal bridge and passed through one deck before it exploded, blasting two holes in her hull and killing five men and wounding twenty-six.

Task Force 58 orders to raid shipping in the Inland Sea reflected Spruance's hunch that the Japanese would attempt another surface attack. When U.S. fliers in the afternoon of the 18th sighted superbattleship *Yamato* and three cruisers at the Inland Sea port of Kure,

Mitscher proposed recalling his planes over Kyushu, hastening
north through the night, and launching torpedo planes against the
giant battlewagon at dawn.

Spruance objected, fearing she might escape by then. By TBS his
new chief of staff, Rear Admiral Arthur Davis, inquired, "Can you
attack and disable her this afternoon?"

"Negative," replied Burke. "All our attack aircraft are airborne."

Yamato apparently made a run for it during the night. In the
morning of the 19th she was beyond reach of the torpedo-carrying
planes, but the American bombers, ranging the Inland Sea, heavily
damaged light carrier *Ryuho* and did minor damage to *Yamato* and
the new heavy carrier *Amagi*.

Meanwhile, Task Force 58 had again come under attack. Carrier
Wasp had just launched a morning sweep when an undetected plane
dived and dropped a bomb that penetrated five decks before exploding in the galley, killing many cooks and mess attendants preparing
to serve breakfast. Total casualties on all decks were 101 killed, 269
wounded.

Hardly had Mitscher and Burke received a radio report of this
attack when they heard six huge explosions from beyond the northern horizon. Presently in the same direction they saw a column of
oily black smoke rising steadily higher, its base repeatedly reddened
by further explosions, whose sound reached them after an interval.

Presently reports came in. The burning ship was heavy carrier
Franklin, flagship of Rear Admiral Ralph Davison, commander of
Task Group 58.2. She had been bombed by an undetected enemy
plane when she was in the most vulnerable of conditions, with
armed and fueled aircraft on the flight deck beginning to take off
and others on the hangar deck waiting to be brought up. Aircraft
still on board had about 60,000 gallons of gas in their tanks and 30
tons of bombs and rockets hanging from their racks. As the flames
spread, ready ammunition in lockers and gun mounts as well as in
planes exploded, and rockets began screaming off in all directions.

Davison, unable to command his task group from the burning,
exploding carrier, transferred with key members of his staff to a
destroyer, from which he reported to Mitscher that he believed
Franklin would have to be abandoned and had so advised her commanding officer, Captain Leslie Gehres. Remarkably enough, in the
midst of the holocaust the carrier's TBS was still operational.
Gehres's voice boomed out a message to Mitscher: "This is the

commanding officer of the *Franklin*. You save us from the Japs, and we'll save this ship."

The distressed expression on Mitscher's face gave way to something approaching a grin. He said to Burke, "You tell him we'll save him."

Though the center of Task Force 58 was within a hundred miles of the Japanese mainland, there was no thought of abandoning the burning carrier. While a skeleton crew of key personnel remained on board and fought to save her, Burke ordered fighter sweeps over Kyushu to keep Japanese aircraft grounded. By noon *Franklin*'s crew had extinguished the worst of her fires and stabilized her list at 13 degrees. Shortly afterward a cruiser passed her a line and, accompanied by the rest of Task Group 58.2, began towing her southward at a stately three knots.

During the night *Franklin* began to regain power. The next morning, 20 March, she regained steering control, and a little after noon she cast off the tow lines and began operating with her own engines. Captain Gehres reported, "Down by the tail but reins up!" Of *Franklin*'s original crew of about 3,200, 724 were killed or missing and 265 wounded. Her hull was bent and blackened, and her flight deck looked like a half-eaten shredded-wheat biscuit. No other carrier of World War II had been so burned and battered and remained afloat.

Burke's efforts to keep all aircraft on Kyushu grounded almost succeeded, but in midafternoon of the 20th several planes attacked Admiral Davison's Task Group 58.2, still covering *Franklin*. One kamikaze, aiming for carrier *Hancock*, missed and crashed into the main deck of destroyer *Halsey Powell*, which had just topped off fuel alongside. Of her crew, twelve men were killed and twenty-nine wounded; her steering gear was jammed, and her speed was reduced to about ten knots. Mitscher, considering a destroyer in this condition of no further use to the fleet, told Burke to order other destroyers to remove survivors and send her down with gunfire. Old destroyerman Burke was shocked. Said he sharply, "You aren't going to do that, are you?"

"What good is she?" replied Mitscher.

"The same good as your airplanes, your aircraft carriers. This is a fighting unit. Let's go back and get her."

"All right," said Mitscher, and they did. Burke turned the whole task force around, and it went back and towed *Halsey Powell* out. Saving one destroyer out of the many in the fleet provided no great military advantage, Burke conceded, but, he insisted, "it had a tremendous effect on morale."

Out of range of Kyushu-based aircraft, *Franklin* was detached and with a single stop, at Pearl Harbor, made the 12,000-mile voyage to New York under her own steam. No capital ship so ravaged had ever before made it back to port. It was, however, her last record. At the naval shipyard she was judged too severely damaged to be worth repairing. *Halsey Powell*, on the contrary, was reconditioned and put back in service.

Air attack and defense over Task Force 58 and over Kyushu and the Inland Sea had been costly for both sides. The task force lost 116 planes. The Japanese, particularly alarmed by the strikes on the remnant of their fleet, had thrown everything available at the Americans, committing even their surviving aces, skilled aviators whom they had retained at home as instructors. Of the 193 aircraft they claim to have sent against Task Force 58, 161 were shot down, and another 50 planes were destroyed on the ground. Because of these heavy losses and extensive damage to installations and communications on Kyushu, the Japanese were unable to strike back again in force for nearly three weeks, and from that point on they had to rely heavily on suicide attacks by virtually untrained aviators.

Meanwhile, Task Force 58 retired to refuel and replenish and then on 23 March returned to begin the pre-assault bombing of targets on Okinawa. The next day, Rear Admiral Morton Deyo's old battleships and Vice Admiral Lee's new battleships from Task Force 58 began the naval bombardment. Admiral Spruance, still suspecting the Japanese would attempt a surface counterattack, had organized Deyo's force as a detachable command to deal with any such threat. Burke now shared Spruance's hunch. "Perhaps," he wrote Bobbie, "this action will bring out their navy in their last banzai charge."

On 25–27 March a U.S. amphibious attack force executed an inspired bit of planning by seizing the Kerama Retto, a group of small islands 15 miles west of southern Okinawa. These provided an anchorage for tenders, oilers, and repair and ammunition ships to service the fleet right in the area of operations.

A British force of four carriers, two battleships, five cruisers, and fifteen destroyers joined the U.S. Fifth Fleet as Task Force 57. Because of possible confusion arising out of operational differences, the Britons did not attach themselves to Task Force 58 but took station between Formosa and the southwest Ryukyus to attack and repel enemy aircraft in that area. To facilitate coordination, the U.S.

and British task forces exchanged liaison officers. Assigned to Mitscher's staff was the Royal Navy's Commander Charlie Owen, a brisk and friendly man, interested in everything and continually asking questions.

While the Japanese were assembling aircraft and pilots on Kyushu for a major strike, individual planes, evidently from airfields on Okinawa or other islands of the Ryukyus, attacked U.S. ships. During the pre-assault naval bombardment, they damaged an LSM, an attack cargo ship, three destroyers, and Admiral Spruance's flagship, *Indianapolis,* then with the bombardment force. Spruance was obliged to transfer his flag to old battleship *New Mexico,* while *Indianapolis* and the most heavily damaged of the destroyers returned to the West Coast for repairs.

On the morning of D-day, 1 April, after the heaviest neutralizing fire discharged against any beach in the Pacific, the U.S. Tenth Army of 183,000 combat troops began going ashore. The Japanese, having in the past experienced the suicidal folly of exposing their forces to naval gunfire, now barely opposed the landing. Instead, the bulk of the 100,000 defenders took position in their main citadel in southern Okinawa. This was a warren of hills, caves, and pillboxes, a sort of king-size Iwo Jima—dug not into soft lava, however, but into solid earth and rock.

On 1 April enemy planes damaged a minelayer, two transports, and an LST. The following day a crashing kamikaze so mangled a destroyer transport that she had to be scuttled. On the same date, suicide planes damaged two attack transports and an LST. The next day kamikazes attacked the escort carriers, putting one out of the campaign, and went after Turner's exposed picket destroyers, damaging one and barely missing another.

On 6 April the Japanese launched the first of a series of major air attacks for which they had been assembling aircraft—any old crates capable of making a one-way trip. Hundreds of bombers and kamikazes approached the American ships that day, but thanks to an alert combat air patrol and expert gunnery, they inflicted no damage to the carrier force. It was not for want of trying. Rear Admiral Jocko Clark, commanding Task Group 58.1, later recalled, "The kamikaze attack against us was almost overpowering. For 40 minutes, commencing at 11:50 A.M., every ship in my task group was firing continuously at seven separate enemy raids. Sherman's Task Group 58.3 ships joined in, and the reinforced combat air patrol had a field day." CAP in fact destroyed much the greater share of the claimed 249

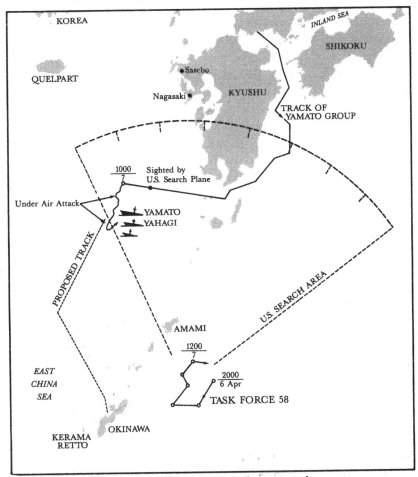

Track Charts of Task Force 58 and
Yamato Task Force, 6–7 April 1945

planes shot down that day by task force aircraft and ships' guns.

Most persistently attacked by the Japanese aircraft were the outlying picket destroyers, which early in the campaign had only their own guns to protect them. Three suicide planes crashed into one picket and three more crashed into another. As Burke had pointed out, a lone destroyer cannot protect herself from such an attack. Both picket ships sank.

Some 200 enemy planes reached the Okinawa area. Here most of the attackers were disposed of by fighter planes and by antiaircraft fire so intense that several American sailors were injured by a hail of falling shell fragments. Nevertheless the enemy planes sank a destroyer transport and an LST, demolished two loaded ammunition ships, and damaged a minelayer and ten destroyers, four beyond repair. The day's attacks killed 367 Americans and wounded 408, mainly by the explosions and gasoline fires that usually accompanied kamikaze strikes. Most men who survived suffered agonizing burns that would require months of hospitalization while their seared limbs and faces were rebuilt.

Toward the end of this terrible day, U.S. submarines reported two large and perhaps half a dozen smaller ships moving southwest out of Bungo Channel, the southern exit from Japan's Inland Sea. Subsequently, perhaps through a check of radioed Japanese call signs, the Americans concluded that one of the big ships was super-battleship *Yamato*, accompanied by a cruiser and as many as eight destroyers. Obviously such a force was not being sent out to take on the whole U.S. Fifth Fleet. It was evidently a continuation of the day's suicide blitz, its objective the "survivors" of the air raid on the U.S. amphibious shipping at the Okinawa beachhead. If the *Yamato* group got that far, it would inevitably be destroyed but probably not before it inflicted a great deal of destruction.

It was unclear whether in the impending action Mitscher or Spruance should assume tactical command of Task Force 58. Mitscher was anxious to have his carrier planes sink the big ship. He believed they had sunk her sister *Musashi* in the Battle for Leyte Gulf, but his aviators had not seen her go under, and there was a tantalizing possibility that submarines had actually sent her down. This new sortie of *Yamato* afforded a chance to display beyond doubt the primacy of aircraft.

After discussing the situation with Burke and Flatley, Mitscher concluded that the approaching *Yamato* group was meat for his carrier planes. Without consulting Spruance, he ordered his task groups to concentrate northeast of Okinawa. Then, exhausted, he retired to his sea cabin, leaving Burke and Flatley to carry on. On Burke's orders, ordnance men began loading the carrier planes with torpedoes and armor-piercing bombs.

Admiral Spruance had plans of his own. He decided that the *Yamato* group should be taken under attack by Admiral Deyo's force of six old battleships, seven cruisers, and thirty-one destroyers. To participate personally in the action, he attached his flagship, *New Mexico*, to Deyo's force. For months his beloved old dreadnoughts had been restricted to humdrum shore bombardments. He now proposed to give them, and himself, a final opportunity to fight a classic daylight surface action.

A little after midnight, Spruance issued radio orders for Mitscher to let the *Yamato* group come south, where it could be demolished by the battlewagons. He further ordered him to concentrate planes in combat air patrols to protect both Task Force 58 and Deyo's battleship force from enemy air attacks. Mitscher was thus being ordered to assume a defensive role rather than carry out the offensive operation he had planned. On the other hand, Spruance had not explicitly forbidden Task Force 58 to attack the Japanese ships.

Flatley appears to have hit the sack at about this time, but Burke remained in flag plot. He had mastered the soldier's technique of staying up as long as necessary and grabbing a little shut-eye when opportunity offered. What he was trying to do now was mentally track the *Yamato* group. He concurred that its objective was the amphibious shipping on Okinawa's west coast, but he was sure it would not head there directly, by the shortest route. Its commander almost certainly knew the general location of Task Force 58 and would try to get past and around it by hugging the south capes of Kyushu and then advancing into the East China Sea until due north of Okinawa, whence he supposedly would head south for the U.S. beachhead. Deyo would no doubt remain in a covering position to prevent the Japanese making an end run past him. Burke was relieved that Spruance had not ordered Task Force 58 also to cover the beachhead, as he had in the Battle of the Philippine Sea.

As dawn approached, Burke had new visitors in flag plot: Commander Charlie Owen, the British liaison officer, and Captain Ray Hege, the staff flight surgeon. Dr. Hege's chief duty was looking after the health of the aviators, but Burke was convinced Admiral Nimitz had assigned him the additional responsibility of keeping Mitscher from overdoing.

Hege looked concerned. "The admiral doesn't feel very good this morning," he said. "I don't think he'll come out. I've advised him to stay in bed."

At first light Burke launched eight planes, which fanned out on a wide arc of search sectors, northwest to northeast, to cover any area the *Yamato* group might have reached during the night. He then put Task Force 58 on course northwest, the bearing toward which he *estimated* the group would head. A little after 0830 one of the search planes reported the *Yamato* group southwest of Kyushu on bearing northwest, course 300°. That course, slightly north of due west, puzzled Burke, but he adhered to his original estimate and launched a sixteen-plane search and tracking group toward a point farther south, where he expected the *Yamato* group to be at the end of the two hours it would take the U.S. planes to reach the same spot. Shortly afterward, at 1000, he began launching the main strike of several hundred dive-bombers and torpedo-bombers.

Commander Owen had been watching these goings-on with increasing bewilderment. Did Burke actually know, he inquired, where *Yamato* would be in two hours?

"No."

"Where are you letting the pilots go?"

"We are taking a chance," Burke explained. "We are launching against the point where we would be if we were the *Yamato.*" He indicated a spot on the chart considerably southwest of the ship's location as reported by the dawn search.

Then why send out additional search planes a few minutes ahead of the strike? Owen wanted to know. Burke explained that these would fan out as they approached *Yamato*'s estimated location. Unless the estimate was utterly mistaken, one or more of the searchers was sure to see the enemy force and coach the strike toward it. The strike planes thus would not have to do any searching themselves but could devote their limited time over the target to the business of sinking enemy ships.

During the two-hour wait, Admiral Mitscher at last came out. "He looked like hell," Arleigh said afterward. Burke suspected that the admiral had had a small heart attack, but he never knew for sure, and Dr. Hege never reported anything of the sort.

As soon as Mitscher had been briefed on the situation, he said to Burke, "Inform Admiral Spruance that I propose to strike the *Yamato* sortie group at 1200 unless otherwise directed."

Spruance, anxious to preserve his options, did not immediately reply. He intended to have Deyo's force take on the *Yamato* group if possible, but he was worried about the group's reported westerly position and northerly course. If *Yamato* was not heading for Okinawa but intended instead to race up the west coast of Kyushu to the safety of Sasebo harbor, she and her escorts would soon be beyond the reach not only of Deyo's battleships but of Mitscher's planes as well. He was relieved when Mitscher reported at 1230 that his planes were in contact with the *Yamato* group, adding, "Will you take them or shall I?"

Spruance reached for a radio message blank and scribbled one of the shortest orders of the war, "You take them."

Take them Mitscher's planes did, beginning at 1241 with two

bomb hits on *Yamato* near the mainmast, followed four minutes later by the first of many torpedo hits in the hull of the great ship. At 1423 this queen of the battlewagons, riddled by torpedoes and blasted by bombs, copiously photographed in her death agony, "slid under completely," unquestionably the victim of U.S. naval air.

Her accompanying light cruiser, *Yahagi*, proved nearly as tough as *Yamato*. It took twelve bombs and seven torpedoes to put her under. Of the destroyers in the group, one was promptly sunk, and three others were so severely damaged they had to be scuttled. The remaining four, heavily battered, made it to Sasebo. American losses in the battle were ten planes and twelve men.

Arleigh, less tight-lipped about operations than he had been earlier, wrote to Bobbie concerning the day's victory: "Another battle down. . . . This was a most remarkable one, for they came out to die—and die they did—without being able to inflict enough damage for the effort, let alone for the loss of their ships."

Japanese air got in a few blows on 7 April. A little after noon a kamikaze penetrated Task Force 58's CAP and crashed into carrier *Hancock*'s flight deck, setting fire to parked planes. In midafternoon an airborne bomb knocked out a turret of battleship *Maryland* in Deyo's force, killing sixteen men and wounding thirty-seven. Kamikazes sank a minesweeper off the Okinawa beachhead and severely damaged two radar picket destroyers.

During the rest of the month, Japanese bombers or kamikazes attacked American ships or landing craft nearly every day, with major attacks on 12–13, 15–16, and 27–28 April. In midmonth the enemy introduced a new little horror called *baka*. Brought to the combat area slung under the belly of a bomber, it was 20-foot-long glider laden with high explosive. Released, it was guided into the target by a suicide pilot.

The kamikaze campaigns were quite simply unlike anything else in the history of warfare. Thousands of healthy young Japanese unflinchingly volunteered to go out alone over the sea in flimsy aircraft to hunt their prey and seek a violent, usually fiery death. Far more were shot down, generally in flames, than reached their targets, yet additional volunteers were ready to follow them. Their naval brothers stepped forward to commit suicide in *kaiten* submarines, one-man craft launched off ports and anchorages by larger submarines and steered in by their lonely pilots, who exploded them against the hulls of Allied ships.

As Burke had foreseen, most of the aircraft suicide pilots dove into the first ships they encountered, which were most often the outlying picket lines of destroyers and destroyer types. On 16 April, picket destroyer *Laffey* underwent twenty-two such attacks from all directions within eighty minutes. By the end of that ordeal she had suffered thirty-one killed and seventy-two wounded and was scarcely recognizable as a destroyer, but she remained afloat and was towed to the anchorage off the Okinawa beachhead. It is unlikely that any other ship ever survived an attack of such intensity, but there were others scarcely less mutilated.

One evening Burke, listening on the circuits, heard "one of those freak communication things." It was an ensign reporting from a picket destroyer, then under attack. The number-one gun was dismounted, he said, the bridge was demolished, and the ship was listing badly. The captain, the executive officer, and the engineering officer were all killed. So far as he could make out, he was the only officer still alive on board, and he had taken command. He could still make five knots, still make steerageway, and he had two guns left in operating condition.

With a blend of horror, pride, and pity, Arleigh listened to the conclusion of the young officer's report, words that would haunt his memory for years.

"I am an ensign," the voice said. "I have only been on this ship for a little while. I have been in the navy for only a little while. I will fight this ship to the best of my ability, and forgive me for the mistakes I am about to make."

At that point the communication snapped off. Arleigh assumed that the attack was resumed and that in all probability the ship was sunk. He never learned the man's fate or his identity, but he never forgot his words.

April 1945 was a rough month for all hands involved. Mitscher's carriers were kept busy providing air cover for Task Force 58 and air cover and support for U.S. operations on Okinawa, which seemed interminable. The admiral took what precautions he could. Whenever he anticipated a major enemy air attack, he beefed up the combat air patrols, canceled the support missions over the island, and had his dive-bombers and torpedo planes disarmed, degassed, and parked in hangar decks. By such means he kept fires and secondary explosions to a minimum. Carriers *Enterprise, Essex,* and *Intrepid* were damaged by air attack, but only *Intrepid* had to be sent to a navy yard for repairs.

The frequent raids against points ashore or at sea kept the crews and especially the commanders and their staffs on almost constant alert. Numerous calls to battle stations interrupted normal duties and often left the men only two or three hours of sleep each night. Some broke under a psychotic condition called combat fatigue and were hauled off to sick bay. Burke, who could stand strain better than most, wrote Bobbie, "The same old pace is being set. It's monotonous now—and it seems perfectly natural that people should always get up at 0330 and be called twenty times during the night."

The strain of ninety days at sea in almost continuous combat, with only one brief and very busy break at Ulithi, showed in the countenances of the men who frequented Mitscher's flag plot—pursed lips, sunken eyes peering out over deepening bags. Most had lost weight. Mitscher now weighed no more than a hundred pounds. At Dr. Hege's insistence, he rose later than before and whenever practical took a rest in his sea cabin.

Mitscher could move about on a level surface, but movement from deck to deck was now beyond his strength. Stairways in men-of-war are not designed for invalids. Rightly called ladders, they are much steeper than stairs ashore, being constructed to permit men in good condition to move from level to level in minimum time using minimum space. In May 1945, when Mitscher and Burke encountered a ladder to negotiate, the latter simply picked up his admiral bodily and lifted or lowered him.

Now rarely occupying the swivel chair, Mitscher when on the bridge most often sat on the less hard transom seat in flag plot. Always soft-spoken, he seldom raised his voice above a whisper. Some officers who had occasion to visit or look in on flag plot reported an impression that Mitscher, left barely conscious by fatigue, had turned command of the task force over to Burke. In fact, Pete Mitscher's mind was as clear as ever. Burke as usual was acting as the admiral's mouthpiece, ordering done what he knew Mitscher wanted done and consulting with him quietly when in doubt.

To ease tension, air squadrons were rotated out and replaced, and task groups were periodically relieved. At the end of April, Jocko Clark's Task Group 58.1 went to Ulithi for ten days of upkeep and replenishment and relaxation for the crews. But Admirals Spruance, Mitscher, and Turner stayed on. They and their staffs could not be spared from the combat zone.

Admiral Nimitz came out to Okinawa to investigate. To General Buckner he said, "I'm losing a ship and a half a day. So if this line isn't moving within five days, we'll get somebody here to move it so we can all get from under these stupid air attacks."

On the morning of 11 May, *Bunker Hill* and the other carriers of

Task Group 58.3 completed launching a little before 1000. Burke felt tense. He had noticed that in warfare the most dangerous times are dawn and dusk and just before 1000. "I don't know why that is," he said, "but nearly everything happens just a few minutes before ten o'clock." He noticed planes coming in on his starboard bow. These began circling the task group, which took them under heavy fire, shooting down several.

A fighter plummeted out of the enemy formation, made a shallow dive on *Bunker Hill*'s starboard quarter, dropped a bomb, and went skidding across the flight deck spraying burning gasoline among the parked planes and then fell over the side. It was followed immediately by a dive-bomber, which released a bomb and crashed through the flight deck near the base of the island and blew apart, spraying more burning gasoline. Its motor, wrenched loose, slammed into the flag office, killing three officers and eleven men of Mitscher's staff. Of the bombs dropped by the kamikazes before crashing, the first went through the flight deck and out through the side of the ship before exploding. The second penetrated to the gallery deck, where it detonated, killing, among others, more staff members.

At the first explosion, Mitscher had stepped out on the starboard side of the bridge to observe the damage. Burke, following him, noticed that the flames had reached the main radio room at the foot of the island. Without a second's hesitation, holding a handkerchief over his nose, he dashed down the ladder into thickening smoke at the base of the superstructure. Here he joined Lieutenant Commander Frank Dingfelder, the communication officer, in half leading, half dragging the radiomen, some barely conscious, out of the hot, smoke-filled room and up the ladder just ahead of the flames. As smoke followed Burke up the ladderwell into flag plot and began to gush from the ventilators there, Arleigh ordered everybody out and, the last to leave, came out coughing and choking and unable to speak for several minutes.

The observers on the bridge could feel the heat of the burning flight and hangar decks below and hear the screams of men engulfed by the flames. Because the ship still had power and steering, her commanding officer, Captain G. A. Seitz, in an inspired maneuver gave his ship a hard turn that threw burning planes off the flight deck and sloshed burning gasoline off flight and hangar decks. At the same time he turned into the wind to help force the flames aft and enable fire fighters to work. Presently a cruiser and several destroyers came alongside to direct their hoses at the hangar deck fire. Other destroyers moved about picking up men who had been blown overboard or had jumped to escape the flames.

Burke ordered Gus Read below to collect and muster members of the staff. Arleigh knew that Mitscher would want to know. These men were his special responsibility, his naval "family." Where respect and warmth exist between a flag officer and his staff, they may become the modern counterpart of Lord Nelson's "band of brothers."

Since the ladder in the superstructure was glowing hot, Read made his way down over the gun-directing system. On the hangar deck and what was left of the flight deck, he saw many burned bodies and men burned but still alive and writhing and whimpering in pain. He found some staff members manning hoses to extinguish the hangar deck fire. Others were helping doctors and corpsmen administer first aid to the injured men. A pair of chaplains moved among the twitching bodies speaking softly.

Read found that at least half the staff had been killed, many by smoke inhalation. Dr. Hege, who had been occupying Burke's abandoned regular cabin on the gallery deck, had been killed by the bomb explosion. Of the surviving staffers, several were seriously burned or otherwise wounded. Mitscher received Read's report with a deep sigh. Beyond that he showed no outward sign of distress. Nor did he raise an eyebrow when Burke informed him that Mitscher's sea cabin had been gutted, all his clothes burned, his letters and other private papers destroyed, and the official papers in the flag office reduced to ashes.

When it was clear that seared *Bunker Hill* could no longer serve as task force flagship, Burke ordered some twenty selected staff officers and enlisted men to collect what possessions they could and assemble on the hangar deck for transfer to destroyer *English*, which he ordered to come alongside. Burke himself never found time to collect anything of his own but went empty-handed, trusting the navy to send his gear after him. It did, two years later.

Meanwhile, the ladder being still too hot for use by Mitscher and the staffers on the bridge, they slung a Jacob's ladder over the side. Hoisting the admiral across the shoulder-high bulwark was the work of several willing hands, but getting him down the Jacob's ladder proved an engineering problem that took the staff's collective ingenuity to solve. That done, *English* headed for the relief flagship, night carrier *Enterprise*. Behind her, fire fighting and rescue work continued on board *Bunker Hill,* but the severity of her damages had put her out of the war for good. Her casualties were 396 killed and 264 wounded. Only *Franklin* had been worse hurt.

The officers of destroyer *English* showed themselves models of courtesy and compassion, though not necessarily of judgment. They conducted the *Bunker Hill* refugees to the wardroom, made them comfortable, brought them ice cream, coffee, and cigarettes. The destroyer's commanding officer asked if they would like to see a movie. They would, of course—anything to take their minds off the horrors they had just witnessed. The skipper himself set up the screen, the lights were dimmed, and the movie began. It was color footage of destroyer *English*'s efforts on behalf of battered *Franklin,* a true action spectacular featuring fire, explosions, and nerve-racking rescue work. At that moment, said Gus Read afterward, he and his fellow staffers would have preferred Mickey Mouse.

At 0800 the next morning, 12 May, Admiral Mitscher, established with the remnant of his staff in *Enterprise,* reassumed command of Task Force 58. That evening at the urging of Burke and Flatley he began a run to the north with two groups to send sweeps and strikes against Japanese airfields and air facilities on Kyushu and Shikoku.

That same evening, Admiral Spruance narrowly missed being killed by kamikaze attack. In fleet flagship *New Mexico,* then off the Okinawa beachhead, he was on his way to flag bridge, his normal station, when a suicide plane slammed into the ship abaft the bridge at a point Spruance would have reached in a few minutes. The resultant explosion and fire killed fifty-four men and wounded 119.

In the morning of 14 May, Mitscher's two groups, having completed their raids on Kyushu and Shikoku, were on the way back to their usual operational area east of Okinawa. A little before dawn, combat air patrol began taking off from the other carriers, but on board night carrier *Enterprise* all was quiet. Her planes were stowed below on the hangar deck, and her flight deck was empty.

Gus Read, who had the duty watch, received word that radar had picked up many bogeys in the distance. Complying with instructions, he called Burke, then Mitscher, then other staffers. All began to assemble in *Enterprise*'s flag plot, which was in an exposed position above the captain's bridge instead of below it as in *Bunker Hill.*

When it was established that the unidentified planes were heading for the task force, general quarters sounded in all ships, and guns were quickly manned. Burke and several staffers, seeking a better view, bounded up to the uncovered observation platform at the top of the superstructure. Flatley rushed out onto the bridge wing outside flag plot.

Most of the oncoming planes, now obviously enemy, were destroyed by CAP, but six broke out of the clouds in full view of most of the ships' gunners, who promptly shot down all but one. The lone survivor began circling the force, darting in and out of clouds, with all the ships' guns groping for him. Burke could see the bullet holes as the plane was repeatedly hit. Afire at last, it turned toward *Enterprise* and dived through a fountain of gunfire from every gun that could bear.

"Hit the deck!" Flatley yelled and dived into flag plot.

The kamikaze crashed into the most vulnerable spot in the ship, the rear edge of the forward elevator. The exploding plane shattered the elevator and peeled back part of the flight deck. Its powerful bomb penetrated deep within the ship, creating more damage and hurling wood and metal pieces of the elevator and flight deck hundreds of feet into the air. The fragments then came raining back down upon the ship.

A big chunk of something hit a man standing on one side of Burke, killing the man instantly. Frank Dingfelder, standing on Burke's other side, had his spectacles shattered by a flying splinter, which dug a gash under his eye. When Dingfelder tottered down the ladder, the remains of his spectacles in hand, he was surprised to see men in flag plot rising sheepishly from the deck. They had reacted automatically to Flatley's cry. Only Mitscher had remained on his feet.

"Flatley," he said, "tell my task group commanders that if the Japs keep this up they're going to grow hair on my head yet."

Enterprise's fires were soon extinguished and she maintained power and steering, but she required such extensive, time-consuming repairs to perform her functions as a carrier that she was out of the war for good. Mitscher and the remnant of his staff transferred the next day to carrier *Randolph*, patched up from that kamikaze attack in Ulithi anchorage. By this time in the campaign, Japanese aircraft had sunk twenty-six ships and damaged 133, and killed nearly 2,000 sailors.

Conquest of Iwo Jima and Okinawa, assigned to the Spruance-Mitscher-Turner team, was proving more costly, risky, and time-consuming than anyone had anticipated. Admiral Nimitz during his late April visit to Okinawa had witnessed a kamikaze attack. That may have convinced him that his top naval commanders and their staffs, who never left the scene of action, would soon reach the limit of their endurance. On his return to Guam he notified Admiral Halsey that he would have to take over from Spruance in about thirty days, whether or not Okinawa had been conquered.

Vice Admiral Harry Hill relieved Admiral Turner on 17 May. Ten days later, Admiral Halsey arrived off Okinawa in his new flagship, *Missouri*, and relieved Admiral Spruance, whereupon Fifth Fleet again became Third Fleet. Spruance, looking remarkably fit and serene for a man who had gone through four months of some of the hottest fighting of the war, would have preferred completing his assignment, but for the sake of his haggard staff accepted relief without protest.

In the morning of 28 May, as Spruance headed for Guam in *New Mexico*, Halsey joined Task Force 58, and Mitscher, Burke, and Flatley came on board *Missouri* by breeches buoy to confer with Halsey and with McCain. All three visitors had lost weight, but Halsey was shocked at Pete Mitscher's appearance. Always thin, he now looked like a walking skeleton.

The conference concluded, Halsey detached Mitscher and directed McCain to take command of the carrier force, again designated Task Force 38. Pete and his staffers were no longer in the shooting war. They returned to *Randolph*, in which they prepared to depart for Guam. As they were getting under way, Mitscher received a final signal from Halsey: "With deep regret we are watching a great fighting man shove off. All luck to you and your magnificent staff from me and my staff and the fleet."

15

EIGHTH
FLEET

IN EARLY JUNE 1945, Arleigh Burke, home from the Pacific, his Fifth Fleet business completed, reported to the Navy Department for duty. He was ordered to establish a new section in the office of Cominch, under Admiral King—a section for anti-kamikaze research and development. Its specific task was to determine what the fleet could do to protect itself better from the suicide air attacks. Since improving the accuracy of antiaircraft fire would be a major means, Burke's reputation as gunnery officer and ordnance expert made him a prime choice for the assignment.

Arleigh was well aware that the science of ballistics had entered the realm of higher mathematics. Gun crews needed to adjust their aim in accordance not only with the range, bearing, and altitude of the target but under varying conditions of wind and temperature. Calculating a single trajectory required hundreds of different multiplications. The results of all this arithmetic and associated mathematics were embodied in artillery firing tables for gunners. One of Burke's jobs was to prepare better tables. He and his assistants compiled the raw numbers and turned them over to secretaries and yeomen for processing by means of swift and fiendishly complicated calculating machines, immediate ancestors of computers.

Burke next had to establish an evaluation task force to test the improved tables and other anti-kamikaze measures. Luckily, Vice Admiral Willis Lee, the navy's most experienced gunnery flag officer, had recently been detached from Task Force 58 and was available to head such a force. Burke arranged to have Lee sent orders to report to Casco Bay, Maine, and take command. Then, to give him something to command, Burke that same evening sent radio orders to certain ships via Admiral Jonas Ingram, commander in chief of the Atlantic Fleet, directing the ships to report to Admiral Lee to serve in his Test and Evaluation Force.

Burke signed the orders "by direction of Cominch," which gave them the force of direct commands from King. He was conscious that he was being a bit high-handed in thus without consultation issuing orders on the authority of a fleet admiral, particularly since on being detached from Task Force 58 he himself had reverted to his "permanent" rank of captain. But Arleigh was accustomed to signing directive and other communications "by direction" of commander Task Force 58, and Mitscher had expected him to do so. Moreover, setting up the Test and Evaluation Force was an emergency operation in which time was vital.

As was his wont, Burke left his office late in the evening and was back early the next morning. On this occasion King arrived still earlier. When Arleigh reached his desk at 0730, awaiting him was an order from the commander in chief to report to his office. Burke complied at once. He found the admiral at his desk going through stacks of papers. Noting Burke's presence, King picked up a sheaf of dispatches and fixed him with a stern expression.

"Did you get any authority to order these ships?" he asked.

"Yes, sir," replied Burke. "You told me to establish a task force."

"But did anybody check these dispatches?"

"No, sir, they didn't. I just sent them out last night. There was a hurry in this thing."

King then proceeded to give Burke unshirted hell for not checking out his dispatches with higher authority. Burke, standing at attention, took the bawling-out with respectful attention. He knew that, strictly speaking, he deserved the reprimand for sidestepping approved procedure, but he recalled that King himself was noted for flouting rules that hobbled performance. It occurred to Arleigh that the old man was simply handing out the routine scolding that was to be expected for his particular misdeed.

When King had finished sounding off, Burke thought he glimpsed a slight twinkle in his eye. Waving his hand in dismissal, the admiral said, "You did the right thing, son," and turned his attention to other papers on his desk.

Arleigh knew that he was in Cominch's good graces because he added a strong endorsement to Mitscher's recommendation that Burke be awarded a second Distinguished Service Medal for his continuing contributions as his chief of staff and a Silver Star medal for gallantry in rescuing the radiomen in *Bunker Hill*'s superstructure. Arleigh was acquiring one of the most bemedaled chests in the navy, had he chosen to wear all his decorations, which he never did.

The Third Fleet began reporting a sharp decline in kamikaze attacks. Evidently the Japanese were writing off Okinawa as lost and hoarding planes and suicide pilots to hurl against the Americans when they tried to invade Japan. The diminishing kamikaze menace coupled with establishment of U.S. airfields on Okinawa at last permitted the carrier task force on 10 June after ninety days at sea to retire to Leyte Gulf for rest and recreation.

The battle of Okinawa was almost over. Mopping-up operations continued until the end of the month, but the island was declared secured on the 21st. All the defending forces except 11,000 prisoners of war had been killed. American dead numbered nearly 13,000, including 3,400 marines and 4,900 sailors. By air attack alone, fifteen U.S. ships had been sunk and more than 200 had been damaged, quite a few beyond repair.

Burke, in common with a number of senior officers, had about concluded that invading Japan would not be necessary. Even the tenacious Japanese would at last have to face the facts. The surrender of Germany on 8 May had removed all hope of a new and decisive weapon from that quarter, and it freed masses of men and arms for operations against Japan. American bombers by the hundreds were turning Japanese cities into ashes. The strangling blockade was reducing production of war materials to a standstill and bringing the people to the verge of starvation. Okinawa, the last offshore outpost, had fallen. In July, Halsey's Third Fleet, 134 ships strong, began parading up and down the Japanese east coast, bombing and bombarding military targets and destroying what was left of the Japanese fleet.

In this period of uncertainty, of a general feeling that a break in the war was imminent, Admiral Mitscher arrived in Washington. He had done a bit of fishing and had been given a triumphant welcome by his small hometown of Hillsboro, Wisconsin. Now he had come to take on his new assignment, relieving Vice Admiral Aubrey W. Fitch as deputy chief of naval operations for air (Op-05). He did so without enthusiasm, because it involved sitting behind a desk.

Hardly had Pete Mitscher got settled in his suite in the Main

Navy building when he sent for Captain Burke, whose office was nearby. Arleigh was pleased to see his old boss comfortably placed, with models of modern aircraft on his desk and paintings of naval air battles on the walls—all placed there by his predecessors. Still, Pete, who was at home in flag plot or perched on his swivel chair on a carrier's bridge, seemed out of place in these comfortable surroundings. He came at once to the point. He wanted Burke to become his deputy.

"Admiral, I can't do that," Burke protested. "I'm not an aviator, and it takes an aviator to run that job. I don't know enough. As a nonaviator I couldn't be effective."

"All right, then," said Mitscher, "why don't you go down to Pensacola and become an aviator?"

"You're kidding," said Burke. "You can't mean that, because you don't like these late-come aviators."

"Yes, but you can fly," Mitscher replied. "You're not so bad. All you have to do is go down and get your wings. We can give you a special course down there."

"It would be an ersatz thing," said Burke. "You've got to grow up in the profession, Admiral, just like you grew up in the profession. I can't become a genuine aviator at this late date."

The "ersatz thing" that Burke referred to was the class of officer designated "aviation observer." The class was concocted in response to mid-1930s congressional legislation requiring commanding officers of naval air stations, seaplane tenders, and carriers to be qualified aviators. But qualified aviators, men whose experience was limited largely to flying, had neither the training nor the seniority to command ships and stations. To fill these commands, selected senior officers were put through a course in aviation and designated aviation observers. The course was no mere subterfuge to evade the law but involved several months of intensive training in engines, radio, aerial navigation, gunnery, bombing, torpedoes, takeoffs, landings, and aerial tactics—everything, in fact, except solo flight.

Admirals King, McCain, and Fitch were all aviation observers. Admiral Halsey was a special case. In order to be permitted to command the big carrier *Saratoga,* he went to Pensacola at age fifty-one. Without being able to pass the pilots' test for eyesight, he managed to be classed student pilot instead of student observer, the usual designation for future aviation observers. As student pilot Halsey was in direct competition with vigorous, keen-eyed young men, aged twenty-two or thereabout. At first, so as not to advertise his nonregulation status, he avoided wearing his spectacles. Without them he couldn't read his instruments and hence never knew precisely how fast, how high, or in what direction he was flying. He nearly killed himself, but he learned to fly. Never an ace, he made himself at least a competent aviator.

Burke was well acquainted with the story and admired Bull Halsey's spirit, but he himself would never assume any title or designation which he had earned by acquiring mere competence. He would not let himself be classed an aviator unless he could become one of the best, and at his age of forty-four that was out of the question.

"Then you won't do it?" said Mitscher.

"No, sir, I'm not going to do it."

"All right, I see your point," said Mitscher, "but you're making a big mistake, because aviation is the future thing."

"It's the future thing," agreed Burke, "but if they need aviators they don't want me."

"Well," said Mitscher, obviously disappointed, "I want you to keep me informed all the time as to where you are. Whenever you are ordered to a new job, I want to know about it. I'm going to sea just as soon as I can go, and I want you to go to sea with me."

Burke grinned. "I'd be happy to go to sea with you, Admiral, anytime, anyplace."

Mitscher grinned back. "Well, okay then," he said.

Captain Burke's anti-kamikaze research and development section early passed beyond preparation of better gunnery tables. Suggestions were solicited, and virtually any recommendation, however bizarre, was given careful scrutiny. Special types of missiles were proposed to supplant guns as antiaircraft weapons. Various designs were offered for improving armor protection of ships. If a proposition showed the slightest promise of prevailing over the kamikaze menace, Burke passed it on to Admiral Lee. Lee would test it, and if it showed any cause for hope, he would send it to the fleet, and they would try it.

In early July 1945, the U.S. Pacific Strategic Intelligence Section developed information implying that all this activity was a possible waste of time, because the war might end more suddenly than anyone expected. The section's code breakers had been regularly listening in on the Japanese foreign minister's enciphered radio communications with Japan's ambassador in Moscow. For some time the ambassador had been instructed to work toward keeping Russia at least neutral with respect to the Pacific war. On 11 July the foreign minister struck a new note—instructing the ambassador "to sound out the extent to which it is possible to make use of Russia with regard to ending the war." The following day the ambassador was informed that "His Majesty is deeply reluctant to have any further blood lost among people on both sides, and it is his desire for the welfare of humanity to restore peace with all possible speed." The foreign minister proposed sending a princely envoy to Moscow, evidently to arrange for Russia to mediate peace terms between Japan and the Allies.

High-ranking government officials in Britain and the United States were not surprised at Japan's seeking and apparently expecting to obtain a negotiated peace. The alternative was the unconditional surrender that Roosevelt and Churchill in January 1943 had announced they would insist upon. Thus far they had not relaxed that stand. Before 1943 was over, the Italians were glad to get out of the war on any terms whatever. By the spring of 1945, when Germany surrendered, the Germans were defeated beyond any capacity to impose conditions. Japan, however, still had a few trump cards—its shores, which no American had yet invaded, many hoarded aircraft, and thousands of young men prepared to give their lives in crashing the planes, bomb-loaded, into any invading enemy. The conquest of Japan would make bloody Iwo Jima and Okinawa look like minor operations. Churchill estimated that it would cost a million American and a half a million British lives.

The Soviets neither informed the Allies of the Japanese overtures nor vouchsafed any clear response to the Japanese initiative. Evidently they had no intention of helping the Japanese get out of the war until they themselves could get into it and partake of the fruits of victory. The Allies had earlier urged Russia to enter the Pacific war and share its burdens. Now with the victory all but won, they had no stomach for confronting the postwar problems raised by Russia as a victor in East Asia.

The Allies had for some time been considering the desirability of offering Japan terms short of unconditional surrender. The stumbling block was whether the Japanese might be permitted to retain their emperor. The Allied leaders were aware to what extent his subjects revered him. Only he had the prestige to order them to lay down their arms, and in all probability only he could assure stability in Japan following the surrender. Hence, Allied governments had avoided officially criticizing him, and his palace in Tokyo had been made off-limits to American bombers. On the other hand, Americans and Chinese citizens in general believed he should be dethroned and tried as a war criminal.

Thus the Potsdam Proclamation of 26 July, the U.S.-British-Chinese reply to the Japanese peace feelers, did not specify the emperor's fate. It stated that Japan was to be stripped of all its territorial gains and possessions except the four home islands and that points in Japan would be occupied until a "peacefully inclined and responsible government" had been established in line with the people's desires expressed in a free election.

The proclamation took the Japanese cabinet by surprise. They had not settled disagreements among themselves, they had not received the reply from Russia on which they pinned their hopes, and they had not begun preparing the Japanese people and the armed services for surrender. Basic to this last requirement was assurance that they could keep their emperor. The promise of a free election implied as much, as it was intended to do, but the Japanese wanted it spelled out before they would capitulate. Meanwhile, on 16 July at Alamagordo, New Mexico, the first man-made atomic explosion had been set off, and within hours the first of two existing atomic bombs was en route to a special airfield on Tinian Island in the Marianas.

On the 28th, Japanese Prime Minister Suzuki, stalling for time, gave the impression in a bumbling press conference that his government would disregard the Potsdam Proclamation. President Truman, taking this statement as a rejection, ordered the first atomic bomb dropped. The order was executed on 6 August by a B-29 flying from Tinian. Hiroshima, the target city, was seared and flattened. To the Soviet foreign minister it was obvious that if the Russians wanted to get in on this fight they had better get cracking. He sent for the Japanese ambassador and handed him his long-awaited answer. It was a declaration of war. Within hours the Red Army marched into Manchuria. On 9 August the second atomic bomb devastated the city of Nagasaki, and the Third Fleet raided airfields in Hokkaido and northern Honshu. On the 10th, Russian forces invaded Korea.

This series of shocks ended the Japanese procrastination. The cabinet by unanimous agreement announced to the Allied governments: "We accept the Potsdam Proclamation, with the understanding that this acceptance does not affect the position of the Imperial Household." U.S. Secretary of State James Byrnes, after checking by radio with London, Moscow, and Chungking, accepted the condition on behalf of the Allied governments but imposed two stipulations: that during the occupation the emperor must submit to the authority of the supreme Allied commander in Japan, and that the Japanese people should decide the emperor's ultimate status through free elections.

From the time Emperor Hirohito on 22 June 1945 had announced to his Supreme War Council that Japan must find a way to end the war, there was really no turning back from the government's search for peace. The jolt of the atomic bombs and the Russian invasion merely hastened the process and lessened the chances of mutiny in the army. "I do not think it would be accurate to look upon use of the atomic bomb and the entry and participation of Soviet Russia into the war as direct causes of the termination of the war," said Admiral Soemu Toyoda, chief of the Japanese naval general staff, "but I think that those two factors did enable us to bring the war to a termination without creating too great chaos in Japan."

Writers in the American press, however, intrigued by the power and mystery of the bomb, tended to give it exclusive credit for the victory. This was too much for Admiral Mitscher, who released to the press his own opinion of how the war had been won.

> Japan is beaten, and carrier supremacy defeated her. Carrier supremacy destroyed her army and navy air forces. Carrier supremacy destroyed her fleet. Carrier supremacy gave us bases adjacent to her home islands. And carrier supremacy finally left her exposed to the most devastating sky attack—the atomic fission bomb—that man has suffered.
>
> When I say that carrier supremacy defeated Japan, I do not mean air power by itself won the Battle of the Pacific. We exercised our carrier supremacy as part of a balanced, integrated air-surface-ground team, in which all hands may be proud of the roles assigned them, and the way in which their duties were discharged. This could not have been done by a separate air force, exclusively based ashore, or by one not under Navy control.

The end of the war of course brought about a quick termination of Captain Burke's anti-kamikaze section and an immediate dispersal of Admiral Lee's Test and Evaluation Force. Arleigh received orders to the Bureau of Ordnance, where in the mid-1930s he had earned a reputation as an expert in ammunition and explosives. Reporting for duty, he looked over the secretarial staff, now mostly

Wave yeomen. Nowhere to be seen was the ingenious Delores, who had engineered his getaway in early 1943. No doubt her talents had taken her to bigger and better fields of achievement. Arleigh hoped so.

Appointed director of research, Burke told the chief of the bureau, Rear Admiral George Hussey, that he didn't want to take a job he couldn't leave quickly, because he had an agreement with Admiral Mitscher to go to sea with him on short notice. Hussey said he knew all about that. Mitscher had telephoned him. He told Burke to go ahead. There wasn't any chance of his being called away soon, and he'd have a standby ready in case something did happen.

Burke found the BuOrd of 1945 a very different place from the comfortable bureau he had served in ten years before. At that time guns and bombs were fairly standardized, and it required no arcane knowledge of physics and chemistry to understand why guns fired and shells and bombs exploded. Now the possibility existed that rockets would replace artillery and that the gun, the main naval weapon for five centuries, would at length give way to the guided missile. The atomic bomb, development of which Roosevelt had assigned to the army, posed new challenges. Could its tremendous destructive power be tamed for use in tactical weapons?

These were some of the problems that confronted Burke as he assumed his tasks as BuOrd's research director. Solving them would take money as well as brains. He knew he could not expect anything like the bounty of wartime appropriations. He may have realized also that U.S. monopoly of the atomic bomb and the recent establishment of the United Nations, which Roosevelt had hailed as a guarantor of peace, would encourage Congress to skimp on defense funds.

The only sure way to fund vital projects was to squeeze the fat out of BuOrd by canceling less-than-vital projects. There were hundreds of them under way in experiment stations in the United States, in the Pacific, in Europe. Some stations, lost track of by BuOrd, were running themselves, wondering what to do next. For Burke, bringing order out of this chaos would have been impossible had he not had a highly capable officer at hand, Commander Kleber Masterson, who knew his way around BuOrd and had the scientific training to evaluate experiments under way or contemplated.

With the support of Admiral Hussey, Burke gave Masterson full power to organize a staff and trim out unproductive and underproductive experiments and experiment stations. Burke challenged him to close down seven projects a day. There were so many obvious duds that at first Masterson could easily attain that ambitious goal, but later when sharp judgment had to be exercised to establish comparative worth he was obliged to move more guardedly. By the end of 1945, however, the fat had been trimmed, and BuOrd was lean and productive, thanks largely to the acumen of Kleber Masterson and to the organizational skills of Arleigh Burke.

In late December 1945, Arleigh got a telephone call from Admiral Mitscher. "Burke," the admiral said, "we are going to sea."

"Good, Admiral," said Burke. "When?"

"By March."

"Where?"

"Atlantic."

"What do we do?"

"We form a brand-new fleet, the Eighth Fleet, and we have it ready for combat by June."

"Good Lord, where?"

"Probably the Mediterranean. You get a staff."

"Aye, aye, sir."

The new Eighth Fleet was being created to fill a vacuum. President Roosevelt had died in April 1945 with the optimistic view, only slightly clouded, that the fine accords reached with Russia at the Yalta Conference of the preceding February would be adhered to. His successor, President Harry S. Truman, soon learned to expect nothing of the sort. Instead of the establishment in Europe's defeated or liberated countries of interim governments "broadly representative of all democratic elements" to be followed by free elections to create "governments responsible to the will of the people," the USSR proceeded to make communist satellites of Albania, Bulgaria, East Germany, Hungary, Poland, and Romania.

In January 1946, Truman, disturbed by Russian threats to Turkey and foot-dragging in withdrawing troops from Iran, wrote his secretary of state, "Unless Russia is faced with an iron fist and strong language another war is in the making. Only one language do they understand—'how many divisions have you?'"

West Germany and the Allied countries of Western Europe were too devastated financially, if not also materially, to resist Russian expansionism. The United States had occupation forces in southern Germany and air bases in France and Italy, but no naval forces were immediately available to patrol the Mediterranean. This militarily empty sea might prove a temptation to the Soviets to build a navy to do the patrolling and thus exert a degree of pressure on the surrounding coastlands. The president ordered the U.S. Navy to fill the vacuum. The navy assigned the task to Mitscher.

The navy had the ships to do the job but not the men. The Japanese surrender had been promptly followed by demands from the American public to "bring the boys home." Complying with the demand, the navy released officers and men so fast that it was often difficult to get ships to ports where they could be decommissioned. By the time Burke arrived at the Norfolk Naval Base in early February 1946 to assume his new duties, the services were in a severe state of disarray for lack of experienced personnel.

Endeavoring to form an Eighth Fleet staff, Burke started calling old shipmates who had remained in uniform, but these experienced officers were hard to pry loose from their current billets. Arleigh particularly wanted Jimmy Flatley and Gus Widhelm, but their commanding officers had enough rank and enough clout to keep a grip on such reliable warriors. Burke was, however, lucky enough to lay hands on three fine officers and former shipmates as a nucleus: Don Griffin for operations, Frank Dingfelder for communications, and Ernie Snowden for air.

With Griffin, Burke went to New York to confer with Admiral Ingram. They took along a shopping list of carriers, cruisers, and destroyers needed to form the new fleet. Ingram told them that the ships were available but lacked sufficient crews to operate them. Particularly wanting were technicians, who were leaving the navy faster than replacements could be trained. Ingram promised to do everything possible to get men with enough training to bring the ships to Norfolk. After that it would be up to Mitscher and his staff to make the ships and crews combat-ready.

On 1 March, Mitscher arrived at Norfolk and took command of the office and couple of ships grimly referred to as the Eighth Fleet. On that date he was promoted to four-star admiral, and Burke regained his former rank of commodore. The admiral, determined to have his fleet ready for combat in record time, set up a breathtaking, backbreaking training schedule to turn raw recruits, of which there were barely adequate numbers, into useful sailors.

Each time new ships arrived, Mitscher called a conference of their commanding officers, and in his name Burke or Griffin laid down the law. As quickly as possible the skippers were to establish a nucleus of trained combatants, even if they had to transfer key personnel from ship to ship. Let these key people train others, who in turn would train still others. Carrier skippers were to go out and take training themselves so that they could fly planes off and on and be able to train their pilots. All the skippers were enjoined to know at all times what their crews could do. The deadline to be ready for a real combat exercise was mid-April. To spur all hands to achieve their utmost, Mitscher through channels invited President Truman to witness the exercise and inspect the new fleet, and the president agreed to do so.

The Russian threat to the Mediterranean was growing. The Soviets were supporting the communist faction endeavoring to take over the government in Greece and were pressing the Turkish government to grant them joint occupation and control of the Dardanelles. To counter these maneuvers, Truman sent battleship *Missouri,* site of the Japanese surrender ceremony, to the eastern Mediterranean, including a visit via the Dardanelles to Istanbul. To arouse American awareness of the threat, the president made use of the famous Churchillian oratory. At his invitation, Winston Churchill, then visiting the United States, went to Fulton, Missouri, and issued a solemn warning to an audience at Westminster College and to the American people: "From Stettin in the Baltic to Trieste in the Adriatic, an Iron Curtain has descended across the Continent. . . ."

Meanwhile, the expanding but still minuscule and untrained Eighth Fleet was struggling to make itself a respectable combat force. It sent men to schools ashore, some hastily improvised. "We ended up with the Atlantic coast shore establishment getting instructors in the most essential schools to teach recruits what to do in various specialties," Burke recalled. "We stripped every experienced man that we could strip from other ships, put ships out of commission in order to get a few experienced people."

In early April the new fleet, now fairly respectable in size if not in training and experience, went to sea to try some dummy runs and find out what it could do. Admiral Mitscher and his growing staff were in the new carrier *Franklin D. Roosevelt* of 52,000 tons standard displacement, an interim type between the 27,000-ton *Essex* class of World War II and the supercarriers that Mitscher was recommending to handle bigger planes to carry bigger bombs greater distances.

Because Burke and Griffin were the only operators on the staff who could handle the details of carrier force operations, they served as staff watch officers, a task assigned during the war to lieutenant commanders. They alternated watch and watch, night and day, and caught a little sleep when they could. Burke had to abandon his rule not to tell an officer how to carry out his assignment. "For example," he said, "I would give an order for a screen to shift position, and the screen commander wouldn't know exactly how to do it, so I'd have to tell him in detail."

Via the press, many senior officers, particularly aviators, were keeping track of the tribulations of the new fleet. Because at this time extensive reorganization of the U.S. armed services was under study, the president's reaction to the forthcoming combat exercise was deemed of great importance. The reorganization program involved both unification and further division. The impetus toward army-navy unification grew out of the need to avoid waste and duplication and possible operations at cross-purposes. The proposed division was based on a demand by the air force for a separate existence apart from the army—a right they believed they had earned by their virtually independent World War II strategic bombing missions against Germany and Japan.

Some air force enthusiasts sought control over all aviation, no matter how used, espousing the simplistic notion that each service should have control of all weapons in its particular field: the air force, all air; the army, all ground forces; the navy, all ships. And since the Soviets at that time had no fleet to speak of, they proposed sharply reducing the navy.

This was not the first time the aviators had proposed taking over what had been deemed naval functions. Following World War I, Brigadier General William "Billy" Mitchell of the Army Air Corps was only the most vocal advocate of the notion that the bomber had superseded the combatant ship. In 1921 he was permitted to have planes drop seven 2,000-pound bombs from low altitude on an undefended, obsolete battleship anchored off the Virginia Capes. That the air attack finally sank the ship was proclaimed by Mitchell as proof that all navies were obsolete. "If a naval war were attempted against Japan," he wrote, "the Japanese submarines and aircraft would sink the enemy fleet long before it came near their coast."

Though Mitchell believed he had proved, as he said, that "airplane carriers are useless instruments of war against first-class Powers," he helped convince American leaders that carriers would in fact be indispensable in any kind of naval warfare. Hence one of the chief effects of Mitchell's demonstration was to spur the U.S. Navy into building the carrier force that in World War II proved the nemesis of enemy land-based air and at war's end was parading up and down the Japanese coast, striking at will. Nevertheless, a good many Americans, especially in the air force, now sincerely believed that the reign of the carrier was at an end, and the sooner this could be proved and the carriers gotten rid of, the better for American defenses.

The air force anti-carrier crowd saw the Eighth Fleet's forthcoming combat exercise as opportunity. They had not been invited to participate, but they could not resist the temptation to launch a surprise strike and in a mock battle demonstrate that carriers could not defend themselves when confronted with recently developed weapons and techniques. They were at any rate anxious to take Admiral Mitscher down a few notches. His postwar proclamation crediting the victory to "carrier supremacy" had not sat well with the fly-boys.

The setting for the proposed mock battle was ideal for their purpose. The president and other dignitaries, including high-ranking officers, would be present—in the very waters where Mitchell a quarter century before had sunk his battleship. This time the target would not be at anchor but moving and manned. The air force planners may have counted heavily on the brevity of its training. If so, they must have been unaware that the training had been carried out by the Mitscher-Burke-Griffin-Snowden team.

At the end of the last dummy run before the combat exercise, Burke concluded that though many things were done poorly, the fleet could get by, because, he said, all hands "were perfectly eager. This thing would have been impossible without the utmost motivation of all the people. They were working their heads off, and those who didn't know were doing everything they could to learn." It had to be a one-shot presentation. Shortage of trained manpower precluded continuous operations. When an operator reached the point of exhaustion there would be nobody to relieve him.

On 22 April the presidential party boarded *FDR* off the Virginia Capes for the scheduled two-day cruise and demonstration. With Mr. Truman, among others, were his chief of staff, Fleet Admiral William D. Leahy; Secretary of the Navy James Forrestal; Fleet Admiral Nimitz, now chief of naval operations; and the presidential aide, Brigadier General Harry Vaughan. Burke was doubtless relieved to note that among the high-ranking visitors there were no carrier veterans. Having never witnessed a carrier battle, none of the observers would know exactly what to expect.

FDR's shorthanded condition left plenty of staterooms to accommodate the presidential group, numbering about twenty-five. Because the weather was unseasonably cool, with rainsqualls, Burke had seen to it that awaiting each visitor in his cabin was a hat, foul-weather gear, and a long aviator coat—all on loan from the ship's store.

Because the fleet demonstration would be carried out within flight range of several coastal air stations, Mitscher suspected that the air force pilots would attempt to do what in fact they were planning to do. He and his key planners also judged the pilots would time their attack with the utmost care in an attempt to demolish the upstart Eighth Fleet before the presidential eyes. To meet the situation Burke set radar watches to observe not merely their own forces but the appearance of bogeys or any long-range activity, and he announced a signal that would require all hands to drop whatever they were doing and assume the planned defense posture.

When the visitors arrived in flag country, clad in their own outer garments or whatever ship's gear they deemed suitable, Burke invited Mr. Truman to take a seat in flag plot, where he could observe the flight deck and the surrounding ships but also watch the radarscopes. Burke then began demonstrating to the president how the officer having the conn used radar to control the fleet. Suddenly he was interrupted by a couple of the radar operators shouting, "Bogeys!" Instantly the signal was sounded, and the fighters not already in the air began taking off.

Snowden had drilled his pilots in using a modification of Joe Eggert's tactical plan that achieved the Turkey Shoot. He lacked fighters to build a defensive wall of planes, but those he had stacked themselves at great height, whence they swooped down upon the oncoming, unsuspecting attackers. Had the carrier planes opened fire, the air force planes would have been clobbered, and their pilots knew it. The rules of the game required them to acknowledge defeat by turning back, and they did. Their attack had ignominiously backfired.

The visitors outside on *FDR*'s bridge wings had seen nothing, the contact having been beyond visual range, but those in flag plot with the president had watched the radarscopes with fascination. Mr. Truman was delighted. "He thought it was a good thing for the air force to do," said Burke afterward. "He thought it was a good experience for us, too. It would have been a hell of a setback for us if we'd been caught not prepared for that sort of monkey business."

The story of the Eighth Fleet's mock victory got around the ship fast. When the fighters returned to the carriers, the visitors crowded out on the bridge wings and received them with cheers. The pilots, inspired by their achievement and the obvious approval of their distinguished guests, outdid themselves that afternoon with demonstrations including mock battles, dive-bombing, and the rest of their bag of tricks.

At the end of the day, Admiral Mitscher and his staff, already dog-tired, had about reached the point of exhaustion, but after dinner they perforce played their expected role of genial hosts to those of their guests who had a mind to party until the small hours. Luckily regulations forbade serving alcoholic drinks on board, or some of the convivial visitors might have stayed up to greet the dawn.

Because the demonstration was being conducted on a war footing, there was a combat air patrol, and Mitscher, Burke, Griffin, and Snowden were up after a couple of hours of sleep to watch the predawn launching. Following breakfast the presidential party assembled to observe gunnery, including shooting from ships and planes at drones and towed sleeves. Most of the officers found this demonstration less than exemplary, but President Truman, though he had served as an army artillery officer in World War I, had forgotten the fine points and praised what he saw.

The president was on the flag bridge standing with Admiral Mitscher when a target drone was launched. It had passed back and forth several times when something went awry with the remote-control system, and it headed for *FDR*'s after flight deck, where a dozen armed, fueled planes were ready to take off. Mitscher and his staffers went tense, expecting a crash and an explosion that would take several pilots' lives and turn the demonstration from a minor triumph into a major disaster. But the drone suddenly dipped down and plunged harmlessly near the carrier's stern. Those in the know breathed again. Mr. Truman, thinking the close pass was intentional, applauded vigorously.

When the visitors at last departed, Burke and Griffin collapsed on their bunks and slept around the clock. Arleigh awakened to bad news. The supply officer was virtually wringing his hands. It appeared that as the presidential party left, most of the issued gear had left with them—evidently carried off as souvenirs. The stuff was worth several hundred dollars, big money in 1946. Admiral Mitscher was responsible for it to the Bureau of Supplies and Accounts, and the supply officer was responsible to the admiral.

"Commodore," said the supply officer, "unless we get this gear back, we've got to survey it. Who's going to sign for it?"

It appeared that President Truman was not among those who had made off with the expensive gear. He had left everything neatly in his stateroom as he found it. That gave Burke an idea. He'd make a dummy run with the president's staff. The obvious contact was the military aide. Arleigh called up General Vaughan.

"General," he said, "your party took some gear by accident when you left."

"The hell I took it by accident," snorted the general. "I'm going to keep it. It's good gear. You gave it to us, and I'm going to keep it."

"Okay," replied Burke wearily. "You keep it."

Arleigh had the supply officer draw up a survey, listing the missing items. Burke signed it under "Stolen by the presidential party." He thought he'd get a squawk from the bureau, but he never heard anything more about the high-level larceny.

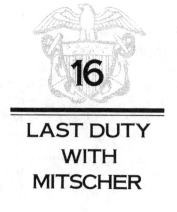

16

LAST DUTY
WITH
MITSCHER

IN A POSTMORTEM discussion of the 22–23 April combat exercise, Admiral Mitscher and his staff were far more critical of the Eighth Fleet's performance than the president and his party had been. The gunnery in particular they judged extremely spotty. Mitscher decreed more weeks of exercises and sought permission to take the fleet to the Caribbean, where the gunners could practice shore bombardment at the bombing ranges on Vieques and Culebra islands.

Chief of Naval Operations Nimitz approved the Caribbean exercise, but he informed Mitscher that the Eighth Fleet would not deploy in the Mediterranean after all. The visit of battleship *Missouri* had been enough to prod the Soviets into backing off. Secretary Forrestal decided that the arrival of a whole U.S. fleet in the Mediterranean at this time might appear an overreaction. In the current situation the U.S. Navy would limit its presence there to one carrier with escorts.

Exercises and instruction continued unabated during the Eighth Fleet's southward voyage. Admiral Mitscher now began shifting the routine burdens of command from his own shoulders to those of his staff, chiefly Burke's. Devoting his own energies to whipping his fleet into shape, he tackled the problem of deficient gunnery from every angle, including aerial observation of bombing runs at Culebra.

On 28 May, Mitscher brought his fleet into New York harbor. He considered it still not battle-worthy, but it was far more capable and professional than it had been in mid-April. He was commanding the only operational force left in the Atlantic Fleet, most of whose ships had been decommissioned and mothballed for want of funds and personnel.

The New Yorkers, delighted to see that the country still had what looked like a fighting fleet, gave the Eighth a rousing welcome, and Mitscher was the man of the hour. He exchanged courtesy calls with Mayor William O'Dwyer, presided at various public functions, and was invited in advance to put a horseshoe of flowers around the neck of whichever horse should win the Belmont Stakes. To show his appreciation for this honor, Mitscher placed a bet. A complete amateur at horse racing, he bet twenty dollars on the nose of a horse named Avenger, a choice he made for no better reason than that its sire had come from Oklahoma, where Pete was born. To everybody's surprise, Avenger, a long shot, came in first, and Pete made a killing.

The admiral now took time off for a little fishing, and Burke brought the fleet back to its home port of Norfolk, where Mitscher soon rejoined. Pete, convinced that talking to people was easier and more likely to get results than writing a lot of letters, had Burke fly to Washington every Thursday on fleet business. If Arleigh saw no one else, he made a point each week of dropping by CNO Nimitz's headquarters and checking with Vice Admirals Mick Carney, Forrest Sherman, and Arthur Radford, deputies respectively for logistics, operations, and air.

Commander in Chief Atlantic Fleet Jonas Ingram fell ill early in July, whereupon Admiral Mitscher, next in seniority, assumed extra duty as acting Cinclant. Admiral Ingram's flagship, amphibious force command ship *Pocono*, was at New York. Mitscher, remaining at Norfolk, had Burke fly up and find out what had to be done and what papers had to be signed. Hardly had Arleigh arrived in New York when Commodore Oscar Smith, Ingram's chief of staff, became ill also, and Burke found himself simultaneously acting as chief of staff to Cinclant, chief of staff to acting Cinclant, and chief of staff to commander Eighth Fleet.

When Commodore Smith recovered, Arleigh dropped one of his titles, but as chief of staff to Mitscher in his capacities as both acting Cinclant and commander Eighth Fleet, he commuted by air regularly between Norfolk and New York, made his weekly flights to Washington, and performed his duties as double chief of staff. Only a man of Burke's extraordinary stamina and soundness of nerves could have carried the load.

In midsummer, Mitscher, informed that he was to succeed Ingram as commander in chief Atlantic Fleet, was in a quandary. He was uninformed about the Atlantic Ocean and its tributary seas, their ports, bases, and lines of communication, and unacquainted with the politics he and his staff would have to consider and the foreign officials with whom they would have to deal.

Some officers facing the problem would have plunged into an orgy of reading. Not Mitscher. He could rarely bring himself to read anything more complex than a detective story—which may explain why his grades at the Naval Academy placed him twenty-third from the bottom in a class of 130. On the other hand, he demonstrated high intelligence by flawless judgment in handling carrier forces, a new form of warfare, which had diminished the reputations of some of his predecessors, Frank Jack Fletcher, George Murray, Charles Pownall—all of whom had earned much higher Naval Academy class standings than he.

Mitscher learned from experience, using eyes and ears, and that is what he proposed to do in preparing himself for his new assignment. He wanted to go to Europe with key members of his staff to look over the geography and consult key officials in order to develop ideas and plans for meeting another crisis like the one that had nearly developed. No letter writer, Mitscher asked Burke to request permission for the tour on his next Thursday visit at CNO headquarters.

Carney, Sherman, and Radford thought well of Mitscher's proposed junket and took Burke in to Nimitz, who approved it. Then a complication developed. Admiral Sherman wanted to go along. As Cincpac deputy chief of staff in World War II, Nimitz had publicly acknowledged Sherman's contribution to the victory by inviting him, along with Admiral Halsey, to stand beside him while he signed the Japanese surrender document for the United States. Thus in the CNO's opinion Sherman clearly had the background and the capacity to profit by the tour, gaining information and perspectives that could prove useful to him in his current duty. Nimitz approved of his going if Mitscher agreed.

Mitscher did not agree. When Burke returned to Norfolk with the proposal that Sherman join their party, Pete reacted with a sharp negative. "Admiral," Burke protested, "you ought to invite him. He's a brilliant man."

"I know he's brilliant," replied Mitscher. "He's too damned brilliant. He'd take charge."

"Well," said Burke, "suppose we arrange with him not to take charge."

"No, you can't do that. He'd violate it. He wouldn't intend to do it, but he would violate it. Besides that, he talks all the time. I don't want to listen to him."

"Suppose we do make that agreement."

"No, nothing doing."

"It's going to be embarrassing," said Burke. "What will I tell Admiral Sherman?"

"Tell him the damned truth. I don't want him to go."

Time was getting short, so Arleigh flew back to Washington at once and called on Admiral Sherman. "Admiral Mitscher doesn't want you to go," he said.

"Do you know why?"

"Not all the reasons probably, but I know some of them," and he repeated what Mitscher had said.

"It's a good trip," said Sherman, "and you're going to learn a lot. I'd like very much to go. Do you think I should?"

"I personally think so," replied Arleigh, "but if Admiral Mitscher says no, then no it is."

Sherman said he'd do his best to maintain a low profile and speak when spoken to. "Will you talk to Admiral Mitscher again for me?" he said. "Or should I talk to him?"

"By no means," said Burke. "Don't you talk to him. He'll freeze on you."

So Burke flew back to Norfolk and had another round with Mitscher. "Admiral Sherman would very much like to go," he said, "and I think he ought to go. I think he'll abide by any rules we lay down."

"Dammit, Burke," said Mitscher, "if you want him to go, you keep him out of my hair. If anything happens, I'm going to call you. I'm not going to have anything to do with Admiral Sherman. You handle it, because you're the one who's going to catch the guff."

So there would be no misunderstanding, Burke went to Admiral Sherman and told him exactly what Admiral Mitscher had said. "Fine," replied Sherman. "I'll go under those conditions."

The touring party, besides Mitscher and Sherman, included staffers Arleigh Burke, Don Griffin, George Anderson, and Charlie Mauro; Captain Ernie Litch, commanding officer of *Franklin D.*

Roosevelt; and, to assist the party, Everett Eynon, Mitscher's flag
lieutenant, and a messboy. They took off from Anacostia Naval Air
Station on 19 August 1946. Besides crew, passengers, and baggage,
their plane carried quantities of provisions. Such cargo was not
unusual at that time, because food shortages were so severe in early
postwar Europe that American parties heading thither for official
visits usually carried foodstuffs, some of which would be served to
them and their hosts at their hosts' tables.

The Mitscher plane refueled at Argentia, Newfoundland, and at
Keflavík, Iceland, and the party inspected the U.S. air bases at each.
On their arrival at an airport near London they were met by a car
from U.S. naval headquarters and driven to their hotel. On the way
they glimpsed the terrible destruction done by air attack. Much of
the city's center was mere rubble, devastation achieved largely by
German rockets fired from the Continent in the last year of the war.

To Burke's dismay the hotel to which they were conducted
turned out to be Claridge's, one of London's finest and most expensive—not the preferred choice of officers traveling on seven dollars
per diem. Arleigh was further shocked when he reached his quarters
in the hotel. It was no mere bedchamber but a palatial suite comprising a spacious living room with vestibule and kitchen alcove and
flanked by two large bedrooms, each with a pair of twin beds and
a bath.

Burke turned to Eynon, the flag lieutenant. "Ev," he said, "who
pays for this?"

"You do."

"How much?"

"I don't know, but the naval attaché here set us up. I don't
suppose it would be outrageous."

"I can't pay for this on any seven dollars a day."

Burke telephoned Admiral Mitscher, who was on the floor above,
stunned to find himself in a similar suite.

"Admiral," said Burke, "we've got to do something about this.
These are suites they save for royalty."

"Well," said Mitscher, "let's double up. I'll move down to your
suite. I'll take one bedroom and you take the other. I'll have Eynon
in my bedroom, and you have Sherman in yours."

The rest of the party, who had been lodged in quarters only
slightly less grand, were equally anxious to double up and avoid
paying sizable hotel charges out of their own pockets. Burke sent
Ev Eynon down to make the best deal he could, placing the members close together, in single beds two to a room.

A couple of hotel managers in morning coats came up, plainly aghast that the commander-elect of the U.S. Atlantic Fleet and his entourage wanted to share space like weekend tourists. Burke did not mention the seven dollars per diem. Rather weakly he explained that they needed to hold frequent conferences, which would be facilitated by the more compact arrangement.

Before long, Claridge's was thrown once more into a dither, this time by a request to the housekeeper to send up an ironing board. The messboy had brought along an iron but no board. Presently there arrived at the suite door a very British valet to collect whatever needed to be pressed. He explained to the messboy that at Claridge's nobody pressed his own clothes. The hotel would do that.

"Oh, no," said the messboy. "I don't let anybody press my admiral's clothes but me."

The valet insisted that ironing was done at Claridge's only in the laundry, never in the rooms. To sidetrack the impending altercation, Burke intervened, using his sternest military command voice. The valet departed, and the ironing board at length arrived, brought by a laundryman.

Mitscher's first conference was with Vice Admiral H. Kent Hewitt, commander U.S. naval forces Europe, and his staff, stationed in London. Hewitt knew the Mediterranean, having commanded an earlier Eighth Fleet, title of World War II U.S. naval forces that landed invasion troops in Sicily, Italy, and southern France. The admiral and his people briefed the Americans on Mediterranean geography and political and military problems.

The Americans spent their second day at the British Admiralty. Here they were guests of Admiral of the Fleet Sir John Cunningham, first sea lord and chief of naval staff. As commander in chief of the Allied Mediterranean Fleet in World War II, he had been Admiral Hewitt's boss.

In the ornate Admiralty conference room, Admiral Cunningham sat at the head of a long green-baize-covered table with Admiral Mitscher on his right and Admiral Sherman on Mitscher's right. Seated at the table also were the other four sea lords, the Admiralty secretary, and a few more highly placed permanent staff people. At the far end of the table opposite Cunningham were charts on an easel. The rest of the official American party and other British officers sat in rows of chairs behind the participants at the table. The Royal Navy had clearly trotted out its stars to receive, inform, and perhaps prevail over the Americans.

Admiral Cunningham led off with a discussion of the political and military problems of the Mediterranean and how the British were trying to deal with them but could not do so without substantial help from the United States. After a break for lunch, each of the other sea lords spoke, explaining his specific responsibility and how he intended, or hoped, to carry it out.

There were no interruptions. Admiral Mitscher had announced to his fellow Americans before the meeting that he would be their spokesman, but thus far he had not spoken. The Americans just sat and listened. The British talked until about 1530, when they had run down. Admiral Cunningham next briefly and adroitly summarized what had been said and then got to the point. The British would like the United States to send over a sizable body of warships and attach them to the small British naval force at Malta. The Americans would use British communications and the British intelligence system. The U.S. Navy would furnish what amounted to the operating ships, but the Royal Navy would run the show.

Burke knew that this suggestion wasn't going to sit well with Mitscher, but the admiral didn't say a word—just sat there. Finally Cunningham said to him, "Admiral, you do agree with me, don't you?"

Mitscher shook his head and said his first word: "No." That was all. Silence reigned. Everybody was embarrassed but Admiral Mitscher, who just sat there, motionless. Cunningham looked around, mortified. At last, after what seemed like a very long wait, he said, "The British have a solution for situations like this. Let us have tea."

So tea was served. Admiral Mitscher now talked cordially enough, but said not a word on the subject that had brought about the recess.

After tea the parties returned to the conference table. After all were settled and quiet reigned again, Cunningham said, "Admiral, why don't you agree with us?"

Admiral Mitscher replied, "The nation that furnishes the forces furnishes the command. The nation that furnishes the commander must have his own intelligence and his own communications so that he knows what's going on. If you furnish the majority of the forces, your command. If we furnish the majority of the forces, our command."

Against this simple statement the British had no argument. It was exactly the position they would have taken for themselves had they possessed the majority of forces. Possessing no such majority, they had still hoped, but scarcely expected, to talk the Americans into accepting their leadership. When Mitscher in four sentences quashed that unrealistic hope, the Royal Navy tacitly dropped its centuries-old claim on the Mediterranean Sea as a British lake—a claim founded on Rooke's capture of Gibraltar in 1704 and confirmed by Nelson's destruction of Napoleon's fleets a century later. The British, denied the leading role, offered their support, and Mitscher agreed to try to bring ships to the Med—the future Sixth Fleet.

After a formal dinner at the Admiralty, at which meat the Americans had brought was served, the Mitscher party got back to Claridge's at 2230 and promptly turned in. They had planned to get an early start for a scheduled inspection trip to U.S. bases at Plymouth and Exeter in southwest England. Burke was ready to go to sleep, but no sooner had Sherman hit the sack than he let loose with all the words he had kept bottled up through the day. His discourse was fascinating, Arleigh conceded, but apparently unending. He was still talking when Burke drifted off to sleep at 0100.

Most of the party was up and ready to go by 0700, but Mitscher and Sherman were remaining in London, the former because he wasn't feeling well, the latter because he had other business. Sherman had reluctantly sat silent while Mitscher got what he wanted, a commitment from the British. Now as deputy CNO for operations, Sherman wanted details, and to get them he spent the day talking with British officers at the Admiralty, while Burke and the other staffers headed southwest in a U.S. Navy car.

The navy had found that when it closed its wartime bases on foreign soil, most or all of its equipment simply disappeared—appropriated, annexed, liberated, or just plain stolen. In abandoning the Plymouth and Exeter bases, the United States planned on leaving much of the equipment to the British, but certain expensive, rare, or secret items, such as communication apparatus, including ciphering machines, were not to be abandoned or left unguarded. The Burke inspection party was to identify such equipment and earmark it for return by secure means to the United States.

From London the Mitscher party flew to Berlin at the invitation of Rear Admiral Roscoe E. Schuirmann, U.S. naval representative. Their plane passed by specified route with Russian permission over the Soviet zone of occupation, later called East Germany. Landing at Tempelhof Airport in the American sector of the city, they were taken by car to Schuirmann's house, a commandeered German residence on Lake Wannsee in southwest Berlin.

The visitors provided most of the raw food that evening, and the

German household servants turned it into a beautifully cooked and served banquet. As one of the servants, the chief housekeeper, was backing out of the dining room into the kitchen with a tray in her hand, Burke noticed that she was looking at the Americans with an expression of absolute hatred. After dinner he said to Schuirmann, "Admiral, your housekeeper is a dangerous woman. She hates you."

"I know," replied Schuirmann. "Wouldn't you under these circumstances?" The house had belonged to the housekeeper's father. He and his family had been ousted, and the Americans had taken over. The daughter and other young women were willing to come as maids only because in the American-occupied house they got enough to eat in the midst of a hungry city.

"They were rich," Schuirmann continued. "Now they have nothing. This young woman sees this beautiful dinner, much better than our normal meals, and she knows that her people are hungry. Of course she hates us."

The American party had come to Berlin mainly to see the desolation wrought by the war. In the city's center it was nearly complete—the product of many months of aerial bombing followed by bombardment from the guns of the Russians, approaching from the east as Hitler blew his brains out in a bunker under his shattered chancellery.

The Berliners were living in basements and in whatever other shelter they could find among the ruins. "Yet," Burke recalled, "the rubble was piled up neatly. The streets were still swept by people who were starving. They were hungry, really hungry. They had achieved neatness in the midst of destruction. That made a bigger impression on me concerning German character than anything else I've ever seen—how they organized themselves into an orderly pattern to do what they could do with what little equipment they had."

Few soldiers of the American occupation forces shared Burke's admiration of the beaten Germans. This was a period of mutual aversion. German arms had swept like a plague over much of Europe, destroying millions of people and their homes and workshops. The conquering Allies closing in on Germany discovered the terrible death camps, where millions more people had been tortured and slain. The U.S. Army had issued to its occupying troops a pamphlet warning them not to trust the Germans. The feeling among the occupiers was that the people of Germany deserved their fate.

But Americans are poor haters. From the beginning, the occupation cooks in their barracks, with the hungry Germans in mind, put out table scraps and other refuse in separate cans marked Edible Garbage and Inedible Garbage. Before the end of 1947, German and Americans were cooperating on every level and the German economy was being restored with the assistance of the U.S. Marshall Plan.

In contrast to dismal Berlin, the Mitscher party found Paris, after a grim four years of German occupation, again conforming to its title City of Lights. The visitors were cordially received by pro-American Vice Admiral Lemonnier, chief of naval staff. He was a close friend of Admiral Hewitt, with whom he had landed in southern France in 1944 at the head of forces of liberation. Now in daylong discussions the French granted the Americans free use of the port of Toulon and the support of what was left of their fleet after wartime sinkings by the Americans at the invasion of Morocco and by the British and the French themselves to keep French ships out of German hands.

For relaxation following the long conference, Admiral Lemonnier had reserved seats for the participants at the Folies-Bergère. He had, moreover, prepared an elaborate surprise, which none of the Americans suspected, though they might have been alerted by the fact that Admiral Mitscher was seated not among his countrymen but up front between two Frenchmen. In the evening's program one of the skits was an acrobatic act featuring girls not in the usual Folies-Bergère nude but costumed to look like little teddy bears with human faces. At the height of the act, one of the bears came swinging out over the footlights, let go, and with the aid of the Frenchmen flanking Mitscher, landed squarely in the startled admiral's lap. At that instant a concealed cameraman snapped a photo that found its way to various unlikely places in the United States, including the hands of Mrs. Mitscher, leaving that estimable lady in a state of shock.

In Rome the Americans dealt mainly with two rear admirals, an American, Ellery Stone, and an Italian, Antonio Ziroli. The American admiral headed an Allied Control Commission, which would handle aspects of Italy's foreign affairs until the county's borders with France, Austria, and Yugoslavia were settled and the peace treaty signed. To Burke it seemed that Stone was "damned near running Italy," but regarding naval decisions Stone always checked with Ziroli, who after Stone's departure might have the power to condemn decisions he didn't care for. Ziroli, however, was anxious to cooperate with the Americans and have them use the port of Naples.

While in Rome, Admiral Mitscher obtained an audience with the pope and permission to bring Admiral Sherman and Commodore Burke along. They were going not merely for the experience. Eugenio Pacelli, Pius XII, besides being a religious leader was one of the best-informed statesmen in Europe, having been papal secretary of state from 1930 until he was elected pope in 1939.

The three Americans drove down to the pope's summer palace at Castel Gandolfo in the Alban Hills south of Rome. In their pockets they carried rosaries and other ecclesiastical objects pressed upon them by their Catholic friends for papal blessing. After presenting their credentials at the palace, they were handed over to a minister of state, who conducted them into the presence of his holiness. Clad in a white cassock, the pope rose from his desk. Tall, lean, erect, he was a majestic figure, his somewhat hawklike face softened by an engaging smile. He paused a moment as if expecting something, then advanced, extending his hand in greeting. As they shook hands, he said, "Well, it's obvious that none of you are Catholics, so we might as well get down to business."

Motioning them to chairs, the pope seated himself and began to talk, using almost flawless English. It was clear he knew who they were and what their mission was. He talked about world problems and Italy's problems in particular, pausing from to time like the well-bred gentleman he was to permit his visitors to ask questions or make observations. When he got into a discussion of ways to meet the problems, specifically what the U.S. Navy might contribute, the Americans were impressed not only with his detailed knowledge but also with the common sense with which he marshaled his arguments.

The pope at length shifted from his discussion of world affairs to such casual topics as his pleasure in his sojourns at Gandolfo, where he could get away from routine. His visitors took this as a gentle hint that the audience was over and presently rose.

Burke, mindful of his other mission, said, "Your Holiness, we have with us a great many rosaries and things that belong to our Catholic friends."

"Fine," said the pope as if that was usual and expected, as indeed it was. He blessed the objects, then turning to his desk, he added, "But you should have one that I give to you." Taking three rosaries from a drawer, he handed one to each of his callers, saying, "You're not Catholic, but this won't do you any harm and may do you some good."

Afterward Burke echoed the sentiments of his friends in saying, "He was a very fine man."

Mitscher, foreseeing that their tour would involve long formal dinners and cocktail parties at every stop, had made an arrangement with Burke to escape at a reasonable hour, before he became tired. He took advantage of the fact that Burke could read his lips—a facility his chief of staff had necessarily acquired because of Mitscher's soft speech. When Pete had had enough at, say, 2230, he would look at Burke and silently say, "Let's get out of here." Burke would then begin making apologies, saying he was awfully sorry but the admiral had to leave. Mitscher would protest that his chief of staff was dragging him off, but away they would go, leaving their foreign hosts wondering about American command relationships that countenanced a commodore ordering a four-star admiral to go home and get to bed. Actually when Mitscher and Burke got back to their hotel they might sit up and talk past midnight. For Burke such occasional quiet conversations were a welcome alternative to Sherman's nightly brilliant but long-winded discussions.

From Rome the American party flew to Naples, where they inspected the harbor. It was almost cleaned up now from the shambles the Germans had left it in when they evacuated the city in the fall of 1944. They had burned or blown up most of the buildings along the waterfront, blocked access to piers and moles, sunk ships in the harbor and piled on them cranes, trucks, box cars, and a few locomotives—not so much to delay the Allied advance as to revenge themselves on the turncoat Italians.

Before the party left Rome, Burke had noticed that Admiral Mitscher was slowing down and appeared uncomfortable. At Naples he attended only what he could not avoid, the official briefings. The night before their departure, Arleigh urged him to see a local doctor, but Pete refused, saying there was nothing wrong with him. The next morning when they got to the airport to fly to Malta, Mitscher got into the plane all right, but he seemed to collapse into his seat. Burke sat beside him.

"Admiral," he said, "how do you feel?"

"Fine."

"Admiral," snorted Burke. "you're a goddam liar. You don't feel fine at all. Something's wrong with you."

"I've got a little trouble," said Pete. "Maybe a little appendicitis."

The flight to Malta took several hours. As they were approaching the island, Burke said, "Admiral, they'll have a battalion here for you to inspect. Do you want me to inspect them? I'd like to. I've never inspected a battalion."

"No, dammit. It's my job to inspect them."

"Admiral, you'd better take it easy."

"No," replied Pete, "these people came down here to meet me, and I owe them the courtesy of inspecting them, and I'm going to do it."

When the plane landed, Mitscher deplaned first, as befitted his rank, and exchanged salutes and shook hands with Admiral Algernon Willis, British commander in chief Mediterranean. Admiral Sherman was supposed to be next in line, but Burke pushed ahead, excusing himself. Sherman, guessing what was going on, let him pass.

Sidling up to Admiral Willis, Burke whispered, "My admiral is a very sick man. Please cut the inspection as short as possible, and let's try to get him to bed."

"Righto!"

Willis with Mitscher inspected the front rank, and that was all. They then climbed into a car and went to the British admiral's quarters, where Pete had been invited to stay. Sherman and Burke followed in the second car. When they got to Admiral Willis's house, Mitscher was already turning in. Burke said to Willis, "I don't know what's wrong with Admiral Mitscher, but there's something wrong, I know. Would you have your surgeon look at him?"

At Willis's call, a medical team of two surgeons arrived and examined Mitscher. Coming out of the bedroom, they announced their diagnosis: acute appendicitis. "We've got to operate right away."

"Have you told the admiral?" Burke asked.

"No, we're telling you."

"Okay, let's go and tell him." Burke went in to Mitscher. "You have appendicitis," he said, "and they're going to operate."

"The hell they are," said Mitscher. "I'm going back. We'll saddle up here and get the hell out and go to the States."

"No, you aren't, Admiral," Burke said. "I'm not going to take a plane, put you in it, and arrive home with a dead commander in chief. You can't make it to the States. These guys are going to get that appendix out of you."

The operation was a success, but it had been a bad case. Mitscher would have to stick around for a while. After the party had inspected the Malta base and their time was up, Burke called on Mitscher at the hospital. He asked Admiral Willis to come along and witness what he told Pete.

"You can't be out of here for two weeks. We can't hang around that long. We're going to take the plane and continue this tour."

"You can't do that!"

"Well, we are going to do it," Burke replied.

Mitscher grumbled, but he knew they were doing the only correct thing. They had been invited to Algiers before they left America. They had accepted. They were now expected on schedule, and provision had been made at the French naval base for their accommodation. Leaving behind Ev Eynon, Mitscher's personal aide, the rest took off. As senior officer present, Sherman took charge. That is what Mitscher had predicted, without foreseeing the circumstances.

From Algiers the party headed back for the United States, pausing to refuel at Port Lyautey in French Morocco, at the Azores, and at Bermuda. During the Bermuda pause, Burke bought two cases of Scotch (eighteen dollars a case) and sent them to the British in Malta as thanks for taking care of the admiral. He had had the foresight to inquire Admiral Mitscher's nurse's stocking size. Back in the States he had Bobbie buy and send her a dozen pairs of nylon hose, a rare commodity in Europe in those postwar days.

At the time of his return to Norfolk in early September 1946, Burke ran into a mare's nest of complications. From Malta he received word that Mitscher felt well enough to travel and wanted to come home. Believing the transatlantic plane ride would be too much for him, Burke turned the problem over to Admiral Sherman, who arranged for light cruiser *Little Rock*, then on a goodwill tour, to pick Mitscher up and bring him to Norfolk, flat on his back if necessary. Jonas Ingram was ill again, and his chief of staff, Oscar Smith, was not feeling well. Arleigh went to New York to see what could be done in that quarter. Ingram and Smith wanted Mitscher to take command of the Atlantic Fleet right away, but that was out of the question, because Pete was by then on the high seas.

Learning that *Little Rock* was to arrive at Norfolk on 8 September, Ingram scheduled the change of command for the 10th. As Arleigh expected, Mitscher arrived too weak to travel to New York, much less participate in a ceremony in which he would have to read his orders and make a speech. It appeared that Ingram was still not well enough to participate either.

"So," says Burke, "I went up and relieved Cinclant. I don't quite know how I did it, but I relieved Cinclant through his chief of staff, and I took over as Cinclant and notified Admiral Mitscher, who really became Cinclant."

Since Mitscher had no intention of going to New York even if he had been able to do so, Burke took flagship *Pocono* to Norfolk. Mitscher was now both commander in chief Atlantic Fleet and commander Eighth Fleet, and Arleigh was his chief of staff and acting deputy in both capacities. With one or two other staffers, Admiral Burke flew to Washington every Thursday, as before, to maintain liaison with the Navy Department. Also as before, he flew regularly to New York to maintain liaison with that part of the Atlantic Fleet staff who, for one reason or another, found it necessary to remain there.

One of the principal duties of a commander in chief is to inspect naval establishments. Ingram because of poor health had been neglecting this responsibility, and now Mitscher for the same reason wasn't up to making the flights up and down the Atlantic coast. Burke and Griffin took turns conducting inspections, but it wasn't the same thing. The base commanders expected the commander in chief.

So Admiral Mitscher set out in late October to visit the establishments not by plane but at a slower pace, in flagship *Pocono*. Because he was tired, running down, his staff generally did the inspecting, but Mitscher would receive the commanders on board his flagship, and that seemed to satisfy everybody.

As *Pocono* approached Casco Bay, Mitscher received from the governor of Maine an invitation to a pheasant shoot. That was not the admiral's sport. He was an expert fisherman, but didn't claim to be much of a shot. Feeling somewhat better, he accepted. He came back elated. His shooting, he said, had improved remarkably. He never learned that the shoot was a setup. The wardens had brought the birds to the spot and fed them grain to the point where they could scarcely rise from the ground.

Back at Norfolk, Burke found that the sudden postwar shrinking of the U.S. Navy plus Admiral Ingram's poor health had left Atlantic Fleet organization records in wretched shape. Working on these, together with other duties, kept the staffs working early and late.

Bobbie drove down from Washington and rented a small apartment, hoping to see more of Arleigh and give him some home life. It didn't work out. At sea, Arleigh and Pete had breakfasted together each morning at seven. Now that Bobbie had provided her husband a retreat ashore, Pete still expected him for breakfast. Because his rapidly aging boss was obviously a sick man, Arleigh couldn't bear to disappoint him, or Bobbie, which meant that he sometimes had two breakfasts. Don Griffin recalls the situation at the end of nearly every day: "Arleigh Burke's wife would come down to the dock to pick Arleigh up and take him home. She would drive up, park her car on the dock, and sometimes she would sit there until eight or nine o'clock waiting for him to come down."

One morning Mitscher said, "Burke, I want you to burn all my papers."

"Where are they, Admiral?"

Mitscher pointed to a pair of filing cabinets. Two or three mornings later, he said, "Did you burn my papers?"

"No, sir."

"All right. I'll burn them myself." He asked Burke why he had failed to carry out the order.

"Because," said Arleigh, "there's a lot of history in there, a lot of things that nobody else has, and they ought to be preserved."

"Yes," said Mitscher, "there is stuff in there that would be useful, but there's also some stuff that's detrimental to people. There are statements I have written without knowing the full story, statements critical of people I now wish I hadn't written and that actually aren't even true. Other things in there are carelessly written, capable of misinterpretation by someone for his own advantage or to vent a grudge. I don't want to leave anything. What I've done is all over. It's all finished. Forget it."

It was clear to Burke then that Mitscher knew he was dying. He had no time to sort out his papers. He destroyed them all.

Dying or not, Mitscher kept himself busy planning the forthcoming winter maneuvers in the Caribbean. With, as always, a dim view of paperwork, he insisted that Burke show him only papers it was absolutely vital he sign in person.

"There shouldn't be more than one or two each day," he said. "If there are any more than that, then something's going wrong that ought to be corrected. Keep your explanations short. If you can't explain a paper in two minutes, it's not clear."

Arleigh did better than that. He wrote across the top of each message a concise statement of the contents. Sometimes Mitscher would read these summaries, but more often he would merely say, "Do I agree with this?" and if Burke said yes, he would sign without looking at either text or summary.

Frances Mitscher came to Norfolk to be with her husband but had no better luck than Bobbie Burke had. As a special concession to his sixtieth birthday, 26 January, which in 1947 was a Sunday, Pete took the day off to spend with Frances. During the afternoon while they were at the Princess Anne Golf Club, he complained of feeling ill. Frances called a doctor, who had the admiral admitted to the naval base hospital. His ailment, at first announced as bronchitis, was subsequently diagnosed as a heart attack. From the White House on 1 February came a message: "This is just a line to tell you I am sorry to hear you are in the hospital. Keep your chin up and get well soon. Harry S. Truman."

When Arleigh Burke visited Pete at the hospital, he discovered that his boss was still at work, planning the winter maneuvers in his mind. He rattled off a series of orders, which were to be followed up. Not long afterward, *Pocono* received a notice from the hospital stating that the admiral was not having visitors. His doctors had learned that when staff members called, Mitscher couldn't resist discussing navy business and making plans. It was important that he conserve his energy toward recovery.

At first even Frances was denied visiting privileges, because she had contracted a severe cold. At last on 2 February the doctors let her come briefly into Pete's room and speak with him but not approach his bed. He died that night of coronary thrombosis. When the news reached Burke, he put out a dispatch to the navy: "The admiral has slipped his cable," like a ship slipping her moorings to put to sea.

Admiral Mitscher had never made arrangements about his funeral and burying place, and Frances, a gentle and impractical soul, had done nothing and had no idea what to do. Burke arranged for funeral services in the Fort Myer chapel and burial in nearby Arlington National Cemetery. On the morning of 5 February, he, Mrs. Mitscher, and key staff members took off by plane in a snowstorm for Washington to pay their last respects to the fallen warrior.

The chapel was packed, with hundreds standing outside in the bitter cold. The president was represented by Admiral Leahy, his chief of staff. Practically all the senior commanders of the Pacific war, from Admiral Nimitz on down, were present, some having flown great distances on short notice. The procession from chapel to grave included a battalion of midshipmen and two platoons each of marines and bluejackets. The navy gave the great commander its final farewell in a seventeen-gun salute.

Much later, in dictating his oral history, Burke said of Mitscher, "He was wise, he was simple, he was direct, he was demanding, and he was ruthless. You wanted to please him, to prove yourself to him, to win his approval." And in an article recalling his years of service with Mitscher, Burke wrote: "I had no desire to serve on Mitscher's staff, no liking for him in the first months of that service—and, yet, he was so good I came to admire and respect his great ability, and within a year I had more affection for him—my demanding, reticent, biased boss—than I ever had for any man."

17

DESK DUTY,
ESCAPE
TO SEA,
AND RECALL

WHEN ADMIRAL MITSCHER was in the hospital, his doctors not only forbade his receiving visitors but ruled that no papers of any kind, including personal letters, were to be brought to his attention. His official mail presented no problem, because Burke and his fellow staffers were accustomed to processing that. Now Mrs. Mitscher asked Burke to handle his private correspondence also. One of the first of his boss's private letters that Burke opened was from Admiral John H. Towers, commander in chief of the Pacific Fleet. Arleigh was surprised to find his own name in it.

It appeared that Towers expected to be appointed chairman of the navy's General Board and in an earlier letter had requested the services of Arleigh Burke, but Mitscher had been reluctant to release him. Towers was now reiterating his request, pointing out that Burke had been with Mitscher a long time. Secretary Forrestal, he said, was counting on Towers to revive the Board from its current state of inertia, and Towers was counting on the energetic, articulate Burke to help him do it.

Burke was both embarrassed at reading mail not intended for his eyes and astonished at Towers's request. The function of the General Board was to advise the secretary of the navy and the chief of naval operations. Arleigh had always thought of it as a place where elderly admirals could make themselves useful while temporarily out of a job, as for example when deserving fleeting up but with no immediate opening befitting their rank. Admiral King and other eminent naval leaders had done a stretch on the Board. Arleigh, in his mid-forties, with a permanent rank of captain, had never dreamed of being so early summoned into such lofty and venerable company.

The General Board, for all its imposing past, had lately fallen into some disesteem. The rapid expansion of the navy in World War II, providing abundant billets for officers capable of filling them, left on the Board only admirals whose services were not in demand—officers whose careers had somehow been sidetracked by the exigencies of modern warfare. Neither Admiral King, nor his successor Admiral Nimitz, nor Secretary Forrestal had felt any great impulse to turn to such men for advice. While anticipating the early retirement of the last of these wartime incumbents, Forrestal was evidently taking steps to restore the Board to its former influence and usefulness.

Burke answered Towers's letter, explaining that Mitscher was in the hospital and thanking the writer for his kind words about himself. He said that while he believed Mitscher was unlikely to return to full active duty, he would remain with him as long as he was needed. If, however, a time came when Admiral Mitscher no longer had use for him, he would be glad to join the General Board if Admiral Towers still wanted him there.

Following Admiral Mitscher's death a few days later, Vice Admiral Thomas L. Gatch, who was next senior in the Atlantic Fleet, became acting Cinclant, but in title only. He left Cinclant administration in *Pocono* and said he hoped he would not have to make any major decisions before the new Cinclant was appointed. Operations being routine at the time, he had nothing to worry about. As during Mitscher's illness, Burke in fact carried on as acting Cinclant.

After nearly a month's delay, Admiral William H. P. Blandy was appointed Cinclant. For his flagship he selected battleship *Missouri* and headed in her to the West Indies. Burke took *Pocono* to the West Indies also and reported to Blandy at Trinidad. Together with the latter's chief of staff, Burke planned the change-of-command ceremony and arranged for transfer of the Atlantic Fleet files from *Pocono* to *Missouri*. On execution of the ceremony, Blandy became Cinclant and Burke became available to take his place on the General Board.

Following the change of command, Admiral Blandy hosted on board *Missouri* a reception and dinner, to which local officials and their ladies were invited. After dinner, Burke politely offered a guest and his severely arthritic wife transportation ashore in *Pocono*'s barge. Once they reached the pier, getting the handicapped lady onto it from the barge presented a problem, for the tide was out, the pier was high, and the lady was portly. While her husband with some difficulty held her upright in the rolling craft, Arleigh scrambled up onto the pier, squatted, reached down, and with his hands under the lady's arms hoisted her topside with a mighty heave.

As she lit, Burke felt his back snap. He managed to see the couple to their car, but as they drove off, he collapsed onto the pier, unable to move. The barge crew bundled him into the boat and took him back to *Pocono*, where the doctor told him he had torn a bunch of ligaments, a painful condition that only time and rest could heal.

In *Pocono* on the way to Puerto Rico, where he was to be detached, Burke spent most of his time in his bunk. On arrival at San Juan, he had improved enough to hobble on crutches over to the officers' club to attend a farewell party the staff was giving him. Under Secretary of the Navy John L. Sullivan, concluding an inspection tour of bases, offered him a ride to Washington in his plane and en route took all his money playing gin rummy.

Burke had a little leave coming, most of which he spent in bed, at first at his Washington home and then, on doctor's advice, at the hospital. Before the accident Arleigh had accepted an invitation to speak on 18 April. When he mentioned this to his doctor, the latter stated flatly, "You can't do it."

Burke demurred. This was no ordinary discourse, he explained, but a formal address to be delivered to the American Society of Naval Engineers at their annual dinner at Washington's Statler Hotel. He persuaded the doctor against the latter's better judgment to accompany him to the Statler. Here they took a room, and just before dinner the doctor injected Burke with a painkiller. He then accompanied him to the ballroom and carefully seated him at the table, saying, "This is going to wear off in about an hour and a half, and then you're going to be in real pain, but I'll be here and will take you back to the hospital. Meantime, don't eat, don't drink, and don't move."

Sitting like a graven image through dinner, Burke turned only his head to exchange a few words with his tablemates. At dinner's end, after being introduced, he rose effortlessly and made his speech to great applause. The doctor was there to catch him and spirit him helpless away, but Burke said he was feeling fine and planned to stay awhile. Though his back remained weak, the severe pain was gone. The doctors were baffled, and Arleigh was delighted.

A little later, when Burke reported at the Navy Department for duty on the General Board, Vice Admiral Charles H. McMorris was acting chairman. An officer of outstanding ability, McMorris had stood sixth from the top in the Naval Academy Class of 1912. His fellow midshipmen, awed by his Socratic wisdom, called him "Soc," a nickname he bore the rest of his life. At U.S. entry into World War II, he was war plans officer under Admiral Kimmel, a post he retained under Kimmel's relief, Admiral Nimitz. In 1943, he commanded the American cruiser-destroyer group in its Battle of the Komandorski Islands, last of the daytime surface actions. Recalled from sea duty, he relieved Admiral Spruance as Nimitz's chief of staff when Spruance took command of the Fifth Fleet.

Admiral Towers, who soon arrived and relieved McMorris as chairman, was another of the navy's superstars. He had been chronologically number three among the pioneers of naval aviation and had been chief of the Bureau of Aeronautics. In the Pacific war, he served as commander Air Force Pacific Fleet and then deputy Cincpac. At war's end, he became successively commander of the Fast Carrier Task Force, commander of the Big Blue Fleet, and commander in chief of the Pacific Fleet and the Pacific Ocean Areas, from which high eminence Forrestal had summoned him to revitalize the General Board.

Towers on Forrestal's advice had assembled an entirely new kind of General Board. Instead of a committee of exclusively high-ranking oldsters, he had brought together a galaxy of gifted officers ranging from commander to admiral, all with combat experience, all able to develop ideas and put them clearly and convincingly into words. Such a sterling group, Burke concluded, should serve as the navy's think tank, its idea factory, providing the SecNav and CNO with information and recommendations on which they could confidently base their leadership.

Instead, he found that McMorris had committed the Board to a study of the navy's shore establishment, with a view to reducing it to square with a shrinking budget and current waning needs. Like the seagoing navy, it had grown tremendously during the war. The navy afloat had already, as we have seen, been diminished by rapid demobilization. As a result, shore installations now included units that were no longer needed.

Since the shore establishment existed to service the fleet, the

Board, to advise intelligently on reductions, had to know the size
and composition of the operational fleet and where it was likely to
operate in peace and war. The Board had to determine how and
where the depots, yards, and bases were to function to remain
efficient in their peacetime support without impairing their ability
to mobilize rapidly and take care of an expanded fleet in time of war.
And it had to take into account economic and political as well as
military considerations. How serious an effect, for example, would
the sudden closing of a base, with cancellation of many jobs, have
on the local population? What could be done about senators and
congressmen who favored reduction but only in other legislators'
areas, never in their own?

Arleigh had lately been unconsciously preparing himself to face
such problems. During much of his career he had applied himself
so vigorously to the problems at hand that he had little energy left
for serious general reading. Within the field of his specialties he was
without peer, but he had become somewhat of a narrow specialist.
Gradually he came to realize that the world of informed citizens was
leaving him behind. Too often he saw references in newspapers or
heard references in conversations to things he did not understand.
To rectify this defect, Arleigh took advantage of the occasional
periods of respite he had been vouchsafed since the war, profiting
by these intervals to devour books and articles that might fill in the
blanks in his knowledge of history, economics, science, politics, and
international relations.

This recent reading helped Burke in some small measure to judge
the future functions of the shore establishment, but it also enabled
him to judge how much he and his colleagues had yet to learn. He
induced Admiral Towers to bring in experts to brief the General
Board on such subjects as the operations of the United Nations and
the navy's experiments toward use of atomic energy for weapons
and propulsion. As for himself, he joined Washington's Brookings
Institution for the study of economic, governmental, and international problems and attended its weekly lectures and discussion
periods. All of these studies had a bearing on what to do about the
shore establishment.

It dawned on Burke that the General Board could not carry out
its assignment unless it could predict with a fair degree of accuracy
what the United States was going to do in the course of, say, the
next ten years. That, he concluded, was just what the Board would
have to do: make a study and draw up a paper on national resources

and developing world conditions to which the United States would probably have to respond, using naval forces.

Burke put his thoughts in a short, carefully worded paper and placed it before his colleagues. They reacted with consternation. "That's not our business," they said. "Our business is the navy."

"Yes," replied Burke, "but we can't make very definite recommendations unless we know what the rest of the government is going to do. We can't make recommendations about the size of the navy if we don't know about the economy of the country and what future administrations are apt to do with our resources."

He couldn't arouse much enthusiasm for his plan among his colleagues, who insisted it was not their billet. But he kept hammering, making himself a nuisance. Finally the Board, to give him something else to think about, elected him mess treasurer. Arleigh took on the new duty without letting up on his hammering. At last his colleagues told him that if he wanted them to take his project seriously, he'd have to give them more than just a general idea. He'd have to give them some examples. "You're the honcho," said Towers. "You run it."

Burke did, or at least he made a start. While carrying out his current regular assignment, which was a study of the Bureau of Ships, he wrote notes to himself concerning what information—navywide, nationwide, and worldwide—he needed to make a judgment about the bureau's future operations. By the time he had finished that assignment, he had written himself a great stack of notes. One unforeseen problem was created by his poor handwriting. When he referred to his older notes, now grown cold, he found there were some he couldn't read.

The course of his studies brought before Burke the problem of strategic resources, raw materials needed for the conduct of war and not available domestically in adequate quantities. The U.S. armed forces had been plagued in World War II by shortages of such resources as chrome, molybdenum, rubber, and quinine. What provision was now being made during this time of uncertain peace to stockpile such resources? He resolved to make that part of his study.

The problem of resources brought him into the matter of oil. At one time the United States, with ample petroleum underground, had been the oil salesman of the world. The war had consumed a tremendous quantity of the domestic product. Eventually Americans would have to look elsewhere for a source of power. Atomic energy could be turned into steam to propel ships and into electricity to move trains and illuminate homes, shops, and factories. But, at least in Burke's day, oil would probably remain indispensable for moving such warmaking vehicles as aircraft, tanks, and trucks. Recognizing another area for study, Burke subscribed to the *World Oil Atlas* and *Oil Weekly.*

Arleigh talked with officers and officials in various government agencies and was surprised to find that apparently nobody was working on the sort of study he had undertaken. It was as if the United States government was feeling its way blindly into the frightening new world that the war had created.

Spurred by his discoveries, Burke wrote an average of twenty pages a day for several months, preparing a skeleton framework for the Big Study. Eventually he got some help. He obtained, for example, the services of a remarkable typist who learned to read his handwriting, even deciphering passages that Arleigh himself had long since given up on.

"By the end of 1947," said Burke later, "Admiral Towers and Admiral McMorris had accepted the general idea that we could do a paper on national security problems of the next ten years, with the understanding that I would guide it. It was my project, but the other members of the General Board would help, and they did. Everybody helped, and they did a marvelous job."

One of several sections Burke assigned to himself was a study of the Middle East. In Palestine the Jews and Palestinian Arabs were at each other's throats, the latter supported by nearby Arab states. In some of the states, discovery of tremendous new reserves of underground oil gave them almost limitless purchasing power for arms. If a general war broke out in the area, Russia might move in "to restore peace" and thus be in a position to close down Middle East pipelines. Rapid demobilization and tight military budgets had left the United States powerless to intervene effectively.

When Burke had finished his Middle East paper, he knew he had done a good job, and his colleagues concurred. He sent a copy to Mr. Forrestal, who was now America's first secretary of defense. Forrestal read the paper and thought so highly of it that he sent copies to the army and air force and personally delivered one to President Truman.

Before the study was completed, some Board members received orders elsewhere and were replaced by carefully selected successors. The new men pitched in and soon shared the general enthusiasm for the enterprise. Through the spring of 1948 the members worked on the various segments of the paper, which had been given the tentative title "National Security and Naval Contributions for the Next Ten Years."

Completion of the paper was scheduled for 1 July 1948, and the Board met the deadline. Members (not including Burke, who had been detached) presented it in outline in mid-July before Mr. Sullivan, now elevated to secretary of the navy. Sullivan ordered his staff to study it to determine how its conclusions could best be applied. Nothing so ambitious had come to the secretary's attention before. An earlier paper, "The Future Employment of Naval Forces," submitted to him by Admiral Nimitz as a legacy before leaving office as CNO, had been widely and justly praised, but Burke's paper, worldwide in scope, was far broader and bolder.

Yet the Burke paper, though generally admired, had little direct effect. It influenced the operations of the National Security Resources Board, but that seems to be about all. There are a number of possible reasons. So ambitious a project was bound to contain a few errors of fact and judgment, and these may have made the rest suspect in some quarters. More important, the timing could scarcely have been poorer. The attention of the three services, now uncomfortably combined under the National Security Act, was focused on budget-cutting and on such questions as who was to carry the atomic bomb and whether the navy was to have supercarriers big enough to carry the big planes needed to carry the big bomb.

The carry-the-bomb controversy degenerated into the bitter Revolt of the Admirals, and that was followed by the Korean War. When the war ended and the dust settled, a different political party was in power. As usual in the U.S. form of government, that meant a sharp break in continuity. Even if the Burke paper had still been on the table, a five-year-old, ten-year security plan hatched under a Democratic administration would scarcely have made front and center among Republicans newly arrived in power after twenty years out of office.

The most long-range effect of the Burke paper seems to have been on Burke himself and on his reputation. His year of intense study, discussion, and writing about history, economics, government, and international relations had given him a worldview much beyond that of most naval captains. From the relatively few officers who read or dipped into the paper, word got around in naval circles that Burke was a man to watch, one destined to rise high in the navy.

Burke had managed to delay his impending detachment until his paper was completed, 1 July 1948. He had been ordered to sea as captain of light cruiser *Huntington*, then in the Mediterranean. Nothing could have pleased him more. After fourteen months of mind-boggling labor behind a desk, he thrilled at the prospect of clearing his head with salt air, as captain of his own ship.

Having heard of recent changes in the combat information center (CIC), the section of a combatant ship where tactical information is collected, Captain Burke had written to the Naval CIC Team Training Center in Boston and obtained permission to come up for a few days of instruction. He and Bobbie packed their old family Dodge, and off they went, the backseat fully occupied by their latest Great Dane, the pony-sized type of dog that the Burkes, for reasons best known to themselves, continued to fancy as pets. At Boston, Arleigh enrolled at the Center, while Bobbie, as so often before, went looking for accommodations that were not too expensive and would accept an enormous dog.

Burke had been at the Center a couple of days when he got a telephone call from an old friend, Captain William R. Smedberg, then on duty in Secretary Forrestal's office.

"Where are you?" asked Smedberg. Burke told him.

Rapidly, in a conspiratorial tone, Smedberg went on, "I just heard something, and I'm probably sticking my neck way out in telling you this, but I want to give you a little advice. You'd better get out of the country by tomorrow morning."

"Thank you, Smeddy," said Burke, but Smedberg had already hung up.

Burke knew Smedberg well enough to realize that this was neither a joke nor a joking matter. Smeddy had evidently heard Forrestal say something that was going to affect Burke, and if Smeddy advised getting out of the country, Burke had better get the *hell* out—and fast. There was only one place to go—to his ship, *Huntington*. In his pocket he had orders instructing him to proceed as soon as he finished his course of instruction to the port *Huntington* was in. Arleigh didn't know what port that was. He knew only that she was somewhere in the Med. He telephoned Bobbie at the inexpensive and highly tolerant hotel she had found.

"Bob," he said, "pack up."

Burke then went to the officer in charge of the center and told him a small lie—justified, Arleigh believed, by the emergency.

"I think I've learned everything I can learn here," he said. "I think I've got it." His request to be detached was granted. When he left the building he found patient Bobbie waiting in the Dodge, the car all packed, with the giant canine panting and slobbering in the backseat.

Out they drove to Westover military airfield without taking time to eat. It was getting dark when they arrived, and the place was mostly closed down for the night. Leaving Bobbie in the car, Arleigh went to the passenger terminal, where he found only one man on duty. Burke said he would like to get transportation to the ship *Huntington* in the Mediterranean.

"Where in the Mediterranean?" the man wanted to know.

Burke said he didn't know, but if they could just get him to London or someplace in Europe or North Africa that would be fine. The man said they didn't have anything that night. He suggested that Burke check in at the BOQ and come back about 0900 the next morning.

"I don't think I can get you out tomorrow either," he said, "but look, three days from now there's a flight to Frankfurt. It's a nice flight, passenger seats, a regular passenger plane. It's even got a galley aboard. Why don't you just take that? In the meantime, you can find out where your ship is."

"I can't wait three days."

"Well, I've got one for London in two days."

"I can't wait that long either."

"It's all I've got scheduled. But look, there are always flights going out of here somewhere. Why don't you try the freight terminal?"

At the freight terminal office also Arleigh found only one man on duty. He didn't seem to know much of anything, but he insisted there were no flights available.

Said Burke, "Do you mind if I go through the terminal and take a look?"

"No. Go ahead."

On the huge floor were piles of goods, each marked to go by plane within the next few days. Arleigh started searching down the line. The sign on one pile caught his eye: "Port Lyautey." That was the North African city from which Mitscher's 1946 European investigation tour had headed back to the United States. The sign with flight number said that the pile was due out at 0600 the next morning.

Burke returned to the man on duty. "Can I get out on that?"

"I don't know whether they take passengers or not," said the man. "You can come over and ask the pilot."

"When will he be here?"

"I don't know. All I know is what the sign says. Why don't you go over to the BOQ, leave a call for 0400, and get some sleep? That ought to be plenty of time."

"No," replied Burke. "Do you mind if I stay right here?"

The man looked at him askance. "No," he said. "Stay here if you want to."

Arleigh went out to Bobbie, who in the darkness had been waiting in the car. "I think I've got a way," he said. "I'll get my baggage, and you shove off for Washington."

So off went Bobbie supperless into the night for the 500-mile-drive, transporting a horse of a dog who could certainly protect her but would be unacceptable at any lodgings along the way. Equally supperless, Arleigh returned to the big shed and in his captain's uniform bedded down on the deck next to the Port Lyautey sign. Years later he seemed to remember tying a string from his finger to the sign.

The pilot arrived early, about 0400, and was astonished to find beside his pile of freight a recumbent, slumbering figure in a naval captain's uniform. He poked the figure, who opened his eyes, sat up, introduced himself as Captain Burke, and asked for a ride to Port Lyautey.

"Sure," said the pilot, "but this is a hell of a flight. We've got no passenger seats, but we'll arrange something."

Workmen arrived, loaded the plane, and put in a canvas-bottomed bucket seat on a side of the baggage compartment.

"Have you got anything to eat?" said the pilot.

Burke replied that he had not.

"Well," said the pilot, "we'd better get some sandwiches. We've got to take our own food."

They went over and bought sandwiches, and the plane was airborne and over the ocean by 0900. No telephone call had caught up with Burke. He had evidently escaped whatever horror Smedberg had warned him about.

Smedberg never wrote to explain, but several months later, back in the States, Burke encountered him and put the question that had kept him wondering. "What was the crisis?"

"I overheard Mr. Forrestal asking where you were," replied Smedberg. "He called the General Board to see whether you had been detached. You had been, and he was saying, 'Where in hell is he?' That sent the aides scurrying, and presently I heard one of them announce that he had located you and mentioned a Boston telephone number. Mr. Forrestal told the aide to get you down as soon as possible, and you'd be put to work. I had already picked up a telephone and dialed the number the aide had mentioned. Luckily, we made connections, and I advised you to skip. It was a near thing. At that time I didn't know what the job was. Now I know. Mr. Forrestal wanted you to do the research on his biography for the Forrestal papers."

Arleigh always considered receiving Smeddy's timely warning one of the luckiest breaks of his life. He couldn't have refused the job. If Forrestal had snared him, it would have canceled his sea duty and obliged him, on top of fourteen months of scribbling on the General Board, to spend a couple of years tied to a desk doing research on the papers.

So, thanks to Smeddy, instead of back to Washington it had been off toward Port Lyautey. For Burke it proved to be a miserable two-day flight at 10,000 feet in a cold, unpressurized cabin seated on a perch designed for a younger, less ample derrière. The plane paused at Newfoundland and at the Azores for refueling and to permit the pilot and his passenger to purchase prepared box lunches containing dry sandwiches.

Burke arrived at Port Lyautey in a state of near-exhaustion. He learned here that his ship, *Huntington*, was with the Sixth Fleet, the ships that Admiral of the Fleet Sir John Cunningham had requested and Admiral Mitscher had advised the U.S. Navy to send to the Mediterranean. In command was Vice Admiral Forrest Sherman, Burke's erstwhile talkative roommate and traveling companion.

The officer in charge at the Port Lyautey airfield did not know the exact location of the Sixth Fleet but had reason to believe it was somewhere off Malta. He had no aircraft heading for Malta, but he had one going to Tunis, which lay in the same general direction. Burke said he would take it, and would they please send Admiral Sherman a radio dispatch, announcing his destination and time of arrival. The officer in charge was glad to oblige, but he pointed out that the plane was leaving early next morning, and they might not have an answer by then.

"You're liable to be stuck in Tunis a long time," he added.

Burke said he'd take the chance.

In fact, the plane while in flight received a dispatch from commander Sixth Fleet ordering it after discharging its cargo at Tunis to proceed on to Malta to deliver its passenger.

Arleigh took command of light cruiser *Huntington* at the fleet

base of Taranto inside the heel of the Italian boot. It was against the
ships at this base that the British in November 1940 launched a
carrier attack that set the example for the December 1941 Japanese
raid on Pearl Harbor. In the summer of 1948, *Huntington* was at
Taranto on the peaceful mission of representing the U.S. Navy at
the Italian Navy Day celebration.

When time for *Huntington*'s departure drew near, Captain Burke
took the conn. All eyes were on the American ship, eyes not only
in the Italian fleet but also among *Huntington*'s ship's company,
who were curious to see how "31-Knot Burke," the hotshot destroyerman of 1943, could handle a cruiser after five years' service in flag
country.

Commander David King, *Huntington*'s operations office, a holdover from the previous command, describes the scene:

> A stiff wind of 25 to 30 knots was blowing, and a moderate sea was
> running outside the breakwater. The breakwater entrance lay one
> or two points abaft the port beam. The engine room was warned
> to stand by for 20-knot speed as soon as under way. As the ship
> guard left, and the moor was slipped, the ship fell off rapidly to
> port and set down from the buoy. By the time the forecastle had
> all the gear on deck partially secured, the ship had turned 90
> degrees left and was steaming with the wind now on her starboard
> beam, and the breakwater entrance was sharp on the port bow, all
> engines ahead full, with first bell ordered with steady as she goes.
> The ship rapidly gained way and sped through the entrance with
> only enough windset effect to require no course change at all. The
> Italian "Well Done!" flew from the flagships.

Huntington had been in the Mediterranean nearly a year. In
accordance with current practice, she should soon be returning to
the United States. To the disgust of her crew, who expected early
stateside leave, she was ordered to undertake an extensive voyage via
the Indian and Atlantic oceans, with numerous stops that would
consume months. Hence when *Huntington,* on being detached
from the Sixth Fleet, headed east instead of west, there was considerable glumness on board.

This was only the gloomy beginning of what turned out to be a
fabulous cruise that everybody enjoyed. After transiting the Suez
Canal, the ship made goodwill calls at most of the east coast African
and South American ports. The calls were all by invitation issued

via Washington, and since the visitors arrived as representatives of a nation whose recent victories made the whole world less apprehensive, the host ports tried to outdo one another in demonstrations of hospitality.

The crew worked hard keeping the ship spotless despite quantities of visitors welcomed aboard at every port, but the trips ashore more than made up for the hardship. In addition, Captain Burke, under no wartime pressures, endeavored to maintain a comradely atmosphere on board, putting into practice his growing belief in the importance of communications between officers and men. At intervals he called the crew together, usually on the fantail, to explain the ship's mission or to give them information about the port they were approaching. He invited and answered questions, a practice that produced some spirited sessions. The question initially most asked he was at last able to answer with assurances from Washington: "We'll be home by Christmas!"—a reply that evoked cheers from officers and men.

As for Arleigh himself, only the presence of Bobbie could have added to his happiness. Long ago Gelzer Sims had figured that Burke was "the kind of man who had to have his *own* cannon." Now he had it. Except for the thin thread of radio linking him to Washington, Arleigh was as much monarch of his little waterborne kingdom as any windblown skipper in the age of wood and sail.

From Cape Town, *Huntington* crossed the broad South Atlantic to Buenos Aires. The Argentines gave the crew a tumultuous welcome, topped by the hospitality of a single citizen, Señora María Ema Santillán de Aignasse, a red-haired woman, aged about forty-five, of German extraction—either very rich or with access to considerable wealth. She invited *Huntington*'s crew to a barbecue in Buenos Aires's main public park. The ship could not of course be stripped of its entire ship's company to attend a social event, but some 500 officers and men, including Arleigh, attended and were regaled by the featured beer and splendid beef. The señora also offered the Americans tickets for theater, opera, and the races.

Touched by her boundless generosity, Burke tendered Señora Santillán his calling card, saying, "If you ever come to the United States, please let us know," and he also sent her a thank-you letter—courteous gestures he afterward had cause to regret. His senior officers likewise offered their cards and sent letters but apparently with some unstated reservations.

With respect to the fabulous Argentine beef, however, there were no reservations in any of the Americans' minds. When they found that tenderloins could be purchased at a ridiculously low price in U.S. dollars, the senior officers proceeded to stock up, filling the half-empty freezers of their undermanned cruiser with meat to take home.

Their great holiday at Buenos Aires concluded, the Americans took *Huntington* down the Río de la Plata for a brief visit at Montevideo. On their departure, Burke, again taking the conn, further endeared himself to his crew by inadvertently demonstrating that as a shiphandler he could be less than perfect. The cruiser, moored bow-away from the entrance, just about filled the small harbor. Hence to move out bow first the ship had to be twisted in her own water, on a dime as it were. Burke drew the ship carefully away from the wharf and had her swinging very well when, becoming a trifle overconfident, he ordered the engines two-third ahead starboard and two-thirds astern port when he should have done just the reverse.

"The stern's going the wrong way!" shouted a bluejacket stationed aft to watch. Thus warned, Burke ordered engine directions reversed starboard and port just in time to save the ship from going on the rocks.

The rest of her South American calls completed, *Huntington* headed northwest away from the coast, threaded the Lesser Antilles, skirted the Bahamas, and entered the Gulf Stream off the U.S. East Coast. A few days before Christmas 1948, as scheduled, she entered the Delaware River and proceeded to her assigned wharf in the Philadelphia Navy Yard. Here wives and family members were waiting to greet their long-absent men. Bobbie Burke was there, having rented a nearby furnished apartment where she and Arleigh could stay a month or so before the ship put to sea again. This time she was dogless, their latest pet having died.

Captain Burke released half his crew for two weeks of Christmas leave. On their return the other half would depart for a leave of similar length. Among his many responsibilities related to returning his ship from overseas, Arleigh called in government inspectors to pass on the frozen Argentine meat he and his officers wished to import.

By late afternoon, Friday, 24 December, everything was squared away. In a happy mood, Arleigh closed his desk and was about to leave his ship for a long Christmas weekend with Bobbie when the shoreside telephone rang. The caller was Rear Admiral Charles

Wellborn, on duty in the CNO's office in Washington. After saying he was glad Burke was in the States again, he came to the point.

"It is necessary that you report to Washington as soon as possible."

Burke was shaken. "How long do you suppose this temporary duty is going to last?" he asked.

"I'm not talking about any temporary duty," replied Admiral Wellborn. "This is permanent duty."

"But I'm captain of a ship," Burke expostulated. "I can't leave until I've been relieved as commanding officer, and that takes time. Why don't you get somebody else? I just completed a couple of years of shore duty, and I want to finish my sea cruise."

The admiral cut him short. The CNO had determined that Burke must come ashore as soon as possible, he said, and there was no way that could be changed.

Realizing he had no choice, Arleigh asked who his relief was to be and when he would be in Philadelphia. Admiral Wellborn said he didn't know, but the department had furnished the names of three captains believed to be in the Philadelphia area. He dictated their names and addresses. Burke was to locate one who could relieve him at once and then notify BuPers, which would issue the necessary orders. After concluding the conversation with a none-too-cheerful "Aye, aye," Arleigh started telephoning, while Bobbie, waiting on the wharf in the newly acquired family Plymouth, wondered what on earth was holding him up.

Two of the telephone numbers Burke dialed failed to answer. Whoever answered the third said that the captain was expected back Monday sometime. By telephone Burke next got into touch with Captain Joe Daniel, a former shipmate, now captain's detail officer at BuPers. Informed of the situation, Daniel told Burke to keep trying. BuPers was sure the three captains were in the area.

On Christmas Day, Arleigh finally made contact. Captain Harold R. Stevens, whom he reached by telephone but didn't know, said he'd be eager to take command of the fine cruiser and thought he could be relieved of his present job early Monday morning. Burke promptly sent a dispatch to BuPers nominating Stevens.

"Early Monday morning, 27 December," Burke recalls, "Joe Daniel called me by phone, saying that orders would be forthcoming for me and for Captain Stevens but to insure there would be no delay due to nonreceipt of orders I was to write my own orders based on this telephone conversation. By that time I was used to peculiar procedures, so I had no misgivings about Burke writing orders to Burke detaching Burke and ordering him to other duty."

The orders, a little odd, were characteristically short. This is what he wrote:

> From: Commanding Officer USS *Huntington*
> To: Captain Arleigh Burke
> Subject: Change of duty.
>
>   1. In compliance with telephone orders received from Captain J. C. Daniel, BuPers, when relieved you will regard yourself detached from duty as Commanding Officer, USS *Huntington* (CL-107) and from such other duty as may have been assigned to you; you will proceed to Washington, D.C. and report to the Chief of Naval Operations for duty without delay.
>
>   Signed,
>   A. A. Burke

Captain Burke was fortunate that he and his team had everything shipshape on board *Huntington* and that his very efficient executive officer had not departed on leave with half the crew. When Captain Stevens arrived a little after noon they were ready for him. Drills and inspection demonstrated to the new commanding officer that the ship was properly trained, and there were enough officers present to break out reports and other papers that convinced him all was in order. They scheduled the relieving ceremony for 0800, the next morning, Tuesday, 28 December.

Now at last Burke began getting his personal affairs in order. He was astonished how much gear he had on board. He hoped the Plymouth would hold it all, plus whatever gear Bob had brought to Philadelphia. The main problem now was what to do about all that meat Arleigh had bought and brought home—nearly 200 pounds of Argentine tenderloin. How was he going to keep it from spoiling in the car? He finally arranged to have it packed in ice in two big boxes that he hoped would fit in the trunk.

Long before dawn next morning, Arleigh and Bobbie were up packing the car with their belongings from the apartment. They were on the wharf by 0730 putting in all of Arleigh's shipboard gear except the meat and a suitcase with his uniforms and toilet articles. Bobbie waited in the car during the change of command, which was over by 1000. Arleigh soon descended to the wharf with his suitcase followed by a pair of husky bluejackets bringing the two heavy meat boxes. They loaded the boxes into the car and wished Arleigh well in getting them out when he got to D.C.

On the way down to Washington, Burke drove slowly and carefully, because the springs of the overloaded car were nearly flat. Now at last he and Bobbie had time to speculate on why he had been so hurriedly summoned to Washington. Admiral Wellborn had impressed on him the importance of speed and the requirement to report to the chief of naval operations promptly. "Without delay" was the phrase he had used and Burke had repeated in his orders to himself. That meant no pausing to find lodgings or to unload but driving straight to the Pentagon by the shortest route.

Though they arrived long after dark, the huge building as usual was well lighted. Burke hopped out of the car and dashed inside. Bobbie waited. And waited. This sort of thing had happened so many times before. No telling when Arleigh would be out. It was up to her to find a motel where they could spend what was left of the night. Knowing the navy's demands, Bobbie guessed it would also be up to her to unload the car. And to find some way to preserve the meat from spoilage. And to serve notice of eviction on the tenants to whom they had rented their home. Bobbie had dedicated her life to looking after Arleigh, and willingly so, but there were moments like this when she felt her allegiance to the navy slipping.

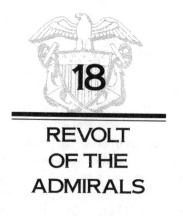

18

REVOLT
OF THE
ADMIRALS

WHEN CAPTAIN ARLEIGH BURKE arrived at the Pentagon in the evening of 28 December 1948, he reported at once to his new boss, Rear Admiral Wellborn, deputy chief of naval operations for administration. With Wellborn were a couple of other officers, on hand to brief Burke on his duties. Now at last Arleigh learned what his new job was to be. He was to relieve one of the officers present, Captain Lyman A. Thackrey, in charge of the CNO's Organizational Research and Policy Section, short-titled Op-23 (i.e., CNO office No. 23). Op-23 was fact finder and adviser to the chief of naval operations on matters concerning unification of the armed services.

Burke was aware that unification was a subject on which the services were at odds. An intruder into this controversial area could make powerful enemies. Arleigh asked the obvious question: "Why me?" Admiral Wellborn replied that he was selected on the basis of his record in successfully filling a variety of demanding posts in the navy.

The next morning, Wellborn took Burke to see Chief of Naval Operations Louis E. Denfeld. The CNO, an affable gentleman, shook Burke's hand warmly. An expert chiefly in personnel operations, Denfeld had been selected by President Truman from among a field of candidates mainly on the assurance that he would be the easiest to work with.

"The navy's in a very tough spot on this unification problem," said Denfeld. "We can't seem to get our story across. We're lambasted in the newspapers. We think our positions are reasonable and in the best interests of the country, but nobody seems to want to pay any attention. It will be up to you to do what's necessary, correct, and ethical to help. You and your small staff will be our chief advisers on unification matters. Do what you can."

Burke had kept reasonably abreast of the unification controversy during his duty on the General Board and earlier, but he had been at sea when the National Security Act was passed, supposedly putting an end to the debate. He was informed, however, that the services were now bent on modifying the act—obviously a process on which the navy would count on Op-23 for advice. To refresh his memory, Burke drew out a copy of the original hearings before the Senate Armed Forces Committee and began studying it.

What the committee had under consideration at that time were two related army proposals: (1) to detach the army air forces from the army ground forces, enabling the former to operate as a separate U.S. Air Force, and (2) to unite the U.S. Army, the U.S. Navy, and the newly independent U.S. Air Force under a single Department of National Defense. The navy opposed both programs on the basis of the old argument "If it ain't broke, don't fix it." The U.S. armed forces had just emerged the major victors over three world powers. Why change such a winning combination?

The army's air officers argued that so far as their command was concerned there was no change contemplated. Army air was already a separate service, a fact needing only to be recognized by law. Over the years the air units, under different names, had been increasingly detaching themselves from the ground forces. In March 1942 the units merged, as the army air forces. Their commanding general, Henry H. Arnold, was one of the Joint Chiefs of Staff, coequal with General Marshall and Admiral King. The army air forces' subsequent quasi-independent strategic bombing of the cities and industrial centers of Germany and Japan had earned them, the air officers insisted, a right to independent existence.

President Truman, who had been an army artillery officer in World War I, favored the army's plan for unification of the services. During World War II he had come to national attention as organizer and chairman of the Senate's so-called Truman Committee, which saved the government a billion dollars by uncovering waste and inefficiency in defense procurement and spending. This achievement brought Truman to the vice presidency, and the death of Franklin Roosevelt catapulted him into the presidency, an office he assumed with a determination to employ whatever means necessary to forestall wasteful duplication and conflicting operations in the armed services. To attain that end, in his capacity as armed forces commander in chief he ordered unification. The main purpose of the Senate hearings was to decide what form the unified services should take. The committee called numerous witnesses, mainly officers who had held senior wartime army and navy commands.

The services agreed that America's only possible enemy for years to come would be the Soviet Union or a Soviet satellite. Since the Soviets had only a minuscule fleet, the maintenance of any large number of U.S. combatant ships was widely considered unnecessary and wasteful. This view was based on a popular notion that navies exist mainly to fight fleet battles, whereas these are only incidental to their main function, which is to maintain the sea safe for one's own ships and unsafe for the enemy's and to convey armed forces and their logistic requirements across the sea to confront the enemy.

The army air forces tended to rely on the atomic bomb to deter a potential enemy and, if deterrence failed, on strategic bombing to conquer him—a view that persuaded many people that the atomic bomb, and the big new B-36 bomber to deliver it, had rendered all other weapons obsolete. Such a view left no means of settling international disputes between diplomatic protest and atomic devastation.

Some extremists argued that when, in the near future, bombers were developed with enough range to carry the atomic bomb to any point in the world and return, the air force would become America's first line of defense. Then forward bases would be unnecessary, fleet carriers would be obsolete, and the marine corps could be absorbed into the army, whose function would be to occupy territory conquered by the bombers. The task of a greatly reduced navy would be to fight enemy submarines, using escort carriers and destroyers, and to ferry troops and supplies. Aircraft and aviators not involved in antisubmarine work would be absorbed into the air force. All the nation's armed forces would be commanded by a single chief of staff and administered by a single civilian secretary of defense.

Secretary of the Navy James Forrestal, wisely voicing no opposition to a separate air force or unification of the services, undertook to outmaneuver the extremists and to educate the president, Congress, and his countrymen regarding the sort of limited unification and balanced forces that would best serve the national defense. By sheer logic and hard campaigning, he succeeded in having all the navy's traditional operations protected by the National Security Act, which cleared Congress on 23 July 1947 and was signed into law by President Truman three days later.

The act provided for a National Military Establishment under the president and headed by a secretary of defense, of cabinet rank, who would coordinate the separately administered departments of army, navy, and air force, each with its secretary, not of cabinet rank. As before, the chief of naval operations and the chiefs of staff of the army, of the air force, and (if any) of the president formed the Joint Chiefs of Staff. Their duties were to serve as principal military advisers to the president and the secretary of defense and to plan and direct military operations. The army's functions were virtually unchanged, and the navy retained its carrier and land-based air and a marine corps with its own air wing.

President Truman nominated Forrestal to be the first secretary of defense, and Senate confirmation came almost immediately. The president then ordered the newly appointed defense secretary to shift his headquarters from the Main Navy building on Washington's Constitution Avenue to the Pentagon, which became the physical embodiment of the National Military Establishment. As secretary of defense, Forrestal was entitled, of course, to the Pentagon's No. 1 suite, but the army had built the Pentagon for its own use and reserved the best suites for the secretary of the army and the army chief of staff. Rather than disturb these occupants, the new defense secretary moved himself and staff into a rather cramped set of offices overlooking the mall entrance.

Forrestal, who had done most to shape the National Military Establishment, now had the task of making it work. He supposed that the nation's chief defense organization problems were settled, and that all that remained was to put the provisions of the Security Act into effect. The economy-minded Truman, however, decided that this was the time to begin slashing the military budget. He cut it in a single year from $45 billion to $14.28 billion. As the budget continued to shrink, the tentative peace produced by the National Security Act was replaced by a sometimes acrimonious struggle among the services to get a larger share of the available funds. "It was," said Stuart Symington, the newly appointed secretary of the air force, "like throwing a piece of meat into the arena and letting 300 hungry tigers go in after it."

John L. Sullivan, the navy under secretary, succeeded Forrestal as secretary of the navy. He and Denfeld solved the problem of the reduced naval budget by mothballing many ships and slashing the shipbuilding program in order to concentrate on building what they considered the navy's primary need, a flush-deck supercarrier—a project proposed by Admiral Mitscher at the end of World War II. Displacing 65,000 tons, she would be the largest naval ship afloat and could serve as a base for the new, heavy long-range planes capable of carrying the atomic bomb.

Fleet Admiral Nimitz, chief of naval operations in 1946–47, had supported the Mitscher proposal, and the big carrier was approved for planning purposes. When the designs were completed, Secretary Sullivan made it the centerpiece in his proposed building program, and early in 1948 Secretary Forrestal and the Bureau of the Budget approved it.

There was an immediate outcry from the air force generals, who considered strategic bombing exclusively their business and the dropping of the atomic bomb strictly strategic. The admirals replied that it was necessary to break the air force monopoly because its longest-range bomber, the vaunted B-36, was not truly intercontinental. What the land-based bombers could not reach was accessible, however, by planes based on carriers, which could bring them to within 1,700 miles of any target on earth.

Secretary Forrestal undertook to resolve the dispute by reason and persuasion, but without much success. Convinced that forcing military leaders to accept measures in conflict with their experience and judgment could only miscarry, he wished to bring about unification by evolution rather than revolution. In any case, his power to impose a solution had been strictly limited by Congress.

From Captain Thackrey, Burke learned the history of Op-23 and its predecessors. Agencies of this type originated with SecNav Forrestal, who planned to attach to his office a committee of the ablest officers then serving in Washington to advise him on unification problems. For its chairman he chose Vice Admiral Arthur W. Radford, who during the war had commanded one of Admiral Mitscher's carrier groups and later relieved Mitscher as deputy chief of naval operations for air. The first officer Radford thought of for his committee was Arleigh Burke, but Mitscher, ordered to form and command a new Eighth Fleet, wanted Burke to serve again as his chief of staff, and such was Mitscher's prestige that what he wanted he got.

Despite problems of obtaining suitable personnel, the Radford group was soon in business, calling itself the Secretary's Committee of Research and Reorganization (Scoror). Forrestal made good use of advice from Scoror, but serving on the committee was temporary, extracurricular duty for its officer members, who came and went. Long before the original unification battle was over, Radford himself left to command the U.S. Second Fleet. When the National Security Act was passed, Forrestal, supposing his battle won, thanked the officers of Scoror for helping the navy to attain such favorable terms and sent them back to their regular duties.

When it became apparent that the air force, backed by the army, was determined to change the Security Act, Navy Secretary Sullivan reactivated Scoror, gave it official status, enlarged it, and made membership long-term. At the same time, to dissociate it from the bitter clashes that preceded passage of the Security Act, he changed its title to the Secretary's Committee on Unification, a name its members quickly shortened to Unicom.

In late August 1948, Secretary Sullivan moved his office from the Main Navy building to the Pentagon, followed by CNO Denfeld and other key and top-level naval offices, including Unicom. These moves completed the concentration of major commands of the National Military Establishment under one roof. This cozy arrangement, however, did little to quench the flames of the continuing interservice battles.

In autumn the press, especially in the persons of several widely read columnists, began supporting an army–air force move to revise the National Security Act by adopting more inclusive forms of unification. Apparently air force personnel had won over the journalists by providing them with choice news items, including authorized and unauthorized leaks. Noting the success of this method, Unicom undertook to attract a few pet journalists of its own and supposed it had made a good beginning when it gained the apparent support of Jim Lucas, Scripps-Howard military correspondent.

This snug compact backfired. Lucas, more interested in putting out sensational stories than in championing causes, made unforeseen use of official letters trustfully leaked to him. Instead of capitalizing on the material for the greater glory of the navy, he artfully manipulated it to produce one story that made the secretary of defense look ridiculous and another that made the secretary of the navy and the chief of naval operations appear underhanded and conniving.

All hell broke loose in the National Military Establishment. Investigators from the navy's inspector general descended upon Unicom and determined that at least one of the letters misused by Lucas had been given to him by Captain Thackrey, by then Unicom chairman. Thackrey's intentions had been of the best, but his judgment was considered defective. Secretary Sullivan wrathfully ordered Unicom disbanded and withheld Thackrey's commission as rear admiral, a rank to which he had just been promoted. He remained an acting captain during the remainder of Sullivan's incumbency, which fortunately for Thackrey was fairly brief.

In the continuing battle of the services, the navy had to have some agency to carry on the Scoror-Unicom advisory function. Conforming to the inspector general's advice that any such agency should be attached to the CNO's office, Admiral Denfeld ordered Op-23 set up. The selection of Captain Arleigh Burke to head the new office may have been at the suggestion of Vice Admiral Radford, now serving as vice CNO. If so, a check at that time would have found Burke at sea commanding light cruiser *Huntington*. Op-23, with eight officers temporarily headed by Captain Thackrey, came officially into being on 15 December 1948. A few days later, Admiral Denfeld, informed that Burke was in Philadelphia, had him ordered to Washington at the earliest practical date.

Arleigh faced the fact that he was undertaking a difficult, fairly thankless, and perilous job. One of Op-23's main duties was to provide information to others, including members of the press, with no control over how the information was to be used. Captain Thackrey was a victim of that system. At Burke's request, Thackrey remained a little longer in charge of Op-23. Arleigh, in addition to thoroughly reviewing the unification controversy, conferred at length with Radford and with Secretaries Sullivan and Forrestal. Finally, in mid-January 1949, he felt sufficiently informed to relieve Thackrey.

Forrestal, conceding that the National Military Establishment did in fact need reorganizing, took personal charge of the program to guard against weakening the nation's defenses. To centralize command, the Establishment was to be converted from a vague catchall setup into an executive branch of the government called the Department of Defense. It was to be headed by a secretary of defense with broadened authority, while the Departments of Army, Navy, and Air Force were to be reduced from executive to military departments. One of Op-23's duties was to keep an eye on the reorganization movement and prepare position papers on the various alternatives under consideration.

As always, Forrestal was working fourteen-hour days under constant pressure and under repeated verbal attack by certain air-minded newsmen, who automatically opened fire whenever the air force failed to get what it wanted. The strain was beginning to show. "Jim is looking badly," said General Eisenhower. "He gives his mind no rest, and he works hours that would kill a horse."

Among his other concerns, Forrestal was aware that he was losing the president's confidence. During their early association they were mutually admiring, but in the course of the unification controversies, the secretary had so often opposed the president that the latter became annoyed. To a man of Truman's decisiveness, moreover, Forrestal's habit of probing every issue from several angles and his capacity to see more than a single solution seemed weak and vacillating. "Poor Forrestal," he once commented. "He never could make a decision."

Above all, Mr. Truman was exasperated by the incessant battling among the armed services. He felt he needed somebody tough enough to knock heads together and make all parties settle down. The intellectual Forrestal was obviously incapable of such methods, but Truman thought he had his man in Louis Johnson, a hard-nosed West Virginia millionaire lawyer. Johnson was more than willing to take over as defense secretary. Champion fund-raiser for Truman's long-shot 1948 election campaign, he was expecting a first-class reward. As a World War I army officer, a former assistant secretary of war, and a former director of the aircraft corporation that produced the air force's B-36 bomber, he considered himself well qualified to be defense secretary.

Though the exhausted Forrestal suspected that he was about to be relieved and rather looked forward to retirement, receipt on 1 March 1949 of an abrupt request from the president for a letter of resignation left him shattered. He stayed in office till the end of the month to oversee completion of the defense reorganization. On his departure he was invited to the White House, where the president awarded him the Distinguished Service Medal, and to the Capitol for a farewell reception in his honor. Unable to rest, his imagination overheated, he was presently admitted to the Bethesda Naval Hospital for psychiatric treatment. Here he jumped to his death from a sixteenth-floor window.

The tall, big-framed, 250-pound Johnson, on assuming the post of secretary of defense, scorned the second-best Pentagon offices

Forrestal had occupied. He ordered the secretary of the army out of the No. 1 suite and moved in himself. That was certainly his right, but his abrupt eviction of the tenant was mainly, as he said afterward, "to show who was boss."

Johnson announced plans to build up the air force and trim the navy. He asserted his determination, moreover, to keep the armed services within a shrinking budget by eliminating waste and duplication. The supercarrier, to be named USS *United States,* on which construction had begun at Newport News, Virginia, seemed to him a contrivance for doing what the air force could do better and more cheaply. He asked the opinion of General Eisenhower and the Joint Chiefs on whether to go ahead with building the ship. Only Admiral Denfeld argued for completion. Johnson, after clearing his decision with the president, on 23 April 1949 ordered construction on the supercarrier to cease at once.

Johnson's high-handed cancellation, without detailed study, without giving the navy a chance to present its case, without consulting or even notifying Secretary Sullivan, Admiral Denfeld, or interested congressional committees, infuriated naval leaders and aroused adverse reactions in Congress. Secretary Sullivan, learning of the cancellation while on a trip to Texas, promptly submitted his resignation in a letter expressing dismay over the defense secretary's decision and indignation at his arbitrary manner of imposing it. Many naval officers believed that Admiral Denfeld had no choice but to follow Sullivan's example, but Denfeld, a conciliator by nature, believed he could make a greater contribution by remaining at his post and working to reconcile the services.

To replace Sullivan, Johnson nominated and Truman appointed Francis P. Matthews, an Omaha lawyer-banker, who had worked closely with Johnson in the fund-raising for the Truman campaign. When Matthews freely admitted that the nearest he had ever come to naval experience was rowing a boat on a lake, the Navy Department dubbed him "Rowboat Matthews," and when it became increasingly apparent that he was less a navy advocate than Johnson's loyal lackey, the department ceased routing essential information his way. Several months elapsed, however, before the new SecNav realized he was being bypassed.

Johnson was resolved to put an end to the public bickering among the military departments. Supporting this aim he had a formidable ally in Representative Carl Vinson, chairman of the House Armed Forces Committee. Soon after Johnson took office, Vinson published a warning:

The Armed Services Committee wants it clearly understood that if persons in the armed services or in their employ continue to pass statements to the press which are calculated to deprecate the activities of a sister service, and which, at the same time, jeopardize the national security, the committee will step in with a full-scale investigation.

Not long afterward, one Cedric R. Worth, a civilian assistant to the navy under secretary, called on Captain Burke with some hot information—nothing less than evidence of corruption in the renegotiation of B-36 contracts. Secretaries Johnson and Symington both appeared to be illegally, if not criminally, involved. If the information could be substantiated, it would remove from office the navy's two most formidable opponents.

Burke agreed to have Op-23 help Worth prepare a paper on his findings, but only if it was retained strictly within the Navy Department. After all, Op-23 did not have adequate means of confirming or disproving the allegations, some of which were suspect because provided by a disgruntled airplane manufacturer who had lost business as a result of the renegotiation.

The paper completed, Worth broke faith with Burke by giving copies of it to several congressmen, through whom some of the major accusations reached the press. Congressman Vinson, his patience exhausted by this disclosure, prepared for his threatened showdown.

Before the investigation got under way, as if in defiance of Vinson's warning, a contentious article titled "An Admiral Talks Back to the Airmen" appeared in the 25 June 1949 issue of *The Saturday Evening Post.* Written by famed naval aviator Rear Admiral Daniel V. Gallery, it posed the question "Does the prevailing doctrine that we can win the next war by air power alone court national disaster?" Secretary Johnson, learning in advance about the article, tried unsuccessfully to block its publication. Through inquiry he learned that the article was based on material provided by Op-23.

The first phase of the Armed Services Committee's investigation, which lasted from 9 to 25 August 1949, dealt with the rumors and allegations of fraud and corruption in Cedric Worth's paper. Two weeks of hearings, including reports by professional accountants who examined all pertinent records, turned up no evidence of wrongdoing—an outcome that cast strong doubts on the navy's credibility. Concerning the committee's findings, Chairman Vinson expressed himself satisfied that there was not "one iota, not one scintilla of evidence . . . that would support charges that collusion, fraud, corruption, or favoritism played any part whatsoever in the procurement of the B-36 bomber." He recommended Mr. Worth's dismissal from government employment, and this was duly carried out.

After the committee recessed, an embarrassed Navy Department set up its own fact-finding board to determine who, if any, among its officers or other personnel had collaborated with Worth. Several officers admitted having done so, conspicuously Burke's first assistant in charge of Op-23. None of these, it turned out, had intended or expected Worth's paper to be publicized. So far as they were concerned, it was to serve only as a guide for further investigations should any of the allegations prove true. This being established, the board exonerated all the collaborators. Nevertheless, Op-23's association with Worth's false charges implanted in some minds the notion that Burke was presiding over some sort of underhanded activity.

That, of course, was far from Burke's intention. To Op-23 he had issued as a sort of motto or guiding principle the phrase "Scrupulousness, and let everybody know." By these words he meant that the agency was to adhere strictly to the law, to regulations, to truth, and to fairness, and that all of its operations were to be made public. In the Worth case, however, the agency had inadvertently dealt in fabrications, and it could not let everybody know in advance material it was providing officers to use before the Vinson or any other committee to rebut charges.

Burke soon had evidence that he had fallen into disfavor with Secretary Johnson and his satellite, Secretary Matthews, but he refused to be intimidated. Drew Pearson and a few other newspaper writers, having lost Forrestal as a target, began to zero in on Burke, suggesting that his Op-23 was a secret rumor mill grinding out deceptive propaganda. Arleigh noticed that a few ambitious lightweights among his officer acquaintances were avoiding his company.

The Vinson committee's endeavor to curb interservice rivalry was suddenly undermined by Secretary Johnson's announcement of a $353 million cut in Navy Department funds. This disclosure followed his scaling down of an already shrunken defense budget and his stated intention to cut navy aviation in half. Many naval officers, suspecting he had something even more drastic in mind, began to take seriously an oft-repeated comment he had once made to a shocked Admiral Richard Conolly. "Admiral," Johnson had said, "the navy is on its way out. There's no reason for having a navy and a marine corps. We'll never have any more amphibious operations. That does away with the marine corps. And the air force can do anything the navy can do nowadays, so that does away with the navy."

Johnson had made his announcement of the cut in navy funds while the board of inquiry in the Worth case was in session. Scheduled to give evidence was Captain John G. Crommelin, veteran naval aviator and longtime opponent of unification. He concluded that the cut in funds was just another move toward eliminating the navy and thereby fatally weakening the national defense. He decided to use the board of inquiry as a forum to air his deep concern, but the board closed hearings before he was called.

Frustrated, Crommelin the next day, 10 September, called newsmen to his home and unburdened himself in colorful language, insisting that the navy was being "nibbled to death" by its opponents, mainly the secretary of defense, assisted by the Joint Chiefs of Staff, where the army and air force representatives with a "landlocked concept of national defense" could always outvote the CNO.

High-ranking officers all over the navy sent Crommelin messages praising his action and supporting his views. Several, including Fleet Admiral Halsey, publicly endorsed his statement. Crommelin's outburst launched the so-called Revolt of the Admirals. It also set the stage for the second phase of the Armed Forces Committee investigation, which began on 6 October. Its main purpose was to compare the military capabilities of the B-36 bomber and the canceled supercarrier.

The whole strategic concept on which the arguments pro and con were to be based had now been nullified by a single new fact. Russia had the bomb! It was no longer an American monopoly. On 23 September 1949, President Truman had issued a statement to the press: "We have evidence that within recent weeks an atomic explosion occurred in the USSR." The officers participating in the hearings, though knowing this, were to utter a good deal of nonsense, because among them the fact had not sunk in that so far as atomic warfare was concerned the United States and the Soviet Union had reached a standoff. The phrase "mutual assured destruction" had not yet been coined.

Secretary Symington and Air Force Chief of Staff General Hoyt Vandenberg had coached the air force witnesses and coordinated their presentations. Normally their opposite numbers, Secretary

Matthews and Admiral Denfeld, would have performed the same service for the navy witnesses, but Matthews did not concur with their views, and Denfeld was holding himself aloof in his chosen role of conciliator. Admiral Radford and Captain Burke therefore took on the task of orchestrating the naval presentation, ably assisted by Rear Admiral Oswald Colclough, the judge advocate general, a skilled lawyer. Radford, now Cincpac and a four-star admiral, had been summoned from Pearl Harbor at the request of Chairman Vinson to serve as technical consultant, making use of his experience while heading Scoror.

Secretary Matthews, at his own insistence, was leadoff witness. He opened his presentation by announcing that he would not censor any navy man's testimony or penalize him for what he testified. As for the controversy, he played it down, calling it the grumbling of "several naval aviators," like Crommelin, who could never bring themselves to accept unification. "In my opinion," he concluded, "they do not reflect the views of anything approaching a majority of naval officers." If that is what he believed, he must have been shocked by the parade of technicians and senior officers who in the next few days, testifying before the committee, condemned the B-36 both as inadequate for its announced function and as the chosen instrument for the misguided strategy of atomic bombing.

The second witness, Admiral Radford, testifying on 7 October, led off with a blast against the B-36, which he called a billion-dollar blunder and a popular "symbol of a theory of warfare, the atomic blitz, which promises . . . a cheap and easy victory." Among the witnesses following him were naval leaders of World War II: King, Nimitz, Halsey, Spruance, Kinkaid, Conolly, Carney, Burke. Every one of them endorsed Radford's testimony, appearing in person or, if unable to come, sending in statements.

The air force claimed that the B-36's ceiling of 40,000 feet put it beyond reach of attack by fighter planes, but Burke, suspecting otherwise, had tests run that proved the navy's new Banshee fighter could lock on and shoot down anything at 40,000 feet. Obviously the B-36, thus proved vulnerable, would need long-range fighter escort, which the air force could not provide. The B-36 would require also a reliable backup system, the navy witnesses pointed out, and this was a need the supercarrier could have filled admirably.

Captain Burke in appearing before the committee limited his testimony to a comprehensive advocacy of the supercarrier. Beginning with the observation that the United States as a maritime nation needed to command the sea, he pointed out that assurance of sea command required a navy employing the most advanced weapons, including aircraft of up-to-date design, and the trend toward greater power and greater range would produce planes too large for launching from World War II–type carriers.

"It takes several years to design and build a new carrier," Burke said. "She is usable for twenty or more years. Consequently, a new carrier must be capable of operating planes foreseeable within her lifetime."

Carrier-based air, Burke asserted, is more versatile than land-based air and thus in certain circumstances is more effective in neutralizing enemy capabilities. Its effectiveness would have been magnified by more powerful planes operating from a larger carrier such as the canceled *United States.* "The navy believes," he continued,

> that both the army and the air force would have found the prime striking power and the close support ability of the powerful naval aircraft flown from this carrier a great asset in their own operations. These carrier planes could support our sister services under some circumstances in which they could obtain the help from no other sources, as is now the case in the Mediterranean. Such a valuable carrier won't be available for war unless it is built in peace.

Admiral Denfeld was scheduled to testify on the 13th as the concluding naval witness. After hearing Secretary Matthews state that dissatisfaction with current trends in the Defense Department was limited to "several naval aviators" and then hearing a week of testimonials to the contrary, Denfeld concluded that he was serving the navy ill as a would-be conciliator. He decided to join his naval brethren in protest, and called on Radford and Burke for advice in framing his remarks.

Matthews, beginning to suspect that Denfeld was shifting his position, asked the latter what he intended to say, to which Denfeld truthfully replied that he had not yet prepared his testimony. In fact, the last page came off the typewriter at 0300 on the 13th.

Seven hours later, in the presence of a hushed audience, Denfeld began presenting his paper before the committee. His opening sentence gratified Radford and his supporters but stunned Matthews. "As the senior military spokesman for the navy," Denfeld began, "I want to state forthwith that I fully support the broad conclusions presented to this committee by the naval and marine officers who have preceded me."

Since as a nonaviator he would be an unconvincing critic of the B-36 or advocate of the *United States,* Denfeld confined his comments mainly to Defense Department methods of administration, on which he could speak authoritatively. The navy must, he said, retain its "ability to keep any war on the far side of the ocean," and experience had taught it what weapons would best enable it to do so. He sharply condemned the action of officials without naval background in dictating how the navy was to spend its limited defense budget.

As the CNO finished testifying, Secretary Matthews, visibly flushed, hastened out of the committee room, while naval officers crowded around Denfeld, congratulating him.

Beginning on Tuesday, 18 October, Symington and Vandenberg, in their rebuttal for the air force, ably restated their arguments previously offered. The surprise testimony, on the 19th, was that of General Omar Bradley, speaking in his new capacity as chairman of the Joint Chiefs of Staff. His handling of forces in Europe had shown him a master of land warfare, but he seemed to have not even a reader's knowledge of how the war against Japan had been fought. Because naval officers before the committee had been warning of the danger of neglecting naval power, Bradley angrily branded them " 'fancy Dans' who won't hit the line with all they have on every play, unless they can call the signals."

Secretary Johnson, convinced he had won his case, in his testimony on the 21st took a lofty, conciliatory line. After the committee adjourned that afternoon, he warned the services not to penalize any officer for what he had testified.

Secretary Matthews, disregarding his own and the SecDef's warnings about reprisals, set out at once to even a few scores. On his orders the navy inspector general descended on the offices of Burke's Op-23 with a team of investigators and a body of marine guards. They put all hands under what amounted to overnight house arrest and held them incommunicado, even among themselves, while all files were impounded. Apparently the inspector general was seeking evidence to quash Op-23 as he had produced the evidence for disbanding Unicom.

When an exhaustive two-day search of all Op-23's papers revealed nothing actionable or even new, Matthews canceled the investigation. Burke then went storming into the secretary's office demanding that he be charged with whatever offense the secretary thought he had committed so that he could "enjoy the rights of a criminal" and defend himself in a court-martial. Matthews loftily replied that Burke was overreacting.

Matthews next wrote a letter to the president asking permission to transfer Denfeld from the post of CNO "to other important duties." It was an obvious reprisal for his testimony, but Matthews based his request on what he called Denfeld's lack of "loyalty to superiors and respect for authority," and gave the president the choice of accepting Matthews's resignation or transferring Denfeld. Mr. Truman, as president of a nation committed to civilian supremacy, had no alternative to granting the secretary's petition. Denfeld, instead of accepting the transfer, retired from the navy and let off steam in an article, "Reprisal: Why I Was Fired," published in *Colliers* the following March.

Matthews wasn't through. The Navy Selection Board had unanimously selected Burke for promotion to rear admiral. When their list reached Matthews, he reconvened the board and, with Johnson's concurrence, ordered it to mark out Burke's name. They were inflicting on Arleigh a penalty similar to the one the previous SecNav had imposed on Thackrey, but Matthews's procedure was illegal. The list of selectees, though forwarded via the secretary, must by law be submitted unaltered to the president. Ignorant of this legality, Matthews sent the amended list to the White House.

After relieving Denfeld as CNO, Mr. Truman had telephoned Admiral Nimitz, one of the few senior naval officers he liked, trusted, and admired. He was being pressured, the president said, to return Nimitz to Washington to resume duty as chief of naval operations.

Nimitz begged off. It would be a mistake in time of peace, he said, to return an older officer to that job when there were plenty of able young officers available.

Who, the president wanted to know. Nimitz recommended Forrest Sherman, then commanding the Sixth Fleet. Truman acted promptly. Sherman, summoned from his headquarters in Lebanon, flew to New York. His plane landed there at 0430 on 1 November, and he went directly to Washington, where he was informed that he had been appointed chief of naval operations.

Meanwhile, Captain Burke, in his Op-23 office, had received a surprise telephone call. The caller was Vice Admiral William Fechteler, deputy chief of naval operations for personnel.

"You're in real trouble," said Fechteler. The secretary of the navy, he explained, had had Burke's name removed from the selection board's list of recommendations for promotion to rear admiral.

"You're right," said Burke. "I'm in real trouble, and I know what will happen. I'm out of the navy very fast."

"That's probably right," said Fechteler. "What do you want to do?"

"I want to go on a month's leave."

Burke got his leave, and he and Bobbie packed up the Plymouth and, in an emotional state combining disgust and despair, headed south. Arleigh was in a mood to retire from the navy and never return to Washington, the scene of his humiliation. In this dark frame of mind he continued driving more or less southward, vaguely looking for a place, possibly in Florida, where he and Bobbie could live in retirement and never again hear even an echo of interservice rivalries.

Secretary Matthews's letter with the altered selection list was forwarded to Mr. Truman at Key West, where he was taking a breather at his "summer White House." Captain Robert L. Dennison, the president's naval aide, routinely opened the envelope and was surprised to see Burke's name marked off the list in red ink, "by order of the secretary of the navy." In Dennison's opinion the omission was an injustice, and it was a clear case of malfeasance, a point lawyers Matthews and Johnson had overlooked. In the library Dennison found the statute about the inviolability of official selection lists. Then, carrying the book of statutes and the list, he went and stood at attention before the president's desk. Looking up, Mr. Truman said, "What's on your mind?"

"I want to talk to you about a selection board report," said Dennison, "and I'd like to have you let me do some special pleading and separate myself for the moment from being your naval aide and simply speak to you as a naval officer."

"Take the stuffing out of your shirt and sit down and tell me what the problem is," Truman said.

Dennison showed the president the report with Burke's name deleted. "This man is a classmate of mine, senior to me," he said, "and I have no personal ax to grind in this at all, but we are friends. This is clearly an injustice, and besides that, it's illegal." He reminded the president of the law that had been broken.

"Give me that report," said Truman, and he stuck it in his desk. Then he said, "You know, I think I remember Burke. I went to Norfolk once and went aboard Admiral Mitscher's flagship, a carrier. I was very much impressed with Mitscher, and Burke was his chief of staff."

"Yes, that's right."

"I remember meeting Burke. I think anybody Mitscher would have as chief of staff must be good."

"I agree."

In Washington somebody leaked to the press the story of Burke's promotion and demotion. The sharp, unfavorable reaction jolted Matthews and Johnson into realization that they were dealing with an officer highly respected in and out of the navy. Citizens wrote letters, congressmen made telephone calls, newspapers published articles—all condemning the shabby treatment accorded Burke. Several prominent people, including the new CNO, intervened with the president in Burke's behalf. Probably also someone pointed out to Matthews that he had broken the law.

The president returned to Washington. Usually he forwarded the promotion lists promptly. Not this time. A worried Matthews got on the phone to Dennison. What had happened to the report, he wanted to know.

"I don't know, Mr. Secretary," replied Dennison. "I gave it to the president. He has it, as far as I know."

Not long afterward, Truman sent for Dennison. "Secretaries Johnson and Matthews want to come up and talk to me," he said. "I think I know what it is. It's this selection board report. I want you to be out of here when they come. I'll handle this."

"I'm sure you will, Mr. President."

"You go into the cabinet room, and I'll call you when they leave."

After a while Mr. Truman opened the door. "Come on in," he said, grinning broadly. "Well, your friend Burke is back on the selection list. The best part of it is that Johnson and Matthews are taking the position now that this happy solution is their idea!"

On his first Sunday out of Washington, Arleigh's bitter mood began to change when he picked up a copy of the *New York Times* and saw a featured article indignantly reporting the deletion of his name from the list, followed by a glowing sketch of his naval career. He was able a little later to lay hands on a *Washington Post* with a story still more partisan in his favor. Arleigh turned the car around and headed back north. He and Bobbie were in the Washington area at a cocktail party with other navy couples when the radio announced the restoration of Burke's name to the list. The news was received with cheers.

One of Admiral Sherman's early acts as CNO was to disband

Op-23, which was still controversial, though it had outlived its usefulness. He then appointed Burke to the prestigious post of navy
secretary (i.e., navy representative) on the Defense Research and
Development Board. There was nothing casual about his choice of
this new job for Burke. It was purely technical and hence unlikely
to become controversial. In it Arleigh would be out of the public
view, with little danger of becoming conspicuous again. Arleigh was
well qualified for the job by virtue of his degree in chemical engineering and his extensive researches in the Bureau of Ordnance. It
particularly suited him because it brought him abreast of recent
developments in guided missiles, nuclear weapons, and propulsion
systems.

On 1 March 1950, the House Armed Services Committee issued
its report on its investigation of unification and strategy. It pointed
out that "the air force is not synonymous with the nation's military
air power. Military air power consists of air force, navy, and marine
corps air power, and of this, strategic bombing is but one phase."
The committee called on the services "to resolve their professional
differences fairly and without rancor and to perform their professional duties not only with efficiency and effectiveness but also with
dignity, with decorum, and with full receptivity to one another's
professional judgments."

The committee recommended joint training activities and an increase in interservice war games to resolve disputed questions "in
order to eliminate or at least reduce the tensions between the services, as well as contributing to their combat readiness." In order to
cancel the imbalance against the navy in the Joint Chiefs of Staff,
the committee proposed adding the commandant of the marine
corps as a member.

The committee expressed no opinion concerning the relative
merits of the B-36 and the *United States* but recommended that the
government accept the advice of its military professionals of each
service regarding weapons. In the spirit of this recommendation,
Congress at the request of Admiral Sherman on 25 April 1950 approved construction of a supercarrier to take the place of the canceled *United States*. The new carrier was to be named *Forrestal*, after
the defense secretary who had authorized her predecessor.

19

KOREAN WAR

(1)

THE THUMBLIKE PENINSULA named Korea juts southward from northeast China between the Yellow Sea and the Sea of Japan. It touches the Soviet Union narrowly in the northeast and is separated from Japan to the southeast by the Korea Strait. For centuries the battleground of rival sovereignties, Korea has been called the "sore thumb of Asia."

Japan's defeat of China in 1895 ended Chinese influence in Korea. Japan's defeat of Russia in 1905 ended Russian influence there and enabled the Japanese to annex the country against its will. In the Cairo Declaration of 1943 and the Potsdam Proclamation of 1945, the Allies guaranteed Korean independence. In the last days of World War II, the Soviet Union, also committing itself to Korean independence, declared war on Japan and invaded Korea from the north. After the Japanese surrender, U.S. troops entered Korea from the south. As a dividing line between the Soviet and U.S. zones of temporary occupation, the occupying powers chose the 38th parallel.

When a United Nations commission announced plans to hold national free elections to establish an independent Korean government, the Soviet Union refused to participate and, treating the 38th parallel as a boundary, barred the UN representatives from entering North Korea. So the commission held elections in South Korea only, forming a Republic of Korea (ROK). An elected general

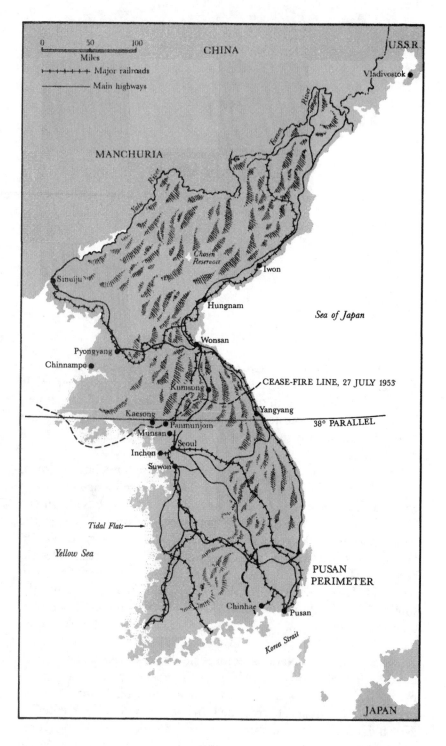

Korea

assembly then chose Syngman Rhee to be president and selected Seoul, the traditional national capital, to be the capital of the new republic. The Soviet Union, branding these proceedings illegal, recognized in North Korea a puppet communist People's Republic of Korea with its capital at Pyongyang. The main body of troops of both occupying powers withdrew from the Korean peninsula, leaving behind advisers to train North and South Korean armed forces.

The Americans, in drafting the peace treaty for Japan preparatory to withdrawing their occupation forces from that country, failed to acknowledge Russia's paramount role in Korea's future. The Soviets, chagrined, decided they had better have their puppet North Korean government take over the whole Korean peninsula before the departing Americans let the Japanese back in. They were emboldened by the fact that American officials had announced a postwar policy placing Japan and the Philippines (but not Taiwan or Korea) within the U.S. defense perimeter.

So the Soviets got busy training a formidable North Korean army that by June 1950 numbered 130,000 men armed with Russian tanks and supported by Russian aircraft. The South Koreans, belatedly discovering the warlike preparations to the north, with American help assembled an army of recent recruits numbering about 94,000 men. These were but feebly backed by U.S. forces afloat and ashore, because most of America's armed might that had not been dissipated by the harsh Truman-Johnson economies had been committed to the North Atlantic Treaty Organization (NATO).

American military strength in the western Pacific consisted mainly of General MacArthur's occupation forces in Japan. These comprised Lieutenant General Walton H. Walker's U.S. Eighth Army of four undermanned, undertrained divisions and Vice Admiral C. Turner Joy's U.S. Naval Forces Far East, made up of a light cruiser and four destroyers. Not under MacArthur's command but available in the Philippines was Vice Admiral Arthur D. Struble's U.S. Seventh Fleet, comprising carrier *Valley Forge*, a heavy cruiser, a squadron of destroyers, and a division of submarines. Luckily for these puny naval forces, the North Korean navy boasted only forty-five small craft.

In the forenoon of 25 June 1950 the North Korean army without warning poured across the 38th parallel in a full-scale invasion. The hurriedly trained South Korean troops, not yet provided with tanks, planes, or adequate artillery, fell back on their capital, Seoul. The

North Koreans and their Russian and Chinese sponsors apparently anticipated no sharper international response to their act of naked aggression than diplomatic protest. Instead, the United Nations intervened. Its Security Council condemned the North Korean invasion as a breach of world peace and ordered military sanctions. Because the Russian delegate to the council was out on boycott, there was no veto.

President Truman, acting as agent for the United Nations, ordered the U.S. Joint Chiefs of Staff, in what he called a "police action," to commit American armed forces to the defense of South Korea. The Joint Chiefs appointed General MacArthur commander in chief Far East (CincFE) and added the Seventh Fleet to his command. The United Nations called on its member states to assist the United States, and ultimately sixteen of them provided combat elements. Several others sent medical units.

MacArthur at once provided air and naval support for the retreating South Koreans, and after the fall of Seoul he committed three of the Eighth Army's four divisions. Several Eighth Army battalions promptly crossed over to Korea from Japan. These joined the demoralized ROK troops south of Seoul in facing the vanguard of fifteen well-equipped Red divisions. The Americans, by blowing up bridges, setting up roadblocks, and fighting suicidally, slowed the Red advance and won enough time to build up UN forces through the southeast Korean port of Pusan. Around this city General Walker was thus enabled to establish a defense perimeter, within which he held back superior forces by skillful use of his interior lines. Nevertheless, the world was bemused by the spectacle of Americans, late chief victors over three major powers, thrust into a corner by the armed forces of one third-rate power, a result of American military penny-pinching.

In Washington, Captain Arleigh Burke fretted at his desk. With the country again at war, he like many another sailor wanted to go to sea. But he was grateful to be where he was and considered himself in no position to ask favors. He was consoled by the fact that on 15 July 1950 he made his number and attained permanent flag rank.

Six weeks later, on 28 August, Admiral Sherman's aide telephoned Burke that the CNO would like to see him in his office at 1400. Curious, Arleigh responded to the summons a little ahead of time. Sherman received him in his inner sanctum and invited him to take a seat. He explained that he was just back from Tokyo, where he had gone accompanied by General J. Lawton Collins, army chief of staff, to consult with General MacArthur. MacArthur had informed them that the opposing forces at the Pusan perimeter were approaching a delicate balance, thanks to General Walker's interior position and to the support of Admiral Struble's Seventh Fleet, to which British warships were now attached.

Planes from U.S. carrier *Valley Forge* and British light carrier *Triumph* had joined U.S. Air Force planes in wrecking the enemy's bridges, marshaling yards, hangars, oil refineries, and fuel storage depots and in wiping out the small North Korean air force. At the Pusan perimeter the naval aviators had provided close support to the UN ground forces, something air force aviators were not trained to do. Most important, the gunnery ships, operating in the Sea of Japan, kept the east road and railroad unusable for supplying the North Korean forces, which now were utterly dependent on munitions, foodstuffs, and other supplies shipped through Seoul on the west side of the central mountains.

In this situation General MacArthur saw an opportunity to turn defeat into victory. He proposed landing troops at Inchon, the port of Seoul, to advance inland and block the North Korean supply line to the perimeter. So delicately balanced was the stalemate at the perimeter that the North Koreans could not hold their position there and adequately defend Inchon at the same time, and if their supplies were blocked they could not hold their position at the perimeter.

There was just one flaw in the general's strategy: Inchon's natural and man-made defenses were among the most formidable in the world. The port sits behind many square miles of islands, shoals, and mud flats and is approachable from seaward only via a couple of narrow, winding channels, both of which can be readily mined. A ship disabled by mine or bomb in one of the channels would trap those ahead and block those behind. Ships heading for the main invasion point would have to pass under the guns of the fortified island of Wolmi Do. The city of Inchon had no beaches. The invading troops would have to clamber over a high seawall into an industrial area and probably fight their way from building to building. The tidal range of Inchon, averaging 30 feet, is one of the world's greatest. Only twice a day, three days out of each lunar month, would the tide be high enough for the troop-bearing LSTs, which required a minimum of 29 feet to maneuver. MacArthur had selected 15 September, when the tide would be high enough at sunrise and again at sunset.

It was MacArthur's announced decision to assault Inchon despite the obstacles that had brought Sherman and Collins to Tokyo. They wanted to check the facts and if necessary attempt to talk the general out of so quixotic an enterprise. Instead, MacArthur in an eloquent thirty-minute monologue won them over. His argument was that precisely because an assault on Inchon was deemed unachievable, the North Koreans would leave the port underdefended rather than weaken their precarious hold on the Pusan perimeter. He had no plan for overcoming the obstacles of the approach. He was leaving that to the navy, which he said had never let him down.

After the meeting with MacArthur, Sherman called on Admiral Joy and found him worried. His headquarters was simply unprepared for warfare, much less for organizing a complex amphibious assault. His staff was small, trained for occupation duties, completely inexperienced in military operations. Admiral Joy's own World War II experience was limited to commanding cruiser fire support units. He needed a senior officer with high-level combat experience to advise him and take charge of the headquarters' wartime responsibilities.

When Admiral Sherman had completed his recital of the facts, he paused, looking directly at Burke. "Will you go?" he said.

Arleigh said he would.

"You will become deputy chief of staff to Admiral Joy," said Sherman. Then he added almost apologetically, "That is a title less than you had quite a few years ago when you were chief of staff to the biggest fighting force in the world. Will that bother you?"

Arleigh replied that it would not. What concerned him was how he would be received. At least this time he was not being forced onto the staff of an admiral who did not want him, but might not the other staffers resent him as a self-styled expert sent in from headquarters to tell them how to run their show?

Admiral Sherman admitted that as a possibility, and he had a still more ticklish assignment for Burke. "I want you to keep me constantly informed of the situation in Korea," he said. "Send a personal radio dispatch to me directly at least once a day. I want you particularly to study the plan for this upcoming Inchon assault. If you think it likely to fail, let me know and I can block the operation."

Sherman placed a metal box on his desk. Burke recognized it as the usual container for code wheels used with the Electric Ciphering Machine. Burke was to use these wheels, or have a trusted communicator use them, to encipher his dispatches to Sherman, who had the only duplicate set.

Burke's head had been set awhirl, not only by the confidence placed in him by the CNO but also by the distasteful prospect of going to Tokyo as a sort of headquarters spy. He gingerly took the box of wheels. "One thing I must do," he said. "I will not send you a dispatch unless I first show it to Admiral Joy. I want him to know everything I send to you. If he doesn't agree with it, I will still send it. Then I will send you another dispatch stating why Admiral Joy disagreed with my report and what I think of his objections."

This plan was agreeable to Sherman. As Burke rose to leave, Sherman said, "When you have finished with this job, which I don't think will take more than three or four months, you can have any job in the navy that a rear admiral can have."

"That's wonderful," said Burke, perfectly aware that no one, not even a chief of naval operations, could fulfill such a sweeping promise. Anyway, for Arleigh the job he was going to was reward enough.

Problems of air transportation delayed Burke's arrival in Tokyo till 3 September. From his plane he went directly to commander naval forces Far East (ComNavFE) headquarters and reported to Admiral Joy, who received him cordially and introduced him to Rear Admiral Albert Morehouse, chief of staff, and to other staff members. Joy told Burke that his gear was being taken to his hotel, and he personally conducted Arleigh to his assigned office, where a yeoman was awaiting him.

Hardly had Arleigh settled himself at his desk when a messenger arrived from the operations department with an armload of papers— dispatches, orders, and whatnot. Burke knew that this was just the first installment of a mountain of paper he would have to master, and master fast, if he was to be of any use to ComNavFE or to the CNO.

With the aid of his yeoman, Burke sorted the papers and drew out the ones he probably needed to study first. Within half an hour he knew that the Inchon assault was definitely in the works, scheduled for 15 September—twelve days away. The landing was to be carried out by the Seventh Fleet, which, unlike ComNavFE, did not lack combat-experienced officers. The fleet commander, Admiral Struble, had participated in or commanded more than a score of World War II amphibious operations, including Normandy and Leyte.

Rear Admiral James H. Doyle, commanding the amphibious force, had been on Admiral Turner's staff in the South Pacific. Commanding the 1st Marine Division, which would spearhead the Inchon assault, was Marine Major General Oliver P. Smith, who had commanded a regiment in the assault on Cape Gloucester and had participated in the Peleliu and Okinawa invasions.

The plans, though in a preliminary stage, were well thought out. During the morning high tide, marines would storm the guardian island of Wolmi Do and silence its guns. During the afternoon high tide, marines, using prepared ladders, would scale the seawalls of Inchon from LSTs and lead the way into the city. Subsequently the invaders would seize Kimpo Airfield and capture Seoul. That evening Burke sent his first report to Sherman. The Inchon assault, he said, had a good chance of success.

During the next few days, Burke worked with Admiral Joy's staffers on a ComNavFE plan for supporting the Inchon invasion. They reversed the usual procedure of the top command's issuing a general plan to the lower echelons for working out details. Instead, Burke and his colleagues worked out a ComNavFE plan based on those of Doyle and Struble. ComNavFE's responsibility would be coordination of the 71,000-man landing force and the hastily assembled 230-ship international fleet that would transport and support it. The tight schedule permitted no rehearsal.

Burke was pleasantly surprised to find himself accepted in a friendly and respectful manner by the ComNavFE staff. His candor and good nature disarmed them, and his reputation impressed them. What Arleigh could never quite grasp was that he had become a celebrity, particularly in the navy. Every navy man had heard of the feats (some mythical) of 31-Knot Burke, who went on to become the right-hand man of the great Mitscher. Though they usually had their facts askew, most naval officers knew that Burke's removal from and restoration to the promotion list had embarrassed Secretary Johnson. Since Johnson was heartily detested throughout the navy, anybody who had mortified him was every sailor's friend.

Several days after his arrival in Japan, Burke learned that typhoons were beginning to develop in the Marianas. He promptly went on a personal alert, knowing what typhoons could do to ships. Under Spruance and Mitscher, the Big Blue Fleet had managed to sidestep them, but under Halsey and McCain it had twice run into typhoons that inflicted damage comparable to that received in a major battle. Burke now took time out to check weather maps and

consult aerologists. By 9 September, he was convinced that if the
fleet and convoy left port on the 12th, as scheduled, one of the
typhoons boiling up from the south would batter the ships as they
rounded southern Kyushu and headed into the Yellow Sea. At this
point only General MacArthur himself had the authority to change
the schedule. Burke dashed off several dispatches and headed for the
general's office.

He was not too surprised to be stopped by members of the general's staff, it being a function of the staff to protect the commander
from unnecessary interruption, leaving him undisturbed to make
major decisions. When Burke insisted that he had to have an important decision from MacArthur himself, they handed him over to
Major General Edward Almond, MacArthur's chief of staff, who
said condescendingly, "You can tell me what you want to bring to
General MacArthur's attention."

Arleigh knew better. If he told Almond what he had in mind,
there would ensue an extended debate over whether to bring it to
the big boss's notice.

"I'm sorry, but I can't do it," said Burke. "I'll go back to my
office."

It was a calculated move that worked. Burke's reputation for
sound judgment assured that he would not be shrugged off. Hardly
had he reached his office when the phone rang. He was asked to
please come back.

This time he was ushered directly into MacArthur's presence. To
the general Burke explained about the typhoon. If the fleet was
overtaken by it, the ships would be in no condition to stage the
invasion on the midmonth high tides. If they waited till the typhoon
passed, they would be too late to make the tides.

"Well, what do we do?" said MacArthur.

"We sail early—at dawn on the 11th."

"All right, Burke. You prepare the dispatches."

"I just happen to have them here."

"Fine," said MacArthur and ordered them put out right away.

Arleigh was strongly impressed by the alacrity with which the
general grasped a situation and acted upon it. As Burke recommended, the assault shipping left Kobe before light on the 11th.
Subsequently, with other GHQ spectators, MacArthur flew to
Sasebo at the southwest tip of Japan. Here Admiral Doyle's flagship
received them on board as the convoy passed by.

Despite the lack of rehearsal and the bad weather kicked up by the passing typhoon, the Inchon operation was executed to perfection. ComNavFE had no coordinating to do. On 15 September, Admirals Joy, Morehouse, and Burke sat at their command post in Tokyo and listened to the radio traffic. After the marines, going ashore on the morning tide, had conquered Wolmi Do with no marines killed and only seventeen wounded, MacArthur radioed, "The navy and marines have never shone more brightly than this morning."

The marines were equally successful in their assault on the city in the afternoon high tide. The North Koreans at Inchon put up a determined defense, but they were too few. The marines all but wiped them out while sustaining casualties of only twenty-one killed and 186 wounded. In the late afternoon Admiral Struble sent in his report to Tokyo and to Washington: "Our losses are light. . . . The command distinguished itself. The whole operation is proceeding on schedule."

On 16 and 17 September the marines cleared Inchon, captured Kimpo Airfield, the largest in Korea, and advanced to liberate Seoul. On the 18th the follow-up 7th Infantry Division landed at Inchon. Together with the 1st Marine Division, already ashore, it constituted the X Corps, commanded by General Almond, who also retained his post as General MacArthur's chief of staff. While the marines laid siege to the capital, the soldiers headed south toward Suwon, which they captured on the 22nd. Seoul fell to the marines on the 26th.

On schedule, General Walker had opened his campaign to break out of the Pusan perimeter on 16 September, the day following the Inchon assault. The North Koreans at the perimeter, despite the imminent blocking of their main supply route, held on grimly until the 22nd, when their line gave way, and the Eighth Army began advancing on several roads. Republic of Korea troops moved up the east coast, and an armored spearhead, heading for Seoul, made contact south of Suwon with the 7th Infantry Division.

General MacArthur had from the beginning assumed full responsibility for the risky Inchon gamble. When it paid off triumphantly he rightly got the credit. Admiral Halsey's telegram of congratulation called it "the most masterly and audacious stroke in all history." Burke said to his colleagues, "This operation really shows the greatness of that man."

*　*

For living quarters Burke had been assigned a small room in Tokyo's Imperial Hotel, taken over as housing for U.S. occupation personnel but run by Japanese. Here he slept and usually break-fasted and dined. The hotel people and the guard outside were the first native Japanese with whom Burke had come in contact. It gave him an eerie feeling, because he still thought of them as enemy. During the Pacific war he had seen them fire at Americans descend-ing in parachutes, he had read about the Bataan death march and other examples of atrocious Japanese conduct, and of course he had been influenced by Admirals Halsey and Mitscher, both champion Jap haters.

In their dealing with Burke, the Japanese hotel people were polite and helpful, and he was polite to them but determinedly distant. It occurred to him, however, that as military adviser and trouble-shooter he might be more effective if he had a better understanding of the Japanese—and the Koreans and Chinese too, for that matter. He turned for advice to his friend Captain Edward H. Pierce, also stationed at Tokyo. Before World War II, Captain Pierce had par-ticipated in the navy's Japanese language program, which required him to spend three years in Japan, first to master the language and then to live among the people, learning their customs and ways of thinking.*

Burke asked Pierce to suggest somebody who might have the knowledge, the skill, and the leisure to teach him how to understand the Japanese and other Orientals. Pierce thought a minute, and then recommended retired Admiral Kichisaburo Nomura. Nomura had been Japan's foreign minister and later ambassador to the United States, where he was struggling mightily to preserve the peace when to his dismay his fellow countrymen attacked Pearl Harbor.

A couple of days after the conversation with Pierce, a Japanese gentleman appeared at Burke's office in ComNavFE and introduced himself as Admiral Nomura. An Americanophile, he was happy in this postwar period to again become acquainted with Americans. He

---

*Graduates of the navy's Japanese language program rendered invaluable service in the Pacific war. The most useful undoubtedly was that provided by Joseph Rochefort and Edwin Layton, who first met and became friends on the language program. In World War II, Rochefort headed the Pearl Harbor Combat Intelligence Unit. Layton, also stationed at Pearl Harbor, was Pacific Fleet intelligence officer. Between them, profiting by the intelligence unit's codebreaking, they predicted when and from what direction a Japanese four-carrier force would attack the U.S. naval air station on Midway Atoll. The Americans, making use of this information, placed their inferior force in an advantageous position that enabled them in the Battle of Midway (June 1942) to sink all four of the enemy's carriers and thereby turn the tide of the naval war.

had developed a friendship with Admiral Joy, on whom he had just paid a call. Speaking excellent English with just a trace of accent, Nomura said Captain Pierce had relayed Burke's request to him. He would, he said, be very happy to teach Burke what little he knew about Japan, the Japanese, the difference between Japanese, Chinese, and Koreans—how they thought and how they arrived at decisions. For a first lesson he invited Arleigh to his home, which proved to be a small house in the outskirts of Tokyo.

Most of the succeeding lessons consisted of hour-long conversations in Burke's office. They provided Arleigh insights that helped him mightily in his later dealings with Orientals. Nomura in his person, moreover, demonstrated that there were high-minded Japanese one could admire. His example prepared Arleigh to accord due respect to Japanese Prime Minister Shigeru Yoshida and members of his cabinet, whom on occasion he helped brief on the situation in Korea.

The situation portended a new phase in the war as the Eighth Army joined the X Corps at Seoul, and the ROK troops, advancing rapidly up the east coast, crossed the 38th parallel into North Korea. At this juncture, Chinese Premier Chou En-lai, using the Indian ambassador as his mouthpiece, issued a warning. Summoning the ambassador to Peking, the premier told him that if any UN forces other than ROKs, crossed the 38th parallel, Chinese troops would enter North Korea to repel them.

The UN command did not take the threat seriously. The Chinese, they concluded, would hardly give advance notice of their intention, and if they meant to intervene they would have done so earlier, while the UN forces had their backs to the sea at Pusan. Burke, not convinced by this line of reasoning, asked Admiral Nomura his opinion.

"If you go north of the 38th parallel, they'll come in," Nomura replied. "They'll have to do that now to save face, live up to their own words."

"Well, what do you think?" Burke said. "Do you think we should cross over?"

"Yes, I do. You've got to defeat them now. They started this thing, so they have to be punished."

That is exactly what the UN command proposed to do—cross the 38th parallel and destroy the remnant of the communist army. The North Koreans had taken appalling losses in killed and captured, but a flaw in the UN Inchon operation was failure to trap the survivors.

As many as 40,000 had made their way homeward through the mountains or along secondary roads. On 27 September the Joint Chiefs authorized MacArthur to cross the parallel in pursuit.

MacArthur planned to ensnare the enemy by means of another amphibious end run followed by a double envelopment. He would send the Eighth Army north from Seoul toward the communist capital of Pyongyang, while he reembarked the X Corps and dispatched it by sea around the tip of the Korean peninsula for a 20 October landing at the east coast port of Wonsan. From Wonsan the corps would drive west to Pyongyang to link up with the Eighth Army.

Admirals Joy and Burke opposed the plan, because they rightly suspected that the spacious harbor of Wonsan was heavily mined. When MacArthur refused even to discuss any change, Burke undertook on his own a highly irregular course of action, which had it been proposed through established channels might have been canceled at the outset by protracted debate.

The problem was that ComNavFE had only twelve minesweepers. These, operating at 5 knots, had not the slightest chance of sweeping a channel by 20 October through the hundreds, perhaps thousands, of mines in the approaches to Wonsan. Japan now had no fleet to speak of. Of its major ships, those not destroyed by submarines or fleet action had been blasted by guns and planes of the Big Blue Fleet operating off Japan in the final weeks of the Pacific war. But Japan had about a hundred minesweepers, and these had been busy since 1944 sweeping the thousands of mines the U.S. B-29s had sown in every Japanese port in the final year of the war. Burke set out to obtain use of some of those sweepers.

The Japanese minesweepers, Burke knew, were manned and commanded by sailors, but they operated under something called the Maritime Safety Agency. In the severely antimilitaristic mood of postwar Japan, no officer could be allowed to occupy so senior a naval command. The agency's general director was a civilian, Mr. Takeo Okubo, who had a former naval officer as adviser.

It was 2 October when Burke got the brainstorm about the Japanese sweepers and telephoned Mr. Okubo, whom he had met at the prime minister's briefings. Okubo suggested they meet in Burke's office at ComNavFE, and Burke invited him by all means to come. When the general director learned the nature of Burke's request, to borrow manned Japanese ships, he was taken aback. The Japanese, he pointed out, were not at war with North Korea, and in fact by the terms of their new constitution they had renounced war.

Arleigh argued that sweeping the mines would not be a hostile act. It would not be hurting anybody. It was comparable to neutral cargo ships delivering noncontraband materials to ports of a nation at war. Mr. Okubo insisted it was beyond his competence to make a decision in this matter. Only the prime minister could do that.

When, after polite exchanges in the Japanese manner, Okubo left, Burke got into his car and went to see Mr. Yoshida, confident that Okubo would have telephoned ahead word of his mission. It was a delicate undertaking, in which Arleigh applied some of the lessons he learned from Admiral Nomura. He did not order the sweepers sent. Yoshida would know that Burke, personally, lacked authority to do that. A request to have them sent would invite a "no" on constitutional grounds. What Burke did was point out the serious need and suggest that a United Nations defeat in Korea would have unpleasant consequences for Japan. In the end the prime minister granted his *assent* to the loan but withheld his *consent*—apparently a practical difference in the Japanese language though nearly meaningless in English.

Burke had hoped to borrow at least fifty of the Japanese minesweepers. Instead, just twenty of the sweeper crews were given permission to volunteer their services, and all but one of the crews did so. The first of the U.S. minesweepers arrived off Wonsan on 10 October. On that date the ROK troops arrived overland at the port and quickly wrested it from its outnumbered defenders. The X Corps would not have to fight its way ashore as at Inchon.

As more U.S. and Japanese sweepers arrived, the crews gradually realized the immensity of their task. In 400 square miles of the shallow approaches to Wonsan, the North Koreans, supervised by Soviet technicians, had planted about 3,000 contact and magnetic mines. When the ships bringing the marines arrived off the port on the 19th, the channel was far from swept, and two American and two Japanese minesweepers had been sunk by mines. For a week the transports steamed back and forth off Wonsan, a voyage to nowhere the disgusted marines tagged Operation Yo-Yo. They finally got ashore on 25 October. The 7th Infantry Division, comprising the rest of X Corps, proceeded far up the coast and landed unopposed at Iwon on the 29th.

Mines had to be cleared also from Chinnampo, a west coast port through which the Eighth Army at Pyongyang could be supplied. Here the task was easier, because the tidal characteristics of the

Yellow Sea, as at Inchon, generally exposed the mines at low water.

The delay in landing the X Corps at Wonsan permitted the retreating North Korean army elements to elude MacArthur's intended trap by retreating northward across the Wonsan-Pyongyang line. MacArthur therefore canceled his intended drive westward from Wonsan and ordered all UN forces to advance northward to round up the refugee troops before they could re-form and reorganize.

At one of the daily CincFE conferences, which Burke was at pains to attend whenever possible, he protested the drive to the north and suggested forming a strong Pyongyang-Wonsan line across the narrowest part of the Korean peninsula. Here it could be easily supplied and reinforced through Chinnampo and Wonsan. North of the narrows, the peninsula, increasingly rugged and mountainous, broadens steadily all the way to the Yalu River, which separates Korea from China. If the Chinese crossed the Yalu, as they probably already had, the place to repulse them would be the secure Pyongyang-Wonsan line, rather than in the northern mountains, which the approaching winter would soon turn icy.

Burke repeatedly advocated his strategy among his fellow officers in Tokyo and in his reports to Admiral Sherman, but he was defeated by assurances from MacArthur's intelligence staff that the Chinese threats were a bluff and that Chinese soldiers would never cross the Yalu. Oddly enough, no one on the staff seems to have asked himself what the United States would do if a Chinese army invaded Mexico, captured the Mexican capital, and headed northward toward the Rio Grande. Had MacArthur sent reconnaissance planes beyond the river to have a look, his staff might have been disabused, but the Joint Chiefs, anxious to avoid spreading hostilities, forbade American aircraft to violate Chinese airspace.

When he could not sell his strategy, Burke set about preparing to evacuate forces following the inevitable retreat. One problem was having transports and cargo ships available on short notice. That meant defeating the ground forces' lazy tendency to immobilize the ships by using them as warehouses. Instead of emptying them on arrival, they would take out supplies they needed when they needed them, thereby tying the ships up for weeks.

The main UN drives, that of the Eighth Army, north from Pyongyang, and that of the X Corps, north from Hungnam, were separated by 80 miles of mountains. Elements of each had reached the Yalu when on the night of 25 November the Chinese hurled a

180,000-man offensive against the Eighth Army's right flank, smashing three ROK divisions. To avoid encirclement by the enemy, General Walker ordered a retirement that turned into a rout as his army fell back, abandoning equipment, past Pyongyang, across the 38th parallel, and past Seoul.

The retreat of the X Corps was more orderly because the 120,000-man Chinese attack in its area was directed against the highly disciplined 1st Marine Division and because the marine ground controllers made skillful use of the close air support afforded by carrier planes and by marine corps planes based on Yonpo Airfield near Hungnam. The marines, "attacking in a new direction," fought their way 60 miles to the sea. Their withdrawal, bringing most of their equipment over difficult terrain, through ice and snow, under constant attack and harassment, has been called one of the great retreats of history.

Promptly on learning of the Chinese attack, Admiral Joy sent Burke to Yonpo to check on the needs of the marine air group operating from there. While at Yonpo, Burke once flew out in a plane sent to pick up wounded marines at a rough airstrip their buddies had scratched out. Having observed the marines in the mountains and again as they came down from the heights, Arleigh later remarked, "I've never seen anything like it. I don't know how the hell they did it. That was the most wonderful display of spirit, discipline, and mutual support I have ever seen."

In mid-December the last of Almond's X Corps reached Hungnam, where they were safe under the protection of Seventh Fleet guns and planes. Some 100,000 troops, with their equipment, and almost as many civilian refugees were evacuated by sea. Carried south, the X Corps was integrated into the Eighth Army, which in late January 1951 stabilized on a firm defense line just south of Seoul.

20

KOREAN WAR
(2)

THE PRIMARY MISSION of the supreme commander for the Allied powers (SCAP), initially MacArthur, was to enforce the terms of the Potsdam Proclamation. These included the elimination "for all time" of "the authority and influence of those who have deceived and misled the people of Japan into embarking on world conquest." As steps toward attaining that end, SCAP disarmed and demobilized Japan's armed forces, and in a general "purge," barred all former commissioned officers in Japan's army, navy, and air force from government aid and access to public office.

Japanese civilians generally supported the purge. In their view, the generals and admirals had initiated the war and then lost it, leaving the people impoverished, their young men lost in battle, their homes destroyed by bombing, and supposedly about to be ground under the heel of the conqueror. Former high-ranking officers, thus excluded by the Americans and rebuffed by their fellow Japanese, became destitute. Members of the gentility, unused to manual labor, they were reduced to selling newspapers, digging ditches—anything to keep body and soul, and family, together.

One American who felt compassion for the starving officers was Captain Pierce. He personally was in no position to better their lot, but he had an influential friend, Admiral Burke. In conversation with Burke, he brought up the subject indirectly.

Did the name Kusaka, Pierce asked, mean anything to Arleigh?

"Yes, indeed," replied Burke grimly. He had never met the man, but as Japanese naval commander at Rabaul, Vice Admiral Jinishi Kusaka had been his wartime enemy, sending ships and planes into the Solomons to attack Americans, including Burke and his Little Beavers. In Solomons night battles, Arleigh had had the satisfaction of destroying several of Kusaka's ships.

"Tiny bit of a gray-haired fellow," said Pierce, sighing. "You know what he's doing? He's working on the railway, swinging a sledge. His wife's selling flowers on a street corner. They're starving. He won't accept charity, but if you can arrange it, perhaps I can get food to him."

"To hell with him," said Burke. "Let him starve."

As Pierce doubtless anticipated, Arleigh, for all his negative words, could not get the plight of Kusaka and his fellow officers off his mind. The situation, Burke concluded, was ridiculous. The Japanese commanders, confronting the overwhelming power and abundant resources of the United States and its allies, had fought nearly four years before suffering defeat. It was an incredible achievement. Yet their reward was hunger and the scorn of their fellow countrymen. Burke went into action. From the commissary he had a box of groceries delivered anonymously to the Kusakas.

"Okay," he said to Pierce. "You win."

Burke was not as anonymous as he imagined. A few days later the door to his office was flung open, and in stormed the little admiral spouting Japanese. Arleigh reached in the drawer for his pistol. He would shoot through the desk if he had to. With his other hand, he rang for an orderly, who presently appeared. They got an interpreter. Through him Kusaka expressed his indignation. He had, he said, been grossly insulted. He would accept charity from nobody, certainly not from Americans. He wanted nothing to do with Americans, he concluded, and coldly stalked out.

Burke was favorably impressed. Kusaka had done exactly what Arleigh would have done—chosen starvation rather than accept charity under such circumstances.

Trying another tack, he had Pierce invite Kusaka and a couple of his hard-up fellow admirals to dinner at the Imperial Hotel. The dinner took place in a private dining room on 26 December 1950, shortly after Burke's return from Hungnam. Captain Pierce arrived accompanied by Admiral Timioka and Vice Admirals Sakano and Kusaka. They wore formal dress, now threadbare, and held themselves aloof. Pierce had warned Burke this would happen. In their view they had been summoned by the occupying power and were obliged to come, but they would keep their distance.

Burke managed to get Pierce aside. "Look, Eddie," he said, "we've got to get some liquor in these men to loosen them up."

"I don't know that they can hold it, Arleigh. They've been too poor to buy liquor."

"I leave it to you. You speak Japanese."

On an inspiration, Eddie got some tiny ceremonial sake cups and filled them with whiskey. The cups added a formal note and also limited the amount that could be drunk without pause. When the guests declined the proffered drink, Eddie said, "You can't be rude to your host."

It took a while and several formal sips, but eventually the three guests were chattering away. It turned out they could all speak English, and Kusaka, who had spouted only Japanese in Burke's office, spoke it especially well, having been a naval attaché in London before the war.

The dinner was the best the hotel could prepare and good by any standard. The Japanese admirals, animated by the whiskey and the good food, shed their frostiness and turned a not unfriendly eye on their host. At the meal's end Burke rose and offered a toast to his guests.

Kusaka then stood up and raised his cup, saying, "I want to give a toast to our host, but not just to our host, who has been very kind to have us for this dinner. I want to give a toast also to the time when I failed to do my duty, because if I had done my duty I would have killed our host, and then we would not have had this fine steak dinner tonight."

Burke then got up and lifted his cup. "Admiral," he said, "could I drink to that toast too?"

They all drank to the toast. Then Arleigh continued, "I would like also to propose a toast to the time when I also failed to do my duty, because if I had not failed to do my duty I would have killed Admiral Kusaka, and therefore neither of us would have enjoyed this fine steak dinner."

Everybody laughed. The ice was broken, and Arleigh's war with the Japanese was amicably concluded.

Shortly after the outbreak of the Korean War, which drew most of the occupation troops out of Japan, the Japanese increased their national police force from 15,000 to about 60,000 men and took over from the occupation forces the job of maintaining order in the country. Japan's sea approaches and coastal waters, however, remained generally unprotected. Japan had never had a coast guard, its functions having been assigned to its navy, which no longer existed. Japan's only remaining combatant ships were the little minesweepers and a few other small craft. The Japanese had no way of stopping large-scale smuggling at sea, no way of detecting approaching invasion forces until they got on the beach, and no way of protecting their fishermen, whose boats were often stripped and sometimes seized outright by Koreans, Russians, or Chinese. Admiral Joy and other officers at ComNavFE discussed this undesirable situation. Burke discussed it too, but at first he was the only one who did anything about it. He began by talking it over with his Japanese mentor, Admiral Nomura.

SCAP, enjoined to both democratize and demilitarize Japan, had prepared the constitution of 1947, which the Japanese accepted without question, including the famous article 9:

> Aspiring sincerely to an international peace based on justice and order, the Japanese people forever renounce war as a sovereign right of the nation and the threat or use of force as a means of settling international disputes.
>
> In order to accomplish the aims of the preceding paragraph, land, sea, and air forces, as well as other war potential, will never be maintained. The right of belligerency of the state will not be recognized.

Burke read the article to Admiral Nomura and shook his head. "How can a nation become viable without the power to protect itself?" he asked.

"This article was suggested by your country," said Nomura, "and it was accepted by my country. You will have to protect us."

"That can't be," replied Burke. "That's all right for a year or so or even for a few years, but it can't go on forever. No nation can take on the sole support of another nation. It can't be done."

"It's a burden you asked for."

"You've got to change, reinterpret, or cancel that article."

Nomura smiled. "You're right," he said. "As a self-respecting nation, we should have a navy. Someday we should."

In a later visit to Nomura's home, Burke was introduced to an

Admiral Zenshiro Hoshina and learned that a number of Japanese naval officers recognized the need to establish a national navy and had formed a planning group to that end headed by a Captain Ko Nagasawa. Included were officers of the Maritime Safety Agency. Arleigh was aware that these men had been quietly depurged in order to command the agency's minesweepers and to advise Okubo, its civilian head. He learned now that the agency also had a few officer-commanded subchaser types patrolling from coastal cities to do what they could against smuggling.

The Japanese thus had a small nucleus for a navy, and Burke had an idea how to expand it a little. At Vladivostok and other nearby Siberian ports were a number of old, beaten-up frigates that the United States had lend-leased to the Soviets during the war. Russia had decided it could now return them and planned to hand them over to ComNavFE. It struck Burke that though these ships were in poor condition, if they were turned over to Japan the Japanese could cannibalize them and make a couple of pretty good frigates out of them. At least they would be useful for training.

Burke discussed the possibility with Admiral Joy, who fully approved, but they were far from certain how the suggestion would be received by authorities in the United States. It was clear, however, that the request should not come from Americans lest it appear they were forcing something on unwilling Japanese. The request had to come from the Japanese themselves, and Burke believed he had the man to do the requesting—Takeo Okubo. Okubo had a dignified yet pleasant personality, he was of subcabinet rank, and he had the confidence of the prime minister.

Okubo was reluctant to undertake the mission, having no idea how he would be received in the United States and fearing antagonism. But Burke paved his way with convincing letters to the officials he would have to visit. Probably Arleigh's most useful letter was the one to Bobbie, asking her to be Okubo's guide in Washington to the offices he should visit. Okubo left for the United States on 10 January 1951 and returned triumphant a month later. He had been granted everything he sought: transfer of the battered frigates to Japan, possession and use of an airplane to locate floating mines, right to increase size and speed of the antismuggling patrol boats, and permission to load their guns.

During the first months of 1951, planning for a Japanese navy went apace under the guidance of Burke and former officers of the Imperial Japanese Navy. Burke played a major role based on his varied experience and his extensive study of naval and military history. The planners had actually picked the ten officers to head the new navy, with Nagasawa as its first chief of operations, when the U.S. State Department got wind of what was going on and ordered a halt. Talk of a new Japanese navy had better be hushed on the eve of a peace conference at which forty-eight nations had to be persuaded to sign the treaty.

The peace treaty, which recognized Japan's right to self-defense, was signed in September 1951. When it went into effect the following April, the Allied (almost wholly American) occupation officially ended. Instead of the barbarous crushing the Japanese had feared, it had been firm but fair, fostering liberty and encouraging commerce. The Korean War, for which the UN forces purchased abundant services and products from Japan, had restored the nation's economy. In this hopeful atmosphere, the Japanese depurged most of their purged officers and officials, and a miniature Japanese navy, the Maritime Self-Defense Force, came into being with Admiral Ko Nagasawa at its head. The Japanese naval officers, then and later, acknowledged Rear Admiral Arleigh A. Burke of the U.S. Navy as its "mighty benefactor."

The indefatigable Burke took an interest also in establishing a Korean navy. Early in 1951 he accepted an invitation to visit the new Naval Academy of the Republic of Korea at Chinhae. The midshipmen of the struggling young school had enthusiasm and spirit but lacked nearly everything else—mainly books. Arleigh at once wrote an appeal, "Books for Korea," which was published in the June 1951 issue of *U.S. Naval Institute Proceedings.* In response to this one article, American schools, colleges, universities, libraries, naval organizations, and individuals contributed more than 20,000 books, which became the foundation of the new academy's library.

While Burke was performing the major role in establishing the new Japanese navy and soliciting books for the ROK Naval Academy, he was also carrying out his duties at ComNavFE and making his daily reports to the CNO. At the same time the outnumbered Eighth Army, thanks to naval support, superior air support, and a more efficient, motorized supply system, was beginning to push the communist hordes back toward the 38th parallel.

In May 1951, Admiral Sherman made good his assurance that Burke's Tokyo assignment was temporary duty by ordering him to the command of Cruiser Division 5. Arleigh flew to Pearl Harbor, where he picked up his flagship, heavy cruiser *Los Angeles.* The other cruisers of the division being committed to duty elsewhere, Burke headed for the Sea of Japan with only his flagship and her accompanying destroyers.

By this time there were several major changes of command, made and contemplated. In September 1950, President Truman sacked Secretary of Defense Johnson, replacing him with General of the Army George Marshall—a change hailed with relief and thanksgiving throughout the army and navy. At the time of Johnson's dismissal, his conduct had become so offensive that several other officials were unwilling to deal with him. The explanation came later when he died of a brain tumor.

While the president was striving to keep the war from spreading, Secretary of the Navy Matthews made a public speech calling for a preventive war against the Soviet Union. To get him out of the Pentagon and off the front pages, Truman was preparing to ship him off to Ireland as ambassador. In late December 1950, during the retreat from North Korea, General Walker was killed in a road accident. Washington sent out Lieutenant General Matthew B. Ridgway to replace him in command of the Eighth Army. In April 1951, Truman sacked General MacArthur for gross insubordination that risked spreading the war and undermining confidence at home. General Ridgway took over all of MacArthur's commands, and Lieutenant General James Van Fleet succeeded to command of the Eighth Army.

When Burke arrived off Korea, the Eighth Army's right had pushed the enemy well past the 38th parallel, while its left lagged behind—partly because along the east coast the big UN ships, including Burke's, unhindered by the shallows, mudflats, and huge tidal ranges that mark the west coast, could approach and provide gunfire support for the troops.

Burke was teamed up with the ROK I Corps, his cruiser and destroyers providing the corps' only artillery. Vice Admiral Lee Song Ho, later ROK chief of naval operations, remarked that "Burke's gunfire support was so deliberate and effective that friendly forces could easily resist enemy attacks along the coast line." Burke, the ordnance expert, was less satisfied, because in his opinion his guns were too often aimed at poor targets. He had a rule against interfering with the skipper of a ship, but on one occasion he managed to intervene with a sporting proposition. *Los Angeles*'s skipper, Captain Robert MacFarlane, had spotted an enemy railroad bridge and was preparing to open fire on it with his 8-inch guns.

"Bob," said Burke, "you'll be wasting your bullets. You can't hit a bridge with 8-inch guns. The thing to do is to knock out the abutments at each end."

"I can hit it," replied MacFarlane grimly.

"I'll make you a bet," said Burke. "I'll bet you can't hit that bridge with your first ten shots. If you hit it with your first shot, I'll buy you nine cases of Scotch. If you hit it with your second, you win eight cases of Scotch, and so on to ten shots. But for every shot over ten that it takes you to hit it, you have to buy me a bottle of Scotch."

MacFarlane was only too happy to shake on a one-sided proposition that appeared wholly in his favor. His satisfied smile gradually faded, however, as he fired thirty shots at the bridge without scoring a hit.

"It's hard to hit a bridge," Burke commented mildly while the captain made out an IOU for twenty bottles of whisky.

Making use of his connections at CincFE headquarters, Burke cadged a helicopter, together with pilot, for use on his cruiser. In it he frequently flew to the front, sometimes with MacFarlane, sometimes with commanding general I Corps, looking for suitable targets. Because the corps had no ground-control parties, Burke sent half his staff over on a rotating basis to the general's headquarters.

"Take portable radios," he said, "and tell us what the general needs and where to put our fire, and direct that fire."

Commanding the ROK I Corps was the diminutive Paik Sun Yup, a phenomenon in any army. With somewhat the look of a friendly small boy, at age thirty-one he held the rank of major general, a rank he had fairly earned in World War II fighting the Chinese while serving in the Japanese Manchurian army and more recently fighting the Chinese and North Koreans while serving in the ROK army, of which he was destined to become chief of staff. Besides Japanese and Korean, he spoke good English. He and Burke frequently exchanged visits.

On one occasion while a guest of the I Corps, Burke decided to join a night patrol into enemy territory to see what it was like.

"Well, hell," said Paik, "if you want to go, I'm going with you."

Burke said, "This is quite a scouting patrol, with two flag officers."

Off they went in silence and darkness. Unfortunately Arleigh had forgotten to remove or reset his wristwatch, which had an alarm. At 0200 the alarm went off, shattering the deep hush of the night like a tocsin. The area was full of foxholes, and everybody dived in fast.

A lot of fire came their way, but nobody was hurt. Anyway, General Paik decreed that Admiral Burke was not to accompany any more patrols with his corps.

Nothing, however, prevented Paik from inviting Burke to his headquarters when General Van Fleet came for a briefing. After G-1, G-2, and G-3 (assistant chiefs of staffs, respectively, for personnel, for military intelligence, and for operations) had presented their prepared reports, General Paik, springing a surprise, said to Van Fleet, "Now I want you to be briefed by my artillery commander, Arleigh Burke."

To everyone's amusement it was obvious that Arleigh was unprepared, but he gave a briefing off the cuff. Afterward, knowing that Van Fleet was fond of ice cream, Burke invited him out to his flagship to have some.

"We can go in my helo," said Burke. "It'll only take fifteen or twenty minutes."

"That's a good idea," said Van Fleet, and away they went. The pilot came onto the cruiser too low and crashed the helicopter, which flipped over on the edge of the deck, spurting gasoline.

"What do we do now?" asked the general, who was on top.

"We get that window out."

"How?"

"Kick it out."

He did. "Now," said Burke, "Let's get the hell out. There's going to be a fire here in a minute."

Van Fleet, using Burke's hips as a stepping-stone, led the way out through the opening, followed by Burke and the pilot. Fortunately the spilled gasoline didn't ignite. Sailors had rushed up to hold the battered helicopter until the passengers were out, then dropped it over the side. Burke and Van Fleet, battle-hardened veterans, took the accident in stride, but the pilot was ashen-faced, probably not so much from his own narrow escape as from realizing he had nearly killed two flag officers.

"What do you want on your ice cream?" said Burke. "Pineapple or strawberry?"

"Pineapple," replied the general. Then he added, "That young pilot seems kind of shaken up by what just happened. Maybe we ought to give him some ice cream."

"Good idea," said Burke.

Van Fleet had his fill of ice cream—about half a gallon, Burke recalled. Then, lacking the helicopter, they headed for shore in a landing boat. Burke said to the boat officer, "There's a pretty bad surf in here. Do you know how to take one of these things in through the surf?"

"No, sir," the young officer replied. "I'm just the junior officer of the deck. I don't know anything about boats."

Burke turned to the coxswain. "Have you ever landed through a surf?" he asked.

"No, sir," replied the lad. "I'm a coxswain, but I've never had any amphibious experience at all."

Burke shouted, "Does anyone aboard know anything about landing through surf?" No reply. Apparently their only landing practice consisted of the tame maneuver of bringing a boat alongside a wharf.

"Well," said Burke, turning to Van Fleet, "you are going to witness something very few people have ever seen. You are going to see an admiral bringing in a landing boat."

"Do you know how?" asked the general.

"I'm a sailor, dammit," snorted Burke as he seized the tiller. "I'll take this boat in all right."

In went the boat through the foaming waves and thrust its bow into the sand, and Burke and Van Fleet waded ashore like MacArthur landing in the Philippines. A jeep was waiting for the general.

In early July, Burke was surprised to receive orders for temporary duty ashore—nothing less than participation in peace talks. There had been some word lately that a truce was in the making. The Eighth Army's right had now reached a point some 40 miles north of the 38th parallel. The left still lagged a little south of the parallel, but the entire UN battle line from the Yellow Sea to the Sea of Japan was in a strong defensive position. The UN forces had no desire to push farther north, suffering more casualties while shortening the enemy's supply lines and lengthening their own. The Chinese and North Koreans wanted to halt their costly retreat. The situation seemed ripe for a quick armistice.

General Ridgway accepted the enemy's proposal to hold negotiations at Kaesong, the ancient capital of all Korea, and afterward regretted having done so. The city, a little below the 38th parallel, had recently been in UN hands. It was currently occupied by communist forces but so tentatively that it could be considered in a no-man's-land between the contending armies. To provide a clearly neutral zone for the talks, General Van Fleet withdrew his forces southward from the city and understood that the communist forces had pulled away similarly to the north.

The UN negotiating team, headed by Vice Admiral Turner Joy, assembled at a small tent village near the town of Munsan, 18 miles southeast of Kaesong. The other members were Burke; Major General Henry Hodes, deputy chief of staff of the Eighth Army; Major General Laurence Craigie, vice commander of Far East Air Forces; and Burke's friend Major General Paik Sun Yup, delegate representing President Syngman Rhee. The opening meeting was scheduled for 1000, 10 July 1951.

The day dawned damp and cloudy. The UN staff, interpreters, secretaries, and other auxiliaries headed early for Kaesong by winding road in a motorcade of mostly jeeps. The delegates themselves left later by helicopter. To see them off was the big boss himself, General Ridgway, and other officers from the UN command. Also present were photographers and reporters asking unanswerable questions. As he left for Kaesong, Arleigh was aware that he was headed for perhaps the most important mission of his life. He was conscious also of the high honor of serving as spokesman for the United Nations.

The UN motorcade had arrived and was waiting for the helicopters at the Kaesong airport. It was immediately apparent that instead of the scrupulous ambience of neutrality the UN delegates had expected at Kaesong, the Reds intended to make the conference appear a communist production, with the UN delegates coming hat in hand to solicit peace terms. The ten-minute ride from the airfield to the house assigned the delegates was along a road lined with communist armed guards and photographers. The house itself was surrounded by machine-gun-bearing guards. To get up the front steps, Arleigh had to push aside the muzzle of one such gun held by a North Korean lad.

From the UN house the delegates proceeded to the conference house, a mansion now gone badly to seed. The communist delegation consisted of five generals, three North Korean and two Chinese, headed by General Nam Il, chief of staff, supreme headquarters, North Korean army. The five were standing stiffly in the foyer as Joy entered, followed by the UN delegation and staff. The tallest of the communist officers said, "I am Nam Il." Joy nodded and said, "I am Admiral Joy."

The two delegations proceeded to the conference room and seated themselves on opposite sides of a green-cloth-covered table.

Interpreters took seats behind their respective delegations, and the UN and North Korean secretarial staffs took station on opposite sides of the room. Thus began for Arleigh in some respects the most fascinating and certainly the most exasperating experience of his career.

Because of the unneutral atmosphere at Kaesong, which the Reds milked for propaganda purposes, Ridgway considered demanding that the negotiations be shifted elsewhere. Instead he instructed Admiral Joy that unless the Western press was admitted to Kaesong, he should recess the talks. On 12 July, when a UN group of newsmen and photographers was barred, Joy walked out, leading his delegation. Thereafter the Western press was freely admitted.

The UN delegates had been warned that communists were impressed only by strength put into action and regarded all concessions as evidence of weakness to be exploited. The communists must have been warned to expect these same attributes in noncommunists. The result was that the conference, expected to last a few days, turned out to be a hardheaded contest of endurance that dragged on for two years.

One strong advantage the UN possessed was military superiority based not on numbers of troops but on an efficient supply system, naval support, and superior air power. When the communists became recalcitrant at the conference table, the UN could apply a persuader by bombing a communist target or driving back the communist line, inflicting heavy casualties. Van Fleet thus had the unwelcome mission of fighting a highly limited kind of warfare merely to apply the appropriate degree of military pressure to gain a point at the table.

One point on which neither side would give way was the location of the dividing line between North and South Korea. The communists wanted it on the original 38th parallel. But as the war had shown, this was an indefensible frontier, and it did not take into account that the Eighth Army had pushed considerably past that line everywhere except in the extreme west. Hence the UN delegates held out for the current battle line as the frontier.

In hopes of facilitating agreement on this point, the opposing delegation heads in mid-August 1951 appointed a pair of two-man "subdelegations" to debate placing of the demarcation line—a North Korean and a Chinese general on one side, General Hodes and Admiral Burke on the other. When this subcommittee failed to reach agreement by 23 August, the communists abruptly broke off the negotiations.

Along with negotiating, Arleigh had applied himself to one of those extra jobs his well-known energy always earned him. At Munsan, it was running the camp, a task assigned him by General Ridgway. Arleigh proceeded to find himself a third job—barber. Assuming that the negotiations would last only a few days, the delegation, sponsored by the Eighth Army, had not listed a barber in its Table of Organization and Equipment, so nothing along that line was to be had from the army.

After a couple of weeks, when the delegation began to look distressingly shaggy, Burke appealed to ComNavFE, which sent out a set of barber tools. Arleigh, who had had no tonsorial experience, tried his hand on Chief Yeoman George Guzowski. The results didn't look so good, but as Burke continued barbering he at length began giving a pretty good haircut. Finally, when Arleigh was the only shaggy delegate left, he accepted an offer from General Hodes, equally inexperienced, to give him a trim. After that, Admiral Burke and Yeoman Guzowski wore their caps most of the time.

Burke always kept in mind that the communist army might attempt another southward drive that would quickly overrun the camp. Hence he held defense drills and had every camper dig a foxhole alongside his tent. During the two-month recess, after the communists broke off negotiations, Burke stepped up the drills, particularly with the enlisted men, as much as anything else to give them something to do.

When it appeared they would still be at Munsan during the cold Korean winter, Burke got wooden floors and oil stoves for the tents and, also for additional warmth, extra tents to lay over the original ones. Remembering the freezing December nights he had experienced at Yonpo and Hungnam, Arleigh had Guzowski buy him an electric blanket the next time he was sent to Tokyo on official business. The camp got its electric power from generators run by diesel engines on trucks. After the evening movie was over and the tent lights were out, one generator kept running to supply a few all-night lights and in event of emergency. There was enough excess power from this source to provide for the electric blanket, and Burke plugged it in and enjoyed a good night's cozy sleep.

When Hodes caught Burke plugging in his blanket, the general was indignant. "Only a pampered sailor would use an electric blanket in camp," he snorted. "A soldier would never stoop to such a thing. I wouldn't have one of those baby covers." Not long afterward, however, when Burke was called away for several days on an errand, the general borrowed the admiral's blanket.

When the communists persisted in boycotting the negotiations, Van Fleet ordered an attack all along the battle front. UN casualties were not light, but enemy casualties were appalling. The communists, hurting militarily, dreading another winter campaign, indicated a willingness to resume talks. General Ridgway was agreeable but refused to send his delegates back to Kaesong and its guard of North Korean troops. He suggested Panmunjom, 5 miles east of Kaesong, and specified that negotiations be carried on in a tent under guard by both sides. When the communists acceded to these demands, the talks resumed 25 October 1951.

The UN delegates were gratified to find that the communists had dropped their demand for dividing Korea along the 38th parallel. They were willing to accept the battle front as it then stood. General Ridgway proposed a somewhat more detailed peace plan. He wanted possession of Kaesong, because it was the ancient capital, because topography made it the strategic gateway to Seoul, and because he considered the Reds had tricked him into withdrawing forces and leaving the city in communist hands to generate propaganda. In return for a Red withdrawal from Kaesong, Ridgway offered to have the Eighth Army withdraw from positions along the east coast and from Kumsong. The precise demarcation line between Kaesong and Kumsong was to be achieved by negotiation, but there would be no cease-fire until the remainder of the armistice terms were settled—concerning exchange of POWs and withdrawal of foreign forces from Korean soil.

While the rest of the delegates debated the major issues, Burke and Hodes dickered with their opposite numbers on setting the demarcation line between Kaesong and Kumsong. Hodes, the senior on the UN subcommittee, afterward said of Arleigh's negotiating skills, "Burke contributed as much as anyone on the team. He was always strong, and he understood communist ways of attacking any subject. There are not many people in the United States, or in the world, who understand communist tactics. If I ever had to head up another delegation or subdelegation, you may be sure that I would want Burke first."

The Americans had the advantage of direct telephone connections via Munsan to every point in the UN battle line. For several weeks the operations along that line were literally controlled from the truce table at Panmunjom. The Reds would be holding out for moving their line forward to, say, Hill 718. The hill, as Hodes and Burke knew, was in UN hands, but the communists' insistence implied they expected it very soon to be in their own hands. Burke picked up the telephone and got in touch with the X Corps on the east coast.

"We're just starting to talk about Hill 718," he said. "There's going to be an attack on it in a short while. Hold it. No matter what, hold it."

On another occasion Hodes and Burke laid a map on the table, and one of them pointed to a location. "Today we'll settle here for our present battle line," he said, "but if you don't accept that today, tomorrow we're going to be two miles farther north."

The communists scoffed at the threat, but Hodes and Burke got on the telephone to the appropriate commander, who launched an attack that pushed back the Reds a couple of miles and a little more. The next morning the communists, apprised of this loss, hastened to the conference table and expressed a willingness to accept the proposed position.

"Oh, no," said Burke. "We distinctly said that that position held only for yesterday. Today the position is here. Do you accept that now? If you don't, we're going to take some more territory before tomorrow."

After several days of this sort of thing, the communist delegates came to the table dragging. They were being outmaneuvered and knew it. A little more adjusting of the line northward and the Reds would be glad to accept Ridgway's Kaesong-Kumsong exchange. Then one morning the atmosphere changed. The Reds came to the table cocky as the devil. Hodes and Burke discussed the battle position of the day for fifteen or twenty minutes, but their opponents made no requests or offers—just sat and grinned at the UN delegates. Finally through an interpreter Hodes said, "Could we have a recess of five minutes? I've got to go to the head."

Their opponents agreeing, Hodes and Burke withdrew.

"Those bastards have got something," said the general. "They know something we don't know. This is the first time they've been cocky in a long while. Today we dribble. Don't try to drive anything today because they're going to be hard to argue with. We'll dribble back and forth, but we don't give anything either. Let's find out what's happening here. Something is happening. That's quite obvious."

That evening, when the delegates got back to Munsan, they found a dispatch from the Joint Chiefs, actually from the U.S. State Department via the Joint Chiefs. It was an order to accept the current battle line as the final line of demarcation.

All hands concerned with the negotiations were stunned. The

UN delegates had stated that under no circumstances would they accept such a solution. The corollary of a stationary battle line is a cease-fire, because so long as there is firing, the line is bound to move one way or the other. On the other hand, with a cease-fire the UN forces would have no means of spurring the Reds toward agreement on the other items on the agenda, concerning which there were wide disagreements. The negotiations could drag on for years.

General Ridgway sent a protest to Washington, explaining his views. He was ordered to do as he was told. He sent a final appeal. It was denied. Meanwhile, Hodes and Burke met daily with the Red delegates. These, far from dragging, were now gleefully self-confident. Though the communications between Ridgway and Washington were classified top secret, it was obvious to Hodes and Burke that their opponents knew exactly what was going on. The only possible explanation was espionage. Somebody with access to the decision-making or at least to classified communications was passing the word to the communist delegates, probably via the Soviets.

Hodes and Burke said they would not comply with the orders from Washington. If the Joint Chiefs wanted to yield on the demarcation question, they'd have to find somebody else to do the yielding for them. Admiral Joy took a similar position. On 15 November, General Ridgway flew to Munsan and called a meeting of the negotiating team.

"You are military people," he said. "I dislike these orders as much as you do, but we are military people. We have stated our position as clearly as we know how. We have now been instructed to do something we believe is unwise, but you are military people, and you will carry out your orders."

He of course was right. Hodes and Burke agreed to go back to the truce table one more time—to settle on the agreed-upon line of demarcation, as it existed on 27 November 1951. They asked to be relieved after that. Having been discredited by the orders from Washington, they felt that their usefulness as delegates was nullified. Ridgway saw their point of view and agreed that they should be relieved.

Burke's relief, Rear Admiral Ruthven Libby, arrived at Munsan on 30 November, no more enthusiastic about his new assignment than Burke had been five months earlier. Arleigh sold him his electric blanket and lightheartedly took his departure. He had an interesting job awaiting him in Washington and was eager to tackle it.

The men he left behind had a dreary time of it. As the delegates had predicted, the negotiations dragged on month after month. On 27 July 1953, more than a year and a half after Burke's departure, the armistice was signed at last in an apathetic, silent ceremony in the moldering tent at Panmunjom.

The homeward-bound Burke paused at Tokyo to say farewell to friends he was able to see and to write notes to the others, including Admiral Nomura. He left for the United States about midnight. At such an hour he scarcely expected anybody to see him off, there being very few private cars in Japan at that time. In fact, no Americans were there, but Admiral Nomura came to the airport. It must have taken him two or three hours by bus and streetcar to get there.

21

STRATEGIC PLANS AND FINAL SEA DUTY

ARLEIGH BURKE arrived in Washington in early December 1951 determined to air his complaints regarding the situation in Korea. "There were several things I was angry about," he said. "One was why we would accept the communists' position when it was so obviously not in our country's interest. Another was their knowing about our orders."

Told that he might take a week's leave before reporting for duty, Arleigh chose to use the free time sounding off. First he went storming to the office of the chief of naval operations. The current occupant of that post was his friend Admiral William Fechteler, who as deputy CNO two years earlier had tipped him off that his name had been expunged from the promotion list.

Fechteler listened quietly while Burke set forth in emphatic language his opposition to the Korean cease-fire and his indignation that the North Koreans at the negotiations table knew about it before the American negotiators did. Who the hell, he demanded to know, was running the show in Washington?

Fechteler smiled and assured Arleigh that the armed forces were not running the Washington show. They merely executed the commands of the president as advised by the State Department and the National Security Council. It appeared to Burke that the CNO was not much concerned about the situation, but when Arleigh asked if he might express his views to the Joint Chiefs of Staff, Fechteler readily consented and made the arrangements.

Arleigh told the chiefs the negotiations in Korea had taught him that the only thing the communists pay any attention to is power— not just potential power but power put to use. The United States had power, he said, military power, economic power, and political power, but we were not using it. A prime example was the UN agreement to a cease-fire before other agreements were reached, mainly concerning humane exchange of prisoners of war.

The chiefs listened politely but wearily. They had been through all this several times before. Power, they said, had to be used judiciously. Its immoderate use could expand a war, ultimately bringing on World War III, with the chief antagonists devastatingly armed with atomic weapons. They pointed to the example of General MacArthur. The president on the unanimous recommendation of the Joint Chiefs had dismissed him from his commands when he risked dangerously expanding the Korean War by his insistence on blockading the China coast, bombing points in China, and permitting the Nationalist Chinese troops on Taiwan (Formosa) to open a second Asian front.

The demand for a cease-fire, they said, had originated among the public, in the press, and in the State Department. The decision was reached on 12 November at a meeting of representatives from the State Department and the Pentagon. The UN now had the demarcation line it had been fighting and negotiating to attain. The five months of power-backed talks it took to achieve it had cost the UN an additional 60,000 casualties, of which a third were American. The cease-fire would probably prolong the negotiations, but the public was convinced, not without reason, that it was better for a few men to argue endlessly in a tent than for thousands to continue shooting at each other.

As for Burke's suspicion of espionage, it was well founded, as demonstrated by the imprisonment of former State Department officer Alger Hiss on espionage-related charges, by the conviction of Julius and Ethel Rosenberg for espionage, and by the recent defection to the USSR of British diplomats Guy Burgess and Donald Maclean. On the other hand, espionage might not have been what tipped off the communists. Enough had appeared in U.S. newspapers for intelligence experts at the Russian embassy to reach a pretty accurate estimate of American intentions. On 11 November, for example, an editorial in the *New York Times* had inquired why the delegates at Panmunjom were "backing and filling over a seeming trifle" when they had already reached agreement on the "big issues" concerning the line. Whatever the source, the chiefs pointed out, the only ill effect of the North Koreans' advance information in this instance was the annoyance it caused General Hodes and Admiral Burke.

When Burke had heard these explanations, he assumed that further argument was useless, and the chiefs assured him that such was the case. However, he left the meeting still angry, convinced that the United States could have used far more power without bringing on an atomic holocaust, that by responding sparingly to Soviet-backed aggression the Americans were inviting the Soviets to stir up trouble elsewhere to their own advantage.

Arleigh's assumption that his crusade had come to an end was belied a couple of days later when he received a call from the navy's public relations officer. Would he please come in? They had a program for him.

It appeared that Admiral Fechteler, far from being uninterested in Burke's criticisms, had agreed with them completely and felt his views should be carried to the public—by Burke himself. On the CNO's orders the information office had worked up for Arleigh a program of television interviews, speeches, and press conferences that would keep him on the circuit for quite a while. The staff would help him write speeches and coach him for his television appearances.

Bewildered, Burke said, "If this is what Admiral Fechteler wants me to do, this is what I will do." And he went home to ponder this surprising turn of events.

On the morning of 17 December, Burke received another startling telephone call. It was from his Academy classmate Captain Robert Dennison, still the president's naval aide. Would Arleigh like to see Mr. Truman?

Evidently someone had reported Arleigh's complaints to the president and piqued his interest. Here was an opportunity for Burke to plead his convictions before the highest authority.

"You bet I would," he replied.

Dennison told him to come to the White House at 1400 that afternoon. When he arrived, Dennison told him Mr. Truman would like to see him for about fifteen minutes. At the end of that time, Arleigh was to say, "Mr. President, my time is up," and leave—unless the president asked him to stay.

Mr. Truman received Arleigh cordially, motioned him to a chair, and began asking him questions that implied he was aware of Burke's complaints. Burke repeated them; then, warming to the subject, he brought up other Washington-originated orders that he considered not in the nation's best interests.

Suddenly he burst out, "Mr. President, who the hell is—are you giving these orders?"

"No," replied Mr. Truman. "I accept what the chiefs agree to."

"Who originates them?"

"The State Department."

"Who in the State Department?"

"I don't know exactly."

It dawned on Burke that he was grilling the president, something one was not supposed to do. He changed the subject.

"Mr. President," he said, "I am convinced that somebody in this government is leaking information. The communist North Koreans at the negotiations got our orders before we did. I can't prove it, but I know it."

Arleigh described what had happened. Mr. Truman seemed interested and said he would look into the matter. Then the president came back to the conduct of the war in Korea and asked Burke what he thought should be done. Before Arleigh got immersed in the subject, he glanced at the clock, said, "Mr. President, my time is up," and rose from his seat.

"Sit down," said Mr. Truman.

Instead of fifteen minutes, the meeting between the president and the rear admiral lasted more than two hours. Burke reviewed the Korean War as he had seen it, being careful to avoid denigrating the performances of any of his fellow officers. Mr. Truman listened with obvious interest.

From time to time Burke revived his favorite recommendations: cancel the cease-fire unless the North Koreans accept reasonable provisions for exchange of POWs and enforcement of the armistice; exert all available power against the enemy to achieve a clear-cut victory. Burke got the impression that Mr. Truman concurred with both proposals, but it is probable the president was not saying all he thought. After all, he had authorized the cease-fire and subsequently disapproved every move to cancel it, and he had sacked MacArthur for trying to expand the war.

"Mr. President," said Burke, "General Ridgway is a wonderful man. He submits recommendations he feels are for the best interests of our country, but nobody pays any attention."

Mr. Truman said, "I confer with him, and I agree with him, but we've got to do the things that are best for the government as a whole, and he doesn't know all of it."

Burke went home convinced that he had won over both the CNO and the president to his point of view. That evening, however, he got another telephone call. It was the public information officer. "It's all off," he said. "You're not making any speeches."

Evidently the president, or perhaps somebody in the State Department, had called Admiral Fechteler. Burke was never given any clear reason for the gag order, but the explanation seems obvious. This was the period of the great American communist hysteria. Seizing the opportunity, Senator Joseph McCarthy of Wisconsin asserted in a speech that the State Department was infested with communists who were "helping to shape our foreign policy." Using the theme of communists in the U.S. government, he gained wide publicity, chiefly through television. At the same time the dismissed General MacArthur was flying about the country making speeches in which he hinted darkly at incompetence and disloyalty in the administration. In the circumstances, it would not be desirable to have a U.S. rear admiral running around calling the State Department soft on communists—particularly as the upcoming 1952 was a presidential election year.

Admiral Burke had been summoned to Washington to head the Navy Department's Strategic Plans Division (Op-30). Director of strategic plans was as senior a navy post as a rear admiral could hold as a rear admiral, that is, without being temporarily promoted. In some respects the billet was second in importance only to that of chief of naval operations and could prove a stepping-stone toward attainment of that top naval command.

The directorship was Admiral Sherman's promised reward for Burke's exemplary work in Tokyo and Korea. Sherman had intended for Arleigh to report to Washington for the duty in the summer of 1951, following negotiation of the armistice, expected to be completed in a week or ten days. But the negotiations, as we have seen, dragged on for months.

Toward the end of July, Admiral Sherman died, a victim, it was widely believed, of overwork. In less than two years he had restored order, morale, and central authority in the navy, repaired the navy's relations with the other U.S. services, improved the navy's liaison with NATO and with foreign navies, and established a healthy shipbuilding program. He died of a heart attack while in Naples on a naval mission. He was fifty-four years old.

The post of director of strategic plans, far from being a sinecure, was a brain-racking, onerous grind. Thus it was the sort of duty Arleigh thrived on, but most incumbents were glad to be relieved when their two-year tours were over. The current director, another Burke classmate, was Rear Admiral William O'Regan. When Arleigh was unable to relieve him on schedule, O'Regan gritted his teeth and stayed on.

Burke, shortly after his interview with President Truman, at last reported to Op-30. He came, however, not as director but as a learner. The work of the division was far too complex for him to assume its leadership without extensive preparation. Much later, toward the end of his tour, he said that he could expect to get no more than a year's work out of any officer assigned for the usual two-year duty, because the officer had to spend his first year learning how to do the work. Burke, however, after devoting just six weeks to investigating the puzzles and problems of the directorship, relieved O'Regan early in February 1952. Arleigh had trained himself to be a fast learner. Moreover, this was not his first think-tank job. With different objectives, its methods were not unlike those of the General Board, on which he had served fifteen months.

The Op-30 staff consisted of about sixty officers, mostly commanders and captains, all very bright. In addition to special intelligence assignments, they had two regular duties: (1) to assure that U.S. Navy plans were sound and (2) to determine how the navy would fight its next war. Their main task under duty (1) was to analyze and evaluate plans worked up by commanders and their staffs, including papers of the Joint Chiefs. An important task under (2) was to determine the problems to be overcome and advantages to be seized in attacking or defending geographical points or areas around the world. Few of the studies in the latter category were likely ever to be put to use, but all had to be prepared, reviewed, and kept up to date so that when one became needed, it would be ready, current, and useful.

As staffers completed their tours in Op-30, Burke was alert to bring in equally intellectual replacements. These he located mainly through recommendations from his own staffers. Bright men knew bright men. "We ought to get Joe in here," one might say. "I know Joe, and he's pretty good at this stuff." If Joe had a job, his boss wasn't going to let go if he didn't have to. So Burke was on the lookout for men about to change. Op-30, and he himself, had enough prestige usually to get first claim on these short-timers.

Another source of smart officers was the war and staff colleges. Burke would write, not always to the head man, and ask for a list of names, arranged in order of excellence, of students who had shown outstanding potential as thinkers and planners.

The period of Burke's directorship was a particularly busy time for Op-30 because it was during a rapid change in the national defense as the services, whittled down by Truman's early economies, rearmed in response to the Korean War. In meeting the challenge, Burke was an exacting taskmaster. He operated on his conviction, not shared by all his colleagues, that men work better when they are overworked, at least to a certain degree.

Rear Admiral Henry L. Miller, recalling his duty in Op-30, said, "I think Admiral Burke operated on the theory that the busiest people always produce, so he gave them the work. He never let up. He was a driver. He had tons of energy. He was absolutely dedicated to the navy. He knew no hours. One never knew what assignment he was going to get next, day or night."

Duty in the brainy Strategic Plans Division conferred a certain prestige, but it was a prestige for which some able officers preferred not to pay the price in tension and drudgery. An exception was Captain Draper L. Kauffman, who asked the Bureau of Naval Personnel's detail officer to assign him to Op-30.

"I do not detail people to Op-30," the detailer wrote back. "Admiral Burke asks for somebody, and unless I can prove strong reasons otherwise, Admiral Burke gets him."

So Kauffman wrote to a friend serving in Op-30 and asked him to put in a good word for him with Admiral Burke. Burke took the suggestion, and Kauffman got his orders. Believing it wise to keep on good terms with the detail officer, Kauffman wrote and thanked him.

"Don't thank me," replied the detailer. "Anyone crazy enough to ask for that sweat shop has only himself to blame."

Incredible as it may seem, Admiral Burke engaged in considerable activity outside of Op-30. For one thing, he and Bobbie went house hunting. Sale of the old Gorsuch home on Fulton Street enabled them to make a substantial down payment on a larger, newer house a few blocks away on Hawthorne Street, and they moved in.

Not long afterward a letter arrived from Admiral Nomura. He said he had sent his son, Tadashi, a former lieutenant in the Imperial Japanese Navy, to do graduate work at Northwestern University. Believing that the future of Japan depended on close cooperation with the United States, he wanted his son to speak English fluently and become familiar with American customs. The young man was not doing well, however, and was not able to adjust. His father asked Burke to find out what was wrong and advise him what to do.

Too busy to go to the university, outside Chicago, to investigate, Arleigh called the commander of Northwestern's NROTC unit and asked him to look into the situation without letting Tadashi know about it. After checking, the officer reported back that the young Japanese was shy, spoke English poorly, had made no close friends, took no part in extracurricular activities, and was above all lonely. He suggested that Tadashi's wife be sent over to go to school too.

Burke passed the suggestion on to Nomura. He knew that it might not be easy for Nomura financially but that he would do it if possible. Sure enough, in a couple of weeks, Nomura wrote that Miyoko was on her way. Burke asked the captain in the NROTC to look out for them without their being aware of it and let him know if there were any money problems.

Miyoko had learned English in Japan and spoke it well. After her arrival, the NROTC captain continued reporting to Burke. He said Tadashi's English and his grades were improving, and he and Miyoko were apparently enjoying life. Bobbie wrote and invited them to come down to visit them during their Easter vacation, and Arleigh sent them railroad tickets.

The Burkes met Tadashi and Miyoko at the station. Tadashi was polite but uneasy, restrained, and humorless. His little wife, on the contrary, was outgoing and entered into everything with pleasure. Though the Japanese couple would be in Washington only a week, the Burkes set out to Americanize them as much as possible. They laid out a schedule of activities ranging from sightseeing to housework.

Although Arleigh regarded housework with distaste and generally avoided it as scrupulously as Japanese husbands did, he knew that many American husbands help around the house. So to set an example, he overcame his aversion to the extent of making beds and setting the table and insisted that Tadashi help. To Bobbie's alarm, he and Tadashi even tried to help with the cooking. Through it all, Arleigh cracked jokes, a practice that tended to slow the work, because he, Bobbie, and Miyoko then had to stop and explain them to Tadashi. Arleigh even played a few practical jokes, a practice that Bobbie regarded with disfavor, considering it in poor taste.

After a couple of days of the Burke treatment, Tadashi began to loosen up. On the fourth day, as they sat down to breakfast, he announced, "Now I tell a joke." He then preceded to tell his story with much shredding of the king's English. When he came to his punch line, the shredding became so acute that it came out pure gibberish. Arleigh and Bobbie, in an act of affectionate deceit, laughed immoderately. Tadashi, pleased at his supposed success, grinned. He had arrived.

One morning Arleigh arose early and had started down the stairs quietly when he observed Miyoko silently fingering the keyboard of the Burke piano. After watching her a few moments and noting that she was actually touching the keys, albeit lightly, Arleigh crept back upstairs and then came down noisily. Asked if she played, she admitted that she used to do so but had not been near a piano since the war. After some urging, she performed, now actually pressing down the keys. She showed considerable skill.

On the day of his guests' departure, Arleigh was walking with them down his front walk to their taxi when Miyoko stopped and, turning to him, said, "I have learned many American customs too," and she put her arms around him and kissed him.

Arleigh could not forget the longing look in the girl's eyes when he first saw her sitting on the piano bench. Later, when Bobbie's sister's piano became available, he had it shipped to Miyoko in Japan.

A subsequent guest in the Burke home brought problems in addition to language difficulties. She was red-haired María Ema Santillán de Aignasse, the Argentine señora who at Buenos Aires in late 1948 had lavishly entertained the officers and men of Burke's cruiser *Huntington*. In gratitude Burke and his senior officers had tendered her their calling cards and afterward sent thank-you letters offering help and hospitality should the gracious señora ever visit the United States. In December 1952 came letters from the señora announcing that she was coming to visit in the following spring and would like to renew those friendly relations. All but one of the officer addressees were safely at sea. The exception was Burke, who felt obligated to make good for all.

Knowing very little Spanish, Arleigh had to have the señora's letters translated into English and his replies translated into Spanish for María Ema Santillán, who knew no English. In the next three months considerable correspondence, all requiring translation, passed between the señora and the admiral. She announced that she would spend three days in New York, where her ship would land, and then come to Washington for a visit with the Burkes—also for three days, at least so Arleigh surmised.

As the date for María's visit approached, Arleigh's correspondence on her behalf multiplied. He wrote to her New York hotel to check on her reservation and room number. He wrote to the steamship company to ascertain on what date, at what hour, and at what pier her ship was to be met. Most of all, he wrote to his navy friends in New York, beseeching them to assemble a Spanish-speaking committee to get the señora from her ship to her hotel and three days later from her hotel to some Washington-bound transportation.

When word came that the señora would arrive in Washington by Greyhound bus, Bobbie enlisted the aid of a fellow officer's wife who spoke passable Spanish. They met the bus together and were intrigued to see María dismounting laden with a huge carryall. She announced that she had more baggage, to be picked up at the baggage counter. The three women loaded the Burke car, and Bobbie's helpful Spanish-speaking friend stayed with the party until María was safely installed in the Burke guest room. Here María revealed the contents of the carryall: a handsome vicuña bed coverlet, which she had brought as a gift for the Burkes.

From the beginning, difficulties confronted María's endeavor to be an agreeable guest and the Burkes' resolve to make her feel welcome. First, there was the language barrier. What little Spanish Bobbie knew was residue from a two-week cram course she had once taken in preparation for a trip to South America. Arleigh was a virtual stranger to the language. Foreseeing trouble, they had armed themselves with Spanish-English dictionaries. These in hand, they painfully undertook to communicate with their visitor, who never learned to say so much as hello in English.

The Burkes staged parties for María, at first inviting their Spanish-speaking friends and then, when these begged to be excused, inviting anybody reputed to know any Spanish, acquaintance or not. The señora was gracious but condescending to all the guests, but the barrier between herself and the Burkes remained.

Second, María was accustomed to wealth and leisure in a Latin-

American setting, to being waited on hand and foot, not to the daily life of a hardworking American couple with limited means.

"She had absolutely no knowledge of people without servants," said Burke, "and here we were, the only servant I had I'd married, and the only cook I had was the same girl. At our house María did have her own bedroom and bath but no bells to push."

In lieu of servants, María tried to make do with Arleigh as butler and Bobbie as maid and chauffeur. Said Burke, "She was polite, courteous, and demanding as hell. She wanted everything done exactly her way."

One day María said to Arleigh, "I understand you have commissary privileges, and I want to buy some things."

Burke had no intention of evading commissary regulations, but if what she wanted was not too expensive he could buy it and pass it on to her as a gift.

"Buy?" he said. "Like what?"

"Like refrigerators."

Burke was stunned. Evidently María expected to procure some American equipment for her Argentine mansion via his commissary privileges. "I can't do that," he said, and he advised her that if she was planning to import anything of value into Argentina she would do well to check with the Argentine embassy.

Lastly, María had come to stay for a while. Her stop in New York had been merely an episode on her way to the Burkes'. Here she evidently planned to follow the leisurely Argentine custom of making a visit a friendly sojourn of some duration. This was something the busy Burkes had not anticipated and were not prepared for. After a couple of weeks, Bobbie had had as much as she could take. The Burkes had run out of parties, out of money, and out of patience. "When is she going to go?" wailed Bobbie.

"I don't know," replied Arleigh. "She said she was going to stay just a little while."

"Well," said Bobbie, "one of us is going to go pretty soon."

She asked María politely how much longer she was staying, but the señora could not, or would not, understand. The Burkes asked their Spanish-speaking friends to try to find out María's intentions, but she evaded their questions.

Since the Burkes could not bring themselves to ask María to leave, one day while she was visiting friends in Baltimore, Bobbie in desperation went for help to the Argentine embassy. She asked the secretaries if they could find some means to move the señora to a hotel, since the Burkes could no longer entertain her. The secretaries replied that María was traveling with a valid passport, and hence there was nothing they could do. However, somebody at the embassy apparently found a means to help without appearing to do so. In some manner, word was passed to María of Bobbie's visit there, whereupon the señora wrathfully packed her belongings and departed, leaving the Burkes with mixed feelings—sorry to see her leave in anger, but immensely relieved to see her leave at all.

In early May 1953, Admiral Fechteler sent for Burke. "I want you to go with me to Europe," he said, "to attend the coronation. Unfortunately, it's just you." Fechteler was taking his wife and daughter, but, his retinue being strictly limited, he could not invite Mrs. Burke.

Though Fechteler was friendly enough, Burke knew he wasn't being taken along out of friendship but to do the work. Arleigh said he'd be very happy to go. It was not that he was particularly interested in Queen Elizabeth's coronation, which he didn't expect actually to see, but the two-week junket would allow him to gather useful data by consulting U.S. officers and officials stationed in Europe.

"I came home," Burke said, "and told Bob I was going to the coronation. She took it very nicely, but she's of British extraction and she wished she could go. She came down to the plane. I'd fought a couple of wars and left her on the dock, and I'd never seen her cry, but when I left on that airplane great big tears came down. I've never seen her want anything so much as to go to that coronation."

Burke attended most of the London functions, mainly to corner naval officers and talk navy business. On coronation day, of their party only Admiral Fechteler had a seat in Westminster Abbey. Burke was invited to join staffers of commander in chief U.S. naval forces in Europe upstairs in Selfridge's department store, whence they could look down on the parade passing along Oxford Street. Said Burke, "We had the best place in all London for that."

Burke considered this trip one of the most hectic he had ever taken. He was tour guide and general factotum for the Fechteler party, making all arrangements for them and for himself, yet he had no yeoman and no possessions or equipment he could not carry. In Paris he had a talk with General Ridgway, who had been relieved in Tokyo by General Mark Clark and had relieved General Eisenhower as supreme commander of Allied forces in Europe. In Naples he consulted with old friend and fellow Big Blue Fleet veteran

Admiral Mick Carney, now commander in chief of Allied forces in southern Europe. The party visited Germany and Scandinavia, then returned to London, whence they proceeded back to Washington, arriving in a state of exhaustion.

In January 1953, General Eisenhower succeeded Harry Truman as president of the United States. Having won the election partly on a promise to bring the Korean War to a victorious close, Eisenhower set out to make good that pledge. He canceled the cease-fire, renewed attacks against North Korean forces, had bombers destroy irrigation dams and thus flood North Korean rice fields, repeated some of the threats that had cost MacArthur his command, and even threatened atomic warfare against China. These jolts, or perhaps sheer weariness, induced the North Koreans at last to accept UN terms, and on 27 July 1953 they signed the armistice. Admiral Burke felt vindicated in that the measures that finally brought the war to an end included those he had been advocating since 1951.

Because Eisenhower had called his presidential campaign a crusade to "clean up the mess in Washington," he felt called on to weed out a good many of President Truman's appointees. This included a clean sweep of the Joint Chiefs of Staff who had conducted the stalemated Korean War. Admiral Fechteler, not ready to retire, exchanged billets with Admiral Carney, going to Naples, while Carney came to Washington as CNO.

The mood of the new administration included a determination to avoid further Korean Wars. The past U.S. policy of containing communism with conventional armament could beget more such limited, inconclusive, and expensive conflicts. The quest for a means to protect American interests at a bearable cost, to secure, as the current phrase had it, "a bigger bang for a buck," led to reliance on nuclear weapons to deter aggression through threat of massive retaliation. This was part of the Eisenhower Defense Policy, which came to be known as the New Look.

To Admiral Carney this aspect of the New Look appeared disturbingly like the view held by many persons during the unification battle—the belief that all that was needed for American defense was the atomic bomb and a long-range bomber to deliver it. That dangerous notion had threatened the navy and helped touch off the Admirals' Revolt. The country had doubtless outgrown such naive assumptions, but Carney considered it his responsibility to keep vividly before the public and government the contribution of sea power to the national defense. To help him find arguments and state them vividly, he turned to Arleigh Burke, who as head of Op-23 had superintended the idea factory for the resisting admirals.

To the usual naval functions of controlling the sea, defending the state against seaborne attack, and carrying the attack across the sea to the enemy, Carney and Burke stressed the value of ships as mobile nuclear launching pads. In the race for nuclear superiority, there would be the constant, nervous temptation on the part of the Soviets to avoid national destruction by striking first. Such an attack could be deterred by knowledge that retaliatory strikes could still be launched from ships at sea. These would be carriers, nuclear-propelled to lessen reliance on bases and large enough to launch long-range planes carrying atomic bombs.

Carney and Burke tried to avert the likelihood that a victorious general elected president would impose the army's general staff system on the navy. Burke's extensive study of military history had convinced him that the centralized control imposed by a general staff would seriously inhibit naval operations. The navy is a complex organization with many ways of carrying out its functions, and a seagoing force meets a variety of unforeseeable and often changing challenges. Hence naval headquarters orders the *what* of prospective operations but rarely the *how*. The high command supplies the intelligence and prescribes the goal but usually leaves the method of execution to the fleet or force commander at the scene of action. The naval officer is trained to solve his problems as he meets them and not rely on orders or advice from headquarters.

The function of Op-30 as strategic planner and critic of plans, including those of the Joint Chiefs of Staff, made it a proper but not the only conduit of such concepts. Carney and Burke used every available forum, especially including the press, to communicate their ideas to the public and the government. By the time Burke completed his two-year tour as director of strategic plans, he and Carney had won their crusade for keeping the navy and its command system intact, and the supposedly indefatigable Burke was exhausted. On 19 March 1954 his friend and classmate Robert Dennison, now a rear admiral, relieved him as head of Op-30.

Admiral Carney appointed Burke commander Cruiser Division 6, part of the Sixth Fleet in the Mediterranean. Now more than ever, Carney was convinced that Arleigh was destined for high command, and this stretch of sea duty could be an important step toward his promotion to vice admiral and his fleeting up to a more senior billet. On the other hand, the new command would not be nearly so demanding as the two-year grind Burke had just completed. The function of the Sixth Fleet was mainly to be present, to train the crews, and to "show the flag." Unless some unforeseen threat arose, it would spend much of its time in port.

In short, compared to his duties of the past five years, since in fact he left *Huntington* at Christmas 1948, the forthcoming tour would be for Arleigh something of a vacation. It would be a holiday for Bobbie too, because, like a number of other officers' wives, she would go to Europe in order to join her husband during his stays in port.

Shortly after Admiral Burke boarded his flagship, heavy cruiser *Macon*, she was temporarily detached from the Sixth Fleet and attached to Task Group 40.1, consisting of battleship *Missouri*, wearing the flag of commander battleship-cruiser force, U.S. Atlantic Fleet, battleship *New Jersey*, heavy cruisers *Macon* and *Des Moines*, an escort carrier, seven destroyers, and three minelayers. Its assignment was to conduct the midshipmen's practice cruise of 1954.

In late May, Task Group 40.1 anchored in Chesapeake Bay off Annapolis. During the next several days, Burke, joined by Mrs. Burke from Washington, participated in several of the Naval Academy's June Week activities. After the graduation ceremonies on the morning of 4 June, 1,692 midshipmen of the Academy's first (senior) and third (sophomore) classes and 1,337 NROTC midshipmen began coming on board the ships. Early on the 5th, Task Group 40.1 headed down the bay and out into the Atlantic for the usual at-sea training routines. Meanwhile, Bobbie and several other navy wives headed for Europe in naval aircraft.

As Task Group 40.1 approached the Iberian Peninsula, it split into sections to visit the peninsula's Atlantic ports—Lisbon, Portugal, and La Coruña, Vigo, and Cádiz, Spain. Burke's *Macon*, a destroyer, and a minelayer put into the southern port of Cádiz. When Arleigh left his ship, he found Bobbie waiting for him. That day the city fathers had a party for the midshipmen, and that evening Cádiz held a formal reception for the fleet officers and their ladies.

The reception was at first rather stiff, a consequence of typical Spanish reserve aggravated by the language problem. Burke, after a chilly passage down the receiving line, noticed that Bobbie was surrounded by several Spanish ladies, and still others were gathering around her. Drawing near, he discovered that his wife was making use of her cram-course Spanish, as mildly enhanced by her recent efforts at getting the word across to Señora María Santillán. Bobbie's rather painful efforts had aroused the sympathy and appreciation of the other women, who were trying to help, an effort in which the husbands soon joined. After this friendly overture, the company, lubricated with choice Spanish wine, was soon chattering away, nobody much concerned about understanding or being understood.

On 24 June the task group was again at sea for training exercises, and on 3 July the four sections put into the ports of Cherbourg and Le Havre, France; Antwerp, Belgium; and Rotterdam, the Netherlands. From these and earlier from the Iberian ports, the midshipmen and whatever officers could be spared from the ships spread out for sightseeing excursions all over the Continent and as far west as Ireland. Task Group 40.1 left Europe 10 July, returned to the United States via Guantánamo Bay, Cuba, and put into Norfolk on 3 August, whence transports conveyed the Naval Academy midshipmen back to Annapolis.

Admiral Carney, keeping Burke's interests in mind, left him with his cruiser division through the rest of the year—long enough to boost his service record, provide him some travel and social life with Bobbie, and above all afford him rest and refreshment after years of drudgery.

In January 1955, Carney transferred Burke to a post he had long coveted, that of commander destroyer force Atlantic Fleet (Comdeslant). This appointment as "king of the tin cans" enabled him again to serve the ships he loved best and the sailors with whom he was still most comfortable, even after years with carriers and associating with aviators and with the big brass.

Rear Admiral Charles C. Hartman, whom Burke relieved as Comdeslant, had a little fun with his staff before his replacement arrived. At their regular Saturday-morning conference, after hearing a long inventory of material casualties, Hartman told his staffers that he was being relieved. He wanted them to hear it from him, he said, before they read about it in the newspapers. He said his relief was to be the famous 31-Knot Burke. "From what I have been hearing this morning," he added with a twinkle, "you're just the boys to slow him down to fifteen."

The staffers knew better, as did practically everyone else in Deslant. From the fountain of energy known as Burke, vibrations were quickly felt throughout the command. He questioned closely everyone who came within questioning distance, and many who did not come as a matter of course he sent for. He wanted to know about anything that was not operating at maximum efficiency, and he wanted suggestions on how they might make it do so. Sometimes his reach extended outside his command. One example will suffice.

Chaplain Glyn Jones in visiting the naval hospital at Newport, Rhode Island, was shocked to see what passed for a waiting room—hard chairs lining the sides of a dark, damp cellar passageway. He went to one of the officers in charge and said, "Can't you do better than this—especially for the wives of seagoing people?"

"Gee, Chaplain," said the officer, "we would, but we just don't have a place."

The next day, Chaplain Jones had occasion to visit Admiral Burke's flagship, *Yellowstone,* a destroyer tender, then at Newport. Burke saw him and invited him to his office. "Come on in," he said. "How are things going?"

The chaplain said, "I wish they could do something in the hospital for a waiting room." He described the place, adding, "A lot of our wives are going there and waiting in that miserable dungeon."

Burke's lips were compressed in anger. "Get your hat," he said. He strode off the ship, Chaplain Jones trotting after him. They jumped into Burke's car and drove to the hospital. When the admiral saw the dimly lighted passageway he said, "This is a disgrace," and he kept on walking, up to the office of the hospital commander, who by this time was shaking in his boots.

Burke said to the hospital commander, "I've just been down in your cellar passageway, and I do not accept this treatment of the wives of my men. You find a proper waiting room and find it immediately." Then he turned on his heel and walked out. To Chaplain Jones, Burke said, "I want you to come here a week from today and come back and report to me."

One of the hospital commander's proud projects was a greenhouse located in a room near one of the lower doors. When Jones peeped in a week later it had been converted into a fine, well-lighted waiting room, with up-to-date magazines and decent chairs.

Chaplain Jones, in relating this story, said, "Be careful what you say to Arleigh Burke. He may do something."

Admiral Carney expected to leave Burke in command of the destroyers for about a year and then have him promoted to vice admiral and appoint him to command of one of the four numbered U.S. fleets. This was a major post indeed for an officer who would then be only fifty-four, but Carney was convinced that the appointment would be in the best interests of the navy. He could be sure of putting this plan into effect, however, only if he was appointed to a second two-year term as CNO, and that was becoming unlikely.

The problem was growing friction between himself and the secretaries of the navy and defense, Charles Thomas and Charles Wilson. The service chiefs—career soldiers, sailors, marines, and aviators—were the commanders of the armed forces. The politically appointed service secretaries—career businessmen, professionals, or politicians—were the managers. But it is not always possible to draw a clear line between command and management. President Eisenhower blurred the line still further by his Reorganization Plan of 30 June 1953, which made the secretaries operating heads of their departments and removed the Joint Chiefs from the chain of command.

Admiral Carney insisted that he should still have the main voice in senior appointments in the navy, because the appointees were officers he had known and observed since his Naval Academy days. He angered Secretary Thomas by continuing his practice of communicating directly and privately with fleet commanders, and he infuriated Secretary Wilson by communicating directly with the president. On this issue, Wilson demanded a decision from the president and got it. Old soldier Eisenhower upheld the right of the chief of naval operations, in his statutory capacity as principal naval adviser to the president, to communicate directly, adding that military command issues might be outside the competence of a civilian secretary. Carney had won a victory, but he knew that from now on he had better not make any mistakes.

One day in March 1955, Comdeslant Burke, relishing what he once called "the most enjoyable job in the navy," arrived in frigate *Wilkinson* at Key West. Shortly afterward he received a telephone call from Admiral Radford, now chairman of the Joint Chiefs of Staff, who asked how soon he could get to Washington. Arleigh asked if this trip wasn't something he could postpone. Radford said no, Secretary of the Navy Thomas and Secretary of Defense Wilson wanted to meet with him as soon as possible.

Burke flew to Washington and, in a short meeting in the defense secretary's office, answered questions put to him by Radford, Wilson, and Thomas. After that, he spent an hour in Secretary Thomas's office talking with him about destroyers but without discovering the purpose of the discussions. Burke next dropped in on his friend Admiral Carney, who said he had no inkling what the meetings were about, but they sounded to him like job interviews. Perhaps, Carney suggested, the secretaries were considering Arleigh for a place on the Joint Staff.

Burke, mystified, flew on to his Newport headquarters. When weeks passed and he heard no more from Washington, he assumed he had failed to impress the secretaries and the job, whatever it was, had gone to somebody else.

Meanwhile, communist China, fulfilling MacArthur's and Burke's prediction that an inconclusive peace in Korea would encourage the communists to make trouble elsewhere, began attacking offshore islands garrisoned by the Nationalist Chinese based on Taiwan. Congress thereupon granted Eisenhower emergency powers to protect Taiwan itself.

Admiral Carney flew to Taiwan to assess the situation. On his return, he invited a group of journalists to dinner and gave them what he warned was to be a strictly off-the-record briefing. Among other frank disclosures, he told them that he and other military advisers had urged the president to send American planes to bomb communist China's industrial centers if the attacks continued.

Such candid backgrounders for trusted newsmen are far from uncommon. Even Admiral King, generally believed to be distrustful of the press, in fact during World War II held no fewer than sixteen secret, highly informative briefings to groups of trusted journalists, none of whom betrayed his trust. Carney was not so lucky. One well-known newsman published Carney's disclosures, and the others followed suit.

Secretary Wilson, angered, promptly put out an order directing military personnel to submit for clearance all information intended for the public via the press or otherwise. Secretary Thomas notified Carney that when his two-year term as CNO ended he would not be reappointed.

Shortly afterward, on the evening of 9 May 1955, Burke was attending a dinner when he was called away to accept a telephone call from the secretary of the navy.

"Where are you?" asked Secretary Thomas.

"Newport."

"Can you come to my office before 1000 tomorrow?" Thomas asked. "I've got to be on the Hill in the morning."

Burke replied that there might be a problem about transportation. Would noon be all right?

"Okay," said Thomas and hung up.

When Burke's plane arrived at National Airport the next morning, one of the secretary's aides was waiting for him with a car. They drove to the Pentagon and went at once to Mr. Thomas's private office. The aide said that the secretary had left instructions that Burke was to remain there until he returned from testifying before a congressional committee. Meanwhile, Burke was not to see anybody in the navy, not even members of the secretary's staff. Presently the aide went for a couple of sandwiches, and he and Arleigh lunched together. The aide said he didn't know why Burke had been sent for.

At 1330, Secretary Thomas returned to his office. After greeting Burke he led him by a private passageway to the office of Under Secretary of the Navy Thomas Gates.

Secretary Thomas got down to business at once. "There are things going on," he said, "that I do not know about and for which I feel responsible." Admiral Carney, he explained, excluded him from his communications with fleet commanders and denied him information on which to base decisions. He said that while he held Admiral Carney as a person in the highest regard, he could not work with him in the SecNav-CNO relationship and therefore was not going to reappoint him.

Under Secretary Gates said that Carney and the officers on whom he most relied had been great in World War II, but since 1945 had largely been marking time. They did not fully appreciate that a changing world and advancing technology meant a new kind of warfare that would require a new kind of navy. The air force was adapting to the change, he said, but the navy was up to its old habit of preparing to fight the last war.

What was needed above all, said Thomas, was a CNO who could provide leadership to revive the navy's sinking morale, one with a technical background and the imagination and vigor to lead the way in bringing the navy and its weapons abreast of ongoing scientific developments. The CNO he had in mind would know how to adapt the navy to meet changing international problems. He would recognize competence in younger officers and give them all the responsibility they could handle. What he had in mind, Thomas concluded, was a CNO who with everything else was willing to cooperate closely with the navy's civilian leaders.

The secretary paused, then, looking directly at Burke, said, "Do you know of any reason why you should not be CNO?"

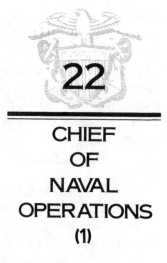

22

CHIEF
OF
NAVAL
OPERATIONS
(1)

DID BURKE KNOW of any reason why he should not be CNO?

Arleigh needed a few seconds to absorb that startling question. Then a half-dozen reasons popped into his head, the foremost being that he would be supplanting a friend and patron. He told Secretary Thomas he could not accept the post if it meant that Admiral Carney was departing under a cloud. Thomas assured Burke the admiral would leave office with full honors. He said the reason for Carney's relief was simply that his differences with the civilian secretaries hampered cooperation.

Burke wondered if the secretaries thought they were replacing a stubborn Carney with a docile Burke. He told them that while he agreed in general with what they had been saying, he was a man of strong opinions, freely expressed. He reminded them that his views had so exasperated a previous secretary of the navy that he had raided Burke's office and expunged his name from the promotion list. Such treatment had failed to silence him, Burke pointed out, and he added that unless his opinions were proved false, he would continue to sound off in the same vein, even though it made him suspect in the air force and to some degree also in the army.

Burke said that while basing appointments solely on seniority would be a mistake, going too far down the list of eligibles also could backfire. There were ninety-one admirals senior to himself, and most of them were eligible to be named CNO. Had the secretaries thought, Burke asked, of the possible effect of appointing him over the heads of all these officers who had devoted their lives to the navy?

Secretary Thomas told Burke he had brought up nothing they had not fully considered. He and Gates and Wilson had examined the records of the top eligibles, had explored the ideas and skills the CNO needed, and had concluded that Burke was the man for the job. They were aware that he was no yes-man but believed he and they could reason away their differences.

The interview concluded, Arleigh made his way to Admiral Carney's office and, embarrassed, told him what had happened. It was no news to Mick. He knew he was being passed over and suspected his replacement would be Burke. He was chagrined and humiliated but not resentful. Secretary Thomas, he said, was a man of intellect and character who had sacrificed a princely income to serve his country. He had taken great pains to master his job and had learned probably more about the navy than any previous secretary. Yet some naval matters he tried to control were simply beyond his competence. One was promotions to flag rank. What the secretary knew about a candidate had to be based on hearsay or on conversations with him at cocktail parties. The candidate's fellow officers, however, had been serving with and observing him since his early Naval Academy days.

In this and other areas, Carney said, a lifetime of observation and personal involvement outweighed a couple of years of fact-cramming. Hence, on the basis of his professional experience, he had felt obliged to take strong exception to some of Mr. Thomas's decisions and recommendations. The secretary thereupon seized on the admiral's supposed indiscreet revelations to the press as grounds for removing him.

At Carney's invitation, Burke drove home with him to the CNO's current official residence, Admiral's House, on the U.S. Naval Observatory grounds. En route through Washington, Arleigh expressed his misgivings. "Secretary Thomas seemed to agree with everything I said, but I'm not sure he hoisted aboard the real import. After all, I don't know Mr. Thomas or Mr. Gates or Mr. Wilson or the president, and they don't know me. I'm afraid they are selecting me because they think I'm a pushover."

"If that is what they think," said Carney with a wry smile, "they are due for a hell of a surprise."

When they got to the residence, Mick gave Arleigh a welcome

drink and took one himself. Burke was worrying again. He said he wasn't ready for the job, wasn't prepared to deal with matters of national policy. Carney agreed with him. He said he had been grooming Arleigh for CNO but had hoped to give him a couple more years of seasoning before recommending him for the top job.

He advised him nevertheless to accept the appointment. He had observed that Arleigh was a quick learner, and he could depend on Mick for help. Burke's being promoted over so many heads would cause some shock, Carney said, but even if he had not been appointed, no more than two or three of the eligibles could be CNO before the others reached retirement age. When they got over the first shock and realized that the appointment was for the good of the navy, as loyal navy men they would rally round.

On the morning of 15 May, Secretary Thomas took Burke to meet the secretary of defense, former president of the General Motors Corporation Charles Wilson—popularly known as "Engine Charlie," to differentiate him from "Electric Charlie" Wilson, president of the General Electric Company. White-haired and affable, Engine Charlie ran his department with quips, hard work, and an ever-present slide rule.

As Thomas had advised, Burke told the defense secretary what he understood the navy expected of him: to train younger officers for positions of responsibility, to ensure that all billets were filled by capable people and that a flow of good prospects to fill them was maintained, to assure that all hands "got the word," to speed development and installation of new weapons, and to improve the navy's spirit and combat effectiveness.

Engine Charlie said these were excellent objectives but attainable only through effective leadership. Then he proceeded to tell 31-Knot Burke of the Solomons campaign how to be a leader. At General Motors, said Wilson, he had found that a man appointed to a key position could not be effective unless he obtained "the cooperation of his associates and the loyalty of his subordinates."

The secretary paused as if to let that sage observation sink in. Then he added with emphasis, "That's the problem in the navy. There must be better cooperation between the military and the civilians."

If, Burke thought, Wilson meant he expected him to be more tractable than Carney, fairness required that the secretary be promptly disabused. Burke said he appreciated Mr. Wilson's advice but he had "a bad quality of having strong opinions at times and of being ready to fight for those opinions while laying them on the table."

Secretary Wilson rather absently said that was fine and indicated the interview was over.

On 17 May, Burke, Wilson, and Thomas were driven from the Pentagon to the west entrance of the White House, whence they were ushered into the president's reception room. Mr. Eisenhower came in almost immediately, and Secretary Thomas introduced Burke as the officer under consideration for CNO.

Six years earlier, when Eisenhower, then president of Columbia University, was called into consultation regarding unification of the services, Burke had briefed him on carrier warfare. Eisenhower obviously did not now recognize him, and Burke saw no point in reminding him of their earlier meeting.

Secretary Thomas did a good job of selling Burke to the president, citing Arleigh's achievements and his popularity in the service and praising his judgment and reliability. Mr. Eisenhower was interested to learn that Burke was fifty-four, young for a CNO, and that he was being recommended over nearly a hundred more senior officers. The president said that while selection by seniority ought to be the general rule, it was a rule that should be broken from time to time. The rapid promotion of outstanding officers benefited the service and at the same time demonstrated that selection for the top job was not automatic but something to be earned. He said he hoped the selection of a relatively junior admiral could be presented as solely for the good of the navy and in no way an adverse reflection on the abilities and contributions of the officers passed over. Burke was pleased to hear the president express this considerate attitude.

Though Mr. Eisenhower failed to recognize Burke, he had by no means forgotten the circumstances that had brought them together. He mentioned the unification battle, calling it a disgrace that military officers had brought their claims before the public via the press. Government personnel, including the armed services, he said, formed a team. He expected Burke to fight hard for his ideas "within the family," but once a decision had been reached he expected him to support it. This presidential attitude Arleigh found less pleasing. He feared it could be stretched into a demand for mindless docility.

On one point Mr. Eisenhower was most specific. He advised Burke to delegate the greater part of his service functions, so that as a member of the Joint Chiefs of Staff he would be able to devote most of his thought and energy to shaping military policy. The president then turned to the others and said that he would send Burke's name to the Senate, where he expected confirmation would come as a mere formality. He then shook hands with Burke and told him he was on the team.

Though this last and previous conferences had all been private, and no announcement of the appointment was to be made until after confirmation, Rear Admiral Burke noticed that in his official rounds people now seemed to be treating him with unaccustomed deference. To arrange for his relief as Comdeslant he needed to return briefly to Newport. A plane was promptly made available to take him there. When the plane had to turn back with engine trouble, a replacement was waiting, ready to take off. Burke, mystified, wrote a friend, "The skids are greased. Those people *knew*—but how the hell it happened I don't know."

Burke's appearance before the Senate committee was so brief and routine that he could not afterward recall what he was asked. That business concluded, he flew to Norfolk to confer with Vice Admiral Jerauld Wright, commander in chief Atlantic, and to attend a symposium at the Norfolk Naval Base. In the morning of 25 May, Burke was seated in an auditorium listening to a briefing on the nuclear-weapon capabilities of the Atlantic Fleet. It was being presented by Captain Thomas Moorer, a forty-three-year-old rising star, destined himself to become CNO twelve years later. Out of the corner of his eye, Moorer saw first Wright and then Burke being called away. Presently, Wright returned, walked up the aisle and onto the platform, excused himself, took the microphone, and announced that Admiral Burke had been appointed and confirmed as chief of naval operations. There was a brief, breathless silence. Then the audience of officers burst into applause.

Burke decided he had better get back to Washington. First, however, he put in a call for Captain George Miller. Their conversation was brief.

"This is Burke speaking. Where are you?"

"I'm down here aboard destroyer *Robinson* in Norfolk at pier six."

"Well, come on up to Cinclant headquarters right away."

When Miller arrived fairly breathless at the headquarters, Burke said, "I've just been nominated as chief of naval operations, and I want you to report to me for temporary duty."

Burke and Miller had served together in Korea, where the latter was Seventh Fleet plans officer. Subsequently Miller had served under Burke in the Strategic Plans Division and as a division commander in the Atlantic Fleet destroyer force. In the course of many long talks, Burke had come to appreciate Miller's good judgment and complete honesty—he would never say anything he did not believe. Now as Burke thought out his initial agenda as CNO he wanted this sensible, honest officer nearby for discussions. Recently Miller had written Burke advocating placing nuclear-armed ballistic missiles on ships. That was a subject Arleigh particularly wanted to discuss.

Burke's appointment received wide coverage in the press, partly because of his relative youth and partly because episodes in his career had kept him in the public eye, but mainly because the prefix "31-Knot" was usually attached to his name when it appeared in news stories and thus kept the public conscious of his identity.

The appointment was generally well received by the public and was greeted with some enthusiasm by Burke's naval juniors and contemporaries. Understandably most of the adverse criticism came from the three-star admirals who had been passed over and from their friends and supporters. "A premature appointment," one said. "Not enough top-policy experience," said another. Precisely what Burke had said about himself.

Senior air force officers were concerned but less vocal. They held Burke largely responsible for abolishing their monopoly of the atomic bomb. Burke's arguments, they recalled, had done much to nullify the cancellation of the first big carrier by assuring the construction of other big carriers able to launch the big planes that could carry the big bomb. What would he do next?

As soon as Burke had settled in Washington, he plunged furiously into preparing himself for his new job, which he would assume when Carney completed his term in August. He visited all parts of the Navy Department, asking questions, and inspected navy yards and bases, asking more questions.

Part of his time Burke spent in a small temporary office assigned to him in the Pentagon. Here he received callers, including members of Carney's staff and officers holding major billets in the navy—men over whose heads he was being catapulted. In a sense, Burke would be senior to them all once he assumed the post of CNO, but, from another point of view he would always be junior to officers who had graduated from the Naval Academy before Arleigh's class of 1923. Burke treated his seniors with respect, then and later rising when they entered his presence. He also listened respectfully to their suggestions, which usually included advice not to "rock the boat" and to retain experienced officers at their posts.

Burke was glad to receive these callers, with whom as CNO he would have to work in close harmony, but, sensing that there were others who, for appearance's sake or reasons of their own, preferred not to visit the new appointee, he called a meeting and issued a general invitation to senior officers on duty in the Washington area. In view of the sort of advice he had been getting, he opened the proceedings with an announcement that on assuming the post of CNO he intended to "take the helm."

Burke did not fail to notice that this manifesto evoked ill-concealed smiles. In the discussion following his brief lecture, Arleigh received from Opnav* staffers more of the advice he had been getting—in effect, "Don't rock the boat. We've got a good staff here. Everything is fine, and we'll work for you. Just come with us." Arleigh Burke, born boat rocker, thus had his warning: Make haste slowly.

Captain Miller, who had witnessed these proceedings, saw trouble ahead. He suggested to Burke that he follow President Eisenhower's example in taking office by cleaning house, replacing officers in senior positions with others of his own choosing. Keeping these senior officers at their posts could make it difficult for the new CNO to put into effect new plans or fresh initiatives. Each of the officers had his funded project and would be tempted to oppose any fresh enterprise that threatened to draw appropriations from his own department. Their opposition could be formidable. Part warriors and part bureaucrats, they could circumvent the chief of naval operations by means of delaying tactics or through friends in Congress, in the Joint Chiefs, or in the executive branch.

While admitting the cogency of Miller's argument, Burke decided to retain Carney's staff and senior heads of activities and replace them with officers of his own choosing only as their tours of duty ended. A humble man, he could not bring himself to oust men he regarded as his seniors. Humane, he shunned dismissals that could suggest those dismissed were incompetent. After all, these men in general had made themselves experts in their jobs, and

*Opnav: The CNO's extended (not merely personal) Pentagon staff.

Burke, by leaving operations in their experienced hands, hoped to avoid the blunders that many of his bypassed peers expected, and some even hoped, he would make.

The navy Burke was about to inherit had made striking technical advances over the fleet he and Pete Mitscher had led to the shores of Japan. Submarine *Nautilus,* the world's first vehicle to be propelled by nuclear energy, had completed her maiden voyage, and Burke now made it his business to go briefly to sea in her. From that experience he envisioned nuclear-propelled fleets able to remain at sea for long periods without refueling.

Burke learned that the army and the air force were racing with the Soviets and with each other to build long-range ballistic missiles—rockets that would soar from ground level hundreds of miles into the air and deliver their payloads many hundreds of miles away. The general aim was to produce two types—an intermediate-range ballistic missile (IRBM) that could strike a target 1,500 miles from the launching point and an intercontinental ballistic missile (ICBM) with a range five or six times as great.

Each of the two American services argued that the other was intruding in its own proper domain. The air force generals maintained that ballistic missiles, as strategic weapons, were an extension of air power and should be controlled by their Strategic Air Command. The army brass claimed that missiles were only an advanced form of artillery, and they cited the German "Big Bertha," a huge cannon that in World War I fired shells into Paris from 80 miles away.

The navy was making no bid for participation in this race. Admiral Carney, stoutly supported by his department heads, was convinced that at their present stage and in any foreseeable future ballistic missiles were too big and their liquid fuel too dangerous to be handled on board surface ships or submarines. The current army design, developed from the German V-2, envisaged a cylindrical rocket, six stories high, to be fueled in a vertical position. On the deck of a wave-tossed ship, such an operation would be perilous, particularly as liquid oxygen, used to burn the fuel (alcohol or kerosene) inside the rocket, is highly explosive.

Such arguments did not convince Burke. His scientific education and his experience with ordnance and explosives left him with the conviction that the impediments that discouraged Carney and his admirals were precisely the sort hard, well-directed brainwork could overcome. The deterrent effect of sending the missiles to sea was worth the effort. On the trackless oceans, covering nearly three-quarters of the earth's surface, a missile-bearing surface ship or, better, a missile-bearing submarine would be hard to find. The Soviets could not hope to spare Russia all nuclear retaliation through a first, preemptive strike at the United States. The U.S. missile ships at sea, or under the sea, would still be there to strike back.

Burke wanted to know more about the possibilities of squeezing a ballistic missile into a smaller space and operating it with something less hazardous than liquid oxygen. In seeking information, he decided to steer clear of factions with vested interests—officers and civilians in the army or air force missile programs. Miller, who had investigated, advised that he was most likely to get unbiased answers from scientists at the General Electric Company, which had wide experience in designing and building rocketry. Burke's inquiries quickly became known to the air force generals, who suspected that this busybody naval officer, who had broken their monopoly of the atomic bomb and sent it to sea, was now bent on making a seafarer of their ballistic missile.

At Miller's request, one of Admiral Carney's staffers who had contacts with General Electric called there and asked if Admiral Burke came up could they give him a briefing on the possibility of putting a ballistic missile on board a ship. They agreed to set up such a briefing and a week later called back and said they were ready, so Burke flew up to General Electric's Heavy Electronics Division at Syracuse, New York. On his return he was met by Captain Miller.

"How did it go?" asked Miller.

"Well," said Burke, chuckling, "I went up there and met an air force general at the airport, and he wasn't too polite. He said, 'What are you doing here?' I said, 'I came up here to have a beer.'" In a more serious vein, he told Miller that he was now more convinced than ever that a seaborne ballistic missile was a possibility.

Before taking office, Burke set out to visit potential trouble areas, make important contacts, and gather information. With a small staff he headed by plane across the Pacific. At Pearl Harbor he called on the current Cincpac, Admiral Felix Stump, an old friend who had commanded carriers in World War II. After being briefed by Stump and the Cincpac staff, Burke and his group headed for Asia and toured weak and strong spots adjoining or near communist China—Japan, South Korea, Taiwan, South Vietnam, Laos, and Thailand. In each country senior officers briefed him on the state of their national defenses.

In Taiwan he conferred with President Chiang Kai-shek, in

South Vietnam with Premier Ngo Dinh Diem, and in Thailand with Premier Pibul Songgram. In Japan, Korea, and Taiwan he found time to make calls on old friends. In the Philippines he inspected American bases and visited the Seventh Fleet. Heading back to the States, Burke paused again at Pearl Harbor, where he was given another briefing.

After hasty visits at home and at the Navy Department, Burke was off again, this time to Europe with the twofold aim of visiting U.S. Army headquarters for briefings on the military situation in Europe and of paying calls on the chief officers of Western Europe's navies. He invited the latter to visit the United States as his guests, and he stated his intention of setting up a radio network whereby he and the other navy chiefs could readily confer.

Burke asked that the change of command, scheduled for 17 August 1955, be held on board an aircraft carrier to remind the American public that sailors do not spend all their duty time behind desks. Carrier *Ticonderoga*, berthed at Norfolk, was designated as site for the swearing-in ceremony, but Hurricane Diane intervened, sending *Ticonderoga* scooting for the relative safety of the open sea. The ritual was hastily shifted to the Naval Academy. Here under threatening skies Secretary Thomas, Admiral Carney, and Admiral Burke were accorded full honors, and Burke took the oath as CNO in Dahlgren Hall, where thirty-two years earlier, in the company of 412 other graduating midshipmen, he had been graduated and had taken the oath as ensign.

Senior officers from all over, including Admiral Stump from Pearl Harbor, were on hand to see their new boss take office and hear what he had to say. Burke unstintingly praised the achievements and legacy of his predecessor and pledged "to push with all my energies those policies which Admiral Carney has initiated to contribute further to the combat-readiness and fighting trim of the U.S. Navy."

Burke took advantage of the presence of key personnel, particularly Admirals Wright and Stump, to discuss a problem that had concerned him since his first days as Comdeslant, the navy's severe manpower shortage. Burke attributed it to the G.I. Bill of Rights, which provided war veterans unemployment benefits, educational expenses, and low-interest loans for buying homes, farms, or small businesses—all of which made civilian life more attractive to war veterans than a service career.

The army and air force maintained their authorized strength by means of Selective Service, i.e., the draft, whereby youths were conscripted for two years' service. The draft had been scheduled to end 1 July 1955, but the president had proposed and Congress had confirmed its continuation till 1 July 1959. The navy had not been included. It prided itself that except in time of war it was a volunteer service. Before the 1955 draft-continuation plan was sent to Congress, Admiral Carney had advised and the president and the secretaries of navy and defense had concurred that the navy, as before, should admit only volunteers. The naval authorities had not supposed they were making too great a sacrifice. Their decision might require taking a few ships out of service, but they anticipated that the volunteers would level off at a rather high figure. It had not turned out that way. The navy's manpower shortage was becoming critical.

Burke's discussions with senior officers convinced him that something drastic had to be done. Too many ships were being laid up for want of crews. Back in Washington, Burke reviewed the situation with Vice Admiral James Holloway, chief of naval personnel. The situation was such that Holloway had begun to think the unthinkable—the navy would have to go to the draft.

Burke, after further consultations and study of the figures, came to the same conclusion. To carry out its functions acceptably, the navy needed 56,000 draftees. Armed with convincing facts and figures, Burke called on Secretary Thomas and said the navy had to participate in Selective Service.

The secretary was shocked at the suggestion. "No," he said, "we've settled that question. This has been a very serious thing. We've worked on it, we've studied it, and we have decided not to go to the draft."

"Well, I think it's wrong," said Burke. "I think we should."

"Your predecessor agreed that we should not go to the draft, that we should have a volunteer navy."

"The situation's different now."

"No," said Thomas hotly, "it hasn't become much different. Now you just go back and work on those problems you can do something about. Don't worry about this one. This decision's been made."

Burke returned to his office. He did some more thinking. He sent for more data, all he could get. The more he thought and the more he investigated, the more he became convinced that without a healthy infusion of personnel, the navy simply could not much longer operate its fleets and bases. He went back to the secretary's office with more arguments, more figures. Mr. Thomas was adamant. He set his jaw and said between clenched teeth, "No draft."

"Then, Mr. Secretary," said Burke, "I must see the president."
"You can't do that."

"Yes, I can. According to the law, the professional service chiefs have a right to see the president whenever they consider it necessary. I think what's being done is wrong and serious enough that the president should know."

Secretary Thomas by this time must have been wondering what kind of deal he had made in exchanging Carney for Burke. "Well," he said, "let's go down and see Charlie Wilson." And down they went to lay their differences before Engine Charlie.

Secretary Wilson received them smilingly and heard first Burke's point of view and then Thomas's, which of course was his own view also. He tried to get Burke to change his mind, but to no avail.

"No," said Burke. "I want to see the president."

Charlie shrugged and threw up his hands in acceptance of the fact that the secretaries were up against a stone wall. He telephoned, made an appointment for them to see the president that afternoon, and took Thomas and Burke to the White House in his own car.

They arrived a little early and had a wait of about twenty minutes in the president's outer office. Burke couldn't sit still. Walking up and down, he pondered the situation he had created.

"What am I doing?" he asked himself. "The president, the secretary of defense, and the secretary of the navy have made a decision that they still think is right. Who am I to pit my judgment against theirs? Maybe I'm wrong and shouldn't have done this."

For a fleeting few moments he considered asking the secretaries to forget the whole thing and join him in making excuses and leaving. He banished the thought. He had brought up the subject, he had taken a stand. If he backed down now, no one would ever again have confidence in his decisions.

A summons brought the three callers into the Oval Office, where Mr. Eisenhower greeted them cordially. When they were seated the secretaries asked Burke to explain his position to the president. Arleigh did so, courteously but without apology or misgivings. Thomas and Wilson then set forth their own point of view and stated why they thought Burke was wrong.

As the discussion developed, Mr. Eisenhower's face began to redden. Burke, hot-tempered himself, recognized the symptom. It was dawning on the president that the admiral was putting him in an awkward position. This upstart CNO, barely a week in office, was asking the president of the United States to withdraw his public statements, revoke his decision, and ignore the advice of his secretaries of defense and navy. It was asking a great deal, but Burke, as a professional officer, foresaw the outcome. In internal matters concerning the services, old soldier Ike would trust the judgment of a fellow serviceman. With respect to this naval problem he would trust a sailor's advice over that of civilians.

When each of the visitors had had his say and answered the president's questions, they expectantly awaited his decision. After a pause, Mr. Eisenhower, very red-faced, announced, "We'll go to the draft."

"Thank you, Mr. President," said Secretary Wilson. The visitors rose and prepared to leave, but Mr. Eisenhower asked Burke to stay behind for a moment. The president remained silent and grim-faced until the two secretaries were out of hearing. Then he swung on Burke. "Admiral," he growled, "you put me in a hell of a spot! Don't you ever again embarrass your commander in chief like this!" Then, turning away, he dismissed Burke with a wave of his hand.

Secretaries Thomas and Wilson had departed in the latter's car, evidently having no immediate desire for more of Burke's company. Arleigh had to telephone for a car to take him back to the Pentagon. When he and Mr. Thomas met later, the secretary was cold and official. Burke, like Carney before him, knew that henceforth he had better not make any mistakes. After one week as CNO, he was evidently in as bad odor with the secretary of the navy as Carney had been after two years. It seemed to him that his chances for reappointment were slight. Whatever programs he hoped to introduce had better be fully operative within a single two-year term. For the moment, however, he had the satisfaction of having saved the navy from the dire consequences of severe undermanning. Using the draft for the first time since World War II, it was scheduled, between November 1955 and May 1956, to call in its needed 56,000 draftees.

When Admiral Burke had occasion to call on the president again, he was not surprised to be greeted amiably. Mr. Eisenhower, like himself, tended to give vent to his anger with one blast and not hold grudges afterward. Besides, it was now abundantly clear that Burke had been right. The navy sorely needed men, and the draft was the only way to get them. The president treated Arleigh with respect, and that was understandable too. Burke had been a deep selection of Thomas and Wilson, who had presented him to Eisenhower as their boy. The draft incident had demonstrated to the navy, to the secretaries, and to the president that Burke was nothing of the sort but was in fact the independent and stubborn bastard he had kept telling them he was.

This was the beginning of a growing friendship between President Eisenhower and Admiral Burke. The president would invite Arleigh to the White House at about five o'clock of an afternoon. They'd have old-fashioneds, which they both favored, and sit and talk. At first they discussed naval problems, then military problems in general, and at length problems that had nothing to do with the armed services.

"Mr. President," Burke once protested, "I'm not familiar with all the details."

"I don't want you to be," said Eisenhower. "I want to get an off-the-top-of-your-head opinion."

It is not to be supposed that Burke, as adviser on domestic matters, in any sense superseded the president's chief of staff, Governor Sherman Adams, or, as mentor on international affairs, displaced his secretary of state, John Foster Dulles, or that there were not others besides Burke whom the president consulted informally. But he obviously valued Arleigh's advice. What Eisenhower got from him was straightforward, completely honest opinion based on varied experience, wide reading, and the orderly thinking he had developed by service in two think tanks.

The president did not match the admiral in intellect or depth of knowledge and certainly not in capacity for hard work. Arleigh recognized these presidential shortcomings, but Ike's obvious integrity, patriotism, good judgment, high standards, and public-spiritedness won Arleigh's admiration. "He had a hell of a lot of character," said Burke.

In the Pentagon, as Burke immersed himself diligently in his CNO duties, conferring with the SecNav each morning and keeping him fully informed, Mr. Thomas gradually dropped his cool and formal manner toward his CNO. They were both ardent to bring the navy abreast of scientific developments, and they had much to discuss. A second nuclear-propelled U.S. submarine had been launched and a third had been laid down. In this category the Americans were clearly ahead of the Soviets, and Burke and Thomas were determined to keep them ahead. The first postwar U.S. carrier, the 59,650-ton *Forrestal*, was to be commissioned that fall. A second, to be christened *Saratoga*, was soon to be launched. Burke and Thomas

decided the time had come to start campaigning for a nuclear carrier. To deal with the threat of air attack, at that time considered the
navy's gravest challenge, they proposed pushing cruiser conversions
armed with surface-to-air guided missiles, chiefly the so-called three
Ts—Terrier; lighter, less expensive Tartar; and big Talos, with a
range of 75 miles.

The president's blue-ribbon Technological Capabilities Panel,
headed by Dr. James Killian, president of the Massachusetts Institute of Technology, warned that the United States was becoming
increasingly vulnerable to Soviet thermonuclear attack. It recommended speeding up work on the air force's ICBM and called for
army development of a 1,500-mile IRBM and the parallel development by the navy of an IRBM capable of being launched from ships
at sea. In September 1955 the National Security Council endorsed
the panel's recommendations and President Eisenhower ordered
them put into effect.

Burke, with Thomas's eager support, now had his green light. He
also had an idea. He called on his opposite number, Air Force Chief
of Staff General Nathan Twining, and proposed a move that, he
said, would save time and money. He recommended collaboration,
a navy–air force pooling of information and expertise in developing
a land-sea ballistic missile. Twining appeared cool to the suggestion
but said he would take it up with his staff and with Air Force
Secretary Wilbur Brucker. In a few days he sent Burke a memorandum politely declining the navy's offer.

Burke next made the proposal for a joint effort to Army Chief of
Staff Maxwell Taylor. The army, whose missile, called Jupiter, still
existed only on paper, was more receptive to Burke's suggestion.
With the navy's cooperation, the army might yet outspeed the air
force. Shortly afterward, over cocktails at Admiral's House, Burke
and Thomas brought the matter up with Secretary Wilson. Thomas
urged the army-navy collaboration as a great money saver. That was
one argument that always appealed to Engine Charlie. The next day
he published an order directing the army and navy to pool their
efforts toward developing a land-sea missile.

In a contest resembling the army–air force missile race, the Bureau of Ordnance and the Bureau of Aeronautics began squabbling
about which would get the navy's missile job. Burke and Thomas
decided to give it to neither. They created a Special Projects Office,
which would be responsible solely for developing the nuclear ballistic missile.

To head the Special Projects Office, they needed a special kind of officer. He had to know enough about missilery to make decisions and provide general guidance. He had to be an organizer and a leader. Above all, he had to be a salesman, able to make good men not only willing but eager to join the enterprise and attain its goals.

Arleigh selected his man on the recommendation of Rear Admiral John H. Sides, head of his own Missile Division. The selectee was a newly made rear admiral, William F. "Red" Raborn, Jr., then operations officer for Admiral Wright at Norfolk and formerly Admiral Sides's deputy director of guided missiles. As a carrier pilot he was a veteran of the war against Japan. Since then he had been a pioneer in developing the navy's air-launched missiles. Burke ordered him to Washington and demonstrated his own salesmanship by arousing Raborn's enthusiasm for his new assignment and instilling in him a conviction that he would succeed. Burke also convinced himself that Red Raborn would do exactly what he wanted him to do and not let his efforts be diverted toward some unproductive goal.

Burke felt he had one more faction to align before he could launch his ballistic missile campaign with peace of mind. He wanted the unstinted backing of his CNO Advisory Board. These were vice admirals, department heads, men older than himself and until lately his seniors—officers whose cooperation he had been courting. He had been treating them with deference, soliciting and respecting their opinions. He now called them into conference and spelled out for them the details of his ballistic missile program. Then he went around the table for their opinions. To a man they opposed the project. They were against it because each of them knew it would take money out of his own program, which he considered more important and more realistic. They revived the old arguments about the impracticality of operating ballistic missiles from ships—arguments that had killed the program under CNO Carney.

Burke was becoming red-faced, a danger sign. He turned to Raborn, who was sitting off to one side. "Red," he said, "what do you think?"

"I think we ought to go for it, Admiral."

Burke pounded his fist down on the table with violence that made the vice admirals wince.

"All right, dammit," he shouted, "we'll do it anyway!"

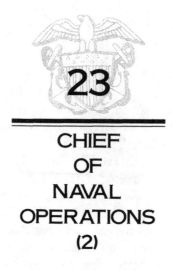

23

CHIEF
OF
NAVAL
OPERATIONS
(2)

ARLEIGH BURKE was now vested with the top professional job in the navy, but he still did not have the cannon of his own that Gelzer Sims had said he had to have. The navy was too linked together by a network of communications and authority for any one person to be in exclusive command of any part of it. Arleigh had come nearest to unshared command with his Little Beavers and in cruiser *Huntington,* but even then he had taken his basic orders from a faraway headquarters, to which he was linked by radio.

Now he shared control of the navy with the Joint Chiefs of Staff, with the secretaries of the navy and defense, with the Bureau of the Budget, with Congress, with the president, and with the American people through their representatives. Burke saw that this was as it should be, and through his mature years he steadfastly opposed excessive concentration of authority in government and in the armed forces. Meanwhile, for the good of the navy and of the nation he intended to employ to the hilt such powers as had been placed in his hands.

At age fifty-six, Arleigh Burke was an impressive man. Though he was simple and direct in speech and manner, years of authority had endowed him with an imposing command presence. In conversation he was habitually courteous and discreet, but when incited by wrongdoing or carelessness he could discharge a volley of billingsgate that rolled the offender back on his heels. His curly blond hair, now tinged with white, surmounted a high, broad forehead and a round, only slightly lined face. His penetrating blue eyes often twinkled with mirth but could turn glacial with disapproval. From his strong white teeth there usually protruded one of his straight-stemmed briar pipes, of which he usually kept a choice at hand. A vigorous six-footer, Burke had retained the broad shoulders and erect bearing of his youth, but their effect was diminished by over-weight, which he had fought since his Naval Academy days. In his long and largely sedentary tour as CNO, the extra flesh settled mostly in his hips, giving his frame somewhat the shape of a bass violin but slowing him down not in the least.

Each morning at 0715, a venerable Chrysler driven by a petty officer picked Burke up at Admiral's House. As CNO, he rated a new limousine, but he preferred to avoid ostentation and found the old car adequate. Arriving at his Pentagon office a little after 0730, he went through his routine morning briefings and conferences and then proceeded to the day's projects.

While all officers who served under CNO Burke praised his achievements, not all approved of his habits. Most frequently cen-sured were his failure to control his hot temper and his excessive working hours, which he expected his staff to emulate. His temper he admitted to be a flaw, and he strove to control it, but he gloried in overwork and stuck to his singular theory that an overworked man achieves better results than one who puts in reasonable hours.

Admiral Burke's workday almost never ended after eight hours and often not after twelve. He not infrequently worked at his desk until 2100 or 2200. For him, Saturdays and Sundays were additional opportunities to get things done. "The only man who ever had his work done by Friday," he used to say, "was Robinson Crusoe."

Admiral Burke's toiling staffers sometimes envied their army counterparts. General Taylor, army chief of staff, set no Burke-like example of endurance for them to emulate. Taylor was usually out of his office by 1600, played a game or two of tennis, took a leisurely shower, and enjoyed an early dinner, yet no one found cause for complaint.

When Burke remained late at his office, as he usually did, Bobbie might telephone an aide to get some estimate of when she should have his dinner ready. She was used to such eccentric behavior and accepted it, having devoted her life to "looking after Arleigh."

It is not to be supposed that Admiral Burke spent so many hours at his desk because he was doing work his subordinates should have been doing. In fact, no officer encouraged more initiative from or delegated more authority to his subordinates. It was just that the more tasks he passed on to others the more he found for himself. He had no children, no hobbies. His loves were Bobbie and the navy. Bobbie asked little beyond the privilege of looking after Arleigh, but the navy could be ever-demanding of an officer who was glad to give everything. What made Burke a hard taskmaster was that he expected others to have the same devotion.

If Burke left his office at the end of twelve hours or less, it was probably because he had house or dinner guests, or was invited to some official or quasi-official function he thought he should attend. The latter might require a 35-mile drive to the marine corps schools at Quantico or an equally long drive to Annapolis for some ceremony or reception at the Naval Academy or the Naval Institute, of which Burke was *ex officio* president. Far from resenting such interruptions, he looked forward to and enjoyed group gatherings. He and Bobbie, who usually accompanied him, liked people, liked socializing, and were charming hosts or guests, though Arleigh had some tendency to talk shop.

Even Burke's warmest admirers conceded that working for him was no picnic. He was demanding. He blew his stack at regular intervals, pouncing on laxity and every other shortcoming. He withheld praise except for outstanding performance, though of course the rarity of his compliments made them all the more treasured. His style of command stimulated some individuals and discouraged others. Most officers who served under CNO Burke recalled the experience as one of excitement and professional growth. Some good men, however, remembered it as a dismal interlude in their careers.

Possibly the unhappiest staffer at Opnav was Commander Ray Peet. As a junior officer he had been with Burke's Little Beavers and had distinguished himself in the battles of Empress Augusta Bay and Cape St. George. 31-Knot Burke, who had discovered the publicity value of a catchy name, advised Peet to call himself Ray instead of his given name, Raymond. "It's unfortunate," Burke had said, "but you need to be noticed in order to accomplish something."

Peet cherished the memory of his seagoing service with Burke, and when at length with the rank of commander he took command of destroyer *Barton,* he set out to emulate his former mentor. Serving with the Sixth Fleet in the Mediterranean, *Barton* had little opportunity to exhibit the devil-may-care dash that had been the hallmark of the Little Beavers, but she was known as a snappy, well-handled ship, and she developed an outstanding reputation as a clean ship, kept that way by a proud crew.

At length, Vice Admiral Charles R. Brown, commander Sixth Fleet, came to inspect. He was so gratified by *Barton*'s spotless, shipshape condition that he had her crew assembled on the fantail, where he congratulated, first, their captain, then the crew, for their achievement and announced that he would inform the chief of naval operations. *Barton* received a copy of the admiral's message, which included the words "This is the finest ship that I have inspected in all my tour in the Sixth Fleet."

It so happened that Admiral Burke had been casting about for a good personal aide to replace his current one, who was being transferred to other duties. Upon receiving Admiral Brown's report, he radioed back: "I have read with interest your comments about Captain [i.e., commanding officer] Peet and the *Barton*. I hereby order Captain Peet detached. If he has such a fine ship, his executive officer can take over. I order him to report back to the United States immediately to be my personal aide."

Commander Peet received this order with mixed feelings. He was pleased at the prospect of serving at the navy's nerve center and of rejoining Burke, his old shipmate and companion in adventures. Nevertheless, he saw the change as a drastic letdown. Here he was king of his own ship, publicly praised by his admiral. In Washington, as an aide, he would be a kind of errand boy, keeping track of appointments, arranging meetings, handling travel details, and such.

After clearing his personal papers and effects from his office and cabin on board *Barton*, Peet packed his belongings and took a flight back to the United States. Here he arranged for the sale of his home and bought fresh uniforms. He then proceeded to Washington and reached the Pentagon three days after his detachment in the Mediterranean. With lively anticipation he made his way to the CNO's office and presented his orders to a secretary, who said he was expected and waved him toward the inner sanctum. Entering, he smilingly approached the desk where the admiral was reading some papers.

"Sir," said Peet, "I am reporting for duty."

Looking up briefly, Burke muttered, "What took you so long? Get to work."

This was Peet's introduction to a tour he would afterward rather forget. An admiral and his aide often develop a relationship like father and son, less often like master and servant. The Burke-Peet association was generally of the latter type. According to Peet, Burke discouraged familiarity and demanded unremitting, top performance of duties. "He was," said Peet, "the most difficult man I ever worked for. He tended to expect the impossible from the aides and from others who worked closely with him. In the early morning, when he came to work, that's when I would generally hit him with the tough problems, because then he was usually pleasant and helpful, but as the evening wore on he got mean and difficult to work with."

More than once, Burke gave him a thorough chewing out for what seemed to Peet a minor lapse. "He's the only officer," says Peet, "that brought tears to my eyes."

Weeping Peet at the time of his service with CNO Burke was no mere stripling but an experienced officer in his mid-thirties with, as noted above, a fine service record. On leaving Burke after two unhappy years, he resumed his brilliant career and eventually, as a vice admiral, commanded a U.S. fleet.

The foregoing account of Peet's service as an aide is based on his recollections recorded some twenty years later. Other, contemporary staffers remembered Burke somewhat differently. There was, for example, Captain George Miller, whom, it will be recalled, Burke had summoned for temporary duty directly upon being confirmed as CNO.

As soon as Miller was available for a regular tour, Burke recalled him to Washington for a new, highly offbeat assignment. His job was to keep Burke under more or less constant observation during the workday. He was to listen in on any of his conversations or conferences, sitting inconspicuously in the back of the room. He was free to monitor his telephone calls and read his correspondence. He was to go where he pleased in the Opnav area and ask anybody anything, saying that Burke sent him.

Miller was to keep notes and from time to time send Burke critical comments on his performance as CNO or sit down with him and tell him how he believed he could make improvements. Burke told him he was giving him the duty because he respected his judgment and knew he could count on him to tell him the truth. It was a ticklish assignment that produced not a few explosions, but Miller took the scoldings in stride, and Burke soon cooled off and held no grudges.

"Admiral Arleigh Burke and I developed a mutual regard for one another," said Miller. "His regard for me was getting up and yelling at me, throwing me out of the office. My regard for him was the tremendous amount of work and dedication the gentleman had and my desire to help. He's the type of person I was going to do anything possible to help. Despite all the yelling, we got along very well."

Captain Miller's other job was to write studies, reports, and letters as assigned. Admiral Burke, said Miller, would "call me up on the phone and say, 'George, I need something by ten o'clock tonight,' or 'I need something by eight o'clock in the morning,' which meant I had the privilege of working all night. Still, it was flattering to know that when he had a hot one or a big one he'd throw it to me, a very junior captain in the organization."

Miller later summarized his CNO duty thus: "Working closely with the chief of naval operations, particularly an individual of Admiral Burke's knowledge and energy, is a very exacting type of duty. It's the type of duty which you can't get away from anytime during the day or weekends. Many of your weekends and nights are spent in the office because of the long hours that Admiral Burke himself kept."

Of all officers in Opnav, none was better situated to observe Admiral Burke in action or better equipped to assess his qualities than Rear Admiral Thomas Moorer, who was himself destined a few years later to serve as chief of naval operations and chairman of the Joint Chiefs of Staff. In the five years Moorer served under CNO Burke, first as special assistant in the Strategic Plans Division and then as assistant CNO for war gaming, he saw Arleigh almost daily.

Asked his opinion of Admiral Burke, Moorer replied, "Well, of course I can't say enough good about Arleigh Burke. He's the salt of the earth. I don't think anybody in this century has made the impact on the navy that he has. He combined an aggressive fighting spirit, technical competence, and an understanding of people. He had a terrific feel for people, and he won the respect and indeed the love of all who served with him.

"Admiral Burke knew how to select people to carry out the task at hand. He indicated the end to be achieved and gave them their heads. So it was easy to work for him. I thought it was a very stimulating experience, because he didn't tell you how to run your business. He wanted certain results, and he would say, 'I think we ought to go in this direction' in the broadest sense, allowing you latitude to make the best use of people under you. That was his strong point. He was a good manager.

"Of course," Moorer added, "you can't say anything about Arleigh without also mentioning his wife, Bobbie. She's a great person in her own right and certainly a perfect match for Arleigh Burke."

Bobbie was so gentle and unassertive that few people discerned the vital role she played in her husband's career. Moorer, however, through his long association with the Burkes, recognized that Arleigh, in any circumstances a great man, was a greater one thanks to Bobbie's advice and support. She was his steadying influence, cheering him out of his glooms and restraining his impulsiveness. He consulted her on all matters, social, professional, and administrative. She lacked his technical training and his broad, hard-earned knowledge, but she was unusually gifted with patience, common sense, and inner strength, and she devoted herself unstintingly to her husband's needs.

When Burke took over as chief of naval operations he had his head full of reforms he wanted to make, but he at once encountered another, less discerning brake on his impetuosity. This was his inherited vice chief, the elderly Vice Admiral Donald B. Duncan, a holdover from the Carney regime. Duncan counseled caution. "He kept advising me not to make changes," Burke recalled, "not to eliminate something until I was sure it wasn't needed or that the replacement would work."

Such advice was useful to a point, but following it too strictly could bring progress to a halt. Burke liked Duncan but was not sorry when he reached mandatory retirement age. Arleigh wanted another kind of brake, not an assistant who was opposed to all change, but an officer of experience and rank who would supplement Miller's critical advice by coming down hard on what he considered Burke's faulty decisions. "I needed somebody to make sure I didn't make any serious mistakes," said Burke, "or if I made any, it would not be without knowing that somebody thought they were mistakes."

Burke searched the navy's flag list and came upon what he believed to be a topnotch choice in Admiral Don Felt. Felt was small, tough, irascible, and brilliant and completely devoted to the navy. As vice CNO, he took charge of Opnav routine. More to the point, when he thought Burke was wrong, he had not the slightest hesitation in telling him he was making a fool of himself. Soon sparks were flying as these two hotheaded officers had it out. Still, Burke kept Felt on, appreciating his hard work and valuing his honest opinions and his utter frankness, not to say insolence, in expressing them.

To other personnel in Opnav, Admiral Felt quickly made himself anathema. His harsh words bounced off Burke but provoked outrage or terror in everybody else. Vice Admiral William P. Mack, recalling that period, said of Felt, "He would grab three-star officers by the lapels, literally shake them, and say, 'Why don't you do so and so or such and such?' They'd be thirty or forty pounds heavier than he was, but that didn't bother him at all. He was there for two years, which was probably about a year too long, because morale was getting pretty low. As I told Admiral Burke, it was just a question of time before somebody was going to slug him. You can't operate like that. Admiral Felt wasn't big enough to defend himself. I said that one of these days he's going to come at someone who's going to wipe up the corridor with him, regardless of how many stars he has."

At the end of two years, Admiral Burke concluded that he had had about enough of Felt. Of that period he later said mildly, "It isn't pleasant to fight continually with a good friend, and after a while you wonder whether he's all that good a friend." In fact, Arleigh was beginning to suspect that Felt's constant faultfinding had become a mere habit. If so, his expressed opinion was worthless. An automatic no-sayer is as useless as a perpetual yes-man.

Fortunately for all hands, a fleet command opened up and Felt was in line for it. Burke said, "I couldn't hold him back just selfishly to keep him in the vice chief's job." So, with a small push from Burke, Felt got his fleet. His relief as VCNO was Admiral James Russell, who sometimes disagreed with Burke but could do so without raising Burke's hackles. A congenial man, Russell became a favorite at Opnav.

Foremost among Burke's goals as CNO was developing a functional fleet ballistic missile (FBM). To Admiral Raborn, on his assuming his duties as head of the FBM project, he sent a letter that came to be called "Red Raborn's Hunting License." It stated that if Raborn "runs into any difficulty with which I can help, I want to know about it at once, along with his recommended course of action. . . . If there is anything that slows this project up beyond the capacity of the Navy and the department, we will immediately take it to the highest level."

Subsequently Burke attached an addendum: "Anytime it looks as though you're batting your head against a technological wall—if you see the job isn't technically feasible—it will be cut off dead."

In conversation, Burke warned Raborn not to depend too much on the letter. To supplement the authority thus bestowed, he would have to use his powers of persuasion.

"You cannot order people to think," said Burke. "You cannot order people to cooperate. People have to want to do these things."

Burke told Raborn that he could recruit a staff of no more than forty officers, of his own selection, from anywhere in the navy. There was just one exception. He was to steer clear of Rear Admiral Hyman G. Rickover. That cantankerous little genius had charmed Congress and the press into backing him to head the navy's nuclear propulsion program. In that capacity he had produced *Nautilus,* which made him unassailable.

Burke fully supported Rickover in his role as nuclear-propulsion chief, but he did not want him in the FBM program. In his Congress-backed race for power, Rickover had tended to take command of any department he invaded. He already controlled a large portion of the U.S. defense establishment. For him the FBM was a secondary interest. If he intruded himself into the program, he would be sure to impede Raborn's single-minded drive.

Burke warned Raborn that unless he met a series of tight deadlines, the program might be canceled. "If the program is a success," he added, "it will be to your credit and the credit of your organization. On the other hand, if you fail . . ." He took a puff on his pipe. ". . . it will be your neck."

Raborn carried what he called "Burke's magic letter" in his pocket for months, but he rarely had to use it. He was known as Burke's representative, and his enthusiasm for his program and obvious expectation of success were contagious. On the couple of occasions when he exhibited the letter, he did so with unfeigned embarrassment, saying it was something the boss said he had to do, and he hoped it wouldn't cause too many problems.

The Raborn committee and the army missile engineers cooperated fully in their efforts to produce a mutually satisfactory IRBM. They tried widening the diameter of the Jupiter rocket to reduce its height, objectionable for navy use. Several months of experiment taught all hands a great deal about rocketry. For the navy, the most important breakthrough was devising a system for *guiding* a missile launched from a moving, rocking platform to a target 1,500 miles away.

Meanwhile, the Atomic Energy Commission was succeeding in reducing the size of nuclear warheads, and the Office of Naval

Research was getting more specific impulse, more "oomph," out of relatively small rockets using solid propellants. Raborn and his committee at once perceived the advantage of wedding the reduced warhead and the solid-fuel body. The combination would be a practical fleet ballistic missile, small enough and safe enough to be carried in and launched from ships, small enough in fact to be carried in and launched from submarines. Submarines would be hard for an enemy to find, and, unlike rolling, storm-tossed surface ships, they would when submerged serve as stable launching platforms.

Raborn's staff's computations convinced them that development of a solid-propellant ballistic missile with a 1,500-mile range was feasible. To convince other interested parties, Raborn had colored slides made showing the shrunken warhead and solid-fuel rocket and how they could be united and fired from a surface ship or submarine to hit points in Russia. He easily convinced Secretary Thomas and Admiral Burke, and the former arranged a slide show for Secretary Wilson and high-ranking officers of all the services.

Raborn accompanied the show with an enthusiastic lecture. Besides arguing the feasibility of the solid-fuel fleet ballistic missile, he demonstrated that it would save money. Ships armed with these safer, smaller rockets would be cheaper to build, and fewer would be required because each ship could carry more missiles. Savings could amount to $50 million.

On seeing this figure thrown on the screen at the end of the show, Engine Charlie beamed. "Well, Admiral," he said, "you've shown us a lot of sexy slides this morning, but I tell you that last slide, where you showed that tremendous saving, was the sexiest one of all."

Wilson dissolved the army-navy missile partnership and directed the navy experts to develop their own solid-fuel ballistic missile. Raborn named it Polaris, after the north star, which through the centuries had guided mariners across the seas. Thomas and Burke, acting on the assumption that the country's survival was at stake, gave the new missile and its carriers, surface and subsurface, top priority. In common with many Americans, they believed that the Russians, unless deterred by sure and dire retaliation, were prepared to bombard the United States with the terrible hydrogen bombs, which would destroy its cities, inflict millions of casualties, and turn the country into a wasteland. Burke considered the FBM the most nearly invulnerable of the possible deterrents to such an attack.

Burke was involved in many other projects. Among these was fulfilling his promise to make sure all hands got the word and informing himself fully about the current status of the navy. In pursuit of the former objective, he personally wrote a periodic newsletter for flag officers. He issued frequent navy-wide bulletins explaining not only what was being done but why, and he cut a long-playing record on the navy's functions and its growing importance and sent copies to all ships and stations.

As means for passing the word and also keeping informed, he welcomed letters addressed to himself and saw to it that each one was answered. When this open-mailbox policy produced a greater load than he could handle, he parceled the letters out for answering by staff members. The assignment might easily consume a staffer's entire weekend. The letters were to be answered promptly, completely, clearly, accurately, and succinctly. The staffers turned in their answers together with the letters they were answering. Burke might merely glance over the letters, but he scrutinized the answers submitted for his signature, and great would be his wrath when he found one he considered sloppy. He would call in the writer, give him a Burke-size raking over, and demand an instant rewrite.

In pursuit of information, Burke visited ships and bases and asked questions—not the routine queries concerning operations and equipment, matters about which Burke probably knew far more facts than he was likely to elicit. He might, instead, ask a commanding officer what he was most proud of, least proud of, in the navy, in his ship, in his crew. What was he doing, or what could be done, to improve combat effectiveness and evoke pride in the service? What measures would he take to sustain a threatened nuclear attack? Or he might ask an officer, however junior, if he had observed any time-wasting, money-wasting, or antiquated activities that might profitably be canceled, abridged, or updated.

In Pentagon corridors, Burke would buttonhole startled individual officers and put them through quizzes about their activities and the activities of their departments. He liked to pick up hitchhiking sailors, somehow put them at their ease, and draw from them their attitudes regarding their food, their quarters, their weapons, their treatment, and their daily routine. He sent several bright, hand-picked young officers through the navy, not as spies but as conduits of informal communication, using quiet, intimate discourse to spread Burke's ideas about the navy and to pick up facts and ideas which the navy wished to share with its chief of naval operations.

From his think-tank experiences, Burke had come to realize how vague are most people's ideas and how putting them into words, preferably written words, tends to bring the ideas into focus. In his interrogations, he now perceived that some high-ranking officers, men on whose mental acuity the national survival could depend, were unable to give any clear verbal description of their responsibilities. As they rose in rank they had assigned to staffers or yeomen the writing of their required reports, and Burke had long been aware how unreadable and hence unread these could be. Many officers had not since their Naval Academy days put anything but their most casual ruminations into writing.

To the astonishment of his senior officers, Burke frequently assigned them essays to write on subjects relating to or affecting their duties: international relations, weaponry, personnel problems, discipline, and the like. He intended these assignments both as exercises in thinking and as tests. He invited writers on key subjects to present their papers at a meeting of their peers. A conscientious but inept paper brought the writer under Burke's close scrutiny. Careless work, as always, earned Arleigh's wrath.

One punishment for apparent carelessness was long remembered. A captain was presenting a paper Burke had given him three weeks to prepare. This officer either did not take the assignment seriously or he was incredibly inept, not to say stupid. To the gathered officers, the paper sounded slipshod and silly.

Finally, Burke had had enough. "Damn!" he roared. "This is no good. You'll have to do it over again."

The captain stood on his dignity. "Well, Admiral," he said, "if you want this done over, you're going to have to get somebody else."

"All right," said Burke, "you're fired. I'll get somebody else."

An officer who was present said afterward, "Because of that one firing, I would suggest that a thousand captains woke up, took their feet off their desks, and put their shoulders to the wheel."

The admirals took notice too. Mr. Nice Guy, who rose when his chronological seniors entered his presence and showed them such deference, had a tough side and could shoot from the hip. They became alarmed when they learned what else he was up to. Burke was writing to certain rear admirals and vice admirals asking them to retire. They were occupying responsible posts for which their main qualification was seniority. He wanted them to clear out so he could move up bright young officers with better qualifications.

But Burke was encountering an old navy problem. By law, there can be only so many admirals, full, vice, and rear, and the naval organization provides only so many slots for each rank to occupy. If all the slots for a given rank are filled, officers of the next-lower rank, however bright and efficient, have no place to rise to until somebody above them dies, retires, or is otherwise removed. An obvious solution is early retirement—before the mandatory age, which for admirals was at that time sixty-four. An officer who has shown ability by attaining flag rank can usually, after retirement, find well-paying employment in business or industry. Having reached his peak in the navy he now has an opportunity to reach other heights and make further contributions as a civilian, and his civilian salary added to his naval retirement pay can provide him with the handsomest income of his career. It should have been a tempting prospect, but Arleigh learned that many vice admirals would rather back down to rear admiral, and many rear admirals would rather back down to captain, than leave the navy.

Admiral Burke made a major point of keeping in touch with and exchanging visits with the senior officers of other navies, beginning with Admiral Louis Mountbatten, first sea lord of Britain's Royal Navy. In the past, some of the foreign admirals, bringing their wives with them, had treated their junkets to the United States as vacations, featuring a reception, a dinner or so, some pleasant conversation, perhaps a game of golf or a bit of yachting, then off to New York for some Broadway shows before returning home. For Burke, whether as host or guest, such visits were strictly professional, friendly but occupied chiefly with meaningful conferences and inspections.

With respect to the naval ambitions of some maritime states, Burke, wanting to be helpful, developed a kind of parental relationship. What the states chiefly wanted from him was ships, to start a navy or enlarge what they had. He was authorized in certain circumstances to make gifts of older American men-of-war, decommissioned and headed for scrapping but still serviceable. To West Germany, stripped of what was left of Germany's fleet at the end of World War II, he gave three destroyers, veterans of his own Desron 23.

To Greece he gave two destroyers and settled a royal dispute. When Queen Frederika came to the United States to accept the gift, the Greek ambassador aroused her fury by opining that it was inappropriate for a woman to take official possession of men-of-war. It required all of Burke's powers of persuasion to constrain her majesty from sacking the offending diplomat on the spot.

Ethiopia wanted a yacht for the use of His Imperial Majesty Haile Selassie. Burke denied the request, but the Joint Chiefs overruled him, wishing to keep on good terms with a nation so strategically located. They sent a small tender, which with a little fancy work could pass for a yacht.

At the earnest entreaty of the Brazilian naval minister, Burke made a twelve-hour flight to Brazil to settle an argument. For reasons best known to itself, the Brazilian navy had bought a used British aircraft carrier, and now Brazil's naval aviators and air force aviators were in a battle over which should have the right to fly planes off it.

Ecuador wanted a naval academy. Burke wasn't willing to build them one at U.S. expense, but he provided used equipment and sent craftsmen and technicians to show them how to build it themselves. They did a fine job, of which they were proud. The grateful Ecuadorean government invited Burke down to commission the new institution. They named it the Burke Ecuadorean Naval Academy, as attested by a brass plate at the door. After Burke had left, they renamed the academy after one of their own dignitaries and sent Burke the brass plate as a souvenir.

Admiral Burke, despite President Eisenhower's advice to devote most of his time to his Joint Chiefs of Staff duty, never gave it more than a third of his attention. This was not neglect. A third of Burke's concentrated effort more than equaled many men's full daily output.

At Joint Chiefs' meetings Burke picked up where he had left off on quitting the Strategic Plans Division in 1954, that is, opposing the creeping centralizing of national defense authority and the "massive retaliation" strategy of relying on nuclear weapons at the expense of conventional forces. Instead of banging the table, however, he now pursued his goals obliquely. Years had taught him a degree of prudence and even of patience.

As CNO he was reluctant to split with the administration, and he preferred not to take up the cudgels with his friend Admiral Radford, now Joint Chiefs chairman. Radford, erstwhile unyielding spokesman for the navy view, was now showing appreciation for the air force contention that the hydrogen bomb alone was adequate for national defense and that the air force should have a monopoly of the bomb. Burke realized that Sailor Radford, now in a neutral post, was leaning over backward in an effort to be fair, but he wished he would not so far forget his neutrality as often to take over Burke's role and speak for the navy.

On the question of strategy, Burke limited himself to pointing out that Soviet progress in weaponry would soon produce a nuclear deadlock, which would in effect neutralize nuclear forces, leaving them unavailable for any purpose but to maintain a "balance of terror." Meanwhile, neglect of conventional weapons would leave the United States incapable of defending its interests against aggression short of all-out war.

On 26 July 1956, an example of such a lesser aggression occurred when Gamal Abdel Nasser, Egypt's nationalist dictator, seized the Suez Canal. Though entirely within Egypt's borders, the canal was internationally owned. England and France, principal stockholders in the Suez Canal Company and heavily dependent on Middle East oil, brought by tanker through the canal, threatened military action.

Admiral Burke, acting in his capacity as CNO and member of the Joint Chiefs of Staff, informed President Eisenhower that the Egyptians were capable of operating the canal, which had no locks, was sea level throughout, and required only dredging of windblown sand to keep it operational. He expressed his opinion, however, that "Nasser has to be shown that international thievery is unprofitable, that violation of international commitments is dishonorable and therefore cannot be looked on with approbation." He recommended that the United States lend support to England and France in their operations against Egypt, at least to the extent of lending naval landing craft for Britain's proposed November amphibious landing at Port Said. Secretary of State Dulles, however, urged the British and French to negotiate instead of resorting to arms. He suggested that the combat-ready U.S. Sixth Fleet, which Burke had moved into the eastern Mediterranean, take station off the African coast to block any Anglo-French attempt to invade Egypt. Burke flatly opposed using the fleet for such a purpose.

While the negotiations dragged on fruitlessly, Burke prepared for the worst scenario by sending an amphibious task group into the Indian Ocean and a carrier task force into the eastern Atlantic and putting the Atlantic Fleet on the alert for submarines deployed out of northern Russia. Israel, provoked by stepped-up Egyptian raids and the growing strength of Egypt's army, for which the Soviets were providing arms, decided the time had come to act. With the sympathy and probable connivance of Britain and France, the Israelis on 29 October invaded the Sinai Peninsula, routed the Egyptian forces there, and within a week controlled the area.

The British and French, who had assembled forces on Cyprus, ordered the Israelis and Egyptians to stop fighting and announced that they would themselves occupy the Canal Zone. The next day, Cyprus-based British and French planes began bombing Egyptian military bases, destroying large quantities of the Russian-supplied armament.

On 30 October, Admiral Burke radioed commander Sixth Fleet, Vice Admiral Brown, "Situation tense; prepare for imminent hostilities."

Brown signaled back, "Am prepared for imminent hostilities, but which side are we on?"

Burke's reply was a classic: "If U.S. citizens are in danger, protect them. Take no guff from anyone."

On 5 November the British and French landed troops at Port Said and began the occupation of the Canal Zone. It was an operation for which they were ill prepared. Like the Americans at the outbreak of the Korean War, the British and French had allowed their conventional armed forces to shrink below what was needed to protect their national interests. Moreover, their forces gathered on Cyprus had not been given advance warning of what was expected of them. The slow progress of the unready invaders against the Russian-armed Egyptians allowed time for international reaction. The Russians threatened to intervene, and the United States, anxious to remove any pretext for such intervention, backed the United Nations in demanding a cease-fire. Under these pressures, the British and French withdrew.

The U.S. Navy had not become directly involved, but the fleet had had a useful exercise in readiness, and Burke was provided with another cautionary demonstration of the need for a nation to keep well armed.

Arleigh campaigned vigorously for funds to build nuclear surface ships, especially carriers, and more nuclear submarines, and above all for funds to support the FBM program. He carried his campaign to the Hill, whither he was frequently summoned to testify before congressional committees. Admiral Rickover, similarly summoned, echoed Burke's drive for wider use of nuclear propulsion in the navy. The two admirals consulted but did not join forces. Rickover's prickly personality deterred fellowship, and his monumental ego forbade his teaming up with a mere CNO. Each, however, testifying alone, made a first-rate witness. Rickover fascinated congressmen with his reasoning and his icy intellect. Burke earned their trust through his reputation, his mastery of his subject, his enthusiasm, and his obvious sincerity.

Burke and Rickover won over the majority of the members of the House Appropriations Committee to the extent that the committee recommended construction of a nuclear cruiser and at least one nuclear carrier. The chairman, Clarence Cannon, dissented. A persistent critic of navies, he had never grasped their function in the postwar period. He sounded off in a statement reminiscent of the discredited views of Billy Mitchell and Louis Johnson. "If war should come," he said, "could warships protect us? Ridiculous! Enemy bombers would fly right over them. With the exception of our submarines the navy would cease to exist in a matter of hours. A carrier is the most expensive machine the world ever saw. It consumes more skilled labor, more strategic material, and more steel than any human contrivance the sun has ever shone upon. And yet in war it would be worse than useless."

That was quite an opinion to express before an officer who, as Pete Mitscher's chief of staff, had sailed in the Big Blue Fleet carrier force to the shores of Japan. The newer carriers, with armored flight decks and armed with antiaircraft and antisubmarine homing missiles and swift, high-flying, missile-equipped fighter aircraft, were far tougher customers than the old *Essex*-class carriers that had raided Tokyo and come away unscratched. Even a nuclear ballistic strike would do far less damage to a fleet with the modern spread-out formation than to a city crowded with buildings. Enough ships would be left, particularly after development of the FBM, to stage a devastating counterattack.

Congressman Cannon's remarks reminded Arleigh of the never-ending necessity of educating the public on the purposes of sea power. He and Secretary Thomas had already begun such educating along with stumping publicly for a nuclear carrier. In his speechmaking Burke had no set text, but varied the content to keep himself alert and avoid falling into a flat, memorized delivery. No orator, he held attention by what he had to say rather than how he said it. The results varied, depending on how much time he had given to preparation. After each speech he appraised his performance with Bobbie, who was generally in the audience. One evening, after Arleigh had done somewhat less than his best, he dismissed his fumblings with the remark "Well, nobody threw an egg."

"Nor laid one?" said Bobbie sweetly.

Arleigh chuckled. "You married a sailor," he said, "not William Jennings Bryan."

"I'm glad," she replied, patting his hand.

To sell the sea-power story to a broader American public, Burke organized a team of eloquent and attractive speakers, naval officers for whom it was extra duty. Headed by Captain John S. McCain, its members were available to speak before audiences—Navy League, Naval Reserve Association, American Legion, Veterans of Foreign Wars, or whatever—all over the United States.

One evening Burke witnessed a pageant staged by marines of scenes from U.S. Marine Corps history. Much moved and ever alert for ways to instill pride of service in naval personnel, he decreed that every base and major station in the navy should stage a pageant of scenes from U.S. naval history, with naval personnel in the acting roles.

Implementing Burke's brainstorm proved quite an undertaking. A professional writer prepared the script: scenes ranging from John Paul Jones shouting, "I have not yet begun to fight!" in the 1779 Battle off Flamborough Head to Pete Mitscher saying, "Turn on the lights," in the 1944 Battle of the Philippine Sea. For guidance each base and station received a movie of a pilot production with professional actors, together with a stern warning that this was not to be shown in place of the live pageant. To lessen the temptation to show it, the movie was made impossibly dull by photographing it with a stationary camera, in black and white and without sound. The project, though formidable, was a success. The live pageants, staged more or less simultaneously throughout the navy, were generally well done and well received.

In January 1957, at the beginning of President Eisenhower's second term, Thomas submitted his resignation as secretary of the navy and recommended that Under Secretary Gates be promoted to succeed him. Gates urged Thomas to recommend the appointment of Burke for a second term as CNO. Thomas replied that he had no intention of doing otherwise.

Instead of experiencing the tension that sometimes exists between the secretary of the navy and the chief of naval operations, an outcome of their overlapping responsibilities, Thomas and Burke had operated smoothly in tandem and had become close friends, and they had made a major contribution toward the building of a new kind of navy, armed with missiles instead of guns and increasingly nuclear-propelled. When Thomas tendered his resignation, nine new nuclear submarines and a nuclear-propelled cruiser were authorized or building.

In a farewell letter to Burke, Thomas wrote, "If I did nothing else for the navy, your appointment should earn me their thanks."

24

CHIEF
OF
NAVAL
OPERATIONS
(3)

WHEN ADMIRAL BURKE began his second term as CNO in August 1957, the United States supposed it was comfortably ahead of the Soviet Union in all forms of rocketry. Then came a pair of surprises that shocked and mortified the Americans. At the end of August, the Soviets announced that they had successfully launched an intercontinental ballistic missile (ICBM), the world's first. On 4 October the Russians achieved another first by placing a satellite, called Sputnik, in orbit around the earth.

Following Sputnik, Burke made a fact-finding inspection trip to the far Pacific. More than two years had passed since he talked with his Seventh Fleet commanders. He needed to make another check to see for himself how prepared they were for combat and to what extent the Japanese, the Koreans, the Nationalist Chinese, and the British at Hong Kong could defend themselves should the communists attack. He had been trying for six months to get away, but always some crisis obliged him to cancel. Now seemed as good a time as any, while the Pentagon was catching its collective breath from the Sputnik jolt.

Burke's navy plane took off from Washington's National Airport half an hour before midnight on 8 October. The admiral had brought Bobbie this time, and she shared a private cabin with him. On board also were Commander Ray Peet and a marine aide, several other naval and marine officers selected to assist the CNO in his inquiries and inspections, a couple of Filipino stewards, and a civilian journalist, sent along with Burke's permission by *The Saturday Evening Post* to get the story for its readers.

When the plane was airborne, Admiral and Mrs. Burke emerged from their cabin in the rear. Bobbie chatted a few moments, then said good night and withdrew. The admiral, however, took a seat, filled and lit his pipe, and initiated a line of navy talk that lasted until long after most of the others would have opted for a little shut-eye.

Burke and his party landed on Oahu and remained two nights and a day at Pearl Harbor, where Burke spent many hours conferring with old friend Admiral Felix Stump, now nearing the end of his tour as Cincpac. A major subject of their discussion was money, or lack of it. President Eisenhower's firm policy, second only to deterrence, was maintaining a balanced budget. To forestall a possible deficit, he had sharply reduced military appropriations for fiscal year 1958. How with slashed resources could the navy contain a militant communist China?

On his previous trip to the Orient, Burke had been treated with courtesy. This time as CNO he was treated with ceremony. Waiting to greet him as his plane landed at Atsugi Airport near Tokyo were a number of dignitaries, including old friend Admiral Ko Nagasawa, commander of Japan's Maritime Self-Defense Force. Also present by their own request were two more old friends, now members of the Japanese Diet, retired Admirals Kichisaburo Nomura and Zenshiro Hoshina.

In Tokyo Admiral Burke was a guest of Rear Admiral Roscoe Good, commander of U.S. naval forces in Japan. At dinner the evening of his arrival, Burke brought up one of the main themes of his visit to the fleet. He said he intended both to advise and to seek advice on how to pare down American Far East naval forces without dulling their fighting edge. He assured Admiral Good that though budget commitments might oblige him to withdraw some ships from the Seventh Fleet, he would send the best men available to man the rest.

The next morning Admirals Nomura and Hoshina arrived at Good's guest house to pay a call on Burke. Nomura was now eighty and almost blind but keen-minded as ever. The three admirals recalled their experiences in organizing the Maritime Defense Force. They discussed ways in which the United States and Japan could cooperate for their mutual benefit.

The following day Burke had an hour-long conference at the

Imperial Palace with Emperor Hirohito and a longer discussion at the Admiralty with Admiral Nagasawa and his top deputies. Both emperor and admiral expressed alarm about the Soviet Union's recent ICBM and Sputnik and sought reassurance. This was a subject Burke would have to deal with at each stop on his itinerary.

To Nagasawa and his officers Burke contended that Soviet missiles were less of a danger to Japan than the Red Fleet, especially its submarines prowling off the Japanese coasts. He urged them to strengthen their Self-Defense Force and assume more responsibility for their national security. He suggested moving their ships in to share Japanese bases now being occupied by U.S. naval forces so that when the latter pulled out, the Japanese could completely take over their own defense.

In South Korea, Burke found fierce old President Syngman Rhee looking forward to the day when he had the military strength to send his army north to unseat the communist government of North Korea and unite his country. Burke said advice on Korean unification was beyond his competence. He had come, he explained, merely as a sailor to assess the South Korean navy's potential for contributing to free world defense.

From Seoul, Burke flew to the Korean naval base at Chinhae. He was accompanied by another old friend, General Paik Sun Yup, now chief of staff of the Korean armies. They recalled adventures together in the Korean War, especially the night patrol when Burke's wristwatch alarm began ringing within hearing of the enemy.

"I'll bet you could have knocked my brains out with a gun butt," said Burke.

Paik grinned. "Wouldn't have stopped little bell," he said.

The South Korean fleet, composed of old U.S. subchasers, patrol craft, minesweepers, and LSTs, was capable of little beyond coast guard, inshore patrol, and limited escort duty, but the ships were clean and well handled and the crews were full of spirit. The nearby Korean Naval Academy, shabby and battered when Burke visited it in 1951, had been repaired and enlarged, and the library, which he had helped found, now contained a respectable number of volumes.

From Korea, Burke flew to inspect the Seventh Fleet, then at sea. This was the main purpose of his tour, and he had been looking forward to it. From the flagship, cruiser *Rochester,* and carriers *Bon Homme Richard* and *Kearsarge,* he spent four days moving through the fleet by helicopter and highline. At each arrival on board he was greeted by the time-honored rite of sideboys standing at attention while the bos'n's pipe shrilled. Whenever practical, he gave the ship's officers a pep talk, stressing the advantages of a naval career.

After a brief stop at Okinawa, Burke proceeded to Taiwan, where he was a guest of President Chiang Kai-shek. Chiang was vehemently resolved to lead a triumphant army back to mainland China—as unrealistic an ambition as Syngman Rhee's plan to unite Korea. Burke inspected Chiang's miniature fleet of destroyers and patrol craft and found it shipshape, its crews smart and efficient.

In a speech to the Nationalist Chinese leaders, Burke made clear his position. "I am a United States naval officer," he said. "I work for the United States Navy and my country. I do not work for the Chinese navy or the Nationalist Chinese. But here in this area of the world our two countries are mutually dependent upon each other. The better you operate as a navy, the less we have to do here; the more of our strength we can assign to other danger areas in the world."

One such area was the British crown colony of Hong Kong, last stop in Burke's itinerary. The British officers described the territory's defenses, and Burke explained how U.S. naval forces might help. The unspoken conviction, however, was that the crown colony, a mere peninsula of mainland China with adjacent islands, was untenable should China, from which the British had wrested it, choose to reannex it. This circumstance was acknowledged in 1984, when the prime ministers of Britain and China signed an accord formally granting China sovereignty over the British colony of Hong Kong in 1997.

Burke's return to Washington coincided with the launching of another, larger Russian satellite, Sputnik II, carrying a live dog. This new Soviet achievement, confirming earlier successes, provoked near-panic in Congress. The media sounded off with a blend of ridicule and alarm. What was wrong with our military establishment and with our research and development programs? Articles demanded compulsory science courses in high school and college, retraining of science teachers, rewriting of science textbooks—a publishing program that actually was carried out, at the cost of a billion dollars.

Neil McElroy, late president of Procter & Gamble, who had recently relieved Engine Charlie as secretary of defense, asked the services for proposals on how, despite the president's economies, they could accelerate their missile projects. In the general cutback even the high-priority Polaris program had had its funding reduced 5 percent.

The Science Advisory Committee, which had been studying problems posed by the new emergency, on 7 November issued a memorandum, known generally as the Gaither Report, that provided guidelines. It recommended accelerating U.S. missile programs and developing a system to provide warning of oncoming enemy missiles early enough to enable American missiles to be launched in a counterstrike.

The Gaither Report strongly endorsed the relatively invulnerable Polaris system, advocated striking for eighteen instead of the proposed six operational Polaris submarines by 1964, and urged efforts to achieve the goal at an earlier date. The committee suggested that the Soviets, undoubtedly recognizing the advantages of firing ballistic missiles from submerged submarines, probably had a Polaris project of their own, possibly already had FBM submarines in operation. Hence it behooved the Americans to increase their antisubmarine warfare capability.

Finally, the report recommended consolidating the Department of Defense by integrating research and development programs, streamlining the activities of the military departments, and centralizing command under the secretary of defense.

Navy Secretary Gates and Admiral Burke were in full agreement regarding acceleration of the Polaris program. Admiral Raborn's calculations showed that by temporarily accepting missiles with a range of 1,200 (instead of the targeted 1,500) miles and firing them from converted nuclear submarines, Polaris submarines could be in operation by early 1960. Conversion from nuclear-propelled submarine (SSN) to nuclear-propelled strategic-missile submarine (SSBN) would be achieved by slicing the former in half across the middle and inserting a 130-foot section to accommodate two rows of eight missile tubes and missile fire control and inertial navigation systems.

The air force tried to downgrade the accelerated program, expressing skepticism about its success, but Secretary McElroy gave it the green light and appropriated the necessary funds, "borrowed" from other naval projects.

Other "borrowed" funds were allocated to a stepped-up antisubmarine program, bringing into operation improved sonar, antisubmarine patrol craft and helicopters, and antisubmarine rockets. Burke set up an Atlantic Fleet Antisubmarine Defense Force to test such weapons together with hunter-killer and escort-of-convoy tactics. Such measures could not, however, guarantee that one or more Soviet submarines would not slip through and wreak devastating damage on U.S. targets.

It turned out that in rocketry the Soviet Union had attained a slight lead over the United States because U.S. Army missilemen had been developing a smaller, more manageable rocket to carry the smaller warhead then under development. The Soviets built a big rocket to carry the old, bulky warhead, and the extra power thus generated enabled them to achieve a propaganda victory by hoisting the Sputniks. The first American satellite, the army's Explorer, was sent into orbit 31 January 1958, four months after Sputnik I. The U.S. Navy sent its first satellite, Vanguard, into orbit on 17 March. By the end of 1959, the United States had put fifteen satellites into orbit, Russia only three.

Admiral Burke strongly opposed the Gaither Report recommendation to streamline and centralize the nation's military establishment. In a speech on 6 January 1958 in Washington before the National Press Club, he warned that assigning control of all U.S. combat forces to "one man, a military Solomon," would risk defeat in combat.

He favored retaining the Joint Chiefs of Staff unchanged because, he said, "it is particularly responsive to the requirements of modern global war. It is in harmony with our form of government. The dual status of the JCS members, who are also the uniformed chiefs of their services, is the inherent virtue of the system. Their dual status combines authority with responsibility to carry out plans. It assures reality. It avoids the ivory tower."

He disparaged the report's proposals for centralizing command under the secretary of defense. "These are proposals," he declared, "all leading toward more and more concentration of power, more and more autocracy by military policy and military decision, more and more suppression of differences of judgment, and more and more of what is described as 'swift efficiency of decision' as a substitute for debate and discussion of the military aspects of national policy."

Burke's speech made headlines all over the country, but it failed to impress President Eisenhower, who on other military matters valued Arleigh's judgment. On 3 April 1958, Eisenhower sent to Congress a special message on reorganization of the Department of Defense. Its chief recommendations were (1) to remove the service chiefs from the operational chain of command; (2) to restrict service secretaries to administration, relieving them of responsibility for military operations; (3) to restrict duties of Joint Chiefs of Staff mainly to advising the secretary of defense; (4) to enlarge the Joint Staff; and (5) to limit control of operating forces to the president and secretary of defense.

The president, probably with Burke in mind, told Secretary McElroy he expected all senior officers and officials to back his bill, and McElroy saw to it that the word got around, particularly to Burke. But Arleigh put duty to country over duty to the commander in chief. Summoned before the Senate Armed Services Committee, he said he could not support all the recommendations of the president's Pentagon reorganization bill. Concentrating power in the hands of the secretary of defense, he said, could lead to merger of the services or creation of a national general staff.

Secretary McElroy, queried by reporters, called Burke's testimony "regrettable." He said Burke was "a fine officer" but added he was disappointed that the admiral could not unreservedly support the administration's proposals. When a false rumor got around that Burke had been rebuked and was expected to resign, McElroy hastily called a press conference. "Admiral Burke is a man," said the secretary. "He has a right to make a decision. I wish he had supported the president's position, but nobody's going to tell Admiral Burke what to say if he doesn't believe it."

When the Defense Reorganization Act of 1958 was passed on 6 August, Burke and others of like mind were relieved that it did not pave the way for merger of the services or establishment of a national general staff. It did remove the navy's operating forces from direct control of the CNO, but that was to be expected. By previous law, the chief of naval operations executed the decisions of the Joint Chiefs of Staff. However, a series of strong CNOs, Admirals King, Nimitz, Sherman, Carney, and Burke, had, without protest from the JCS, increasingly taken operational control of the naval forces into their own hands. This was a concentration of power that Burke would have deplored in anyone's hands but his own. By odd coincidence, while Congress was still debating the issue, Burke exercised that power in two major naval actions, the Lebanon landings and the Formosa Strait crisis.

These U.S. interventions were in response to commitments President Eisenhower had made with the consent of Congress. As part of his policy to contain communism, he signed with the Nationalist

Chinese government a treaty by which the United States pledged itself to defend Taiwan and its adjacent Pescadores Islands. Following Gamal Nasser's seizure of the Suez Canal with Soviet-supplied weapons, the president obtained what became known as the Eisenhower Doctrine: authority to defend any Middle East country requesting help against communist aggression.

From the time he became CNO, Admiral Burke had taken meticulous pains to assure that the navy and the marine corps were in constant readiness to carry out national policy and presidential commitments. He recognized the defeat of British and French forces opposing the canal takeover as the outcome of the sort of laxness he resolved to preclude. When a coup d'état in Iraq upset the power balance in the Middle East, Burke alerted the Sixth Fleet and all other affected commands to prepare for trouble.

Trouble came promptly. Communist agents from Syria, now part of Nasser's United Arab Republic, instigated revolution in Lebanon. Lebanese President Camille Chamoun thereupon appealed to the United States for military aid pending a lawful election in his country. His request reached President Eisenhower at approximately 0700, 14 July 1958.

After daylong deliberation with an enlarged National Security Council, Eisenhower at 1648 queried Burke: "Can you land marines over the beaches of Beirut at precisely 0900 tomorrow morning, Washington time?" Burke's reply was an instantaneous "Affirmative."

Admiral Burke now began flashing get-ready dispatch orders worldwide. It had occurred to him that involvement of the Sixth Fleet in the Middle East might tempt communist China to make a grab for advantage in the Far East. Accordingly, he put the Seventh Fleet on a four-hour alert and activated the General Emergency Operation Plan, whereby all major naval units put to sea and took positions of maximum strategic advantage. The plan, devised to forestall another Pearl Harbor–type debacle, placed the Seventh Fleet where it could support Taiwan or reinforce the Sixth Fleet via the Indian Ocean.

A little before 2200, Burke turned flag plot over to his deputies, called for his car, and had himself driven to Admiral's House. Invitations had long since gone out for an intimate dinner party that evening at the Burkes', a social obligation that Arleigh did not take lightly. At home he greeted his guests affably, exhibited no signs of the strain under which he had been laboring, and did not mention

Lebanon. When he could politely do so, he excused himself and raced back to the Pentagon, where he remained at full alert for the next twenty-four hours.

At 0330, Washington time, on the morning of 15 July, Burke received a dispatch stating that elements of the Sixth Fleet were nearing the Lebanese coast and that the 2nd battalion, 2nd marines, would hit the beach near Beirut at 1500 Lebanon time (0900 Washington time). Backed by Sixth Fleet carriers, the marines landed on schedule against no resistance and took over the nearby airfield. Here planes, flying from the United States via Europe and Turkey, soon landed and disembarked several thousand more marines. This prompt and massive show of strength stabilized the situation in Lebanon, where peaceful elections were held in September. The last of the American forces were pulled out the following month.

Meanwhile, the Red Chinese were assembling forces as if planning to assault the island of Quemoy, just off the Chinese coast but still held by a 60,000-man Nationalist Chinese garrison. The Red Chinese regarded Quemoy as a stepping-stone toward their conquest of Taiwan, and the Nationalists clung to it as a way station for their return to the mainland.

Quemoy was not included within the U.S. guarantee of protection, and the American government had no intention of sponsoring a Nationalist Chinese assault on Red China. However, simply permitting the Reds to take Quemoy would surely embolden them to attempt further troublesome aggressions. Admiral Burke, therefore, with the approval of President Eisenhower and the Joint Chiefs of Staff, proposed to support the Nationalists in their defense of Quemoy by all means short of combat.

To beef up the Seventh Fleet striking force, Burke attached to it carriers *Hancock* out of Hong Kong, *Shangri-La* from Yokosuka, *Midway* from Pearl Harbor, and the Sixth Fleet's *Essex*, which raced 8,000 miles from the Mediterranean to join. From their decks, fighter aircraft flew defensive missions over Taiwan, thereby freeing the Nationalist air force to take on the Red Chinese air force. The Nationalist fighter aircraft, armed with the U.S. Navy's heat-seeking Sidewinder missiles, played havoc among the communist MiGs sent against Quemoy. To supply Quemoy's embattled garrison, Seventh Fleet combatant ships, at which communist gunners were careful not to fire, convoyed Nationalist landing craft to a point whence they could make a quick run to shore without heavy losses. Under the Nationalist counterattack backed by American sea and air power, the communist forces at last withdrew, leaving the Nationalists on Quemoy more firmly entrenched than ever.

The navy's prompt and effective interventions in the Lebanon and Taiwan crises of the summer of 1958 served as exemplary models of how such emergencies could be handled. They also provided an instructive alternative to Secretary Dulles's strategy of massive retaliation. The U.S. fleets had carried both strategic and so-called tactical nuclear weapons, which they never used and scarcely contemplated using.

Burke had from the beginning opposed massive-retaliation strategy. General Taylor, of like mind, had expressed his opposition before the Joint Chiefs, and Burke had seconded him. The notion of an all-out nuclear attack was unthinkable. The United States and the Soviet Union each had the might to devastate the other. The United States could not pledge itself, as the Soviet Union eventually did, not to be the first to strike with nuclear weapons. That would free the massive Red Army to roll over western Europe. So long, however, as the United States possessed the means of nuclear retaliation to employ in response to a general attack, the communists would restrict their aggressions to local and peripheral operations, and these could be contained by conventional weapons, as had been demonstrated in Korea, Lebanon, Quemoy, and elsewhere.

To study such problems, Admiral Burke upgraded the Navy Department's Long-Range Objectives Group, organized by Admiral Carney. He assigned to it some of the navy's brightest junior flag officers and moved it physically to offices adjacent to his own, where he could influence and be influenced by it.

The Objectives Group suggested that questions of U.S. nuclear strategy would be simplified if consideration of the retaliatory mission was separated from that of the preemptive-strike mission. Their conclusion was that the navy's primary missions in the foreseeable future would be (1) nuclear deterrence, (2) deterring or fighting limited wars, and (3) antisubmarine warfare. Since the navy's principal nuclear-deterrent weapon would be Polaris, which would supplement or partially replace the Strategic Air Command's vulnerable long-range bombers, the Objectives Group proposed building forty Polaris submarines instead of the eighteen recommended by the Gaither Report. The primary weapon for deterring and fighting limited wars, said the group, was the carrier strike force. These conclusions served to guide the navy's building program during the next several years.

Admiral Burke was still maintaining his mankilling schedule, on top of which he and Bobbie kept up a busy social life. Often after an early reception or cocktail party, Arleigh would return to the Pentagon and work till midnight. He and Bobbie entertained almost as often as they were entertained. Every two weeks, assisted by Burke's staffers and their wives, they hosted dinner parties for officers of all ranks and their ladies, mainly so that Arleigh could explore their views and expound his own. When the weather was fair and the guests could spill over into the observatory grounds, the Burkes held receptions for as many as 500 people. Such activities imposed an additional burden on Arleigh and Bobbie, of course, but one they enjoyed.

Sometimes even prospects for an enjoyable social gathering failed to penetrate Arleigh's professional concentration. One evening he was conferring with Secretary Gates, something of a workaholic himself, when Gates suddenly looked up at the big navy clock, which showed 2015. "Oh, my gosh, Arleigh," he said, "I was due at some damned black-tie dinner at eight o'clock." Turning to an aide, he asked, "Where am I having dinner tonight?"

Before the aide could check the log and answer, a look of dismay suffused Burke's countenance. "My God, Tom," he gasped, "it's *my* damned black-tie dinner you're due at, and we're both deep in the doghouse."

Once when Burke was planning to take a business trip, a friend living in the area he was to visit sent him a letter inviting him to stay at his home. Arleigh was most happy to accept the invitation, but he was puzzled over the letter's concluding words: "Bring your Ken Smiths." He didn't know what Ken Smiths were, and he was hesitant to ask lest they should prove to be something of a private, not to say intimate, nature.

Burke called in a trusted aide and showed him the letter. The aide was equally unable to identify Ken Smiths. Burke asked him to make discreet inquiries, on his own, not revealing on whose behalf he was investigating. The first golfer the aide queried had the answer. Ken Smiths were custom golf clubs made and sold by the well-known sporting-goods firm of Kenneth Smith. Burke's friend had assumed that he would be glad to take off time from his business to play a round or so of golf, but Arleigh did not play golf or any other game. The only game he ever observed was an occasional navy football contest. Ever devoted to the Naval Academy, he even participated, vigorously, in pep rallies preceding the Army-Navy game.

Even busy Secretary Gates became appalled by Burke's relentless work habits. Fearing that Arleigh, whom he genuinely liked, would suffer a breakdown under the load he put on himself, he once *ordered* him to take a vacation—get away from Washington, stay away at least a week, longer if he felt like it. Burke, a stranger to such junketing, was at a loss where to go. Finally he and Bobbie, on a colleague's advice, set out for the Homestead, a gracious vacation hotel at Hot Springs, Virginia. Here one played golf and tennis, swam, rode horseback, or hiked through the mountains. In the afternoon one might sit on the wide veranda, rocking and enjoying the splendid view. Then there was tea and, usually, a concert, followed by a formal dinner and dancing. The combination was calculated to cool the most overheated brain. Not Arleigh's. He was miserable. He did a good deal of pacing. On the third day he fled the place, and on the fourth he was happily back at his desk in Washington.

Captain William Mack relieved George Miller as Arleigh Burke's observer and critic and writer of special letters and reports. Since there is no record of any knock-down-drag-out fights between Mack and the admiral, it must be assumed that Burke had mellowed, which is unlikely, or that Mack was uncommonly tactful, or that the record is incomplete.

Arleigh's one recorded outburst against Mack occurred over a sore subject. One day in March 1959 the admiral came frowning back to his office.

"I've just been to the White House," he said. "I have always paced myself, as has my wife, to a four-year tour as chief of naval operations, and now they want me to take on two more years. I don't think I can do it."

No other CNO since World War II had served more than a single two-year term, and none had ever served more than two such terms. Burke had reluctantly accepted appointment for a second two-year term only because he had not yet attained all his original objectives. Now the Polaris system seemed a sure thing. The nuclear-propelled guided-missile cruiser *Long Beach* was scheduled to be launched in July. Building of the first nuclear-propelled aircraft carrier, *Enterprise,* was nearing completion. He had gotten younger flag officers into positions of high responsibility. His Naval Leadership Program was bearing fruit. His efforts opposing the massive-retaliation strategy, merger of the services, and establishment of a national general staff had been successful. Arleigh had been looking forward to retirement at the end of his second term in mid-August.

"You go down to your office," he said to Captain Mack, "and write down all the reasons why you think I shouldn't accept a third term."

Mack was back in about an hour. His list, some ten items, contained the standard reasons for Burke's not accepting reappointment: he had essentially completed his program, a new officer with new ideas was needed in the top billet, staying in office overlong held up promotions all down the line, and so on.

Burke ran his eyes down the list, muttering "Uh-huh, uh-huh, uh-huh" at each item. Then he got to a "but," followed by a list of reasons why he *should* stay. As his eyes ran down *this* list, his face became redder and redder.

"Dammit!" he roared. "I didn't tell you to do this."

"No, sir, you didn't," replied Mack smoothly, "but it's something you ought to think about."

Arleigh grinned but didn't commit himself. Other officers whose opinions he respected urged him to stay. Their advice only stiffened his intention to do otherwise. When he had assembled every good reason for not accepting reappointment, he went and recited them to President Eisenhower. The latter was not impressed. If he, despite declining health, had committed himself to carrying the presidential burden for eight years, robust Arleigh could stand being CNO for six.

Ike said simply, "It's your duty."

That ended it. Arleigh accepted the appointment. He was sworn in for a third term on 17 August 1959.

Burke had his triumphs during his final term. One was the first successful underwater launching of Polaris. On 20 July 1960, off Cape Canaveral, SSBN *George Washington,* converted from SSN *Scorpion,* submerged and with compressed air launched two successive Polaris missiles. On board a nearby ship, naval officers, newsmen, cameramen, congressional staff members, and representatives of industry observed the white-nosed rockets one after the other burst out of the water, ignite with an earsplitting blast, and trailing white tongues of flame streak off out of sight on their programmed courses toward their targets.

During operations the Polaris submarines would remain submerged, mostly cruising off the Eurasian continent, where their missiles could reach Soviet targets. Because duty in these submarines, in such circumstances, would be at best tedious, each would have two crews, called Blue and Gold, who would relieve each other at thirty-day intervals.

The feat of putting this new weapon system into operation only four years after its initial conception is paralleled only by the production of the atomic bomb in a similar span of time. Polaris was the achievement of many men, and Red Raborn gets chief credit. On the other hand, it was Arleigh Burke who launched the program. He was its motivator and to some extent its guide. He got the money for it. He promoted it at the secretary of defense level. He was continually behind it, goading, encouraging, financing, and defending it. Development of the Polaris system is rightly accounted one of CNO Burke's major achievements.

The air force, which had attempted to block development of Polaris, now tried to take it over. General Thomas S. Power, commander of the air force's Strategic Air Command, had submitted to the Joint Chiefs a plan whereby operations of the Polaris submarines would be put under his control. His argument was that all U.S. nuclear forces should be unified under the Strategic Air Command, which would direct the retaliatory response to an early radar warning of oncoming Russian nuclear missiles.

Admiral Burke, outraged by the proposal, fought it within the Joint Chiefs, before Congress, and in the press. He argued that turning Polaris over to generals with no experience in handling naval forces, let alone submarines, would be inefficient and dangerous. The Polaris submarines, while remaining under naval control, could join the Strategic Air Command in trading big bang for big bang. Or they could hold off at least in part and fire later, an option for delayed response denied bombers and land-based missiles because of their vulnerability.

Thomas Gates, now promoted to secretary of defense, bought the air force argument for a unified nuclear command. He proposed originating a Single Integrated Operational Plan (SIOP) for the employment of all strategic nuclear weapons in the American arsenal, including those on Polaris submarines and on attack carriers. The SIOP would be developed by a Joint Strategic Target Planning Staff so as to carry out the policies of the secretary of defense as approved by the president and the National Security Council.

To make the Target Planning Staff truly joint, at least in appearance, Gates appointed a naval officer, Vice Admiral Edward N. Parker, deputy director, and an officer from each of the services, army, navy, air force, and marine corps, as members. For director he appointed none other than General Power himself, wearing a second hat while still commanding the Strategic Air Command. To keep the Target Planning Staff from becoming too joint, Power so organized it that no matter how much it expanded, no fitness report on any officer would be written by anybody but an air force officer. He established it at Strategic Air Command headquarters in Omaha, Nebraska, about as far from salt water as any place in America.

To Admiral Burke the setup looked like an air force plot to deprive the navy of control of its carriers and Polaris submarines. He was not far wrong. General Power expected to run the whole operation with his SAC staff and a mere token effort from the other services. The token effort would supposedly be exerted in an Omaha conference on the SIOP, to which he invited the armed services and the Central Intelligence Agency to send representatives. Power had not been specific, but he expected each service or agency to send no more than three or four representatives. Burke packed the meeting by sending forty of the navy's savviest officers with instructions not to be "soft on the air force."

The result was pandemonium, and no chance of meeting the deadline set by President Eisenhower, who had ordered the Planning Staff to have the SIOP prepared and ready to implement before he left office in January 1961, just four months away. The navy's Captain Gerald Miller and the air force's Colonel Bill Crum, friends and members of the Planning Staff, decided to take matters into their own hands. Leaving the temporary representatives to their endless arguments, they slipped off to the BOQ and got to work. From their studies and their attendance at scores of earlier meetings, Miller and Crum knew what was available, how to find or calculate the parameters of everything, and what would be acceptable to the president and the secretary of defense. Thus informed, the captain and the colonel produced a practical plan well ahead of the deadline.

Regulations required them to pass all official information upward and outward through their commanding officer, who of course was General Power, but Captain Miller felt he owed his other boss, the CNO, advance data on measures that would affect naval operations. So, skirting regulations a little, he sent Admiral Burke a message he was coming and why and then flew to Washington. The CNO received Miller not in his office but in the big CNO conference room, crowded with navy brass and navy planners. Burke was in the chair, seated behind a big table. Because he already had some inkling of the unwelcome news he was about to hear, there was fire in his eyes.

Miller, at the end of the table, began his briefing, using a series of flip charts. As he proceeded, Burke's face grew ever redder. At last with a bang he brought his fist down on the table and began anathematizing Miller in potent and pungent language. When Miller had heard enough, he in his turn banged the table and shouted, "Goddammit, Admiral, I'm on the firing line. I'm out there waging this battle. If you don't like the way I'm doing it, fire me. Get another guy."

"No, by God," thundered Burke, "I'm not going to fire you. You're going to get back out there and do the job right."

"Okay," said Miller. "Get off my back."

Some of the younger officers present held their breath. They had never expected to hear a junior captain talk this way to the chief of naval operations. They had heard of officers being sacked or court-martialed for less blatant insubordination. The older hands, who knew Arleigh well, took it all in stride. Burke never hesitated to sound off in defense of what he believed or strongly felt, and he never held it against another man who did the same thing.

The integrated operation plan devised by Miller and Crum was approved with little change by General Power, by Secretary Gates, and finally by President Eisenhower. Thereafter Admiral Burke loyally kept his objections to himself, but he could not suppress his anxiety. The president passed the plan on to his successor, President John F. Kennedy, who had a committee of his own tinker with it and make minor revisions before he put it into effect. The SIOP, never used, remained in force for fifteen years and was canceled at last by President Carter, a former naval officer.

In his campaign for the presidency, Kennedy had made a major issue of the national military organization, which in its current form, he charged, bred duplication, waste, inefficiency, and incapacity for making decisions. As soon as he was elected, he appointed a committee to draw up proposals for reforming the defense establishment. Heading the committee, of all people, was Senator Stuart Symington, first secretary of the air force, and still a major air force spokesman.

In December 1960, Symington delivered his report to the president-elect, who released a summary to the press. Burke read it with horror. It called for complete reorganization of the armed forces along "functional" lines—army, navy, marine corps, and air force being replaced by monolithic entities comprising all infantry, all air, all amphibious, all carrier, all supply units, etc., the whole headed by an all-powerful chief of staff, responsible only to the president—

everything Arleigh had been battling against since World War II.

Burke called in Rear Admiral William C. Mott, judge advocate general of the navy. "Bill," he said, "we've got to do something. It looks like we're in for some kind of reorganization for sure. If all we can do is oppose the Symington plan, I think we'll lose. What we need is a constructive counterproposal. How about putting some of your lawyers to work on this?"

Mott handed the job to three of his brightest legal officers, who worked on it a month. They scarcely realized what a worked-over field they were plowing or how many previous such studies had come to naught. After preparing a voluminous survey of the national defense structure, they concluded that the Reorganization Act of 1958 required no revision, but that the secretary of defense needed an expanded staff to enable him to exercise the full authority vested in him by the act.

Admiral Mott, pleased with the report, sent one of its authors to summarize it for Admiral Burke at a meeting attended by top Opnav staffers. When the speaker argued for retention of the individual services, Burke smiled and nodded. He beamed when the speaker excoriated the national-chief-of-staff plan, but when he advocated reinforcing the authority of the secretary of defense, Burke looked stern. When the speaker recommended expanding the secretary's staff to facilitate his reaching decisions without input from other agencies, Burke leaped to his feet, roaring, "Bullshit!"

The lawyers' report went into the wastebasket. So, fortunately, did the Symington report, after Kennedy had time to read it and think it over.

Mott's lawyers had noticed in the course of their studies that Gates as secretary of defense had not exercised the full authority of his office. Perhaps his long association with the navy and with Arleigh Burke had imbued him with distrust of omnipotence.

Gates's successor, Robert McNamara, suffered from no such distrust. Brilliant and energetic, he had risen spectacularly to the presidency of the Ford Motor Company, from which position Kennedy appointed him to be his secretary of defense. Taking full advantage of the powers inherent in the office, McNamara, with little understanding of military operations, made himself in effect chief of staff of the U.S. armed forces. In this role he was to manage the Vietnam War, which ended in America's only defeat.

Senator Kennedy, in his campaign for the presidency versus Vice President Richard Nixon, criticized the Eisenhower-Nixon administration for permitting Fidel Castro's communist Cuban government to thrive "eight jet minutes from the coast of Florida." Kennedy pounded so hard on the theme of the Republicans' failure to act against Castro that former Secretary of State Dean Acheson warned him he was making things impossibly hard for himself. If he won the election through such criticisms, the public would expect him to do promptly what he had censured the preceding administration for not doing.

In fact, the Eisenhower administration had an eliminate-Castro project under way. Richard Bissell of the Central Intelligence Agency had proposed training a brigade of Cuban exiles to stage an amphibious landing on Cuba, on the mistaken assumption that anti-Castro elements in the country would flock to their banner. Eisenhower consented, provided the brigade was trained elsewhere than in the United States and the fact of U.S. sponsorship was concealed.

Bissell's proposed expedition was properly a job for the Department of Defense—to execute, to supervise, or at least provide advice. But the CIA spooks kept the project to themselves, presumably on the novel theory that high-ranking military officers cannot keep secrets. As it turned out, the Cuban brigade and their goal became the worst-kept secret of the decade. Newspapers told their story around the world, and in movie houses news reels showed the brigade training in Guatemala.

Had the CIA project toppled Castro before election day in November 1960, Nixon, riding in on a wave of public gratification, might have become president eight years earlier than in fact he did. But the brigade of exiled Cubans was far from ready, Castro remained in power, and Kennedy won the election. The CIA gave the president-elect a briefing, but there was not much the CIA could tell him he didn't already know from reading the papers. Anyway, he realized he had been handed a very hot potato that he couldn't drop—not after all the things he had said during his campaign.

Following President Kennedy's January 1961 inauguration, CIA spokesmen at last gave the Joint Chiefs a briefing. But the CIA men talked so long without saying what really needed to be said that the officers, puzzled and slightly stunned, remained silent, and Kennedy took their silence as approval. Spokesman for a subsequent Joint Staff task force, which studied the plan a little more completely, said its chances for success were "fair," an imprecise term, generally misinterpreted.

Burke called the CIA proposal "weak" and "sloppy." Afterward he reproved himself for not seeking a private meeting with the president to express sharp disapproval of the way the invasion was being planned and organized. In fact, however, he had not been told enough, and could not find out enough, to know how to frame a constructive criticism.

The invasion was scheduled at last for the night of 16–17 April 1961. A U.S. carrier task force would escort the small transports of the invaders from Guatemala to the waters south of Cuba and remain out of sight of land, never revealing its presence, while the transports moved in under cover of darkness to an inlet in the Cuban coast named the Bay of Pigs. As part of the elaborate pretense that Washington knew nothing about what was happening off Cuba, the White House went ahead with its annual Congressional Reception, which began at 2200 on the evening of the 16th.

Midway through the reception, Robert Kennedy, the president's brother, pale, entered the East Room. He drew aside Florida's Senator Smathers, who had been briefed on the Bay of Pigs expedition. "The shit has hit the fan," said Kennedy. "The thing has turned sour in a way you wouldn't believe."

When the reception broke up at midnight, President Kennedy, Vice President Johnson, Secretary of State Rusk, and Secretary of Defense McNamara, in white tie and tails, and Joint Chiefs Chairman General Lemnitzer and Admiral Burke, in dress uniform with medals, left the East Room and proceeded to the Oval Office. Here the CIA's Bissell and several White House staffers were waiting with a sheaf of dispatches full of bad news. Bissell said the situation was desperate but could still take a favorable turn if the president would authorize sending in aircraft from the carrier.

Burke concurred. "Let me take two jets and shoot down the enemy aircraft," he urged.

"No," said Kennedy and reminded them that he had said "over and over again" that he would not commit U.S. forces to combat. He apparently did not want the world to find out what the world already knew, that the whole expedition had been conceived, planned, and armed by the United States.

Burke suggested sending in a destroyer from the task force. It could arrive in the Bay of Pigs in less than two hours. Its guns could knock out Castro's tanks and might change the whole course of the battle.

The president, annoyed, raised his voice. "Burke," he snapped, "I don't want the United States involved in this."

"Hell, Mr. President," Burke snapped back, "but we *are* involved!"

As the world knows, the Bay of Pigs expedition ended in total failure with every invader killed or captured.

For Burke, though not directly involved, the debacle was deeply distressing, more so than for any other operation of what had been for him a generally unsatisfactory third term in office. He had previously accomplished all he was likely to accomplish. He was tired and discouraged. He had submitted his resignation before the election of 1960. Since then Kennedy had several times offered to reappoint him, but Burke each time declined the offer. When it was clear that Burke's days as CNO were numbered, the president offered him the ambassadorship to Australia. Burke declined that too, considering himself unqualified.

On 25 July 1961 in a ceremony at the White House, President Kennedy awarded Burke a third Distinguished Service Medal. A week later, 1 August, at the Naval Academy, where six years earlier he had been sworn in as CNO, Burke relinquished the office to Admiral George W. Anderson. He then, after forty-two years of naval service, had his four-star flag hauled down for the last time. Excusing himself, he retired briefly and returned in civilian clothes, to say farewell as a private citizen to his assembled friends.

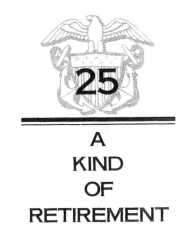

25

A
KIND
OF
RETIREMENT

AT THE TIME of Burke's retirement, Secretary of the Navy John B. Connally sent him the usual formal letter listing and praising his major achievements. He sent Burke also a less formal note according praise he felt equally deserved:

> Dear Admiral Burke:
>   When a man achieves greatness, he is almost always backed and aided every foot of the way by a wonderful and devoted wife. It is beyond my official power to award Mrs. Burke the decoration she so richly deserves; however, I want to say that you have been most fortunate in your wife's choice of a husband.
>   To Mrs. Burke and to you, may the best of everything be yours for many years to come.

For some time the Burkes, chiefly Bobbie, had been looking for a new home conveniently and attractively located. In the spring of 1961 they found what they wanted on Fenway Drive in Bethesda, Maryland, just outside the beltway encircling Washington. On 1 August the Burkes drove directly from Admiral's House to the change of command ceremony at the Naval Academy and from there to Fenway Drive, where they found to their dismay that their stored furniture had not been delivered. That evening Secretary and Mrs. Connally had the Burkes in for dinner. After the delicious meal in pleasant surroundings with good friends, the late chief of naval operations and his lady returned to Fenway Drive and slept on the floor.

Arleigh, realizing that after a career of intense activity he could not bear a life of mere idleness, sought council from friends outside the navy on how to use his time after retirement. Their advice, which he followed, was to apportion his pursuits about equally between business employment and public service. He had already received a number of offers to enter business and had tentatively decided to accept one from Texaco, Inc.

First, however, Arleigh and Bobbie took a vacation, their only extended leave since their wedding thirty-eight years before. Prior to leaving, Burke moved his personal papers into a temporary office assigned to him in the old Main Navy building. Here he posted Commander C. R. Wilhide, his public relations officer, to answer his mail, which continued to arrive in such quantity as to leave the commander no long stretches of idleness.

Arleigh and Bobbie departed in their ancient Plymouth for quiet, sleep, and fishing at the town of Cedarville, population 300, on Michigan's Upper Peninsula near the Straits of Mackinac. The trip there was not entirely uneventful. While they were tooling along through Ohio, an axle of their car broke and left them immobile in the highway. They were towed to a Plymouth sales and service agency, where they were informed that repairs on their car would take some time. Arleigh received the news philosophically. After dickering for a good price for his wreck, he bought a new Plymouth. He had, he said, been planning to buy one at the conclusion of the trip.

Before they could resume their journey, word got around among the townspeople that 31-Knot Burke was in their midst. A newspaper reporter and a photographer arrived, and a crowd began to gather. Bobbie, after excusing herself to comb her windblown hair, posed with Arleigh and the new car, and the Burkes drove off waving to the assembled public.

At Cedarville the Burkes stayed with friends who owned a cottage there. How many fish Arleigh and Bobbie caught is not recorded, but they enjoyed the novel experience of quiet and rest. In September they bade farewell to their hosts and left Michigan for a leisurely automobile tour of eastern Canada and the U.S. East Coast. Refreshed and happy, they returned home in early October.

Shortly afterward, Burke reported to Texaco's Washington head-quarters as a director, elected by shareholders, and a member of the corporation's executive committee. As a participant in the board of directors, he was responsible for resolving such questions as what part of the company's income should be distributed as dividends. The executive committee had the related function of allotting funds and approving expenditures. Having a man of Burke's reputation in such key fiduciary roles helped Texaco maintain shareholder confidence. Arleigh, however, had no intention of serving as a mere symbol of integrity. As he had done so often before in the varying duties to which the Navy assigned him, he applied his skill as a quick learner to mastering his new responsibilities.

Because his duties with Texaco were part-time, Burke could further apply his new practical expertise by accepting directorships with additional firms—Chrysler Corporation, Thiokol Corporation, Capital Radio Engineering Institute, and Newport News Ship-building and Dry Dock Company. He met with his fellow directors of each of these companies at intervals, usually quarterly, to provide services and advice. Such employment earned Burke income considerably handsomer than the navy pay he and Bobbie had subsisted on through the years. The only noticeable change in their deport-ment, however, was that they now could contribute more liberally than before to causes they believed in.

In the area of public service, Burke did duty on advisory commit-tees for educational institutions, patriotic groups, and veterans' or-ganizations. Possibly because he never had any children of his own, he derived particular satisfaction from his service from 1962 to 1974 as president and executive committee member of the National Capi-tal Area Council of the Boy Scouts of America.

Burke considered himself launched on a new career. In this new life he hoped as before to attain recognition and advancement solely through merit and effort and not from past reputation. He did not expect to use the office of chief of naval operations as a springboard. On his new stationery he identified himself simply as Arleigh Burke. He suggested that his business and service associates address him or refer to him as Arleigh or Mr. Burke. His scheme did not work. He had made too deep an impression on the public mind to be anything but Admiral Burke, or perhaps 31-Knot Burke.

In an interview, Bobbie had this to say about Arleigh's new career:

I think he was very happy with his initial offer from a big company, and before he knew it he seemed to be having many opportunities. I think he has never ceased to have a sort of naive wonder, and this made it difficult for him to refuse. However, I think at last he has found that he really cannot be more than two or three people, and he has learned to say no.

It's good for him that he has been able to have such adventures in the business world, because he entered it knowing nothing. Very few service people know much about business. They are away so much that their wives take care of things, in the main. So he has had a great adventure and a challenge, and that's important to a man like Arleigh. I think he has been happy and never looked back. With it, he's been traveling a bit, and that gives him variety and compensates for the old cruise time. Also he has found, to his delight, that in a number of these big companies important people are retired navy people, and that makes him very happy. He feels that they are still proving their worth.

Late one afternoon in the autumn of 1961, Burke received in his Navy Department office a caller with an idea. It was David Abshire, a 1951 graduate of West Point who had served in the Korean War and subsequently earned a 1959 Ph.D. from Georgetown University. Married to the daughter of Admiral George Anderson, commander Sixth Fleet and Burke's friend and successor as chief of naval operations, Abshire had met Burke, but only socially. Now he had come on business.

Abshire and a few associates had interested Georgetown's dean of the graduate school and its chairman of the department of government in organizing at the university a center for studies in strategic problems confronting free societies. It would be set up to mobilize the nation's best minds toward helping the American public and its leaders to maintain a strategic view of the world and their role in it.

To launch such a project the group needed a director who was both dynamic and contemplative, a strong leader who was also an intellectual, a man known to the military, to scholars, to politicians, and to the general public. Abshire said he and his friends had concluded that the description uniquely fitted Burke, and they invited him to head their program.

Burke, who had learned to say no, declined the invitation. The proposed association, he agreed, could prove immensely useful, but it needed a full-time director. He himself was already committed to too many enterprises to do it justice. He suggested that it should be headed by an academic. Abshire did not concur. A professor at the helm, he said, might incline it toward abstruseness and the ivory tower. To be useful, its output had to be comprehensible and convincing to public, Congress, and administration. Burke said that while he was too busy to form or guide the suggested organization, he was interested and would like to be kept informed. Abshire left, convinced he had his man.

After waiting a reasonable spell to let Burke sort over his priorities, Abshire called on him again. He now had a name for the organization: the Center for Strategic Studies. Burke liked it. Abshire said he had discussed the problem with friends whose opinions he respected, and all were agreed that the center could not be formed without Burke. Nobody else, they said, at least nobody out of national office, had the background and stature that would persuade the nation's brightest thinkers to submit papers, or prompt the nation's leaders to heed the advice the papers contained. Burke gave in. He would head the center, he said, but only if Abshire served as executive director and really executed the center's business. Abshire delightedly agreed.

During the planning stage, before the actual establishment of the center, Burke and Abshire exchanged memoranda and conferred from time to time. They discussed how to guide their authors toward common goals without dictating their approaches. The center would do government work without working for the government. That is to say, it would make itself useful to the government but accept no government contracts, because the government, as employer, could then call the tune. Instead, it would rely on the foundations for financial support.

As for structuring of the center, Burke hearkened back to the successes of the Navy Department's small, low-budget General Board and Strategic Plans Division. "This should be a lean organization," he wrote. "It should be hungry. It should not have too much money. People should be overworked rather than underworked. There should be too small a staff. The reasons for this are that many organizations have become so overorganized, and their administrative staff has become so elevated, that the output becomes either mediocre or poor."

In the summer of 1962, Abshire, with advice from Burke, set up an executive board to serve as a sort of steering committee, to guide the writers they were enlisting, and an advisory board to keep a

critical eye on the whole operation. The former consisted of Arleigh
Burke, as director, David Abshire, as executive secretary, Georgetown's graduate school dean and government department head, and
two other men with backgrounds both academic and managerial.

The advisory board was a carefully calculated eleven-man mix:
Neil McElroy, former secretary of defense; John H. Sullivan, former secretary of the navy; Robert Anderson, former secretary of the
treasury; Karl Bendetsen, former under secretary of the army; Arthur Radford and Nathan Twining, former chairmen of the Joint
Chiefs of Staff; a Republican and a Democratic senator and a Republican and a Democratic congressman; and the director of the National Science Foundation.

Georgetown University provided the Center for Strategic Studies with office and conference space. Abshire, with Arleigh Burke's
name to flourish, had no trouble extracting operating funds from the
foundations. Burke, his interest aroused, began spending as much
time at Georgetown as he could spare from his other commitments.
He conferred with Abshire almost daily and with the other executive board members frequently.

The initial topic for study was Development of Political, Military,
and Economic Strategies to Win the Cold War Without Resort to
Armed Conflict, concerning which pundits of national reputation
would be invited to submit essays. Since writing the papers would
take time from their professional activities, the participants would
receive appropriate remuneration.

To get the Center for Strategic Studies off to a healthy start, it
was imperative that the opening panel and its products be first-rate.
Each member of the center's executive board was acquainted with
at least two or three top writer-thinkers who could be counted on
to produce outstanding essays and defend them professionally, but
Burke's contacts with the nation's sages far outnumbered the rest.
In the course of his studies with the General Board, the Brookings
Institution, and the Strategic Plans Division, and in his personal
search for enlightenment, he had made contact with many of the
country's brightest pen-wielding intelligentsia. He and the rest of
the board, making use of their connections, assembled an extraordinary panel of thirty-six authorities, ranging from Edward Teller,
"father of the hydrogen bomb," to Henry Kissinger, future secretary of state.

As the writers finished their essays, they circulated them among
themselves, and the executive board selected from them key debat-

able issues. These became the basis for discussion at a conference at Georgetown, 23–25 January 1963. The meeting, which opened with an address by Senator Henry M. Jackson, was attended by all the participants, by the center's executive and advisory boards, and by a large audience. The essays and discussions were subsequently published in a volume, *National Security: Political, Military, and Economic Strategies in the Decade Ahead,* for which Burke wrote a penetrating introduction.

Having thus been launched with great éclat, the center grew rapidly, changed its name to Center for Strategic and International Studies (CSIS), detached itself from Georgetown University, and at length occupied seven floors in an office building in the heart of Washington's business district. Usually managing to keep a step or two ahead of current world problems, it had an increasing influence on the national government. Its advisory board expanded to more than 150 men and women, all national leaders, including a dozen U.S. senators and a cardinal of the Roman Catholic Church.

Arleigh Burke, who had played a major, probably indispensable, role in founding, organizing, and developing the CSIS, eventually resigned as director, remained several more years on the staff as a counselor, and then withdrew altogether. Perhaps he felt that he had done his part in getting so useful a project under way, and that his services were no longer essential and might be more usefully employed in other pursuits.

Burke never ceased giving speeches, some out of duty without charge, most for a fee, handled through a lecture bureau. His subjects generally related to areas he knew best—the Soviet threat, the cold war, and military strategy—but his extensive reading and writing enabled him to venture into other fields. His speaking career reached a sort of pinnacle in his delivery in the spring of 1962 of the Walter E. Edge Lectures at Princeton University.

Burke's Princeton lectures were in several respects a remarkable achievement. That a leading university would invite a military man to deliver them and that Burke had the self-confidence to accept attest to his recognized intellectual stature. A mystery is how he found time to prepare them while he was busy organizing the Strategic Center, along with his numerous other projects. There was nothing slapdash about the lectures. They were clear, carefully worded, and convincing, and they show a firm grasp of history. *Orbis: Quarterly Journal of World Affairs,* published by the Foreign Policy Research Institute of the University of Pennsylvania, saw fit in its summer 1962 edition to print a condensed version of what Burke had to say.

Burke titled his lectures "Power and Peace." They were about how to win the cold war, roughly the topic assigned to the writers for the Strategic Center. None of these, however, had submitted their essays when Burke spoke at Princeton. His speeches were based on his own observations and conclusions while wrestling since World War II with the problems posed by communism.

The enemy, Burke pointed out, was not the Russian or Chinese people but the communist movement and its advocates, whose aim was to participate in what they regarded as the ruthless process of history by destroying the existing order and supplanting it with world communism. The communist movement, said Burke, could be stopped by the exercise of power, which he defined as influence, ranging all the way from pure persuasion to pure force, including armed force.

"A state has power," he stated, "when it has the ability to compel other states to pattern their behavior after its own ideas." He gave two examples, the *Pax Romana* and the *Pax Britannica*. The Roman Empire, he said, "was maintained by a combination of justice, interest, advantage, penalties, pressure, persuasion, and at the margin, force. The entire structure became dependent on the Romans' will to use the power available to them—military power if necessary, economic or psychological power if that sufficed. Those who accepted the leadership of Rome became prosperous. Those who did not were penalized economically, politically, socially."

The British Empire similarly exercised power, said Burke. "Under the *Pax Britannica*," he added, "the order of the world depended on the Royal Navy." Trade was the heart of the system, and the British navy kept the trade routes open. In fact, if not in name, the pound sterling served as the world currency. "England controlled the course of events. By trade preferences, by persuasion and cajoling, by the sheer power of prestige, and by shrewd manipulation of the ambitions and desires of leaders and peoples, England was able to convince the world that what England wanted was beneficial, not only for England but for everyone else as well."

Burke pointed at the period following World War I and during the Great Depression, when major nations through disarmament and laxity created a power vacuum in which total dictatorships emerged. "Thus," said Burke, "World War II was caused by a failure of the Allies to use their power responsibly. Consequently a small group of men used the lesser power available to them so effectively that it took the combined resources of the world to defeat them."

In conclusion, Burke got down to his basic proposal. "Our earlier policies," he said, "envisaged two major territorial powers facing each other in the traditional way. From this basic error derived such territory-centered policy proposals as containment, rollback, and withdrawal." On the contrary, he said, "The American policy here envisages the destruction of an ideological movement. This policy depends, not on any particular form of power, but on all forms of power. It is oriented to a world order guaranteed by the power of the United States in cooperation with the wider base of power of the North Atlantic Community. With the North Atlantic Community as its core, the free world can defeat communism and bring peace and order to the whole world."

In the decades following Burke's lectures, Japan, South Korea, Taiwan, and Hong Kong came to rival the Atlantic Community in wealth and productiveness. The industrial, noncommunist countries of both the Atlantic and the Pacific communities then exercised power against communism by their evident prosperity, their exercise of freedom, their regard for human rights, and the practicality of their politics.

The people of the Soviet Union and its satellite states, of China, and of Vietnam, after decades of shortages, shoddy goods, poor living conditions, injustice, and despotism, at last began facing the fact that communism is based on unworkable economics and a false interpretation of history. Among their other vexations was the sight of hundreds of thousands of foreign tourists annually visiting Moscow, East Berlin, Beijing, Leningrad, Shanghai, and other cities within the communist sphere while they themselves, even if they had the means, were not permitted to travel outside their country or even outside their neighborhood without very special permission.

In the late 1980s, Burke and the rest of the free world watched with hopeful interest the reforms initiated in the Soviet Union by Mikhail Gorbachev and the Polish free elections that turned communist leaders out of office. They observed with compassion the flight of Vietnamese by boat from their destitute communist homeland to prosperous Hong Kong, and they recoiled in horror from the brutal suppression by a frightened communist Chinese government of student-worker demonstrations for democracy and an end to corruption. Did these developments, they wondered, herald the imminent end of the communist experiment, or were they mere incidents in a frustrated people's progress toward their eventual casting off of the Marxist albatross?

Among Burke's post-retirement exercises of civic duty was his testimony before the Senate Armed Services Committee in August 1963 in opposition to the nuclear-test-ban treaty, his support in 1964 for Republican Senator Barry Goldwater's campaign for the presidency, and his journey to his ancestral homeland in September 1973 as President Richard Nixon's representative and head of the U.S. delegation to the funeral of Sweden's King Gustavus VI. The Swedes, despite their national mourning, paid much attention to one of their countrymen twice removed who had made good, very good indeed, in the United States.

On 10 January 1977, in recognition of Burke's many post-retirement contributions to his country, President Gerald Ford conferred upon him the nation's highest civilian award, the Medal of Freedom. Foreign countries bestowed on Burke no fewer than twenty-six decorations, some during his frequent travels abroad, others in ceremonies at Washington embassies.

The foreign recognition Burke at first found most puzzling was an invitation to join the Rabaul Kai, an organization of Japanese veterans who, based on Rabaul, had fought against both MacArthur's Southwest Pacific and Halsey's South Pacific forces, including Burke's Little Beavers. The Rabaul Kai was headed by Vice Admiral Jinishi Kusaka, Burke's adversary in the 1943 Solomons campaign and his toast-offering guest at dinner in Tokyo.

Burke, mystified, wrote to Kusaka, "I don't think you want me there. I don't think your organization understands. I fought as hard as I could against you. I wouldn't want to come under false pretenses."

By return mail, Kusaka wrote back, "We know all about you, and that's why we want you."

Burke tells what followed:

> So I went over there. I went through this whole Shinto ceremony at the Yasukuni Shrine, complete with cleansing, sake toasts, and palm leaves, and became a member of their society. I had to make several speeches, of course. The Japanese love to make speeches, and they love to have other people make speeches, too, so I had to make many speeches to this organization—at the ceremony, at the dinner, at a meeting that they had. I became a kind of blood brother.

Burke listened with great fortitude to the Japanese talks, of which he didn't understand a word. Even the speech-loving Japanese must have found the proceedings a test of patience, since chances are that very few of them had any idea what Arleigh was saying.

After the ceremony, Burke, in conversation with a couple of English-speaking members, at last learned why he was there. It was in response to an event of 22 February 1943 in the Bismarcks (chapter 6, above). Burke with five destroyers had encountered a Japanese tug and by signal demanded her surrender. Instead, the Japanese captain opened fire with his one small gun, and Burke's destroyers promptly sent him down with their twenty 5-inchers. The Americans picked up a good many survivors from the water. When it was clear that their gallant captain was not among them, Burke ordered a one-minute prayer service in his memory.

After the war, the survivors brought the story home to Japan. The Japanese were much impressed, because Burke had done exactly what they would have done. They honored gallantry, even among the enemy. When a U.S. plane crashed in Japan, with the fliers killed, the Japanese gave them honorable burial because they had done their duty.

Arleigh Burke, as long as he was able, continued to carry heavy responsibilities and do a prodigious amount of work. In his early eighties, however, nature at last called a halt, or at least a slowdown. In May 1983, invited to attend meetings of the CSIS Advisory Board, he replied in part:

> Your very kind and most generous invitation to meet with your distinguished committee in June and September is a great honor and I'm proud that you would consider including me in your deliberations. Naturally, I was strongly tempted to accept regardless of my misgivings [but] since my eyes have deteriorated to the point where I cannot drive at night and need a very strong light and a magnifying glass to read ordinary print, I have resigned from every responsible position I held because I have a dread of having obligations I can no longer meet. . . . I must reluctantly conclude that I cannot contribute anything worthwhile to your meetings. I am not now familiar with the present day projects. I am not up to date on the subjects with which the Center must deal. I cannot read myself into the picture now. It takes me an inordinately long time to accomplish small tasks. I have noted other people being "carried" on a board to which they did not contrib-

ute, and that is not a desirable situation. It would be unfair to your committee and to the Center for me to accept your very generous invitation.

Becoming increasingly blind, Arleigh gave up reading altogether, and Bobbie read to him. To the ever-patient Bobbie, he dictated answers to his many letters received. She wrote them in her neat handwriting, and he signed them in a big scrawl. In 1986, deciding that maintaining their Bethesda home had become too great a burden for them, they moved into an apartment in the Virginian, an attractive retirement community in Fairfax, Virginia, a few miles west of Washington.

Though Arleigh had left the main stage of history, he was far from forgotten. To those who loved the navy and knew his contribution to it, he was a living legend, and to those who knew the Burkes as a couple, Bobbie was very much a part of the legend. They received many invitations, including to dinners at the White House. They received far more bids than they could accept, but they were no stay-at-homes. Arleigh even attended symposia and other meetings where he was not expected to be an active participant. At the Virginian the Burkes were hosts to many callers, famous and not so famous, who came to pay their respects.

A chair was established at the Center for Strategic and International Studies "in honor of the co-founder and first director." The Arleigh A. Burke Chair in Strategy would "support an outstanding authority in the field of strategy, resources and maritime affairs whose work and character will serve to promote the principles of public service and the ideals of freedom to which Admiral Burke has dedicated his life."

In April 1989, the navy flew the Burkes to Newport for the dedication of Admiral Arleigh A. Burke Hall, a new classroom building at the Naval War College. After Secretary of the Navy Lawrence Garrett and Burke had spoken, Bobbie cut the ribbon across the entrance, thus opening the hall for use.

In mid-September of 1989, the Burkes were flown to Bath, Maine, for the launching at the Bath Iron Works of the Aegis guided-missile destroyer *Arleigh Burke,* first of her class. After remarks by Chief of Naval Operations Carlisle Trost, Governor of Maine John McKernan, and other dignitaries, Secretary Garrett and Admiral and Mrs. Burke spoke. Then Bobbie christened the destroyer in her husband's name, and the ship, cheered by some 10,000 guests and other onlookers, slid majestically down the ways into the Kennebec River. That evening Admiral and Mrs. Burke were guests of honor at a dinner of Little Beavers and their families in the main ballroom of a Bath hotel. The one-time dashing young destroyermen of the battles of Empress Augusta Bay and Cape St. George, now white-haired, many on canes, but spirited as ever, were united by the memory of their Solomons adventures and by their loyalty to Burke.

Clara and Oscar Burke's firstborn from the hardscrabble farm at the foot of the Rockies had dedicated his life to the navy with almost unparalleled devotion. In the Solomons as 31-Knot Burke he had emulated the dash and fury of his Viking ancestors. As Pete Mitscher's right-hand man, he had played a major role in conducting the Big Blue Fleet across the Pacific to the shores of Japan, storming enemy strongholds along the way. In the following years he had made major contributions to every aspect of the navy, from strategy to shipbuilding and weapons development and, above all, to the formulation of ideas, which served not only as beacons for the navy but as wise suggestions to the national government. Now, with Bobbie at his side, the old Viking was savoring the honors he had justly earned.

ACKNOWLEDGMENTS

I COULD NOT have completed this book in anything like the time available without the active participation of my wife, Grace. She was my chauffeur to sources of information, a meticulous note-taker at interviews, and my partner in every phase of the research, from copying data from ships' logs at the National Archives to digging through the daunting files of Burke papers at the Naval Historical Center. Her biggest project, carried out with the cooperation of Alice Creighton and her assistants of the special collections section, Nimitz Library, U.S. Naval Academy, was combing through more than fifty oral histories and copying out for my use everything any of the interviewees said about Arleigh Burke. Another of her contributions, no less valuable, was reading and commenting on my chapters as I completed them. Lastly, she was my collaborator in the preparation of the index.

Dean Allard, director of naval history, and his assistants at the Naval Historical Center, particularly in the operational archives and the photographic center, have, as always, been obliging and efficient. At the U.S. Naval Institute, Paul Stillwell and Patty Maddocks and their assistants were helpful in providing, respectively, copies of oral histories and of naval photographs.

At Random House, Robert Loomis, vice president and executive editor, kept in touch and encouraged me throughout the composition of this book, then read the text and suggested minor but useful revisions before the pages went to the copy editor.

My former colleagues, sharp-eyed Edwin Hall and Arthur A. Richmond, have again, as for previous books of mine, devoted many hours to scanning the proofs for misprints and other slips.

SOURCES

BOOKS

Abshire, David M., and Richard V. Allen. *National Security: Political, Military, and Economic Strategies in the Decade Ahead.* New York: Frederick A. Praeger, 1963.

Acheson, Dean. *Present at the Creation: My Years in the State Department.* New York: W. W. Norton, 1969.

Adams, Henry H. *Witness to Power: The Life of Fleet Admiral William D. Leahy.* Annapolis, Md.: Naval Institute Press, 1985.

———. *Years to Victory.* New York: David McKay, 1973.

Albion, Robert Greenhalgh, and Robert Howe Connery. *Forrestal and the Navy.* New York and London: Columbia University Press, 1962.

Baar, James, and William E. Howard. *Polaris!* New York: Harcourt, Brace, 1960.

Bartley, Whitman S. *Iwo Jima: Amphibious Epic.* Washington, D.C.: Historical Branch, G-3 Division, Headquarters, U.S. Marine Corps, 1954.

Blair, Clay. *The Forgotten War: America in Korea, 1950–1953.* New York: Times Books, 1987.

———. *Silent Victory: The U.S. Submarine War Against Japan.* Philadelphia and New York: Lippincott, 1975.

Belote, James H. and William M. *Titans of the Seas: The Development and Operations of Japanese and American Carrier Task Forces During World War II.* New York: Harper & Row, 1975.

————. *Typhoon of Steel: The Battle for Okinawa.* New York: Harper & Row, 1970.

Borklund, Carl W. *Men of the Pentagon: From Forrestal to McNamara.* New York: Frederick A. Praeger, 1966.

Braun, Wernher von, and Frederick I. Ordway III. *History of Rocketry and Space Travel.* New York: Thomas Y. Crowell, 1969.

Bradley, Omar N., and Clay Blair. *A General's Life.* New York: Simon & Schuster, 1983.

Bryan, J., III. *Aircraft Carrier.* New York: Ballantine Books, 1954.

Buell, Thomas B. *Master of Sea Power: A Biography of Fleet Admiral Ernest J. King.* Boston: Little, Brown, 1980.

————. *The Quiet Warrior: A Biography of Raymond A. Spruance.* Boston: Little, Brown, 1974.

Cagle, Malcolm W., and Frank A. Manson. *The Sea War in Korea.* Annapolis, Md.: United States Naval Institute, 1957.

Caraley, Demetrios. *The Politics of Military Unification: A Study of Conflict and the Policy Process.* New York: Columbia University Press, 1966.

Clark, J. J., and Clark G. Reynolds. *Carrier Admiral.* New York: David McKay, 1967.

Coffin, Tristram. *The Passion of the Hawks: Militarism in Modern America.* New York: Macmillan, 1964.

Coletta, Paolo E., ed. *American Secretaries of the Navy.* 2 vols. Annapolis, Md.: Naval Institute Press, 1980.

Davis, Vincent. *The Admirals Lobby.* Chapel Hill, N.C.: U. of North Carolina Press, 1967.

Dyer, George Carroll. *The Amphibians Came to Conquer: The Story of Admiral Richmond Kelly Turner.* 2 vols. Washington, D.C.: U.S. Government Printing Office, 1971.

Eisenhower, Dwight D. *The White House Years: Waging Peace, 1956–1961.* Garden City, N.Y.: Doubleday, 1965.

Field, James A., Jr. *History of United States Naval Operations: Korea.* Washington, D.C.: U.S. Government Printing Office, 1962.

————. *The Japanese at Leyte Gulf: The Sho Operation.* Princeton, N.J.: Princeton University Press, 1947.

Forrestel, E. P. *Admiral Raymond A. Spruance, USN: A Study in Command.* Washington, D.C.: U.S. Government Printing Office, 1966.

Geffen, William, ed. *Command and Commanders in Modern Warfare.* Colorado Springs: U.S. Air Force Academy, 1969.

Goldberg, Alfred, ed. *History of the Office of the Secretary of Defense.* Vol. I, Steven L. Reardon, *The Formative Years, 1947–1950.* Washington, D.C.: Office of the Secretary of Defense, 1984.

Hammond, Paul Y. "Super Carriers and B-36 Bombers: Appropriations, Strategy and Politics," in Stein, below.

Higgins, Trumbull. *The Perfect Failure: Kennedy, Eisenhower, and the CIA at the Bay of Pigs.* New York: W. W. Norton, 1987.

Hubbard, Douglass, ed. *The Best of Burke.* Fredericksburg, Texas: Admiral Nimitz Foundation, 1986.

Jones, Ken. *Destroyer Squadron 23: Combat Exploits of Arleigh Burke's Gallant Force.* Philadelphia and New York: Chilton Books, 1959.

Jones, Ken, and Hubert Kelley, Jr. *Admiral Arleigh (31-Knot) Burke: The Story of a Fighting Sailor.* Philadelphia and New York: Chilton Books, 1962.

Kerr, "Andy" (Alex Arthur). *A Journey Amongst the Good and the Great.* Annapolis, Md.: Naval Institute Press, 1987.

King, Ernest J., and Walter Muir Whitehill. *Fleet Admiral King: A Naval Record.* New York: W. W. Norton, 1952.

Layton, Edwin, Roger Pineau, and John Costello. *"And I Was There": Pearl Harbor and Midway—Breaking the Secrets.* New York: William Morrow, 1985.

Lewin, Ronald. *The American Magic: Codes, Ciphers and the Defeat of Japan.* New York: Farrar, Straus & Giroux, 1982.

Lockwood, Charles A., and Hans Christian Adamson. *Battles of the Philippine Sea.* New York: Thomas Y. Crowell, 1967.

Love, Robert William, Jr., ed. *The Chiefs of Naval Operations.* Annapolis, Md.: Naval Institute Press, 1980.

Mammarella, Giuseppi. *Italy After Fascism: A Political History, 1943–1965.* Notre Dame, Indiana: U. of Notre Dame Press, 1966.

Mason, John T., ed. *The Pacific War Remembered: An Oral History Collection.* Annapolis, Md.: Naval Institute Press, 1986.

Millis, Walter, Harvey C. Mansfield, and Harold Stein. *Arms and the State.* New York: Twentieth Century Fund, 1958.

Millis, Walter, ed. *The Forrestal Diaries.* New York: Viking, 1951.

Morison, Samuel Eliot. *History of United States Naval Operations in World War II.* Boston: Little, Brown, 1947–62. Vol. 5, *The Struggle for Guadalcanal, August 1942–February 1943* (1949). Vol. 6, *Breaking the Bismarcks Barrier, July 22, 1942–May 1, 1944* (1950). Vol. 7, *Aleutians, Gilberts and Marshalls, June 1942–April 1944* (1951). Vol. 8, *New Guinea and the Marianas, March 1944–August 1944* (1953). Vol. 12, *Leyte, June 1944–January 1945* (1958). Vol. 13, *The Liberation of the Philippines, 1944–1945* (1959). Vol. 14, *Victory in the Pacific, 1945* (1960).

Morton, Louis. *Strategy and Command: The First Two Years.* Washington, D.C.: Office of the Chief of Military History, Department of the Army, 1962.

Newcomb, Richard F. *Iwo Jima.* New York: Holt, Rinehart & Winston, 1965.

Palmer, Michael A. *Origins of the Maritime Strategy: American Naval Strategy in the First Postwar Decade.* Washington, D.C.: Naval Historical Center, 1988.

Polmar, Norman, and Thomas B. Allen. *Rickover: Controversy and Genius.* New York: Simon & Schuster, 1982.

Potter, E. B. *Bull Halsey.* Annapolis, Md.: Naval Institute Press, 1985.

——. *The Naval Academy Illustrated History of the United States Navy.* New York: Thomas Y. Crowell, 1971.

——. *Nimitz.* Annapolis, Md.: Naval Institute Press, 1976.

——, and others. *Sea Power: A Naval History.* Englewood Cliffs, N.J.: Prentice-Hall, 1960.

——, and others. *Sea Power: A Naval History.* Annapolis, Md.: Naval Institute Press, 1981. Revision of the 1960 edition.

——, and others. *The United States and World Sea Power.* Englewood Cliffs, N.J.: Prentice-Hall, 1955.

Pratt, Fletcher. *Night Work: The Story of Task Force 39.* New York: Henry Holt, 1946.

Radford, Arthur W. *From Pearl Harbor to Vietnam: The Memoirs of Admiral Arthur W. Radford.* Stanford, Calif.: Hoover Institution Press, 1980.

Reardon, Steven L. *The Formative Years, 1947–1950.* Washington, D.C.: Office of the Secretary of Defense, 1984. Vol. 1 of Alfred Goldberg, *History of the Office of the Secretary of Defense.*

Reynolds, Clark G. *The Fast Carriers: The Forging of an Air Navy.* McGraw-Hill, 1968.

Richardson, James O., and George C. Dyer. *On the Treadmill to Pearl Harbor: The Memoirs of Admiral James O. Richardson, USN (Retired).* Washington, D.C.: Naval History Division, Department of the Navy, 1973.

Roscoe, Theodore. *United States Destroyer Operations in World War II.* Annapolis, Md.: United States Naval Institute, 1953.

Ross, Bill D. *Iwo Jima: Legacy of Valor.* New York: Vanguard Press, 1985.

Sapolski, Harvey M. *The Polaris System Development.* Cambridge, Mass.: Harvard University Press, 1972.

Sherman, Frederick C. *Combat Command: The American Aircraft Carriers in the Pacific War.* New York: E. P. Dutton, 1950.

Spector, Ronald H. *Eagle Against the Sun: The American War with Japan.* New York: The Free Press, 1985.

Stafford, Edward P. *The Big E: The Story of the USS Enterprise.* New York: Random House, 1962.

Stein, Harold, ed. *American Military Decisions: A Book of Case Studies.* Tuscaloosa, Ala.: U. of Alabama Press, 1963.

Sweetman, Jack. *The U.S. Naval Academy.* Annapolis, Md.: Naval Institute Press, 1979.

Tarr, Curtis W. *Unification of America's Armed Forces: A Century and a Half of Conflict, 1798–1947.* Ph.D. dissertation. Ann Arbor, Mich.: University Microfilms, 1962.

Taylor, Maxwell D. *The Uncertain Trumpet.* New York: Harper & Brothers, 1960.

Taylor, Theodore. *The Magnificent Mitscher.* New York: W. W. Norton, 1954.

Toland, John. *The Rising Sun: The Decline and Fall of the Japanese Empire, 1936–1945.* New York: Random House, 1970.

Williams, T. Harry, Richard N. Current, and Frank Friedel. *A History of the United States (Since 1865).* 2nd ed., rev. New York: Alfred A. Knopf, 1964.

Wallin, Homer N. *Pearl Harbor: Why, How, Fleet Salvage and Final Appraisal.* Washington, D.C.: Naval History Division, Department of the Navy, 1968.

Wheeler, Gerald E. *Admiral William Veazie Pratt: A Sailor's Life.* Washington, D.C.: Naval History Division, Department of the Navy, 1974.

Woodward, C. Vann. *The Battle for Leyte Gulf.* New York: Macmillan, 1947.

Wyden, Peter. *Bay of Pigs: The Untold Story.* New York: Simon & Schuster, 1979.

Y'Blood, William T. *Red Sun Setting: The Battle of the Philippine Sea.* Annapolis, Md.: Naval Institute Press, 1981.

ARTICLES

Burke, Arleigh A. "Admiral Marc Mitscher: A Naval Aviator." *U.S. Naval Institute Proceedings,* April 1975, pp. 54–63.

———. "The Hazards of Negotiating with Communists." *Reader's Digest,* October 1968.

———. "Power and Peace." *Orbis,* Summer 1962.

———. "Unforgettable Bull Halsey." *Reader's Digest,* September 1973.

Bush, George. "A Boy Goes to War." *Life,* September, 1989.

Gallery, Daniel V. "An Admiral Talks Back to the Airmen." *Saturday Evening Post,* 25 June 1949.

Hayler, William B. "USS Franklin (CV-13): What a First Year Out of the Academy!" *Shipmate,* March 1984.

Martin, Harold H. "On the Prowl with '31 Knot' Burke." *Saturday Evening Post,* 18 June 1958.

Rosenberg, David Alan. "Officer Development in the Interwar Navy: Arleigh Burke—the Making of a Naval Professional, 1919–1940." *Pacific Historical Review,* November 1975, pp. 503–26.

U.S. GOVERNMENT PUBLICATIONS

Annual Reports of the Navy Department
The Battle for Leyte Gulf, October 1944: Strategical and Tactical Analysis. Newport, R.I.: U.S. Naval War College, 1957–58.

The Campaigns of the Pacific War. Naval Analysis Division, United States Strategic Bombing Survey. Washington, D.C.: United States Government Printing Office, 1946. Valuable chiefly for translations of important Japanese wartime military and naval documents.

Combat Narratives. Washington, D.C.: Office of Naval Intelligence. Accounts of battles and other combat operations issued to U.S. naval officers during World War II. Solomon Islands Campaign: IX, "Bombardments of Munda and Vila-Stanmore, January–May 1943" (1944). X, "Operations in the New Georgia Area, 21 June–5 August 1943" (1944). XI, "Kolombangara and Vella Lavella, 6 August–7 October 1943" (1944). XII, "The Bougainville Landing and the Battle of Empress Augusta Bay, 27 October–2 November 1943" (1945).

Dictionary of American Naval Fighting Ships. Navy Department, Office of the Chief of Naval Operations, Naval History Division, Washington, D.C.

Interrogations of Japanese Officials. 2 vols. Naval Analysis Division, United States Strategic Bombing Survey. Interrogations of Japanese officers and other officials by U.S. naval officers in Tokyo during October–December 1945.

King, Ernest J. *U.S. Navy at War, 1941–1945: Official Reports to the Secretary of the Navy.* Washington, D.C.: United States Navy Department, 1946.

U.S. Naval Academy, Executive Department, Memorandum for the First Class, 7 March 1923.

U.S. NAVAL DOCUMENTS (Logs in National Archives, Washington, D.C.; war diaries in Naval Historical Center, Washington Navy Yard)

USS *Antares* (AG 10) log, 1933
USS *Argonne* (AG 31) logs, 1934–35
USS *Arizona* (BB 39) logs, 1923–28
USS *Charles Ausburne* (DD 570) war diaries, 1943–44
USS *Chester* (CA 27) logs, 1932–33
USS *Conway* (DD 507) war diary, 1943
USS *Craven* (DD 382) logs, 1937–39
USS *Denver* (CL 58) war diary, 1943
USS *Farenholt* (DD 491) war diary, 1943
USS *Maury* (DD 401) war diary, 1943
USS *Montpelier* (CL 57) war diary, 1943
USS *Mugford* (DD 389) logs, 1939–40
USS *Procyon* (AK 19) logs, 1928–29
USS *Saufley* (DD 465) war diary, 1943
USS *Waller* (DD 466) war diary, 1943

BURKE STATEMENT

Burke, Arleigh. *The First Battle of the Philippine Sea: Decision Not to Force an Action on the Night of 18–19 June.* Transcription from microfilm in Nimitz Library, U.S. Naval Academy.

BURKE PAPERS (Naval Historical Center)

Burke's orders, telegrams, official and private correspondence, and other documents. Of particular interest are several hundred letters from Burke to Mrs. Burke, beginning with his first notes to her as a midshipman and continuing through life whenever they were separated.

INTERVIEWS

U.S. Naval Institute Oral Histories (Those by Burke consulted on loan from the Naval Institute; all others consulted in the Nimitz Library, U.S. Naval Academy)

Anderson, Admiral George W., Jr., USN (Ret.), Vol. II
Austin, Vice Admiral Bernard L., USN (Ret.)
Baldwin, Hanson W., Vol. I
Bauernschmidt, Rear Admiral George W., USN (Ret.)
Beshany, Vice Admiral Philip A., USN (Ret.), Vol. II
Bogan, Vice Admiral Gerald F., USN (Ret.)
Burke, Admiral Arleigh A., USN (Ret.), CNO volume and Special Series, Vols. I–IV
Chew, Vice Admiral John L., USN (Ret.)
Colwell, Vice Admiral John Barr, USN (Ret.)
Cooper, Rear Admiral Joshua W., USN (Ret.)
Dennison, Admiral Robert Lee, USN (Ret.)
Duncan, Admiral Charles K., USN (Ret.), Vols. I & III
Felt, Admiral Harry D., USN (Ret.), Vol. I
Gallery, Rear Admiral Daniel V., USN (Ret.)
Griffin, Admiral Charles D., USN (Ret.), Vols. I & II
Hedding, Admiral Truman J., USN (Ret.)
Hooper, Vice Admiral Edwin B., USN (Ret.)
Irvin, Rear Admiral William D., USN (Ret.)
Jackson, Vice Admiral Andrew McBurney, Jr., USN (Ret.)
Johnson, Vice Admiral Felix L., USN (Ret.)
Johnson, Admiral Roy L., USN (Ret.)
Jones, Captain Glyn, USN (Ret.)
Jurika, Captain Stephen, Jr., USN (Ret.), Vol. II

Kauffman, Rear Admiral Draper L., USN (Ret.), Vol. I
Kenyon, A. Prentice, Naval Personnel–Naval Training
Kerr, Captain Alex A., USN (Ret.)
Lee, Vice Admiral Fitzhugh, USN (Ret.)
Libby, Vice Admiral Ruthven E., USN (Ret.)
Loughlin, Rear Admiral Charles E., USN (Ret.)
Mack, Vice Admiral William P., USN (Ret.), Vols. I & II
Masterson, Vice Admiral Kleber S., USN (Ret.)
Miller, Rear Admiral George H., USN (Ret.), Vol. I
Miller, Vice Admiral Gerald E., USN (Ret.)
Miller, Rear Admiral Henry L., USN (Ret.), Vol. I
Minter, Vice Admiral Charles S., Jr., USN (Ret.), Vol. I
Moorer, Admiral Thomas H., USN (Ret.), Vol. I
Morton, Rear Admiral Thomas H., USN (Ret.)
Peet, Vice Admiral Raymond E., USN (Ret.)
Pirie, Vice Admiral Robert B., USN (Ret.)
Raborn, Vice Admiral William F., Jr., USN (Ret.)
Price, Rear Admiral Arthur W., Jr., USN (Ret.)
Ramage, Vice Admiral Lawson Paterson, USN (Ret.)
Reich, Vice Admiral Eli T., USN (Ret.), Vol. I
Rivero, Admiral Horacio, Jr., USN (Ret.)
Royar, Vice Admiral Murrey L., USN (Ret.)
Ruckner, Rear Admiral Edward A., USN (Ret.)
Russell, Admiral James S., USN (Ret.)
Salzer, Vice Admiral Robert S., USN (Ret.)
Sharp, Admiral U. S. Grant, Jr., USN (Ret.), Vols. I & II
Smedberg, Vice Admiral William R., III. USN (Ret.), Vol. II
Strean, Vice Admiral Bernard M., USN (Ret.)
Thach, Admiral John S., USN (Ret.), Vols. I & II
Ward, Admiral Alfred G., USN (Ret.)
Wertheim, Vice Admiral Robert H., USN (Ret.)

Others

Abshire, David M., by the author
Burke, Mrs. Arleigh A., by Stanley E. Smith
Jackson, Comdr. Virginia E., USN, by Grace Potter
Mack, Vice Admiral William P., USN (Ret.), by the author

Several times during the composition of this book, the author and his wife, Grace, visited Admiral and Mrs. Burke in their home and interviewed them. From time to time the author telephoned Admiral Burke to get a fact straight.

CHAPTER
NOTES

References are shortened, usually to the last name of the author (or one of the authors). Where necessary a short title has been added.

Chapter 1. Early Years of an American Viking

Interview: Author with Adm. and Mrs. Burke, 18 June 1986.

Letters: Burke to Mrs. Burke, 28 Dec. 1920, 12 & 26 Jan., 6 & 13 Feb., 14 Mar., 4 Apr. 1921; Bernard C. Duncan to Bobbie, 1 Feb. 1921.

Books: Buell, *Quiet Warrior*, 12; Jones, *Burke*, 27–59; Love, 265–66; McCandless, 34–36; Sweetman, 171–72.

Midshipmen's yearbook, Lucky Bag, 1921–1923.

Chapter 2. Junior Officer

Letters: Burke to Mrs. Burke, 3 & 14 Jan., 7 & 15 Feb., 15, 17, 18, & 19 Mar. 1924, 12 Jan. 1927.

Article: Rosenberg, 511–13.

Books: Jones, *Burke*, 63–78; Morison, XV, 34; Potter, *Nimitz*, 137–40; Wheeler, 155, 219–31.

Other: Arizona log; Navy Dept. Rpt., 1924, 1925, & 1926; U.S. Naval Academy, Executive Dept. Memorandum for the First Class, 7 March 1923.

Chapter 3. The Road to Command

Oral History: Ruckner, 25.

Letters: Burke to: Lt. Comdr. H. A. Flanigan, 13 June 1928; Comdr. A. D. Denny; Comdr. Leighton Wood, 18 July & 9 Aug. 1928; Mr. Allen, Seaboard Motor Co., San Pedro, 22 Aug. 1918; Capt. M. G. Cook, 27

Aug. 1928; Comdr. A. D. Denny, 1 Nov. 1928; Lt. Comdr. Kerr, 21 Nov. 1928; Lt. Horgaard, Staff, CinC, U.S. Fleet, 20 Jan. 1934; Lt. Comdr. Jacobson, 12 Mar. 1934; Mrs. John Paul Jones, 7 Apr. 1934; Mrs. Burke, 24 Apr. 1934; Dr. Mees, 29 Apr. 1934; Lt. (j.g.) W. C. Holt, 30 May 1934; Lt. Wells C. Fields, 30 May 1934; Capt. A. C. Stott, 15 June 1934; Carol Victor, 25 June 1934; Kenneth Walker, 7 Sept. 1934; Rear Adm. Thomas J. Senn, 13 Sept. 1934; Prof. C. C. Bramble, 5 Dec. 1934; Lt. T. H. Tonseth, 31 Jan. 1935; Lt. George Nold, 23 Mar. 1935; Lt. J. S. Smith, 26 Dec. 1938; Ken, 25 Jan. 1939; Comdr. George F. Hussy, 8 Sept. 1937 & 27 Jan. 1939; Lt. Comdr. Harold D. Krick, 16 Mar. 1939; Mrs. Burke, 12, 14, 15, & 21 Jan. 1943. To Burke: Comdr. Leighton Wood, 3 Aug. 1928; Lt. H. A. Flanigan, 6 Aug., 6 Sept., & 15 Nov. 1928; Capt. M. G. Cook, 10 Oct. 1928; Camera Craft Publishing Co., 9 Mar. 1934; Lt. George F. Kraker, 8, 20, & 25 July 1934; Carol Victor, 13 July 1934; Comdr. A. D. Denny, 24 Oct. 1934; Prof. C. C. Bramble, 5 Dec. 1934; Lt. Comdr. H. J. Hansen, 4 Jan. 1934; Lt. T. H. Tonseth, 15 Jan. 1935; F. N. Loria, 11 Mar. 1935; Mable, "Slave 1," 21 July 1938; Comdr. George F. Hussy, 6 Oct. 1938; Lt. J. S. Smith, 4 Jan. 1939; Lt. Comdr. Harold D. Krick, 20 Mar. 1939. *Other:* Lt. Comdr. H. A. Flanigan to BuNav, 15 Nov. 1928.

Article: Rosenberg, 518–23.

Books: Adams, *Power*, 68–70; Buell, *Master*, 114–17; Coletta, 636; *Jane's Fighting Ships*, 1928; Jones, *Burke*, 78–90. Gelzer Sims's long monologue beginning on page 51 of this book is taken from Jones, *Burke*, pages 83–84. It sounds realistic and natural, but I was curious to know how a discourse like this came to be recorded. Sims was dead, and Burke could not recall the incident, so I wrote to Sims's son, Gelzer Sims, Jr., a retired navy captain living in Georgia. Sims could not confirm the conversation but said his father was a fine storyteller, and the discourse as reported was typical of the tales he would tell. "I brought the passage to my father's attention in the fifties," Sims wrote. "He had suffered a stroke and was unable to speak. He did, however, nod and laugh when he heard it. I do not know if he was acknowledging the passage took place as reported or simply agreeing with the sentiments expressed."; Love, 267; King, 228–29, 288–93; Potter, *Halsey*, 142–46, *Nimitz*, 137–69, *Sea Power* (1960), 491–95, 646; Richardson, 223, 236–50; Wheeler, 348.

Logs: Procyon, Chester, Antares, Argonne, Craven, Mugford.

Other: Lt. Comdr. J. H. Jacobson to Burke (telegram), 22 Dec. 1928. Burke deposition, State of New York, County of New York, 12 July 1932. Burke, "Notes on the U.S.S. *Argonne*," 12 Sept. 1934.

Chapter 4. South Pacific

Letters: Burke to Mrs. Burke, 22 and 26 Jan., 4, 6, & 17 Feb. 1943.
War Diaries: Denver, Waller.

Government Publications: American Naval Fighting Ships, vol. V, 374. According to this source, *President Monroe,* built for American President Lines and launched 7 Aug. 1940, had vacationing passengers on board and was "just clearing San Francisco Bay on her maiden voyage around the world when word was flashed to her Master to return as Japan had just attacked Pearl Harbor." She was transferred from the War Shipping Administration to the U.S. Navy in July 1943. *Combat Narratives,* Solomon Islands Campaign: IX, Bombardments of Munda and Vila-Stanmore, 33–43.

Books: Jones, *Destroyer Squadron,* 117–19, 120, 123–26, 180. I use this source with caution. In his preface, Jones says, "In the matter of dialogue the words spoken may be accepted as interpreting reliably the personality of the speaker and the sense of the situation portrayed. All TBS transmissions are recorded word for word as they appear in the official record compiled at the times the conversation took place. All other dialogue is substantially supported by log entries, by signed battle reports, by war diaries, or by official memoranda, or else reported orally to the author by the speakers." Since Jones, in researching his book, published in 1959, interviewed at length several participants who have since died, I have made use of a very limited amount of his dialogue but only if clearly supported by other sources. I have used Smith's quotations of Burke only after checking with Burke himself. Obviously the admiral's memory of what he said is not as clear at the time of this writing as it must have been nearly three decades earlier, but I have accepted the quotation if Admiral Burke agreed that it was what he probably said or is not contrary to what he meant. After all, that is probably as close as we can get to dialogue recollected from the distant past. Morison, *Struggle for Guadalcanal,* 326–29, 345–47, 359–71, *Bismarcks Barrier,* 96–106; Potter, *Halsey,* 33–55, 160–82, 199–200, 238, 251, *Sea Power* (1960), 705–7, (1981), 289–96, 302–12; Roscoe, 210–14.

Chapter 5. Central Solomons

Letters: Comdesron 43 to CTF 19, 7 May 1943, "Employment of Destroyers"; Burke to Moosbrugger, 9 Aug. 1943; Burke to Wilkinson, 24 Aug. 1943; Merrill to author, 18 Feb. 1953, in response to a request for information while I was working on *United States and World Sea Power;* Burke to author, 28 Jan. 1953, containing Burke battle plan and Simpson's letter saying plan was used by Moosbrugger in Battle of Vella Gulf; Burke to W. H. Russell, 27 Feb. 1956. In 1956, while I was working on *Sea Power* (1960), in conversation with Admiral Burke following a meeting of the U.S. Naval Institute at Annapolis, I asked him a number of questions about his night tactics in the Solomons campaign. In his reply he mentioned the influence of the tactics of Scipio Africanus as reported by Polybius. I repeated his remarks to my Naval Academy colleague Professor Russell, who was teaching a class in the history of ancient warfare. Deeply interested, Russell wrote to Burke, requesting further details. I quoted a key passage in Burke's reply in a footnote in *Sea Power* (1960), 721, and have repeated most of that quotation in this chapter.

Government Publications: Combat Narratives. Solomon Islands Campaign: IX, Bombardments, 48–74, X, New Georgia, 48–54.

War Diaries: Farenholt, Montpelier, Waller.

Books: Isely, *Amphibious War*, 172; Jones, *Destroyer Squadron*, 127–29, 134–35, 137–39; Morison, *Bismarcks Barrier*, 97, 110–16, 120–24, 156–59, 202–4, 212; Potter, *Halsey*, 212, 223–31, 250, 252, *Sea Power* (1960), 717, 721, 722, *U.S. & World Sea Power*, 750–51.

Chapter 6. 31-Knot Burke

Letters: Burke to Sims, 23 Mar. 1944; Fladm. Halsey to Chief of Naval Personnel, 24 Feb. 1947, recommending award of Distinguished Service Medal to Harry Raymond Thurber (probably written by Thurber; copy sent by Thurber to author 3 Mar. 1957), 12.

Dispatches: Desron 23 to BuPers 222200 of Oct. 1943. BuPers 141658 to Burke of March 1944. The version quoted in the text (p. 103) is expanded from the verbal shorthand used to save space and transmission time. The original read: "DET DUTY COMDESRON 23 DUTY COMDESDIV 45 PRO FAG AIR PORT COMCARDIV 3 MAY BE DUTY HIS CHIEF OF STAFF." Halsey (mailgram) to Burke, 21 Mar. 1944.

Government Publications: Battle of Cape St. George Action Report. Combat Narratives, Solomon Islands Campaign: XII, Bougainville, 11–25, 37–71. *Destroyer Squadron 23 Doctrine.*

War Diary: Ausburne.

Books: Jones, *Destroyer Squadron*, 171–73, 212–37, 242–63, 269; Mason, 196, 202–3 (Burke's oral history, quoted here, incorrectly places these sinkings off Kavieng in November 1943); Morison, *Bismarcks Barrier*, 293–304, 323–36, 352–59, 363–65, 378–81, 412–21, 423–24; Potter, *Halsey*, 55–58, 262–63, *Nimitz*, 238, 245, *Sea Power* (1960), 723–27, 730–31.

Chapter 7. Bald Eagle

Oral Histories: Burke, Special Series, Vol. I, #4, 238–41, 245–48; Hedding, 53–64.

Article: Burke, "Admiral Marc Mitscher," 54–55, 57–58.

Books: Buell, *Master*, 101–2, 356, 371, *Quiet Warrior*, 247–48; Jones, *Burke*, 111–13; Morison, *Bismarcks Barrier*, 99n, *New Guinea*, 29, 31; Morton, 652–53; Potter, *Halsey*, 140, 204–5, 214–15, 241, 248–49, 269; Potter, *Nimitz*, 248–49, 264–67; Potter, *Sea Power* (1960), 731, 738–40, 749–55, 757; Potter, *SeaPower* (1981), 188, 193–94, 203, 238, 302, 323–25; Spector, 278; Stafford, 300–1; Taylor, Theodore, 144–45, 157, 159, 161–67, 174–89, 193.

Chapter 8. Supporting MacArthur

Oral Histories: Burke, Special Series, Vol. I, #4, 248–51, 262, 268–71, 273–74, 277–78; Hedding, 70–71, 80, 82.

Books: Buell, *Quiet Warrior*, 248–49; Morison, *New Guinea*, 13, 32–33, 36–37, 38–41, 69; Stafford, 319–29; Taylor, Theodore, 192–94, 205–6.

Chapter 9. Assault on the Marianas

Oral Histories: Burke, Special Series, Vol. I, #4, 266–67, 279–80, 283; Hedding, 79.

Statement: Burke, "First Battle," 6–8.

Op Plan: Cincpoa Operation Plan No. 3-44, dated 23 April 1944.

Government Publication: Campaigns of the Pacific War, 221.

Books: Blair, *Silent Victory*, 638–39, 650–51; Buell, *Master*, 337, 439–40, *Quiet Warrior*, 259–62, 267; Forrestel, 37, 126; Holmes, 179–80; Jones, *Burke*, 116; Morison, *New Guinea*, 116–19, 131, 169, 174–80, 209–10, 233–34, 243, 252; Lockwood, 90; Potter, *Halsey*, 248, *Nimitz*, 282–83, 287–89, 295–99, *Sea Power* (1960), 759–60, 763, 765; Reynolds, 153–54, 174, 177; Spector, 293; Stafford, 319–20; Taylor, Theodore, 208, 210, 219–23; Y'Blood, 14–15, 31–47, 55–56, 65–70, 89–93.

Chapter 10. Battle of the Philippine Sea

Oral History: Burke, Special Series, Vol. I, #4, 319–25.

Statement: Burke, "First Battle," 13–16.

Books: Bryan, 13–18, 23, 73; Lockwood, 92; Morison, *New Guinea*, 104, 257–74, 278–85, 290–92; Potter, *Nimitz*, 300–2, *Sea Power* (1960), 760, 768; Reynolds, 195, 201, 204; Stafford, 337–57; Taylor, Theodore, 225–26, 229–33, 325; Y'Blood, 106–51, 179–80, 194–98.

Chapter 11. From the Marianas to the Philippines

Oral History: Burke, Special Series, Vol. I, #4, 327–28, 335–36, 343–45, 371–72, 374, 377–78, 387–88, 409–10.

Letter: Spruance to author, 21 Feb. 1954.

Op Plan: Cincpoa Operation Plan No. 8-44, dated 27 Sept. 1944.

Articles: Bush, "A Boy Goes to War," 72; Burke, "Admiral Marc Mitscher," 56, 59–60.

Government Publication: War College, *Leyte Gulf*, Vol. I, 510–35.

Books: Adams, *Victory*, 157; Blair, *Silent Victory*, 746–47; Bryan, 202–9; Buell, *Quiet Warrior*, 27; Clark, 196; Geffen, 236; Dyer, II, 914; Jones, *Burke*, 84, 121–22; King, *Fleet Admiral*, 557–58; Morison, *New Guinea*, 291, 311–15, *Leyte*, 12–15, 86–87, 90–109; Potter, *Halsey*, 118, 128–29, 258–85, 317, *Nimitz*, 3, 18, 267, 303, 313, *Sea Power* (1960), 769–73; Reynolds, 16, 40–41, 236, 240–46; Sherman, 274–75; Stafford, 368–79; Taylor, Theodore, 245, 248–49, 251–52; Y'Blood, 212, 286–87.

Chapter 12. Battle for Leyte Gulf

Oral Histories: Burke, Special Series, Vol. I, #4, 398–401; Royar, 180–81.
Radio Dispatches: Com 3rd Flt (Halsey), 240612, 240829, 250027; CTF 77 (Kinkaid), 240315, 242123; CTF 38 (Mitscher), 240817, 240942, 242335; CTG 38.1 (McCain), 250125.
Government Publication: War College, *Leyte Gulf,* Vol. II, xiv, 1, 4, 8, 9, 37–38, Vol. II, 431–41, Vol. III, 341, 363, 365, 768–73.
Books: Blair, *Silent Victory,* 746–49, 753–54; Field, 66–71; Halsey, *Story,* 297–98; Morison, *Leyte,* 126, 175–82, 192–96, 318–28, 357–41; Potter, *Halsey,* 219–21, 287–310, 403, *Nimitz,* 330, *Sea Power* (1960), 774–92; Reynolds, 270–71; Sherman, 292–95; Taylor, Theodore, 257–62, 267; Woodward, 43–44, 48–74, 136–58, 479.

Chapter 13. Iwo Jima and the Tokyo Raids

Oral History: Burke, Special Series, Vol. I, 34, 406–23.
Letters: SecNav James Forrestal to Burke, 6 Nov. 1944; Navy Department Memorandum, 7 Nov. 1944; Dudley Harmon to Burke, 20 Nov. 1944.
Article: Burke, "Admiral Marc Mitscher," 60–61.
Books: Buell, *Quiet Warrior,* 312, 322–42; Costello, 547–52; Forrestel, 164; Jones, *Burke,* 134–38; Morison, *Leyte,* 117, *Philippines,* 5, *Victory,* 11–13, 21–38, 52–59; Newcomb, 92–93, 263–64; Potter, *Halsey,* 309–26, *Nimitz,* 318–22, 356, 362, *Sea Power* (1960), 824–28, *Sea Power* (1981), 347; Spector, 502–5; Reynolds, 333; Ross, 61; Taylor, Theodore, 268–74.

Chapter 14. The Fleet Under Suicide Attack

Oral History: Burke, Special Series, Vol. I, #4, 435–36, 451–54, 465–56.
Article: Haylor, "USS Franklin," 12–13.
Books: Belote, *Titans,* 39–41; Bryan, 57–58; Buell, *Quiet Warrior,* 307–19, 344–61; Clark, 213, 224–25; Dyer, 1106–7; Halsey, *Story,* 250; Jones, *Burke,* 139–45; Morison, *Victory,* 18, 94–100, 182–211, 235–36, 248–49, 262–63, 390; Potter, *Halsey,* 332–36, *Nimitz,* 281–82, 374–75, *Sea Power* (1960), 813, 829; Sherman, 360; Stafford, 440–45; Reynolds, 336–338; Taylor, Theodore, 275–87, 299.

Chapter 15. Eighth Fleet

Oral Histories: Burke, Special Series, Vol. I, 469–502; Griffin, 152; Masterson, 128.
Article: Burke, "Admiral Marc Mitscher," 62.
Government Publication: Interrogations of Japanese Officials, Vol. II, 320.
Books: Lewin, 277–88; Potter, *Halsey,* 128–32, 340–43, *Nimitz,* 384, *Sea Power* (1960), 635–36, 833–34, (1981), 237, 354–60; Spector, 545–59; Taylor, Theodore, 303–13, 331; Toland, 741–850.

Chapter 16. Last Duty with Mitscher

Oral Histories: Burke, Special Series, Vol. I, 380, 503–549; Griffin, Vol. I, 178.

Articles: Burke, "Admiral Marc Mitscher," 58; *New York Times,* 6 Feb. 1947.

Books: Mammarella, 159; Morison, *Sicily,* 310–11; Potter, *Nimitz,* 359; Taylor, Theodore, 332, 336, 338.

Chapter 17. Desk Duty, Escape to Sea, and Recall

Oral Histories: Burke, Special Series, Vol. II, 3–12, 19–21, 29, 45, 56, 58–60, 62, 63, 70–73, 82–94, 281–82, 300–2, Vol. III, 1–9.

Books: Coletta, 751–54; Jones, *Burke,* 149; Love, 195–97; Potter, *Nimitz,* passim.

Chapter 18. Revolt of the Admirals

Oral Histories: Bauernschmidt, 227; Burke, Special Series, Vol. I, 12–13, Vol. III, pt. 1, 11, pt. 2, #11, 1–3, Vol. IV, 74–75, 98–123; Dennison, 195–99; Griffin, Vol. I, 190–91; Kerr, 292; Henry L. Miller, Vol. I, 180; Minter, 415–16.

Books: Blair, *Forgotten War,* 14–15; Borklund, 26–34, 39–51, 71–74; Bradley, 509–11; Coletta, 737–42, 800, 804–5; Davis, 288–89; Hammond, 491–98, 505–8, 513, 518, 525–34, 548–51; Love; 193–97, 200–5, 217–18, 272; Potter, *Nimitz,* 407–8, 443–48, *Sea Power* (1960), 846–49, (1981), 354–58; Radford, 26–37, 73–86; Reardon, 49, 411–18.

Chapters 19 and 20. Korean War

Oral Histories: Burke, Special Series, Vol. I, 8–234 and selection from Takeo Okubo's book following index; Vol. II, 95–115; Libby, 181; George Miller, 142.

Letters: Rear Admiral Seizaburo Hoshino, JMSDF, to author, 10 Sept. 1967; Burke to author, 15 Aug. 1988; Vice Admiral Nobuo Fukuchi, JMSDF (Ret.) to author, 3 Sept. 1988.

Books: Blair, *Forgotten War;* Cagle, *Sea War in Korea;* Field, *Korea.*

Chapter 21. Strategic Plans and Final Sea Duty

Oral Histories: Burke, Special Series, Vol. II, 95–99, 115–342; Kauffman, Vol. I, 412; George Miller, 143; Henry Miller, Vol. I, 178, 185–86.

Chapter 22. Chief of Naval Operations (1)

Oral Histories: Burke, CNO Years, 16–35, 229–30; Duncan, Vol. III, 454; Hooper, 246–47; George Miller, 180–86; Henry Miller, Vol. I, 208–9; Moorer, Vol. I, 1595–96; Raborn, 13–17; Sharp, 145–47.

Books: Baar, 15–36; Braun, 120–26, 143–45; Coletta, 869; Jones, *Burke,* 166–77; Love, 263–77.

Chapter 23. Chief of Naval Operations (2)

Oral Histories: Burke, CNO Years, 62–65, 182–205; Duncan, Vol. III, 1387; Mack, Vol. I, 273–74, 298–99; George Miller, 162, 188, 238; Henry Miller, Vol. I, 210, 227–28; Moorer, Vol. III, 355, 402, 1524, 1595; Peet, 36–41, 94–98, 121–25; Raborn, 19–23.

Article: Martin, "Prowl," 36–37.

Books: Baar, 36–48, 69–72; Coletta, 861, 871; Jones, *Burke,* 179–83; Love, 275–81; Polmar, 11, 255–56, 539–40; Potter, *Sea Power* (1960), 876–79; Sapolsky, 64–65.

Chapter 24. Chief of Naval Operations (3)

Oral Histories: Burke, CNO Years, 207–10; Kauffman, 427; Mack, Vol. I, 275–76; Gerald Miller, Vol. I, 272–78, 283–91; Peet, 126–27, 131–32, 141–42, 536.

Recollections of the author.

Books: Baar, 236–39; Braun, 164; Coletta, 885–86; Higgins, 58–94; Jones, *Burke,* 2–21, 189–93; Kerr, 84–87; Love, 284–93, 302–5, 310–14, 317; Potter, *Sea Power* (1960), 879–81; Wyden, 86–92.

Chapter 25. A Kind of Retirement

Interviews: Author with Adm. & Mrs. Burke, 5 Apr. 1989; author with David M. Abshire, 25 Apr. 1989; Stanley E. Smith with Mrs. Burke, n.d.

Letters: Burke to: George M. Clark, 6 Nov. 1961; Capt. Wm. S. Busik, USN, 14 Mar. 1962; Capt. E. Robt. Anderson, USNR (Ret.), 29 July 1963; Anne Armstrong, 14 May 1983. To Burke: Floyd D. Akers, 4 Aug. 1961; Joseph D. Ardleigh, 12 Apr. 1963; David M. Abshire, 21 Apr. 1972; Anne Armstrong, 3 May 1983. Comdr. C. R. Wilhide, USN, to Rear Adm. Arthur A. Ageton, USN (Ret.), 7 Sept. 1961.

Memorandum: Burke to David M. Abshire, 19 June 1963.

Lecture: Burke, "Peace and Power," condensed in *Orbis,* Summer 1962.

Books: Love, 317–19; Mason, 201–3; Abshire, passim.

INDEX

Arleigh A. Burke is abbreviated AAB. Ships, unless otherwise noted, are U.S.

Burke (*cont'd*)

Greek, Ethiopian, Brazilian, Ecuadorean, 412–13; the nuclear deadlock, 414; reaction to Nasser's seizure of the Suez Canal, 414–15; relations with Admiral Rickover, 408, 416; stuggles to build the new navy, 416; and instill spirit, 417; Secretary Thomas's retirement, 418; Soviets put Sputnik in orbit, 419; AAB's 1957 visit to Pearl Harbor, Seventh Fleet, and threatened friendly Pacific powers, 419–22; accelerating the Polaris program, 422–24; AAB and the Defense Reorganization Act of 1958, 424–25; the Lebanon landings, 426–27; the Formosa Strait crisis, 427–28; problems of deterrence, 428; social life and work habits, 429; AAB reluctantly accepts unprecedented third term as CNO, 430–31; successful underwater launching of Polaris, 431–32; AAB's unsuccessful fight against Single Integrated Operational War Plan (SIOP), 432–34; his continuing fight against excessive centralization of U.S. warmaking power, 434–35; the Bay of Pigs, 436–38; resigns as CNO, 438–39

IN RETIREMENT: on vacation, the Burkes' first extended leave in 38 years, 440; business employment and public service, 440–42; founding, organizing, and directing Center for Strategic and International Studies (CSIS), 442–45; lectures (especially those at Princeton) forecast breakup of communist bloc, not through conquest or containment but by forced recognition of impracticality of Marxism, 445–48; supports Goldwater's campaign for presidency, 448; heads U.S. delegation to funeral of Swedish king, 448; joins Rabaul Kai, 448–49; deterioration of his eyesight, 449–50; chair in honor at CSIS, 450; Admiral Arleigh A. Burke Hall at Naval War College, 450; launching of guided missile destroyer *Arleigh Burke*, 450–51; dinner in his honor by Little Beavers, 451

Burke, Clara (AAB's mother), 3, 4, 6, 10, 14, 20, 58, 451

Burke, Gus (AAB's grandfather), 3

Burke, Oscar (AAB's father) 3, 9, 14, 451

E. B. POTTER graduated from the University of Richmond and the University of Chicago. He served in World War II in the U.S. Naval Reserve, attaining the rank of commander. At the end of the war, he joined the civilian faculty of the Naval Academy, becoming chairman of naval history, a post he held for twenty years. In that capacity he led his colleagues in writing *Sea Power: A Naval History,* which in a new edition was still being used as a textbook at the Naval Academy and elsewhere when this book was published. He retired from the Naval Academy faculty in 1977 and was awarded the title of professor emeritus by the secretary of the navy.

Potter has lectured at the Army, Navy, and National war colleges and on TV (a series of 45 lectures on naval history for the Westinghouse network). His previous naval biographies have won him the Author Award of Merit from the U.S. Naval Institute, the Alfred Thayer Mahan Award for Literary Achievement from the Navy League of the United States, the Samuel Eliot Morison Award for Outstanding Contribution to the History and Traditions of the U.S. Navy from the Naval Order of the United States, and the John Lyman Award for Best North American Memoir, Autobiography, Biography from the North American Society for Oceanic History.